ALSO BY JOE JACKSON

Black Elk:
The Life of an American Visionary

Atlantic Fever:
Lindbergh, His Competitors, and the Race to Cross the Atlantic

The Thief at the End of the World:
Rubber, Power, and the Seeds of Empire

A World on Fire:
A Heretic, an Aristocrat, and the Race to Discover Oxygen

A Furnace Afloat:
The Wreck of the Hornet *and the Harrowing 4,300-mile Voyage of Its Survivors*

How I Left the Great State of Tennessee and Went On to Better Things

Leavenworth Train:
A Fugitive's Search for Justice in the Vanishing West

Dead Run:
The Shocking Story of Dennis Stockton and Life on Death Row in America

SPLENDID LIBERATORS

SPLENDID LIBERATORS

HEROISM, BETRAYAL, RESISTANCE,
AND THE BIRTH OF AMERICAN EMPIRE

★ ★ ★

Joe Jackson

Farrar, Straus and Giroux
New York

Farrar, Straus and Giroux
120 Broadway, New York 10271

EU Representative: Macmillan Publishers Ireland Ltd, 1st Floor,
The Liffey Trust Centre, 117–126 Sheriff Street Upper, Dublin 1, DO1 YC43

Printed in the United States of America
First edition, 2025

Star ornament by Anna Timoshenko / Shutterstock.com.

Library of Congress Control Number: 2025012963
ISBN: 978-0-374-19190-0

Designed by Patrice Sheridan

10 9 8 7 6 5 4 3 2 1

AS ALWAYS,

TO KATHY AND NICK,

BUT THIS TIME TO LUCIE AND ROSEBUD TOO

Life is warfare, and a visit in a strange land.

—MARCUS AURELIUS, *THE MEDITATIONS*

★

Contents

PART III: LIBERATORS

PART IV: THE AMERICAN CENTURY

Dramatis Personae

AMERICAN MILITARY, CIVILIAN OFFICIALS, AND OTHERS

Henry Adams: Grandson of President John Quincy Adams who presided over a Washington, D.C., social set dubbed "the Pleasant Gang." An astute observer, he cast a cold eye on the Washington rise of Theodore Roosevelt.

Russell A. Alger: Former governor and U.S. senator from Michigan, lumber baron, and William McKinley's first secretary of war, from 1897 to 1899. He resigned in the wake of the Dodge Commission investigating the War Department's record during the War with Spain.

Frederick W. Alstaetter: Young Signal Corps lieutenant captured in August 1900 in Central Luzon by David Fagen. Both Alstaetter and Buffalo Soldier George Jackson would state in the press that they were humanely treated by Fagen when others called him "savage."

J. Franklin Bell: The commander of U.S. forces in the Philippine provinces of Batangas and Laguna, responsible for the concentration camp policy directly resulting in the deaths of tens of thousands of Filipinos. Bell would serve as the U.S. Army chief of staff from 1906 to 1910.

Magdalene Blankart: Frederick Funston's sister-in-law, present at Funston's headquarters in San Isidro during his unsuccessful campaign against David Fagen and successful capture of Emilio Aguinaldo.

John R. Brooke: Major general during the Puerto Rico campaign, he would be appointed the first military governor of both Puerto Rico and Cuba at the end of hostilities. He was succeeded, rather acrimoniously, by Leonard Wood in Cuba in December 1899.

John W. Calloway: A sergeant major in the black U.S. Twenty-Fourth Infantry, whose written crisis-of-conscience to a Filipino friend, plus his relationship with a Filipino woman, led to his arrest and dismissal from the army in January 1901. Calloway witnessed David Fagen's recruitment, served beside him on San Juan Hill and the fever camp in Cuba, and with him in the Philippines.

Allyn K. Capron: A captain in the Rough Riders from the Oklahoma Territory, Capron was the first U.S. Army officer to die in the Spanish-American War, during the Battle of Las Guásimas. Capron's father—also named Allyn Capron—commanded an artillery battery during the Battle of El Caney.

Adna R. Chaffee: Major general in the U.S. Army who fought in Cuba, the Boxer Rebellion, and the Philippines during the years of the Spanish-American War. The fourth commanding general in the Philippines, after Wesley Merritt, Elwell Otis, and Arthur MacArthur, Chaffee assigned Jacob H. Smith to conquer Samar and J. Franklin Bell to conquer Batangas, both with disastrous results.

Grover Cleveland: The twenty-second and twenty-fourth president of the United States, his terms separated by the election of Benjamin Harrison in 1888. The Panic of 1893 occurred during his second term, as well as the growing insurgency in Cuba.

Leon Czolgosz: Professed anarchist from Detroit who assassinated President William McKinley on September 6, 1901, in Buffalo, New York. Seven weeks later, Czolgosz was executed in New York's electric chair.

George Dewey: U.S. Navy admiral best known for his victory over the Spanish Asiatic Fleet on May 1, 1898, at the Battle of Manila Bay.

Henry A. Dobson: First sergeant of Company D, First D.C. Volunteers, who contracted typhoid during training at Camp Alger in Falls Church,

Virginia, carried it through Tampa and the Santiago campaign, then died in New York, largely because of misdiagnosis. Typhoid would be the main cause of death during the Cuban campaign.

David Fagen: Buffalo Soldier from Tampa who served with the U.S. Twenty-Fourth Infantry in Cuba and the Philippines until defecting to the guerrilla army in November 1899. He would be one of the two most hunted men in Luzon and called a Philippine "general" on the front page of *The New York Times.*

Hamilton Fish: Wealthy New Yorker who joined the Rough Riders as a sergeant in Captain Allyn Capron's L Troop. Killed in an ambush while on point during the Battle of Las Guásimas.

Eda Blankart Funston: Wife of Frederick Funston, from Oakland, California. Joined Funston in Manila and Nueva Ecija during the hunts for David Fagen and Emilio Aguinaldo. Died at age fifty-seven of a heart attack in 1932.

Frederick Funston: By the end of his life, a major general in the U.S. Army. Also known as "Fighting Fred" and the "Little Guy," he served as a "filibuster" during the Cuban Revolt, then captured Emilio Aguinaldo during the Philippine-American War.

Jack Ganzhorn: Silent-film actor and scriptwriter, he wrote the 1910 memoir *I've Killed Men*, which details his service with Funston's Headquarters Scouts. It is one of the few firsthand accounts of the contest between Funston and David Fagen.

William W. Grayson: Private in the First Nebraska Volunteers who on February 4, 1899, fired the first shot in the Battle of Manila, thus initiating the Philippine-American War.

Charles V. Gridley: Commander of Commodore Dewey's flagship *Olympia* during the Battle of Manila Bay.

Marcus "Mark" Hanna: Ohio businessman, U.S. senator from Ohio, Republican Party chairman, and campaign manager for William McKinley during his successful presidential campaigns of 1896 and 1900.

Joseph H. Hawkins: Marine private in the ill-fated march across the island of Samar. His handwritten diary is the only soldier account to describe the sacrifice of native porters by Americans in an act of "survival cannibalism," though the suppressed notes of a journalist allegedly echo his diary.

JOHN M. HAY: U.S. ambassador to Great Britain, he coined the famous phrase "splendid little war" to describe the Cuban phase of the Spanish-American War. He later served as secretary of state under both William McKinley and Theodore Roosevelt.

ROBERT P. HUGHES: Brigadier general tasked with suppressing rebels on the islands of Leyte and Samar; his tactics led to what was famously called the "Rape of Samar."

HENRY WARE LAWTON: U.S. officer famous for capturing the Apache chief Geronimo, then assigned to take the Cuban fortress town of El Caney during the first phase of the July 1, 1898, attack on San Juan Heights. Later killed in Luzon by a Philippine sharpshooter.

FITZHUGH LEE: U.S. consul general to Havana during the Cleveland and McKinley presidencies. His duties included saving U.S. journalists and naturalized citizens thrown into prison by Spanish officials. The highest American official in Cuba when the USS *Maine* exploded.

HENRY CABOT LODGE: U.S. senator from Massachusetts and good friend of Theodore Roosevelt; a strong proponent of U.S. intervention in Cuba in 1898, and later, of U.S. imperialism worldwide.

JOHN D. LONG: Secretary of the navy under William McKinley, significantly increasing the size of the navy during the Spanish-American War; Theodore Roosevelt was his assistant secretary before going to San Antonio to train with the Rough Riders.

ARTHUR MACARTHUR: Brigadier general in the U.S. Army. Named military governor of the Philippines in 1900, he lost his post the next year to the newly appointed civilian governor William Howard Taft.

ALFRED THAYER MAHAN: U.S. naval officer and historian whose two books on the influence of sea power on history encouraged the development of dreadnought battleships worldwide.

WILLIAM MCKINLEY: The twenty-fifth president of the United States, serving from 1897 until his assassination in Buffalo, New York, in September 1901.

WESLEY MERRITT: U.S. major general of the army who became the first military governor of the Philippines following the fall of Manila to U.S. forces on August 13, 1898. He relinquished his post to Major General Elwell Otis two weeks later, on August 30.

Nelson A. Miles: Veteran of the Civil and Indian wars, Miles was commanding general of the U.S. Army during the Spanish-American and Philippine-American wars.

James A. Moss: David Fagen's immediate superior in the U.S. Twenty-Fourth Infantry, Lieutenant Moss's punishments are generally credited with influencing Fagen's decision to join the Philippine rebels on November 17, 1899.

Elwell S. Otis: U.S. Army major general and second military governor of the Philippines. Generally unliked by his officers and men, who called him "Grandma Otis."

Herman Hoffman Philip: American ambassador and career foreign service officer, he served in the Spanish-American War as a private in the Rough Riders. Wounded in battle, he was taken to the field hospital, where he was piled among the dead.

Charles Johnson Post: Cartoonist for the *New York Journal* who joined the Seventy-First New York Volunteers in 1898 and fought in the Santiago campaign. His *The Little War of Private Post* is considered one of the best accounts of soldier life during the war.

E. Spencer Pratt: U.S. consul general to Singapore from 1893 to 1899. Emilio Aguinaldo said in his memoirs that both Pratt and Commodore Dewey promised Filipinos freedom if they fought with the United States against the Spanish Empire, a charge both denied.

Theodore Roosevelt: Assistant secretary of the navy, Rough Rider, William McKinley's second vice president, and twenty-sixth president of the United States following McKinley's assassination. An active proponent of U.S. imperialism.

William T. Sampson: U.S. Navy rear admiral known for his victory over the Spanish fleet in the Battle of Santiago Bay during the Spanish-American War.

Winfield Scott Schley: U.S. Navy commodore commanding the "Flying Squadron" blockading the Spanish fleet in Santiago Bay. When the Spanish ships began to emerge on July 3, 1898, he pressed the battle, for which Admiral Sampson never forgave him.

William Rufus Shafter: Commander of the U.S. Fifth Corps tasked with the attack on Santiago. Though he never feared defeat by Spanish troops, he feared decimation of his troops by tropical climate and disease.

Charles D. Sigsbee: Captain of the USS *Maine*, which exploded for unknown reasons in Havana harbor on February 15, 1898.

Jacob Hurd Smith: U.S. Army general infamous for ordering indiscriminate retaliation on the island of Samar following the Balangiga Massacre on September 28, 1901. After telling subordinates that he wanted Samar turned into a "howling wilderness," his men called him "Howling Jake."

William Howard Taft: First civilian governor of the Philippines, and twenty-seventh president of the United States, after Theodore Roosevelt.

Littleton Waller: U.S. Marine Corps major who led an ill-fated expedition across the island of Samar. His court-martial revealed the depredations ordered by General Jacob H. Smith, and in the end he was acquitted.

Leonard Wood: Career army officer placed in charge of the First U.S. Volunteer Cavalry, better known as the "Rough Riders." Appointed military governor of Santiago after its surrender, then military governor of Cuba after John R. Brooke.

CUBAN REVOLUTIONARIES AND OTHERS

Demetrio Castillo: Cuban revolutionary general whose troops secured Siboney and Daiquirí from Spanish troops before American troops landed for the Santiago campaign.

Evangelina Cosio y Cisneros: Imprisoned Cuban rebel who escaped from a Spanish jail with the help of a reporter from William Randolph Hearst's *New York Journal.* The resultant publicity ran for days in his paper and initiated a nationwide tour.

Tomás Estrada Palma: First elected president of Cuba, from 1902 to 1906. Before that he was leader of the New York–based Cuban Junta after the death of José Martí.

Calixto García: Cuban general in three successive uprisings that eventually turned into the Spanish-American War. Most closely worked with American forces during the Santiago campaign.

Maximo Gómez: Cuban Dominican *generalissimo* commanding all Cuban rebels during their 1895–1898 War of Independence from Spain. Known for his scorched-earth policy, which laid the countryside to waste.

Antonio Maceo: Cuban general and Maximo Gómez's second-in-command of the Cuban army of independence, killed on the battlefield in December 1896.

José Martí: Cuban poet, nationalist, and journalist who almost single-handedly developed and promoted the philosophy of *Cuba Libre*. Killed soon after landing in Cuba at the Battle of Dos Rios on May 19, 1895.

PHILIPPINE REVOLUTIONARIES AND OTHERS

Felipe Agoncillo: Emilio Aguinaldo's chief diplomat and representative to the negotiations at the Treaty of Paris that ended the Cuban phase of the Spanish-American War.

Emilio Aguinaldo: Philippine revolutionary leader who became the first president of the Philippines.

Anastacio Bartolomé: Filipino deer hunter who supposedly brought in the severed head of deserter David Fagen, later proven untrue.

Andrés Bonifacio: Founder of the revolutionary Katipunan devoted to the end of Spanish rule in the Philippines. Executed in 1897 by Emilio Aguinaldo's First Philippine Republic on charges of sedition and treason. Went by the title "El Supremo."

Josephine Bracken: Irish American common-law wife of the nationalist author José Rizal.

Antonio Luna: Commanding general of the Philippine Revolutionary Army and Emilio Aguinaldo's secretary of war, assassinated in Cabanatuan on June 5, 1899.

Apolinario Mabini: First prime minister of the Philippines, considered one of the principal intellectual architects of the Malolos Constitution. Exiled to Guam when he refused to take the American oath of allegiance.

Gregorio del Pilar: One of the youngest generals in the Philippine Revolutionary Army, his doomed stand at the Tirad Pass in Northern Luzon allowed Emilio Aguinaldo to flee his American pursuers and disappear into the mountains of the Central Cordillera. Affectionately known as "Goyo," del Pilar is one of the great tragic heroes of the revolution.

José Rizal: Philippine nationalist, writer, and scientist, his two anti-Spanish novels and execution inspired the Philippine Revolution. Considered one of the greatest Philippine heroes today.

Simeon Villa: Emilio Aguinaldo's chief of staff who kept a daily diary of their flight through the mountains of Northern Luzon.

SPANISH MILITARY, OFFICIALS, AND OTHERS

Basilio Augustín: Governor-general of the Philippines when it fell to the United States.

Ramón Blanco: Governor-general of Cuba during the Spanish-American War. Ordered Admiral Pascual Cervera to break out of Santiago Bay, initiating the destruction of his West Indies fleet.

Arsenio Martínez Campos: Governor-general of Cuba who refused to cast Cubans into "reconcentration" camps, thus relinquishing his imperial post to Valeriano Weyler.

Pascual Cervera: Spanish admiral who fought a last stand against the American fleet at the Battle of Santiago Bay.

Camilio García de Polavieja: Governor-general of the Philippines who ordered the execution of José Rizal.

Queen Isabella II: Queen regent of Spain during the Spanish-American War, known as "She of the Sad Destiny."

Arsenio Linares: Commander of the Spanish Fourth Army Corps at Santiago when the American forces invaded.

Patricio Montojo: Commander of Spain's Pacific Squadron during the Battle of Manila Bay.

José Toral: Major general in charge of Spanish forces at Santiago after Arsenio Linares was seriously wounded. "Capitulated" to Rufus Shafter after extensive and elaborate negotiations.

Valeriano Weyler: Governor-general of Cuba after the departure of Arsenio Campos. Called "the Butcher," he was the author of the despised *reconcentrado* policy designed to starve out the rebels.

MEMBERS OF THE PRESS, AND OTHER WRITERS

Stephen Crane: Famed author of *The Red Badge of Courage* and "The Open Boat," he wrote for various papers during the Santiago and Puerto Rico campaigns.

James Creelman: Star reporter for William Randolph Hearst's *New York Journal* during the war. Seriously wounded at the Battle of El Caney.

Richard Harding Davis: American journalist and author. Probably *the* most famous reporter in Cuba during the period of the Santiago campaign. Covered Theodore Roosevelt and the Rough Riders so exclusively that he was often called Roosevelt's press agent.

William Randolph Hearst: Controversial owner of the *New York Journal* and principal rival to Joseph Pulitzer's *New York World.* Their rivalry and frequent overreach spawned what was even then called "yellow journalism."

George F. Kennan: Famous journalist who covered the American Red Cross and also sat on its board of directors. A friend of Clara Barton, he also clashed with her frequently.

Rudyard Kipling: British imperialist poet whose poem "The White Man's Burden" urged the United States to assume the burdens and responsibilities of imperialism.

John Mitchell: Firebrand editor of *The Richmond Planet.* Opposed the enlistment of black soldiers because they could not choose their own officers.

Frank Norris: Author of *McTeague* and *The Octopus* who covered the Battle of El Caney, where he discovered the horrors of war.

Joseph Pulitzer: Controversial owner of *The New York World*, locked in a press war with William Randolph Hearst's *New York Journal.*

Carl Sandburg: Premier American poet of the twentieth century and Lincoln biographer. He didn't even know he wanted to be a poet yet when he invaded Puerto Rico with his friends in the Sixth Illinois Volunteers.

Charles Scott: Frederick Funston's college friend, and owner of *The Iola Register.* The paper was often the prime source for news about Funston's exploits in Alaska, Cuba, and the Philippines.

Sylvester "Harry" Scovel: Groundbreaking reporter for *The New York World* who covered Maximo Gómez's rebels so extensively that an enraged Valeriano Weyler put a bounty on his head.

Mark Twain: Called "the American," he was probably the most famous American writer of the era, and then the most famous anti-imperialist as well.

William Allen White: Frederick Funston's college friend and chronicler. Pulitzer Prize winner for his famous anti-Populist column "What's the Matter with Kansas?"

DOCTORS, NURSES, RELIEF WORKERS, AND MEDICAL RESEARCHERS

Clara Barton: Founder of the American Red Cross and one of the most famous American relief workers of her day. Plagued by depression and thoughts of suicide.

Carlos Finlay: Cuban epidemiologist and yellow fever researcher who determined the disease was transmitted through the mosquito *Aedes aegypti.*

Dr. William C. Gorgas: Chief sanitary officer of Havana who worked to eradicate yellow fever at the end of the Spanish-American War. Summoned Clara Maass to help in the effort.

Dr. Juan Guitéras: Cuban pathologist and physician instrumental in the yellow fever trials.

Janet Jennings: American nurse and reporter famous for her work aboard the "horror ship" *Seneca.* Testified about the medical care of U.S. soldiers before the Dodge Commission.

Jesse Lazear: American physician who died of yellow fever during the yellow fever trials.

Clara Maass: German American "trained nurse" who volunteered to be bitten during the yellow fever trials. Her death by yellow fever was featured in a long, somber editorial on the front page of *The New York Times.*

Dr. Walter Reed: U.S. Army physician leading the yellow fever trials.

George M. Sternberg: Army surgeon general during the Spanish-American War and the yellow fever trials.

CUBA AND ENVIRONS

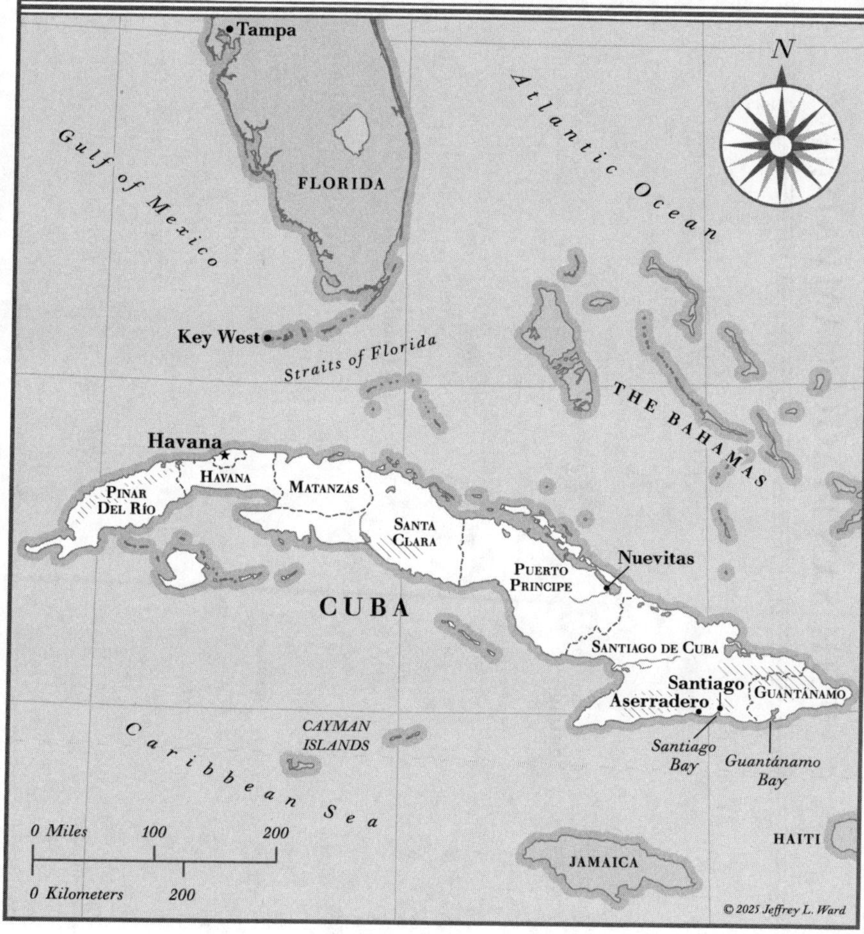

THE SANTIAGO CAMPAIGN

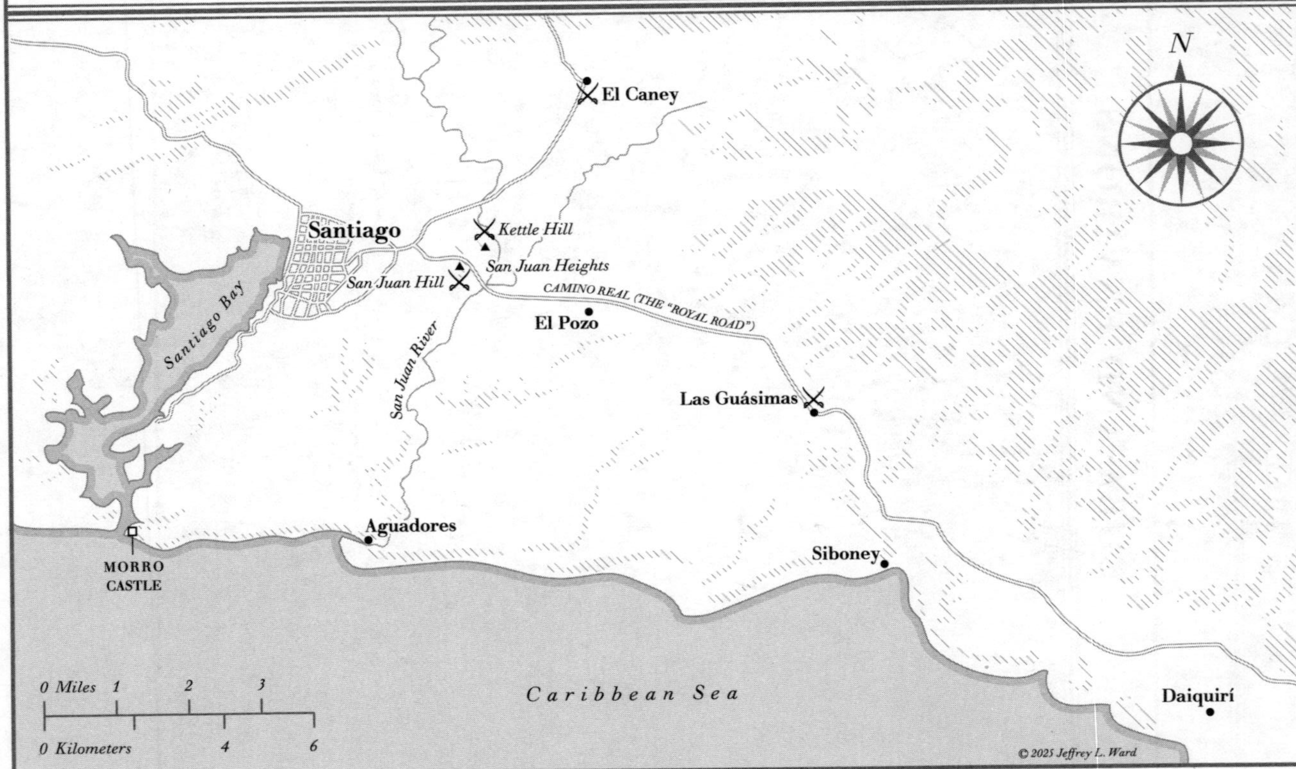

THE PHILIPPINES
N
South China Sea
Candon
Palanan
LUZON
Philippine Sea
Malolos
Manila Bay
Manila
Cavite
Batangas
MARINDUQUE
PHILIPPINES
LITTLETON WALLER'S "HIKE" ACROSS SOUTHERN SAMAR
MINDORO
ROMBLON
MASBATE
SAMAR
Calbayog
Catbalogan
Basey
Llorente
Tacloban
Balangiga
PANAY
CEBU
LEYTE
PALAWAN
BOHOL
NEGROS
Sulu Sea
Dapitan
MINDANAO
0 Miles 100 200
0 Kilometers 200
Celebes Sea
BORNEO
© 2025 Jeffrey L. Ward

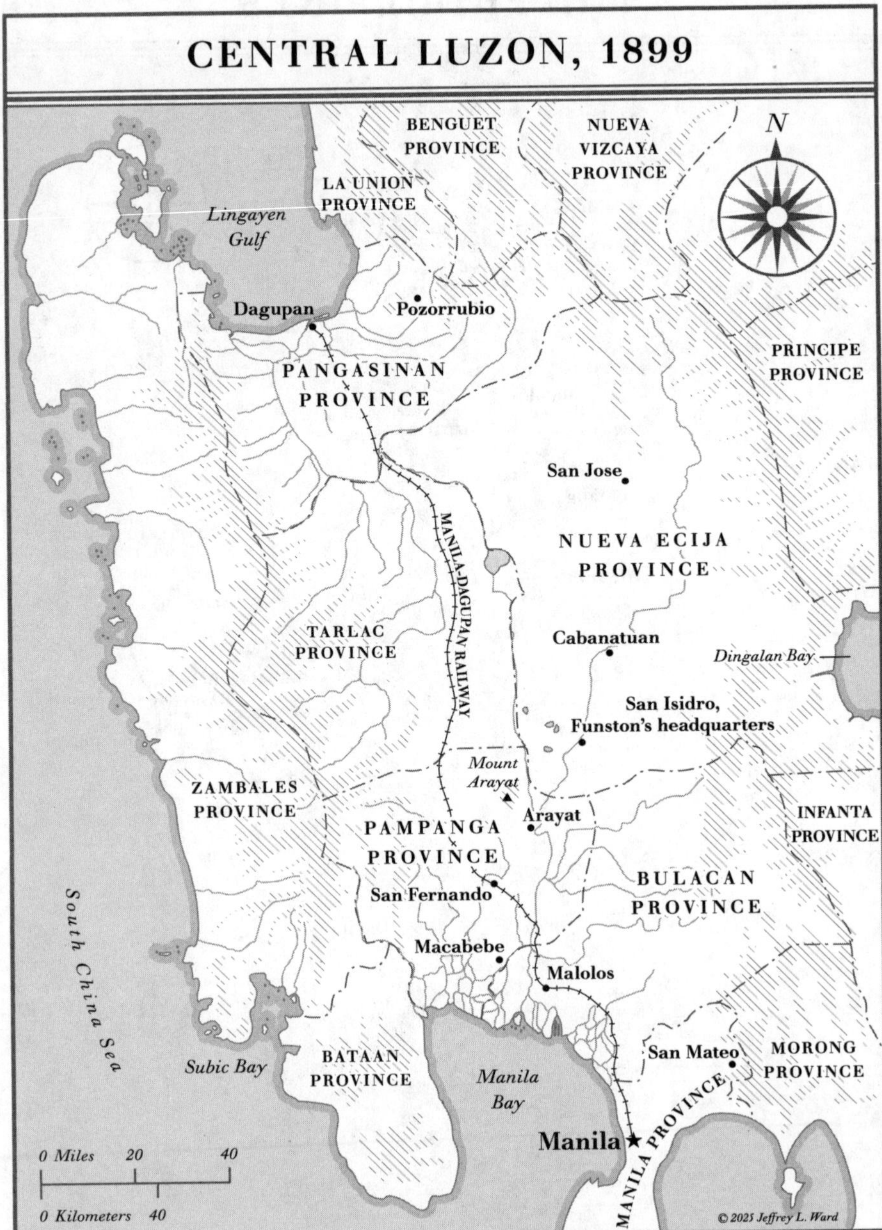
CENTRAL LUZON, 1899
BENGUET PROVINCE
NUEVA VIZCAYA PROVINCE
N
LA UNION PROVINCE
Lingayen Gulf
Dagupan
Pozorrubio
PANGASINAN PROVINCE
PRINCIPE PROVINCE
San Jose
MANILA-DAGUPAN RAILWAY
NUEVA ECIJA PROVINCE
TARLAC PROVINCE
Cabanatuan
Dingalan Bay
San Isidro, Funston's headquarters
Mount Arayat
ZAMBALES PROVINCE
Arayat
INFANTA PROVINCE
PAMPANGA PROVINCE
South China Sea
San Fernando
BULACAN PROVINCE
Macabebe
Malolos
Subic Bay
BATAAN PROVINCE
Manila Bay
San Mateo
MORONG PROVINCE
MANILA PROVINCE
Manila
0 Miles 20 40
0 Kilometers 40
© 2025 Jeffrey L. Ward

SPLENDID LIBERATORS

PROLOGUE

"Had the Nation Gone Mad?"

At 9:39 p.m. on February 15, 1898, Clara Harlowe Barton was one minute away from a moment that would change her nation forever. That Tuesday night, she sat at her desk at Havana's Hotel Inglaterra, plying through the pleas for relief in the world's newest abattoir. Her seventeen-year-old American National Red Cross had just come home from aiding Turkey's beleaguered Armenians; now stories of "starving Cuba" filled the news. Revolution pummeled the island for the third time since 1868; in order to starve out rebels, the Spanish Crown drove peasants into "concentration camps" and burned their farms. During eighteen months in 1896 and 1897, more than 225,000 *reconcentrados* died from disease and starvation. The Red Cross put the death toll closer to 425,000.

That Christmas, Barton had turned seventy-six. She still toured disasters the way high society toured the Wonders of the World. Since the Civil War, relief efforts had taken her to wars, floods, fires, famines, cyclones, and earthquakes. The world revered the straight-spined spinster in the black dress who stood five feet tall; she focused disaster in her bright black eyes and saved lives. But miracles have a cost, and after each occasion she'd collapse and dream of death, its eventual release "the sweetest hour in my whole existence."

She'd been in Havana six days. On February 9 she'd visited the Palace of the Governor and paid her respects, then boarded the sleek white USS

Maine. The solemn, bespectacled Captain Charles Sigsbee squired her around his twenty-four-gun battleship—the soaring bridges connecting three deckhouses, black-painted guns, gilded bow. Sailors in dress whites stood at attention like dolls. The ship had anchored in the harbor as a "friendly act of courtesy" to Spain, but U.S. Consul General Fitzhugh Lee believed she could protect American lives and property in this war-torn land. Away from the ship, Barton was spending much of her time in a warehouse called Los Fosos, four long buildings housing hundreds of *reconcentrados* who were dying so quickly their graves went unnamed. A "grim, terrible pile of black coffins" stood guard at each entrance; inside, she faced "death-pallid mothers lying with glazing eyes."

At least for the moment, she enjoyed a brief lull. The hotel was still, one of those colonial donjons lush with tropical flowers, a fountain, and gardens. Her window peered south toward a dark sea. To the right lay the harbor, its narrow entrance guarded by the grim Morro Castle. At nine p.m. she'd heard the melancholy strains of Taps, no doubt from the *Maine.* How many times had she heard a bugle play that beautiful, sad tune?

Afterward, many recalled their exact location at 9:39 p.m. At the redbrick German Hospital in Newark, New Jersey, twenty-one-year-old Clara Louise Maass had just been promoted to head nurse; she supervised the student nurses, who lived in shoebox rooms in the colonnaded Trefz Hall. Three years earlier she'd been like them: rising at 5:30 a.m., leaving the wards fifteen and a half hours later. Hard work, but an honor, for in 1890 the United States boasted only thirty-five nursing schools with a mere 471 graduates; this, at a time when doctors realized that the two greatest life-saving advances in medicine over the past thirty years had been aseptic surgery and trained nursing. Maass traced her rounds, dressed in crisp blue-and-white stripes, white muslin cap with a black ribbon, thermometer pushed through a buttonhole. This was *her* uniform—the army of her heroes Florence Nightingale and Clara Barton.

In tiny Iola, Kansas, thirty-two-year-old Frederick N. Funston signed on the dotted line. From August 16, 1896, to January 10, 1898, the five-foot-four-inch congressman's son had fought in the same conflict Barton now tried to relieve. In his eighteen months combating the Spanish imperial army, he'd survived seventeen battles; had seventeen horses shot from under him; been wounded in both lungs, an arm, and a hip; and contracted malaria. When he returned to New York, he weighed two-thirds of his normal 120 pounds and coughed up blood. The next morning, he'd hop the Kansas City Express to formalize a three-and-a-half-month lecture contract with the theatrical manager J. A. Young. The "little fellow" who'd soon become one of turn-of-the-century America's most controversial characters had decided to mount the stage.

Within sixty seconds, events were set in motion turning two strangers into Funston's prey. Both would be famous, both see themselves as liberators, and both be disparaged with racial slurs. The younger, David Fagen of Tampa, was a nineteen-year-old phosphate miner who worked hellish ten-hour shifts for one dollar a day. He wanted out, and saw that escape through the army. He'd travel the globe while proving to whites that the "Buffalo Soldiers" were anyone's equal.

Another man, older by six years, argued with fellow patriots in a Hong Kong café. Emilio Aguinaldo y Famy, the Philippine Revolution's unlikely embodiment, had evolved from an unknown provincial mayor to become the leader of eight million Filipinos. He was slim, stubborn, clever, and a little vain: even today, historians cannot agree on the man who became the Philippine George Washington. Nonetheless, in 1896–1897 his army fought Spain to a standstill, and he'd accepted exile in exchange for an end to the war. Now he wanted back, debating how to return. At the moment, all doors seemed closed to him. In an instant, Fate showed the way.

Events of the next minute sucked American writers into its slipstream. More famous and soon-to-be-famous writers would be crammed together in thought and proximity than in any other sixty-six-day span in U.S. history, and it changed the way Americans saw themselves. "There is precious little glory in war," an unknown Frank Norris would write in six months: "I've made a roof for myself to sleep under, out of boards that were one glaze of dried blood, though I didn't find it out till morning." Within a year, he wrote *McTeague*, the ultimate condemnation of the American Dream. "I heard somebody dying near me. He was dying hard," wrote Stephen Crane, already famous for *The Red Badge of Courage*. Where he'd plucked that novel from his imagination, the death rattle of a nearby army surgeon in a Cuban firefight would be all too real. The next sixty seconds would embitter Mark Twain against "his" America, place reporter Sylvester Scovel within hours of execution, and make handsome Richard Harding Davis a household name.

One writer did not yet know he wanted to write: twenty-one-year-old Carl August Sandburg, son of a blacksmith's helper in Galesburg, Illinois. In time he would be among America's most celebrated poets, lauded for lines critics called biblical. This Tuesday night, he went to bed at 9:30 p.m. and was asleep nine minutes later. In two months he would enlist in the rush of patriotism that swept up nearly every boy he knew in town.

If one person welcomed the approaching moment, it was Assistant Secretary of the Navy Theodore Roosevelt Jr., age thirty-nine. In almost exactly one year, on February 12, 1899, Brigadier General Samuel B. M. Young, Roosevelt's commander and friend, would write about these days. "I often recall with much pleasure our luncheon a year ago at the Metropolitan Club in Washington, when you were Assistant Secretary of the Navy and told us that the Battleship Maine was ordered to Havana," Young wrote in a private letter. "How we were unanimous in the belief, and I doubt not in hope, that War with Spain was inevitable . . . My assurance turned out as we predicted and desired. How we talked it over like enthusiastic college boys, and how particularly gratifying that it all came out, even rosier than our enthusiasms had pictured it." It is not a letter often found in the heroic biographies that would come.

The night had been inauspicious for the *Maine*'s Captain Sigsbee. A south wind breathed across Havana Bay. The Spanish man-of-war *Alfonso XII* bobbed to one side, the Spanish mail boat *Legazpi* to the other. Nearly four hundred yards astern lay the American steamer *City of Washington*: her passengers leaned on the rails, the air so motionless they could hear accordion music drift from Havana.

At eight p.m. the watch reported "All secure." The crew had turned in. Sigsbee sat at a table on his cabin's port side and about thirty minutes later finished a report to Roosevelt about the wisdom of placing torpedo tubes aboard warships. He then started an apologetic letter to his wife. Just that day he'd discovered in the pocket of his thin civilian coat a letter to her from an old friend that he'd forgotten for ten months. His mess attendant, James Pinckney, had just helped him don the coat; Sigsbee described Pinckney as "a light-hearted colored man, who spent much of his spare time in singing, playing the banjo, and dancing jigs." Sigsbee realized that the man playing Taps was a marine bugler named Newton, "given to fanciful effects" when playing standard bugle calls. Both men were part of that comfortable onboard routine that barely brushed his consciousness. In another thirty minutes, both were dead.

At 9:40 p.m. Sigsbee hoped he'd apologized to his wife sufficiently. He sealed the envelope, and a huge explosion tore from amidships, followed by a sickening lurch. A "bursting, rending, and crashing sound or roar of immense volume" filled his ears. The *Maine* trembled and angled up, then listed to port, throwing him from his chair. The cabin's eight electric lights snuffed out. Smoke and blackness enfolded him. Then he heard screams.

"Every war is ironic, because every war is worse than expected," wrote the critic Paul Fussell—and even those who welcomed what spun from this moment's cataclysm would stand aghast at the consequences. All three young nations snared by the conflict were more similar than any cared to admit, their volunteer forces born in waves of sentiment, each convinced it alone promised freedom—the second and most merciless of man's ancient creeds.

All three believed themselves liberators—*and* made choices that echo today. Americans broke promises implicit in the way they imagined themselves. Cubans hoped to manipulate the northern giant, and learned otherwise. Filipinos were the most tragic, naïve in their choice of saviors, realizing too late that they'd exchanged one master for another.

What Cubans call the War of Necessity, Americans call the Spanish-American War. The difference suggests the fraught nature of memory. U.S. historians describe it variously as America's first true war of empire, a commercial recasting of "manifest destiny," a global assertion of machismo, or an adolescent *yowp* of "war fever." The diplomat John M. Hay called it a "splendid little war," proving once again that "winning" was a natural outcome of America's virtues. The "manifest destiny" that swept away Native Americans to create a transcoastal nation fulfilled Heaven's plan:

"Away, away, with all these cobweb tissues of rights," wrote the newspaperman John O'Sullivan, referring to the rights of Indian tribes. "The American claim is by the right of our manifest destiny to overspread and to possess the whole of the continent which Providence has given us." If Providence gave Americans the right to civilize a continent, why not the world?

The short war in Cuba gained the United States the Philippines, Guam, and Puerto Rico; turned the nation into a Pacific power; and created beliefs that America was a stern yet benevolent country tasked by Destiny to enforce peace and bring prosperity to the world. If Cuba's liberation created for Americans a vision of themselves as emancipators, the Philippine "liberation" turned so savage that the public shut it out of mind. It is easier to forget unsavory truths than to face them. The new Philippine Republic believed that the United States would deliver them from Spain, as it had the Cubans. Instead, the war that resulted transformed the archipelago into a postapocalyptic wasteland of famine, disease, ecological disaster, and hundreds of thousands dead.

The Splendid War created this, becoming the template for every American "small war" in the twentieth and twenty-first centuries. It was a "war of choice" that started in a wave of idealism and disintegrated into brutality. America's dependence on overwhelming force would form the assumption that, as in Cuba, war should be quick and relatively bloodless. Instead, outgunned opponents became an insurgency: the U.S. response throughout the coming decades would proceed with such near-identical ruthlessness as to seem scripted. Though usually treated as separate conflicts, the wars in Cuba and the Philippines should be seen as a continuum—one that begins with two similar Cuban and Filipino poet-martyrs who shape their nations' identities and ends with the United States entering as a savior, only to become a scourge. One is reminded of the opening of T. E. Lawrence's *Seven Pillars of Wisdom*, where the ideal of a people "devoted to freedom" heats first to an "unquestioning possession" and then to an "overmastering greed" for victory. "By our own act," Lawrence wrote, "we were drained of morality, of volition, of responsibility, like dead leaves in the wind." As we'd already done to Native Americans, in order to save them, we had to kill them.

How did this happen so quickly, affect the individual American, and shape the national character? The consequences were as momentous as casualties were light: overnight it seemed the nation morphed into an imperialistic power in the mold of the European empires it disparaged. This was the war in which General Jacob Smith demanded, "I want no prisoners. I wish you to kill and burn"; in which American doctors and a nurse martyred themselves against yellow fever; in which black Americans watched prejudice grow worse; in which an exhausted Clara Barton wrote, "Had the nation gone mad?" Others felt uneasy about a change they did not understand. On October 12, 1899, Minnesota governor John Lind tiptoed around his misgivings when welcoming home state volunteers from the Philippines: "The mission of the American volunteer soldier has come to an end. For the purposes of conquest he is unfit, since he carries a conscience as well as a gun."

The United States was born in revolt; it survived the cataclysmic rebellion of 1861–1865. But not until the conflict in Cuba and the Philippines did America's love of war become so bold that one can track the transformation. On June 2, 1897, Theodore Roosevelt told students of the Naval War College: "All the great masterful races have been fighting races, and the minute that a race loses the hard fighting virtues, then . . . no matter how skilled in commerce and finance, in science or art, it has lost its proud right to stand as the equal of the best . . . No triumph of peace is quite so great as the supreme triumphs of war." The speech was published to glowing reviews and would be, in one form or another, justification for military buildup throughout the twentieth and twenty-first centuries.

With the events in Cuba and the Philippines, the United States increasingly became a "culture of war" with a sense of global purpose, prone to jingoistic eruptions. The rhetoric of war became that of patriotism: "God has not been preparing the English-speaking and Teutonic peoples for a thousand years for nothing but vain and idle self-contemplation and self-admiration," claimed the Roosevelt ally Albert Beveridge. "No, he has made us the master organizers of the world" in order to govern "savages and senile peoples." Even the Pulitzer Prize–winning newspaper scribe William Allen White would rationalize the change: "It is the Anglo-Saxon's manifest destiny to go forth in the world as a world conqueror. He will take possession of all the islands of the sea. He will exterminate the peoples he cannot subjugate. That is what fate holds for the chosen people. It is so written. Those who would protest will find their objections overruled. It is to be."

The culture of war became indelible: a new Orwellian world in which, according to Paul Fussell, war becomes "peacekeeping" and the acceptance of any act "in the name of freedom" a citizen's duty. "Those who challenged the authenticity of American altruism were by definition evil-doers and mischief makers," observed the historian Archibald Cary Coolidge. "So fully were Americans in the thrall of the moral propriety of their own motives as to be unable to recognize the havoc their actions often wrought on lives of others."

It's easy for moral certitude and blindness to be one. At its heart lay a darker certainty: those who needed our help were lesser beings—because they were not American. It lay in the order of things that they accept American guidance; dissenters were not only misguided but corrupt, and thus enemies. The myth plays out often—in my life, from the Bay of Pigs to Vietnam, Iraq, and Afghanistan. The leaders we elect always act surprised when things go awry.

Since one classical definition of mental illness is the tendency to repeat obviously self-destructive behavior, one wonders how deeply our cherished myths make us willfully blind and mad. Though those in power rarely heed historical lessons, neither do the Americans who vote them in. "A people unaware of its myths is likely to continue living by them," warned the cultural historian Richard Slotkin, "though the world around that people may change."

There are places where resentment shapes our image. Cuba and the Philippines rank high. Three nations forged modern identities in those years; each saw itself as freedom's messenger. If the memory of the two wars is barely preserved in the United States, it lives in the collective consciousness of Cubans and Filipinos. In both nations, anger prevails for the injustices of those calling themselves saviors. The bitterness of the broken promise persists through centuries.

Most narratives of the Splendid War adopt an American viewpoint, yet doing so turns a blind eye to its wider truths. In the summer of 2018, I traveled through Cuba to retrace the footsteps of Frederick Funston, Theodore Roosevelt, the Cuban rebel Calixto García, and the two Claras—Maass and Barton. My wife, Kathy, and I followed in the footsteps of Carl Sandburg as he marched through Puerto Rico. In the spring of 2019, I flew to Manila and its surrounding provinces, tracking David Fagen and Emilio Aguinaldo, their pursuer Funston, Philippine patriots who contributed to an apocalypse, American patriots who asked "What have we done?" In each place, I collected narratives and documents unavailable in the United States, hoping to see the drama from all angles. I meant to finish earlier, but in February 2020 a drunk driver nearly killed us in a nighttime crash. Yet that delay allowed the unfolding of events that cast the reckoning in sharper focus—the January 6, 2021, attack on the U.S. Capitol; Cuba's nationwide protests and incarcerations; the election of the son of the dictator Ferdinand Marcos to the Philippine presidency and his recasting of fact and history. All speak in some fashion to warring impulses in the three cultures, and the way narratives change given time and ideological need.

It begins with the *Maine*. Four nations would be pulled together beneath the still surface of Havana harbor in a catastrophe that can still be felt and heard. Individuals who believed in the purity of the dream of freedom learned instead that they had become its captive.

Part I

"WHAT IS A NATION?"

The guerilla is like a poet.
He moves with the green brown
multitude.

—"THE GUERILLA IS LIKE A POET,"
JOSE MARIA SISON

1

Martyrs

On Holy Tuesday of April 1895, nine members of a secret society called the Katipunan plunged into the craggy San Mateo Mountains southeast of Manila. The range forms the heart of the West Valley Fault system, a twelve-hundred-kilometer tectonic fracture stretching from Northern Luzon, through Metro Manila, and south to Mindanao. From 1608 to 2016, at least 25,100 earthquakes were recorded along this fault; Filipinos fear it will spawn the "Big One" that kills them all. After three days, the climbers reached the limestone caves of Mount Tapusi, 1,397 feet above sea level. Andrés Bonifacio, their baby-faced "El Supremo," declared that in these caves—where the mythic freedom fighter Bernardo Carpio was entombed—they must pledge their lives to founding a new nation. He dug some charcoal from his pocket and scratched on the wall "Long live Philippine Independence!" Each Katipunero signed his name, some with trembling hands, others with tears in their eyes.

Bonifacio had a fine sense of theater. Carpio was said to possess the strength of Samson; like Samson, he'd been betrayed, in his case by Spaniards, then trapped between two giant boulders, perhaps for eternity. In some versions, he separated the mountains, just as the Greek Titan Atlas held up the sky. In others, he forever tried to break free. Earthquakes rumbled with each attempt; escape would mean his death as the mountains fell. Thousands would die. But what, Bonifacio asked, was the life of any one man in the name of freedom?

Be ready, he warned. The time of martyrdom nears.

Martyrdom infused the Cuban and Philippine revolutions, a fact few Americans understood. The word stems from the Greek *martys*, "witness": the martyr watches the signs. Speaking of Mahatma Gandhi, the psychoanalyst Erik Erikson said that it is easy "to kill or be killed," but the martyr shapes death into a lens, allowing others to see why they must live and fight on.

Cuba and the Philippines were similar in more ways than in their rebellions. Both were Spanish possessions, discovered nearly thirty years apart during Spain's great age of nautical exploration. Cuba was the richest island of the West Indies, the Philippines the lushest of its Asian possessions. Both lay athwart vast continents, making them gateways to treasure. The archipelago was blessed with its famous "Manila hemp," used for the rope essential for ocean empires; Cuba was rich with sugar and tobacco. By 1896 the United States bought most of Cuba's tobacco, while 90 percent of its hemp came from the Philippines.

Even Oscar F. Williams, the neglected U.S. consul in Manila, noted the similarities. "Conditions here and in Cuba are practically alike," he wrote to his State Department handlers: rebellion could exist because Spain was a shadow of her former glory. Once Earth's greatest empire, her dominion had included the Low Countries, parts of Italy and Germany, most of Central and South America, the islands of the Caribbean, the Philippines, the Marianas, Guam, and parts of North America. Peruvian gold and Mexican silver assured power; for two centuries great treasure fleets assembled in Havana to sail to Cádiz under heavy guard. Yet by the eighteenth century the Crown reeled from war to disaster and back, draining its resources at home and abroad. When France occupied Spain at the turn of the century, the resistance spawned a new guerrilla warfare that became the model for the world's outgunned. By 1826 every Spanish possession had gained independence except Cuba, Puerto Rico, the Philippines, and some tiny Pacific islands; by 1895 nearly 64 percent of Spain's 18.5 million inhabitants were poor and illiterate, with no real future before them and only fading glory behind.

Cuba and the Philippines were also deeply Catholic. Every Sabbath, peasants heard Holy Scripture; every Holy Week they watched passion plays of Jesus of Nazareth's crucifixion and resurrection, an act of defiance in the face of death. The Kingdom of God was always at hand: martyrs arise to change the world. The Cuban journalist José Julián Martí y Pérez and the Philippine novelist José Protasio Rizal Mercado y Alonso Realonda may have died a year apart and a world away, yet their deaths molded the Cuban and Filipino characters. Today the two are honored in monuments, holidays, and popular culture; streets are named for them in every city and village. As my Cuban guide Benito Albino Sr. said as we rolled east across his island, "We use Martí for everything." The same can be said of Rizal.

In Havana today, Martí's portrait seems to glower from everywhere: the high forehead with a widow's peak, thick brows and Groucho mustache, oddly translucent skin. He appears frail and tubercular, a common look among nineteenth-century intellectuals. He was indeed host to many ailments, but not TB. In Revolution Plaza, he gazes at traffic in the pose of Rodin's *The Thinker*; his marble statue, erected in 1905, would be the first of thousands across the country.

Born on January 28, 1853, in a modest two-story stucco house at the western edge of "Old Havana," Martí was the oldest child of eight and the only son. His Spanish parents moved to Cuba in 1850, his father a low-level police officer from Valencia, his mother from the Canary Islands. The nineteenth century was not a peaceful time: in 1848 all of Europe had convulsed when revolution rocked nearly fifty nations from the Atlantic Ocean to the Caucasus Mountains. It was hard for a young man in the rising "middle" class not to sympathize.

Such was Martí's bad luck to come of age during civil war. His mother believed in upward mobility and in 1865 enrolled her precocious son in the Municipal School for Boys in Havana, the prestigious home of the Cuban poet Rafael María de Mendive. The poet schooled Martí in the revolutionary creed of Simón Bolívar and such antislavery texts as *Uncle Tom's Cabin.* Martí's practical father finally laid down the law: the school was vain and high-priced, beyond their means. How could a boy make a living spouting Harriet Beecher Stowe? He apprenticed his son as a shopkeeper, but Mendive engineered a scholarship that allowed his prize pupil to continue his studies into his fifteenth year.

The year 1868 seemed electric with change. A two-year war by liberals against Queen Isabella II ended in September with her defeat and exile to Paris: she'd be remembered forever as "She of the Sad Destiny." Some hoped the "Glorious Revolution" would spread to the Caribbean, and on September 23, Puerto Rican separatists declared independence in the mountain town of Lares. The Spanish Army crushed them in four days.

Puerto Ricans never revolted again on such a significant scale, but in Cuba *Grito de Lares* was reborn. Oriente Province in the remote east was a perfect place to rebel. Every important Cuban rebellion started in Oriente's rugged 14,641 square miles, from the first in 1523 to Fidel Castro's Revolution of 1959: far from centers of power, it was filled with those at both ends of the economic spectrum who had plenty to gain from change. Landowners especially had contemplated revolution since the American Civil War. Wars of independence are often started by economic or political elites seeking better control of their fortunes: such was the case in 1776 in Philadelphia; such was the case now in the Oriente town of Bayamo. Sugar was king in Cuba: by 1867 the island was the world's largest sugar producer, its output at six hundred thousand tons. More than half was shipped to the United States, but Spain set such heavy customs on that market that in one famous case, $73,000 in duties were levied on a shipment worth $91,000. Left unchecked, Spain might bleed the Cubans dry.

Two weeks after the death of Puerto Rico's freedom movement, a forty-nine-year-old poet and sugar planter called for independence from Spain and slavery's end. On October 10, 1868, Carlos Manuel de Céspedes rang the morning slave bell at his La Demajagua sugar mill. When his slaves assembled, he read aloud his own *Grito de Yara* and told them they were free; if they chose, they could join him in a war of liberation against Spain. His proclamation echoed that of Puerto Rico; his flag mirrored the one flown over the Alamo—a lone star beside fields of red, white, and blue. Five hundred rebels and freed slaves disappeared with him into the Sierra Maestra Mountains between the coast and Santiago; when they emerged a month later, their numbers had grown to fifteen hundred. With this, Céspedes made liberation central to his vision of a free Cuba while also assuring himself of an army. Though razed by time and troops, La Demajagua still overlooks a long green valley rolling west toward the Gulf of Guacanayabo—an idyllic place from which to launch the Ten Years' War. By the time it ended, the economy lay in tatters, with hundreds of thousands slain or dead from starvation or disease.

In 1868 Martí still studied under his mentor, Mendive. Céspedes's revolt enflamed Havana, and on October 21, 1869, a letter signed by Martí in support of Céspedes fell into Spanish hands. Martí was thrown into jail for six months and, on March 4, 1870, sentenced to six years hard labor in a prison quarry outside the city walls. He was barely seventeen. An appeal by his parents lowered the sentence to exile, and in January 1871 Martí landed in Madrid. *Madre* and *Padre* hoped that the university studies might be calming, but the quarries had destroyed his health, and he walked with a cane. There could be no forgiveness: "Blood, always blood!" he wrote: Spain had "too much blood upon her head."

As he studied, the war dragged on. Céspedes had seen his revolt as part of a worldwide struggle, and Cuban archives mention English, Italian, Chinese, and even Spanish mercenaries joining the rebels. Few of them left accounts: most died from wounds or disease. But above all others, Americans joined. Such "filibusters" had a long pedigree in joining Latin American wars—for idealism, for adventure, to spread slavery outside the South, or to create personal empires. So many expatriate Cubans lived in New York, Florida, and New Orleans that from 1868 to 1898, patriot groups would pool funds, hire an American ship, and attempt to land men and arms. In June 1869 Spanish authorities executed two Americans trying to join Céspedes; in November 1873 fifty-three suspicious passengers ripped from the filibuster ship *Virginius* were shot in the back, beheaded, their heads mounted on spikes, bodies trampled by horses. The arrival of a British man-of-war saved the remainder.

In 1874 Céspedes died in battle, and leadership fell to the Camaguey rancher Salvador Cisneros Betancourt and the Bayamo educator Tomás

Estrada Palma. Since neither were soldiers, two generals arose: the Dominican commander Maximo Gómez, who'd learned his craft in Spain's war against France, and his seemingly indestructible lieutenant Antonio Maceo.

The thirty-eight-year-old Gómez cut a dashing figure, with jet-black hair, handlebar mustache, and rattail goatee hanging below his collar. He was Cuba's most feared *insurrecto*, the inventor of the devastating "Machete Charge." On October 26, 1868, he charged from ambush at Pino de Baire near Santiago, killing at least 200 soldiers; on February 19, 1874, his 700 rebels defeated 2,000 troops; a month later, 2,050 Cubans obliterated 5,000 Spaniards with only six casualties. Gómez was shot twice, in 1875 and 1896. The 1875 bullet plowed through his neck and never properly healed; he plugged the open wound with cotton and covered it with a bandanna, an easy way to pick him out on the battlefield.

In contrast, Antonio Maceo y Grajales was shot twenty-seven times yet seemed to shrug off injury. Born in 1845 near Santiago to a black Cuban woman and a white Venezuelan veteran, he knew the racism of Spanish rule. Maceo rose in the ranks, a rarity in the nearly all-white Cuban officer corps, yet he exuded a style and gentleness that commanded intense loyalty. In one apocryphal story, he considered releasing a female spy until his brother José completed the "sad but necessary task" of execution; in another, he shared an egg with a correspondent despite his own hunger. A "fierce fight" loomed, he said, "and you will need a clear head." Cubans called him the "Bronze Titan"; Spaniards, the "Greater Lion."

Yet without Céspedes to bind them, the rebels splintered into two broad factions: landowners hoping for economic and political freedom, and farmers and laborers seeking greater rights for the common man. In 1876 Spain sent 70,000 fresh troops under the newly appointed Governor-General Arsenio Martínez Campos, but war, attrition, and disease had worn them all down. By 1878, 91,095 Spanish troops, 50,000 rebels, and 100,000 civilians had died. Campos offered concessions, and in February 1878 combatants signed the lackluster Peace of Zanjón. After ten years of fighting, not one of the rebellion's original causes was resolved. Gómez went into exile; Maceo refused to sign and became a hunted man.

By then, Martí had returned to the New World: in 1874 he finished his studies and fled to Paris, where he met Victor Hugo; two years later he rejoined his family in Mexico City, where he married fellow expatriate Carmen Zayas-Bazán and wrote for liberal newspapers. Peace meant amnesty, and in August 1878 the couple returned to Havana, where their son, José Francisco, was born.

But ceasefire did not mean reform. That fall, Martí became Havana's voice for New York's Cuban Revolutionary Committee, better known as the Junta, soon *the* driving force behind continued revolt. The Junta sheltered Maceo and Gómez lieutenant Calixto García; it bankrolled the August 1879 *La Guerra Chiquita*, or Little War. Again Martí was deported to Spain; again he escaped and went to New York, where on January 9, 1880, the Junta made him a director. War must continue, he wrote, but those in its path had been drained by more than a decade of blood and ruin. In December 1880 the Little War wheezed to an end.

During this period, Martí woke to what he called a greater threat than Spain. Los Estados Unidos and her presidents had been drawn to Cuba for decades, an attraction composed of idealism, fear of the future, and greed. In 1805 Thomas Jefferson had considered annexation for an undisclosed sum; John Adams felt that the island would "fall like a ripe fruit" if severed from Spain. In 1848 James K. Polk offered $100 million; in 1854 Franklin Pierce bid $130 million. The interest had everything to do with slavery: the 1841 Cuban census recorded four hundred thousand slaves, and Southerners hoped the institution would flourish in an annexed Cuba.

The dream lingered after the Civil War, driven by commerce, not slaves. During the last forty years of the nineteenth century, America experienced unprecedented growth: her raw materials seemed inexhaustible; the technology to transport and convert them always improved. From 1865 to 1895, wheat production increased by 256 percent; corn by 222 percent; coal by 800 percent. Miles of operable railway grew sixfold. The United States expanded outside her coastal borders: first with the 1867 purchase of Alaska from Russia; second by American businessmen's steady takeover of Hawaii, an encroachment later furthered by the 1893 coup d'état.

In Cuba, U.S. dominance was more subtle. By 1880 most sugar plantations, cattle ranches, coffee estates, and tobacco farms that survived the war owed massive debt to U.S. banks, merchants, and shipping firms; a law passed that year allowed creditors to seize the land of those in default.

In 1884 the U.S. consul reported that "out of the twelve or thirteen hundred planters on the island, not a dozen are said to be solvent," a situation that worsened when Europe's sugar beet industry flooded the market with cheap sugar, driving down Cuban prices. When many planters declared bankruptcy, U.S. investors scooped up their properties at rock-bottom prices.

Realizing this, Martí cast himself as Cuba's Jeremiah. What good did it do, he warned, to break Spain's yoke, only to become a U.S. colony? He sounded the alarm from what he called the belly of the "monster," yet the Monster seemed uncertain. A huge body of public opinion still opposed the idea of empire, and though many called Spain the "sick man of Europe," its imperial army was sizable: 200,000 troops in Cuba; 8,000 in Puerto Rico; 30,000 in the distant Philippines. The United States, by comparison, could barely field an army of 25,000 men.

For the next fifteen years, New York was Martí's base. He wrote about Native Americans, the Statue of Liberty, a Hungarian Party of Christ, and America's lynchings; he founded several magazines; and he wrote one novel, two books of poetry, dozens of short biographies, and hundreds of English and Spanish newspaper articles. But always he wrote about "poor suffering Cuba," which "must be considered an altar for the offering of our lives." He believed that only a war of independence could forge a *patria* uniting all classes and races. "Cubans do not live as Spaniards do," Martí claimed. Spain was a parasite sucking them dry. The two peoples shared no common goals or memories. "Peoples are joined only by bonds of fraternity and love."

This idea of *patria* was a powerful global concept in its day, its most renowned expression an 1882 lecture by the French scholar Ernest Renan. "*Qu'est-ce qu'une nation?*" he asked: What is a nation? He replied in mystical terms: "A nation is a soul, a spiritual principle" bound by "a rich legacy of memories," driven by "the desire to live together, the will to perpetuate the value of the heritage that one has received in an undivided form." Just as important was the need to *forget*: a people could not live together in peace unless they forgot the violence often inherent in nation-building. To Renan, overcoming common grief bound a people as one.

For Romantic nationalists, the genius of a given people was paramount: they loved the idea of "national essence." When was France most

French, the United States most "American"? Martí shifted the frame forward, from "What is Cuban?" to "What will Cuba be?"

Ironically, the "Monster" was the only place where he could explore such ideas. In Cuba and other Latin countries, he would be exiled, imprisoned, or killed. He envied Americans' freedom of speech and was amazed when he heard speakers call for "the destruction of the capitalist system." Yet he feared his adopted home: feared its restless drive to expand, often for profit; its pervasive racism and abuse of its ideals. In a heartbeat the United States could absorb smaller countries around it. "The scorn of our formidable neighbor who does not know us is Our America's greatest danger," he wrote, thus predicting a century of U.S. intervention.

Prophecy comes with a price. Martí's wife hated New York; she moved back to Havana, obtained a divorce, married a Spanish veteran, and raised their son to be loyal to the Crown. Martí's fellow exiles neither liked nor trusted him. General Gómez thought he was more poet than rebel—all talk, no action. Maceo believed him a schemer. Martí worried that the two planned a military coup should Cuba become free. "A nation is not founded as a military camp," he wrote in an October 20, 1884, letter to Gómez: it sprang instead from those mystical elements he dubbed *Cuba Libre*. Cuban veterans reviled him for the perceived insult to their hero. Tensions escalated until Martí challenged one detractor to a duel, an event headed off by cooler heads.

Florida's cigar industry saved him. Since 1878, thousands of cigar workers had settled in Key West and Ybor City outside Tampa; by 1895 Florida's 515 cigar factories had rolled 161,084,191 cigars. Martí's first trip to Ybor City, on November 25, 1891, was a revelation. Florida's Cuban society was more diverse than New York's, a mixture of white owners and black workers espousing racial equality. Martí's writing began to reflect as much: the coming revolution would be for "all Cubans, regardless of color," he wrote, and Junta rolls swelled. Each week, cigar workers and their trade groups donated a day's wage to the cause. They pulled in so much money that by 1895, thirty boatloads of arms and ammo were purchased solely by cigar makers and smuggled to Cuba.

A successful revolution needs four ingredients: a complaint, a solution, a leader, and a means to carry out goals. Complaints and solutions were obvious, and Martí's "voice" made him the leader. The Floridians' numbers, money, and fervor supplied the means. But to rebel a third time, Martí must swallow his pride. In the fall of 1892, he visited Gómez in the Dominican Republic, and in 1893 he met Maceo in Costa Rica. On February 24, 1895, when war broke out, cigar makers flooded Tampa's streets, crying, "*Cuba Libre! Cuba Libre!*"

Short of seeing Cuba freed, Martí had accomplished every goal. But how could he maintain credibility if he did not join the war? "I promoted the war," he wrote to a friend on March 25, and "with it my responsibility begins, not ends." That day, he wrote several letters, all resembling goodbyes. To his mother: "In the anger of your love, the sacrifice of my life hurts you." To his son José: "I am leaving for Cuba tonight, leaving without you, when you should be at my side." He wills him his watch and chain. Photos show a wan, skeletal man: it was hard to eat with decayed molars; he had cirrhosis of the liver, some undiagnosed "brain problem," a cancerous spot on his right testicle. Over the Junta's objections, he set out with Gómez by boat on April 9; the next night, the party landed on a remote, stony beach on the island's eastern point and clambered uphill through thorns and mud. There was no going back. Five days later, on April 15, Gómez promoted him to major general in the new Cuban Liberation Army.

A few days earlier, Maceo had landed near coastal Baracoa, Cuba's oldest and most isolated town. The plan was to meet at Guantánamo, gaining adherents along the way. But Gómez and Martí got lost in the peninsular wilderness, and for ten days Martí shouldered his rifle, hung his machete from his belt, and marched. He carried a bag with a hundred cartridges over one shoulder, a tube with maps over the other, a knapsack with fifty pounds of medicine, clothing, books, a hammock, and a blanket on his back. He felt happy because he felt useful; he ate heartily at night and woke sore in the morning. "How affectionate" the stars seemed to him, he wrote—a simple joy he had never known.

By May 17 they'd joined with Maceo, and their ranks swelled to three thousand, but with those numbers came Spanish attention. Martí tended the wounded: one shot through the thigh, another through the shoulder, a third in the back. He wrote, always wrote. The recruits were young and hungry: one is timid, another "honest and stuttering," a third vain about his college degree.

On May 18 Martí starts a letter to Manuel Mercado, a lawyer in Mexico City. He muses on his life and warns of America: "I have lived in the monster, and I know its entrails; my sling is David's." But he leaves the letter unfinished, and it will be his last piece of writing. The Spaniards have captured a courier carrying letters that reveal Gómez's position—they march through the night and surprise the Cubans. Skirmishes surround the village of Dos Rios, where the rivers Cauto and Contramaestre join.

It is midday, May 19, 1895, and Martí is alone in the middle of shooting. He spots a young courier and yells, "Young man, charge!" then leads him on a suicidal charge straight at the Spanish lines. He wears a black jacket and tie and rides a white horse, a perfect target, if rather strange. The Spaniards cut him down. The courier is lucky: he loses his horse but staggers to tell Gómez the news.

Was Martí driven to prove himself? Did he choose a battlefield suicide rather than face his maladies? No one knows. Neither did the Spanish know at first whom they had killed. In some reports, Martí's body was buried on the spot; in others, Martí was still aboveground when rebels counterattacked, trying to save their prophet's body. But the Spanish pushed back, slightly wounding Gómez, and in the chaos the Spanish captain realized whom they had slain. They retreated to the fortress town of Remanganaguas, where Martí's corpse was embalmed; they hastened to Santiago, and his body was exhibited at Santa Ifigenia Cemetery. He lies there today, between Céspedes and Fidel Castro. One man who talked to Martí before his death told the press that he was "astonished to find in him at times a Christlike silhouette." Some claimed his death was "predetermined," and even Martí hinted at this in his letters.

By accident or design, Jose Martí's martyrdom had begun.

On the day of Martí's death, thirty-three-year-old José Rizal wrestled with the complexities of modern love. Three years earlier, Spanish authorities had exiled the slight novelist to Dapitan, a remote coastal town on the isle of Mindanao, about as far south as one could go and still be in the Philippines. This was a far cry from his native Calamba, the playground of rich Spaniards, thirty-one miles south of Manila and known for its hot springs.

Indeed, Dapitan was a charming place, far from Spanish crowds, with an acacia-lined square and coral beaches facing north on the Sulu Sea. Rizal planned the city's waterworks, drained marshes to eliminate mosquitoes, and discovered three new animal species that still bear his name. But it was the free eye clinic that brought international renown as the blind and half-blind from across Asia streamed to Rizal's clinic for cataract surgery. In February 1895 the American businessman George Taufer arrived from Hong Kong with his Irish stepdaughter, Josephine Bracken, in tow. Within a month, José and Josephine had planned their vows.

Such things were not done in the Spanish Philippines. The nineteen-year-old Bracken was described as "slender, a chestnut blond, with blue eyes, dressed with elegant simplicity, with an atmosphere of light (gaiety)." Rizal was an *ilustrado*, the native-born "intelligentsia" educated in Spain and exposed to liberal ideals. The Philippines of 1895 was just as racially repressive as Jim Crow America, and such unions were not permitted. It appalled Bracken's father, who returned to Hong Kong uncured and alone. It scandalized the Catholic Church, which refused to marry them. So they lived instead in common-law union at the beachfront clinic away from town. They were "very very happy," Bracken wrote: she got pregnant but would miscarry. The boy, named after Bracken's father, lived three hours.

Though most chronicles describe Rizal's romance as a brief interlude, it illustrates why he was revered by Filipinos and hated by Spain. If Cubans martyred Martí after his unnecessary death, Rizal *chose* that path on his own. Both were beatified for their writing, but where Martí invented Cuban identity as a mass upwelling of souls, Rizal's two novels satirizing Spaniards made him a marked man.

Rizal's hatred for the Spanish ran as deep as Martí's. When he was young, his mother was falsely accused of trying to poison a friend; she languished in prison for two and a half years before her acquittal. His family was thrown from their land in Calamba, where brutality was common. But his hatred did not exist in a vacuum. His childhood overlapped with what the historian Nick Joaquin called the "beginning of a nationalist consciousness" in the Philippines. On January 20, 1872, when Rizal was just ten, two hundred Filipino soldiers mutinied at Fort San Felipe Arsenal, not far from his home. Within seven days, most were executed;

three Filipino clergymen, known by the acronym *GomBurZa*, were garroted before forty thousand witnesses on February 17, 1872, at Manila's central park, the Luneta. This single act sank deeper than most, proving Spain capable of anything.

One thought apparently obsessed the young Rizal: How could one escape such a world? But he was a stellar student, and he soon realized that freedom might lie abroad. On May 3, 1882, he enrolled at the university in Barcelona, then transferred to Madrid's Central University to study medicine. Twelve years separated Martí's and Rizal's studies, but Madrid was still the insurgent capital of the Spanish Empire. The city had a history of street barricades, underground cells, and popular fronts; its annals were filled with young colonials schooled in Enlightenment ideals. Cuban radicals preached rebellion: "Liberties are secured by bullets," they taunted young Filipinos, "not by kneeling!" Indeed, 1880s Madrid was for them what 1920s Paris was for the "Lost Generation"—a glimpse of life *as it should be*, and the ideas they sent back radicalized the Philippines. Rizal and others launched the Propaganda Movement: its biweekly voice, *La Solidaridad*, carried articles of the same flavor as Martí's cries for *Cuba Libre*. "We suffered from an incurable patriotic madness," one member recalled. Their headquarters at 43 Atoche was awash with dandies dressed in coats, top hats, and canes; they indulged in long nights of drinking and the favors of *las cholas*, party girls from such "low" barrios as Chamberí and Lavapiés. Within a decade, most of these young Propagandists would be dead. Rizal became friends with such future revolutionaries as Antonio Luna, who, in a drunken argument over a woman, challenged Rizal to a duel, and José Alejandrino, one of the few to survive the coming war.

Rizal had his romances but was something of a prude, and by 1886 he'd moved to more sedate studies in Paris, Heidelberg, Leipzig, and Berlin. Yet freewheeling Madrid had made an impression, and in 1887 he published in Berlin the first of two novels that made him a famous, marked man. *Noli Me Tángere* (Touch Me Not) is a satire of the Spanish priests and government officials who ruled the Philippines; it starts as a love story, but does not end well. Juan Crisóstomo Ibarra, a young *ilustrado* like Rizal, returns home after seven years in Europe to marry his childhood sweetheart, Maria Clara. He has a rosy picture of his country, and as in Voltaire's *Candide*, the naïve and optimistic Crisóstomo slams hard against the real world. His father dies in jail; Maria Clara rejects his love and enters a convent; friends are killed in a rebellion. Crisóstomo is excommunicated and ends up as an outlaw.

No native son had ever dared create such a picture of Spanish rule. Written in Spanish and self-published, *Noli*'s effect back home was huge: it seemed to act as a focal point, triggering the old hatreds that linked the generations. Smuggled copies surfaced in Manila, and within weeks, barrio leaders petitioned for the expulsion of all friars. Instead, twenty-eight signers were jailed. Priests condemned *Noli* from the pulpit. One wonders how many Filipinos actually read the book, since only 10 percent of the population was literate. Yet those who did held important positions—and their condemnation or praise mattered. The Church consigned the work to the banned list of "*impias y pestilenciales novelas*" that included Balzac, Victor Hugo, and Zola. This only made *Noli* better known.

By the early seventeenth century, five religious orders had carved out huge spheres of influence in the Philippines. The Augustinians, Dominicans, and Franciscans took over Luzon; Jesuits and Recollects divided up Mindanao and the Visayas. They acquired massive estates, which they leased and ran in a tenant system. The largest structure in any town was the central cathedral, the true seat of power. Civil authority came and went, but friars stayed for life, and their word was God's. They controlled the parish budget, conducted the census, directed tax collection, chose recruits for military service, controlled the jails and police, held veto power over all native government, and could banish people without trial. As discontent grew in the provinces, the friars were cited as the main cause.

After *Noli*'s publication, Rizal returned to Europe to finish his studies and publish *El filibusterismo* (*The Reign of Greed*), a bitter sequel to *Noli*. He stayed with his friend and mentor Ferdinand Blumentritt, a professor of history and anthropology at Austria's University of Leitmeritz, where Rizal completed a thesis on the moral questions of anthropology. Were there true differences between races? he asked, concluding that biology had no basis in the current world order, which lay instead in the harsh logic of conquest and control. "No feeble persons wander to exotic lands," he wrote, only those "with the firm conviction that they have been called upon to exercise dominion" over native races. The conqueror always found fault in the conquered, largely because of that subjugation.

Something changed in Rizal after his second novel. In January 1891 he left Europe for the last time. Before leaving, he told Blumentritt of his intention to return home. "I am a fatalist in many things and I believe that we shall never see each other again in this life," his mentor replied. Rizal had hinted as much in a character sketch written after the publication of *Noli*. Even as a child, when his mother tucked him in at night with the tale of "the moth and the flame," he'd grown fascinated by the moth's predestination. "All my attention was fixed on the fate of the insect. I watched it with my whole soul," he wrote. "I gave to it my every thought. It had died a martyr to its illusions."

By the summer of 1891, he'd returned to Hong Kong, where the Filipino dissidents, who also called themselves a Junta, pushed him to lead a rebellion. The time was not right, he argued back, but could he be wrong? He'd heard about José Martí's Cuban Revolutionary Party in New York, and it dawned on him how much leverage the United States might have. The fact that the Propagandists never started a New York branch seemed a huge mistake. In March 1892 he wrote to Blumentritt, and his old professor warned, "One who would start a revolution must see at least the probability of success if he does not wish to burden his conscience with the futile shedding of blood." The colonies that had successfully rebelled had also received aid: the United States from France, Spain, and Holland; Latin American colonies from the United States; Greece from England, France, and Russia; Belgium from England and France. Luckily, those aiding rebels never conquered the countries themselves.

Rizal kept his thoughts close. He asked Governor-General Eulogio Despujol y Dusay for permission to come home. Despujol granted safe conduct if he promised not to preach revolt, and on June 26 the thirty-one-year-old writer stepped off the ship in Manila. Before doing so, he wrote a short piece, which was not published until after his death: "I wish to show those who deny us patriotism that we know how to die for our country and convictions." Within days, he set up La Liga Filipina, a mutual aid society seeking independence by gradual legal means. Spain believed that La Liga was another name for Propagandists, and on July 6 Rizal was exiled to Dapitan.

The exile had an unintended consequence: when La Liga disbanded, a twenty-nine-year-old member founded a more violent society. Andrés

Bonifacio had risen from Manila's vast slums, called the Tondo. His parents died when he was fourteen, leaving him in charge of two younger siblings. He sold paper fans to survive; became a clerk; read the latest French novels; and, like many others, joined the Masons. One night after Rizal's arrest, he attended a meeting at No. 64 Azcarraga of "The Highest and Most Respected Association of the Sons of the Country," or *Kataastaasang Kagalang-gagalang na Katipunan ng mga Anak ng Bayan*, better known as the Katipunan, or KKK.

Secret societies were inescapable in nineteenth-century revolutions; blood oaths, ceremonies, and iconography all appealed to the century's romanticism. If La Liga attracted moneyed classes, the Katipunan drew from the poor. Within a year, it had fourteen thousand members in Manila alone. The KKK borrowed symbols from the Catholic Church, the Masons, and Chinese triads; they performed mystic rites, used covert names and passwords, wore masks at meetings, and promised a horrible death for any member who revealed them to authorities. By 1893 Bonifacio had separated from conservative groups; two years later, he climbed to the reputed grave of Bernardo Carpio. "Reason tells us that we cannot expect anything [from Spain] but more and more sufferings, more and more treachery, more and more insults, and more and more slavery," he wrote in his "What the Filipinos Should Know." Revolt was the sole option: victory was certain, "for righteousness and the sanctity of duty are on our side."

Yet Filipinos were more likely to rally around a known hero like Rizal. On June 21, 1896, Bonifacio sent a deputy to see him, accompanied as cover by a blind man. They met at his eye clinic, spoke of the Katipunan, and Bonifacio begged for his support. But Rizal refused. The revolt was premature, the common people not ready, the Katipunan could not wage a sustained war. Where was the money? he asked. Where were the arms?

Yet the request must have unnerved him. He'd already sent a request to the newly appointed Governor Ramón Blanco, volunteering to serve as a surgeon in Cuba's yellow fever hospitals. Blanco's acceptance, dated July 2, gave him a pass to Manila and then aboard the monthly mail boat to Spain, where he'd receive an assignment from the war minister. Rizal took with him Josephine Bracken, some family members, and six students, but escape was not in the cards. His steamer missed the monthly mail boat, and from August 7 to September 2, he stayed aboard a Spanish cruiser anchored in the bay while awaiting the next mail packet. During this wait, he had no contact with the mainland.

And during this wait, the rebellion started without him. Two versions of the trigger exist, both occurring on August 20, two weeks before Rizal sailed. In the first, a terrified parishioner exposed the Katipunan's plans to Father Mariano Gil, the Augustinian curate of the Tondo slums. In the second version, rival supervisors at *Diario de Manila* revealed stacks of Katipunan propaganda printed and stored in the newspaper office. The results were identical: police arrested and tortured those on the discovered membership lists; vigilantes took to the streets, killing suspected conspirators. Hundreds of prisoners were packed into Fort Santiago, where at least one hundred died of suffocation.

Bonifacio took four days to react: on August 24 he appointed himself president of the Katipunan, making widespread his appellation "El Supremo." August 29 was set as the first day of war. But again, he waited too long. Skirmishes on the 25th and 26th warned Blanco of approaching peril. Bonifacio planned to dim the Luneta's lights on the 29th to signal the attack, but the lights never flickered. Waiting Katipuneros crept off, confused. The next morning, he led an attack on a powder magazine in the suburbs, but that fizzled, too. Blanco pressed his advantage and drove Bonifacio into the mountains outside Manila, bottling him up, never considering him enough of a threat to pursue.

Yet in places where El Supremo did not lead, revolt succeeded. Two days after his failed attack on August 31, three towns in Cavite Province south of Manila fell to the KKK. As the rebellion spread, Bonifacio became an irrelevant spectator, trapped on the sidelines.

During these two weeks, Rizal stayed apart on the cruiser, unable to participate if he'd desired. It is uncertain how much he knew of events, and on September 3 the mail boat arrived and he sailed away. But he was still blamed. As his ship plied west, tortured captives cried out that they'd used Rizal's name as a rallying point. Recruitment speeches ended with the words "Long live the Philippines! Long live Liberty! Long live Dr. Rizal!"

Rizal's mail boat had barely left the Suez Canal and entered the Mediterranean when, without warning or explanation, he was confined to his cabin. On October 5 they reached Barcelona: he was thrown into a dungeon and later that day transferred to a ship for Manila. As he steamed back, torturers amassed "evidence" from fifteen witnesses. One was probably his old classmate Antonio Luna. On November 12 Luna said, "The 'Katipunan' is the Liga Filipina"—a mistake, but a good indication of the rumor mill. He added, "The founder is Don Jose Rizal," also mistaken. But such statements were enough. Rizal was thrown into a cell in Fort Santiago on his return, and on December 3 the Crown charged him with treason, sedition, and forming illegal societies. The chief magistrate called him the "living soul of the insurrection."

Yet Blanco knew that martyrdom fuels resistance, so he decided to block a death sentence, a decision that displeased the mocked friars. Dominicans lobbied the queen to replace Blanco, and on December 13 the ultraconservative General Camilio García de Polavieja filled his shoes. Rizal denied the accusations, and on December 15 he even urged Katipuneros to stop fighting, since revolution without financial support was hopeless. It didn't matter: the court blamed him for everything, and on December 26 he was condemned to death by firing squad.

Shortly before his plea to the Katipunan, Rizal composed "Mi ultimo adiós," his final farewell, a long poem kept hidden in the pan of his cell's alcohol stove: "I'll go where there are no slaves, tyrants, or hangmen, where faith does not kill and where God alone does reign." At daybreak, Josephine Bracken was led to his cell. A Jesuit confessor married the two in a simple ceremony; Rizal told Josephine to take the alcohol stove when he was gone and bequeathed her one of his few books—Thomas à Kempis's *The Imitation of Christ.* Then she was led away.

Sometime later, the confessor and Rizal talked. Accounts are varied. In one version, Rizal exclaims, "What is death to me? I have sown the seed, others are left to reap." The priest says he took Rizal's confession and returned him to the fold, a suspect story, as a plea for forgiveness only served the Crown. He added that Rizal made two statements, both doubted to this day. "My presumption has ruined me," he mourned, which the Jesuit interpreted as regret for writing *Noli.* And, "It is in Spain and in foreign countries that I was ruined"—as though, if he'd only stayed in the Philippines and accepted his lot, this never would have happened.

Around seven a.m. Rizal was led from his cell. He'd donned a black suit, white shirt, and derby hat. His elbows were bound behind him as he marched a mile from Fort Santiago and through the walled gates of the Intramuros. Soldiers with fixed bayonets marched in front; two priests flanked him. The drum corps followed. The slow, steady walk took about twenty minutes. The route was hung with bunting and flags.

Rizal had been on this earth for thirty-five years, six months, and eleven days. The morning was crisp and bright, with a cloudless blue sky, but the young drummer Hilarion Martinez would remember the hour as overcast and cold. They reached the Luneta, where the three Filipino priests had been garroted. Thousands packed the field: chatting *peninsulares* in holiday garb, quiet supporters, gloating friars smoking fat cigars. A colonel announced, "In the name of the King, he who raises his voice in favor of the criminal will be executed." Deep silence descends. Rizal is led between two light poles: from this spot, he can see the bay. Twenty-seven miles south sprawled Cavite, where even now the revolution he'd tried to stop is being fought in his name.

Decades later, in the 1920s, a grainy black-and-white photo surfaced that seemed to show the last seconds of José Rizal's life. It depicts a small man in a dark suit and bowler hat, resembling Charlie Chaplin; he stands several paces from a firing squad, their guns raised. Tall, straight trees tower in the background; beneath them, spectators, clad in hats and gowns, fade into the distance. A dog plays near the line of troops, possibly the band mascot. The man who might be Rizal looks away from his executioners. His arms hang loosely by his sides.

Several legends surround these moments. In an 1890 letter to fellow Propagandist Mariano Ponce, Rizal wrote, "One only dies once, and if one does not die well, a good opportunity is lost and will not present itself again." As the rifles were loaded, a surgeon asked Rizal if he could take his pulse for a physiological study of the condemned. He'd found that their heart rates usually accelerate, but Rizal's was normal. He looked up, astounded: How can this be? Rizal barely smiled. The doctor leaves and Rizal is turned away from the firing squad, a stance reserved for traitors. He objects, but he is neither blindfolded nor forced to kneel, the ultimate shame. Six Filipino soldiers step up; behind them, a line of Spanish troops ready to shoot should they disobey orders. As the drummer Martinez watches, Rizal plucks off his hat; his head bobs up and down, lips moving as if in prayer. The colonel raises his saber; his men take aim. In some accounts, Rizal repeats Christ's last words, "*Consummatum est!*" ("It is finished!"), but Martinez does not mention this and it is probably an embellishment. Martinez feels his own heart beat faster. The saber drops; the crack of rifles. Rizal whirls as the bullets strike, and he falls, his face to the sky. There is silence; then the band's small dog runs circles around the body, barking, whimpering. The squad calls this "a premonition of coming misfortune."

Rizal was buried in an unmarked grave in Manila's Paco Cemetery. His sister Narcisa searched the graves that night and found one mound with newly turned earth and guards posted nearby. She paid the caretaker to mark the site with her brother's reversed initials, "RPJ."

In the church register, Rizal's death was recorded as a suicide, ensuring in the eyes of the Church that he is eternally damned.

2

Watchmen

Martí's dreams of *Cuba Libre* would have died with him if not for the men he'd distrusted for so long. After the poet's death, Maceo rode south to the slums and small farms of Santiago; Gómez rode west with twenty-five men into Oriente's sugarcane, the heart of the Ten Years' War. When local leaders said they did not want war in their state, Gómez replied that it had already come: as hundreds of volunteers materialized, he attacked isolated garrisons, rode rings around Spanish columns sent to destroy him. Each victory brought more horses, supplies, and men. By June 27, 1895, his forces numbered fifteen hundred, and he incinerated the towns and garrisons of El Mulato and San Geronimo, victories that "caused a very uneasy feeling in official circles," the Louisville *Courier-Journal* declared.

No one felt more uneasy than Governor-General Arsenio Campos, who wired Spain for fourteen thousand more men. This was Campos's second anointment as viceroy: the Crown had returned him to Cuba on April 14, four days after Martí's landing, apparently expecting the same miracles he'd used to end the Ten Years' War. But Campos was older, fatter, and wiser, and he knew Gómez had not mellowed with age. The old fox was too smart for a frontal attack; the only winning strategy Campos could see was to separate him from food. The only way to do *that* was to force neutral peasants, called *pacificos*, off their farms into designated zones. "Yet the misery and hunger would be horrible," he wrote to Madrid, and

Cuba's resentment would never end. "We will have another war within ten years," this followed by "another and another." Campos said he could not go that far.

With each success, rebel numbers grew. They called themselves *mambisi*, a Spanish racial slur they'd appropriated as their own. Their ranks swelled to several thousand: poor blacks from Santiago, whites from Puerto Principe, multiracial recruits from everywhere, all flocking to *Cuba Libre*'s red, white, and blue banner and the old impossible dream given a new mystical aura by the death of José Martí.

Such early success probably determined Gómez's strategy of total war. Outnumbered rebels should avoid direct conflict with Spanish columns, instead attacking the supply chain. On July 1, 1895, he told planters: "Sugar plantations will cease their labors, and those that try to produce sugar will see their cane set afire and their facilities destroyed." He banned farmers from selling any foodstuffs or basics in Spanish-held territory; anyone caught violating this edict could be "treated as traitors" and executed. Maceo was more apocalyptic: "Destroy, destroy, always destroy," he said. As long as Cuba turned a profit, Spain would stay. Profits would only stop flowing once the "Ever-Faithful Isle" was "drowned in blood and devoured by flames."

Gómez called his strategy *la tea*, "the torch," modeled after Sherman's March to the Sea through Georgia. By the summer of 1895, peasants around coastal Manzanillo fled their homes when Gómez gave them no other choice, the informal beginning of *reconcentrado*, the unhappy fate Campos had foreseen but refused. To ensure success, Gómez and Maceo must march toward Havana, where more than half of Cuba's sugar was grown. *La Invasion* would thrust west from Santiago along most of the 780-mile length of the island. They must destroy Cuba to free her. Only then would she be "redeemed."

To do this they must cross *la trocha*, a military railway that stretched about fifty miles from coast to coast at Cuba's narrowest point, from Júcaro in the south to Morón in the north. This was essentially a cleared space, 150 to 200 yards across, with a railroad running its length, guarded on its western side by a line of forts and barbed wire. Small forts of various size lined the route every quarter mile, and between them lay five-man redoubts; outside the wire lay the jungle, dense, impenetrable, and unknown. By 1895 the *trocha* had suffered years of neglect, and the soldiers manning the forts felt like prisoners. By day, hidden snipers picked them off. By night, the watchers yelled obscenities from the trees.

They did not want to be there. Many were conscripts, drawn from the poorest strains of Spanish society: one observer recalled seeing "herniated, one-legged, one-armed, asthmatic, tubercular and even blind" conscripts in Cuba in 1895. Their officers were schooled in past Spanish glories rather than practicalities like engineering or pathfinding; they suffered from "stupid confidence and Quixotic pride," one governor mourned. But they did have one advantage—the 7-by-57-millimeter-round Mauser, called "one of the best balanced cartridge designs ever made." The 175-grain bullet came loaded in a five-round clip, used smokeless powder, flew from its rifle barrel at more than 2,300 feet per second, and penetrated the human body with horrifying results. The Crown ordered 250,000 from the designer Paul Mauser and awarded him the Grand Cross of the Order of Military Merit, a rarity for arms manufacturers.

But neither Gómez nor Maceo intended to get within range. As conscripts sat in their forts, rebels flowed around them like fish past desert isles. Gómez crossed the line first with six hundred riders; Maceo followed with four thousand men. Once they joined, *La Invasion* could begin.

Since few observers had ever chronicled guerrilla war, you hitched a ride in this early stage by whatever means possible. On November 30, 1895, young Winston Spencer Churchill, fresh from the Royal Military Academy at Sandhurst, rode with Spain in a place called Arroyo Blanco to observe for British Military Intelligence the effects of this unknown Mauser. Churchill saw the results up close: as Cubans unleashed a "ragged volley" at his group, "a circle of dark red" spread on the "bright chestnut coat" of the horse behind his. The horse was put down.

Sylvester "Harry" Scovel rode in the same battle, but with the *mambisi.* A Presbyterian minister's son, Scovel, twenty-six, had already bounced through several jobs. On October 4, 1895, he sat opposite the *New York Herald* head editor Horatio Rubens, who tried to dissuade him from obvious suicide. But Scovel envisioned covering the conflict from the guerrilla perspective, and this unusual angle won the day. He'd be a freelancer, not regular staff, paid $24 per story. Rubens provided a contact in Cuba, shook the young man's hand, and figured he'd never see him again.

There *were* reporters in Cuba in the fall of 1895, but most reported from curbside tables at the Hotel Inglaterra, where the *New York Journal*'s "traveling commissioner" Murat Halstead deemed the steaks "as tender as Delmonico ever served." Horse-drawn carriages creaked across granite stones in the square outside. Commissioners received their "news" from Junta sources they called "Laborantes," Cuban slang for the "technicians" serving a well-oiled propaganda machine. Stories generated by Laborantes strove to move news of the rebellion to the front page: they left Havana via telegraph or the fast steamers plying the ninety miles between Key West and Havana. The Laborantes told wild stories of rebel success and Spanish incompetence, with headlines proclaiming "Five Hundred Men Landed in Cuba" and "Cannon Made from Trees!" First drafts were polished by the Key West Junta, then wired to New York: reporters called early at the Manhattan Life Building at 66 Broadway, which they dubbed the Peanut Club. Each morning, the legal counsel provided an ample supply of peanuts as he read the latest "news." They liked the way he cleared his throat when he lied.

Scovel wanted to see the fighting firsthand. He landed in southern Cienfuegos in mid-October and on his second attempt slipped through Spanish lines. He blundered into Gómez on November 1 as the general prepared to cross *la trocha*, and he was not inspired: like Churchill, he considered the *mambisi* an "undisciplined rabble" and figured he'd be slaughtered with the rest of them. But for some reason Gómez liked him, a rarity given the general's infamous temper, and allowed Scovel to tag along. On November 30, outside Arroyo Blanco, they met Maceo as well as the Spanish column hosting Winston Churchill.

Scovel thought he understood the Old Man. The point of guerrilla warfare was not to win territory, but to wear down and demoralize the foe. In time he understood how Gómez's rabble did much with very little. He followed as they wove west through central Matanzas Province, hiding by day, marching by night, torching miles of sugarcane. Widespread executions did not happen as threatened, as most landowners had fled and those who didn't were condemned to death in mock trials, then pardoned. Thousands joined as they marched past Cienfuegos and coastal Matanzas on toward Havana. On December 23 a force under Governor Campos nearly trapped them near Coliseo, but Gómez slipped free. On January 6, 1896, when the Old Man reached the Havana suburb of Hoyo Colorado, rumors flew that the capital was overrun.

But rather than enter Havana, Gómez raided the countryside while Maceo marched on to the far western province of Pinar del Río. Scovel rode as far as that border and turned back, hoping to sneak into Havana to check whether his dispatches ever made it out of the country. He felt "mentally desperate," he wrote, and hoped to creep into a hotel like the Inglaterra, where American newspapers were sold. On January 12 he masqueraded as a Spanish journalist to bluff the sentries, but they were not fooled. He was thrown into Morro Castle, his small cell lighted by one high window. Worse, he was mistaken for "El Inglesito," an English-speaking mercenary who probably didn't even exist. His jailers told him that in four days his cellmates faced a firing squad.

Then they grinned. *You will accompany them*, they said.

Another war took shape as Scovel faced his Maker. Today the press is seen as a main cause of the Splendid War, but in the fall of 1895, the contest between Joseph Pulitzer and William Randolph Hearst that defined "yellow journalism" had hardly begun. Ground zero for the approaching press war was New York's Printing House Square at Park Row and Spruce Street, where the statue of Benjamin Franklin hopefully reminded journalists of high-minded goals. Charles Dana's *New York Sun* faced Franklin; near it squatted the lagging *New York Times.* One block north rose the glittering Pulitzer Building, where every day presses rolled out half a million copies of *The New York World.*

America was a nation of newspaper junkies, with 14,000 weeklies and 1,900 dailies: 89 percent of its sixty-nine million citizens could read, and many subscribed. New York boasted eight morning dailies, seven evening dailies, and twice as many weeklies. The dailies' combined circulation stood at two million. At the top stood Pulitzer's *World*, home of the legends Nellie Bly and James Creelman. Pulitzer was tall, thin, tyrannical, and probably brilliant; his "New Journalism" emphasized the sensational—human interest, disasters, crime, and scandal, all subjects that he said spoke to the "common man." Entertainment news and reform crusades were staples, as were lurid headlines like "How Babies Are Baked" for a story on the heat-wave-related deaths of 392 children. A new innovation was the color Sunday supplement, featuring Richard F. Outcault's comic *Hogan's Alley* and its main character, the anarchic Yellow Kid.

In 1895 a new kid came to town. On September 25 William Randolph Hearst acquired formal title to *The New York Morning Journal* for $180,000; owned until 1894 by Pulitzer's brother, Albert, this was originally a scandal sheet known as a "chambermaid's delight" that had sold for $1 million to the *Cincinnati Enquirer* publisher John R. McClean. But it did so badly that McClean slashed the price to $360,000, then slashed *that* in half when Hearst came knocking. Hearst did not announce his ownership until November 8: he lowered its price to a penny and increased its size to sixteen pages. By year's end, circulation swelled from 77,000 to more than 100,000.

Sixteen years younger than Pulitzer, Hearst was rich and intelligent, and he suffered from an almost pathological shyness. Photos show a tall man in love with flashy suits, facing the camera with the sad face and eyes of a basset hound. Though Pulitzer and Hearst seemed aloof, both were admired by their staffs; though isolated by their psyches, both used their papers as the nation's loudest and most powerful voices of the century's end.

Hearst had apprenticed at the *World* as a reporter: he studied Pulitzer's style and then turned those lessons against his former master. When Hearst returned to his native San Francisco after his apprenticeship, he took over the moribund *San Francisco Examiner* from his father, who'd made millions on the Comstock Lode. "Willie" reshaped the *Examiner* in Pulitzer's image—gigantic headlines and illustrations, outrageous stunts and stories. A clergyman married a young couple in a hot-air balloon; a reporter trekked to Southern California to trap a grizzly bear. Hearst brought that formula to New York. He also lured Pulitzer's writers and editors with huge salaries, the most famous of these Richard Outcault and his Yellow Kid. Pulitzer ordered a second Kid for his pages, inspiring a wag to dub the style of Pulitzer and Hearst "yellow journalism."

Though Hearst would not send correspondents to Cuba until the fall of 1896, others had already arrived. They included the *Herald*'s redheaded

George Bronson Rea and Pulitzer's Dr. William Shaw Bowen. Both visited Scovel in Morro Castle, and Bowen convinced the governor to release him, as executing a preacher's son might be bad publicity. He then convinced Pulitzer to hire the kid full-time. Rea, for his part, informed Scovel that although his stories had made it to New York, none had ever run. He also begged for an introduction to Gómez. Sure, Scovel said, amazed by the guy's chutzpah. But you'll have to get there on your own.

Rea left Havana on January 18 and wandered lost for six days. On the seventh, he stumbled into some rebels headed to meet Gómez. They rode to an abandoned plantation southeast of Havana, where several thousand rebels had gathered. The numbers impressed Rea; the Old Man did not. Though Scovel had called Gómez a military genius, Rea was reminded of "a resurrected Egyptian mummy," the general's thin white goatee and mustache so long he finally understood why Spaniards called him the Old Chinaman. These whiskers were weather vanes: whenever Gómez tugged at them violently, his men murmured, "The Old Man is bad today."

And there, beside the mummy, rode Scovel, who made the promised introductions. To Gómez, this new reporter was just another "mercenary American" hoping to make his name at Cuba's expense. And Rea's reports, which ran in the *Herald* from January to March 1896, were not laudatory. To Rea, the general was an "insolent" fool who didn't charge the enemy, a contradiction of nineteenth-century norms. Some stories trickled back to Gómez, and in March the inevitable occurred. One evening the Old Man glanced up from dinner and saw Rea sitting at the far end of the table. "Mr. Rea," he snapped, "by what right do you sit at my table and eat?" The table fell quiet. "How do I know but that you are a Spanish spy in disguise?" It was "as if a bomb had exploded in the room," Rea wrote.

Everyone knew Rea wasn't a spy, but something deeper was going on. Rea wore his entitlement like armor: he was more than a reporter, he was an *American* reporter, and Cubans should be grateful that he was there. By early 1896, U.S. readers did not quite know what to think of this feud at their doorstep: true, the *mambisi* were sympathetic underdogs, yet the outlandish tales of the Laborantes hindered fair appraisal. Though Rea thought his duty was that of a skeptic, Gómez saw that skepticism as one more proof of American condescension.

Rea did not grasp any of this. Instead, the outburst confirmed his suspicion that Gómez was mad. The general offered Rea "the ten gold pieces I have in my purse" to head west to Maceo and get out of his hair. Rea refused the money, grabbed his hat, and rode west the next day.

An annoying tenet of storytelling informs Rea's break with Gómez. In the eyes of readers, clear moral choices are best. Complexity muddies a tale. Scovel's and Rea's differing views of Gómez were an example. To Scovel, the Old Man was a brilliant "liberator" embarked on a holy cause; to Rea, he dragged innocent peasants through hell in his lifelong obsession to cast out Spain. What if both views were correct, and Gómez brought freedom *and* ruin? A true villain was needed to make the narrative more palatable.

Such a villain had been expected since January 7, the day Governor Campos wired his resignation to Spain. As far back as July 1895, he'd told the Crown that the only way to beat Gómez was to create such misery that the hatred would never end. He was not willing to do that, but he knew someone who was: "If you prefer his system, do not hesitate to replace me," he wrote. "We are deciding the fate of Spain, but I have scruples that come before everything else."

On January 21, 1896, Campos left for Spain. Twenty days later, Valeriano Weyler y Nicolau arrived. Born in 1838 to a Prussian father and a Spanish mother, the man called "the Butcher" had a knack for crushing revolts, first in Spain, next around Santiago, and finally in the Philippines from 1888 to 1891. "I know I am merciless," he once told a reporter, "but mercy has no place in war." When Campos returned to Spain, he told friends that "even the dead will rise out of their graves to fight Weyler."

He was also different in style. Campos was "fat, good natured, wise, philosophical"; Weyler was "lean, diminutive," and "ambitious for immortality, irrespective of its odor." Campos was drawn to gold lace and pomp; Weyler was "an apparition of blacks—black hair, black beard, dark, exceedingly dark complexion." The *Journal*'s Kate Masterson described a small man, barely five feet, long face, square chin. Once, when she asked about the treatment of prisoners, his "eyes glinted dangerously." When she asked what would happen if she were caught interviewing rebels, he replied, "You would be treated the same as a man."

One American who did like Weyler was Consul General Fitzhugh Lee. The big, burly nephew of Robert E. Lee had been posted to Havana two months after Weyler arrived. Lee called at the Palace, expecting trouble, but instead found an "affable, pleasant, and agreeable" fellow who'd been Spain's military attaché to Washington during the American Civil War. Lee was always happy to reminisce about his days in the secessionist cavalry; Weyler said that one day he'd like to go back to America, and Lee said he should. But Weyler shook his head: he could never go, he said, because "the people of the United States would kill him."

Weyler inherited an island where Spanish troops controlled the cities but six thousand insurgents controlled the countryside. The rebels were well-supplied with arms and provisions, thanks to some two thousand *pacificos* who were "insurgents at heart," wrote George Rea. They "made their trips into the towns, smuggled out provisions," and acted as spies. Every Spanish move was reported to guerrillas; in contrast, Spanish troops operated blind.

Soon after arriving, Weyler rode into the country surrounding Havana. Burned fields stretched in all directions, but a few had escaped *la tea*, as their owners regularly paid a blackmail "tax." Weyler ordered a halt to all sugar grinding to deprive rebels of this revenue, but how could he cut off *all* support and starve the rebels?

The answer lay in an intensification of Gómez's own method. Rural residents would be uprooted into *zonas de reconcentración*, controlled areas near fortified cities and towns. If moved to such zones, peasants could no longer furnish *mambisi* with food and support; they could not serve as spies; their sons could not join the rebels. In fact, they were hostages.

Weyler issued his first *reconcentrado* order on February 16, 1896, six days after arriving. This early stage applied only to the eastern provinces of Santiago and Puerto Principe, plus the Sancti Spiritus district in Santa Clara. Rural residents had eight days to move to the zones. No food could be removed from *las zonas*; cattle must be herded into these areas; anyone failing to obey could be shot. Anyone found outside would be deemed a rebel and executed. Weyler recruited scores of Cuban-born irregulars, dubbed *guerrilleros*, to enforce the edicts, and they quickly became more hated than Weyler. "How do they want me to wage war?" Weyler once snapped during an interview: "One does not make war with bonbons." In one stroke, Weyler did his part to help create two hallmarks of modern war: the concentration camp and the "free-fire zone."

Everything went tragically wrong in the zones. On paper, Weyler made provisions to feed and house refugees, to let them farm designated tracts, but housing often consisted of abandoned warehouses, lacking sewage, and there was never enough room. Families slept in doorways or crowded into courtyards; beggars fought over scraps; children, bodies swollen from starvation, seemed to be everywhere. Some Spanish commanders looked the other way when *reconcentrados* slipped through the lines to forage. If the *guerrilleros* shot them, it was a more merciful fate than this lingering death in the zones.

At heart, the *reconcentrado* order attempted to isolate *mambisi* from every form of contact, including the press. Weyler made all communication with rebels punishable by expulsion or death. The *World* correspondent Charles Michelson was thrown into Morro Castle for trying to cross military lines; the *Journal*'s Murat Halstead was deported. When Scovel's February 23, 1896, profile of Gómez ran in the *World*, it so enraged Weyler that he offered a five-thousand-dollar bounty for the reporter's capture.

The world paid attention. On February 20 Henry Cabot Lodge, the forty-five-year-old Republican senator from Massachusetts, rose in Senate chambers to demand that America intervene in Cuba for humanitarian reasons. A slight and sickly Boston Brahmin who'd been Roosevelt's close friend since Harvard, Lodge was considered the architect of the expansionist stance dubbed "the large policy" and in June 1895 had authored an article in *The North American Review* that stretched the Monroe Doctrine to claim America's "rightful supremacy in the Western Hemisphere." In March 1896 the Senate passed, 64 to 6, a resolution recognizing Cuban guerrillas as legitimate belligerents, and the House passed a mirror image in April. The cautiously neutral President Grover Cleveland refused to sign, but he did offer to act as mediator between the two sides. As always, Spain refused.

Yet nothing filled the headlines like *reconcentrados*. Images of Cuba as a starving woman with sunken eyes and fleshless ribs first appeared in print in 1896; by 1898 there was no escaping her. In town halls and civic leagues, song, pulpit, and stage, the appeal was relentless: How are we the World's Hope if we let *reconcentrados* die? The play *The Last Stroke*, set in insurgent Cuba, opened in February 1896 in St. Paul, Minnesota: "The house was draped with American and Cuban flags [and] American sympathy for the struggling Cubans gave vent in a mighty shout when the American Consul of the play said: 'No. We don't want diplomacy! Where would America have been if we had had diplomacy instead of Bunker Hill?'"

Over the next two years, Weyler extended the policy in steps across the entire island. Thousands of homes sat empty; women and children went to camps as their men joined the *mambisi*; by mid-1896 the economy ground to a halt. In Cienfuegos, smallpox and yellow fever infested the *zonas*. In Havana, typhus, cholera, dysentery, and measles raged through 100,000 internees. In Guadalupe, 3,000 *reconcentrados* "lay everywhere under the broiling sun," a visitor observed. His mule "picked his way between human heaps that looked like so many mounds of rags." He heard sobs in a pile beneath him, but in his profound horror rode on.

No one knows how many *reconcentrados* died. Census figures show that Cuba's 1894 population stood at 1,631,696; in 1899, one year after America's invasion, it dropped by 58,851 to 1,572,845. Death emptied the countryside, dropping population density from 42.05 people per square mile in 1896 to 36.68 two years later. Even this is debatable. According to an 1897 fact-finding mission by the Spanish newspaper editor José Canalejas, "at least a third of the rural population," or 400,000 Cubans, had already died, and another 200,000 faced death before Weyler's policies could be reversed. If true, this would be proportionally higher than Russia's death toll during World War II. Fitzhugh Lee estimated 75,000 deaths in Havana alone, and 300,000 across the island. Today the best estimate seems based on the census and the work of the Spanish historian Jordi de Motes, who concluded that 155,000 to 170,000 *reconcentrados* died. Though not quite the 300,000–400,000 of legend, this is still enormous, accounting for nearly 10 percent of Cuba's total population.

Mass death changes everything. Nations react like individuals: they pass the horrors on as nightmare lessons to their progeny. In Cuba, historians ask what could explain an evil organized on such a scale? One thing is certain: horrors replicate once unleashed. *Reconcentrado* camps appeared throughout the twentieth century—in South Africa, the Philippines, Axis-held Europe and Asia, Vietnam, Cambodia, Rwanda, Native American reservations, the Russian gulags, China, Bosnia, Darfur. Always in the name of security. Always under another name. The daily parade of horrors confirmed the Americans' belief in Old World decadence—and their absolute certainty that they themselves could never sink so low.

3

The Wanderer

Weyler's ascendance marked a major shift in the war. Spanish morale improved, and an aide to Gómez noted that the enemy's "activity and aggression" increased the moment Weyler arrived. On February 19, 1896, Spaniards descended on Gómez and Maceo, killing and wounding one hundred *mambisi*, forcing the generals to flee. They met again on February 23, the war's first anniversary, and would never meet again. Weyler's men harried Gómez back east to Puerto Principe; his men died "of hunger and exhaustion" during the retreat. On March 9 fighting came so close that the Old Man lost sixteen of his forty-man escort. Their gains fell apart quickly.

Weyler's arrival also marked a shift in war reporting. Until that point, Americans saw the rebellion as colorful rather than tragic, and editors were slow to grasp its importance. Though coverage during 1895–1898 is now called yellow journalism, the bulk of such reporting occurred from 1895 to spring 1896. The most prolific fabricator was the *Journal*'s Frederick W. Lawrence, who spun tales of imaginary battles and victories from his table at the Inglaterra. On March 29, 1896, he began a six-week saga about Maceo's capture of Pinar del Río and Santa Cruz del Norte on the same night, towns separated by 122 miles. He invented a platoon of beautiful Amazon warriors wielding machetes. Even Weyler believed the yarn: when Kate Masterson asked about them, he said that at least thirty rode with Maceo and "are fiercer than men."

Pulitzer worried about the ridicule attending such tales, so he sent the first of journalism's big guns. James Creelman was thirty-six, stocky, and known for his black goatee and rapid-fire questions. He'd grilled everyone from Count Leo Tolstoy to the Sioux holy man Sitting Bull. He'd dodged bullets during the feud between the Hatfields and McCoys, lectured Pope Leo XIII on Catholic-Protestant relations, and considered himself the "conscience of the fourth estate." Quipped his future boss Hearst, "The beauty about Creelman is the fact that whatever you give him to do instantly becomes in his mind the most important assignment ever given any writer."

Creelman arrived in Havana in late March, just after the *Harper's Weekly* photographer Thomas Dawley was caught crossing the *trocha* and sent to Morro Castle in chains. Weyler hated U.S. journalists as much as he hated Gómez. "They poison everything with falsehood!" he snapped as Creelman presented his papers: in his opinion, half were Junta agents, half were liars, and all should be banned!

Creelman was there to check that rumors of Weyler's men slaughtering peasants was not just another Laborante fiction. One night he crept from Havana with two guides and rode to the village of Campo Florido, where some *pacificos* were said to have been shot. The guides stopped outside the village, pointed at a fresh mound of dirt, and then dug up the bodies as Creelman held their horses. "The hands of the slain Cubans were tied behind their backs," he wrote, a sight that "would have moved the hardest hearts." It certainly moved his: he abandoned all pretense of objectivity and vowed to help "extinguish Spanish sovereignty in Cuba."

Creelman's account, with the names of thirty-three victims, ran on May 1 on the *World*'s front page, filling nearly four columns. An accompanying editorial proclaimed that genocide worse than Armenia's was occurring ninety miles south of Florida. "Intervention has become a duty," it cried. Creelman walked a copy to the Governor's Palace, handed it to Weyler, and demanded an investigation. In response, Weyler signed deportation orders for Creelman and the imaginative Frederick Lawrence, too.

That left Scovel, who'd returned to New York after his release from Morro Castle and signed a contract with Pulitzer for $60 a week plus $400 in expenses. By May 18 he was back with the rebels, determined to prove or disprove Creelman's story. At first he suspected that the reporter exaggerated, but as he rode through a land of abandoned farms and bloated corpses of livestock, he learned otherwise. In the town of San Pedro, he upset a flock of vultures feasting on human remains that were piled in the village square: "The skulls of all were split to pieces down to the eyes. Some of those were gouged out. All the bodies had been stabbed by sword bayonets and hacked by sabres until I could not count the cuts; they were indistinguishable. The bodies had almost lost semblance of human form." The desecration seemed Gothic: severed limbs woven into crude five-pointed Cuban stars; one man's tongue stuck to his forehead like a horn.

"Blood on the roadsides, blood in the fields, blood on the doorsteps, blood, blood, blood!" Creelman had written back in New York. Now Scovel's report, printed in the May 27, 1896, *World*, discounted all claims that the stories were lies. A barrage of reports by Scovel followed, each running from two to five columns, signed with his name. Both series of reports ran in time for the Junta's Grand Cuban-American Fair in Madison Square Garden during the last week of May. "Cuba Appreciates Sympathy," proclaimed the colorful banners outside.

It was purely by chance that Fred Funston strolled by Madison Avenue and Twenty-Sixth Street on that pleasant spring evening. Stanford White's Byzantine dream glowed with electric lights, its pilastered entrance choked by a crowd. He needed to forget that despite a decade of striving, life had gotten him nowhere.

The crowd swept him through the flag-bedecked hall. Stalls sold green cocoa, cigars, sugarcane, and other delights from the "Queen of the Antilles." Originally planned for May 25–30, the fair was such a success that the Junta extended it a second week; though earnings were ostensibly slated for "quinine and bandages," Funston later concluded that it went to "dynamite and cartridges." The Junta called this a "Sympathy Meeting," and similar fundraising fairs had been held since October 1895 in Philadelphia, Chicago, Cleveland, Cincinnati, Columbus, Detroit, and Kansas City. Madison Square Garden was the biggest and gaudiest, and the night's featured guest was General Daniel E. Sickles, the seventy-six-year-old

Medal of Honor winner whose leg had been blown off at Gettysburg. The white-bearded soldier whipped his audience into a patriotic frenzy: Could America remain silent? he asked. Had we not received God's mandate to save humanity?

It seemed as if Sickles spoke to Fred personally. The old soldier's drooping mustachios inflated with each shout, his eyes glittering behind his pince-nez. Funston returned to his rooms; by dawn he'd decided to go to war, and he hurried to the Junta's 56 New Street office to volunteer.

The Cubans were underwhelmed. A "Mr. Zayas" praised Funston's intentions, but said they were raising funds, not men. Funston's guilelessness became clear: the Junta must preserve a façade of obeying U.S. neutrality laws to continue its "fundraising." What made him think they'd accept a complete stranger? He could be "a fugitive from justice seeking a hiding place, a worthless adventurer, or, worst of all, a spy in Spanish pay." He'd have to find another way.

The moment characterized Funston perfectly. In classic American fashion, he was the "Little Guy" made bigger than life, the Plainsman trusting his gut because his instincts were pure. Roosevelt would see in him an expression of his own deepest beliefs—a Midwestern mini-me. But the newsman William Allen White was mystified by his lifelong friend. He knew of no one else who *attacked* the world as Funston did: he was a "pudgy, apple-cheeked fellow," barely standing five feet, who "had absolutely no sense of fear, physical or spiritual." If anything, Funston was ruled by dangerous impulse, countered by a lucky star: he could do the most stupid thing imaginable and survive. A popular nineteenth-century saying was "God looks after children, fools, and the United States." Funston seemed a flesh-and-blood confirmation.

He was born in Ohio on November 9, 1865, six months after the end of the Civil War; his parents, the big, blaring Union artillery veteran Edward Hogue Funston and the cultured Ann Eliza Mitchell, who resembled a china doll. Two years after Freddie's birth, the family moved to Iola, Kansas, on the fringe of the Lower Plains. He watched prairie schooners carry settlers west to the unsettled lands. The Battle of the Little Bighorn raged to the north before Freddie turned eleven; to the south, the Apache

Wars went on from 1871 to 1886. The children were told to run for a hole behind the hedge should strangers approach. "Scratches from thorns were nothing to the horrors of a scalping knife," Freddie's sister recalled.

Freddie's future pal White called Kansas "hardly a state but a kind of prophecy," since anything fated to happen in America "happens first in Kansas." From the mid-1800s to the Depression, that seemed true. The "Bloody Kansas" of 1854–1859 preceded the Civil War; the state gave birth to Prohibition, Populism, and agrarian protest. Change always loomed on the horizon. Funston witnessed prairie fires, locust plagues, droughts, and twisters; White watched Kansas turn "poorer and ornerier and meaner than a spavined, distempered mule."

But what, exactly, did this prophesy? In 1859, before White or Funston were born, Charles Darwin's *On the Origin of Species by Means of Natural Selection, or the Preservation of Favoured Races in the Struggle for Life* posited that all life evolved through natural selection. Its offshoot, social Darwinism, came straight from the title. Strong races would triumph over weak, and the strongest were Anglo-Saxons, their highest embodiment Americans. The March 1885 *Harper's New Monthly Magazine* article "Manifest Destiny" by the historian John Fiske argued that a New Manifest Destiny lay at hand. The civilizing mission of the "English race" had been honed by their Yankee scions; the federalist system of government was their greatest invention, and the time would come when it would be possible "to speak of the United States as stretching from pole to pole." Only then would mankind finally witness the "ultimate triumph of good over evil."

Fiske's thesis filled the public sphere. Where was America going? What was its *destiny*? The subject drove Theodore Roosevelt's four-volume *The Winning of the West*: its theme, an epic racial struggle spanning centuries in which barbarians gave way to "civilized" races. That struggle, he wrote, was "elemental in its consequences to the future of the world":

> The most ultimately righteous of all wars is a war with savages, though it is apt to be also the most terrible and inhuman. The rude, fierce settler who drives the savage from the land lays all civilized mankind under a debt to him. American and Indian, Boer and Zulu, Cossack and Tartar, New Zealander and Maori—in each case the

> victor, horrible though many of his deeds are, has laid deep the foundations for the future greatness of a mighty people . . .

In Roosevelt's world, the mystique of privilege excused all sins. Progress took no prisoners: the conquered must be raised into his conqueror's image. Only then could he earn admission into "the fellowship of doers," the most glorious fellowship on Earth.

A third voice agreed with Roosevelt and Fiske but tried to replace racism with need. On July 12, 1893, Frederick Jackson Turner delivered his address on "The Significance of the Frontier in American History" to fellow historians at the World's Columbian Exposition in Chicago. The United States stood at the end of its first formative era, when triumphs in democracy and wealth stemmed from its spread west. But that epoch ended in 1890, when the census declared that the vast reserve of undeveloped land called the frontier had been filled. The frontier was gone. *Wilderness* shaped the nation, Turner claimed, not racial conquest: one saw in the long march west an evolution of attitudes, practices, and institutions that defined everything American—its intellect, character, and soul. Turner's "frontier thesis" posed a central problem: if we wished to remain ascendant, we must conquer the next frontier—wherever and whatever that was.

By 1896 social Darwinism and Fiske's call to arms came to seem like articles of faith, at least among large swaths of America's educated classes. Yet at this moment when the nation needed them most, a psychic malady sapped their will. "Neurasthenia" was a vague, probably psychosomatic nervous disorder characterized by insomnia, melancholy, lassitude, fainting spells, and general aches and pains. First called a woman's disease, then an "American nervousness," the infirmity by 1896 had entered the ranks of American men, especially in the leisure classes. Theodore Roosevelt suffered its effects, as did his confidant Henry Cabot Lodge. A free-floating anxiety plagued neurasthenics, fueled by reports of increased impotence, homosexual liaisons, and loss of virility. The "New Woman," who wore trousers and smoked cigarettes, seemed poised to supplant them; a mysterious poison flowed in their veins even as Providence demanded that they reshape the world. Exercise might help, and across the nation middle- and upper-class men threw themselves into weight lifting, crewing, football, and other outdoor activities. But exercise merely addressed the symptoms. Something must attack the cause.

How about war?

Roosevelt believed that war could heal. He saw it "as an ideal function," wrote the Harvard psychologist William James to his novelist brother, Henry, "necessary from time to time for national health." Even before this January 1896 observation, Roosevelt yearned for a scrap, the more global the better. In August 1886, when Mexican troops killed an American army captain at the border, Roosevelt wrote War Secretary William Endicott that he could raise companies of cowboys: "I think there is some good fighting stuff among these harum-scarum roughriders out here." In 1894 he said he yearned for a "general national buccaneering expedition to drive the Spanish out of Cuba, the English out of Canada." In March 1895 he begged New York's governor for a commission with the state's National Guard should war begin with Spain. "But, of course," he ended forlornly, "there won't be any war."

Funston, like Roosevelt, was always ready to fight. He was like his father, though Edward Funston warred in the political arena. Foes called him "Foghorn" for his thunderous voice and habit of hogging the stage. A staunch Republican, he served three terms in the Kansas State Legislature, one as house speaker; won a four-year term to the state senate; and in 1884 landed a seat in the U.S. House of Representatives, where he served five terms.

Tales of this period stress Fred Funston's overcompensation for his size: he lifted weights, developed the body of a bantamweight fighter, and "trounced" the school bully who pulled a pistol on the "new little teacher" during his single term in charge of the rural "Stony Lonesome" school. He traveled to Mexico, returned to earn his diploma, applied to West Point but didn't meet the height requirement, and failed the entrance exam.

He enrolled at the University of Kansas in Lawrence in the fall of 1886. A mere sixty miles north, this was another world. The Jayhawk campus attracted prairie gentry, all entitled in their minds to that glorious "inland empire" rising from the Plains. When Funston left campus for good, he told a professor that he might have been better off anywhere but this "hungry land of theories and dreams." But KU opened doors. He joined the Phi Delta Theta fraternity, where he met fellow initiates "Billy" White and Vernon L. Kellogg, a state senator's son who became a famous entomologist at Stanford University. The three became lifelong friends. Because of a clerical error, Funston was listed as "Timston," and "Timmy" became notorious for failed romances, growing aggressiveness, and unparalleled "blue language" composed of Old English, Kansan, Texan, and Mexican phrases pulled from his reading and travels.

More than anything else, he was known for his drinking. The Phi Delts kept a ready supply of homemade wine and hard cider, and Funston developed a taste for liquor. Two drinks and "Timmy was off," White recalled. Though usually "affectionate by nature," he could at such times be consumed by murderous rage. "Timmy" was a mean drunk, and "with two drinks it took three men to hold him," White said.

In 1889 Funston left before graduating and jumped between jobs. At twenty-four, he seemed lost and asked his father for help. Foghorn, now chairman of the House Agricultural Committee, advised Fred to take the Civil Service exam. He landed a spot as assistant botanist in a nine-month survey of Death Valley. Little was known about the forty-by-ten-mile trough running north-south near the California-Nevada border, and from January to September 1891, his eighteen-man party collected 2,160 plant samples and discovered 150 new species. The trip nearly killed Fred—three times: once from starvation, once from dehydration, and once when his horse stumbled and slid into a thousand-foot gorge. At the last minute, he grabbed a small shrub. Several legends arose about this expedition—that one man went mad, that several died, that by May 1901 "Funston is the only one now living who is still sane." All were untrue, and may have come from Funston.

In 1892 the U.S. secretary of agriculture chose him for a two-year trip to Alaska and the Yukon. The United States lacked scientific data on "Seward's Icebox," and from 1892 to 1894, he embarked on two separate expeditions, tasked to survey plant life and write up details of climate and terrain. He traveled 3,000 miles to the Arctic Ocean and back on dogsled and foot, paddled a canoe 1,500 miles down the Yukon River, endured winters registering 70 below. He lived with trappers, prospectors, and Inuit

Indians; slaughtered a sled dog for meat; watched arrows arc at him from a riverbank; turned morbid in the silence and slightly mad. "I nearly died of loneliness," he later said.

The isolation also drove his drinking to new dimensions. On August 15, 1894, an Interior Department survey group encountered Funston at St. Michael, a small trading post with a Russian church and some houses. The expedition member George Rudolph Voss called Funston "a short stoutly built little fellow, active as a cat," who vowed vengeance when a Russian priest named "Father Orloff" stole and drank a bottle of Scotch they both enjoyed. Funston beat him severely and threatened to "thrash him some more" if he didn't apologize. Voss thanked God when the priest relented, "for there seems to be a sentiment among the natives against striking a Priest," he said.

On August 21, 1894, Funston started home. But home had changed. During his absence, Lizzie Borden killed her mother and stepfather with an axe; President Grover Cleveland won a second term; the four-year depression launched by the Panic of 1893 shut five hundred banks and fifteen hundred businesses. Strikes, riots, and protests dotted the nation. Funston had changed too, emerging from the cold silence a devout believer in the Church of Fred. Like Jack London's Yukon wanderers, he'd learned that his life meant little in the grand order of things. Such realization brings a kind of freedom: everything gained in this life must be wrested alone.

And now he wanted fame. He gave lectures about Alaska, but auditoriums did not fill; hatched plans for a five-thousand-acre coffee plantation in southern Mexico, but few invested. Friends advised him to seek his fortune in New York. He arrived in March 1895, and the family friend Charles Gleed, one of the richest men in Kansas, arranged a post as deputy comptroller, signing "several thousand bonds" of the Atchison, Topeka, and Santa Fe Railway, which was undergoing bankruptcy reorganization. Funston took long walks, seeking inspiration, until that evening when he entered the Cuban Fair and heard Dan Sickles's fiery call.

Somewhere in that pinball existence lay the ingredients to make him Someone. The day after the fair, he wrangled an introduction to Dan

Sickles, probably through Charles Gleed. Funston appeared at the general's doorstep and left with a letter of introduction to Estrada Palma: though Sickles said he did not know the young man *personally*, he was impressed by his zeal.

Like "Mr. Zayas" before him, Palma was underwhelmed. Funston's offer violated section 5286 of the Revised Statutes of the U.S. Code. Though filibusters sustained the revolution, they also compromised U.S. neutrality statutes and created friction with Spain. Even as Funston tried to sign up, President Cleveland signed, on July 27, a second neutrality pact warning that any American citizen caught violating section 5286 could be charged with criminal conspiracy. The Junta knew it was watched by Treasury agents, so caution was key.

Still, the young stranger seemed too naïve to be a spy. When Palma asked about military experience, Funston said, "I've read considerably along military lines and feel I have it in me to make good." Spanish? "I have a fair reading, but no speaking acquaintance with your language, no." Was anyone *less* prepared for this war? Palma explained that to avoid breaking U.S. law, the Junta must never receive applicants in New York. But he *could* embark on an expedition and offer his services upon arrival. Palma handed him back to Mr. Zayas, who took his address and said to check in weekly.

Funston prepared, convincing *Harper's Weekly* to commission him as their Cuban "war correspondent," assembling a kit that included a "large camera" for articles. He read the newest atrocity stories. On June 3 Scovel wrote of a young Cuban mother, babe in arms, who failed to adequately answer a Spanish officer's questions. "I'll make you," he cried, then tore off her clothing, slashed her with his saber, and watched as his men beat her and her baby with rifle butts and finished the job with gunfire. On June 22 Funston wrote his father that he was going to Cuba for about four months. On July 5 he answered Foghorn's objections: "[I] did not expect you to look at the project very favorably, but I was pretty sure for a number of reasons that it was a good thing for me to do."

Funston wrote to his college friend Charles Scott, now sole owner of the hometown *Iola Register*. Freddie'd lived too long in his father's shadow and now planned "to see a real live war for my own satisfaction." He wanted to "get away from some of my disappointments and bitterness against things in general." Scott had chronicled Funston's exploits in Death Valley and

Alaska, and in a July 10 article titled "Fred Funston Gone to Cuba," he wrote, "The ordinary dangers of war would be enough to deter a less courageous soul. But in addition to the chance of being killed in battle, he faces the certainty of being put to death if made prisoner, and the possibility of contracting the fatal fevers of that country. We wish he were not going."

Funston felt otherwise. During one weekly check-in, Mr. Zayas mentioned a need for artillery. If Funston could remedy this, it might "add to [his] welcome." The closest Funston had come to a cannon was "once having seen a salute fired to President Hayes" at a Kansas county fair. Yet he vowed to learn. Zayas wrote a letter to the arms supplier Schuyler, Hartley & Graham, and an expert introduced Funston to the "Hotchkiss gun," the small, mobile breech-loading cannon that fired twelve-pound shells. They gave him an instruction manual filled with tables of shell velocities and allowed him "to fondle that ugly looking instrument of death to my heart's content and take it apart and put it together again."

The fifteen-hundred-pound "Hotchkiss mountain gun," or "Kipling's little brown pet," was a deadly tool for its time. But it had problems. A simple "quick-fire" piece that could be disassembled in the field and lugged into battle by pack animals, it belched ready-to-use "fixed ammunition" or "shells" whose timing was adjusted by rotating a section of the "warhead" clockwise or counterclockwise. Yet shells were sensitive to moisture and rough handling, and the cannon was made for short-range, flat-trajectory fire. This meant that a gunner must get in close and aim down the barrel, within range of Spanish Mausers.

In New York, Funston trained fifteen young Cubans in the gun's use; he attended a demonstration of the new Sims-Dudley dynamite gun, a two-barreled tube using compressed air to fire a two-pound brass cylinder filled with five pounds of nitroglycerin. One afternoon in early August, the wait ended. A telegram ordered him to "Be at Cortland Street Ferry at 7 p.m., ready to leave the City." He packed his valise and borrowed money from J. Willis Gleed, the younger brother of his Kansas benefactor. "Why are you joining this fight?" Gleed asked. "Cuba must be cleaned up," he answered, "and I am footloose and I may as well help as anybody else." He'd led a charmed life. It was time to take "nasty chances."

Of the seventy-one filibustering expeditions to Cuba from 1895 to 1898, the Spanish intercepted five and the United States stopped thirty-three. Based on such figures, Funston had less than a fifty-fifty chance to get through. The Spanish used 67 ships and more than 200,000 soldiers in the effort, while the United States fielded coast guard, naval, and revenue ships as well as federal agents and private detectives. Funston was one of forty-three volunteers to sign on to the expedition of General Rafael Cabrera, a veteran of the Ten Years' War. Their evasions were variations of the hat trick, using railways sympathetic to the Junta and three seagoing vessels: the tug *Dauntless*; the steamer *Commodore* from Charleston, South Carolina; and the tug *Three Friends* of Jacksonville.

Funston stepped aboard the New Jersey ferry and met his fellow mercenaries: a former Canadian Mountie who would die in Cuba, an Englishman whose legs would be shattered so badly that he'd spend a year in a "bush" hospital, and an American and a former British marine whose fates Funston never learned. They all sped through Jersey City to a Pennsylvania Railroad sleeper car bound for Charleston, then hustled to a downtown hotel where the other thirty-eight members of their party waited. All were well-dressed Cubans, all upper crust. Cabrera—a "considerate and kindly old gentleman" returning from exile "to renew the struggle of younger days"—shook Funston's hand.

They weren't alone. Another fifteen to twenty guests hung around the lobby: federal agents, Pinkerton detectives, some in Spain's pay. Two steered him to the bar: "There's nothing like a mint julep to beat the August heat," one said. The former Mountie muscled in and warned that he'd thrash them both if they didn't leave his buddy alone.

Funston left Charleston the next morning aboard a Plant Line special hooked to the rear of a Jacksonville-bound train. As Funston recalled it, several detectives tried to board but were told that this was a private excursion and they must take seats in the car ahead. The train clacked through the night, reaching a sidetrack deep in the Georgia woods. Funston's car was quietly detached; the main express sped on to Jacksonville, still carrying the unsuspecting detectives. After a while, Funston felt a soft bump, and his car joined a Florida Central and Peninsular engine heading in the opposite direction. They retraced their route north and stopped at a second siding, where the locomotive picked up three freights of arms and ammo. In the early hours of August 12, they puffed into the secluded crossing of Woodbine, Georgia, on the Satilla River, where the *Dauntless* awaited their arrival.

Tugs like the *Dauntless* had become the Junta's mainstay: they moved fast, jettisoned cargo in a wink, and sped home for another sub-rosa run. She carried seventy-six tons of cargo, boasted a crew of seven, and was captained by the infamous "Dynamite" Johnny O'Brien, so-called because he'd transported sixty tons of dynamite to Colombia through a hurricane. "Dynamite" was ready to go. At sunrise, the recruits unloaded cargo labeled "sawmill machinery" from the boxcars to the tug: this included the Hotchkiss gun, 800 shells, 1,300 Mauser and Remington rifles, 800 pounds of dynamite, and sundry small arms, ammo, medical supplies, and saddles. By midday, O'Brien gave several blasts on the whistle and the *Dauntless* steamed unnoticed into the Atlantic, thanks to the Junta's decoys. While the closely watched *Three Friends* remained in port, the *Commodore* steamed north in a false run to Norfolk, pursued by federal cutters.

Funston would write that the transit took four days, but records indicate that the trip stretched from midday August 15 to the night of August 16. It's possible that time and constant seasickness dulled his memory. What is certain is that after dark on August 16, O'Brien approached Cuba's northeast coast, cutting his engine a half mile from shore. Fifteen miles west lay the garrison town of Nuevitas, where the Spanish torpedo gunboat *Galacia* rested in a deepwater bay. He anchored near an inlet called Nuevas Grandes, separated from the sward by a shallow coral reef and hidden from Nuevitas by a western embankment. South of the beach lay a salt marsh and a tidal inlet peppered with flamingos; beyond that, miles of mangrove forest.

The *Dauntless* carried eight flat-bottomed skiffs, each equipped with two oars for rowing and one to steer. Funston and the four other "Americans" loaded the cannon piece by piece, then dragged it over the reef and up the shelving beachhead. All went smoothly until the sixth trip, when O'Brien spotted a white light sweeping over the embankment; he weighed anchor and steamed to sea. Three-quarters of the cargo had landed; Funston and the others spent the rest of the night hiding in the dunes.

But no one came. The *Dauntless* returned at eleven a.m. with the remaining cargo. All had been safely delivered but ten Remington rifles and some waterlogged Hotchkiss shells.

They waited four days amid mangroves and mosquitoes. Cabrera sent four men to alert Gómez of their arrival; on the fifth day, they spotted a lone figure walking on the beach. "*Alto! Quien va?*" they called. "Cuba," he said, the proscribed reply. He was one of Gómez's scouts, so relieved to find them that he hugged everyone. An advance guard followed, then six hundred men with pack animals. They spent the night loading every horse and before dawn began their march thirty miles south to a pasture Funston called *Las Angeles de Salviol*. That night, Funston discovered four more Americans around the campfire: a fellow from Massachusetts who'd be wounded in Cascorra; a Washington native who lost a leg; William Smith, second-in-command of Gómez's personal escort; and a New Yorker who stayed in Havana after the war.

Funston met Gómez the next morning. The "grizzled and silent old chieftain" picked through the mail brought on the *Dauntless*. He thanked them for leaving their homes to help, then turned and asked Funston what he knew about cannons.

Just what he'd learned from the instruction manual, he replied.

"Well," Gómez scowled, "you couldn't know any less than another American who came down here and said he knew it all." He put Funston in charge of the Hotchkiss gun and called him "Capi," short for *capitán*. Only later did Funston realize he'd been made commander of the entire artillery, though that would not be official until he "made good."

4

Making Good

The war that made Funston famous began a week after he met Gómez. It started in the Philippines, a place unknown to most Americans, 8,104 miles from Iola, his hometown. Though thousands of Katipuneros had heeded Bonifacio's call to arms, he proved an inept general. His bungled attacks in Manila on August 29, 1896, and later could have been the end, just one more slaughter in the archipelago's long chronicle of failed rebellions.

Yet in Cavite Province, to the south, a different kind of revolt evolved. Where Bonifacio appealed to the poor, Cavite's leaders—like Rizal—hailed from the middle class: artists, intellectuals, and merchants. They planned ahead, built trenches and forts, trained leaders, established an army. Bonifacio's rebellion was "plebian, instinctive, and in vain," observed the Filipino writer Nick Joaquin, but that in Cavite was "bourgeois, sophisticated, and effective." The first failed from the start; the second gained territory and pushed forward, both in battle and in the idea of creating a nation.

No one embodied this difference more than twenty-seven-year-old Emilio Aguinaldo. A slight figure, his cherubic face scarred by smallpox, he was the seventh of eight children and the youngest boy in a well-to-do Chinese *mestizo* family. His father, a lawyer and mayor of Kawit, Cavite's capital, died when Aguinaldo was nine, forcing the boy to drop out of school to help run the family farm. By 1896 he'd inherited his father's office, one that brought him to Bonifacio's notice. Aguinaldo adopted the code name *Magdalo*, for Mary Magdalene, Kawit's patron saint; Bonifacio's speeches and Rizal's writing fired his blood.

Like Rizal, Aguinaldo believed that he was "destined for martyrdom." It meant something that he was born on Holy Monday, the day of Christ's anointing in Bethany; that his father named him for Saint Emilius, a sad little martyr who'd renounced his faith under torture, only to repent and be burned to death for refusing to recant again. His soldiers saw him as the Revolution incarnate. Reporters asked, "Who is the real Aguinaldo?"

He is an enigma today. Of all Filipino leaders, he was "quiet, with little to say," wrote the American journalist O. K. Davis, "but saying that little in a plain, straight-forward way." Americans took the "high-sounding language" of his proclamations as proof of grandiloquence, but these were written by his more educated prime minister Apolinario Mabini, or the older cabinet member Felipe Buencamino, who was trained as a lawyer. In the end, Aguinaldo chose action over words, and many thought him rough-hewn. He could barely converse in Spanish, the language of educated Filipinos, preferring Tagalog, his native tongue. He was happiest dreaming of elsewhere while watching ships sail from Manila Bay.

In fact, Aguinaldo's lack of education may explain his hold over the peasantry. He did not put on airs. Peasants could relate: he was one of them. Instead, he was "terrible" in battle and *muy valiente*, descriptions also used for Gómez. Perhaps he was protected by an *anting-anting*, an amulet said to make him invulnerable. Edwin Wildman, the U.S. vice consul in Hong Kong who wrote a book about Aguinaldo, heard followers swear that the Santisima Trinidad medallion hanging from his neck was its source. One legend claimed that when a doubter questioned this, Aguinaldo "posed while a squad of six sharpshooters took aim at his heart and fired." The bullets bounced off. The soldiers adopted his *anting-anting* to the man.

According to the scholar Reynaldo Ileto, Aguinaldo probably did not believe in *anting-anting*, but he knew he must conform to what his soldiers believed "a man of power should be and have." This was a peasantry deeply versed in Catholic mysticism, a land where images of Christ and the saints were believed to emit an unworldly glow from wide, staring eyes. He'd created an armed state, so a powerful magic must be at work:

his followers believed "he could foresee the future; he was invulnerable; he had a magic sword by waving which he could turn bullets in their flight." That saber glowed like the fiery blade of the Archangel Michael.

Unlike Bonifacio, Aguinaldo never assumed success, and thus he planned ahead. One day after Bonifacio's failure in Manila, Aguinaldo visited Cavite's Spanish governor to pledge his loyalty to Spain. He asked for a detachment of marines to ward off the coming chaos, when in fact he planned to strip them of their guns. Impossible, said the governor—all but one of his companies had been ordered to Manila that morning to defend the city. Aguinaldo left without arms or troops, but with the knowledge that Kawit's fort was practically empty.

Aguinaldo returned to Kawit and told his coconspirators that they must begin the revolt immediately. By three p.m. his men had overpowered the three Guardia Civil left to guard the armory and acquired 17 rifles, two 2½-pounder cannons, and 1,900 pesos in silver and gold. By five p.m. thousands of people collected in the central plaza to hear him proclaim "the end of friar and Spanish rule." He raised his arms. Today's uprising, he said, "is a miracle of heaven, overthrowing empire, erecting the Tagalog flag, dragging down the Spanish emblem." The multitude cheered.

He sent out messengers to neighboring towns, and by the end of that day, Aguinaldo's Katipuneros controlled neighboring Noveleta and San Francisco de Malabon. He sent his cousin Baldomero to subdue the important town of Imus, but the attack failed, and during that sleepless night he grew certain that his martyrdom was nigh. By dawn, he'd organized a second attack and marched at the head of six hundred rebels, their numbers swelling to two thousand by the time they crossed the Imus Bridge. The Spaniards had retreated to a *casa hacienda* belonging to the friars, and when the rebels surrounded the house, priests and soldiers started shooting. Aguinaldo set fire to an adjoining grain warehouse, and the defenders staggered out, overcome by smoke. Imus was his.

The most serious threat came the next day. On September 2 Katipuneros in neighboring Bacoor asked for help against one hundred well-armed Spanish soldiers. Though Aguinaldo led five hundred men to block them at the strategic Zapote Bridge, they carried only the blunt machetes, called "bolos," and nine guns. They charged and were cut down. "Fire! Lie Flat!" Aguinaldo shouted. "Crawl! Fire!" But when he looked back, there were just the wounded and dead. The cavalry charged, and he fell as if shot; he covered his face with blood, played dead, and crept through surrounding swamps to rejoin his troops in Imus. They gasped when he rose from the muck: they'd seen him fall in front of them. Tales of his *anting-anting* began.

At this critical moment, Brigadier General Ernesto de Aguirre returned to Manila for reinforcements. If he'd pressed on a few more miles, he could have crushed the outgunned revolution in its third day. Instead, Aguinaldo had time to fortify Imus. His Katipuneros dismantled the bridge into town, something the Spaniards would not know about until they turned a right angle in the road and faced the chasm over the river, a cannon pointing at them from the other side. On September 3 Aguirre marched back with his five hundred men. His lead soldiers discovered the trap; the cannon fired; Aguinaldo and others lying in wait fired into their flank. Panicked Spaniards fled through the rice fields, where ambushers hacked them to death with their bolos.

Within a week, nearly every town in Cavite Province was liberated. Thousands of Filipinos from surrounding provinces carried their possessions into "the little Republic of Cavite." This new labor force turned Cavite into a stronghold. Trenches connected the towns; roads were barricaded; improvised cannons, made of iron hoops and water pipes, were filled with scrap iron. Aguinaldo divided the provinces into five "zones of war," each responsible for its own army. Though Governor Blanco had 6,000 men, he believed that Aguinaldo had 105,000.

Few had accomplished so much so quickly. Other revolts had flared and failed: Mindanao in 1620, Bohol in 1622, Negros in 1844. Aguinaldo inspired hope, and among those streaming into the Little Republic were *ilustrados* schooled in republican ideals.

A republic is a government founded on the consent of the governed; it embodies its people's aspirations. When Bonifacio and Aguinaldo first rebelled, they did not know enough of the outside world to understand such ideals. For the greater mass, the word "republic" held no meaning. There was no word for it in Tagalog, Ilocano, or any other Philippine language. They longed for a world where friars no longer ruled, but they were uninterested in international standing or legalities. They simply responded to one of mankind's oldest urges—they wanted to be free.

Yet by early October 1896, a rough draft of nationhood began to form in Aguinaldo's mind. He might not believe in *anting-anting*, but he would not discount the power of inner being, or *loob*, best described as a spiritual essence woven through ideas of power. Gómez had *loob*; so did Theodore Roosevelt. Only a man of strong *loob* could shape a nation out of disparate tribes: educated *ilustrados*, rural peasants, enraged Katipuneros from the urban slum. All were united in their hatred for Spain's centuries of abuse, but that hatred needed a voice, and as October unfolded, the uneducated mayor from Kawit emerged as an orator. "Filipinos!" he called them, the first time anyone had done so, just as Martí turned "Cuban" into an expression of group soul. "His words produced an effect upon his hearers which [those] who have read them in translation will not understand," wrote the American observer J.R.M. Taylor. Aguinaldo tapped into something deep: "There is a strong love for music and poetry among Filipinos and Aguinaldo's florid speeches moved them strongly." Aguinaldo's imagery struck a chord in his listeners: "We are all children of a single Mother, of Mother Filipinas." Every social class represented a "single child of God," all of the same soul and spirit, all "one in *loob*."

On October 31 Aguinaldo issued a manifesto declaring complete independence from Spain, his first truly revolutionary proclamation. He wrote in Tagalog and sealed it with the sunrise emblem of Magdalo, his Katipunan code name. "Liberty, Equality and Fraternity," he declared, the motto of the French Revolution. He proposed a government "like that of the United States of America," where towns chose delegates who elected a president, who picked a cabinet to advise him. A revolutionary army of "ten thousand men" would be drawn from separate regions and towns: "Every town which adheres to the cause of the revolution will be defended and protected by the revolutionary army against any attack of the enemy."

During these months, Governor Blanco marshaled his forces as the insurrection spread north and east of Manila through Central Luzon. There it was less organized, composed at most of five thousand men who primarily harried the northbound railroad. In fact, clerics, not *insurrectos*, would prove to be his greatest enemy. As friars fled to Manila from all over Luzon, they brought lurid tales of murder and outrage. In Imus, thirteen friars were captured: one was cut to pieces; a second soaked with petroleum and lit; a third pierced through the length of his body with a bamboo splint, doused with oil, and turned over a fire like a roasted pig. On the Bataan Peninsula, friars were hitched to carts like *carabao*. The Church took out its anger on Blanco: he was too lenient with captives; he refused to execute the despised Rizal. The last Spanish archbishop of Manila led the attacks—fifty-two-year-old Bernardino Nozaleda y Villa, arguably the most powerful man in the Philippines. Portraits depict an imposing man, as solid as a boulder; when he later sat for an interview with the American reporter Murat Halstead, he smiled and called the rebels "ungrateful" children who'd been "lifted from savagery by . . . the very men whom now they persecuted." On October 31, 1896, he wired Madrid: "Rebellion spreading. Apathy of Blanco inexplicable. In order to avert danger immediate appointment of a commander necessary."

Blanco attacked the next day, personally leading two thousand men in an amphibious assault at what is now Cavite City on the province's north shore. He amassed stores on the coast, and from these points sent out three columns on November 9. Aguinaldo fell back, drawing them deep into a maze of swamps; their lines stretched five miles when rebels burst from the mangroves, hacking and stabbing with bolos and spears. By dusk, five hundred Spanish troops lay dead or wounded; the rest fled back to the coast, where they stayed until year's end.

Blanco left in disgrace, replaced by Camilio Polavieja, a colonial-war veteran believed to be as brutal as Weyler. Upon arrival he told troops to "wash all offenses in blood." A people who had been "a model of tranquility and repose" had been turned into brainwashed masses by the "criminal ambition" of a few. Aguinaldo and his traitors could only expect death, their names expunged from memory.

Polavieja's words lit a fire in his army. "The cannibals are still in the forests," a Spanish officer declared in a toast. "The wild beasts are hiding in their lairs. The time has come to exterminate the savages. Destroy! Kill!" They did so with a vengeance, primarily on those in easy reach. Polavieja relieved prison overcrowding with executions; by December 31 about a thousand Filipinos were deported to penal colonies, their property seized. Rizal's execution on December 30 was the capstone: Archbishop Nozaleda and his friars rejoiced as they watched. That same day, twenty-four other prisoners were executed.

While Aguinaldo's victories inspired the Little Republic, they also spawned a threat from within. The Katipunan had split between Bonifacio's supporters, called the Magdiwang, and Aguinaldo's Magdalo. The Magdiwang were ruled by the Alvarez clan, to whom Bonifacio was related by marriage: they ran the south, while the Magdalo ran the north, where all fighting was centered. The Magdiwang feared that Aguinaldo's triumphs shifted power—after all, Bonifacio started the revolution. To set matters right, they brought him down from the mountains.

El Supremo arrived in Cavite on December 19, 1896, ostensibly to mediate the feud. Instead, his allies elected him *hari*, or king. He ordered one of Aguinaldo's lieutenants jailed for causing his August 29 defeat; this was ignored. Both sides launched smear campaigns. On December 28 a meeting was called in Imus to unite the sides, but Bonifacio insisted that he'd head any new government. This, too, was ignored. Each time the sides tried to meet, the attempts dissolved into insult—until finally the insults went too far.

One night after New Year's Day, Aguinaldo and his secretary Mariano Trias faced Bonifacio and his brother Procopio in an alley in San Francisco de Malabon. Each man carried a gun. They stood two feet apart under a tree, argued one last time, and aimed. It would have ended badly if an officer who'd shadowed them hadn't thrown himself in their midst and shouted, "Shoot me first before you proceed with what you intend to do!" Others appeared from the shadows: they called a priest, who made them embrace, kissed each man on the cheek, and blessed them in the name of God and the Holy Trinity. But even divine intervention could not heal these wounds.

Polavieja was unaware of such poison; if anything, rebels seemed of one mind. The once-meek peasants had turned into devils, wrote Lieutenant Colonel Federico de Monteverde, gripped by a bloodlust the likes of which he'd never seen. Every battle "ended only when the last defender had been killed," he said. "In all parts the struggle was desperate, viscous blood formed pools on the floor, and there was no knife that was not dyed red, or hollows without corpses of the enemy." In the opinion of the Filipino scholar Reynaldo Ileto, Catholicism, the creed that once made them docile, now fueled their resolve. These were a people raised on the Passion of Christ, the eternal struggle of light against dark; they were part of that same cosmic struggle, expressed by their journey from "the dark, miserable, dishonorable age of Spanish rule to a glowing era of freedom" called *kalayaan* in the native tongue.

Aguinaldo talked inspirationally of *kalayaan* in town after town. But they were still outgunned. By late January 1897 Polavieja commanded 36,000 soldiers, with 30,000 of them in Luzon. Aguinaldo knew the odds were not favorable. As Ferdinand Blumentritt had told Rizal, few revolutions succeeded without help, yet the Katipunan had lunged ahead anyway.

As popular will in the United States crept closer to war in Cuba, not a word was uttered in Congress about the Philippines. Yet there *had* been one appeal to the U.S., shortly after New Year's. On January 3, 1897, the Filipino Junta sent a rambling missive to William E. Hunt, the U.S. consul in Hong Kong, begging him "to implore the government of your nation to extend its protection over the Filipinos who are now suffering under the tyranny of Spain." The five-page letter listed Spanish corruption and "gross stupidity," but it also enumerated the great profits to be made on the islands. The Junta showed a clear-eyed grasp of the Yankee instinct for turning a buck; it listed agriculture, railroad profits, and vast, untapped mineral wealth: "coal, lead, copper, iron and petroleum . . . the immense riches of which are not taken advantage of." If the United States aided the rebels, they promised "to gratefully grant such concessions as may be desired in return for protection so generous and humane."

Hunt's response is unknown, if it even exists. One gets the feeling that those few Americans even aware of the Little Republic considered it none of their business. In fairness, Hong Kong was gripped by the second year of a bubonic plague that, from 1894 to 1901, would kill 8,600 residents, with 95 percent mortality. No action was taken on the Junta's pleas.

In September 1897 Hunt would rotate from his post and go home to his native Greenville, Mississippi. But when he left, he did mention the strange proposal to his successor. Rounsevelle Wildman would be very interested in the schemes of the Junta, and his enthusiastic attentions would lead to broken promises that determined the fate of the Philippines.

On November 3, 1896, William McKinley Jr. was elected twenty-fifth president of the United States. Nearly 14 million people voted out of an estimated 75 million; the fifty-three-year-old Republican, crowned "the advance agent of prosperity," won by 601,331 votes over the handsome thirty-six-year-old Democrat William Jennings Bryan. McKinley promised stability after the Panic, "sound money," and a return to prosperity. The man who hoped to be called the Business President is remembered instead for sending America down a path no one anticipated.

McKinley has been called "one of the most enigmatic figures ever to occupy the White House," with good reason. There's little in his papers to reveal his feelings; his public statements were so ambiguous that even allies were left guessing. In 1891, when asked about Cuba, he said, "In my position it were better that I say nothing now." History, like Nature, abhors a vacuum. McKinley is painted as a "good man without greatness"; the model of a "Christian statesman" beset by doubt; a mystery defined by "the masks that he wore." The enduring judgments are those forged by memorable quotes. Most famously, Roosevelt's famous critique that McKinley had "no more backbone than a chocolate éclair" has prevailed: a good man but a weak president, pushed by popular opinion into an unnecessary war. "Why is McKinley's mind like a bed?" ran a contemporary joke. "Because it has to be made up for him every time he wants to use it."

Yet this was not the day's majority opinion. McKinley was the "Accessible President," wrote the historian Gerald Linderman: it was how he saw himself and how others saw him. West Virginia senator Stephen B. Elkins boasted that he introduced a thousand men to the president; the necessity of the handshake never lost its appeal. "I feel better" after the ritual, McKinley said. More than that, voters trusted him. He was one of them.

Few have traveled the same social distance from McKinley's straitened origins to 1600 Pennsylvania Avenue. Born on January 29, 1843, the seventh of nine children in small-town Niles, Ohio, he studied hard, was quick and pious like his mother, and entered college at seventeen, bound for the ministry. But his father's ironware business failed, so to keep the family afloat, he took jobs as a postal clerk and teacher. Then came the Civil War, and McKinley joined what would be known as the Ohio Guards. He'd be cited three times for courage. At Antietam, he drove his mules through heavy fire to deliver food and hot coffee to the men in the front lines. In the retreat from Kernstown, Virginia, he delivered orders for an exposed company to retire. In the same campaign, he led volunteers to save some artillery abandoned by its crew. In each case, he preserved or protected the group, acts that earned commendations from his commander, the Cincinnati lawyer Rutherford B. Hayes.

After the war, McKinley studied law: he hung out his shingle in Canton, joined the Masons and the Knights of Pythias, helped the county Republican committee. When German and Irish miners were arrested during a strike, he won their acquittal and refused to take a fee. Labor supported him after that, regardless of party, and in 1867 he parlayed that support to the post of county prosecutor. The same election swept his old commander into the Governor's Mansion, and over the next thirty years, Rutherford Hayes's patronage would buoy him in his slow, upward trek from governor to congressman and finally president. In 1871 he married Ida Saxton, daughter of a prominent Canton banker and publisher: their first daughter lived three and a half years, their second five months, and by 1876 depression and epileptic seizures filled Ida's days. He took care of her as he had cared for his fellows during the war. Americans knew of this when he ran for high office, and they translated that into a similar care for the nation.

A vote for McKinley was a vote for no surprises. He regularly attended church, was a teetotaler, had no known sexual flings or rumors thereof. He lived in the White House just as he had in Canton: dinner at 6:30, maybe a game of euchre, a scan of the newspapers as Ida knitted. He adhered to the belief that national power resided in Congress, not the White House, and gently willed others to do his bidding. His party's platform also held no surprises: financial stability, annexation of Hawaii, enlargement of the U.S. Navy to protect the coasts, Cuban independence by "peaceful means." McKinley's portraits gaze upon a changing world—pensive gray eyes set deep within a square, expressive face. Slight melancholy is the abiding effect, as if he knows that even an assassin's bullet cannot save him from the judgment of history.

McKinley's campaign was run by Mark Hanna, the millionaire kingmaker from Cleveland. Every national paper except Hearst's *Journal* and the party's Southern conservatives abandoned Bryan over his risky opposition to the gold standard, and Republicans hammered that his policies would ruin the nation. While Bryan canvassed the nation in a "whirlwind" of whistle-stops, McKinley spent the summer on his front porch. People came to him. On the day of his nomination, special trains brought thousands to Canton; it is estimated that from five p.m. to midnight on June 18, 1896, fifty thousand people listened to him speak and many were personally greeted by him. These "front-porch speeches" went on all summer—delegations from across the country marched daily from the train station to his home on Market Street, overflowing his front lawn. In fact, he addressed millions, since Mark Hanna guessed that he'd mailed out 120 million copies of these speeches to newspapers nationwide. McKinley showed a talent for sustained discourse and a solid command of facts, dispelling Bryan's contention that he was a "man of one idea." His landslide victory surprised no one.

The period from McKinley's election to his inauguration was filled with the onerous duty of choosing a cabinet and making hundreds of political appointments. Five were consequential. He chose for the War Department Russell A. Alger, a timber magnate who would be embroiled in scandal before 1898 ended; he chose for navy secretary his former congressional colleague John D. Long, a round Dickensian character whose great loves were visiting his seaside cottage and writing poetry. Neither Alger nor Long knew much about the military. McKinley retained Fitzhugh Lee as U.S. consul in Havana: though a Democrat, Lee knew Spaniards and rebels alike, and McKinley found his intelligence valuable. When Ohio senator Joseph B. Foraker sought a consular post for his friend Oscar F. Williams, McKinley apologized that the only opening at the moment was in a place called Manila, "somewhere way around the other side of the world." It sounded exotic, so Williams accepted.

And there was Teddy Roosevelt, chafing on the sidelines. McKinley thought the New Yorker too hotheaded, while Roosevelt considered the Ohioan staid. Though initially backing House Speaker Thomas B. Reed, Roosevelt stumped vigorously for McKinley. Born to riches and a Harvard graduate, Roosevelt had already authored, among other works, *The Naval War of 1812* and all four volumes of *The Winning of the West*; he'd read navy captain Alfred Thayer Mahan's *The Influence of Sea Power upon History, 1660–1783* and claimed that it opened his eyes to the clockwork of empire. He'd been elected to the New York State Assembly from 1882 to 1884, attended the 1884 Republican National Convention in Chicago, served on President Benjamin Harrison's U.S. Civil Service Commission, and was now New York City police commissioner. Few people could pack so much into thirty-eight years of life, and he'd seen tragedy, too. On the morning of February 14, 1884, his beloved mother died of typhoid fever; eleven hours later, his first wife, Alice, succumbed to kidney failure masked by her pregnancy. He scrawled a huge "X" on that page in his diary and wrote "The light has gone out of my life." He retreated to his North Dakota ranch, where his path to resurrection lay through "the strenuous life" preached by third-century Desert Fathers, but with cowboy overtones. For the rest of his life, he rarely mentioned Alice, even in his autobiography or after his second marriage to his childhood friend Edith Kermit Carow.

Through triumph and tragedy, Roosevelt had one constant wish: the United States would become a world power, and he would be involved. A war with Spain was one means. As early as March 9, 1896, he wrote to his sister Anna that such a war would force the United States to build a proper navy. On March 30 and April 5 he said he really wished Americans would interfere in Cuba, and on January 2, 1897, he said he hoped Grover Cleveland might send the fleet to Cuba despite McKinley's pending inauguration only two months away.

Roosevelt's hope was to be appointed assistant secretary of the navy, an influential post in an age of empires. To argue his case, he enlisted his old friend Henry Cabot Lodge, to whom McKinley owed favors. Lodge drafted a powerhouse group to lobby for his friend—future Secretary of State John Hay, Speaker of the House Thomas Reed, Vice President Garret Hobart, *New York Sun* editor Charles Dana, and Sixth Circuit court judge William Howard Taft, called the most popular man in Washington. Lodge told Roosevelt that the president-elect feared his notorious fire eating. "I hope he has no preconceived plans which he would wish to drive through the moment he got in," McKinley had said, and Lodge assured him that "he need not give himself the slightest uneasiness on that score."

But McKinley was unsure. "I want peace," he told the wealthy Washington hostess Maria Storer, "and I am told that your friend Theodore—whom I know only slightly—is always getting into rows with everybody." McKinley was firm about this. He'd seen the dead in Antietam and the Shenandoah Valley, and he did not want a war with Spain. On the night before his inauguration, he sat with Grover Cleveland in the White House and said, "Mr. President, if I can only go out of office at the end of my term with the knowledge that I have done what lay in my power to avert this terrible calamity"—what he saw looming in Cuba—"I shall be the happiest man in the world."

The next morning, Thursday, March 4, 1897, McKinley rose at six and told Ida that this was her first day as the nation's First Lady. She didn't need to be reminded, she said. It was a crisp, beautiful day: "Not a cloud cast its shadow over any part of the inaugural proceedings," wrote *The New York Times.* Shortly after 12:45 p.m., McKinley gazed from the inaugural platform overlooking the Capitol's east lawn and saw forty thousand spectators staring back; he placed his hand on the large gilt-edged Bible to affirm that he would "preserve, protect, and defend" the Constitution. He'd not yet made up his mind about Roosevelt, and would not for another month. He kissed the Bible and stepped to the lectern: he promised strong financial policy, extolled America's commitment to freedom and equality, though the commitment was flawed, especially for black Americans. "Lynchings must not be tolerated," he declared. He sought a "firm and dignified" foreign policy: "We want no wars of conquest; we must avoid the temptation of territorial aggression." And he added, "Peace is preferable to war in almost every contingency."

Peace was the last thing on Fred Funston's mind. He quickly learned the uncomfortable realities of Cuba's guerrilla war. He'd thrown in with a poor lot, and over the next sixteen months he discovered *how* poor. In their white cotton uniforms and straw hats, they resembled tramps; only the machetes and crossed bandoliers separated an officer's uniform from that of an enlisted man. Theft was rampant. He lost his camera, with which he'd hoped to illustrate his *Harper's Weekly* articles, and most of the gear he'd bought in New York. Soon all that remained was a Spanish grammar book, a ragged hunting coat, and a pair of worn corduroys, attire that would be his trademark among the guerrillas.

Funston stayed in camp a week, then on August 24, 1896, marched into the interior. He was "in ecstasies" over the miles of "primeval forest," spotted with clearings growing with squash, yucca, and other vegetables that served as their grocery store. They marched past free-roaming herds of "fat, sleek cattle" that became their butcher shop. But such a life brought shortages. If they stayed too long in one place, they stripped it like locusts; to offset this, they divided into groups of fifty to five hundred and scattered through the countryside.

By early September, Funston learned that they planned to lay siege to Cascorra, a garrison town manned by tough Catalonians. They turned west onto the Camino Real, the great "Royal Road" running the island's length; all along this route, they saw cut barbed-wire fences, burned houses, and residents resembling refugees. Scouts described Cascorra as a ghost town invested in its center by 170 soldiers, among them twenty-seven-year-old Eloy Gonzalo, a conscript who'd become Spain's only hero of this war. Tall, big-shouldered, with a mustache, goatee, and close-cropped black hair, Gonzalo had been orphaned early, and he wandered Madrid with packs of homeless boys. He enlisted in 1889, one of the few upward routes open for those with no future. After four years, he was given permission to marry; one year later, in February 1895, he caught his betrothed in bed with a lieutenant, whom he threatened to kill. In response, the Spanish Army found him guilty of insubordination and sentenced him to twelve years in Valladolid Prison, a pit from which few emerged.

But he got lucky. Spain had grown so desperate for recruits that it granted clemency to convicts willing to fight in Cuba. In November 1895 Gonzalo pledged to "cleanse himself [by] shedding his blood for the nation." He boarded a steamer for Havana, and by early 1896 he manned Cascorra's garrison. Weyler had said the place had no strategic value and planned to abandon it, and then Gómez arrived. Outside the walls, three thousand angry *mambisi* wandered unchecked; inside, Gonzalo and others endured shortages and contracted malaria, dysentery, typhus, and yellow fever. As Funston peered from the bush, Gonzalo stared back, figuring his chances looked slim.

Eight hundred Cubans surrounded Cascorra. That night, Funston listened to Gómez's engineers raise a wood-and-earth parapet four hundred yards from the tavern and cut a door-size opening in its front. At four a.m. on September 22, 1896, the five "Americans" crept into the little *trinchera* housing the Hotchkiss gun. At dawn, the tavern took shape in front of him. Three of his squad opened the breech and loaded the shell; Funston squatted behind the gun to take the sighting and turned the elevating screw to lower the muzzle. A fifth man moved the "trail" right or left as Funston indicated. He climbed atop the parapet and yelled "Fire!" but forgot to cover his ears. The blast deafened him. Flame and smoke erupted from the tavern; bricks rained down. Funston jumped from the parapet onto a *mambi*'s back, causing the battle's first casualty.

Of Funston's five days at Cascorra, the next hour was his most memorable. They reduced the upper floor to rubble, then shifted their sights to the church and city hall. Fifteen years later, he'd grow poetic recounting the sounds of return fire: "The air was suddenly full of those peculiar popping noises that we were soon to know so well, leaves dropped from the trees, there were odd movements in the grass, a patter against the opposite side of our shelter." Mauser fire rained down during the seconds it took Funston to aim. A bullet struck a gun wheel like a hammer; a *mambi* standing by him was shot through the thigh; a round knocked off Funston's left heel, and backward he fell.

He'd entered the fugue state that only combatants know. "War is a joyous thing," wrote the medieval soldier and author Jean de Bueil. Time slows down. The Wehrmacht soldier Guy Sajer felt an "almost drunken exhilaration" during battle; the frenzy that gripped the Vietnam War correspondent Michael Herr was almost sexual, like the "feeling you'd had when you were much, much younger and undressing a girl for the first time." Blind fury transforms to ecstasy—a "daemonic lightness" Greeks called "the dance of Ares." One felt invincible and untouchable, until there was a sudden shock and, looking down, you saw the blood.

For all his joy, Funston knew that without exploding shells, they weren't hurting the Spaniards. He asked Gómez to move two hundred yards closer. The Old Man consented. They moved up in the dark, and again Funston appeared before Gómez. Even at two hundred yards their damage would be minimal. They should reduce the church bastion to rubble, he pleaded, then send waves of *mambisi* through the breech. Gómez knew this would be suicide: his men were guerrillas, not regular troops; their job was to outwit and outlast, not engage directly. The slaughter Funston suggested would spawn mass desertions.

More days of cannon fire; more days of ruined church walls. Eloy

Gonzalo kept his head down and did not get hit, but others were not so lucky. A smaller Hotchkiss, stationed to the north, lobbed 219 shells during the siege and killed or wounded twenty-one comrades. During the fight, Gómez politely offered terms of surrender, and the Spanish commander, Captain Francisco Neila, just as politely declined. Gonzalo and his fellows began to starve. At one point, some Cubans moved into a building 150 feet from the main redoubt and picked them off with deadly accuracy. Captain Neila asked for a volunteer to creep up and set the building afire. Gonzalo stepped forward. Success would wipe clean his slate, if he survived.

That night, he crawled up, carrying his rifle, a tin of gasoline, and a match. His comrades tied a rope to his waist so they could drag back his body if he were killed. But no one saw him: he set fire to the building, then picked off backlit Cubans who tried dousing the flames. Gonzalo crawled back, and the heartened defenders held out until October 7, when a 2,500-man relief column approached and Gómez withdrew.

Gonzalo gaped at the forest, amazed that he still lived. His officers recommended him for the Silver Cross for Military Merit, the Spanish equivalent of the Medal of Honor. The former convict was hailed as "the Hero of Cascorra," and Spain was inspired: if this unknown orphan could prevail against such odds, maybe they could, too. No one mentioned that the column marching toward them had come not to reinforce Cascorra, but to shut it down.

Gonzalo never fought again. Spaniards worldwide collected money, though it's unclear whether any reached him. On April 29 a royal order granted him a modest lifetime pension, but he had little time to enjoy it. Like many Spaniards fighting in Cuba, disease laid him up: while fewer than 4,000 died in battle, 41,288 fell to disease. On June 19, 1897, the Hero of Cascorra succumbed to an undiagnosed fever and died in bed.

Cascorra changed Funston, and he wondered whether he'd erred badly in going there. Cuban losses had been high enough that Gómez decided to turn east, away from Spanish reserves. At the far eastern end of Camaguey Province lay Guáimaro, a point on the map where the first Cuban Constitution was penned and the Cuban flag designed. Gómez hoped to join forces there with another veteran of the failed first revolt, the unsmiling Calixto García.

Though Funston had never seen García before October 13, he'd heard of him. Three years younger than Gómez, his life had been "one long tragedy of war and prison." He stood at six feet and was rather heavy; his receding hair and thick mustache were easy to spot on the battlefield. The most commanding feature was the hole in his head. On September 3, 1874, midway through the Ten Years' War, he'd been surrounded and had decided to escape by the only means open to him. He placed a large-caliber revolver beneath his lower jaw and pulled the trigger. The bullet traveled straight up and exited the center of his forehead, right above the brow. When Spanish authorities informed his mother, Lucia Íñiguez replied that it could not be her son. She'd raised him never to surrender. He'd tried to commit suicide, they replied, but had failed; she screamed back, "Better dead than captured!" The wound never healed properly and he plugged the open wound in his skull with a wad of cotton. As Gómez and Maceo sped west, García had raised two thousand volunteers and kept the Spaniards pinned down in the eastern end of the island. History would judge him as the Cubans' most important general during these last two years of the war, for it was with him the Americans dealt, not Gómez.

Fred Funston came to revere García. He seldom saw him smile and never heard him laugh but once, when he fired six times at a sleeping rodent called a *jutía* without once "disturbing its slumbers." While those who served under Gómez "regarded him with something akin to awe or fear," García's men "had for him a feeling of affection." Gómez handed Funston and the other *Americano* artillerymen to García with unbridled praise; for the next fourteen months, Funston reported directly to the well-loved general.

García already had a squad of American gunners, led by Winchester Dana Osgood, one of the era's most famous college football players. "It was downright uncanny to watch him run," groused an opponent; his body "undulated like a snake's" and tacklers missed by inches. "Major" Osgood outranked Funston and took command, but Funston didn't mind. Now the Cubans had four working field guns, a fact that gave them confidence to attack three hundred well-entrenched Spaniards.

The siege began at seven a.m. on October 17, 1896, and lasted until the

Spaniards surrendered ten days later. Death became personal. On the first day, Cubans overran a blockhouse called Gonfu: on the second, the gunners set their pieces inside, thinking they would be safer there. Since Osgood held rank, he sighted the Hotchkiss, which meant the enemy targeted him. "I think that will do," he said while leaning forward to correct for windage; at that moment, a bullet caught him between the eyes. He died hours later, the first American to fall.

They froze: for a while "we did nothing but sit in the blockhouse, well back from the fatal port-hole, and gaze in awe at the splatter of blood." They'd all seen death, but it happened to Cubans and Spaniards, not them. Pain, even the enemy's, no longer seemed removed. One night after surrender, Funston walked through the medical tent and heard a Cuban officer speak to the Spanish commandant, who'd been wounded in a cannonade. "That American is the man who gave you your wound, as he personally sighted every shot at the church on the last day," he said. The commandant, "a very handsome and dignified man with snow white hair and beard," looked at Funston in a "reproving and wondering way." Funston felt like dirt. "I slunk out of sight."

Despite his guilt, he'd done as Gómez advised and "made good." Two weeks after the surrender of Guáimaro, he was promoted to major of artillery, in charge of all four artillery pieces under García. With this he earned two servants—one for his horse, one to cook meals. He dined on fresh beef, fried plantains, sweet potatoes, and the "bric-a-brac peculiar to the tropics." He'd never been in better health, figuring he'd go home in top condition. On November 9, 1896, he wrote a letter to his newspaper pal Charles Scott, one he knew would run in the *The Iola Register:* He anticipated coming home and scooting "my feet under your mahogany desk as I have done many times of yore." He could comfortably predict that "next Spring will see Cuba [a] free and independent nation."

5

The Voice of America

By late 1896 Gómez's *La Invasion* had mixed results. His guerrillas controlled Cuba's countryside from Guantánamo in the east to Pinar del Río in the west, and the nation's economy had ground to a halt. Yet that success brought Valeriano Weyler, and with him came *reconcentrado* camps, mass starvation, death, and ruin. Even Gómez's men were starving. By 1896 his forces had fled east. Only Antonio Maceo stayed in place, his freedom absolute in Pinar del Río.

But if Weyler could not catch the elusive general, neither could Maceo leave. Weyler hoped to trap the Bronze Titan there by building a second *trocha*—a 232-mile barrier stretching from Majana in the south to Mariel in the north, complete with electric lights, artillery, and fifteen thousand soldiers. Maceo had crossed this easily while it was still under construction, but now it was finished, the most elaborate man-made barricade Cuba had ever seen.

Until November 1896, this wasn't a problem. Maceo had free run of the country. The *trocha* was an afterthought—until a letter from Gómez arrived.

Come east, his commander said. An old problem had emerged. The racism that plagued Carlos Céspedes during the Ten Years' War festered once more: Maceo's success in the west had rekindled in planters the old fears of a black republic. Gómez needed Maceo to help settle their fears.

In late November 1896 Maceo rode east with two hundred men, but he slammed into a six-thousand-man force led by Weyler. He escaped, but still had to cross the wall. On December 4 he rounded the *trocha* by boat with seventeen others and landed on the far side. His party included his aide, Francisco "Panchito" Gómez Toro, Gómez's youngest son. They could have vanished, but Maceo could not resist tweaking Weyler one last time. On December 7 he attacked a small town outside Havana when suddenly reinforcements appeared. Nevertheless, he charged, driving Spaniards before him. "This is going well," he said, leaning forward in his saddle, when one Mauser round went through his chest and a second entered his jaw, penetrating his skull. His companions tried to drag him back, but the fire was too great; Panchito Gómez rushed to his side and was shot in the leg and the arm before dragging his general behind a low stone wall.

The Bronze Titan was dead, and Panchito vowed not to be taken alive. He wrote a short note to his parents with the one hand that still worked:

> Dear Mamma, Papa, Dear Brothers: I die at my post. I did not want to abandon the body of General Maceo, and I stayed with him. I was wounded in two places, and as I did not fall into the hands of the enemy, I have killed myself. I am dying. I die pleased at being in the defense of the Cuban cause. I wait for you in the other world.

He grabbed his dagger but was too weak to drive it home; instead, Spaniards slit his throat, nearly severing his head. They stripped the two, unaware of their identities, and left them by the wall. *Mambisi* later sneaked back, buried the bodies, and carried the news and note to Gómez.

On the day Maceo died, Grover Cleveland delivered his last address to Congress. He'd been president twice—in 1885–1889 and 1893–1897, divided by Harrison's presidency. He'd watched Cuba slide from bad to worse, and he detailed his growing fears: the 30 to 50 million dollars in American investments that could be lost; the annual trade worth nearly 100 million dollars shot to hell. He warned Spain that America's patience was limited.

"Weep, weep, Maria, for both, for you and for me," Gómez wrote to his wife with news of their son. He announced Maceo's death to his army on December 28, but did not mention Panchito's. He asked his wife to grieve, "since for this unhappy old man, the privilege of relieving his innermost grief by . . . a flood of tears is not possible." In Key West and Tampa, thousands of cigar workers mourned in the streets. When word reached Weyler, he pushed east and west, sweeping rebels from his path; he expanded the *reconcentrado* orders, destroying anything left behind in farms. By mid-March 1897 the revolution was in deep trouble. Funston realized that his sunny prediction sent to Iola was way off mark. He wasn't going home soon.

For the past year, Citizen Hearst had contemplated war. In December 1896 he sent questionnaires to every state governor asking how many soldiers they could field if war broke out. He gave Ralph D. Paine, a young *Philadelphia Press* reporter, the impossible task of presenting Gómez with a $2,000, jewel-encrusted sword, which ultimately traveled five thousand miles and never reached Gómez until war's end. The *Journal* became known as a place for daring young men to risk their lives in harebrained publicity schemes.

By December 1896 reporters were flocking to Florida in unprecedented numbers. Some came with assignments, some without, all hoping to board a filibuster boat and join the rebels. On New Year's Day, three of the most famous tried to cross the straits in bad weather. One succeeded. One turned back. One barely escaped alive.

Sylvester Scovel succeeded. On January 1, 1897, he crossed in a small boat named *Scooter* and landed in Pinar del Río, determined to confirm Maceo's death. He crept the next day into Havana and met with Fitzhugh Lee, who asked him to find Gómez, and Lee sent a note asking how Gómez felt about a truce followed by Cuban home rule. Scovel crept off and wrote, "I have been fortunate enough to get into Havana, get out of it again, and to find an insurgent force, all within twelve hours." When the front-page story ran on January 7, 1897, Weyler doubled the old $5,000 bounty on Scovel to $10,000 and ordered him captured or killed.

The reporter who turned back was a celebrity. Richard Harding Davis's clean-cut good looks epitomized the "muscular Christianity" so in vogue; his square jaw and aquiline nose seemed everywhere after the artist Charles Dana Gibson used him as the model for a male counterpart to his stylish "Gibson girl." Davis was a high-society fixture, had written several short stories and novels, and served as managing editor of *Harper's Weekly*. His fictional characters and public persona were one. His popular book *Gallagher* convinced thousands that working for a New York daily was the height of glamour; his *Soldiers of Fortune* was finished in the Santiago home of Jennings Cox, inventor of the daiquiri. With this voyage, he hoped to become a true soldier of fortune.

Davis was born to society and the pen. His father edited a Philadelphia newspaper; his mother wrote uplifting novels. He attended classes at Lehigh University wearing English-cut suits and kid gloves, carrying a cane. He referred to himself in the third person or by his initials, RHD. All contributed to his reputation as a notorious snob, yet many found him likable and oddly touching. He was now thirty-two: for all his accomplishments, he never felt good enough and for the last two years had been periodically bedridden with "nervous storms," bouts of painful sciatica accompanied by feelings of worthlessness. The doctors called it "shattered nerves"; Davis called it "morbidness." All he wanted was to "turn my face to the wall."

But few saw that side of him, only the surface glamour. Hearst coveted his literary style, the sharp eye for detail threading through clear prose, and offered Davis $3,000 a month plus all expenses. It seemed surefire: send the nation's most flamboyant journalist to a superheated story, accompanied by the artist Frederic Remington, famous for his depictions of cowboys and Indians. Hearst bought the 112-foot steam-powered yacht *Vamoose* to get them across: the ship could steam between Key West and Cuba in four hours. After a month of waiting, the *Journal*'s team attempted the ninety-mile sprint on New Year's Day.

They didn't get far. The sea was so rough that Davis and Remington hung on to the rails. They watched as a Chinese cook lashed together a door and some boxes to make a raft, and Davis suggested they do the same. "Let him make his raft," Remington said. "If we capsize, I'll throttle him and take it from him." Twenty miles out, the captain declared the voyage too dangerous and turned about. The frustrated Davis lay on the deck and cried.

That left Stephen Crane. The twenty-six-year-old novelist sat in an open boat pounded by waves. He'd always suspected that he'd die young, but not this way. His frail, spindly body, racking cough, and sallow complexion suggested that he'd contracted tuberculosis. In 1897 TB was a death sentence: the slow-growing *Mycobacterium tuberculosis* ate the lungs from inside, causing the chest to fill with blood and the lungs' liquid remains, decreasing oxygen exchange until the sufferer drowned. So many artists died of TB in this era that it was called the "romantic disease": Crane's wall plaque of Mozart, dead at thirty-five of the "white plague," reminded him of that fate each morning. Before he became famous, he told Willa Cather of his doubts about his future. You'll be famous in ten years, she said. He countered, "I can't wait ten years. I haven't time."

He was more famous than he'd ever imagined. From 1892 to 1896, he'd published the scandalous *Maggie, a Girl of the Streets*, the free verse *The Black Rider and Other Lines*, and *The Red Badge of Courage*, which made his name. He still wrote for newspapers, which he'd done since the age of sixteen. The man who'd penned the ultimate American war novel had never been to war; now the small Bachelder-Johnson newspaper syndicate, which first published *Red Badge* in serial form, paid him $700 in Spanish gold to report it from the rebel side. He kept the gold buckled around his waist in a money belt. He'd see war firsthand.

But only if he got there. He'd hung out a month in Jacksonville with his lover, Cora Taylor, who in time would be called the first female war correspondent, but for now ran the city's popular house of ill-repute, the Hotel de Dreme. Scovel joined them. Both loved roulette and horses; both were "bad boy" sons of preachers. The similarities ended when Crane tried to cross the straits: he'd not be as lucky as his friend. After midnight, he boarded the filibuster tug *Commodore*, loaded with 400 rifles, 1,000 pounds of dynamite, 200,000 rifle cartridges, 300 machetes, 1,000 cannon rounds, 2,000 rounds for dynamite guns, and 27 or 28 passengers. They were probably overloaded, though official reports said the pumps went bad. Two miles from Jacksonville, the tug beached on a sandbar in the foggy Saint John's River. It beached again at Mayport, causing a leak in the boiler room. She lost power sixteen miles from the Mosquito Inlet Lighthouse near New Smyrna and lowered her lifeboats. By seven a.m. on January 2, 1897, she slipped beneath the waves.

Crane's ordeal had just begun. As the volunteers and crew piled into lifeboats, Crane, the captain, the cook, and the oiler jumped into a ten-foot dinghy still tied to the ship by a forty-yard line. They drifted leeward, and the captain announced, "Boys, we will stay right near the ship till she goes down." At that moment, the first mate and six others whom they'd watched board a lifeboat appeared back aboard the sinking tug. Crane's dinghy rowed close, and the first mate yelled that their boat had foundered. They'd made some small rafts: Could the captain tow them? Three grabbed their rafts and paddled for the larger dinghy; Crane watched the mate jump in without a life belt, and "even when he did this horrible thing, I somehow felt that I could see in the expression of his hands, and in the very toss of his head, as he leaped to his death, that it was rage, rage, rage unspeakable that was in his heart at the time."

The last three men did not move from the tug; they stared at Crane as the boat went down. A black stoker paddled up in his flimsy raft and panicked as he tried boarding Crane's dinghy: "He had turned into a demon," Crane wrote. "He was wild—wild as a tiger. He was crouched on this raft and ready to spring," a leap that would sink them, so the cook dropped the line and the stoker's raft drifted away. The last two rafts were sucked into the "frightful maw of the ocean" as the tug sank. Only silence remained.

The captain steered toward the lighthouse that "stuck up above the horizon like the point of a pin." They rowed and bailed for thirty hours off Daytona Beach as holiday-goers waved, thinking they too were on holiday. Crane hated them all. In desperation, they turned to shore and rowed through the breakers. The waterlogged dinghy pitched up, and they spilled out; Crane unbuckled his gold-filled money belt, terrified it would drag him down. He, the captain, and the cook were tossed onto the beach, exhausted but alive. The oiler, strongest of the four, lay "with his forehead in sand that was clear of the water, and he was dead."

New York newspapers announced Crane's death as he washed ashore that Sunday, January 3. "When I die I hope I will face Death as manfully as you did," wrote one literary colleague. Crane wired his paper: "I am unable to write a thing yet, but will later." Three days later, he wrote his "Own Story." Five months after that, his fictionalized account appeared in *Scribner's Magazine* for $700, the same amount of gold he lost off Daytona's Main Street Pier.

"The Open Boat" is today among the most widely anthologized short stories in American letters, considered a bridge between nineteenth- and twentieth-century literature. The "correspondent" fills in for Crane; as he labors in the tiny boat, he understands for the first time Nature's indifference to his survival. She is neither cruel nor kind; God and Fate are neither treacherous nor merciful. They just don't care: "When it occurs to a man that nature does not regard him as important, and that she feels she would not maim the universe by disposing of him, he at first wishes to throw bricks at the temple, and he hates deeply the fact that there are no bricks and no temples." He saw this when the first mate jumped to his death: in the man's eyes and "expression of his hands," Crane grasped the unspeakable final truth of the mate's "rage, rage, rage."

Crane was not alone. Death focuses a writer. The roots of twentieth-century American literature sprang from the Splendid War: its literary chroniclers parted the patriotic mists, and their writing burned with rage. The literature of the Romantics and realists before them—of William Dean Howells, Henry Adams, Henry James, Whittier, and Longfellow—stylistically sheltered man in a continuum: its phrasing was mannered and dense, sentences complex, characters playing out dramas within an elegant syntax of "tireless proselytizing" to suggest that, although it might be beyond our ken, order and meaning exist in this world.

Not so in Crane's. Suddenly the style was less baroque, the imagery jarring, dialogue direct, and for the time profane. The seeds had already been planted: in Pulitzer's "New Journalism" and in the enraged slices-of-life of Jacob Riis, Lincoln Steffens, and Nellie Bly. Now American literature catches up. Suddenly no higher meaning or old truths intercede, only the lonely struggle to survive amidst a revelatory rage. The rage of Carl Sandburg, Frank Norris, Sherwood Anderson, an older Mark Twain, and at times Richard Harding Davis leaks down to their spiritual descendants: Ernest Hemingway, Sinclair Lewis, John Steinbeck, Eudora Welty, and "hard-boiled" writers like Raymond Chandler and James M. Cain. Each chronicles a loss that is filled, like Crane's endless ocean, by an all-consuming rage.

The new voice of America insisted on being heard, and Crane may have set it in motion. But he would be absent for the rest of the year. His near death had left him broke and dispirited. He returned to New York, completed "The Open Boat," visited family, and sold his short story to *Scribner's.* He still wanted to be a war correspondent, but blockades by the U.S. Navy and the Revenue Cutter Service convinced him that Cuba was not in the cards. "It can't be done," he wrote to his brother in March. "I am through trying." He signed with Hearst's *Journal* to cover the conflict between Turkey and Greece. War stirred something within him. "It is a great thing to survey the army of the enemy," he wrote. "Just where and how it takes hold upon the heart is difficult of description." But this war was brief—a stalemate by May, armistice by June. He hopped a steamer back to England, where he lingered for the rest of the year.

Davis and Remington reached Cuba on Saturday, January 9, 1897, though not with the drama they'd intended. They took the *Olivette*, the regular packet boat to Havana, and landed in Spanish-controlled Cuba, where journalists were carefully attended. The next day, Fitzhugh Lee took them to meet Weyler; to his surprise, Davis found "a dignified and impressive soldier" who received them with "courtesy and consideration." Weyler granted them permission to travel, but only on the Spanish side of the lines; he assigned them a translator, and they headed southeast to a sugar plantation close to the southern coast near the first *trocha*.

Davis might be impatient to leave, but not Remington. Though a former cowboy, army scout, and failed rancher, Remington by 1897 was renowned, grossly obese, and allergic to physical exertion. He filled his time with drink and complaining. Alcohol unleashed his racism: any war in Cuba would be tragic because Americans would die "to free a lot of d— niggers who are better off under the yoke." His desire to go home also led to one of the most apocryphal yarns of the war. On January 15 the grumbling Remington wired his boss: "Everything is quiet. No trouble here. There will be no war. I wish to return."

"Please remain," Hearst replied. "You furnish the pictures, and I'll furnish the war."

This probably never happened, but it said reams about both men. Both had little patience; both thought their presence got things done. The anecdote's sole source was James Creelman's memoir *On the Great Highway*. Davis and Remington hopped the Spanish armored train to Cienfuegos; halfway there, in Matanzas, Remington turned back to Havana and returned to New York with a portfolio of sketches under his arm. Davis was glad to see him go.

Davis could observe the effects of war without Remington. He encountered his first *reconcentrado* camp in Cardenas, a coastal town east of Matanzas. The refugees were packed into abandoned warehouses built on crumbling wooden posts, set back fifty feet from the water's edge. High tide was the sewer system; through gaps in the planks he spotted an undisturbed pool of "green slime, colored blue and yellow." About three hundred women and children lived here, organized for survival. The children went out by day to beg for food; what they gathered was cooked that evening by the women. A "fat little doctor" took Davis on his rounds; they came upon babies covered with sores, skin drawn so tight "that the bones showed through as plainly as the rings under a glove."

Davis felt his "professional neutrality" weaken. He took pride in dispassion; he'd seen people die. That was the nature of war. But here the innocent died like cattle. At what point, he wrote, must America intervene?

It was also in Cardenas that Davis realized he'd never meet the rebels. He'd arranged a secret meeting in his room with Scovel and Rea, who hoped to sneak Davis across the lines. But when Scovel arrived, he handed Davis a copy of the January 17 *Journal*: the front page trumpeted that Davis and Remington had "reached the insurgent army on the island of Cuba" and ran a photo of Davis in riding breeches astride a giant white horse. "Your paper has queered you, Davis," Scovel said. By now, his photo was probably in the hands of every Spanish officer in Cardenas. His chances of slipping through the lines with Scovel and Rea had plummeted to zero.

His entire Cuban junket had been "a failure from the beginning," Davis wrote to his mother. "I haven't heard a shot fired or seen an insurgent." And he doubted he would. He continued east in disgust, and on January 19 witnessed the execution of a twenty-year-old rebel—in the process writing one of the great classics of American war journalism in this or any other war.

"The Death of Rodriguez" was written in the straightforward, spare style that would echo thirty to forty years later in Hemingway's fiction or the war reporting of Ernie Pyle, John Hersey, and Richard Tregaskis's *Guadalcanal Diary*. "Adolfo Rodriguez was the only son of a Cuban farmer, who lives nine miles outside Santa Clara, beyond the hills that surround the city to the north," he began. The Guardia Civil had captured him a month earlier; a military court sentenced him to death, and he was thrown into prison with thirty other *mambisi* awaiting identical ends. Rodriguez would be first; the remainder, "one after the other" on each successive morning. The condemned led the way, trailed by a band playing a "jaunty quickstep," then three hundred volunteers. "I witnessed his execution," Davis simply declared, "and what follows is an account of the way he went to his death. The young man's friends could not be present [since they too would be shot] . . . and I like to think that, although Rodriguez did not know it, there was one person present when he died who felt keenly for him, and who was a sympathetic though unwilling spectator"—an aside that makes the reader a witness, too.

They marched half a mile to a field lit by a full moon. As they stopped and awaited the dawn, Davis glanced back and spotted a "mass of people" hurrying from town, led by two priests who'd stayed all night with the condemned. In the new light, Davis could study Rodriguez's features: "He had a handsome, gentle face of the peasant type, a light, pointed beard, great wistful eyes, and a mass of curly black hair." His white linen shirt was open at the throat, and around his neck hung a new scapular. To Davis, he seemed "shockingly young for such a sacrifice," but life was cheap here. As Rodriguez passed, he held a cigarette between his lips with such nonchalance that Davis felt humbled; in this hour of death he'd let "his enemies see that they can kill him but can not [*sic*] frighten him." Rizal had died only a week or two earlier: the theater of rebellion demanded calm from its sacrifices. Rodriguez was led to the edge of the square, and the commanding officer turned him to face away. As the commander raised his sword, a mounted officer rode up and pointed out something "which I had already observed with some satisfaction"—the firing squad was so placed as to shoot into another group of soldiers at the edge of the square. The commander placed his hand on Rodriguez's shoulder and spoke into his ear.

Davis could only imagine the effect on a man who had just heard the click of rifle locks, "but this boy turned his head steadily, and followed with his eye the direction of the officer's sword." He took a new position, faced away from the riflemen, and straightened his spine.

Davis had never seen such resolve: "This man was alone, in sight of the hills he knew, with only enemies about him, with no source to draw on for strength but that which lay within himself." He became for Davis every *mambi.* The officer raised his sword, let it drop, and his men fired. Rodriguez's head snapped back, "but his body fell slowly, as though some one had pushed him gently forward from behind . . . He sank on his side in the wet grass without a struggle or sound, and did not move again." Priests ran up; soldiers marched off; Davis fell in behind them. He was a guest of the nation and must go, but he glanced back at the young Cuban "who was no longer a part of the world of Santa Clara." He seemed asleep, his arms still tightly bound, "with the scapular twisted awry across his face and the blood from his breast sinking into the soil he had tried to free."

More than one hundred years later, "The Death of Rodriguez" proves the power of words. One stands in Davis's shoes and marvels at the courage of the condemned, feels the guilt of continued existence while watching another die. Any war correspondent will speak of the complex emotions that settle in an intimate cloud: guilt, sadness, anger, exhilaration—and, above all else, a sense that you must get this moment right and people must see. Davis did it all, and for all his faults, you like him for his talent and honesty. The *Journal* published "The Death of Rodriguez" on February 2, 1897; it was picked up nationwide and would be the most anthologized of Davis's Spanish war stories, focusing American anger, reverberating today about the waste of war.

Davis left soon after that, sailing again on the *Olivette*, and during the trip chanced upon a scoop that became his most controversial. As he sat for dinner, he talked to Clemencia Arango, a young Cuban woman whose brother commanded a *mambisi* unit operating near Havana. Because of that kinship, the Spaniards suspected her of aiding rebels and expelled her from her home. Cultured and well-heeled, she was "dressed as you see girls dress on Fifth Avenue after church on Sunday." This was the kind of society belle Davis liked, and he took her seriously. On the day of departure, she was strip-searched three times—in her home, in the customhouse, and in her cabin on the *Olivette.* Arango was outraged; Davis, too. He filed an overwrought story when the *Olivette* docked: a young woman's strip search was salacious enough, but Davis failed to mention that police matrons conducted the searches, not men.

Davis's tale of outraged femininity was one of the most incendiary newspaper pieces of the war. Hearst's flagship had been building to this: the *Journal* had already run lurid tales of arrested nuns, captive women trussed like geese, and female *reconcentrados*. But such horrors paled to those of Senorita Arango. Run under the headline "Does Our Flag Shield Women?" the story filled two pages. On the second page, Hearst ran a Frederic Remington drawing of three male Spaniards surrounding a naked young woman. One stands in profile; a second turns away. The third faces the "invisible wall" and leers at the spectator, making him complicit: *You like this, too.* With his goatee and pencil-thin mustache, he is the embodiment of the devil. Remington was too smart not to know what he did.

The story and drawing affected the nation in a way no other had. Congressman Amos Cummings called for an investigation. The Senate drafted its own fact-finding resolution. The *World* interviewed Arango in Tampa. She and the other young women were indignant, not because of the outrages themselves but because of the way the searches were portrayed. No lecherous men had ogled their naked flesh; women carried out every search; they'd been searched two times, not three. And despite Davis's claims, international law actually *did* allow Spain to search vessels docked in its harbors. Congress dropped its investigation. A mortified Davis fired off a letter to the *World*: "I never wrote that she was searched by men," only that they were "undressed and searched . . . to the length of taking off their shoes and stockings." Yet the normally detail-rich Davis had neglected to mention the searchers' gender, so Hearst filled in the details and Remington proved again that a picture was worth a thousand words. With "Does Our Flag Shield Women?," coverage reached an unprecedented level of shrillness, and cascading cries for intervention became the new norm.

Sex and violence fueled that norm. Previously, the horror stories shocked U.S. readers, but these involved Cubans and Spaniards, and did not directly affect folks at home. It was like family strife—you might know that your neighbor beats his wife or children, but that was their business, not yours. Editors in the Midwest had lectured that the rebellion interrupted trade, destroyed property, and stymied the "natural expansion" of capitalism—yet they rarely counseled invasion. Strategy and capital did not touch their readers' lives. But sex crimes and violence involving fellow Americans did. From February 1895 to February 1897, the solutions debated for the "Cuban question" included neutrality, arbitration, and charitable donations to lessen *reconcentrado* suffering. Rarely did newspapers call for war.

Then, in the month of "Does Our Flag Shield Women?," four Americans were arrested and thrown into prison. The first was Sylvester Scovel. He'd contacted Gómez as Lee asked, sounding him out about an American peace plan. "And now you have come to demand my surrender," Gómez groused, reiterating that Cubans would settle for nothing less than independence. Yet the death of his son and Maceo, and the unabated suffering of the *reconcentrados* had shaken his resolve. Scovel came away believing that if the United States dealt with Spain, then sent an official peace delegation to Gómez, he might accede. Scovel tried to get his report to Thomas Alvord Jr., the *World*'s accredited reporter in Havana, but on January 13, 1897, Alvord heard that a cadre of officers planned to ambush Scovel, dump his body in a cane field outside the city, and collect Weyler's $10,000 reward. He told Scovel to flee: they'd meet on the southern coast, in the town of Trinidad. But this was filled with Spanish troops, so Alvord suggested a second town, six miles north of Tunas. Somehow, Weyler knew their every move.

Life on the run had worn Scovel down. His shoes were falling apart, his clothes ragged. He'd traded his favorite derby for one that correspondents called a "hippy-happy," a style popular in the interior. On February 2 an officer with the Guardia Civil studied him in the train station, then laid a hand on his shoulder: no one wears a hippy-happy on the southern coast, he said. Guards hustled Scovel to the provincial capital, but during the train ride, he noted so many chances for escape that he thought it must be a setup: one false move and they'd shoot him down. On February 5 Fitzhugh Lee wired Washington about the arrest; two days later, the *World* printed the news. On February 14 authorities charged Scovel with communicating with the enemy, punishable by death. Two days later, the mutilated body of his Cuban guide was found dumped beside a road.

Scovel was not alone. On February 4 the military commander of Guanabacoa arrested Dr. Ricardo Ruiz in his home. Ruiz had fought in the Ten Years' War, studied dentistry in Pennsylvania, become a naturalized U.S. citizen, and opened a practice in Cuba. Naturalized citizens were thought to aid rebels, using their status as a shield, but these days it served more as a spotlight. Ruiz was charged with train robbery, a common charge, since rebels plagued government trains. He handed over proof of his citizenship, then disappeared for thirteen days.

Other Americans vanished. On February 6 Francis J. Cazañas was arrested in Sagua and thrown without trial into jail. By now, Fitzhugh Lee was wiring the State Department. All he knew about Cazañas was that he owned a plantation worth $39,843, now forfeit, and some property in New York City. Then, on February 9, Charles Scott—employed by an American gas company—was arrested in Regla and held like Cazañas and Ruiz. Scott wasn't even a property owner; his crime, Lee wired, was "having [a] Cuban postage stamp in his house."

Scovel's treatment was never an issue: Lee wired that he was "treated like a king." His cell boasted a carpet, a nightstand, a cozy bed, and even a rocking chair, sent by admirers. He might be headed for the firing squad, but until that moment he'd live comfortably. Many admirers were young ladies: they sent baskets of food and stayed to chat when they delivered them. The *World* campaigned for his release: "Scovel May Die, but His Death Will Free Cuba," it trumpeted. Eighty-seven editors and reporters, including Davis and Remington, wrote statements demanding his freedom. Congress denounced his arrest; resolutions for his release were drafted by the Senate, seventeen state legislatures, the Oklahoma Territory, the city council of Columbus, Ohio, and the University of Michigan's alumni association. "How long shall the United States sit idle and indifferent within sound and hearing of rapine and murder?" Pulitzer demanded on February 13. Scovel's daily letters were smuggled out of jail by the wife of a U.S. consular official. They appeared in the *World* datelined "Calaboose #1." The paper's circulation climbed by eight thousand.

Conditions were different for Ruiz, Scott, and Cazañas. Jailers threw Ruiz into a three-by-five-foot cell with a stone floor, no window, and a six-inch slot in the door for food. Scott's cell was slightly larger, five by eleven, but damp with standing water; he was "not allowed anything to sleep on or [a] chair; discharges of the body removed" once every five days, Lee wired. Scott regularly went twelve hours without water. Little was known about Cazañas, but Lee assumed the worst.

Then the worst happened. On Wednesday, February 17, Ruiz was found dead in his cell. His wife, Rita, was informed by Guanabacoa's clerk of civil court, who let her view Ruiz's body. She asked jailers for a lock of his hair and a folding "steamer-recliner," the only chair in his cell. It seemed a strange request, but she must have been forewarned that on the bottom her husband had scratched a message in his blood: "Adios, I will be killed. Yes, they will kill me if they take me to Havana! Adios, Rita, wife of my soul and my children; adios, my sons; adios, my daughters! Be good and obedient to your mother." Rita Ruiz sent the chair to Fitzhugh Lee as proof of the murder, then fled.

Ruiz's autopsy occurred the next day. Lee insisted that an American doctor be present: two Spanish doctors and the U.S. sanitary inspector of Havana, Dr. H. M. Burgess, attended. Results showed that Ruiz died from cerebral congestion and a blow to the top of the head. Burgess described the wound as "a severe contusion, about an inch and a half long, by an inch wide . . . produced by a blow or blows, which, while not fracturing the cranium, were of sufficient strength to cause the congestion." In other words, Ruiz was beaten to death. The Spaniards disagreed. They described the wound as slight, just a "small abrasion"; although it may have been caused "by a blow with a round club or other instrument," they considered his death self-inflicted, caused by his "butting the head against the door or walls of his cell."

By February 20 Lee's wires sounded panic-stricken: "Can not stand another Ruiz murder and have demanded [Scott's] release." His dilemma was very real. Scovel, admittedly, had goaded Weyler, but the only sins of Ruiz, Scott, and Cazañas were that they were naturalized U.S. citizens. Two owned property that reverted to cash-strapped Spain: Cazañas's plantation was worth $1.25 million; Ruiz owned five properties worth $2.35 million in 2020 dollars. The U.S. secretary of state said it seemed like "American citizens are being murdered in cold blood."

Threats did not intimidate Weyler, and on February 20 he wired Madrid that Cuba was under control. Two days later, he visited Scovel, possibly to gloat. He appeared at the cell door, glanced at the gifts and cozy trappings, and turned on his heel without a word. That same day, the warden was demoted and all visits from smitten young ladies ended. Soon afterward, Madrid ordered Weyler to release Scovel without trial. On March 9, five days after McKinley's inauguration, the celebrity correspondent sailed from Havana to New York to write of his arrest and threatened execution. "Another Triumph for Publicity!!" boasted the *World*. By then, Charles Scott and Francis Cazañas had also been released and sent to the United States, both nearly destitute. Rita Ruiz met with the new president, wearing her widow's weeds.

The Voice of America formed the chorus of her mourning.

6

The Young and the Restless

A strange lull beset America. The Voice of America calmed down. Hostilities waned with the rainy season. In April, war broke out between Turkey and Greece over the island of Crete, and Crane, Davis, Scovel, and Creelman scribbled furiously for the short month of shooting. On April 15 the *World* claimed that 200,000 "dying wretches" starved in Weyler's camps, 60 to 70 per day; Spanish troops regained ground in Cuba and the Philippines. Such stories made the front page, but more exciting things were happening. On July 15 four lucky prospectors from Alaska stepped off a ship into a San Francisco assay office, their valises stuffed with gold nuggets as plentiful as "yellow hulled corn." The Klondike Gold Rush was on!

The "new American" had turned his back on the nineteenth century "before he was done with it," wrote Henry Adams, grandson of President John Quincy Adams. A transplanted Bostonian, he presided over a Washington social set John Hay dubbed "the Pleasant Gang." Roosevelt belonged, as did Henry Cabot Lodge. But what, Adams wondered, was this New American? He seemed a restless creature, preferring action to thought. Once set in motion "the laws of mass could have no other outcome" but that of "crushing equally the good and the bad that stood in its way."

Change seemed everywhere, but who could interpret its meaning or direction? The U.S. population had nearly doubled since 1870 to seventy-five million, with a third of that growth from immigration. The country that achieved its first billion-dollar budget during Benjamin Harrison's administration now surpassed all others in steel, timber, meatpacking, and the mining of gold, silver, iron, and coal. National wealth surpassed $65 billion, more than Russia and Germany combined, while the nation's trade surpassed all others save Great Britain. Such feverish production pushed a search for world markets; McKinley's election reached into Adams's salon, sending members to the ends of the earth in service of expansion. John Hay, a family friend of the Roosevelts, packed off for London as U.S. ambassador; others departed for Athens and Persia. "Only the Lodges and Roosevelts remained," Adams wrote, "but even they were at once absorbed in the interests of power."

Perhaps Theodore Roosevelt was this New American. The idea disturbed Adams. When the group met in his book-lined chamber overlooking Lafayette Square, he sank in his leather armchair and watched the Washington newcomer. He found Roosevelt "repulsively fascinating," as if a caveman had walked into his library. His vitality seemed indecent, his confidence ridiculous: "All Roosevelt's friends knew that his restless and combative energy was more than abnormal." If one word described him, it was "primitive." Roosevelt was "pure act," but Act without Thought creates chaos and ruin.

Roosevelt was just as troubled by Adams. He felt intimidated by the older historian, needing only to glance at his nine-volume *History of the United States of America, 1801–1817* to see that Adams was the writer and thinker he could never be. Since Roosevelt's instinct was to attack at the hint of threat, he consigned Adams to the realm of those "white-livered weaklings" molding American thought after the Civil War. Balding, big-eared, watchful, and shy, Adams walked to work every morning at the State Department Library, then returned at night to socialize. Adams was a thinker, not a doer, everything Roosevelt despised. Where Adams could step back to analyze repulsion, Roosevelt had little patience for such reflection. "He was forever imagining himself as a man of the highest ideals," wrote William Allen White; he saw himself "mirrored in the heart of youth," and America was still young. He found it impossible to forget and forgive, and would say of Adams and the "little emasculated mass of inanity" Henry James that both were "charming men, but exceedingly undesirable companions" for men "of strong nature." Roosevelt, of course, considered himself "strong-natured."

McKinley nominated Roosevelt as undersecretary of the navy on April 6, 1897; the Senate confirmed it two days later. He resigned his post as New York police commissioner and began his new duties on April 19, 1897, at the time the youngest man ever appointed. He prepared by asking Captain Alfred Mahan to his home at Sagamore Hill to discuss naval strategy. He promised Lodge that he'd temper his pro-war opinions, but wrote his sister Anna that he was a "rampant 'Cuba Libre' man" and wanted to "send our fleet promptly to Havana."

Roosevelt stayed quiet during his first weeks in office, but did not sit idle. Navy Secretary John Long showed little interest in naval policy, often leaving the office in Roosevelt's hands. In his first week, Roosevelt drafted a six-hundred-word memo about ship deployments in a Mediterranean crisis, inserting forewarnings about Cuba, the opening salvo of a yearlong campaign. In his second week, he listed talking points: annex Hawaii, build a canal across Central America, add a dozen battleships to the navy's aging fleet. In the ninth week, McKinley sent to Congress a renegotiated treaty making Hawaii a U.S. territory. In his eleventh week, the undersecretary updated the navy's war plan concerning Spain: in this version, most conflicts occurred at sea, and a naval blockade preceded any invasion. He added a new detail: an attack on the Philippines.

During this period, Roosevelt delivered one of his most consequential speeches. On June 2 he addressed the students and faculty of the Naval War College in Newport, Rhode Island, concerning a more modern navy. Colleagues could detect Mahan's hand. The speech used as its theme George Washington's maxim, "To be prepared for war is the most effectual means to promote peace." But the tone was more bloody-minded than Washington's, who'd known the tragedies of war. Roosevelt's was a paean to the gods of combat. All the "great masterful races" were "fighting races," Roosevelt claimed, and once they lost those "hard fighting virtues," their civilization waned. The pursuit of peace through trade or diplomacy was the coward's route, which "in a race, as in an individual, is the unpardonable sin." Diplomacy was "the servant, not the master of the soldier": maybe in some distant future, war would be consigned to memory, but not today. Today, "no nation can hold its place in the world, or can do any work really worth doing, unless it stands ready to guard its rights with an armed hand." He uttered the word "war" sixty-two times, nearly once a minute, before he sat down.

Roosevelt had turned Mahan's theories into Gospel. Sea warfare was changing, but the United States had not changed even as so many great powers pushed ahead. If America wanted to enter that club, a modern navy was the fee. During the 1880s, there had been little public sentiment for expensive "first-class" ships of the line. Newspapers and the *Congressional Record* listed Chile, Argentina, and Brazil as nations whose navies the U.S. should emulate, but this was not good enough, for navies are built with potential adversaries in mind, and the greatest threat now stemmed from European powers. Every great industrial nation except the United States was building fleets of steam-driven, steel-sheathed warships able to cross great stretches of ocean; their huge, breech-loading cannons fired with a range, accuracy, and speed unknown a generation ago. Great Britain and Germany were locked in an Atlantic arms race, while Japan would soon be the Pacific's premier naval power. Most of all, he feared Germany. Kaiser Wilhelm already sought Asian colonies, and Roosevelt could see a future where he would do so in this hemisphere. Roosevelt felt that armed conflict with Germany would break out before century's end.

His speech was printed in all major newspapers, and some editors extolled it as evidence of a new, defiant spirit in American affairs. "Well done, nobly spoken!" praised *The Washington Post*. Roosevelt's words were "manly, patriotic, intelligent, and convincing," said Charles Dana's *Sun*. Secretary Long was not pleased, even less so when Roosevelt repeated the speech in Sandusky, Ohio. It chilled McKinley. "I suspect Roosevelt is right," he said, "and the only difference between him and me is that mine is the greater responsibility."

On June 16, two weeks after the speech, Roosevelt came to the White House to lobby for a bigger navy; on July 18 he met with senators and Cuban sympathizers to discuss the rebellion. On August 2 the sweltering Washington summer drove Long to the cooler Northeast, and Roosevelt found himself the acting "hot weather secretary." He roared through the Navy Department, inspecting battleships, issuing reports, clearing production lines. "I am having immense fun running the Navy," he wrote a friend.

His influence grew. He dined daily at the Metropolitan Club, the men's-only private club close to the White House, on H Street. Founded during the Civil War, its visitors and members included every president since Lincoln; generals, admirals, ambassadors, and cabinet members; and some of America's richest men, including J. P. Morgan and the Vanderbilts. The dark-wood floors and paneling, floor-to-ceiling bookshelves, and crystal chandeliers bespoke power and privilege. Roosevelt started dining there in 1889 when President Harrison appointed him to the Civil Service Commission; he preferred it for Boone and Crockett Club gatherings, a covey of gentlemen hunters he and Lodge had cofounded devoted to hunting and the new idea of conservation. The membership included politicians and industrialists; the historians Francis Parkman and Frederick Jackson Turner; the Western iconographer Frederick Remington; and Owen Wister, author of a number of tales of the West that, in 1902, he linked to form *The Virginian.* Roosevelt now assembled a group of similar luminaries, many from the Boone and Crockett ranks, tied together by the belief that America must free Cuba, annex Hawaii, and exercise dominion over the Western Hemisphere and, eventually, the world.

They called themselves expansionists, a free-floating term in popular culture that they made their own. Though belief that the United States should be a world power was nothing new, it began to crystallize near the end of the Harrison administration. Even then the lobby was loose-knit, until recent "crises" accelerated the "need." In March 1889 tensions between the United States and Germany over coal stations in Samoa were cooled by a giant hurricane; in October 1891 a deadly brawl in Valparaiso, Chile, between American sailors and locals had both sides briefly demanding war. If anything, "war scares" forced a realization that America's armed forces were too weak to wage colonial wars. The world was suddenly a dangerous place, populated by great powers armed to the teeth. Roosevelt became the expansionists' de facto leader and started recruiting new allies.

The first was Captain Leonard Wood, the president's attending assistant physician. Roosevelt had only met Wood in June, but had worshipped him for years. Wood had won the Medal of Honor for his part in the Apache campaigns and had been part of the force that ran Geronimo to ground. Wood was unassuming wit to Roosevelt's bluster, but both were Harvard men. Roosevelt was two years older than Wood, though he seemed younger; both were great expansionists. When Roosevelt invited Wood to the Metropolitan, he could not hold back: Cuba's plight tainted the national conscience. It was our duty to intervene.

Roosevelt's second important recruit that summer was Commodore George Dewey, president of the navy's Board of Inspection and Survey. If ever a man resembled a raptor, it was Dewey: piercing eyes, beaklike nose, restless despite his sixty years. He'd sailed during the Civil War as a lieutenant in Admiral David Farragut's Mississippi River campaign, participated in the Chilean crisis, and after three decades of peacetime service strained to return to war. Like Wood, Dewey was an ardent expansionist, and Roosevelt mulled over ways to name him commander of the U.S. Asiatic Squadron once Rear Admiral Fred V. McNair, the current occupant, retired.

One target of Roosevelt's charm offensive is especially interesting, both for the fact that he lay outside traditional realms of power and for his description of Roosevelt's pursuit. In the fall of 1897 Frederick Funston's newspaper pal William Allen White came to Washington from Kansas on a patronage mission. White was not yet thirty, blond, pudgy, but famous for his editorial "What's the Matter with Kansas?" that ran in his *Emporia Gazette* on August 15, 1896. White claimed in the piece that Populists were "gibbering idiots" ruining his state; Republican papers across the country reprinted it, and McKinley used it in his presidential campaign. When Roosevelt learned of White's visit, he asked that he drop by his office.

That first meeting resembles a seduction: "I was afire with the splendor of the personality that I had met," White later said. He describes Roosevelt as a caged animal raging with pent-up energy: his countenance could be primitive—"impetuous, imperious, splashing in a reserve of vigor." Or sophisticated—"not ever quite furtive, but often feline." His "grayish blue eyes" glinted behind round glasses; his hair and mustache bristled; his "double row of glittering teeth" clicked and snapped at each word. White returned so frequently to these jaws and teeth—"the hard, wriggling jaw muscles, and snapping teeth"; "when he was excited he worked his jaw muscles with animal ferocity"—that one envisions a predator.

The seduction resumed the next day at the Metropolitan. Roosevelt led

White to his table and gestured for the menu. For the next hour, the two talked and dined on double lamb chops, Roosevelt's favorite. Years later, White remembered that meal with ecstasy: "double mutton chops . . . seas of speculation . . . excursions of delight, into books and men and manners, poetry and philosophy." White must have mentioned Funston, for within two years, Roosevelt told the Kansan that he'd long followed his career. White describes the lunch in almost intimate terms: Roosevelt "poured into my heart such visions, such ideals, such hopes, such a new attitude toward life and patriotism and the meaning of things, as I had never dreamed men had." They ate "heartily but not too heartily; enjoyed with a zest good food . . . drank one glass of sherry and no more." Exit the future Pulitzer Prize winner; enter the swooning paramour. They walked beneath the swaying elms of F Street, and when they parted, White would write, "I was his man."

As summer cooled into autumn, Roosevelt set his sights on bigger game.

But McKinley was not so easily swayed. On Tuesday, September 14, he invited Roosevelt on an afternoon drive in his open carriage. He complimented the undersecretary's tenure during Long's absence and praised his remarks about Japan. Roosevelt had boarded the battleship *Iowa* one week earlier for gunnery practice and now waxed ecstatic about the potential destruction issuing from its 8- and 12-inch guns.

McKinley did not comment, but fixed Roosevelt with his dark, steady eyes. Sometimes his pupils enlarged, and one seemed to fall into their black holes. The stare unnerved Roosevelt; it was the gaze of a sphinx, unreadable. Many found it troubling; Mark Hanna found it powerful; political foes gossiped that the president partook of Ida's medicine cabinet, and thus the weird dilation. Roosevelt's biographer Edmund Morris, who dislikes McKinley, posits that there was little behind the stare: "McKinley stared in order to concentrate a sluggish, wandering mind." Considering the hero worship that follows Roosevelt, it is the image of McKinley that remains.

Yet McKinley had a different kind of intelligence, one that stripped off the extraneous to get to the heart of the matter. He did not indulge in imaginative flights, not like the younger man beside him; he used silence to draw men out. On the same day as Roosevelt's visit to the *Iowa*,

McKinley had attended a reunion of old Civil War veterans in Fremont, Ohio—men who'd served with him in the Twenty-Third Ohio Volunteers. He watched military maneuvers, listened to martial music, was honored by two cannon salutes, and gently reminded his listeners: "My comrades, the memories of the war are sweeter than service in the war." Now he sat in a rattling carriage beside another young man gripped by war fever. He listened to Roosevelt mention a possible war with Spain and agreed that there might be "trouble" there. When Roosevelt said he hoped to enlist should hostilities commence, McKinley laughed lightly and promised the overgrown boy a chance to serve "if war by any chance arose."

Three days later, McKinley invited Roosevelt to the White House for dinner; in another three days, on September 20, the two took a second carriage ride. Now Roosevelt gave the president his own war plan. Within forty-eight hours of formal declaration of war, a squadron of swift cruisers would leave Key West, followed by a fleet of battleships. If the army sent in a small landing force, war would end in six weeks. Meanwhile, the Asiatic Squadron could take Manila. McKinley's response is not known: again, he may have just listened.

Events had occurred to which Roosevelt was not privy. In August, an anarchist assassinated Spain's conservative prime minister Antonio Cánovas del Castillo. Soon the old government fell. In September, the queen regent bowed to pressure and asked Práxedes Mateo Sagasta, leader of the Liberals, to be prime minister—for the sixth time. The Liberals believed in granting the Cubans autonomy, and General Stewart L. Woodford, McKinley's new ambassador, convinced the queen regent that U.S. demands "were so moderate and our cause so just" that public opinion would not support continued Cuban death and ruin.

But on that same day, Gómez rejected an offer of peace, something McKinley did not yet know. "Cuba can not, must not, and does not wish to continue any longer under the sovereignty of Spain," the Old Man declared. "The names of our champions who have fallen and those of the 150,000 defenseless Cubans pitilessly murdered by General Weyler would condemn us from Heaven if we were to treat with Spain." Communications were not instantaneous, and Woodford still cabled hope that Spain had tired of war. Two rebellions at opposite ends of the earth had sucked her Royal Treasury dry; Cánovas's assassination ripped the heart from the nation. Spanish newspapers asked: When will it end?

Woodford was even hearing rumors that Weyler might be recalled. And he was, without fanfare. On October 31, 1897, Weyler ascended the gangplank for Spain—replaced by the former Philippine governor Ramón Blanco, cooling his heels since leaving Manila. Sagasta desired a more conciliatory tone, the very thing the archipelago's friars had condemned. As Blanco quietly replaced Weyler, the *reconcentrado* policy began to ease. He considered making peace with Gómez, something Weyler would never do.

Given all this, McKinley could hope that the very war Roosevelt championed was not inevitable. He refused to commit, not through lack of will or courage, but because the landscape always changed. Clichéd as it seems, he believed in the common wisdom that "Good things come to those who wait." He did not tell Roosevelt any of this. The man had no need to know.

After that second carriage ride with McKinley, Roosevelt changed. He'd entreated the man and got nothing, and as early as that Metropolitan lunch with William White, he'd professed "scorn" for the president. McKinley's "weakness and vacillation are even more ludicrous than painful," he groused in his diary. "The blood of the Cubans . . . lies at our door."

During this time, he did something so conspiratorial that anyone else would have been fired. A week after the second ride, he intercepted a letter to Secretary Long from New Hampshire senator William E. Chandler recommending Commodore John A. Howell for the Asiatic Command. Roosevelt was appalled. Howell was "irresolute," he told Chandler, and "extremely afraid of responsibility." The senator ignored him. Roosevelt sent for Dewey: "You are the man who will be equal to the emergency if one arises. Do you know any senators?"

He did—Senator Redfield Proctor of Vermont, a Republican and a friend of McKinley's. "Senator Proctor is from my state," Dewey added. "He is an old friend of the family, and my father was of service to him when he was a young man." At Roosevelt's suggestion, Dewey sees Proctor; Proctor sees McKinley; and when Long returns from vacation, a note from the president sits on his desk suggesting Dewey for the Asiatic

Command. As insurance, Roosevelt made sure that Long didn't see Chandler's letter until Dewey's appointment was approved.

Though the deception ruffled his feathers, Long again forgave his assistant. To many, Roosevelt seemed charmed. But McKinley had looked inside him and was not pleased. White House invitations dwindled. After September 20, there were no more carriage rides.

Carl August Sandberg was desperate to be a real American. As a child, he called himself Charles or Charlie, which sounded more American to him than the Swedish "Carl." In grammar school, he changed his surname to "Sandburg"; in time the rest of the family followed. The family history was one of reinvention: his father, August, had changed *his* name to Sandberg when he emigrated in 1869, erasing all clues of his ancestry. For thirty-five years, August worked fourteen to sixteen hours daily, six days a week, in the roundhouse shop of the Chicago, Burlington and Quincy Railroad in Galesburg, Illinois. He spent the day "swinging sledges and hammers on hot iron on an anvil" till a hump formed on his right shoulder and he came home "fogged and worn." Boys see what they want in their fathers—what they want, and don't want to be.

In June 1897 Charles Sandburg was nineteen. Lean, tall, blond, tanned dark from outdoor work, he had flashing blue-gray eyes; he laughed a lot; and people liked him, girls especially. But he grew tongue-tied in their presence and loved them from afar. He was the oldest boy of seven siblings, and must set an example. But what did that mean?

In 1892 hard times hit Galesburg, and Charlie quit eighth grade to help his family survive. He took several jobs: sweeping floors at the drugstore, emptying spittoons at a real estate office, delivering milk from the local dairy. In October 1892 he caught diphtheria and passed the disease to his two youngest brothers, Emil and Fred. In days the two fought for breath, then died within an hour of each other. The dairy owner had little sympathy: no work, no pay, including the day Charlie watched his brothers' small white coffins lowered into the ground.

Was this what it meant to be American—work till you drop, then die? He thought about the small coffins, about his father's quest to own "proputty." In 1883 August had put $100 down on a house and lot on

South Street and paid it off in six years, only to learn that the mortgage was encumbered by an older loan, something the seller had not divulged. He borrowed $807 to pay it off, a terrible burden for a man raising seven children on a $35 monthly salary. At night, he'd sit by the kitchen's west window, drop his eyes to the floor, raise them, over and over, ensnared by the American Dream.

Charlie thought of the "small-frame house" half a block away that he must have passed a thousand times. He'd never really noticed it until a buddy spied black crepe draped from the front and a passerby said, "A young fellow hanged himself in the basement last night." *Suicide!* With that the house took on a meaning that was "dark and strange." This guy was not much older than Charlie. Maybe he'd lost his job; maybe he was sick of living. How would you do it, anyhow? Carbolic acid, drowning, jumping from a high window? Gunshot, and "it's all over in a second." When Sandburg passed the little house, he felt "a queer blur" in his head.

This suicide opened his eyes. Galesburg had been his world, an upright bastion of work and temperance, where churches outnumbered taverns and the town's eighteen thousand inhabitants lived by the pulse of passing trains. By the 1880s it was the largest city within forty miles, a railroad hub filled with Swedes, blacks, and Scots-Irish toughs working for the CB&Q. The rail yard stretched five miles, one of the nation's largest; the tracks lay three blocks from his house at 806-810 Berrien Street, his third home. The tracks divided the town into haves and have-nots, the former living north in their stone and gingerbread estates; the latter, like Charlie, relegated to south of the tracks in their cramped frame cottages.

Galesburg was a typical "piece of the American republic"—but what was typical? He'd heard that America was a free country, but "free for what and for whom," he wondered, "and what is freedom?" Hard work was said to define a man in this country, but with his brothers' deaths, father's shackles, and neighbor's suicide, he wondered about that narrative.

Suddenly he saw suicides everywhere. He'd heard of a woman on nearby Lake George who'd jumped from an excursion boat because of "a love affair that had made her want to die rather than live." Today's suicides are rarely reported, but in turn-of-the-century newspapers they overflowed. Due north of Galesburg by 267 miles lay Jackson County, Wisconsin, where for a decade the *Badger State Banner* chronicled daily pain with the same regularity as it reported the latest crop failure. August 3, 1885: "The 60-year old wife of a farmer . . . killed herself by cutting her throat with a sheep shears." October 30, 1890: "Frederick Windey, an aged farmer, [drowned] himself in a pond where his little daughter had been accidentally drowned two years ago." October 10, 1896: "A man who will not give his name was found with his head upon the rails . . . awaiting the approach of a freight train." It was everywhere: in 1900 poisoning was the lead cause of death; men outnumbered women. Suicide stalked Boston society so relentlessly that it seemed written into the Brahmin genetic code. On December 6, 1885, Henry Adams came home from the dentist to find his Brahmin wife, Clover, collapsed in the parlor. A budding photographer, she'd drained a vial of potassium cyanide, a darkroom chemical. In the years after her death, Clover's sister leaped before a train. Her brother jumped from a third-story window.

Charlie had to get out of Galesburg, but how? He imagined joining Maceo's and Gómez's "scrabbly little armies fighting against Weyler," but there were no Cuban recruiters in Galesburg. He felt trapped, until the most obvious route stood revealed.

On a bright afternoon in June 1897, Charlie Sandburg joined the migration whose participants numbered up to 600,000. The "great army of tramps" had been part of the American landscape since Reconstruction, at first soldiers who could never go home, then the culture changing with time. The photojournalist Jacob Riis had been one of the early ones, forced on "the road" by the Panic of 1873. By the 1890s they were divided into "hoboes, who worked and wandered; tramps, who dreamed and wandered; and bums, who drank and wandered." Taking to the road was a natural choice in a railroad hub like Galesburg, where tramps gathered in the local "jungle" while awaiting a train.

Charlie's family was not pleased: "Papa scowled. Mama kissed me and her eyes had tears." He left after dinner in the last week of June 1897, nabbing an open boxcar west of the Galesburg terminal. He wore a black shirt, coat, vest, and pants, good shoes and socks, a floppy slouch hat and no underwear; he stuffed in his pockets $3.25 in change and "a small bar of soap, a razor, a comb, a pocket mirror, two handkerchiefs, a piece of string, needles and thread, a Waterbury watch, a knife, a pipe and a sack of tobacco." He'd formed a rough plan. The abundant Western wheat crop of 1897 sold for a dollar a bushel, an unprecedented $500 million harvest begging for threshers like Charlie.

For the next three months, he worked his way west, slinging hash in Keokuk, Iowa; laying track in Bear Lake, Missouri; threshing wheat on Kansas farms. He picked up tips in hobo jungles, read water towers for news. He learned which towns were generous, where one could "kip," or sleep, without a rousting by "bulls." Since you asked no questions about another 'bo's past, all were created equal.

And one could die easily. In 1895, 4,155 hoboes died on the rails. One night on the Colorado Midland to Denver, Charlie almost became a statistic, too. Since every boxcar was filled with tramps, he rode the bumpers, hands wrapped around the brake rods so he wouldn't slip beneath the wheels. But it was cold that night, and he started to nod. He caught himself twice, beating his head with his fists to stay awake. After an hour, the train slowed and he jumped off, thanking God he'd survived.

Man was as dangerous as the elements. Plainclothes cops, called "shacks," could be lethal, some shooting tramps, beating them with saps, throwing them off moving trains. Hoboes adorned the common mutilations with names: "Sticks" for a 'bo who lost a leg; "Wingy" for one who lost one or both arms; "Halfy" for a man who lost both legs above the knee.

By late September, Sandburg had made it as far west as Salida, Colorado. He could continue to the Pacific or turn north to the Klondike and pan gold. But he'd grown "a little homesick," so he turned back toward home. It's hard to say what made him turn. Maybe it happened the morning he'd seen the Rockies and called them "the hand of God." Maybe it occurred that near-fatal night on the bumpers when the Angel of Death brushed past with "soft wing tips" and murmured, "Not yet for this boy." He kept a journal and wrote how mysteries compounded in his mind, rather than answers: "Thoughts incessant, never ending—and what of it? Where to?" The same questions had nagged him before he set out, but after months on the road, he'd discovered a new confidence and "was easier about looking people in the eye."

So he turned back. He paused outside an army recruiting office in Omaha until he recalled the words of a fellow thresher who'd said that his entire three-year enlistment was filled with mowing garrison lawns and mucking out horse stalls. He moved on, riding freights until the afternoon of October 15, when he walked down Berrien Street to the only house in the nation where "I could open a door without knocking." His mother kissed him. They talked past supper, and the clean sheets that night "were not so bad."

But the old questions remained. He'd learned that "movement" and "longing" were two words for the same mystery, but he'd come to rest, which meant he must make money, must be useful, and he knew why a 'bo never stayed still. He got a job as a housepainter's assistant, making thousands of tiny circles with sandpaper, preparing wood siding for the first coat of paint. When would they let him paint? He didn't even want to paint. He was thinking like an apprentice, "and that's what you are, one more apprentice."

And the old longing returned.

There were many kinds of longing, and Clara Louise Maass thought she knew them all. There were the longings of the heart, but these she kept private. There was longing for status and respect, a natural desire for someone raised in penury. And there were longings beyond explanation—the kind that got you remembered because they got you killed.

One would not guess as much, just looking at her. She is a cipher, leaving few hints, and must be judged by her actions. In some ways, she resembles Sandburg—born to immigrant parents, the eldest child saddled with extra responsibility. She is two years older than Sandburg, born on June 28, 1876, three days after Custer dies in eastern Montana. A photo taken in her early twenties shows a prim and pretty young woman, light brown hair pulled in a bun, cross-shaped brooch pinned under a high lace collar. Army documents for 1898 record her height as 5 feet, 4½ inches and weight as 134 pounds, but photos show a smaller woman, almost willowy. She has a heart-shaped face, high cheekbones, and dark brows, but the most striking feature is her expression. She seems kind and friendly, and later pictures show her laughing in the middle of some army prank. Her eyes bore through the camera, dark and unwavering, straight into yours.

She was born in a tenement in East Orange, New Jersey, the first child of ten of recent German immigrants Robert and Hedwig Maass. Her father's job as a hatter was seasonal. Like the Sandburgs, the Maasses lived one step ahead of poverty; like elder son Carl, eldest daughter Clara must supplement the family income. While still in grade school, she took a job as a "mother's helper" in another house: this involved everything from cleaning to feeding newborns at three a.m. She received room and board, time off to go to school, but no pay. At fifteen, she hired on at the Newark Orphan Asylum, earning $10 a month, half of which she sent home.

The Germans of East Orange and Newark formed a separate community, often out of necessity. Many came to the United States after the aborted revolution of 1848, when Germans rose against the rule of Teutonic princes. Ringleaders settled on a two-square-mile plot of steep hillside west of downtown; by 1865 nearly one-third of Newark's 100,000 residents were German-born, like Robert and Hedwig Maass, or first-generation Americans, like Clara. They flocked together, built their own churches, listened to sermons in German, opened German schools; they owned or worked in their own factories, cornered Newark's beer trade. They dubbed this separate place "Schmierkase County" after a cheese spread in the Old Country. A city attorney prosecuting beer gardens that stayed open on Sundays warned owners that if they disagreed with Newark's laws, they could "go back to the Fatherland."

Such dislike extended to medical care: many city physicians turned Germans away. Out of need, the Newark German Hospital opened in December 1870 after four years of fundraising. Every doctor was German; nurses trained in the Institute for Protestant Deaconesses in Kaiserworth, Germany, where Florence Nightingale trained. German Hospital surgeons performed Newark's first cesarean section, the first resection of the stomach for cancer, and the nation's first resection of the bowel. By 1883 the hospital admitted its four thousandth patient, and by 1887 it needed its own "school for ward women" to maintain a reliable source of nurses. Christina Trefz, the wealthy wife of a brewery owner, donated funds for a three-story house with a lecture hall, fourteen student bedrooms, bathrooms, and a parlor. On Thanksgiving Day 1893 the Training School for Nurses, one of only thirty-five such schools in the nation, opened at Trefz Hall.

Maass applied in 1893 for the school's second class: she was seventeen, three years shy of the minimum, but her entire life had been one of caregiving. Few 1890s professions opened their doors to young women, but the prevailing belief held that women were natural nurses owing to the altruism inherent in their gender. Florence Nightingale believed this fully, but added to the schooling a command of medical science and what she called "sickroom management," the ecological belief that cleanliness, nutrition, fresh air, and sunlight were essential for healing. Nursing should be a spiritual calling, wholly female, answering only to itself and not to men.

Clara rode the trolley uphill to the corner of Newton and West Bank and gawked at the freshly painted white house with green shutters built next to the redbrick German Hospital. A dozen steps led to a decorative veranda supported by three colonnades. She stepped into a wide lobby that had fifteen-foot-high walls. A reception room opened off this, where she asked for Head Nurse Anna Seeber, the school's first director.

Seeber's approval was the school's only entrance requirement, but that didn't come easily. The head nurse held strong opinions about frivolous Gay Nineties girls. The young woman standing before her was small and pretty, but not in a fussy way; she was plainly dressed, no jewelry, and wore cheap rimless glasses for nearsightedness. Her command of English was a plus, though German was required: doctors lectured in that language, and for many patients it was their only tongue. Nurse Seeber asked her to take off her gloves. The girl's hands were calloused from hard work. Maybe she *was* a little young, but she'd worked her entire life serving others. She was hired.

Two grueling years of training followed, yet Maass earned $15 a month and free room and board, plus another $100 upon graduation if she excelled and behaved. Nurses must be quiet, and must manage the long hours in the obstetrics and fever wards and the operating room. She made beds, gave baths, checked temperatures, emptied bedpans. Cleanliness was not left to chance: mattresses were changed every four weeks; bedsheets and clothes every week; commodes, pails, and urine bottles immediately. She learned to apply dressings, set leeches and poultices, give enemas, apply catheters, and give morphine injections on a doctor's order. So it went, life's spectrum from birth to death, day after day, fifteen and a half hours a day, with one afternoon off every other week from two to five p.m. Until, on October 12, 1895, she stood ramrod straight and repeated the Florence Nightingale Pledge: "I solemnly pledge myself before God and in the presence of this assembly to pass my life in purity and to practice my profession faithfully." The head nurse placed on Clara's head a white muslin cap with tiny pleats and a narrow black ribbon; she pinned the nursing shield of the German Hospital on the stiff collar beneath her chin.

Clara's class of 1895 made her one of the school's first five graduates. She was now nineteen, more self-assured, even thought pretty when she took off her glasses and piled her honey-colored hair atop her head in a bun. As a graduate and "trained nurse," she had two options. She could become a private nurse for the princely sum of $15 a week, or stay at the German Hospital. She was a favorite among the doctors and staff, and by 1897, pending the retirement of Anna Seeber, was rumored to be the next head nurse.

By 1897 the world had grown more complicated. Sometime during this period, her father died, making her responsible for the upkeep of her mother and her younger sister, Sophie. The sense of duty that led Maass and others into nursing drove thousands of American women to join purity and temperance societies, fueling empathy for the plight of their Cuban "sisters." End Cuba's suffering, they cried in print and at rallies: "Shame, shame," scolded the magazine *American Home*, that President Cleveland "has allowed the wholesale butchery of women and children at his very door."

But outrage cuts both ways. A woman of influence could be condemned for not doing enough, as Clara Barton learned on September 26, 1897. As she sailed home from a hard year in Armenia, her staff wired that an "open letter to Clara Barton" had been released by some "Cuban patriots" in Tampa. They accused her of "inhumanity" for failing to relieve *reconcentrados*, too. In some ways, her hands were tied: she could not act unless Spain allowed her American Red Cross into the Ever-Faithful Isle. Yet such criticism was galling, and she asked McKinley to let "the Red Cross take steps on its own." By November 18 she received a letter from the Spanish ambassador Dupuy de Lôme: "Spain would offer every facility," she wrote in her diary. "He wants to come see me. Think Spain wants us to go. It might be well!!"

This was the year that violated feminine virtue became provocation for war. The first outrage came with Richard Harding Davis's "Does Our Flag Shield Women?" The second, in August, when Hearst's *Journal* followed the saga of the "Cuban Girl Martyr," and hundreds of thousands of American and English women sent petitions for her release to the Spanish queen.

Evangelina Cosio y Cisneros came from a provincial family in central Camaguey; her elderly father, accused of forming a rebel cavalry company, was sentenced to death but sent instead to mild confinement at the Isle of Pines. She went with him, then hatched a plot to set him free. According to the court, she lured the Spanish commander to her cottage, where he was to be beaten and bound by rebels, but Spanish soldiers foiled the plan. In her version, she screamed for help when the lustful commander took liberties, and friends saved her. Hearst's early stories spun both scenarios but emphasized Iberian carnality over time. Whatever the truth, the seventeen-year-old Cisneros was charged with sedition and sent to the top floor of Havana's Recogidas women's prison to await trial.

Her story got little play until the *Journal* reporter George Eugene Bryson discovered her plight in August 1897. He'd just covered Ruiz's death, and in his hands, the details of Cisneros's incarceration changed. "This tenderly nurtured girl," he wrote, was innocent of all charges; her wanton cellmates were some of "the most depraved Negresses of Havana." He said she'd been sentenced to twenty years, when in truth she hadn't yet faced trial.

Hearst turned the Cisneros story into a holy crusade. He mobilized women across America and claimed that a *Journal* petition for her release had been signed by fifteen thousand women, including McKinley's mother, President Grant's widow, and even Clara Barton, who was still overseas. Julia Ward Howe, creator of "The Battle Hymn of the Republic," wrote to Pope Leo XIII. Spain was astounded: they call *us* excitable, their papers exclaimed. The sheer number of signatures frightened the queen. Cisneros suddenly became the vessel of every wrong visited upon women in her sad, battered isle.

And Hearst would be Galahad: since the letter-writing campaign hadn't freed the maiden, he'd break her out of jail. He hired another expendable adventurer—the blond, six-foot Virginian Karl Decker, son of a Confederate cavalry colonel—who slipped into Cuba and broke her free.

The *Journal* devoted thousands of words to the caper: how Cisneros and Decker passed messages; how Decker rented a room directly across from her cell window. How, on October 8, 1897, she drugged her cellmates' coffee while Decker slid a twelve-foot ladder across the gap and cut the bars with a hacksaw. He smuggled her from Havana dressed as a sailor. One detail was omitted—Decker had bribed the guards to look the other way.

Barton had just returned home on October 10 when the Cisneros whirlwind descended. As always after a mission of mercy, she felt depressed and physically drained: she was seventy-six, and she felt her age. All she wanted was time apart at Glen Echo, Maryland, her home outside Washington, D.C. But on October 11 reporters called for her opinion on Cisneros, and she had to admit that she didn't have one, since she'd just come home. Two days later, the "Cuban Joan of Arc" arrived in New York, hand in hand with Karl Decker. "The girl stands like a beautifully chiseled statue, motionless, awed," the *Journal* gushed. A band played the Cuban anthem; fireworks bloomed in the sky.

"Evangelina Cisneros Reaches the Land of Liberty," trumpeted page one. Hearst planned a reception at Delmonico's and on October 14 sent Barton an invitation. She had a "previous engagement," but did not say that it was picking ripe pawpaws. On October 21 Hearst invited Barton to another event, and again she declined. Cisneros would shake hands with the president, travel across the nation, and tell the story (with Karl Decker) to adoring crowds. The *Journal* devoted 375 columns of type to the circus, while other New York papers devoted less than one. Hearst wooed Barton a third time; again she refused. To return from the wholesale Armenian slaughter to *this* was beyond madness. What, she wondered, had become of America?

By the fall of 1897, Cuba was everywhere in the news. Barton had seen such tensions build before, but for younger Americans like Sandburg and Maass, this was all new. Something momentous would soon break: the young and the restless want to be part of it. The winds tremble. The distant thunder rolls.

If one group supported *Cuba Libre* from the start, it was black America. As far back as the Ten Years' War, prominent blacks like Frederick

Douglass had petitioned President Grant to recognize the guerrilla cause: a free Cuba, Douglass said, meant the emancipation of 400,000 slaves. The Omaha *Enterprise* prodded McKinley to intervene. His continued reluctance could only be due to a "mysterious something" that wasn't hard to determine: fear that a free Cuba would grant "black natives the same respect and rights" accorded to whites—a racial Utopia compared to the United States of America.

American blacks had entered what one scholar called "a vale of tears." Reconstruction's promise lay in tatters; Jim Crow's full weight drew near. Federal courts successively upheld state laws disemboweling equal rights; white supremacists devised elaborate theories of black degeneracy wrapped in the folds of social Darwinism. Lincoln's party, as it reconciled with Southerners, no longer seemed to care about "the Negro question." In 1890 Henry Cabot Lodge pressed in Congress what was called the "Force Bill," designed to protect the voting rights of Southern blacks; it failed under arguments for regional harmony, and it would be the last federal attempt to shield black suffrage until the Civil Rights Acts passed sixty-seven years later. "We have made friends with the Southerners," the Yale social scientist William Graham Sumner wrote ironically in 1899. "The Negro's day is over. He is out of fashion."

The 1890s was the decade in which the violent control of Southern blacks entered a new dimension. Lynching grew in scope: from 1889 to 1923, fifty to one hundred incidents occurred per year. As the price of King Cotton plummeted, lynchings soared in counties where blacks held significant majorities, and with this the myth that white wives and daughters stood in constant sexual danger when surrounded by too many black men. Some control was thought necessary, extrajudicial or otherwise, to head off the carnage. "We have never believed [the Negro] to be the equal of the white man," said U.S. senator Benjamin Tillman in 1900 on the Senate floor, "and we will not submit to his gratifying his lust with our wives and daughters without lynching him."

If you were black in the Deep South between 1882 and 1930, studies suggest that you were lucky to survive. Lynching became a common means of control: 462 men and women murdered in Mississippi; 423 in Georgia; 283 in Louisiana; 262 in Alabama. Florida ranked fifth, with 212. Yet a 1993 University of Georgia study suggested that fifth-place

Florida was actually the nation's most lethal: because she had fewer black residents than other Southern states, her per capita deaths were thus the nation's highest. For every 1,250 blacks living in Florida during this period, at least one was lynched, a death rate seven times higher than North Carolina's and nearly twice the rate of Georgia's. Thirty-nine whites were also lynched in Florida during these years, a Southern rarity. The Sunshine State was a dark place for everyone.

No place was more dangerous than Tampa. Mob violence rarely concentrated in one area, but from 1858 to 1935, three blacks and six whites were lynched, and the city's five lynchings from 1900 to 1940 represented one of the highest numbers in any Southern city. Few other Southern cities grew as fast in one decade as Tampa, where cigars and expatriate Cubans turned an 1880 village of 720 residents into a manufacturing hub in 1890 of 5,532, one-fourth of them black. Unionized Cubans might be protected, but blacks were not, and white vigilantism thrived.

In October 1897 David Fagen turned nineteen. In another five years, *The New York Times* would run front-page stories on "the notorious Fagen," wanted by the U.S. Army, dead or alive. But on that October 23 he married the teenage Maggie Washington, and they set up house at 813 Harrison Street in Tampa's "Scrub," a slum named after the ubiquitous scrub palmetto. Enlistment papers signed in the next seven months paint him as solid and wide-shouldered, 5 feet, 10¼ inches, 140 pounds. As Clara Maass made her rounds, Frederick Funston fought to survive, Theodore Roosevelt dreamed of conflict, and Carl Sandburg came home, David Fagen gazed at his new bride and, like all grooms, wondered what the future might hold.

Hopefully it would improve. Little is known of Maggie, but Fagen's childhood was not easy. His mother, Sylvia, died in 1883, when he was five. His father, Sam, was a laborer who creeps into local legend, yet much of that is contradictory. An 1878 story in *The Sunland Tribune* has him catching an alligator; one in 1881 reports his stealing oats; a story in D. B. McKay's 1959 *Pioneer Florida* calls him "a shiftless old Negro who was never known to work, but had about 20 children," wrong in nearly every way. In McKay's account, he is accused but acquitted of stealing chickens. Yet when young David signed up for the army, he provided two references: one, Samuel Bryant, owned a Nebraska Avenue carpentry shop, was active in Republican politics, and built the Mt. Sinai African Methodist Episcopal Zion Church, a pillar in Tampa's black community. Support like that suggests Fagen came from more than alligator wrestling.

Maggie Washington married a man with a harrowing job. Vast phosphate deposits, dubbed the "Bone Valley," stretched south through the Withlacoochee and Peace river valleys, ending at Charlotte Harbor above Fort Myers. Phosphate was used in fertilizers, baby powder, cleaning compounds, water softeners, and matches, and the 1883 dredging of the Hillsborough River channel had unplugged these riches. Fagen worked for Hull Phosphate Company, ten hours a day at $1 daily, under the blazing Florida sun; he stood waist-deep in stagnant water as he broke chunks of phosphate rock from the riverbed with a crowbar and oyster tongs. Clouds of mosquitoes swirled around him; white foremen supervised from dry land. He heaved the rock into small boats, these hauled to shore, where it was dried, crushed to powder, and sold. Local blacks like Fagen provided 95 percent of the workforce; when numbers dwindled, convict gangs were contracted for forty cents a day. Sometimes Fagen worked close to Tampa and at night could go home. But often, he spent weeks in the phosphate camps dotting Bone Valley, places as mean as the turpentine camps Zora Neale Hurston profiled in *Mules and Men*. Black laborers' attempts to improve conditions met strong resistance from operators. In 1899 an "Anti-Lynch and Mob" club formed by black phosphate workers fought a pitched battle with lawmen, and two miners died. Four years later, a white employee in Bartow killed a black man who was arguing with the company bookkeeper, probably over pay.

By the time Fagen enlisted, his papers document several scars, most likely from the camps and mines. These include an "oval scar ½ x ¼ inch on left cheek," "a livid scar 1 inch on his right wrist," and a "curved scar ¼ inch on chin." Later events would show that he was not one to take abuse lightly. His time with Hull Phosphate apparently conditioned him for two things: life in the toughest of physical environments and contempt for white authority.

Fagen's teenage years coincided with what the Jacksonville *Florida Times-Union* called a new kind of black: the "Winchester Negro," named for his preferred weaponry. The 1890s saw the emergence in popular culture of the black outlaw or "bad nigger," an admiring term among contemporaries. The Winchester Negro was a lone desperado who violated all Black Codes, those strictures that white society said made him a good citizen. He took justice into his own hands and survived against impossible odds—the same legendary space as Robin Hood and Jesse James. The most famous Winchester Negro was the Alabama turpentine worker Morris Slater, better known as "Railroad Bill," who shot and killed a policeman, escaped confinement, and roamed southern Alabama robbing trains and stealing from black and white, rich and poor. Florida's version was Harmon Murray, who led his "Winchester rifle brigade" through Central and North Florida in 1890–1891, killing a number of whites, including a sheriff and his deputy. The gang formed in a turpentine camp near Tampa. The law tracked them across Florida, and once caught, most members were lynched. But Murray stayed on the run until September 3, 1891, when he told a cousin he wanted to "kill some crackers." The cousin agreed, then shot him in the head when his back was turned, just like Jesse James.

The "bad man" lived and died by his own rules, and David Fagen would model himself after the Winchester Negro when the time came. October 1897 was too early. But for Fagen, Sandburg, Maass, Roosevelt, and the other young and restless, the moment drew near.

7

"I Was a Rebel Once, Too"

Philippine rebels would remember the end of 1896 as a time of joy. "The people were truly happy, free to enjoy life in all sorts of ways," wrote Santiago Álvarez, who'd witnessed the aborted duel between Bonifacio and Aguinaldo. Release from Spain was intoxicating. Food was cheap; theft diminished; many tried practicing the Katipunan ideal of brotherly love. *Insurrectos* later called this the "Lost Eden." War raged at the ramparts, and Spaniards bombarded them daily, yet the "whistling cannonballs" came to be regarded "as fireworks in a celebration."

Popular heroes arose. The first was Josephine Bracken, christened "Josefina." In the week following her husband's death, she realized her path. She walked all night from Manila and appeared at the Zapote Bridge connecting to Cavite. A sentry demanded her name, and she replied, "A sister, Rizal's widow." She was whisked to meet Aguinaldo in Imus, where great celebrations ensued. She gave Bonifacio a copy of her husband's last poem, which she'd hidden in her shoe. She tended the wounded in a convent and wrote a short autobiography. Yet she always wanted revenge. When the Spaniards pushed Aguinaldo back from Zapote, she rode with another woman to the front, both armed with Mausers. *Insurrectos* fell around her: she witnessed Spaniards killing women and old men, watched as they seized babies by their legs and dashed them against walls. She charged the enemy, later saying she was "lucky enough" to kill a Spanish officer.

In Cavite, one still runs across cheap prints of this charge, Bracken portrayed as Lady Liberty in Eugène Delacroix's *Liberty Leading the People.* But the horror and bloodshed caught up with her, and she returned to the convent, stricken with fever. She remained until March 25, 1897, when Imus fell.

The second hero was Gregorio del Pilar, known as "Goyo," who would rocket to become one of the revolution's youngest generals. He grew up poor in San Jose, Bulacan, and hawked meat pies to survive. This made him smart and glib. At fifteen, he attended Manila's Ateneo Municipal to earn his *bachillerato*, the equivalent of a high school diploma; he lived with his aunt Deodato Arellano, considered the Katipunan's chief propagandist. Goyo distributed pamphlets and in one early coup slipped them into a pile of anti-revolution material distributed in church each Sunday. In one story, the unsuspecting curate passed them out to his parishioners.

With the revolution, Goyo came home and joined the rebels. The Bulakeños raised three thousand fighters and seized the town of Paombong. Pilar headed to Imus for weapons and an audience with Aguinaldo, but somehow he got sidetracked to the citadel of the supposedly bulletproof Maestrong Sebio, and he was present when Sebio's stronghold near Lake Laguna was breached by Spanish troops on New Year's Eve 1896. Goyo escaped with a head wound and hid in a "cave of lights" where "enormous white rocks" were washed by a "singing" spring.

It's possible he was feverish; possible he knew heroes emerged from magical caves. When he told Aguinaldo of his adventures, the general saw dramatic potential in the young man. He promoted him to lieutenant and sent him to fight back home. One day he ambushed a Manila-bound friar and his escort, killing one guard and taking his Mauser. He watched the churchman and remaining guards flee, but the story evolved to where he killed *seven* soldiers and captured the friar, plus seven Mausers. He *did* grab four coin-filled sacks: he gave each married man in his troop 50 pesos, half of that to the bachelors, and with the rest bought warm cloaks for everyone. He also kept the Mauser, the original point of the adventure. Few believed the account, but his men loved their generous, flashy fabulist and fought for him "like lions."

Just as important were legends of love. Goyo was handsome, charming, well-tailored, and he sweetened the war with rumored lovers in every town. "His traveling bags," wrote the biographer Teodoro M. Kalaw, "were always replete with mysterious and perfumed letters, capricious and artistic memoirs of women." His letters pledged undying love: "I received the amulet you sent me, which will save me from peril," he wrote one *amante*. Responses were usually perfumed.

Heroes might boost morale, but by March 1897 the Little Republic was running dangerously low on ammo and arms. That January, Aguinaldo sent the Propagandist José Alejandrino to Hong Kong, but the British controlled sales, and he shifted to Japan. On February 25 he wrote that investors might help: for $3,000 he could buy ten thousand Murata rifles and charter a small "sail vessel" for smuggling. But by March, Governor Polavieja's fresh troops began to maul the Filipinos. They pushed through the isthmus separating Manila from Cavite, laid siege to Imus, landed on Luzon's far southern coast, and pushed north toward Bonifacio. As Aguinaldo had predicted, bolos could not hold back Spanish guns.

An equally grave threat rose from within. As Spain attacked, the rift between Bonifacio and Aguinaldo deepened. A meeting held on New Year's Eve came to nothing; a second on March 22, 1897, was postponed as Aguinaldo fought outside Imus and his brother Crispulo died. When the two groups met the next day in the little town of Tejeros, Bonifacio's supporters formed the majority, as Aguinaldo's men were still fighting. They named Bonifacio mediator and moved to elect officers; El Supremo apparently felt so sure of the outcome that he declared all results final. Control of the Katipunan—and the Little Republic—seemed in his grasp.

Then the inconceivable occurred. As delegates elected Aguinaldo president in absentia, a roar filled the hall. Cabinet posts in war, finance, justice, and state also went to Aguinaldo. Perhaps as a sop, the single post of director of interior went to Bonifacio. El Supremo's pride was great: he drew a pistol on a man who taunted him, then shouted, "I annul all that has been approved and resolved." His loyalists shouldered their way from the hall.

What had just happened? The kerfuffle embodied in miniature two possible routes for the Little Republic—if it survived. Bonifacio's Magdiwangs were monarchists; Aguinaldo's Magdalo republicans. When Bonifacio came to Cavite from the mountains, the faithful shouted "*Mabuhay ang hari*," or "Long live the king!" He told followers that he was the incarnation of Bernardo Carpio and he could do no wrong. Yet one irrefutable fact overrode all else: Bonifacio, the outsider from Manila, did not win victories. Hometown Aguinaldo did.

Bonifacio moved his headquarters west to the town of Naic to create a rival government. He proclaimed himself the true leader, ordered all Filipino men to enlist in *his* army, and called for a coup. He allowed Spain to roll over towns that Aguinaldo had freed. Day by day, the Spanish juggernaut gobbled up territory: Noveleta and Rosario were taken; Aguinaldo's home in Kawit burned to the ground.

On March 25 Imus finally fell. Josephine Bracken rose from her bed to fight, but she collapsed; she streamed north with other refugees to the mountains of Maragondon. The range lies at the southern entrance of Manila Bay and provides numerous coves for a secret escape north to Luzon or west to Japan or Hong Kong. At some unspecified point, she slipped into Manila, but was discovered and brought before Governor Polavieja. Since she was British, he decided not to execute her, and he freed her but kept close watch. She feared incarceration and torture, so bought a bottle of strychnine. Yet Polavieja paid her passage to Hong Kong, and she threw herself into Propaganda work for the Junta.

Others were not so lucky. While Aguinaldo fell back to the west coast, Bonifacio abandoned Naic and on April 4 headed south to Batangas, hoping to rebuild in its jungles. Old and young came with him, many starving. They were refused when demanding food from the village of Limbon, so he ordered it burned. "Spare no one!" he cried. Yet he lacked the manpower for slaughter and settled into a small fort on the edge of town. In one short month, he'd transformed from idealist to demagogue, content in his anger to burn the world down.

On April 27 Aguinaldo ordered Bonifacio seized. He'd been reluctant to arrest him, but now he threatened his own people. The next day at dawn, his forces surrounded the fortress and overpowered the defenders. Bonifacio and his brother Procopio were wounded in the attack; their brother Ciriaco died. Aguinaldo's men carried the wounded Supremo in a hammock to an abandoned estate outside Naic and threw him into a dark room with his brother. The thick wooden doors were guarded by loyal troops; the two were not allowed visitors. There they stayed as Aguinaldo organized a tribunal.

The court-martial stretched from April 29 to May 6, starting in crumbling Naic and ending in the mountains of Maragondon. The Bonifacios were charged with treason; the main prosecution witness against them, a twenty-seven-year-old lieutenant colonel in Bonifacio's army named Pedro Giron. He testified that one day, while still in Naic, Bonifacio said, "If Mr. Emilio Aguinaldo would not subordinate himself to his authority, he would have him killed." Bonifacio gave Giron 10 pesos and "assured him of his patronage and protection no matter what happened." No further details bolstered this story; no corroborating witnesses. Bonifacio testified in his defense that he "never even once met with Pedro Giron."

On May 6 the court found both brothers guilty of all charges and sentenced "each of them to be shot in an open place, up to five shots for each; that the distance be ten feet according to the graveness of their crimes." Aguinaldo could not stomach this, and he commuted their sentences to "indefinite banishment" on a tiny island, watched over by "wardens." Yet his officers pressured him: if spared, El Supremo might escape and rain havoc on them all.

On the morning of May 10, 1897, the brothers were led to the mountains by a squad under Colonel Lazaro Makapagal. He was ordered to march to the foothills of Mount Buntis, where he must open a letter of instruction. When he read it, he said later, "My lips trembled and I was speechless for some time." He must take the brothers almost to the summit and shoot them; if he disobeyed, "it would be I who was shot upon my return to headquarters." If he fled, he'd be tracked down and executed. He read the orders to the Bonifacios, and Procopio began to weep. He embraced his elder brother: "What are we to do?"

Here Makapagal's memory enters a painful present tense, where heroes are criminals and hope collapses. They are at the summit, and Bonifacio cannot speak. "He bowed his head and sobbed while bitter tears . . . rolled down his cheeks. Not able to bear it, I turned my back; and when I faced them again, the deed was done."

One unpublished account exists: the memoirs of Castor de Jesus, an enlisted man. In this, Bonifacio was carried by hammock up Mount Tala, not Mount Buntis, owing to the pain of his wounds. They reached the top, and Makapagal read the orders: as Bonifacio crawled to the colonel to beg forgiveness, Procopio was led from sight, and shots rang. In panic,

Bonifacio found strength to rise and stagger to a promontory surrounded by a stream. The firing squad caught up and finished the job. They buried him in an unmarked grave, throwing twigs on top as they departed. El Supremo was not yet thirty-four. The revolt he sparked was only eight months old.

With that execution, the "Lost Eden" ends. Bonifacio's death rips the heart from many, and hordes of people return home. The Little Republic is dead.

Only Aguinaldo holds out. He turns to the refugees in his wake and says, "I know that hunger and disease will eventually kill us if we do not do something now." They must go home and seek amnesty while he goes into hiding. But he would return.

So he fled, extracting his last troops from Cavite with remarkable stealth and skill. He led more than a thousand, with their cattle, around the Spanish cordon, marching through streams and jungles until coming to the mountains of Bulacan sixty miles northwest of Manila. Gregorio del Pilar and other allies joined him there. They found an old iron mine in the Biak-na-Bato Valley near the town of San Miguel de Mayumo; the only road in sliced through towering cliffs that could be blocked by boulders. It was nearly impregnable.

Aguinaldo offered to recognize Spanish rule if the friars were expelled and Filipinos were represented in Spain's Parliament. He was refused. He proclaimed the birth of the Republic of Biak-na-Bato, its constitution modeled after the Cuban Constitution of 1895. "Enough of suffering!" he declared. "Viva the free Philippines!" Spain attacked, and five thousand more rebels and their families swelled the fortress state. They were locked in their redoubt, dangerously short of food and water; leprosy and smallpox emerged. But the Spaniards could not get in.

And changes were in the wind. On April 23 Polavieja resigned, citing ill health; his replacement, General Fernando Primo de Rivera arrived two days later. He, too, attacked the redoubt, but this floundered with the start of the rainy season. Like his predecessor, Rivera advised the queen that war would be expensive, and Cuba had already drained Spain's coffers. Instead, the new liberal prime minister, Práxedes Sagasta, ordered Rivera to sue for peace.

So Rivera turned to an old friend. Pedro Alejandro Paterno was a political fixer in every sense of the word, a *mestizo* lawyer able to socialize with Propagandists and hobnob with Spain. For seven months, he trekked from Manila to Bulacan and back, through rivers and mud and mountains, until on December 16, 1897, the two sides reached an accord. Spain would pay the rebels 800,000 pesos in three installments: 400,000 up front, another 200,000 to surrender their weapons, the remainder when a Te Deum sung from the Luneta announced a final peace. Spain also promised to pay 900,000 pesos to Filipinos suffering unjust treatment by Spain. The friars would go home; the press would be free. In exchange, Aguinaldo and his deputies would go into exile and declare loyalty to Spain.

On December 27 Aguinaldo stepped aboard the British steamer *Uranus* with eighteen allies: "All are confident that Spain, impelled by right and justice, will grant reforms without bloodshed or combat, since so much blood has already stained the soil of Luzon," he said. They stepped off the gangplank into Hong Kong on New Year's Eve.

Neither side kept their promises. Aguinaldo and the others immediately plotted to come home; Spain never paid the remaining reparations. Instead, after the new year, she arrested those involved in the revolt and tortured them for the location of hidden arms. A faint pulse of revolution resumed. By March 1898 scattered gunfights erupted throughout Luzon.

By March 1897 Frederick Funston had fought in Cuba for seven months. The romance had evaporated like morning fog. He was sick, injured, and wondering if he'd see Iola again.

And he was hungrier than seemed humanly possible. Weyler's starvation strategy was so effective that every day brought more misery. Funston's rations consisted of "a few sticks of sugarcane." At night, he dreamed of "bacon and kindred things." When he did eat, it would be a yam, served on a banana leaf, and his first thought was always "How I hate yams!"

During this period, Funston also suffered from *paludismo*, a severe form of malaria. Every other day, he'd burn with fever, so delirious he imagined himself "another person." This became a chill so intense he'd "shake his teeth out." A "welcome unconsciousness" was the only relief.

He no longer believed that Cuba would be free by spring. This war would last forever, and Cuba would be his grave.

These were not feelings he could admit to his father. On March 5 the mail finally arrived, and in his return letters he described events in ways to make Foghorn proud: García had made him "chief of artillery of the Department of East Oriente," with two batteries of four guns apiece; his soldiers were Cuban, but all officers American; he'd been through "two long sieges, eight battles and a number of smaller fights without a scratch although I have had two horses killed under me." He does hint at homesickness, but the future is bright, and García "has taken a great liking to me." Once fighting ends, "I have some big schemes" regarding railroad franchises. He tells Foghorn that he'll be paid $1,200, since he's contracted for "$220.00 per month (in) American gold," payment that will end in the same place as the Mexican coffee plantation—in the clouds.

He sits in camp outside Jiguani as he writes: this is a commercial center of bulging warehouses east of Bayamo, manned by eight hundred troops, ringed with trenches, barbed wire, and twenty-two forts of all sizes. The largest was El Castillo, a veritable castle atop a low hill rising eighty feet above the main street, protected by an 8-cm Krupp field gun. The job of taking the castle was given to Funston: the fact that García would even consider such a costly attack bespeaks his absolute desperation to feed his 4,200 starving men.

The attack started on March 13 at six a.m. Funston sent the letter to his father and started a second to his sister Ella, saying he was in "superb health" and felt "coltish" when reading news from home. He breaks off for war. The siege begins with his guns: the great hope is a new long-barreled, twelve-pound Driggs-Schroeder naval gun paid for by Florida cigar workers. Funston calls it "*Cayo Hueso*." But the fuses are so sensitive that shells explode almost upon impact, exacting far less damage than hoped. Funston and the Spaniards commence an "artillery dance"—the Spaniards fire at him with their old Krupp gun, he fires back, realizing that he must knock out this Krupp before he can get close enough to attack other fortifications. Its shells fly through the air so slowly that he can watch their lazy trajectory: he grows cocky and on the second day waits too long before diving aside. He later tells his sister that "an ill-mannered

Spanish shell" exploded nearby and knocked him down, omitting that shrapnel shreds his left arm and breaks a bone.

Doctors tied the arm across his side and chest and sent him back to battle. By now, Funston knew this duel was futile; he did not have the firepower. A direct infantry assault also failed: the Cubans seized posts two hundred yards from El Castillo, but could go no farther. They held this position overnight, then pulled back before dawn. A scout told García that a Spanish column from Bayamo would arrive within hours. García pulled his men back; he'd lost four hundred in the assault and had pushed them too hard. Plus, the scout's intelligence proved wrong.

For the rest of that spring, García kept the Spaniards bottled in their towns. On May 11 they rushed to the port of Sama on the northern coast; the siege netted them a few cattle and horses. During this time, Thomas W. Steep, a Scripps-McRae reporter, interviewed Funston and his men. Funston resembled a tramp: beard and mustache, hair poking through holes in his panama hat. They'd circled their hammocks like a wagon wheel and built a fire in the hub; when Funston spotted Steep, he shouted "Have you got any socks?" then lifted his pant leg to show his naked foot strapped inside a moldering sandal. "I think he never forgave me my having no socks to spare," Steep later said. The little man seemed in good spirits, though Steep noticed that he winced when he laughed and clutched at his shrapnel wound.

The newsman's visit seemed to trip something inside Funston. He finally told his sister of his exhaustion and admitted that his chest was badly bruised. "If [the war] is not finished by October, I am going home anyhow and let them fight it out among themselves," he wrote. "I suppose I was a pretty big fool to come down here and mix up in this war." But it was to Charles Scott that he bared his soul. Scott had written earlier about the weddings of "old chums," and it seemed as if the world had passed him by: "The best years of my life is behind me. Nothing can ever occur that can make me thoroughly happy, that is I mean absolutely happy, but there can come about plenty of hard luck, disappointments and heart aches. Would it be such an awful thing after all if I met the fate of my predecessor, Osgood, who in half a second went from the full vigor of manhood into Eternity."

Steep left soon, carrying the letters. He slid into Jamaica and dispatched his story to the States via cablegram. On May 20 "Funston Starving" ran in *The Iola Register*: "They came there with the most romantic ideas of war, but they are all sick and tired of it, and want to get back home." One month later, the very thing Funston had dreaded occurred. On June 20 he was shot through the body with a Mauser, "the bullet piercing both lungs and missing my heart a scant three-quarters of an inch," he wrote Scott. The high-velocity bullet did not "flatten and shatter" like a slower Remington shell, but drilled straight through him to kill an even unluckier Cuban standing right behind him.

His life teetered in the balance for ten weeks in an *insurrecto* field hospital. Two "Negro Revolutionists" carried him between them in a bull-hide hammock strung beneath a long pole, trekking miles through cane and forest to a remote "mountain hospital." He contracted typhoid fever, but of greater danger were the loyalist *guerrilleros*, who sniffed out such facilities. This may have been the most hated of any group during the war: a mix of young urban loyalists of good social standing, convinced that the *mambisi* threatened their existence, riding beside the locusts drawn to any war. They gave no quarter in the hospitals: they'd charge through and "machete the poor sick and fever stricken wretches and kill the women nurses," Funston told Scott. "But, God, I can't write about such things without cursing."

By mid-August, he felt ready to fight, though coughing fits still made him spit blood. He participated in the two-day assault on Tunas, placed like a bull's-eye in northern Oriente, directly south of the bay where he'd arrived one year earlier. It is a large city now, spreading amoebalike in the Cuban version of urban sprawl. At the time, it was a major garrison, manned by 800 infantrymen, 47 hated *guerrilleros*, and two Krupp guns, all sheltered in 22 city strongpoints and tied together by trenches and barbed wire.

If García couldn't take the smaller Jiguani, Funston wondered how he could conquer Tunas. But several factors worked in his favor. The city lay on an open plain beneath a low southern ridge, which spelled opportunity for Funston's guns. García's nearly six thousand *mambisi* cut the garrison off from all aid, still leaving him two thousand to throw against the town.

Funston's artillery had increased to six guns during his convalescence, including the air-fed Sims-Dudley dynamite gun he'd observed in New Jersey. Its earsplitting blast should unnerve any defender.

The assault began on August 30 and ended the next day. García lost 106 men, half of them officers; the Spanish, around 200. It was an odd affair, colored by Old World chivalry. At one point, the Spanish commander asked for a lull so women and children could flee the dynamite gun. A "sad procession" of about a hundred Spanish residents and family members wove down the road to the right of his battery, "weeping and wailing and wringing their hands." Then, a twenty-four-year-old Cuban officer who'd downed too much looted alcohol staggered to within fifty feet of the Spanish position, waved his machete, and screamed that the defenders "had murdered his father in the Ten Years' War." His comrades begged him to come back, as did the Spanish officers, "shouting that they did not wish to kill him." But he would not stop, and finally the command was given to fire. He'd be the last man killed in the fight, and García did not blame the Spanish commander. But all were not reprieved. After surrender, the captain of *guerrilleros* asked what terms would be given: "The same that you have given the helpless wounded in our hospitals," Cubans replied. Theirs was a choice of manner of death, so they marched from their stronghold, threw down their arms, and stood rigid as machetes cut them down.

The artillerymen were "the heroes of the day." All were promoted, Funston to lieutenant colonel, his highest rank, but that night he wrote Charles Scott that he was done in. "I have been so broken down by the hardships that I have undergone that I am coming home for good," he said. He finally admitted the severity of his wounds, and begged Scott not to tell his parents "for fear of alarming them." He'd lied all along about his injuries, or the malaria that made him pass out until someone doused him with a pail of water. In the past year, he'd survived four sieges and twenty-two battles, but how did one survive this damnable war?

That fall, he was assigned to García's staff; though it was lighter duty, his condition worsened. In October, his mount was shot from under him: the horse rolled atop him, injuring his hip and driving a jagged branch through his leg. This time the doctors found an abscess deep within the open wound. If that got infected, it would kill him. On November 28

Funston finally asked for leave. He promised to seek medical attention, recuperate, and come back; by now, his men acquitted themselves well in battle without him. García was kindly by nature and granted him leave at once, as well as granting leave to another American officer named James Pennie, who suffered a grave case of *paludismo*. They planned to head north to the coast and connect with a filibuster tug.

But, as an officer of staff rank, Funston could not leave the country without permission from the rebel government, sitting in a town Funston called Aquaro. The two rode there on horseback, and on December 4 Funston presented his petition to the Assembly. The secretary of war turned them down, no reasons given besides the fact that he saw no "case of imperative necessity." A new government had been elected in October; the issues of control that had killed Maceo still lingered. Perhaps this was a small proxy fight that allowed the Assembly to flex its muscles. Funston and Pennie lay in a nearby field and debated their options. They were weak, lacked adequate medicine, and hoped the constant sight of them might evoke some pity. But after a week, nothing had changed. If they lingered, they'd die, so they rode north, becoming deserters.

On December 12 Funston and Pennie followed a dusty road between the towns of Nuevitas and Puerto Principe. To the left ran a high railroad grade. They needed to cross these tracks to reach the coast, and Funston pulled a few yards ahead. He topped the grade and found himself face-to-face with "a row of Spanish rifles." He'd blundered upon a Spanish outpost, and he threw up his hands to warn his companion. Pennie rode off: it is unknown whether he ever left Cuba alive.

Funston thought fast: the next few seconds ruled his survival. Yes, he said, he was an *insurrecto*, but a deserter, too, a *presentado*, sick of war. As proof, he could give them important information. That probably saved him, at least immediately, but if they discovered the pass that identified him as an officer, he'd see a firing squad. He was also a prominent American *mambi*: Spaniards were very aware of the "little American . . . who hauled his guns up so close [to Spanish defenses] that they scorched our eyebrows."

He must destroy that pass somehow. He kept denouncing the rebels, and as he did, he ran a handkerchief across his face as if to wipe away sweat. He'd wrapped the pass in the cloth, and when he passed it over his lips, he gulped it down. Though the dirty wad of paper upset his stomach, his captors didn't spot the ruse. They bound him hand and foot, took him to their post in Las Minas and from there to Puerto Principe, the regional headquarters. A board of inquiry interrogated him: Funston "cooperated," always mixing facts about the Liberation Army with fiction, and the board believed him, offering parole provided that he swear never to aid the rebels again. He swore, and late December found him on a ship to Havana, penniless, sickly, and nearly naked, clad only in a linen duster. His hat resembled Swiss cheese; the soles of his shoes flapped as he limped off the boat. His only hope lay with the U.S. consul.

The position of consul general could saddle one with strange duties. You were one of a nation's chief representatives in a foreign port, yet you weren't really an ambassador and did not have official powers. You acted as impromptu business consultant, finder of lost persons, ad hoc diplomat, and unofficial spy. British consuls were famous for finding Distressed Subjects on their doorsteps: in the Amazon, they floated from the jungle filled with madness and parasites; one consul in Siam found a Sad Case in his bed, sleeping off the contents of his liquor cabinet. You fed these lost souls, bathed them, and bought them a suit of decent clothes and a ticket home.

Such duties had assumed added urgency for Fitzhugh Lee. After the death of Dr. Ruiz and the incarcerations of Scovel, Scott, and Cazañas, he'd determined to work on the behalf of any imprisoned or mistreated American on this devastated isle. His efforts seemed to work: the government now saw fit to send all captured Americans to him. But this late December day was unique. Lee was working behind his desk when he heard a noise. He glanced up and saw the most "disreputable-looking character" imaginable. A specter like this could only be a desperado, so he grabbed the revolver in his desk drawer and pointed it at the man. "Identify yourself!" he cried, ordering him to raise his hands. The sorry scarecrow did as told. He muttered his name and narrated his progress through the revolution.

As Funston's story unfolded, Lee's caution fled. The consul may have heard tales of the diminutive American and his Hotchkiss gun without actually knowing his name; his appearance certainly confirmed what Lee had gathered about the sad state of the rebels. By now, Spain controlled the cities; Gómez, the country in between. The stalemate was killing both sides. Lee bought new clothes for this sad little *mambi*, a meal, a ticket home aboard the SS *City of Washington*. He no doubt interrogated Funston about García, as he never got straight answers from the Spaniards. Lee chuckled as the story progressed, and a wistful smile lit his sad walrus face. "I was a rebel once too," he admitted:

"But damme, if I was as bad a looking rebel as you are!!"

Part II

THE MOB

Sometimes I growl, shake myself and spatter a few red drops for history to remember. Then—I forget.

—CARL SANDBURG, "I AM THE PEOPLE, THE MOB," *CHICAGO POEMS*

8

The Spark

Funston watched Havana recede as he stood on the ship's deck, shifting from leg to leg as the pressure built on his oozing wound. Again, all plans had failed: he'd not become famous, Cuba was not free, the wood shards must come out, and he coughed up blood. Maybe his life *was* over, like he'd told Charles Scott. The sea mirrored his thoughts: endless, choppy, gray.

On January 10, 1898, he stepped off the gangway in New York with $6 in his pocket, clad in the white duck suit bought by Fitzhugh Lee. Two people waited. His friend Willis Gleed gasped: when Freddie'd left in the summer of 1896, he'd brimmed with vitality. Now he seemed a corpse, skull visible through the skin, and Gleed ordered him to a hospital. Freddie complied: before this venture, he'd weighed 120 pounds. Now he weighed 80.

The second person to greet him was an unidentified stringer for an unidentified paper. Funston told the journalist of Dana Osgood's death, of the seventeen horses shot from under him, and of his war under Gómez and García. When captured by the Spaniards, he said, "I was released upon my oath that I would never fight against Spain . . . By swearing this I saved my life, after having fought twenty-four battles for Cuba, being crippled for life and all bunged up. I am not going back to Cuba. I shall go to a hospital and then to my home in Kansas." The writer emphasized "crippled for life," and identified him as "Furston."

Funston pored through periodicals in the hospital to kill time. An aggressive belligerence possessed his nation such as he'd never seen, as if he were Rip Van Winkle waking to an enraged land. He'd known nothing of Davis's "Does Our Flag Shield Women?," the arrests of Americans, or the death of Dr. Ruiz. Nothing of the Cisneros drama, the letters of thousands of women, or her staged rescue. America hummed like an angry hive.

Self-righteousness prevailed. That summer, Roosevelt published a series of essays titled *American Ideals* that ranged from "The Manly Virtues" and "True Americanism" to "Social Evolution," and "The Law of Civilization and Decay." Henry James called them puerile; others noted their jingoism, which did little for international accord. To Spanish readers, Americans seemed a shapeless horde "composed of the world's refuse" whose only talent was commerce. They lacked those heroic traits God had given the "Latin race": honor, courage, duty, strength, and dignity. If war arose, light would conquer dark. "We have only to display our virtues" to "roll back and vanquish" such agents of depravity.

Such insults sounded as if the nations were already at war. In some sense they were. Each had turned its opposite into the savage Other lacking all humanity. Cooler heads knew this left little room for compromise. On December 4, 1897, House Speaker Thomas B. Reed rose to his full six feet and two inches (and three hundred pounds) to deliver an appeal dubbed "Empire Can Wait": "The thing which most engages our attention in history is the growth and decay of empires," he intoned. "There seems to be a natural law operating through all time and through all space. By this law, the very extension of an empire seems by its own power and nature to plant the seeds of that decay . . ."

In one breath, he'd addressed the ambitions of Lodge, Roosevelt, and others who pushed a "long" policy. His words sounded biblical: In such ambition we plant our doom. Was the aim of a great nation to conquer all before it or to "use all the appliances of advancing knowledge, to assimilate its peoples to a common standard"? Reed advised calm. "As we grow, we will spread fast enough. Our strength grows with our years. Men who are but of yesterday and will never see tomorrow must seize time by the forelock. But those empires which hope for eternity can wait."

It was a masterful speech, but few listened. Even Reed smelled the winds. When asked later why he could not dissuade his colleagues from war, he shrugged: "Might as well ask me to stand out in the middle of a Kansas waste and dissuade a cyclone." McKinley did listen, within limits. Two days later, on December 6, his first annual message was read to the same Congress, and his words reflected his desire to give Spain's reforms time to succeed. But if nothing changed, America reserved the right "to intervene with force" when needed.

Such warnings were not new: Harrison had said as much, then Cleveland, now McKinley. Fans of *Cuba Libre* called the words weak; the opposite with the anti-war crowd. New York papers seemed split. "We have had enough of war, more than enough of jingoism," wrote the anti-interventionist *Herald*; McKinley's speech was "lacking in virility," timid and "cringing," Hearst's *Journal* complained. Spain received the message in "a spate of intense hostility," reported the U.S. military attaché Tasker Bliss, adding that when Prime Minister Sagasta searched for any hidden encouragement of rebels and found nothing, he seemed mollified.

It was hard to read the signs. On January 1, 1898, the limited autonomy promised to Cuba and Puerto Rico became official, despite Gómez's rejection. When the 55th Congress convened on January 5 and there was "complete abstention" from Cuban matters, the Spanish minister Dupuy de Lôme reported, "Our situation is better every day." Yet two days earlier, when Dewey took command in Hong Kong of the Asiatic Fleet, oracles smelled trouble. On January 8 Fitzhugh Lee told the State Department that Weyler had already moved 400,000 people into his *reconcentrado* camps, and half had died. Relief might be futile. "A daily average of ten cents" of food for 200,000 people would cost $20,000 per day: "The most humane efforts upon the part of our citizens can not hope to accomplish such a gigantic relief, and a great portion of these people will have to be abandoned to their fate."

Even Funston had spotted troubling signs during his brief time in Havana. Vagrants filled the streets; long lines formed for a daily cup of lentil soup called *rancho*. When he sailed home, he couldn't help noticing the 6,682-ton *Maine* moored in Key West. What was *that* doing there?

The *Maine* was an odd-looking ship, modern yet retrograde, as if designers never quite decided what she should be. Launched in the New

York Navy Yard on November 18, 1889, and commissioned in 1895, she'd been intended as the first armored vessel of the "New Navy." Yet her design followed that of the British-built Brazilian armed cruiser *Riachuelo*, then considered the Western Hemisphere's most perfect warship; she sported two unused masts, fore and aft, and a useless ram in the bow. Still, as an artilleryman, Funston admired her guns. She bristled with armaments like a lethal hedgehog. Her four 10-inch guns in twin turrets were set fore and aft of the central superstructure, one to port and one starboard; six 6-inch guns pointed in all directions, two in the bow, two in the stern, two amidships. Thirteen light rapid-firing guns dotted all sides; a one-pound cannon and .50-caliber Gatling gun poked from the two fighting tops; four 18-inch torpedo tubes opened underwater. An armor belt circled the hull, starting three feet above the waterline and ending four feet below. The ship was a statement of U.S. might and will.

That was the idea. Though Fitzhugh Lee may have projected bonhomie to Funston, that lurch when he mistook him for an assassin said otherwise. He felt exposed. Havana's politics were a stew of confusion: there were parties that hated America, others that hated Spain, some who could only accept total Cuban independence, while the Old Guard and the military supported the status quo—with a few more freedoms thrown in. Lee feared that he and other Americans could fall prey to these bubbling passions, and he dared not stroll outside without his pistol. He made his concerns clear: when the *Maine* dropped anchor in Key West on December 15, Captain Sigsbee's orders placed him at "the immediate judgment" of Lee. The two communicated by regular mail and underwater cable: if Lee ever sent the code phrase "Two dollars," the *Maine* must prepare to sail. A follow-up "One dollar" meant come immediately.

On Wednesday, January 12, Sigsbee received the first half of the message. That day, there'd been a small riot when Spanish officers and their supporters trashed the offices of three pro-autonomy newspapers. Counterprotestors materialized. Lee moved among the groups, heard shouts of "Death to Blanco!" and "Death to autonomy," but no threats to Americans. That evening, all seemed quiet. But with morning came more protests, and the Governor's Palace and the American consulate were placed under heavy guard. A mix of nerves and caution led him to wire "Two dollars" and add, "presence of ships may be necessary later, but not now."

New York's papers had a field day. "The riots in Havana mean revolution," predicted Pulitzer's *World*. "Next to War with Spain," headlined Hearst's daily. The news kindled Roosevelt: on January 13 he rushed into Long's office and slammed the door. The fleet was too scattered; the navy *must* prepare for war. The next morning, he produced a twenty-page memo on fleet readiness, and Long feared he'd gone "daft in the matter." It was during this period that Roosevelt begged New York's adjutant general for a commission, that Samuel B. Young and he talked "like enthusiastic college boys" about war. People commented on his bizarre harangues. On February 9 he cornered Henriette Adler, a young Parisian accompanying Mark Hanna and his wife to a party. His arm flailed as he smacked his fists, until he finally swept a silk rose from her bodice. "*Mon Dieu!*" she screamed. He apologized, then harangued her in French: he wouldn't be happy until he saw Spanish and English flags eliminated from "North America before I'm sixty!" Hanna was amazed: "You're crazy, Roosevelt! What's wrong with Canada?"

People made excuses for Roosevelt, but his words and actions can't be ignored. He channeled something seen but barely grasped—the way a mob spews a leader from its gut; or a nation, an angry prophet around whom forms a cult of personality. Mob psychology springs from deep emotions, not logic, and Roosevelt echoed passions he didn't understand.

During this period, a pair of articles in the December 1897 and January 1898 *North American Review* shed light on this combustible national temper. "Why has homicide increased in the United States?" asked the Italian criminologist Cesare Lombroso, who is credited with creating that field. From 1880 to 1890, murders in the nation had increased from 4,600 to 7,500, a 60 percent jump, while the population rose only 25 percent. It was the highest murder rate of any developed Western civilization, and, whereas the "statistics of homicide are a sure guide as to a people's state of culture," the "startling frequency" of homicides would suggest that the United States still sat at that scale's lower end. Yet, Lombroso said, "America prides itself upon being at the head of civilization." Rather than pointing out the irony, he tried to explain the disparity.

Violence is woven too deeply in the history and practice of American culture to be ignored. Lombroso never explicitly stated this, but he raised the point by repeated example. "Those who invaded the territory of the Indian and who based their rights upon conquest thought no more of killing a red-man than a hunter would of killing a monkey," he wrote. "The same may be said of the former slave-holders, who were so used to disposing of the lives of their slaves that no more importance was attached to the life of a negro than to that of a domestic animal in Europe." Under such circumstances, "violence becomes legitimate." Murder is easy, whether for "destroying industrial competition or putting an end to private strifes," or for revenge.

In effect, Lombroso said, murder had become an efficient tool, and newspapers' daily stories of mayhem and death had become the user's manual. A man kills his wife with nitric acid because he's read of similar crimes; in 1851 a New York woman kills her husband, "and it was only a few days later that several others perpetrated the same crime." If war is sanctioned murder used to solve international disputes, one could call war a tool as well. And Roosevelt called for war; expansionists called for it, adherents of manifest destiny, believers that America was chosen to spread God's Word. Sanctioned murder was not sinful, but useful.

Funston tried to understand his new, angry homeland. On January 18 he wired Charles Scott that "18 reporters" had visited his room to ask about Cuba. *Harper's Weekly* and *Scribner's* wanted some articles or a book and "when this cursed pain lets up on me, I shall try to dish them up something." Scott suggested that he run for governor, but Funston rejected the idea. When Scott suggested the lecture circuit, Funston was intrigued. "I believe I could make money of it," he said.

On that same day, McKinley ordered the *Maine* to Havana, despite Lee's earlier caution. Even today, no one knows why. The historian G.J.A. O'Toole suggests that a report by the American minister to Haiti about four German warships cruising through Haitian waters may have triggered him. McKinley knew of Spain's attempts to enlist European allies against the United States, and he'd heard rumors that she would turn Cuba over to a great power before giving it to America. The kaiser wanted a coaling station in the West Indies. It all sounded sinister.

That day, the Spanish minister Dupuy de Lôme huddled in the State Department with Undersecretary William Day. De Lôme was suave, pudgy, and usually unrattled: he'd served in the diplomatic service more than half his life, posted in Japan, Italy, Belgium, Uruguay, Argentina, Germany, and in 1892 to America. He'd found the Grover Cleveland years peaceful, but McKinley irritated him. Four days earlier, on January 20, de Lôme had complained that America's pro-rebel attitude breathed life into the insurrection; if the United States wanted peace, it should silence the Junta. Day had told the minister that he'd speak to the president and get back to him.

Now Day had McKinley's answer. If, as de Lôme said, Cuba was close to peace, tensions must be further eased. In diplomacy, symbols mean everything. There was no reason why routine visits by warships, halted by Cleveland, could not restart. "It is the purpose of the President," Day said, "to resume these visits, and that very soon." In fact, Spain could send her own warship to an American harbor. De Lôme was in no position to object, and Day rushed to McKinley, who summoned Secretary Long: tell Fitzhugh Lee that the *Maine* would come soon.

The *Maine* left Key West at night and pushed south; simultaneously, the Tampa-berthed *Montgomery* headed out on a similar "friendly visit" to Matanzas and Santiago. Sigsbee intended to enter Havana in full light, "when the town was alive and on its feet," and he roused the crew at dawn to make the ship gleam. The crew donned their winter service blues; officers, their frock coats. Sigsbee ran up the ensign and steamed at flank speed to the harbor entrance; the pilot boarded and threaded the *Maine* through the narrow channel.

This entrance has changed little in 120 years. The main concessions to time are a modern gift shop in Morro Castle and a neutered Russian nuclear missile lying at the entrance, rusting testament to the Cuban Missile Crisis. Stone steps descend to the water; soldiers lined the castle side of the one-mile channel as the *Maine* passed, civilians on the city side. Since the channel was three hundred yards across, only one ship could pass through at a time. Now, as then, the bay's two square miles is crowded with ships, fishing boats, and tugs; a ferry crosses the mouth, running from Havana to Casablanca, once home to escaped slaves. The constant flow of sewage from the city never completely diluted; one eddy was such a "festering mass of corruption" that locals called it "dead man's hole": if a ship anchored there for more than a day, its crew contracted yellow fever. The pilot brought the ship to her mooring buoy opposite the *machina*, or "shears," of the navy yard. Lee sent off hourly reports, beginning with "Ship quietly arrived around 11 am today." Late that night, Lee wired, "Peace and quiet reign," then went to bed.

Calm prevailed for three weeks. Spanish authorities sent a case of fine sherry; Sigsbee's days were filled with official and social obligations. He called the Spanish warships anchored around him "admirable," but noted the polished wood decking that would be "all aflame" within ten minutes of "close action." He permitted his officers to go ashore: sightseeing included a dinner with Fitzhugh Lee and a bullfight. Six bulls died that day; the Americans left after the fifth. The only "incident" occurred as Sigsbee entered the stands and someone thrust a small circular into his hand. It excoriated Spaniards for allowing the "taunt" of the *Maine*'s visit and called on them to "protest with the energy befitting a nation worthy and strong." He stuck it into his pocket and didn't read it till later: "Death to the Americans!" it demanded. "Death to autonomy!" Out of caution, he canceled shore leave for enlisted men and increased watches.

Perhaps war *could* be averted through goodwill. Hearst's *Journal* on January 26 headlined "Our Flag in Havana at Last" and urged Washington to send a ship to every Cuban port. That night, McKinley hosted his first diplomatic dinner and invited the Spanish minister to dine with him. "I see that we have only good news," McKinley said, then lit a cigar. "You have no occasion to be other than satisfied and confident." Yet de Lôme may have remained uneasy. In mid-December he'd written a personal letter to his friend José Canalejas y Mendez, editor of the Liberal *El Heraldo de Madrid*. In it, he called McKinley a weak, vacillating politician, "a bidder for the admiration of the crowd." A month had passed without a reply.

The *Maine*'s arrival did not bode well for fifty-nine-year-old Rear Admiral Pascual Cervera y Topete, the recently appointed commander of Spain's Atlantic Squadron. On January 30 he wrote to his cousin: "Today we find ourselves again in one of those critical periods which seem to be the beginning of the end." If war came, Spain would lose, "because we are reduced, absolutely penniless, and [the Americans] are very rich." Defeat would bring down Sagasta's government, possibly even the monarchy, and Cervera knew he'd be the sacrifice on Spain's altar of pride. He asked his cousin to stash this letter away as his last testament in case of disaster. "But as it is necessary to go to the bitter end, and as it would be a crime to say that publicly today, I hold my tongue, and go forth resignedly to face the trials which God may be pleased to send me."

January ended, and Funston left the hospital, entraining 1,160 miles to Iola. He didn't have a penny to his name. Charles Scott and others offered loans, but he would not hear of it. But the lecture circuit did look promising, and his friends made dates in their hometowns. When a Kansas City theatrical manager showed interest, he hoped to fill churches, Odd Fellows Halls, and Masonic temples at fifty cents a head. Funston would tell the "plain, unvarnished, undressed facts" about the revolution—"with the splinters in them," promised his ads.

Sometimes persistence paid dividends. Since Clara Barton's return home in October, she'd found that arranging relief for the *reconcentrados* was like battling headwinds. When she tried to send supplies through a chartered ship, Spain would not let her land; if the ship did land, it could be seized outright and her cargo rerouted to the Spanish Army. She petitioned the queen, but when Her Highness granted access, New York papers spun this as such an act of betrayal that "not one donor" came forward. Had the United States changed for the worse while she was in Armenia? she asked herself. "Had the nation gone mad?"

Since Barton believed that the Red Cross was a "direct servant of the government," she'd need McKinley's permission to begin relief efforts. She'd learned long ago to go to the top rather than deal with government bureaucracy. On February 4, 1898, when she visited the office of Undersecretary Day, she was told that he was with McKinley. Since one could still visit the president unannounced, she walked to the Executive Mansion: though McKinley and Day were meeting, the president's secretary said, "Wait a moment, Miss Barton, and let me present your card." The two looked up as she entered the executive chambers; her first impression of McKinley was of a kindly man who seemed tired and sad. She remembered that his mother had died in December; she'd been through enough death to know what that did to you. McKinley ordered the formation of the President's Committee for Cuban Relief, centered in New York and tasked with soliciting aid for *reconcentrados*: eight to ten Ward Line steamers would off-load supplies to Havana's huge San José warehouse next to the Customs House, all consigned to Fitzhugh Lee as the island's highest-bonded U.S. official. Lee would then appoint "key people of Havana" to hand out food and supplies from their homes. The president asked Barton to go oversee the effort: his order, dated February 4, 1898, directed the American community in Cuba to lend encouragement and aid "wherever her mission may take her."

She left the next day, accompanied by John Elwell, a shipping executive who'd lived the last six years in Santiago and spoke Spanish. Free passes were granted on all railroads, and they sped from Washington to Tampa in three days. On February 8 they boarded the *Olivette*, berthing in sight of the *Maine* the next day.

Barton arrived in time for the newest Cuban crisis. On February 9 Dupuy de Lôme finally learned the fate of his missing letter. It had been plucked from the desk of his friend José Canalejas by a Junta agent and sent to New York. This morning, it appeared on page one of Hearst's *Journal* under the headline "The Worst Insult to the United States in History." In the letter, de Lôme had called McKinley "weak and catering to the rabble" and branded the autonomy effort a sham. Hearst milked the scandal for five days; de Lôme cabled his resignation to Madrid; the Junta raised money. A New York pastor shouted to his congregants, "Let us get at the Spaniards! Let there be war!"

Barton paid little heed. New York manufactured outrage; Havana, the walking dead. Her first days were spent setting up a distribution system. Weekly ration tickets were printed: *reconcentrados* got them at distribution sites, then lined up on the street on the given day. Four stations opened, dispensing among them 6,300 tickets. Sunday, February 13, was tagged the kickoff day. Barton boarded a carriage and visited station after station with John Elwell. In each place, "crowds of gaunt hunger" lined the cobblestone streets, the individuals "orderly, patient, respectful, but pitiful beyond description." Streets were filled with "half clad, eager" skeletons, "waiting, watching, for the little packages, for the little morsel of food."

She wondered, "Where do these people stay?" Someone suggested Los Fosos, a large blockhouse that once defended the city. It may have been one of the worst sights she'd encountered in a life of tragic tableaux. "On these dark, bare, wet, filthy floors, a hundred feet unbroken by partition, with few cots or any other provision for sleeping, were huddled from six hundred to eight hundred human beings, largely women and children, although many feeble men and boys were among them." Spanish rations were a memory; medicine had run out long ago.

She dined that day on the *Maine*. The captain had invited her to afternoon lunch: "His launch courteously came for us; his officers received us; his crew, strong, ruddy, and bright, went through their drills for our entertainment, and the lunch at those polished tables, off glittering china and cut glass, with the social guests around, will remain ever on my memory," she wrote one year later. Barton had a weakness for military trappings, and Sigsbee squired her past the looming white turrets and black guns. She spoke of what she had seen this day, insisting that the *reconcentrados* suffered more than anyone else in this war. Sigsbee was no doubt sympathetic, but he was a navy officer, assigned to keep the peace, not assist the victims of war.

Thus ended the gleaming white dream. Barton headed back to distribute food, and as she left, she spoke to Lieutenant Commander Richard Wainwright, Sigsbee's second-in-command. She thanked him for the delightful lunch and promised her assistance should anything happen to him or his men. Though Wainwright could be stern with visitors, he was not so with her. Barton did not record his response, but he watched as she rode the captain's launch back to shore. No doubt he smiled, thinking of her comment. What could happen to the *Maine*?

Havana on Tuesday, February 15, enjoyed the second day of Carnival, and not even the tensions of the past month could sway residents from enjoying self-denial's last fling. Harry Scovel and George Rea sat in the Hotel Inglaterra's café; Scovel had just wed, and his wife, Frances, made a dinner threesome. It was nearly 9:40 p.m.: they watched revelers in their beaked masks fill the streets outside. In Washington, D.C., late-night dinner parties were in full swing; in Madrid, the café set drifted home as the queen readied for bed. In New York, the morning papers locked up their early editions. In her hotel room overlooking the same square watched by the Scovels and Rea, Clara Barton and John Elwell worked hard at their writing desks, tackling the piles of paperwork generated by *reconcentrado* relief. The great glass doors were shut; music and laughter drifted in, but seemed miles away.

In Havana Bay, music and laughter drifted to the *Maine*. The evening flood tide had gentled the ship around her mooring buoy to point her northwest, bow toward the harbor mouth. It was a breezeless, moonless night, high clouds blotting out all but the brightest stars. The Spanish warship *Alfonso XII* floated to starboard about 150 yards distant; a little farther on, the Spanish transport *Legazpi*. The Ward Line steamer *City of Washington* lay to stern, her passengers taking in the night air.

Lieutenant John Hood, the chief watch officer, sat on the port side, his feet on the rail, puffing an excellent local cigar. Sigsbee wrote in his cabin, first a report on torpedoes, then a letter to his wife. All but four of the *Maine*'s twenty-six officers were aboard, either in their quarters, gathered in smoking quarters, or distributed over the deck; the 302 enlisted men had turned in to their quarters, located forward near the magazines filled with black powder and shells. All seemed at peace, and Hood took another drag on his cigar.

Suddenly the lieutenant "felt more than heard" a blast that sounded like gunshot; it seemed to come from underwater, at the forward end of the starboard deck. He turned his head, and a larger explosion occurred. "I saw the whole starboard side of the deck and everything above as far as the aft end of the superstructure spring up into the air with all kinds of objects in it—a regular crater-like performance with flames and everything else coming up."

Sigsbee was sealing the letter to his wife when his cabin lights went out and he was thrown from his chair. He heard a series of "ominous, metallic sounds, as if the ship were rending itself to pieces"—the crash of falling fragments, a rush of water, and screams of wounded or dying men. The *Maine* seemed to crack in the middle and slough down by the head, then list so badly to port that there was no righting her. Sigsbee realized that his ship had blown up under him. He groped his way from the cabin and in the passageway ran into a marine guard, rushing to tell him that the ship had been wrecked. Together they stumbled to the poop deck, the highest spot aft, where some crewmen had gathered. He saw now what he'd only heard and felt—the *Maine* was sinking, and fast. Forward, he could make out an enormous mass of tangled metal, flames licking throughout, while small-caliber ammo stored in the superstructure popped and banged. He sent an officer forward to extinguish the fire, but the man could not squeeze past the wreckage. Sigsbee realized that the forward magazines must have gone up: most of the crew, whose quarters were close and who had turned in just a half hour earlier, was probably dead.

This was, in fact, what had occurred. The first blast emanated well forward on the port side, against the double-bottomed keel. Two 6-inch gun magazines were located there, one filled with four and a half tons of gunpowder stored in copper casks, the other holding three hundred pounds. The second, gargantuan explosion that ripped the ship in half occurred a little back and to starboard, where lay the starboard 10-inch magazine. This contained eight to nine tons of black powder: in hot weather like this, the compartment's temperature had been measured as high as 110°F. That second blast "was more violent than any explosion I had heard," one officer recalled, and could not liken it to anything "except possibly the explosion of a magazine." Survivors remembered black smoke, superhot steam, and agonized screams. Most were thrown by the blast into the water.

By now, the remaining officers had gathered with Sigsbee: one told him the forward magazine was underwater; another said the aft magazine was, too, which could only mean the ship had folded in half, with both ends submerged. Sigsbee could feel his ship sinking, hear cries from all points, see "white floating bodies" in the bay. Rescue boats from the *Alfonso XII* and *City of Washington* circled about, picking up survivors. There was nothing more to do: he ordered his men to abandon ship. The *Maine* settled gently to the bottom; she came to rest with her poop deck barely awash. Sigsbee stepped off onto one of the circling boats, which took him to the *City of Washington*. True to tradition, he was the last to leave.

The whole of Havana trembled. Rea and the Scovels were enjoying dinner when they noticed the wineglasses beginning to shake. Seconds later, the shock wave hit the café. Windows shattered; revelers in the plaza screamed and ran. The sky shone with a brilliant white light followed by a series of smaller explosions that sounded like war. The two correspondents made sure that Frances Scovel was safe, then sped to Havana Bay.

In the Hotel Inglaterra room overhead, the great glass doors to Clara Barton's balcony flew open and she flew sideways. Everything in her room tumbled or whirled through the air. The roar, she later wrote, was "deafening." She pulled herself up and stepped to the balcony: "The air was filled with a blaze of light," and in that blaze spun "black specks like huge specters flying in all directions." The light subsided, but in its place bells rang, whistles blew, "then all was quiet again." She'd been near enough battlefields to recognize the sound: the "bursting of some mammoth mortar, or explosion in some magazine." She sent John Elwell to find the cause.

Fitzhugh Lee looked up with the first blast in time to see "a great column of fire go up into the air." He climbed into a hansom cab and drove to the waterfront, stopping at the Palace where General Blanco met him: "He had just heard it and was crying; tears were coming out of his eyes." Lee later said that Blanco seemed as shocked as anyone else he met. He hurried to the waterfront and hailed a boat to the *City of Washington*. Wounded men filled the dining room, laid out on mattresses. He found Sigsbee in the captain's cabin, composing a wire to Secretary Long. Lee found it difficult "to repress my own suspicions," but Sigsbee made a point of reserving judgment. He handed the wire to George Rea, who'd barged into the cabin with Scovel. "Maine blown up in Havana Harbor at nine-forty tonight and destroyed," it read: "Many wounded and doubtless more killed and drowned. Wounded and others on board Spanish man-of-war and Ward Line steamer. Send lighthouse tenders from Key West for crew and the few pieces of equipment above water. No one has clothing other than that upon him. Public opinion should be suspended until further report. All officers believed to be saved . . ."

Scovel and Rea jumped into a boat commandeered by the harbor police chief and rowed to shore. On the way, they passed the wreckage. "The superstructure alone loomed up," Scovel would write, "partly colored by the red glare of flames glancing upon the black water." When a searchlight shone from the wharf, they realized they were surrounded by dismembered remains. "Great God!" Scovel gasped. "They are all gone.

This is the work of a torpedo, and marks the beginning of the end." This first impression became *the* rumor that would not go away.

Scovel and Rea dove into the teeming cable office, Rea waving Sigsbee's wire overhead. Others had jammed in before them, but the two skipped to the front. Anticipating such an emergency for several weeks, Scovel had carried a pretyped cable form in his pocket, and now it came in handy. "The injured do not know what caused the explosion," he wrote. "There is some doubt as to whether the explosion took place on the *Maine*." The unsubstantiated rumor reached Pulitzer's *World* in time for the five a.m. edition and colored every investigation to follow.

It was eleven p.m., one hour and twenty minutes after the blast. John Elwell had returned to tell Barton of the disaster; they hailed a cab for the hospitals. As they left, Lieutenant Commander Wainwright and Chief Engineer Charles P. Howell spotted them. "Miss Barton," Wainwright said, "do you remember you told me on board the *Maine* that the Red Cross was at our service?" Many sailors had been taken to the main Spanish hospital, San Ambrosio. They needed her now.

Of the ship's 354 officers and men, a staggering 266 were dead. Many were never recovered, their dismembered remains never identified. Those in the forward quarters, near the blasts, were blown to pieces or ripped to shreds. There were 88 survivors: Sigsbee, 24 officers, and 63 men and marines. Of these, only sixteen escaped uninjured.

Sometime during the night, Barton found time to wire McKinley: "I am with the wounded." She found thirty to forty crew members at San Ambrosio: bruised, cut, burned. Some had been crushed by timbers; others cut by iron, scorched by steam and fire, blown high into the air, or pounded straight through the red-hot furnace room to be plucked, senseless, from the water. She felt overwhelmed. Though more familiar with disaster, perhaps, than any other American alive, she had never encountered these kinds of injuries. In the Civil War, she'd observed bullet and shrapnel wounds, and she knew how to comfort such sufferers—but these men suffered burns from explosion, fire, electricity, and scalding steam, and their pain lay deep and seemed unbearable. Wounds covered their bodies; those who could talk thought the explosion "could have been the result of an internal explosion." She took names to pass to relatives; she'd done this during the Civil War and found it one of the greatest comforts for dying men. One man peered at her from bandages covering his face and asked, "Isn't this Miss Barton?"

"Yes," she said.

"I thought it must be. I knew you were here and thought you would come to us. I am so thankful for us all."

It was too much to bear. "I passed on the pencil to another . . . and stepped aside."

Sigsbee's cable reached Washington before one a.m. on Wednesday, February 16. A Western Union messenger delivered it to the Navy Department, where it was receipted to Secretary Long's apartment at the Hotel Portland. Long and his daughter Helen had dined at the White House that night; then Long returned to his rooms while Helen attended a dress ball. She returned about 1:30 a.m. and found the dispatch at the door. She awakened her father: the *Maine* had blown up, cause unknown. Long scribbled orders to Commander Francis Dickens, acting chief of the Bureau of Navigation, the first to receive Sigsbee's wire: send the gunboat *Fern* and other vessels deemed necessary to Havana. When Dickens arrived to see his chief, the foyer was already crowded with "bright representatives of the press" who'd learned of the disaster through Rea's cable. According to differing accounts, Long either phoned McKinley or sent Dickens with the telegram to inform him directly; the latter is more probable since Dickens would witness the president's reaction. A member of the White House staff woke McKinley, who emerged from his bedroom in a dressing gown. Dickens handed him the cable, and he read it through.

"The *Maine* blown up," he muttered, stunned. "The *Maine* blown up." It was two in the morning, and the battleship still burned.

In New York at about the same time, William Hearst came home from a night on the town to find a staffer at his door. Telephone the *Journal*, he was told—it's important. He reached a night clerk and learned of the *Maine*. "Good heavens, what have you done with the story?" They'd put it on page one, the staffer replied.

"Have you put anything else on the front page?" Hearst asked.

"Only the other big news."

"There is not any other big news," Hearst cried. "Please spread the story all over the page. This means war."

And soon Clara Maass, Carl Sandburg, David Fagen, Frederick Funston, Theodore Roosevelt, and almost every other American asleep that night in their beds would be swept up by the storm.

9

"All I Wanted Was More Time"

Dawn revealed the ruins of the *Maine*. Vultures perched on the twisted steel; bodies floated in the bay or washed against the seawall. The keel had jackknifed up, and she'd settled forty-two feet into the harbor floor. The mainmast thrust from the water like an aerie. Later evidence showed that the blast had blown the ship open forward of amidships; the forecastle separated entirely before capsizing to starboard. A large part of her port side had disappeared, as well as the starboard turret and two 10-inch guns. The steel keel just forward of the foremast, adjacent to the massive explosion, had wrenched up thirty-four feet to deck level in an inverted V.

By midmorning, the injured had been settled into the city's two main hospitals; one ward fixed a sign to its entrance asking visitors to remove their hats out of respect. Sigsbee moved to the Hotel Inglaterra, and throughout the silent city he encountered signs of profound sorrow: ships in the harbor flew their flags at half-mast; shops and firms closed and hung black crepe for mourning. On February 17 Havana turned out for the burial of nineteen crewmen—all who had been recovered so far. Nineteen black hearses wound slowly from the cathedral, caskets draped in flowers; the cortege ended at Colón Cemetery, where they were buried in a grave dedicated in perpetuity to the United States; it still stands today. Anyone who mattered attended: Governor Blanco, the bishop of Havana, the city's mayor, generals, admirals, the Autonomy Council. The bishop read last rites; the coffins sank into the earth; the last rifle volleys faded. It seemed to Sigsbee "inconceivable that a greater demonstration could have been made."

February 16 was "a day of gloom and sadness" in Washington, Long wrote: the entire Spanish legation visited his office as well as the British ambassador and Swiss minister. Crowds gathered outside the White House. McKinley summoned his cabinet and congressmen. "My duty is plain," he told Indiana's senator Charles Fairbanks: "We must learn the truth and endeavor, if possible, to fix the responsibility." Americans must withhold judgment "until the truth is known." This could be the kind of mishap that every warship, "with the tremendously high and powerful explosives which we now have on board, is liable to encounter," Long said, but he feared trouble: "In this, as in everything else, the opinion of the individual is determined by his original bias. If he is a conservative, he is sure that it was an accident; if he is a jingo, he is equally sure that it was by design."

Conspiracies flourished in the absence of hard facts. On the night of the 16th, Roosevelt wrote, "The *Maine* was sunk by an act of dirty treachery on the part of the Spaniards, I believe." The *Journal* and *World* drummed war hysteria. "Cruiser Maine Blown Up in Havana Harbor," the *Journal* announced on the 16th, the last truthful front-page headline it would run for the next two weeks. On the 17th it led with "The Warship Maine Was Split in Two by an Enemy's Secret Machine," the story accompanied by a seven-column drawing of the *Maine* anchored over mines, these attached to wires leading to Morro Castle. This conspiracy theory took root, and Sigsbee, for one, believed it: the drawing seemed proof. The story came so quickly that the paper must have had prior knowledge.

Though the *World* did not mimic the *Journal*'s shrillness, it adopted the same story line: "The *Maine* Explosion Was Caused by a Bomb—Suspicion of a Torpedo." Elsewhere: "Not an Accident, Capt. Sigsbee Says." Pulitzer sent a reporter to Havana to learn the truth, which he never did. Meanwhile, Hearst offered $50,000 for evidence, and circulation climbed. By the 18th, the *Journal* circulation passed the million mark. The deluge of false news flowed as quickly as anything on today's internet, including "Five hundred sharpshooters made up of Westchester businessmen" set to invade Cuba. By February 17 the AP printed a blanket denial of all rumors: "The cruiser New York has not been ordered to Havana; Consul General Lee has not been assassinated; there is no conference of the Cabinet; Congress is not in session tonight, both Houses having adjourned at the usual hour until tomorrow; President McKinley did not go to the Capitol, and the situation is decidedly quiet."

On February 18 McKinley ordered a Naval Board of Inquiry to determine the cause. That Friday morning, a team of navy divers arrived aboard the coastal steamer *Bache*. Scovel's story on February 17 had cut to the heart of the matter: if the divers' investigation showed "that the indentation of the hull is inward, the conclusion that the magazine was exploded by a bomb or torpedo is inevitable. If the indentation is outward, it will be indicated that the first explosion was in the magazine." Though Scovel was no explosives expert, his misguided statement took on traction. It simply was not possible at that time to determine the cause or origin of the explosion by debris alone.

Obstacles beset the divers from the start. First, they could not descend without a Spanish diver. Sigsbee and Lee protested that the *Maine* was U.S. property, but Blanco replied that since she blew up in Spanish waters, Crown law required its own investigation. Perhaps a joint inquiry? Sigsbee doubted that Washington would agree, but had no objection to a separate Spanish probe.

Sigsbee was right. Roosevelt and others opposed a joint investigation. Yet an independent U.S. inquiry had already begun. When Rear Admiral Montgomery Sicard, the North Atlantic Squadron's top sailor, named officers to the five-man court of inquiry, he chose the *Iowa*'s Captain William T. Sampson as its president. The body, thereafter called the "Sampson Board," was scheduled to start on Monday, February 21, aboard the U.S. lighthouse tender *Mangrove*, even then sailing to Havana.

Sampson was one of those new engineer-scientists who'd reached command rank after the Civil War. When Richard Harding Davis wrote that he more closely resembled a "calm and scholarly professor of mathematics" than a combat leader, he touched a raw nerve. Since naval engineers had been of a lower echelon than line officers, promotion was difficult. Yet he'd graduated first in his class and since 1861 had taught physics to midshipmen, commanded numerous ships, served as assistant superintendent of the U.S. Naval Observatory, officer-in-charge at the Naval Torpedo Station, superintendent of the Naval Academy, and chief of the Bureau of Ordnance. Sampson preached adaptation to his students: "Every officer on a modern war vessel in reality has to be an engineer, whether he wants to or not." He'd just turned fifty-eight; his high forehead and gray-whiskered muzzle lent him the appearance of a prickly Scottish terrier.

Like Commodore Dewey, Sampson was Roosevelt's man. Over the years, the captain had become an expert in torpedo specifications, armor plating, ordnance, steel production, and turret design—everything Roosevelt wanted in his "New Navy." On September 7, 1897, when Roosevelt watched gunnery practice aboard the *Iowa*, Sampson was that ship's first commander. The concussions had cracked glass and loosened wooden fittings, and Roosevelt was thrilled.

For Roosevelt, there was good reason for Sampson to lead the inquiry board. The undersecretary's patronage reflected close attention to his beliefs. Though Roosevelt and other jingoes insisted that the *Maine* was the victim of perfidy, a consensus was building that the explosion was an accident. For three days, beginning on February 16, the Washington *Evening Star* took a poll of navy officers on duty in the capital: a large majority called the explosion accidental. That day, Lieutenant Frank Fletcher, stationed at the Naval Torpedo Station, wrote, "Everybody [here] is gradually settling down to the belief that the disaster was due to the position of the magazine next to the coal bunkers in which there must have been spontaneous combustion." Analysts at the Bureau of Ordnance agreed. On February 17 Professor Philip Alger, the navy's lead expert on explosives, told the *Star* that no torpedo then known to man "can of itself cause an explosion as powerful as that which destroyed the *Maine*."

The "accident theory" was backed by strong evidence. The navy's new coal-powered warships—especially first-generation models like the *Maine* and the *Texas* whose keels were laid in 1888 and '89—were designed with coal bunkers set near the ships' magazines. Only a bulkhead separated them, a serious design flaw that was only then being realized. On January 27, 1898—nineteen days before the explosion—a naval board warned of that very danger: "There are some bunkers in which a fire would involve great danger, namely, those adjacent to the magazines." There had been a dozen reported fires in American coal-powered ships in 1897, including the *New York* and the *Cincinnati*, where fire scorched bunkers by the magazines: "If they had not, fortunately, been discovered in time, there might have been in each case a terrible disaster."

Carrying large quantities of coal was a constant hazard. Coaling left a ship covered by fine black dust, a fire hazard unless scrubbed clean. Inspectors had twice reprimanded Sigsbee for violating ordnance protocols and keeping a disorderly ship, a detail that did not appear in the final report. In addition, fresh surfaces of newly broken coal oxidize naturally when exposed to air, producing heat; high moisture content, like that in seaports, increased the likelihood. If the heat did not dissipate, the reaction could double for every increase of 15° to 20°F. At 750° to 800°F., combustion occurred, followed by self-ignition and flame. Though many ships installed alarms in their bunkers, spontaneous fires could smolder deep below the surface without raising temperatures near the alarms. Once started, such fires were nearly impossible to put out: the *Titanic* had one in her bunker on her maiden voyage, and stokers worked days to put it out. If she'd made it to New York, the city fire department planned to meet her upon arrival. But the *Titanic* sailed in frigid waters. The *Maine*, in the tropics, was a disaster waiting to happen.

Roosevelt had good reason to suspect an explosion caused by a design flaw—and just as strong a reason *not* to want it known. Senator Eugene Hale, chairman of the Naval Affairs Committee, had already called the modern explosives-filled battleship a floating "volcano." Since an "accident" verdict could end the dream of a coal-fired navy, some senators worried about a cover-up. When William Mason of Illinois suggested that neither the navy nor Roosevelt could be impartial, Lodge objected: "I think those who know Theodore Roosevelt would be slow to believe he would seek to conceal the truth in regard to this disaster." Even today, the question remains: Evan Thomas's *The War Lovers* and Joyce Milton's *The Yellow Kids* both raise the possibility of a cover-up. Sympathetic biographers tend to skirt the issue.

Though no documentation ever surfaced to prove that Roosevelt doctored evidence or improperly influenced the board, his fingerprints are everywhere. He set parameters for a favorable verdict, beginning with Sampson's appointment as president. He silenced Professor Alger, who'd raised the possibility of a coal-bunker fire to *The Washington Star*, asking his boss at the Bureau of Ordnance, "Don't you think it inadvisable for Prof. Alger to express opinions in this way?" No members of the Bureau of Ordnance sat on the inquiry board, nor were asked to speak. In his influential 1976 analysis, Admiral Hyman G. Rickover concluded that the explosion was "without a doubt" internal, adding that Alger reputedly prepared a report on the tragedy—this, too, suppressed. When the board reached Roosevelt's preferred conclusion, Sampson was promoted to acting rear admiral and made commander of the North Atlantic Squadron when his predecessor, Montgomery Sicard, suddenly retired due to malaria.

Good things come to those who play the game.

When historians speak today of the *Maine*, they overwhelmingly cite its destruction as the cause of the Spanish-American War. Roosevelt described it in absolutes: "When the *Maine* was blown up in Havana harbor, war became inevitable," again demonstrating his choke hold on memory. War Secretary Russell A. Alger believed that the blast "swept away forever" all chances of peace. Contemporary historians buttressed these views: Richard Titherington's 1900 history says war "was largely due to the *Maine*," while a 1906 narrative by Horace E. Flack says that if not for the *Maine*, "peace might have been obtained." Conventional wisdom holds today that the *Maine*'s destruction stoked public wrath into "an unseen and relentless force," said the historian Louis A. Pérez Jr., "that could be calmed by nothing less than war"—as if, as Clara Barton had said, the entire country had taken collective leave of its senses.

It was not seen like this at the time. Bracketed within the inquiry board lay a quieter one that received less press but swayed more people. During that period, Clara Barton was finally distributing relief to the *reconcentrados* outside Havana. From February 28 to March 8, she traveled in a wide, irregular loop along the north and south coasts, with returns to Havana to restock. She was accompanied by Redfield Proctor—the Republican senator from Vermont, patron of Dewey and friend to McKinley—and Proctor's fishing buddy Colonel M. M. Parker. On Tuesday, March 8, Proctor and Parker returned to the States via the Havana packet; on March 17 Proctor stood behind his Senate desk and delivered a low-key thirty-minute speech that so excited the proponents of war and swayed the advocates of peace that it "formulated in the popular mind a proclamation of war" more than a month before it was officially declared. Today Proctor's speech is almost unknown. Historians mention it in passing, but at the time no other speech "in any legislative assembly in the world" for the past fifty years had so powerfully "aroused the nation," said Proctor's old boss, former president Benjamin Harrison.

Tall, gray-bearded, and dignified, Proctor was called "Lincolnesque" by the press, and his long tenure in Washington—first as Harrison's war secretary from 1889 to 1891, then as a senator until his death, in 1908—made him respected. He'd fought at Gettysburg, got rich in the marble trade, and was called the wealthiest man in Congress, with at least $1 million invested in D.C. real estate when he died. He rarely granted interviews and gave few public speeches. He was abrupt, sometimes mean-spirited, "impenetrable to humor," said the historian Gerald Linderman, and "the author of extramarital adventures extensive enough to alienate his wife permanently." Yet his financial success made him trusted among the business elite, and when he said he went to Cuba as a private citizen with no opinions, fellow legislators paid attention.

Proctor also knew that his closeness to McKinley made him the president's emissary. Thus, he should inform the president of his plans. "I didn't ask permission to go," he later said, "but I thought he ought to know. He was President and I was his friend." In the same light, Acting Secretary of State Day wrote a letter to Fitzhugh Lee describing Proctor as "one of the closest friends of the President." Lee arranged an introduction to Blanco, who guaranteed free passage. When Clara Barton set out on her relief effort, Proctor and Colonel Parker tagged along.

She never reveals how this was arranged. Yet Barton was good at luring patrons, and taking along an influential senator was a coup. She'd already been to the town of Jaruco when Proctor caught up: more people had died there than the city's entire peacetime population. She ordered clothes, food, medicine, fresh bedding, "water by the dray load, lime by the barrel," and other cleaning equipment to combat decay.

On Tuesday, March 1, Proctor joined her in Havana. They headed east to Matanzas, looped to Artemisa, returned for supplies. Weyler had herded 11,000 *reconcentrados* into Matanzas, and within a year, 9,000 had died. Twenty-three expired in one day near the governor's residence; it was said that 55,000 died province-wide. "Torn from their houses," Proctor later told the Senate, "with foul earth, foul air, foul water, and foul food or none, what wonder that half have died and that one-quarter of the living are so diseased that they cannot be saved?" Death in the streets was common; one consul told him that the dead were often found in the markets, where they'd crawled overnight in hopes of scavenging food. Children were the worst, their arms and chests emaciated, eyes swollen, abdomens "bloated to three times the natural size." Doctors said to him, "These cases are hopeless." The little group restocked a last time and headed east, where Proctor counted ten thousand Spanish troops whom he did not think "at all equal to our men." They returned to Havana, and on Wednesday, March 9, Proctor headed home.

Eight days later, he rose on the Senate floor. He'd already met with McKinley, who made no move to dissuade him. That Thursday, senators were enduring a debate over public health hospitals when Proctor asked to describe his trip. Pleased to escape the tedium, they agreed.

Delivery is all. Accustomed to long, enflamed speeches about *Cuba Libre*, the senators leaned back. Within a minute, they were electrified. Oratory was still considered a classical art, but Proctor offered no exhortation, recommended action, line of argument, or appeals to greater glory. "I merely speak of the symptoms as I saw them," he said in quiet tones, self-deprecation augmenting his words. He'd met with Fitzhugh Lee, General Blanco, the U.S. consuls of Matanzas and Sagua La Grande, municipal *alcaldes*, Cuban doctors and lawyers, and the Sampson Board; he did *not* meet with insurgents or the Junta. "I went to Cuba with a strong conviction that the picture had been overdrawn," he said, "that a few cases of starvation and suffering" had been sensationalized, and that the photos of starving *reconcentrados* "must be rare specimens, got up to make the worst possible showing."

Instead, he'd witnessed scenes "plenty as bad or worse" than that in the papers, many too horrific to be shown. His voice did not rise or fall: his colleagues craned forward. Every place he saw outside Havana was a charnel house of "desolation," "distress," "misery," "starvation." The towns garrisoned by Spanish troops were "prison yards"; the hospitals, indescribable; the children, deformed with hunger and dying; Cubans, locked in a fight to the death for "deliverance from the worst misgovernment of which I ever had knowledge." He discussed the *Maine*; the military, racial, and political situation; the effectiveness of the Spanish Army should the United States go to war. Yet he was not there to recommend intervention, he said, neither that nor annexation, since Cubans were wise enough to rule themselves. "I merely speak of the symptoms as I saw them, but do not undertake to prescribe." His testimony was that of a convert: he'd gone to Cuba a mild anti-interventionist, only to encounter ghastliness both inhuman and profound.

And then he sat down.

Within two days, the tone of public debate changed. Before, it was between anti-interventionists and jingoes; now it boiled down to good versus evil. Religious institutions that opposed war on moral grounds did an about-face: "A day of the Lord, a judgment day, is at hand," proclaimed the Presbyterian *Interior.* Wall Street, once fearing that war would derail economic recovery, saw no looming financial disaster: Proctor's speech "had converted a great many people on Wall Street," people to whom McKinley listened, wrote *The Wall Street Journal.* The anti-intervention *American Banker* turned 180 degrees. *The Literary Digest* concluded that within ten days the nation's most conservative papers had reversed themselves, including *The Pittsburgh Times*, *The Boston Journal*, *The Chicago Record*, and *The Washington Star.* Proctor had distilled the conflicting and confusing arguments into one question and one answer: "What was this country's duty in the sight of God?" wrote *Scribner's.* "War, for humanity's sake."

The damage to McKinley was real. Americans saw the senator as his surrogate and his speech a sign "that the President has decided to move forward with rapidity," Senator Shelby Cullom told the *New York Evening Journal.* A few days later, Proctor asked McKinley his opinion of the speech, and the president answered simply, "I thought you would wait."

A distance formed between them that Proctor did not immediately recognize. By September, it seemed that presidential invitations had slowed. By November, he noticed increasing resistance to patronage requests that before had been easy. By early February 1899, Proctor would write to Secretary Alger, "The President has no use for my service or opinions on any matter."

McKinley's conscience became a prison. By mid-February, Secretary Long feared that the president looked "more oppressed and careworn" than he'd ever seen him. By March, he needed sedatives at night to sleep. He'd seen "the dead piled up," faceless, nameless, relinquishing all humanity—like Walt Whitman, who'd stood before a "heap" of amputated "feet, legs, arms, hands, &c.," outside a Union hospital and asked, "Who are you?" Both had glimpsed the truth: dreams of glory meant nothing in the end.

Now his countrymen were choosing the same path again. Given his dearth of self-reflective writing, it's hard to know exactly *what* went through the president's mind. He'd been to war and despised it; he'd fought and survived in the political trenches, and developed a certain hard shell. Yet threading through this was his faith in the "public intelligence." He would say many times that "the people know more than any one man"—a faith in a nation's group mind as firm as Rizal's and Martí's—but without the Romantic overtones. He worked hard to understand the electorate, asking questions during public receptions, reading up to a dozen papers daily, sifting through the White House mail. By such methods, he hoped to tap into the national consciousness and through that determine how best to lead. Yet the public's war fever and his experience of its horrors were irreconcilable forces. Many historians have flatly condemned him as weak or cowardly, but such psychologizing is too easy. He'd certainly lost the quiet confidence that had served him well, but the reasons for this are almost tragic: one senses a man trapped between two unmoving rocks of belief, unwilling to act because he sees every choice as wrong.

One anecdote of this period says a lot. Sometimes McKinley invited friends to the White House, and in April he invited his Chicago confidant Herman Henry Kohlsaat to an evening piano recital in the Blue Room.

When it ended, McKinley asked Kohlsaat to join him in the Red Room, where he sank into a huge crimson-brocade couch, placed his elbows on his knees, and cupped his face in his hands. He poured out his soul: Ida's health, a Congress and populace hot for war. To Kohlsaat's astonishment, McKinley "broke down and cried like a boy of thirteen."

And always, the clock ticked to war. Twentieth-century historians belabored the notion that if he'd been more forceful, decisive, courageous, or manly, he could have turned the flood. This assumes that a president controls the elements, a belief in political sorcery that continues unabated today. History and politics create an illusion of meaning, but those caught in its torrent might hear only a deafening roar.

Take, for instance, the most famous single act of insurrection during McKinley's tenure. It began with a case of nerves. Ever since the *Maine* disaster, Secretary Long had been unable to sleep and was beset with aches and pains. At noon on Friday, February 25, he visited his osteopath for a "mechanical massage," a device that agitated his upset stomach and cramped legs. This proved so pleasing that he popped into the corn doctor before ambling home.

As Long ambled, Roosevelt charged—with such alacrity he must have already planned his moves. First, he wired Dewey: "Secret and confidential. Order the squadron . . . to Hong Kong. Keep full of coal. In the event of declaration of war Spain your duty will be to see that Spanish squadron does not leave the Asiatic coast, and then offensive operations in Philippine Islands." Dewey would call this cable "the first step" in America's conquest of the Philippines. Roosevelt sent similar wires to other squadron commanders. He authorized navy coal-buying agents to buy maximum stocks, warned European and South Atlantic stations of possible hostilities, ordered huge supplies of reserve ammo, and sent demands to Congress for legislation recruiting more sailors. He placed the navy in a higher state of readiness than at any time since the Civil War. Long erupted when he returned, writing that Roosevelt "has come very near causing more of an explosion than happened to the *Maine*." He resolved to never again leave his assistant in charge, yet did not revoke any of his orders, even the one to Dewey.

Thus, Roosevelt set in motion the first phase of naval war plans he had drafted over the past four years. The world noticed—especially Spain.

Historians label Roosevelt's move a masterstroke, when in fact it probably derailed any last chance for peace. Spain, like the United States, was balanced between war and peace, and it wouldn't take much to tip her scales. On February 26, as Long exploded and Proctor landed in Havana, the Spanish parliament allocated one million additional pesetas for their navy. That day, Ambassador Woodford wired that Spain's Cuban policy was set, come what may. Autonomy, not independence, was as far as she would go: "They want peace if they can keep peace and save the dynasty. They prefer the chances of war, with the certain loss of Cuba, to the overthrow of the dynasty."

Until the 25th, Spanish public opinion toward the United States had been conciliatory in light of the *Maine*. That changed with Roosevelt's actions. On February 28 Spanish papers reported that the Sampson Board would blame Spain. "What interest could we have in destroying the American battleship?" asked *El País* of Madrid. Spain had nothing to fear from Yankee "bacon-eating pigs": "It is not one ship nor ten ships which might enable the United States to triumph over Spain. Ships have to be manned and there are very few men in the United States. The inhabitants of that country lack the stuff men are made of."

Soon afterward, Spanish spies in Hong Kong wired the new Philippine governor Primo de Rivera that Dewey had orders to attack Manila should war be declared. On March 5 Spain's Caribbean squadron was ordered to assemble in Cádiz under Admiral Cervera. The next day, Roosevelt bragged in a letter, "We are certainly drifting toward, and not away from, war."

McKinley realized this, too. That busy Sunday, he authorized Admiral Charles O'Neil to order an additional four million dollars for ammo. He messaged Congressman Joe Cannon of the House Appropriations Committee to meet him at noon. Even now, he suspected that he could not stem the tide: to prepare for war was to invite it, but not to prepare courted disaster. Despite his best efforts, "it must come," and he feared that the United States was unprepared. "Who knows where this will lead us?" he asked, perhaps thinking of the peripatetic German fleet: "It may be more than war with Spain." How could he get that money, he asked Joe Cannon as he paced the floor.

But Cannon had already calculated whether the Treasury could shoulder a $50 million appropriation without new taxes or bonds, and he suggested that McKinley draft a message to Congress but hold off on any speech while still negotiating with Spain. Cannon wondered whether his committee might not introduce the bill itself. McKinley walked to the table and wrote on a telegraph blank, "For national defense, fifty million dollars." The next day, the famous "Fifty Million Bill" was introduced in the House, and two days later, on March 9—the day Proctor returned from Cuba—the bill passed 311 to 0. The Senate passed it 76 to 0, and McKinley signed it into law. The bill stunned the Spanish; Hearst's *Journal* crowed, "For War! $50,000,000!"; Long and Roosevelt reviewed warships on the international market during a shopping spree.

There seemed to be no turning back. War preparations on both sides assumed lives of their own. On March 11 the House Committee on Naval Affairs released funds to build three new battleships, one to be christened the *Maine*. On March 13 three Spanish destroyers and three torpedo boats left Cádiz for the Canary Islands: the Spanish Navy placed a lot of strategic stock in its torpedo boats, and U.S. naval planners worried about them. Admiral Cervera's squadron steamed to catch up the next day. On March 15 the Liberal party's paper *El Imparcial* welcomed a war with the United States. Its editors proclaimed, "Spain does not scare."

Two days later, Redfield Proctor asked for thirty minutes of his fellow senators' time. By then, the Sampson Board had shifted its court from the *Mangrove* in Havana to the USS *Iowa* in Key West. Officially, the judges met to deliberate evidence; in reality, they'd already reached a verdict. That day, four navy officers sped by rail to Washington to brief Secretary Long. One task remained: to draft a final report, due by March 21.

Evidence had been weighted toward Spanish perfidy since the start, yet weaving a façade of truth proved elusive. Long excluded proponents of the accident theory, while Sampson suppressed evidence that the explosion originated in the ship. Sigsbee certainly believed that the source was external, yet his testimony demonstrated an embarrassing negligence when it came to daily operations. Nevertheless, the board agreed with him that none of his officers or men bore any responsibility. Though divers had explored the wreck for nearly a week, their discoveries proved debatable, as they were not trained in analysis. That duty fell to an ensign.

Wilfred Van Nest Powelson possessed singular skills. Appointed to the U.S. Naval Academy in 1889 at age sixteen as a cadet engineer, he graduated first in his class in 1893 and then went to Glasgow, Scotland, to study naval architecture. After a year, he realized that engineers did not get promoted, so he came home to start over as a line officer. Yet new assignments take time; as he waited at the New York Navy Yard, he watched the *Maine* being built piece by giant armored piece, and he fell in love. He hoped his familiarity would lead to an assignment aboard the *Maine*.

But the navy sent Powelson to the gunboat *Fern*. He was crushed, yet when the *Maine* exploded, the *Fern* was one of the many vessels rushed to Havana. Since duty was light, he hung around the dock as divers brought up the guts of his armored love. His single year in engineer's school made it possible to understand the divers' findings, such an all-consuming puzzle for him that his irritated captain transferred him to the Sampson Board. In an instant, an ensign with one year of engineering became the board's "expert" on the *Maine*.

Powelson's job was to interview divers, compare their observations with the *Maine*'s blueprints, and make sense of it all. The ship's forward part was completely destroyed, he testified: the blast turned the forward superstructure upside down and bent the skeletal frames upward. On Friday, February 25, he reported an enigma: the *Maine*'s starboard keel had bent into an inverted V fifty-nine feet back from the bow, where the blast was centered. Though the keel rested in mud forty feet down, a section of bottom plating twisted up to within four feet of the surface. What does this mean? Sampson asked. Powelson did not know, but he would give it more study.

He returned the next day with plans showing the positions of the vessel's steel ribs, or "frames," spaced three to four feet apart and numbered in ascending order from the bow. The apex of the inverted V was just forward of Frame 17. Powelson believed this meant that the center of impact occurred between Frames 16 and 18: "This was under the ship, a little on the port side."

"How far from the keel?" Sampson asked.

Powelson thought for a second. "Fifteen feet on a horizontal line."

In other words, an explosion under the ship, fifteen feet beneath the keel, had hurled the *Maine* up, folding the hull into a V. Powelson had given the board the first and only evidence of an exterior explosion, and given the fact that spontaneous combustion was never considered or mentioned, it became the blast's *only* explanation. The Sampson Board's final report, dated Monday, March 21, concluded, "In the opinion of the court, the *Maine* was destroyed by an explosion of a submarine mine, which caused the partial explosion of two or more of her forward magazines." Though the court had been unable to fix responsibility "upon any person or persons," the verdict was clear: mass murder by a person or persons unknown.

The next day, Spain's board of inquiry concluded that "the explosion was produced by an internal cause."

What really happened to the *Maine*? In the 125 years since the cataclysm, not a single shred of evidence indicates the presence of a mine. Torpedoing or mining a ship required considerable equipment and many hands, but no responsible Spanish officer would dream of such a thing. Though insurgent sympathizers and anti-autonomy conspirators had reasons to destroy the ship, one doubts their technical expertise or ability to conceal the fact afterward.

It remains one of history's great mysteries, as great as the disappearance of Amelia Earhart, and has thus invited several investigations. In 1911 President William Howard Taft ordered the Army Corps of Engineers to study the wreckage: they reaffirmed the Sampson Board's judgment, but changed the location of the mine. A 1982 book by Louis Gould and a 1992 study by John L. Offner focused on fires in coal bunkers; there were at least thirteen other spontaneous-combustion fires in U.S. ships from 1895 to 1898, a systemic problem rooted in flaws. In 1998 the National Geographic Society commissioned a computer model to be created by Advanced Marine Enterprises (AME): heat transfer studies indicated that within four hours, a coal-bunker fire could raise the temperature of gunpowder to 645° F, enough to trigger a chain of explosions. On the *Maine*, the nearest gunpowder canister lay four inches away on the other side of a quarter-inch-thick plate of steel. In all probability, that sleek white symbol of American might destroyed herself that calm night through no other agency but her own.

But for Americans, the Sampson Board's report was conclusive. Whether or not Spain was responsible became marginal: Spain would be blamed for *creating* the conditions that allowed mass murder. "Remember the *Maine*! To Hell with Spain!" Hearst's *Journal* roared. The "condition of affairs in Cuba was a constant menace to our people," wrote Marrion Wilcox in his 1898 *A Short History of the War with Spain*, one of the first thoughtful histories to appear. Later historians went further. Expelling Spain "appeared to be a necessary act of duty for the health of civilization," wrote James M. Callahan in 1899. Seventy-eight years later, the same thinking applied: "Most certainly Spain was blamed," wrote Charles S. Campbell, "not because she had ordered the deed, but because her crumbling authority in Cuba made it possible."

McKinley and his cabinet reviewed the Sampson Board report on Friday, March 25, and released it to Congress on Monday, hoping the weekend would quell tempers. The delay did not matter. The nation called for McKinley to declare war, but he prevaricated, hoping to engineer a Spanish surrender. He wired Minister Woodford that the United States would not declare war if Spain surrendered to the insurgents and delivered the means for independence into U.S. control. On March 31 three Spanish ministers formally gave Woodford their terms: The *reconcentrado* decree was revoked, and three million pesetas were appropriated to return the people to their land. The government would grant a truce if the insurgents asked, but not unilaterally. Both sides must act: it was a matter of honor and pride. Both sides would rather fight forever than be the first to yield.

In Spain, self-delusion reigns. Spain will face the American juggernaut "with the courage of the race etched on his face and with the smile of the martyr on his lips," her press proclaims. "God, always great . . . will not permit Right, Reason, and Justice to be mocked" by Yankees. Twenty thousand Cubans in Pinar del Río would mobilize to repel invaders. Other Latin American countries would rally; European powers would weigh in. Spain would attack and reclaim Florida with 100,000 men. The Sioux would rebel and 100,000 Mexicans mobilize on the southern U.S. border.

But Spain had no allies—in Latin America, Europe, Indian reservations, anywhere. The great powers were already dividing the spoils. The British hoped to extend their sovereignty over Gibraltar; the French and Russians over the Balearic Islands in the Mediterranean. And who would acquire the jewel at Asia's doorstep—the Philippines?

In Washington, McKinley tells his party he will send his War Message to Congress, but hints from Madrid suggest further concessions. He delays until Wednesday, April 6, then delays again to give American citizens in Cuba time to evacuate. Fitzhugh Lee is formally ordered to leave. Pope Leo XIII offers to mediate with the rebels, but that fizzles. On April 6 ambassadors from England, Germany, Italy, France, Austria, and Russia visit the White House, urging peace. Their concerns, like the pope's, are graciously received and shelved.

On April 6 Clara Barton returned to Havana after a brief fundraising visit back home. She'd thought that "when the papers said I was coming back, things could not be so bad." Instead, she finds among the residents "strong talk of war." Spanish officials advise care; even her friends in the Spanish Red Cross "feel very sore." On April 9 she and twenty Americans leave Havana on the *Olivette*; when she debarks in Tampa, she runs into Fitzhugh Lee. This drives home the fact that she won't be returning to Cuba soon.

McKinley's delays seem to drive Americans mad. During this period, they reveal the ugly face they've tried to hide. Roosevelt flies into theatrical rages at the most printable moments: at the Gridiron Club, he confronts Mark Hanna, a last holdout for peace, and snaps, "Now, Senator, may we please have war?" He delivers his most quotable insult about McKinley's backbone. Mobs in Virginia burn McKinley in effigy; theatergoers in New York hiss at the mention of his name. Something is unleashed that, while not completely new, becomes a more frequent fixture in the American character: patriotism allows malice at home, and in less than a year it excuses murder overseas.

A trigger has flipped, and, as the Nobel laureate Elias Canetti would write in his 1960 *Crowds and Power*, the mob had "erupted." It was a "war crowd," a "double crowd," because both sides decided "I can be killed" and "I myself want to kill this man." Spaniards and Americans may not actually think that death is imminent, but something greater is at stake:

the death of Spanish pride; the stillbirth of America's assurance that it has been chosen by God to save the world. The death of one means the life of the other. The mobs do not see McKinley's delays as stuttering attempts at peace. To Americans, they are barriers to a moral birthright; to Spaniards, endless humiliation. They seek baptism in the "strongest possible feeling of [their] own animal force" and to get that, they will use "whatever social pretexts and demands offer themselves."

On Monday, April 11, McKinley finally delivered his "War Message": huge crowds filled the Capitol, dressed in their Easter finery. "The city is beginning to wear its Spring look," Lodge writes to his mother: the cherry blossoms have fallen; tulips and magnolias are in bloom. "But," he adds, "there is no thought to anything but the Spanish question and the coming war." McKinley's seven-thousand-word message will be ambiguous, asking Congress to authorize armed intervention but falling short of actually declaring war.

William Hearst listened unimpressed as House clerks read the message in relays. The speech "profoundly disappointed the American people," his *Journal* declared the next day. Instead of a "call to arms," the president "sounded a summons to retreat." And another issue was also taking shape: the future relations of the United States and Cuba. The speech hinted that McKinley did not believe Cubans yet capable of self-government. Securing peace meant expelling Spain *and* disarming rebels, a problem that will be repeated in the Philippines.

Neither did the speech mollify Capitol Hill. Congress stewed for a day; then, on April 13, the House revolted. Democrats called to recognize Cuban independence; Republicans yelled to be heard. House Speaker Tom Reed sat calmly in his elevated chair. A Pennsylvania Republican called a Georgia Democrat a liar; the Democrat chucked a hefty volume of the *Congressional Record* at his critic; overexcited members of both parties spilled into the aisles. A congressional page was socked in the jaw. The sergeant at arms grabbed a flagpole topped with an American eagle and waded into the crowd. The eagle was knocked loose and sent flying. A reporter with the London *Times* observed, "Such is the body in whose favour the President on Monday abdicated his rightful authority and to whom he entrusted the fortunes of his . . . country."

Though McKinley did not ask for war, Congress declared it anyway, debating all week as crowds milled outside. The people wanted war, but Congress had no idea what to do with Cuba once fighting ended. Many legislators distrusted the idea of an independent nation; few wanted to annex it as a territory or colony. Reasons varied. Many showed a "general repugnance," wrote the historian Margaret Leech, toward absorbing "an alien and insubordinate people, Roman Catholic in faith, with a large admixture of Negro blood." On Saturday, April 16, Senator Henry M. Teller of Colorado offered an amendment renouncing any "intention to exercise sovereignty, jurisdiction, or control over said island except for pacification thereof," thus leaving "the government and control of the island to its people." In a stroke, the resolution endowed the cause with a high moral purpose the American people could find palatable.

The Teller Amendment was not as high-minded as it seemed. Colorado had a booming sugar beet business, and her profits would be threatened if Cuban sugar did not face the high import tariff that would be stripped upon annexation. In addition, Teller was rumored to have gained a $2 million bribe from the Junta, which, like Martí, did not want Cuba to become an American colony. Teller's amendment might allow Americans to don an armor of virtue, but it also helped create what the historian Evan Thomas called a "policy mishmash" of unclear aims, an ambiguity scarring Cuban-American relations for decades.

On April 20, amid whoops and cheers, McKinley signed a joint congressional resolution and sent the ultimatum to Spain: Get out now! On April 21 Ambassador Woodford closed the U.S. embassy in Madrid, burned and collected his papers, and lit out on the four p.m. Paris express. Spanish mobs stoned his train. On April 22 the North Atlantic Squadron sailed from Key West to blockade Cuba's ports. On April 23 Spain declared war. That Saturday, McKinley called for 125,000 volunteers to swell the 28,000-man Regular Army; a million volunteers would try to enlist. On April 25 Congress made it official but backdated the declaration to April 21 so the blockade was a legitimate act of war.

After McKinley signed the war resolution, his confidence returned. He managed the war with vigor and never publicly doubted Americans' wisdom or morality. He extolled the "magnificent army" that "mustered in less than sixty days." But in private, he never came to terms with what happened. He'd done everything in his power to avert war, he told confidants, yet had lost control. The piles of bodies at Antietam still haunted him, and now more deaths loomed. The "declaration of war against Spain was an act which has been and will always be the greatest grief of my life," he told his private secretary in the fall of 1900. "I never wanted to go to war with Spain. Had I been let [alone], I could have prevented [it]. All I wanted was more time."

10

Promises

In the final days of April 1898, two U.S. naval squadrons sailed for war. At 4:30 a.m. on April 22, the North Atlantic Squadron steamed south from Key West to blockade Cuba's ports; by three p.m. officers and correspondents standing on the flagship saw the island's green hills rising from the sea. Five days later, at two p.m. on April 27, Commodore George Dewey's Asiatic Squadron sailed from Mirs Bay in Hong Kong. Dewey had received Long's cable two days earlier: "War has commenced United States Spain. Proceed at once to Philippine Islands. Commence operations particularly against Spanish fleet. You must capture vessels or destroy. Use utmost endeavor." The sixty-year-old Dewey had waited thirty-six years for this moment. There would be no half measures. The British members of the Hong Kong Club thought the Yanks fine fellows, but shook their heads as they sailed off.

One member spoke for them all: "We shall never see them again."

Oscar Williams had known this day would come. Before February 15, the professorial consul in Manila felt forgotten in a forgotten land. But after the *Maine* exploded, he was an "intelligence officer." Washington knew little about Manila's defenses: all they knew was that Spain's decrepit Asiatic Fleet guarded Manila Bay. It was Williams's job to learn more.

Manila was a sleepy post, its only immediate connection to the world an undersea cable to Hong Kong controlled by Spain. The city rose a foot above high water; those who entered through the Customs House stepped around goats nosing for lumps of wet sugar dropped from cargo. Some 300,000 people called it home, including 50,000 Chinese, 5,000 Europeans, 100 English, and 3 registered Americans. As in any port, lowlifes and lost souls drifted through. Earthquakes were common, and houses were built low, without glass windows. Cloth covered the walls, not plaster, as the latter rained down in chunks or fine powder with every shake. By the same logic, gas pipes were taboo. Typhoons from the China Sea usually landed eighty miles north: a medium-size blow could capsize three thousand houses. Now a typhoon composed of American battleships stood ready to roar through.

Dewey first wrote to Williams on February 17, 1898: his language was cordial but stiff, unused to diplomats' phrasing. Williams read the letter again. The commodore wanted him to send the name of every Spanish war vessel entering and leaving the harbor, plus changes to land defenses. He'd be his eyes and ears.

Williams's heart quickened: suddenly he was a player in the Great Game. Yet in the Philippines, accurate information was hard to come by. Since the press was so heavily censored, he hired informants and took long walks. Manila was a small place, far more negotiable then than now, and as a third of the city's official three-person American populace, he found Filipinos eager to talk. He discovered, for example, that the recently proclaimed peace was a fiction. His predecessor had mentioned skirmishes in Mindanao and other southern islands, but had never explained that fighting between Spaniards and *insurrectos* as ferocious as that in Cuba had raged for at least two years. Hospitals were filled with wounded; the city lay under martial law. On February 19 a bloody battle took place that neither side won. On February 22 Williams described prisoners shot without trial, while rebels were drilling ten miles outside Manila. Rumor held that an uprising was planned for March. Spain must send men or lose the archipelago, Williams said.

Such detail brought the consul considerable attention—from the State Department *and* Spanish authorities. He suspected that he was followed in the streets, so he hired four "detectives" who in turn hired stooges. He flew the Stars and Bars over the consulate and made himself available to Yankees, respectable or not, all frightened by the new hostility. He helped those who wanted out and advised those who stayed to carry a sidearm, in violation of local law.

In late February, he discovered that his reports were no longer secure. Letters were opened; recent cables "excited suspicion." He sent his letters to Dewey on British ships and in this way maintained an almost daily flow of news. The first letter was apparently dated March 1: he'd taken a "long stroll among the gun shells and on the walls" of Fort Santiago, which he believed "very inadequate to protection." Any two warships could "silence the forts and capture the city," he said. He'd seen several Spanish warships: the *Don Juan de Austria*, the *Reina Christina*, the *Isla de Cuba*, and one or two smaller ones he could not identify.

He felt the net tighten. Anything addressed to or from Dewey was "being tampered with"; the telegraph office tried to decipher Dewey's codes. He believed the keys to his consulate safe had been taken by "persons who have no right to them." He warned that his spycraft should be taken with a grain of salt: "I am on the *side track* of the universe," he lamented. "I know little of events." Manila's newspapers were untrustworthy; rumors rarely came true. People told him, "If the U.S. or Great Britain would only take these islands, how happy we would be," but such panegyrics proved misleading.

Throughout March, Williams transmitted news that Dewey considered "highly valuable," though he did suspect him of believing "extravagant rumors." On March 17 Williams told of a mutiny by Filipino troops who refused to fire on their own people; on March 22 he described mines and torpedoes lining the main channels; on March 25 he corrected this, as the electrician charged with connecting mine detonators had not received supplies. The Spaniards were building a cordon of small stone blockhouses around Manila in anticipation of a "surprise attack by natives." When a second native regiment refused to fight, the Spaniards pulled out eight Filipino corporals and "shot [them] to death" in front of their comrades.

Spanish morale deteriorated daily, he said. On Sunday, March 20, all electric lights blinked out during a performance at the Theater Lorillo, and "the men all squatted behind the seats so as to escape the expected volley of bullets from the natives." He wrote two letters to Dewey on the same day. In the first, a meeting of rebels held nearby was raided: twelve were killed, many wounded, sixty captured. All were executed the next morning. The second was an afterthought: he'd run out of funds to pay his spies, "all of small means." His $2,000 monthly salary did not allow for expenses greater than $50. Unable to pay them, he needed a loan.

Williams's letters had effect. On Thursday, March 31, Dewey wrote Secretary Long that, thanks to Williams's intelligence, "I believe I am not overconfident" that Spain's fleet "could be taken and the defense of Manila reduced in one day." That same day, Governor Rivera politely urged Williams to leave. His rooms and the consulate had been searched: nothing was safe, and for this reason he kept the secret ciphers for cables "always on my person."

Williams's handlers in Washington were concerned. One week after Rivera's warning, the State Department told Williams to withdraw and place all U.S. interests in the hands of the British consul or some other neutral power. He shot back: "GO WHERE[?] NO STEAMER." The Spanish had blocked his only route out. What informal protection he'd received from Primo de Rivera ended on April 9, when Lieutenant General Basilio Augustín replaced him as governor. Like Blanco in Cuba, Augustín's job was to establish a new autonomous era of Spanish rule.

By April 10 Williams had reached a crossroads. His men heard rumors that his life was forfeit should war begin. "When Washington cables me to withdraw," he asked Dewey, "is it an order or advice?" If it was an order, he'd haul down the flag. But if it was advice, he'd rather stay. "If I go, you get no information," but if he stayed, "I may gather information saving millions of dollars to our Govt." For the moment, "I will stay here." He thanks Dewey for a $150 check to pay informants, but the consular office had forgotten to sign it and it had to be returned.

By April 19 Dewey took Williams's safety in hand. Come to Hong Kong, he said. He wanted to talk before sailing for Manila. Williams wired the State Department that he was closing the consulate on April 22, one day before Spain declared war. Maybe it was best. He'd woken one morning to find the U.S. coat of arms above the front door daubed with Spain's red and gold; the signs of some American businesses had been ripped down. The few remaining expatriates had found havens, and he'd placed consulate business in British hands. He'd been having the time of his life, but Dewey had spoken. Williams arrived in Hong Kong on April 26—one day before the commodore's squadron left Mirs Bay.

In early 1898 Emilio Aguinaldo watched the peace pact between Spain and his rebels wither and die. Those left in Luzon continued to fight, but their uncoordinated efforts got nowhere. Surrendered guns were often rusty or useless, so Spain refused to pay the remaining 400,000 pesos. No reforms were enacted; arrests were on the rise. Exile stretched before him. Either that, or he'd be turned into a puppet by one of the great powers.

Filipino expats met his little group when they landed in Hong Kong. These people had fled the islands after the 1872 upheaval and were now a moneyed part of the British Crown colony; though nationalistic, they did not spring from the same source and distrusted these young "beggarly rebels." But Aguinaldo needed them: they were rich, and they possessed valuable contacts in Europe, in Asia, and back home.

They too called themselves the Junta, just like the one in New York seeking *Cuba Libre*. Their leader was thirty-eight-year-old Felipe Agoncillo y Encarnación. A lawyer and judge in Batangas, he'd posted a famous sign outside his office: "Free legal services to the poor anytime." This did not sit well with the Church, and in 1896 he was exiled to southern Jolo. He escaped to Japan, then to Hong Kong. Others joined him: Dr. Galicano Apacible, who disapproved of Aguinaldo's lack of learning; Antonio Luna, whose booming voice filled every room. Where others stressed military issues, Agoncillo valued diplomacy: he'd been behind the failed January 1897 letter to U.S. consul Hunt seeking an American alliance, and had tried again in October 1897 with Hunt's replacement—Rounsevelle Wildman, a magazine editor who seemed more fascinated with this strange, exotic place than his predecessor had been. Agoncillo's new offer had intrigued Wildman: an "offensive and defensive alliance" should there be war with Spain. He asked for twenty thousand stands of rifles and ammo, offering the Manila Customs House and two provinces as security. Rather than dismiss the offer, Wildman conferred with Washington. But war did not loom in late 1897, and the State Department demurred.

Aguinaldo occupied the same position as Bonifacio in Cavite: the resented outsider. But unlike his rival, he had *lots* of money. His exiles moved into a sprawling mission-style home on Morrison Hill Road in the Wan Chai district, next door to Agoncillo. January 2 was the first banking day of the New Year, and Aguinaldo deposited 400,000 pesos in the Hong Kong and Shanghai Banking Corporation at 4 percent interest, under the name "Aguinaldo & Company." Two days later, he withdrew half and deposited *this* in the Chartered Bank of India, Australia and China at 2 percent interest, with the provision that he could withdraw up to 50,000 pesos per quarter. He probably did this under Agoncillo's guidance, since he would not have known Hong Kong's financial world. He still expected the Spaniards to honor the peace pact and make their second and third payments. Though this never arrived, the interest on the original deposit yielded 18,582.90 pesos between January 6 and February 16. He placed his exiles on such a strict budget that they must account for every new coat and pair of shoes, a hardship for dandies. But by pinching pennies, they became self-supporting and had to beg from no one.

A challenge soon materialized. Ten days after Aguinaldo left Luzon, the remaining rebels resolved that all future Spanish payments should go to them, not Hong Kong. Rivera acceded: it meant a split in the leadership, and the upstarts quickly received the second 200,000 pesos. On February 14 Aguinaldo told his exiles. They exploded, and placed the reins of the new Philippines Provisional Government squarely in Aguinaldo's hands.

More surprises arose. On Thursday, March 10, an American appeared at the house on Morrison Hill asking for Aguinaldo. He'd come from Captain Edward P. Wood, skipper of the U.S. gunboat *Petrel*, who'd been ordered by Dewey to arrange an interview. Aguinaldo returned with him to the ship, where the executive officer, Lieutenant R. V. Hall, told him that America needed intelligence about Manila. Aguinaldo was no fool. There must be deeper reasons for this meeting, so he got to the point: Would America support their fight for independence? Lieutenant Hall played coy, but did say the United States would arm and return the exiles to the Philippines if they agreed "to help fight the Spanish." This was straight from Dewey, Hall added.

Aguinaldo was wary: the great powers broke promises to "natives" without qualm. Sensing his caution, Hall invited Aguinaldo to meet his captain. Though exact dates are fuzzy, several secret meetings took place on the *Petrel* between March 10 and April 7, their content also debatable. According to Aguinaldo, Wood urged him to return to Luzon, reorganize his army, and liberate his nation. Should the U.S. go to war with Spain—which looked likely—she'd give him arms, advice, and ammunition. Wood also revealed America's plans to attack the Spanish fleet, which Wood later denied.

Aguinaldo's critics would doubt that a U.S. commander would reveal secret plans, yet it was easy by now to link rumors of war to fleet movements and see how it pointed straight at Manila. In fact, a telegram from the Crown to Governor Rivera showed that Madrid had already reached this conclusion as early as March 3. As they talked, Aguinaldo asked Wood what the United States planned to do with his homeland: "The Commander answered that the United States was very great and rich and did not need colonies. In view of this, I [Aguinaldo] suggested to the Commander how much better it would be to have an agreement in writing, and he said that he would lay the matter before Admiral Dewey."

With this, a route had been paved for a meeting between Dewey and Aguinaldo.

Yet greed is rarely convenient, and at this moment, a member of Luzon's Katipuneros appeared without preamble in Hong Kong. General Isabelo Artacho led the faction that had commandeered all future Spanish payments from the exiles; he now demanded 200,000 pesos for "services rendered." This so infuriated the exiles that they stripped Artacho of all rank; in response, the apostate filed suit for the money in Hong Kong Supreme Court. The exiles debated whether they should just strangle the man, but Agoncillo calmed them down. British courts in Hong Kong frowned on murder, he said. Instead, they could smuggle Aguinaldo beyond the court's reach to Singapore, where he could hide out under a false name.

Aguinaldo left on April 7, 1898, with Gregorio del Pilar and his secretary José Leyba. They booked a steamer to Saigon, then Singapore, and falsely let slip that they were bound for Europe and America. During this time, Dewey met with the Junta. His disappointment must have been evident: when he asked for Aguinaldo, the exiles had to have provided details. "They seemed to be all very young earnest boys," Dewey later said. If anything, the intrigue irritated him, and he claimed to have turned them over to his staff. But at least one witness disagreed. The writer A. H. Myers said that when Dewey encouraged his guests to accept American arms and renew the revolt, they asked, "What will be our reward?"

"I have no authority," Dewey replied, "but there is no doubt if you cooperate with and assist us by fighting the common enemy, that you will be granted your freedom the same as the Cubans will be."

Aguinaldo arrived incognito in Singapore on April 23 and moved into the home of the wealthy countryman Dr. Isidoro de Santos. Four hours later, a stranger described as both an "Englishman" and a "Jewish gentleman" knocked on the door. He introduced himself as Howard Bray and asked for Don Emilio. No "Don Emilio" lived here, de Santos said.

Aguinaldo was flabbergasted. Was there no place to hide? If anything, it suggests a wire from Dewey listing Aguinaldo's precise location, most probably revealed by the "young earnest boys." Bray was the kind of "fixer" common in Asia then and today: a former British official in India who sympathized with the rebels, he'd purchased a Philippine plantation, only to watch Spain take it away. He now lived in Singapore, wrote articles on the islands for the local press, and served as legman for U.S. Consul General E. Spencer Pratt.

Bray reappeared the next morning, saying that he bore a message for *El Presidente.* De Santos repeated: Aguinaldo is not here. Bray came back that evening, and again the next morning, finally "declaring with insistence" that there was no use denying Aguinaldo's presence. Dewey himself had wired Consul Spencer Pratt about his location, he said. Hearing that, Aguinaldo stepped forward, and Bray handed him a note from Pratt arranging a secret meeting at a secluded public house called "The Mansion," with Bray and José Leyba serving as interpreters.

The meeting had a real "cloak and dagger atmosphere," Aguinaldo recalled. As before, a series of meetings followed; as before, both sides remembered things differently. The clearest and most detailed narrative is Aguinaldo's: Pratt said that Spain and America had been at war since April 19, a date slightly off, since this was the day the United States declared Cuba's independence, not war with Spain. Aguinaldo was overwhelmed by the news. "Now is the time for you to strike," Pratt insisted. "Ally yourself with America, and you will soon defeat the Spaniards!"

Aguinaldo stayed mum.

"America will help you," Pratt added, "if you will help America."

This was surprising, Aguinaldo later wrote. He asked, "What can we expect to gain from helping America?" Pratt said that the United States would give the Philippines more riches and liberty than ever possible under Spain. Aguinaldo pushed: Cannot an agreement be honored in writing? Pratt countered: only Dewey could sign such a document—and considering the distance, it would be a waste of valuable time. Aguinaldo's doubts must have shown. "You need not have any worry about America," Pratt insisted, telling him about America's promise to leave Cuba "to the Cubans after having driven away the Spaniards and pacified the country. As in Cuba, so in the Philippines. Even more so, if possible. Cuba is at our door while the Philippines is ten thousand miles away!"

Here lay the realization of their dreams—the same powerful backing Rizal had urged! Aguinaldo said that if Dewey would honor him with an official invitation and confirm Pratt's assurances, he'd return to the Philippines "and fight side by side with the Americans!"

They resumed their talks between ten and noon the next day. Bray took Aguinaldo to Pratt's suite at the stately Raffles Hotel. The consul held up a cable from Dewey: SEND AGUINALDO AT ONCE. According to Dewey, the United States would treat an independent Philippines as a "naval protectorate," its ships guarding her from those great power navies even now circling like wolves. No written agreement was needed, because Dewey's words "were sacred and would be fulfilled"—unlike Spain's. Pratt added: "The Government of North America is a very honest, just, and powerful government."

In time, when Dewey and Pratt were questioned about these promises, both claimed they'd been misquoted. Dewey, being Dewey, was exonerated; Pratt, not being Dewey, was not. When pressed, Dewey called Aguinaldo "a soft-spoken, unimpressive little man." Pratt was more generous, but just as firm in his denials. Yet translator Bray would be the thorn in their side, writing to Massachusetts senator George Hoar that Aguinaldo had not lied. "I frankly state that the conditions under which Aguinaldo promised to cooperate with Dewey were independence under a protectorate," he said. "I am fully prepared to swear to this." His account of American promises echoes Aguinaldo's almost word for word.

Not surprisingly, Aguinaldo swooned: "If I can secure arms, I promise you that my people will rise as one man against the Spaniards." Pratt said he would secure those guns.

Is it possible that Aguinaldo was too easily seduced by America's promises? The charge shadows his legacy today. He was a lamb thrown to the wolves, said the biographer Nick Joaquin: "A provincial thrust upon the global stage and forced to deal with the cunning" of Americans who considered themselves innocents but "were about as innocent as Fagin or Machiavelli."

Even this early, America harbored plans for the Philippines. Around the same time that Pratt and Aguinaldo talked, John Barrett, the U.S. minister to Siam, told the Bangkok press, "It is of the greatest importance that the United States should take the Philippine Islands." The archipelago was "richer and far larger than Cuba, and in the hands of a strong power would be the key to the Far East." Aguinaldo's caution reflected a growing suspicion among Asian thinkers that despite America's stated commitment to freedom, the nation had other designs.

One way to hold America to account was to make its promises public, and Aguinaldo visited the *Singapore Free Press* soon after his meeting with Pratt. In an April 21, 1898, interview, he said he'd told Pratt that he wanted "to establish a proper and responsible government on liberal principles" and expected the same terms "as the United States intended giving to Cuba." The *Free Press* added that "General Aguinaldo's policy embraces the independence of the Philippines," something Pratt did not deny.

Aguinaldo was not alone in thinking he'd brokered a marriage from heaven. Suddenly the United States seemed to treat the former mayor as an equal, and back in Hong Kong, the exiles brimmed with joy. "Compatriots!" they proclaimed in a wire back home: "Divine Providence is about to place independence within our reach, and in a way the most free and independent nation could hardly wish for. The Americans, not from mercenary motives, but for the sake of humanity and the lamentations of so many persecuted people, considered it opportune to extend their protecting mantle to our beloved country." The United States was coming by sea: don't fire on them. "Rather blow your own brains out than fire a shot or treat as enemies those who are your liberators," they warned. "There, where you see an American flag flying, assemble in numbers; they are our redeemers."

Not all were smitten—Apolinario Mabini, for one. Dubbed the revolution's "intellectual architect," the self-educated lawyer fell prey in January 1896 to an unknown paralysis; during convalescence, he wrote of the need for revolution before shooting started, in August of that year. The timing proved his undoing, and in October, Spain threw him into prison as a collaborator. He stayed there for seven months as his malady grew worse, finally released in the May 1897 general amnesty surrounding the Pact of Biak-na-Bato.

Thus, between prison and infirmity, Mabini had missed the Little Republic, the Pact of Biak-na-Bato, and exile. Yet his critiques of Spanish rule made him known to both sides. He might sympathize with the Junta, but his legal training disposed him to a hairsplitting that won few friends. Why, he warned in an "Open Letter to All Filipinos," should we trust the Americans? "Do not deceive yourselves," he warned. They, "like the Spaniards and all other European powers, covet this most beautiful pearl of the Orient Seas." Instead, gather forces, seize territory, and bargain from a position of strength. Only then would Americans "be forced to restrain themselves." Might was the only thing "colossi of ambition and power" understood.

Mabini proved right, but no paralyzed Cassandra whispered warnings into Aguinaldo's ear. Now, as before, *El Presidente* found himself without written commitment from a great power. He'd taken Spain at her word, and look what happened! Now the Americans called written agreements cumbersome—and didn't Dewey's promise to return him to the Philippines on a U.S. warship demonstrate America's goodwill? The nation's historic stance against colonialism and its adoption of the Teller Amendment—weren't these adequate proof of U.S. intentions? Unfortunately, neither Aguinaldo nor anyone else understood that the U.S. State Department alone had the power to make such deals. Washington would soon remind Pratt, Wildman, and Dewey of this in the strongest terms. At the moment, however, the United States needed allies, and truth gets omitted when promising dreams.

Aguinaldo left for Hong Kong on April 26, the day after the United States declared war with Spain. The steamer *Malacca* could not go fast enough; Aguinaldo paced her decks as if to hurry her along. They arrived on the night of May 1, but Dewey's launch did not meet them. Aguinaldo sought out Rounsevelle Wildman, who told him the U.S. Asiatic Squadron had sailed four days earlier, bound for the Philippines.

Dewey sipped cold tea on the bridge of the flagship *Olympia* the night Aguinaldo returned to Hong Kong. It was a quiet tropical night, washed with light rain. They'd entered Manila Bay with little fanfare. A white glow to the northeast marked Manila itself; the squadron steamed in line toward that beacon. It had been thirty-six years since he'd been a fresh-faced lieutenant serving under Admiral David Farragut in the Battle of New Orleans. He listened now as a sailor crooned "Just Before the Battle, Mother" in falsetto; a critic poured coffee on the singer and the concert ended. Dawn would break soon.

They'd steamed six hundred miles through the South China Sea for four days—seven warships, 1,743 officers and crew, and three correspondents with Pulitzer's *World*, *The New York Herald*, and *The Chicago Record*. The *Herald*'s Joseph L. Stickney planted himself on the *Olympia* with Dewey. The sight of men-of-war steaming in line to battle took his breath away: the officers standing on the bridge, men going about their tasks, blue sea stretching away on all sides. A ship's routine is familiar, yet every engine stroke brings one closer to possible calamity. Dewey filled the hours with drills. At midnight of the first day, "Quarters for action" sounded and the crew tumbled from sleep to battle stations. Dewey timed the *Olympia* with his pocket watch—they cleared the ship in seven minutes. In their wake floated tables, chairs, every piece of wood deemed unnecessary for combat that might catch fire. On the second day, Dewey had the captain of each ship read a thumping proclamation penned earlier by Manila's new governor, Basilio Augustín y Dávila. "SPANIARDS," it cried: "The aggressors shall not profane the tombs of your fathers, they shall not gratify their lustful passions at the cost of your wives' and daughters' honor, or appropriate the property your industry has accumulated as a provision of your old age." Prepare for the coming struggle! The crews greeted the words with laughter.

But Dewey had concerns. The day before sailing, he'd finally talked to Oscar Williams, who'd learned that Admiral Patricio Montojo had relocated his ships from Cavite to Subic Bay, thirty miles north of the northern channel. Subic lay outside Dewey's route: it was small, narrow, and easily defended. If this was true, Dewey would have to attack Subic first or leave an armed menace in his rear. They'd have to reconnoiter Subic before attacking Manila.

Wherever the Spaniards lurked, the advantage lay with Dewey. The commodore had seven ships: four steel cruisers, decks protected by armor plates; two gunboats; and the revenue cutter *McCullough*. Two colliers stayed back from the action. The picture wasn't totally rosy, since some ships lacked thick armor on their prow and stern. Others lacked light artillery to ward off torpedo boats. American torpedo tubes held one torpedo apiece, compared with the Spanish standard of three.

An earlier study by the great powers had predicted that the Spaniards could win if they attacked first and got in close to the Americans. But this did not take into account the pitiful state of the Spanish squadron. Montojo commanded two small armored cruisers, five "unprotected cruisers," and gunboats of various types and sizes. One was a wooden hulk, unable to move. His largest ship, the *Castilla*, had a wooden hull. And American firepower outclassed them. Dewey's squadron mounted ten 8-inch rifles, twenty-three 6-inch guns, and twenty 5-inch guns. Montojo's ships mounted seven 6.3-inch guns, plus four ancient 5.9-inch cannons in the fort guarding the bay. In layman's terms, this meant that the Americans could pound them from a safe distance while Montojo's shells would fall short. Some guns were even old, useless muzzleloaders.

That left the mines. On April 19 Madrid ordered Montojo to close off the ports with mines, but the admiral found only fourteen of them, many lacking fuses or cables. He cabled his discovery on April 21, hoping the Crown could send more. At Subic Bay, only five mines were in place, while the guns meant to guard the entrance lay on the beach in pieces. Madrid promised to ship seventy mines, but on April 28 Montojo received the Spanish consul's wire from Hong Kong that Dewey's squadron had vanished the previous day—presumably on its way to Manila. The Americans would arrive long before the mines. When Montojo wired Madrid of this fact, he was told to make up his lack of armaments with "zeal and activity."

This seems the moment when he knew he was doomed. His only real choice lay in how best to lessen the slaughter. Subic Bay measured forty feet deep: his sailors stood less chance of drowning in the shallow waters of Cavite. With the crippled *Castilla* in tow, Montojo headed south. He could put his ships under the protection of Manila's guns, but this would put the flammable capital at risk. His only choice was to line his fleet along the shallow Cavite littoral at the southwest edge of the bay.

How had matters grown so dire? The question also concerned Admiral Pascual Cervera in Cuba, who'd already predicted disaster. In broad terms, Spain lay at the end of a path paved with hubris, one the United States had just begun: no race could compete with the descendants of conquistadores—or Anglo-Saxons. But the two diverged in more narrow terms. Both entered the 1880s with nearly worthless navies, but by 1898 a series of political and technical decisions had created two different forces. Though the U.S. Congress had authorized funds in 1883 for its first steel-hulled ships, one can pinpoint change to the following year, when Commodore Stephen B. Luce founded the Naval War College. When Alfred Thayer Mahan became its second president, he turned the school into a pulpit for a "blue water" navy of big battleships at the same time that a world revolution in ship design was fired by new technologies. The sweeping change seduced "Mahanites" like Roosevelt and Lodge. Though every service branch must fight for funding, the U.S. Navy at this time boasted a greater continuity of purpose than ever before in its history.

In Spain, naval planning was always tied to politics. From 1876 to 1898, twenty-six navy ministers shuffled in and out of office, many more than once, wrecking all chance of continuity. In 1885 Minister Juan Bautista Antequera had sent to the Spanish Congress a plan to build twelve new battleships and other vessels for 231 million pesetas over ten years. This went nowhere. Spain was impoverished all century: ship design changed so quickly in the late nineteenth century that a ship could go from "first-class" to obsolete before its keel was laid. Spain gambled that if it waited, design would stabilize: until that happened, it could depend upon a cheap, fast fleet of gunboats and destroyers loaded with a terrifying new weapon everyone overrated. Torpedoes would create a "new equilibrium"; naval warfare would represent a "true guerrilla war at sea."

In Manila, the archbishop who'd ordered Rizal's death urged all countrymen to pray. On Sunday, April 24, 1898, a "patriotic demonstration" marched around the city; two days later, word reached Manila that the

Americans had left Hong Kong and moved to Mirs Bay. By Wednesday, Dewey's ships were en route, and the archbishop exhorted his people to fight this holy war "with prayer and weapons." The Americans, "possessed by the blackest rancor and all the abject passions that heresy engenders," planned to destroy that "which we most esteem, namely, our religion."

Dewey reached Cape Bolinao on the western tip of Central Luzon on April 30 at three a.m. He steamed south, and at daylight two ships reconnoitered in Subic Bay. They reported it empty. "Now we have them!" Dewey said. That night he asked himself, "What would David Farragut do?" He assembled his captains and laid out a plan lifted straight from his old commander's playbook: "You will follow the motions and movements of the flagship, which will lead." The meeting broke up, and Dewey's nephew, Lieutenant William Winder of the *Raleigh*, stayed behind. "Commodore," he said, "I have always made it a policy never to take advantage of our being related." But this time he would. He wanted to take the unarmed collier *Zafiro* ahead into the bay to detonate any floating mines. "Sir," he said, "this is one chance I have to become famous."

Dewey smiled at his nephew, but shook his head. "Billy, I have waited sixty years for this opportunity. And as much as I like you and know you are a fine officer—mines or no mines, I am leading the squadron in myself."

Shortly past midnight, they passed in line through the bay's north entrance between Corregidor and El Fraile islands. Both ships were armed and fortified, but no sound issued from them. To cut the tension, Dewey said to the *Olympia*'s captain, Charles V. Gridley, "A fine night for a smoke, eh, Gridley? It's a pity we can't light up." But nerves played on him, too: cold tea was all he could keep down. The *McCullough* was the last ship; her engine room temperature soared to 170 degrees, and the chief engineer, "a very stout man who took little or no exercise," collapsed from heat prostration. At that moment, accumulated soot in the *McCullough*'s smokestack ignited into a tall pillar of flame. El Fraile opened up, the whistling shells passing over the revenue cutter. The *Boston*, *Concord*, *Raleigh*, and *McCullough* fired back; El Fraile's guns replied twice until a direct hit from the *Boston* silenced them. Corregidor's guns never fired.

Every ship had run the gauntlet unscathed. They turned toward the white glow of Manila, twenty-five miles distant. One hour later, at eight bells, the crew was served coffee, beans, and hard bread. The tropical heat descended; on the *McCullough*, the chief engineer died. No guns broke the silence; no torpedoes, rockets, or mines. Dewey reduced speed so he would come upon Manila in daylight, where he expected to find Montojo. The sun rose behind Manila two hours later: Dewey was a mile off the waterfront and could see the long rows of houses and gray towers of the old fort, but no Spanish men-of-war. A few minutes later, the gathering light revealed a line of gray and white ships five or six miles south, where the hook of Cavite's navy yard jutted into the bay. The flame-red flag of Spain flew over every one.

Dewey's flagship swung to starboard, and all others followed. The line bore south, increasing speed to eight knots. Dewey told the navigator to run close to the enemy; he wanted every shell to count. A Spanish shell passed overhead, a distance of six miles. Two more plunged into the water ahead, while the shells from Manila's batteries passed overhead. Dewey ignored them all. At 5:40 a.m. the *Olympia*'s navigator calculated that they were 5,400 yards from the lead Spanish ships. "You may fire when ready, Gridley," Dewey said.

By now, Manila's waterfront was lined with spectators, watching as the Americans bore down on Montojo, "haughty in their colossal barks," wrote Miguel Saderra Masó, a Jesuit scholar ordered by his rector to record these historic days. A battery in Cavite opened fire, as did one or more of Montojo's ships, some batteries in Manila. The Americans shrugged them off and bore down in silence. To those watching, this was the most terrible thing.

Admiral Montojo saw them coming, too. An ironbound sense of fatalism had filled him since the shambles at Subic Bay. He'd decided to take position in the shallow navy yard and await destruction there. The idea that there could be any other outcome seems to have never occurred to him. Dying well was the most important thing. He'd attended a party in Manila on that last night but returned to his flagship and at four a.m. signaled the fleet to clear for action. Forty-five minutes later, he could see the *Olympia* bearing down, followed by its silent procession. At five a.m. the shore battery to his left started firing.

Captain Gridley did not open up with his 8-inch guns until 5:30 a.m., then all others followed. The American line came up from the Spaniards' east, passed west along its front, and fired at will; the overlapping blasts seemed unending. Suddenly one of the dreaded little torpedo boats steamed right across the path of the *Olympia*. During the trip, the *Herald*'s Joseph Stickney had graduated from newsman to Dewey's aide: he pointed to the boat, and Dewey said, "You look after her. I have no time to bother with torpedo boats. Let me know when you're finished with her." The *Olympia*'s rapid-fire guns and 6-pounders turned on the flimsy craft; even marines began shooting. Soon it was crippled and driven ashore, the battle's first casualty, thanks to a newspaper reporter.

By six a.m. the "cannonading was veritably infernal," wrote a spectator in Manila. Dewey's ships swung around for a second pass, but could not confirm damage because of all the smoke. Some enemy ships had slipped their cables, but they moved aimlessly, getting in one another's way.

Yet American shells *were* doing damage. One exploded on the poop deck of Montojo's flagship, the *Reina Cristina*, obliterating nine men. Another exploded in the officers' quarters, "covering the hospital with blood and destroying the wounded who were being treated there." A third exploded astern in the magazine, disabling the hand-steering gear. Dewey's nephew gave the distance to the Spanish flagship to the gunnery officer: "He plunged a six-inch shell right through, and instantly volumes of steam poured out, showing that a pipe had been struck and, alas, doubtless many poor fellows scalded to death." A half hour later, the ship burst into flames. There was no longer any way to control the fire, and stored shells began to burst. Montojo flooded the compartment so his ship would not go up like the *Maine*.

When Dewey's fleet came around a third time, the leadsman discovered a greater depth than the charts indicated. On this closer pass, Spanish shells hit their marks. One projectile headed straight for Dewey on his bridge, but exploded less than a hundred feet away. A shell passed through the armored cruiser *Baltimore* without hitting a soul; a second ripped up the main deck, disabled a 6-inch gun, exploded a pair of 3-pound shells, and wounded eight men. The *Boston* received a hit in her port quarter; a second passed through the ship's forecastle in front of the captain. The battle overrode one's senses: "I felt absolutely no fear," Dewey's nephew told his mother, a realization that "greatly surprised me." Men on the *Raleigh* heckled shells that splashed nearby: "Try again, Don!" they cried. "I would see a gun fired right at us and wonder, in a sort of stupid way, if it was going to get me," Winder said, "but meanwhile I went along with signals, etcetera, and so did everybody else, to the poorest messenger boy."

Seeing the thick billows of black smoke drifting from the Spanish fleet, Dewey could tell that he'd done considerable harm. And the carnage *was* incredible. On the flagship, fires burned fore and aft, and half the crew was wounded or dead. Montojo was hit in the leg. The *Castilla* caught fire and was abandoned after eight sailors were wounded and twenty-three killed. Lighter ships escaped as Americans sighted the bigger vessels. Out of 1,534 men and officers, Montojo had already lost 381, almost a quarter. In Manila, spectators knew the battle was already lost. Thunder echoed from the surrounding hills.

As Dewey looped back for a fourth pass, a heartbreaking vision pierced the smoke. The *Reina Cristina* limped toward the *Olympia*, probably to ram her. The two flagships drew to within twelve hundred yards apart, but the faster *Olympia* steamed past and the *Reina Cristina* received multiple broadsides. Dark smoke poured from the bow and stern; a plume of white steam shot up when a shell pierced the superheater. She'd lost her steering engine, and most guns were shot away. The chaplain was killed, his head "blown to bits while he was hearing the confession of a wounded Marine." Montojo turned his flagship to shore and ordered her scuttled before fires ignited the magazines. He signaled the *Isla de Cuba* and *Isla de Luzon* to rescue survivors, but the *Cristina*'s captain fell while directing the evacuation. One hundred and fifty men were killed and ninety wounded on the *Cristina* alone; when she was raised five years later, eighty skeletons were found in sick bay.

At 7:35 a.m., as the squadron made its fourth pass, a situation arose that could have turned Dewey's victory into ridicule. Captain Gridley told the commodore that the *Olympia* had only a mere fifteen rounds of 5-inch ammo left for her big guns. This translated into five minutes at the current rate of fire. If this held for the other ships, it would be a disaster: the American fleet was deep in hostile territory, seven thousand miles from home, nearly out of ammo. Dewey looked toward the Spanish ships and saw only smoke. How many enemy ships still remained? He decided to break off, wait out the smoke, and take stock; he turned away to redistribute ammo.

But Gridley had misread an officer's report. Instead of having fifteen rounds of ammo left per ship, they had fifteen rounds per gun. They had plenty of ammo left; not only that, but the *Olympia* had escaped virtually unscathed. Dewey signaled for his captains to come aboard and give their reports: to his amazement, the ships were barely touched, with only six men on the *Baltimore* slightly wounded. The sole fatality was the *McCullough*'s chief engineer, who died before the battle started. Dewey ordered breakfast for his men, an act that enthroned him with a reputation for nonchalance, when in fact he used the time to double-check his ammo.

The lull lasted three and a half hours: at 11:16 a.m. Dewey decided to finish the job. The squadron steamed back to where the Spanish fleet lay, a smoking ruin. Only one tiny torpedo boat, *Don Antonio de Ulloa*, and the shore batteries were left, and they started firing as the Americans neared. By 12:30 all were silenced, and the white flag was raised. Manila's batteries still fired, so Dewey sent a message to Governor Augustín promising to destroy the city if this continued. The guns grew very quiet. Dewey asked to use the Spaniards' undersea cable to wire news of his triumph to the world, but this was more than Augustín could stomach, and he refused. So Dewey ordered the collier *Zafiro* to dredge the cable from the seafloor and cut it. The officers and crew began to realize the extent of their victory. Astonishment reigned. "The Spanish fleet destroyed," wrote Winder, "and as Dewey said, 'No joy is like the joy of victory.'" But such joy had a price: "They'd killed and wounded eleven hundred poor devils" in the "frightful slaughter, men who, after all, had no hand in making the war."

Manila lay silent for seven days. There were rumors, leaks, and one official dispatch wired by the governor during Dewey's breakfast pause. It said nothing and everything: "Our fleet engaged the enemy in brilliant combat," Augustín wrote. "Our fleet, considering the enemy's superiority, naturally suffered severe loss." New York chose optimism: "Victory! Complete!!" blared the *Journal*; "Spain's Asiatic Fleet Destroyed by Dewey," the *Herald* said. But as the week dragged on, the words "severe loss" assumed ominous tones.

At three a.m. on May 7, truth interrupted a poker game at the *World*. The paper's Edwin Harden had wired at the commercial rate of $9.90 a word. He'd witnessed the battle aboard the *McCullough*, which had just returned to Hong Kong. "The great American triumph in Manila," Harden wrote. "The entire Spanish fleet of eleven vessels was destroyed." His story even beat the first word to Washington, which arrived at the Navy Department at 6:15 a.m.

Dewey stayed in place. "The American squadron, mistress of the bay, entertains herself by burning merchant boats," the Jesuit diarist observed. Dewey had sufficient ships to command the bay, but not the men to take the city. To leave would create a vacuum. In Washington there was joy; in Madrid, grief; among the great powers, awareness of opportunity. From Thursday, May 5, 1898, to Tuesday, May 10, predators gathered: two British warships, two German battleships, a warship apiece from France and Japan. It was a waiting game.

No one had waited longer than Aguinaldo. Dewey and the consuls had promised passage back home, but a mix-up delayed his boarding the *McCullough* until mid-May. During the wait, Aguinaldo conferred with Rounsevelle Wildman and bought 2,000 Mausers at $7 apiece, and 200,000 cartridges at $33.50 per thousand, to renew the war. Wildman advised his protégé that upon arrival, he should go to Cavite Province to "establish a Philippine government in a dictatorial form; this would be the best system for waging war, and after victory he could then establish a government in the American mold." Aguinaldo bought a $15,000 steam launch to shuttle between islands, then handed another $67,000 to Wildman for arms and supplies.

On May 15 the *McCullough* returned with its paperwork in order. Two days later, *El Presidente* stepped aboard with seventeen fellow exiles and crates of ammo and guns. This return on a Yankee warship was considered crucial. Arriving as part of the victorious fleet signaled Dewey's support, inspiring potential recruits. They'd remember the charmed general protected by the potent *anting-anting*.

The *McCullough* dropped anchor on the afternoon of May 19. The houses on the waterfront rose like cliffs; beyond that, the green hills of the alluvial plain. Warships from all nations bobbed around Dewey's fleet; Aguinaldo realized that, for this moment, his home was the world's hub. The commodore's launch separated from the *Olympia* and puttered toward him. Aguinaldo took a deep breath and smiled. Just as he'd promised his people, he'd returned.

11

Gathering Tribes

The first news of Dewey came to the State, War, and Navy Building on May 7 at 4:30 a.m. Thomas Cridler, the third assistant secretary of state, was sleeping on a cot when a Western Union messenger handed him a note: "Hong Kong McCullough Wildman." The name of the ship grabbed his attention. He ran up the corridor to the Bureau of Navigation, where they could decode the cipher. By eight a.m. Washington knew that Dewey still lived, though his message would not be deciphered for another two hours. John Long called the president, who authorized its release minus some military details. By then, about fifty newsmen stood outside Long's door.

But when the secretary stepped out, he noticed that their anticipation had dissolved. Roosevelt had beaten him to the punch. On Friday the undersecretary had resigned; this was his last day. Ever since the *Maine* blew up, he'd pleaded for a commission, and on April 25 one finally opened: lieutenant colonel in the First U.S. Volunteer Cavalry, a patchwork of cowboys, Ivy League sportsmen, Indian fighters, and Indians, all organized by Leonard Wood. This morning found Roosevelt cleaning out his desk when he heard the excitement; he peeked over a code clerk's shoulder, then discovered the crowd. He read Dewey's cable to the newsmen, his last act of insubordination to the boss he'd tell in his farewell note "I hate to leave you more than I can say." He also wired Dewey and took credit for his part in his success: "Every American is your debtor," he wrote. "I can't say how pleased I am to think that I had my share in getting you the opportunity that you have used so well." Then he strolled out the door, ordered to training in San Antonio, Texas, eight days away.

Dewey's second report came an hour later: he'd seized and destroyed the Cavite Navy Yard, he said: "I control bay completely and can take city at any time, but I have not sufficient men to hold." Long took his son with him to the White House, where cheering crowds stood outside. "No man could have done better or deserved more," Long said of Dewey: Remember, "had the enterprise failed, it would have been his ruin."

There lay the heart of the matter. Not only would Dewey have been forced to step down, if still alive, but the United States would have been disgraced. The jubilation that spread cross-country suggests relief mixed with pride. If he'd failed, other European powers would have rushed in—as shown by their battleships; if repulsed, all pretenses of "greater destiny" were nullified. But Dewey prevailed, and America felt vindicated. Lieutenant Winder's captain said of Dewey, "I love him." The young lieutenant told his mother, "I guess we all do."

Dewey was deified. McKinley appointed him acting rear admiral on the spot. Two days later, Congress added a new rear admiral to the command list, making permanent a slot he'd earlier been denied. The *World*'s early edition trumpeted "Old Glory Waves Over Manila!" Hearst's *Journal* improvised a star-spangled narrative from the six-hundred-word dispatch sent by the *Chicago Record* reporter. Euphoria stretched from coast to coast, though "delirium" might be more apt. A new brand of chewing gum named Dewey's Chewies hit the market; Dewey's portrait graced "badges, banners, lithographs, and transparencies" as well as "paperweights, pitchers, cups, plates, butter dishes, shaving mugs, teething rings, and rattles." Dozens of popular songs sprang up, inspiring lyricists to rhyme "truly" with "Dewey" and "day" with "Hooray!"

Europe was amazed. Though the great powers recognized that Spain's failure lay in her neglect of the most minimal defense, this defied understanding. In an instant, the United States became one of the world's great naval powers, in the same club with England, France, and Germany. Reactions varied: France, Germany, and Japan seemed inclined to treat it as a fluke. Spain lived in denial: the defeat meant nothing to the army that once beat Napoleon. Only England seemed pleased.

With Dewey's victory, the thought of seizing the Philippines as a war prize formed rapidly. But what did that mean? The "United States is forced to step upon the world's stage and deal with the world's problems," warned *The Philadelphia Press.* The idea of U.S. imperialism suddenly seemed real. Not all welcomed the idea. The *Boston Herald* thought those who favored an imperial route should "read the Monroe Doctrine from top to bottom." *The Washington Star* added, "We belong in the western hemisphere."

As debate progressed, bewilderment turned to pride. George Washington's warning about foreign entanglements no longer monopolized the common wisdom. Perhaps empire was its own justification. "From a nation of shopkeepers we became a nation of warriors," declared Henry Watterson, editor of the Louisville *Courier-Journal*—an image that still holds. No longer were we a "*quantité négligeable*" with "no standing in the councils of the nations," declared Charles Denby in *The Forum.* "We have become a great people."

Yet a Great People needs a Great Army.

The U.S. Army of April 1, 1898, consisted of 2,143 officers and 26,040 enlisted men, hardly a threat to the 150,000 Spanish troops thought to be in Cuba. It did have a decent rifle, the 30-shot, 5-caliber version of the Swedish Krag-Jørgensen, which used smokeless powder, its range slightly less than the Mauser's. But the army barely had enough to arm Regulars, and its stores of ammo would be exhausted after six months. Supplies and food for an 8,000- to 12,000-man division were a fantasy.

If anything, army bureaucracy prevented change. McKinley stood at the top, but coequal beneath him sat the civilian war secretary and the uniformed commanding general. Although the president appointed both, the uniformed post went to the army's senior major general after a long, distinguished career. Orders officially passed from the president to the secretary to the commanding general: while the secretary and his War Department controlled staffing, facilities, and matériel, the commanding general controlled actual fighting and men. Yet the Civil War, and the relationship between Abraham Lincoln and Ulysses S. Grant, had so fundamentally changed both offices that by the mid-1890s Congress and the army considered them equals.

History has not been kind to McKinley's first war secretary, Russell Alexander Alger. A self-made lumber baron, cousin of Horatio Alger, and former Michigan governor, he was handsome and affable, graced at sixty-one with a narrow Van Dyke beard and a charming smile. Yet he suffered from heart disease and had grown frail. Like many McKinley appointees, he was a Union veteran, ending the war as a colonel with service in Gettysburg and the Shenandoah Valley campaign. But impaired health denied him the energy needed to create a modern army able to wage foreign war. His War Department was "a collection of disconnected agencies" loath to cooperate. He did little to correct this, and as a result, "Algerisms" meant incompetence in the 1898 army.

Standing opposite Alger was Commanding General Nelson Applegate Miles, named to that post in 1895. Hated by officers, loved by the rank and file, no one better understood the nuts and bolts of the army. Roosevelt called him a "brave peacock" for his abundant courage and prickly ego. He was fifty-nine when war broke out and had been in the army since the Civil War: he'd been wounded four times, received the Medal of Honor, and rose from private to brevet major general. He was appointed colonel in the Regular Army after the War of Secession, and went to fight in the Indian Wars; he'd learned to respect his Native American adversaries, and sought the court-martial of the officer responsible for the 1890 Wounded Knee Massacre. The officer corps never forgave him for this, since one did not shame fellow officers for tactical decisions. Now silver-haired and sleepy-eyed, he'd planned for a war in Cuba long before its declaration.

Miles detested Alger's cavalier approach to the war. Unlike the navy, the War Department did not get serious about Cuba until the March 8 passage of the $50 million war fund—and then only halfheartedly. When Alger, Long, and McKinley met for their first war council on April 20, Alger's incompetence became obvious. He'd not brought the army up to the same preparedness that Roosevelt and Long had done with the navy, complaining instead that his "prerogatives were being encroached upon"—probably referring to Miles. The meeting made clear that the navy would have to blockade Cuba before the army could fully mobilize. Long wrote in his diary, "At present it seems as if the Army were ready for nothing at all."

More than anything, the army needed men. On April 22 Congress authorized a call for volunteers: Alger thought 60,000 were enough, but McKinley asked for 125,000 to serve two years or until war's end. A month later, he would ask for another 75,000. On April 26 Congress increased the Regular Army's enlistment cap from 25,000 to 62,527; on May 11 it passed a bill permitting the enlistment of 10,000 "Immunes"—men believed resistant to yellow fever—and 3,500 engineers. The Cuban invasion force was dubbed Fifth Corps, and Brigadier General William Rufus Shafter, the senior officer on the lists, was named commander.

Shafter proved to be one of the war's most controversial characters: a gruff Medal of Honor winner, he was sixty-three, weighed 330 pounds, and suffered severe gout in his left leg. He took his discomfort out on the press, which returned the favor. The fact that he hailed from Alger's home state shielded him from health questions. But he was not the only political appointee: McKinley nominated eleven men to major general, four of them civilians, all Republican. Two were former Confederates: Fitzhugh Lee, commissioned as soon as he left Havana; and sixty-one-year-old Joseph "Fighting Joe" Wheeler, a famous cavalry general who'd served as Alabama's congressman for the past seventeen years. Neither was fit for tropical warfare, but both could sway Southerners to vote for the party of Lincoln.

From East to West, Regular Army officers pulled strings to land a combat posting. On April 15 the Army Adjutant General ordered seven regiments to assemble in Tampa and others at Georgia's seven-thousand-acre Chickamauga Battlefield Park. Many had started before this, endowed with a sixth sense for combat. Like Miles, Henry Ware Lawton had survived the Civil War, earned a Medal of Honor, and become an Indian fighter; he'd served with Miles and the surgeon Leonard Wood in the 1886 campaign against the Apaches. Now Lawton was famous, the picture of an "ideal frontier officer," nearly six and a half feet tall, handsome, courageous, and popular with his men. Yet, like many Western officers, he drank: the monotony of the frontier worsened it, leading him at one point to assault an enlisted man. He could have been dismissed, but the incident was hushed up. Posted as inspector general in Los Angeles, he offered Miles his services and boarded a train to D.C. Miles appointed him volunteer brigadier general and assigned him command of the Second Division.

Some traveled much farther. On March 22 Lieutenant Henry Tureman Allen was serving in Russia as military attaché when he began writing letters, starting with Miles. He'd served under him in the 1880s, once exploring fifteen hundred miles up Alaska's Copper River basin—a journey Miles compared to that of Lewis and Clark. But his old commander turned him down: "No one can tell at this point whether we will have war or peace," Miles replied on April 1, suggesting that he stay in Europe. This was not what Allen wanted to hear. On April 21 he wrote his wife that he'd sent off "five pleading letters" and hadn't gotten anywhere. But by June he was given command of Troop D of the Second Cavalry and ordered to Tampa. On June 3 he clacked south in a railroad car.

The call for 200,000 volunteers forced the army to mobilize beyond its experience or means. Some historians claim that a million tried to enlist; others, hundreds of thousands. The Regular Army was forced to reject 77,000 of its 102,000 immediate applicants, while the volunteers rejected 25 percent in pre-muster physicals and an equal proportion after induction. Even then, Miles complained that they'd admitted 100,000 too many. Volunteer units lacked shoes, tents, and blankets; their uniforms were the same heavy blue-wool cloth worn by privates under Grant. They carried single-shot Springfield rifles considered useless in modern combat; these fired black-powder cartridges, producing a cloud of smoke that gave away the shooter's position. Theophilus Steward, chaplain of the all-black Twenty-Fifth Infantry, called it a "popular frenzy," a mob "which could not be directly opposed. Dissenters were branded cowards or unpatriotic, this silencing many. Young men were going to liberate Cuba and in the process prove their manhood before the eyes of the world."

Volunteers funneled through each state's National Guard. No plans existed to train or outfit the men, and McKinley didn't know if he had authority to send Guards outside U.S. borders. So the War Department devised a legal fiction. Each state governor could mobilize his Guards en bloc, and army officers assigned to the camps would call a man's name and ask him to enlist in the federal force for the duration. The recruit then rejoined his pals to reelect their officers. Through this awkward route, the nation turned state units into a patchwork national army.

There was no shortage of volunteers. William "Buffalo Bill" Cody offered to raise an army of thirty thousand Native Americans; the Colorado matron Martha Shute proposed a cavalry regiment made entirely of women. Both were turned down. Young men across the nation signed with their hometown Guards. The New York native Charles Johnson Post, a twenty-five-year-old cartoonist for Hearst's *Journal*, pledged his life to the Seventy-First Regiment of the New York U.S. Volunteers. He'd announced his intentions to "two young maidens" and "a mellow married aunt," who stitched for him some red flannel bellybands, believed to ward off "all forms of pestilence and intestinal fevers." He stripped naked and coughed; aced his eyesight test; and shipped to Camp Black in Hempstead, Long Island, where on May 10 he formally entered the U.S. Army.

On April 26 Charles Sandburg signed with Company C, Sixth Illinois U.S. Volunteers. The company needed a dozen new recruits, and he was among the first. Why are you joining? the recruiter asked. The question puzzled him. Patriotism? A need for adventure? A chance to escape the tedious sanding of unpainted walls?

Sandburg was a typical recruit in a typical Guards unit from a typical small Midwestern town. Recruits must be between eighteen and thirty-five, of good character and habits, free from disease, speak English, have no addictions, and be able to pass a physical exam. Single men were preferred; one's teeth must be good. Enlistment records described Private Charles A. Sandburg as "twenty-one years of age, five feet ten inches high, ruddy complexion, grey eyes, brown hair and by occupation a painter." It was the first time anyone called him "ruddy."

He felt at home. "I knew most of the privates, had worked for Corporal Cully Rowe at the Auditorium, and had gone to school" with Conrad Byloff, first lieutenant and a grade-school friend. His tentmate was Andrew Tanning, a member of the Monarch Dancing Club. Sandburg once danced with Tanning's girl and her sister Tillie, as light on her feet as "a white feather in a blue wind." Three-quarters were Galesburg boys, the rest from farms and villages outside of town.

A Guards unit was as much a social as a military organization. Since they elected their own officers, a common democracy existed between ranks that did not exist in the Regular Army. Lieutenant Byloff might be stern when issuing orders, but then he'd recite the promise of Spartacus to fellow gladiators that a struggle for freedom made all men equal. Woe to the man who acted above his station, as happened in Company C. Their elected captain was Thomas Leslie McGirr, "a second-rank Galesburg lawyer . . . with a distinct paunch, heavy jaws, and a large mustache slightly graying." He kept beside him a yellow-haired Saint Bernard named Smuggler; as the men ate wormy rations, McGirr "fed juicy sirloin steaks" to his dog.

Company C was ordered to Springfield on the day Sandburg enlisted. He shouldered his rifle and marched to the depot; thousands jammed the sidewalks and peeked from windows hung with red, white, and blue. If there must be war, he thought, this was the way to do it, cheered by friends, bound for a noble cause. He spotted his mother, who was crying; he waved and laughed, and "she laughed back through her tears."

At noon the train packed with a hundred volunteers chugged away. They detrained at the state fairgrounds, renamed Camp Tanner after the current governor. Nearly two thousand volunteers from across the state were herded into a building normally reserved for livestock. Illinois was the first state to respond to McKinley, and more than eleven thousand men volunteered. This was enough for eleven regiments, though only three would see combat, including Galesburg's 109 volunteers. Two recruits immediately vanished, "ostensibly for home." Sandburg and the rest were put through company drill and the manual of arms. They stood naked in a large room to file past "a well-meaning surgeon" who listened to their hearts, peered down their throats, and ran his hands "over the scrotums of a thousand privates, corporals, and sergeants." When Sandburg's pal Joe Dunn measured an inch or two short of the required height, tears filled his eyes; the surgeon glanced at an officer, who gave a nod. The doctor "wrapped the measuring tape around a finger, measured again and found that Joe would pass." Joe Dunn grinned.

They roamed around the capital and past Lincoln's home, drilled and marched, grew bored. The restlessness took shape as stolen goods, truant soldiers, disturbances, nights in the guardhouse. On April 30, 110 men from Company B, Fourth Illinois, left for home. Hawkers ran through the camps selling tropical "necessities": remedies for yellow fever; a cloth packet called the "Soldier's Housewife," stuffed with needles, thread, baby pins, and a crumbled cake of "very cooling" starch for heat rash. On May 11 they mustered into service in a massive outdoor ceremony; that same day, the first reports of American casualties came in. The torpedo boat *Winslow* was shelled in the port of Cardenas, killing five crewmen and an officer; at Cienfuegos, the *Nashville* and *Marblehead* tried to dredge up an undersea cable, but Spanish fire injured five and killed two. In the camps, "the bloodthirsty populace" realized they might not come home.

On May 17 they crammed into trains and clicked east to Camp Russell A. Alger in Falls Church, Virginia, a place that would kill and debilitate more of them than the enemy would. All must be fed, housed, and equipped, but the ingredients were in short supply. Tents were few. Soldiers lacked shovels for latrines and garbage pits. There was no disinfectant, no kettles for boiling water.

One narrow stream ran through camp; orders forbidding men to bathe in it were ignored. According to the August 1898 "How Our Boys Died" in *The Kansas City Star*, the army foresaw problems with a single water source, so it pumped river water all over the park for drinking, cooking, and bathing. Major General John R. Brooke ordered eighty carloads of 6-inch pipe from Pittsburgh, which rusted for weeks before being laid. When the pipe leaked, Camp Alger became a sewer. The men dug latrines near field kitchens and hospitals, threw garbage near their tents, defecated in the surrounding woods. An inspector wrote that one could not walk near the Third Volunteer Cavalry's camp "without soiling one's feet with fecal matter."

Typhoid and dysentery spread quickly in such conditions: medical officers especially feared typhoid, recalling its ravages during the Civil War. Nearly twenty-one thousand men contracted it during this part of the campaign. Caused by a variant of the *Salmonella* bacterium, "camp fever" spread when the men ate food or drank water contaminated by infected feces. The Sixth Illinois was not spared. The first to succumb was Private S. L. "George" Bledsoe of Company A, who collapsed in camp on Saturday, May 21, the day they arrived. He died that afternoon. The fact that he contracted the germ in Springfield and carried it with him on the train was worrisome. Sandburg fell ill that day and was assigned to light duty. His diagnosis: dysentery. The "vaults," or latrines, were two hundred yards from camp: they were six feet deep, three feet wide, swarming with flies. He ran to them endlessly. The infected flies flew to the kitchens, and one morning he watched the cook "cut away from a flitch of pork about a quarter of it that was alive with maggots." Five days later, on May 26, Sandburg and four others were "sick in quarters." By month's end, thirty-four soldiers from Sandburg's Company C reported for sick call.

Conditions and disease rates worsened in June's heat: new recruits kept coming—2,000 from June 12 to 15, another 4,000 over the next four days. As soldiers in Tampa finally shipped to Cuba, it looked like they might leave—and none too soon. Swan Bohman of Company C went mad and was sent to an asylum. He'd watched his three small children die violently in the two years before enlisting and hoped war might exorcise his pain. Instead, he'd shown signs of "morbid derangement" as early as Camp Tanner. By June, he called out at night and wandered "continually in the neighborhood of graveyards, mourning the loss of his little ones."

By the end of that month, Sandburg and friends wondered if they'd go mad, too.

One camp ran like silk: Camp Wood, two miles outside of San Antonio, Texas. Its five hundred tents were pitched in orderly "streets"; latrines gleamed. Sheltered by cottonwoods on the state fairground and bordered by the San Antonio River, the quarters of the First U.S. Volunteer Cavalry boasted adequate food, stalls and hay for the mounts, a well-staffed hospital, and exemplary sanitation. Men would not sicken and die here at the same rates as elsewhere, largely owing to the camp's commander and namesake, Leonard Wood. A letter from Secretary Alger dated April 28, 1898, authorized Wood to raise "a regiment of Volunteers possessing special qualifications as horsemen and marksmen." Originally conceived as a "cowboy regiment," it evolved into a hybrid. Wood visited the chief of ordnance to ensure that his men received Krag-Jørgensens; he ordered machetes, not cumbersome cavalry sabers, and lightweight khaki fatigues. He arrived on May 15, weeks before anyone else, but not before a sign was already hung at the station: "This Way to Camp of Roosevelt's Rough Riders."

The story of "Roosevelt's Rough Riders" evolved into the central story of the war. The name changed from the early Teddy's Terrors and Teddy's Texas Tarantulas to its final iteration: it inhabited a front-page position from which it rarely moved. Roosevelt eclipsed even Dewey as the war's great hero; he became for the Splendid War what John Wayne became for the Hollywood Western, more myth than man. Like Wayne, he played to the image. As far back as 1886, Roosevelt had imagined leading a band of "harum-scarum rough riders" into battle, but he'd filed it away as he did so many daydreams. "You must always remember that the President is about six," said Roosevelt's favorite Englishman, Cecil Spring Rice; an early biographer called his life the dream of every American boy: "He fought in a war, became President, killed lions, and quarreled with the Pope." Whatever his faults, Americans never got bored.

The story develops in three phases: the factual history of recruitment, training, and combat; its treatment in the press; its apotheosis in Roosevelt's 1899 *The Rough Riders*, which became historical truth in popular memory. Roosevelt guides the narrative. He shapes the unit with an eye on symbolism: the group becomes what the cultural historian Richard Slotkin called "a utopia of meritocracy" where "distinctions of birth and wealth are set aside in favor of military aptitude." He uses his influence to get the unit assigned to the front line, then gets them home before disease kills them. He shapes press coverage by attention to correspondents, especially Richard Harding Davis. Finally, he authors its official history.

Those accepted to the regiment were telling. They came from the "types" portrayed in Roosevelt's hunting books or *The Winning of the West*: cowboys, hunters, scouts, lawmen, and even outlaws, who defined his vision of the virile frontier. He recruited Ivy League aristocrats and "Eastern dudes," most of them athletes or "gentlemen hunters" belonging to the Boone and Crockett Club: all must be able to shoot and ride, and all but one or two were "straight Republicans." He accepted Native Americans, but segregated them in their own company. Those excluded do not fit into his frontier vision: no mechanics, factory workers, sodbusters, or sharecroppers. No clerks, merchants, or bankers. Most notable was his exclusion of blacks, though the Rough Riders would charge up Kettle and San Juan hills with black Army Regulars.

His friends thought him crazy. “Is he quite mad?” asked Henry Adams. Henry Cabot Lodge thought it the end of his political career. Yet Roosevelt had been planning this for a long time. As early as 1895, he’d written to New York’s governor Levi P. Morton, Colonel Francis V. Greene of the Seventy-First New York, General Nelson Miles, McKinley, and Secretary Alger. On the day Spain declared war, Alger offered Roosevelt a colonelcy and command of the First Volunteer Cavalry. T.R.’s answer shows forethought: Why not give it to Leonard Wood, a man with more battle experience—and make him second-in-command? In his pocket diary, he writes, “Commissioned as Lt. Col. 1st U.S. Volunteer Cavalry. Wood as col., by my choice. The colonelcy was offered to me.”

The Rough Riders eventually numbered more than 1,000, an increase from the 780 allotted in Alger’s April 28 memo to Wood. By May 17 the regiment included men from forty-two states, four territories, and several foreign countries. Though most hailed from the West, some had served with the British Army in South Africa, one with Australia’s New South Wales Mounted Rifles, and the trumpeter was born in Monaco. They ranged from yachtsmen to barkeeps, cowboys to lawyers. About fifty were well-to-do Easterners, many of them friends of Roosevelt’s, a source for him of never-ending pride. The journalist Lincoln Steffens begged him on May 4 to release some of the “swellest names,” but Roosevelt wired back that singling out individuals might be bad for morale. Still, they included men from Yale, Harvard, and the Knickerbocker Club, all “going as troopers, to be exactly on a level with the cowboys.” Later, in *The Rough Riders*, he rattled them off more freely: the America’s Cup yachtsman Woodbury Kane; the Harvard quarterback Dudley Dean; Hamilton Fish, “the ex-captain of the Columbia crew.” He gathered many Easterners around him at the Washington army depot before shipping out and delivered a stern lecture: they mustn’t shirk and must perform every duty “without flinching.” He was serious about this: “No matter what comes, you mustn’t squeal. Think it over—all of you.” The message rang clear: they were not just representing their country, they were representing *him.* No one withdrew.

Not all joined through T.R. Herman Hoffman Philip was a twenty-five-year-old D.C. native and Ivy Leaguer, one of the "gentlemen hunters" belonging to the Metropolitan Club. Photos show a thin man with high forehead, usually in a tux; his eyes and thin lips hold his amusement in check, but in his writing he never takes himself too seriously. He'd been hunting big game in February along Oregon's Snake River when passing cowboys told him of the *Maine*. It took him two months to get home. He'd already been promised an infantry commission, but the Rough Riders were tempting; he'd always liked cowboys and had made friends with several. So he wired Leonard Wood. All commissions were already filled, Wood replied, but he could still sign up as a private. That was fine with him. Wood added that it was too late to come to San Antonio: he'd have to meet the regiment in Tampa and be assigned to a company then.

Most volunteers joined in their state, then entrained in a group to San Antonio and signed with Wood. The first group appeared on May 7, two days after Wood arrived with equipment and 189 mules. These were Arizona volunteers, organized into Company A and led by their captain, the soft-spoken sheriff and newspaper editor William Owen "Bucky" O'Neill. A few hours later, eighty-three Oklahomans arrived. Some Easterners recruited by Roosevelt landed on May 9, wearing expensive suits and carrying fine leather valises. There were four troops of New Mexicans, including the Santa Fe Railroad night telegrapher George Hamner, who'd quit his job and experienced a "most enjoyable trip . . . even the farmers themselves waving a cheery God speed from their plow handles as we sped through the level fields." The week passed that way, filled with men, khaki uniforms, "good-sized cow ponies," McClellan saddles, nose bags, machetes, Krag-Jørgensen carbines, canvas tents and tentpoles—everything comprising a cavalry troop bound for war. By May 11 enough troopers had massed or were on their way that Wood could announce the regiment's makeup: three squadrons of four troops each, the first two made of men already in training. The third was a patchwork of latecomers from Indian Territory, spillovers from oversize troops, and the "Fifth Avenue Boys" whom cowboys called the "society swells" or the "lah-de-dah boys." The very last group arrived on May 17: cowboys and Indians from Oklahoma Territory, led by the blond, blue-eyed boxer Captain Allyn

K. Capron, a fifth-generation West Pointer whom Roosevelt called "the archetype of the fighting man." Stragglers were placed wherever they fit: Herman Hoffman Philip, for example, was placed in Bucky O'Neill's Troop A when he joined later in Tampa.

Roosevelt arrived at 7:30 a.m. on Sunday, May 15. He stepped off a Southern Pacific coach wearing the crisp, fawn-colored uniform with canary-yellow trim that he'd designed, plus his famous grin; his khaki trousers were stuffed into gleaming cordovan boots, his khaki jacket with epaulets bearing the initials "U.S.V." beside crossed sabers. His slouch hat sported the crossed-saber badge. The Westerners didn't know what to think: he looked nothing like the fire-breathing giant depicted in newspaper cartoons, but was squat, bandy-legged, nearsighted, with a high-pitched voice and an explosive one-syllable laugh that came out as "Hah!"

Nevertheless, it was clear within a week whom they considered their leader. Wood seemed standoffish: it took longer to warm up to "Old Poker Face," though most eventually did. On Saturday, May 21, Wood was in his tent when a "big husky chap" entered and blurted, "Say, Col., I want to shake hands with you and tell you that I like you a dam sight better than I expected to; in fact, we are all with you, etc., etc." But Roosevelt was the friend of all. "I realized that if this campaign lasted for any considerable length of time I would be kicked upstairs to make room for Roosevelt," Wood wrote, which is exactly what happened. The Cult of Roosevelt grew. Wood let Teddy train the men, yet did not hesitate to take him down a notch if necessary. One night, in an ebullient mood, Roosevelt bragged that he'd treated the boys to some beer. That night in the officers' mess, Wood described what could happen if officers drank with their men: no officer who did so was worthy of a commission. Silence fell over the table. Later that night, Roosevelt visited Wood's tent: "I wish to say, sir, that I agree with what you said. I consider myself the damndest ass within ten miles of the camp. Good night." The matter never rose again.

Even so, Roosevelt had the time of his life. Cavalry drill was fairly standard, and Camp Wood settled into a routine. Reveille blew at 5:30, followed by roll call and a 6:10 stable call for feeding and rubbing down horses. After breakfast, the men led their mounts to the river to drink and prepare for the day. Lunch was at 1:30, followed by close-order march, target practice, and inspections, until final stable call at four p.m. A dress parade ended the day; dinner at seven; Taps at nine. After that, men snuck out, singly or in pairs, for the fleshpots of San Antonio.

By month's end, Wood wrote that his recruits worked together "most harmoniously." Roosevelt told a reporter that they "could whip Caesar's Tenth Legion" and bragged to Lodge that "there could be no better material for soldiers than that afforded by these grim hunters of the mountains, these wild rough riders of the plains." Yet both bent reality to buff the image of their "democratic utopia." Wood assured McKinley, "we have no drunken men or disorderly men about the camp," but said nothing about the disabled or dissatisfied. There were no serious revolts, but "one poor fellow [who] was thrown from his horse and sustained a fracture of his skull" was getting better. In fact, the "poor fellow," Marshall M. Bird, received a medical discharge. Two others were also mustered out for serious injuries: Cornelius Cronin, of Arizona, for undisclosed reasons, and John B. Alamia, of Texas, for "epileptic fits." Wood did admit that "these men are wild," and if they didn't soon fight the Spaniards, they would fight one another. There was enough dissatisfaction that ten men deserted between May 5 and June 8, the day all shipped to Cuba. The "most thoroughly hated man in the regiment" was the adjutant, First Lieutenant Thomas W. Hall, whose job was to enforce regulations. Allen Coville described him as a "pompous overbearing martinet" who "never lost the opportunity to insult and tyrannize" the enlisted men. "One half of the men had sworn to shoot him at the first opportunity, while the remainder sincerely hoped that some one would."

Finally, on May 25, the War Department asked when the men would be ready. "AT ONCE," Wood said. Troopers emerged from their tents to find Roosevelt and Wood "embracing like schoolboys" and dancing a jig. The wait was over. On May 29, 1,060 men and 1,258 horses loaded into long Southern Pacific trains and rolled across the South to the chaos called Tampa.

12

The Pleasure Dome

All eyes turned to South Florida. At no time in her history had this region received so much national attention; to most, Florida was a blank on the map, filled with alligators, mosquitoes, and unconquered Seminoles. On April 14, 1898, this changed, thanks to the shipping magnate Henry Bradley Plant's grasp of geography.

War creates opportunities. For two decades, Plant had bought Southern railways that had been ruined by the Civil War: by 1898 his Plant Investment Company controlled fourteen lines traversing 2,100 miles of the Deep South, several steamship companies, and at least eight garish tourist hotels. The money funneled south to Tampa, a small town with an 1890 population of 5,500; at its tip lay Plant's port, newly built and dredged to service steamships connecting the U.S. and Havana.

Plant was seventy-eight when war looked certain. Three days after the *Maine* disaster, Tampa's U.S. representative Stephen Sparkman introduced a bill for the War Department to improve the harbor. McKinley, during his April 14 war-planning meeting, considered three bases from which to launch an invasion: Tampa, Mobile, and New Orleans. Tampa was closest geographically, and Sparkman argued that this made it the best choice. Plant's lieutenant, Franklin Q. Brown, personally lobbied McKinley. On April 14 plans were drawn to send seven regiments, and two days later, news reached Tampa that it had been selected.

Tampans had never seen anything like it: people flowed in and out of the city as if a spigot were turned on. On April 7, five hundred Cuban refugees arrived on the Plant steamer *Mascotte*; on April 18, 153 Spaniards left for Havana on the *Olivette*. The first five companies of the Fifth Infantry arrived two days later. On April 22 the twenty-seventh troop train brought the soldier count to 3,000; by May 9 that had increased to 15,000; by May 25 Tampa and Port Tampa were engulfed in a sea of canvas, sheltering more than 23,000 men. Soldiers outnumbered residents two to one; newsmen mixed with prostitutes, moonshiners, and gamblers. Thousands of sightseers arrived in excursion trains.

More money flooded the city than Tampans dreamed existed. The first army payday occurred on May 4 and 5, with soldiers receiving $325,000. The bonanza fell upon merchants and saloonkeepers like manna; the sandy streets clogged with soldiers spending their pay, usually on food to supplement their greasy pork and beans. "Any man or boy can now make money as long as the troops are here," claimed the May 16 *Tampa Times*. Newsboys made $30 per week; a soda fountain cleared $1,100 in a week, lemonade stands $25 in one day. Drinking water was in such short supply that locals charged 2 cents a glass for water reeking of sulfur.

This was pennies compared with Plant's war profiteering. When an officer arrived on April 28 to lease buildings for warehouses, most of them belonged to Plant. He blocked delivery of military goods carried by the rival railway Florida Central and Peninsular, and on May 5 the government warned that unless this stopped, it would seize his railroad. The practice continued another month, until June 3, when the quartermaster general told Plant that his property lay an inch from being seized. Plant stopped the next day.

Within a month, Tampa stood revealed as a poor base for preparing an invasion. It lacked the warehouses, rail sidings, and facilities needed to handle a huge crush of men and matériel. The port could dock and load only two ships at a time. A blizzard of invoices overwhelmed the small post office, making it impossible to quickly determine any one boxcar's lading; a quartermaster's investigation revealed 1,162 unmarked cars clogging sidings, their invoices and contents in limbo. By May, cars were backed up thirty-five miles inland to Lakeland.

Troops arrived to face weeks of boredom, heat, sickness, and bad food.

Volunteers had no experience in military life, so their days were filled with simple soldiering: organizing a campsite, recognition of bugle calls and rank, proper dressage, simple tactics. Many had never picked up a rifle, much less fired one, so they learned how to maintain, load, and aim a firearm. On May 22 Shafter reported that three hundred soldiers of the Seventy-First New York had never fired a rifle, a statistic that included Charles Post, whose company drilled in the palmetto scrub where rattlers and coral snakes lived. When bugles blew skirmish drill, he rushed forward "noisily, giving all snakes notification to get out." No one got bitten: in fact, "not a snake was ever seen."

A typical day chipped at one's reserves: up at five a.m., roll calls, drill, mess, more drills. "Tampa is a bum place," wrote First Sergeant Henry A. Dobson of Company D, First D.C. Volunteers. The lack of clean water and edible food was killing him. The typical meal consisted of hardtack, coffee, and rancid bacon, so his gut constantly roiled. The best one could hope for was a stew called "clean-up," made from three days of kitchen scraps boiled together. Once he vomited up "scrapes of Bacon that I knew I ate at Camp Alger and lots of grease, etc." Afterward, he felt better "than at any time since being home," but then the cycle started again. The poor food was "making the men cross," and he always seemed tired. "We think of home, take a long, long breath, and try to stop thinking."

Dobson had typhoid, though the slow-growing fever was not diagnosed until after the war. He already showed many signs: weakness, abdominal pains, vomiting, and headaches. Its insidious spread would be *the* major cause of death in the Cuban theater, with one in five soldiers falling ill and 30 percent dying. A study later revealed that it decimated the ranks before fighting even began: out of 230,000 new recruits, only 35,000 to 55,000 were healthy enough to fight. The army believed that these weeks in camp prepared its green troops for survival. Instead, it weakened them for the tropical diseases patiently waiting on the Ever-Faithful Isle.

Of all its many problems, the army's great vulnerability was the prehistoric state of its medical care. Four years earlier, Congress had stripped the Army Medical Department of fifteen commissioned surgeons and all "contract surgeons, as well as extra medical transports and stores of ice, medicine, and other necessities." The Fifty Million Dollar War Bill allocated a mere $20,000 to the Medical Corps; when the Americans landed, reporters outnumbered doctors 89 to 71.

One hindrance was a dearth of trained nurses; the Medical Department had no female nurses, while men sent in were often unwilling transfers, a notorious dumping ground for "dregs." These proved dangerous owing to their neglect of basic sanitary procedures. When Congress suggested recruiting women, Surgeon General George Miller Sternberg fought back. "In my opinion, this would be very unwise legislation," he said. Women would be out of place in hospitals, though they might prepare meals. His testimony reflected the army's contempt for women, reflected by an apocryphal tale: When told he would receive ten female nurses, a doctor replied, "Change it to ten Bengal tigers, for the sake of quiet and peace."

The war, as well as typhoid, changed this. It also inserted an influential voice into twentieth-century medicine. Dr. Anita Newcomb McGee was thirty-four when the war broke out: she'd earned her medical degree from George Washington University and studied gynecology at Johns Hopkins. When she heard that Sternberg finally felt forced to recruit women, she convinced him to hire only trained nurses. When she sent out a call for "contract nurses," about five thousand women applied.

Clara Maass was one. The exact date of her letter is unknown, but it was apparently early. McGee and her screening teams focused on qualifications, health, and character. The application stated that only trained nurses, ages thirty to fifty, would be considered, and Clara's age initially worked against her, but as war continued, the fact that she was the German Hospital's head nurse seemed to override her age. She sent back her application and began the long wait. In time, she would be one of 1,563 women hired. Typhoid would strike 140 of them, 12 fatally.

If one person glimpsed the future, it was Clara Barton. She'd witnessed government inefficiency firsthand during the Civil War: too often she'd bound wounds with corn husks, made gruel from scavenged grain, watched surgeons work by candlelight. That conflict had spurred her to found the American Red Cross; thirty years later, she wondered whether the United States was even *less* prepared for this war than for the first one she had known.

Although McKinley granted the Red Cross permission to help *reconcentrados*, the army had refused its aid. Still, Barton didn't need anyone's leave to prepare. The New York–based Central Cuban Relief Committee chartered the 1,800-ton *State of Texas*, a twenty-five-year-old Mallory Line steamer captained by the thirty-four-year-old Frank A. Young. The board had originally planned to use her to aid *reconcentrados*, but with war, the Red Cross loaded an extra fourteen hundred tons of medical and other supplies and called her a hospital ship instead. All was stowed in wooden crates that could be used for firewood: bags of grain and flour cushioned the load. In addition to the captain and his thirty-man crew, her seventeen-member medical staff included Dr. J. B. Hubbell as medical director, four Red Cross nurses, and ten or twelve female volunteers. The ship dropped anchor in Key West on April 28, and Barton arrived the next day. She thought the *State of Texas* a "snug little ship," both "firm [and] sound."

The U.S. fleet waited in Key West, too. On May 2 Barton begged Admiral Sampson to let her cross the blockade to feed "the suffering people of Cuba," but Sampson would not budge. Those supplies would comfort Spanish soldiers, not *reconcentrados*, he claimed.

Attempts to sway Shafter were no more successful. On May 6 the sharp-tongued George F. Kennan headed for Tampa Bay. Kennan was famous for his book about imperial Russian exiles imprisoned in Siberia; earlier in 1898, he'd been elected vice president of the American Red Cross and because of this had been assigned by *Outlook* magazine to cover Barton's efforts in Cuba. Today this would be considered a conflict of interest; back then, it seldom counted as a disqualifier. Kennan liked "Miss B.," but could be hotheaded; they sometimes clashed, since Barton could be just as unyielding.

Kennan arrived in Tampa on a "warm, clear Southern night"; the town struck him as "a huddled collection of generally insignificant buildings standing in an arid desert of sand." The roads were clogged with four-mule wagon trains; the sidewalks overflowed with Cuban volunteers, sailors, and "war correspondents everywhere." His carriage passed through the "dirty, weather-beaten tents" of the army camps, pitched without order; smoke rose in a fog from cookfires.

Above it rose the "Pleasure Dome," Kennan's name for the Tampa Bay

Hotel. It reminded him of the palace in Samuel Taylor Coleridge's "Kubla Khan, Or, a Vision in a Dream." The five-story "red-brick castle" covered six acres, its roof surmounted by silvery domes and thirteen tapered minarets, each tipped with a crescent moon. Mosquelike curves shaped the windows of its massive lobby and five hundred rooms. Modeled after Spain's Alhambra, it was the first Florida tourist hotel to boast electric lights and room telephones. Two regimental bands played waltzes; a walk around its circumference measured exactly one mile. The interior was a "shining bewilderment" of chandeliers, beaded glass, marble statues, and life-size bronze Indian maidens cradling light fixtures. In the restaurant, one could order "consommé Dewey" and "roast turkey with Shafter sauce." As Kennan entered the Grand Parlor, he spotted military grandees "smoking, talking, or listening to music" as "gaily attired ladies" fluttered among them.

Anyone who was anyone in the war effort came to the Pleasure Dome: Brigadier General James Wade and Major J. W. Pope when they set up headquarters; Shafter when he took command; General Miles when he came to advise Shafter. Commander or subordinate, they came to receive their appointment in the "great order"; observers from Great Britain, Italy, Russia, and Germany crowded the bar. Stephen Crane and young Frank Norris arrived early; Richard Harding Davis arrived by train the next day. Hordes of reporters mobbed the refreshment center: Kennan guessed he counted 75 to 100 men, dressed in flannel shirts, knickers, and gray sombreros.

Kennan checked in and sought out Shafter the next day. His purpose was twofold: to interview the commander and to argue for the Red Cross's place on the battlefield. Despite McKinley's letter of introduction, the general would not be moved. The Red Cross was welcome to relieve "the distress of the starving Cuban peasants," Shafter told him, but the Army Medical Corps was "fully competent to take care of all the sick and wounded soldiers in the field." In his opinion, the Red Cross simply wasn't needed. "The best for you to do is to go in with us and under our protection," then help the *reconcentrados*. Miss B won't be happy, Kennan predicted: he stayed two more days, then hustled to Key West to relay the bad news.

He boarded the *State of Texas* on May 9. If Tampa was a study in chaos, the little hospital ship exuded careful planning: he discovered 10 tons of medical supplies, including beds and cots; 50 days' supply of food; 500 gallons of oil; 300 bushel barrels of charcoal; 25 tons of lard; 30,000 tons of bacon; 25,000 tons of pork; 25 tons of rice; 300 bushel barrels of hard bread; 300 tons of cornmeal; 600 cases of clothing; 500 bags of flour; and miles of waterproof canvas for building huts. The difference between the army and the Red Cross was astounding: Barton knew the War Department's disorganization through experience, and she felt that the closer she could be to frontline hospitals, the more lives could be saved.

In fact, the only person unhappy with Miss B was Miss B. The wait from May 7 to May 21 annoyed her: she blamed herself for multiple failings and grew cross with others. She felt that the captain got too familiar with her nurses, though it seems little more than gentle kidding. When a *London Standard* reporter asked why the Red Cross wouldn't be in the battle, she replied calmly—but that night her anger boiled over. She condemned in her diary the U.S. government and the navy for their "lack of compassion" and fumed that if the Red Cross had no status in the coming fight, "let it be known and we will retire." Maybe someday another president, "better informed and with broader views," would see things differently. But by then, she'd be dead and gone.

On May 22 she told Kennan that she'd confront Shafter herself. Kennan had doubts, but he knew there was no stopping her in this mood. Within two days, the *State of Texas* steamed for Tampa: during the trip she hid in her cabin and succumbed to dark introspection. Twenty-four years earlier, her sister Sally had died of liver failure: "Then followed many years of weakness and woe—how I lived then I cannot conceive, and sometimes I find it an equal mystery—why?" Why had she survived when so many friends and family did not, with "not one soul near me that I knew or even heard of then?" The struggle often seemed futile, and in a few years she'd be "what the others are to me . . . A memory—nothing more."

They reached Port Tampa at four p.m. and rolled up to the Pleasure Dome. Someone slipped her a *Herald* story announcing that Surgeon General Sternberg was placed in charge of all Red Cross matters in Cuba. "I have nothing to say," she fumed, "and indeed what should I care? I have done all I could with what I had to do with." Nonetheless, Shafter came downstairs. It was a pleasant call, inconclusive, and if anything, she felt sorry for the man. Shafter "is a large, stout, desperately swelled-out man."

There was no reason to stick around. She'd go to the top, as she had earlier, and from June 1 through 6, she lobbied Washington for permission to cross the blockade. On June 6 Alger granted her wish. She headed back, triumphant, ready to steam off on her God-given mission, only to learn that Spain had refused her permission to enter Cuba, and she must wait, wait, wait again.

All month, the world waited during what Richard Harding Davis dubbed the "rocking chair" phase of the war, named after the white rocking chairs lining the veranda where reporters and officers rocked and awaited The Word. "It was an army of occupation," he wrote, "but it occupied the piazza of a big hotel." The invasion would begin in two days, then Monday, Tuesday, on and on. By early May, the Regular Army had camped and the volunteers drifted in; they all lived on a war footing, ready to go at any minute, but as the days wore on, it felt like a summer holiday. "Officers who had not met in years" spun old war stories. Soon they unpacked their evening clothes and summoned daughters and wives.

There were good reasons to wait, but that made it no easier. The location of the Spanish fleet remained a mystery. On April 19 Admiral Cervera assembled his squadron at Saint Vincent and stayed for the next two weeks for repairs. "I am in despair," he wired Madrid. His force consisted of four armored cruisers—the *Infanta Maria Teresa*, *Almirante Oquendo*, *Vizcaya*, and *Cristóbal Colón*—and six torpedo-boat destroyers. Of the latter, three were useless, the other three nearly so. The *Colón*—the newest, fastest, and best-armored of his cruisers—lacked a main battery; the *Vizcaya*'s hull was so fouled that it hampered her speed. Since ammunition was short, his crews forfeited gunnery training. Cervera had not even received war plans from Spain.

On April 24 he received orders to sail. He would set off once his ships finished coaling, he said. On the 25th, the United States declared war. Four days later, he wired, "Am going north," and sailed. U.S. correspondents watched the fleet disappear over the western horizon, then cabled that Cervera was on his way.

The hunt for the admiral's "phantom fleet" became Sampson's obsession. Without knowledge of its location, the invasion could not proceed. For Cervera to suddenly materialize and sink a troopship was the ultimate nightmare. With each day, Sampson grew testier. He guessed that the Spanish admiral would use Puerto Rico as a coaling station, so led seven warships from Key West on May 4 and reached San Juan at dawn on May 12. No Cervera. He shelled the capital anyway, killing two, then circled back to Key West. A later analysis determined that the attack probably drove Cervera deeper into hiding. On May 13 the mystery fleet was observed near Martinique; on May 15 near Curaçao; on May 20 sailing to the Philippines. The fleet was a threatening wisp, hovering everywhere.

Davis arrived at the Pleasure Dome during the endless wait and paid six dollars a night for a room and adjoining bathroom. Some twenty-five thousand soldiers came to Tampa in May. "RHD" entered the tent city looking for stories, interviewed "Joe" Wheeler, Fitzhugh Lee, and the men of Troop G, Third Cavalry, whom he'd met out West. At night, he drank sweet tea with ice and danced with beautiful women as the band played Latin airs. One officer grinned at the colored lights and said what they all felt: "Gentlemen, as General Sherman truly said, 'War is hell.'"

In the absence of anything else, reporters watched one another. The most unusual development was the presence of two "lady correspondents": Kathleen Blake Watkins of *The Toronto Mail & Empire* and Anna Northend Benjamin of *Leslie's* magazine. Both received a cold shoulder from male counterparts, so they dove into the sprawl instead. Benjamin broke the first details of the *Gussie* expedition, a failed attempt to land arms and supplies for the *mambisi* that led to the war's first blanket attempt at censorship. Since bored officers talked to bored reporters, the *Gussie* expedition was so well-known that both *The New York Herald* and the London *Times* ran detailed stories of her destination even as she sailed—so detailed that Spanish troops awaited her arrival. Afterward, Shafter ordered his aide John Miley to take over the Tampa telegraph station and censor everything the reporters sent or received.

Correspondents covered the naval blockade. On Friday, May 6, Crane, Scovel, Frank Norris, and one or two others boarded the *Three Friends* to cruise off Havana's coast with the battleships *New York*, *Indiana*, and

Iowa. The *World* paired Crane with his buddy Scovel and chartered the tug for the duration; Norris was a guest, attached to the First U.S. Infantry Regiment from San Francisco's Presidio, writing for *McClure's*. Though he was still at the beginning of his literary career, Norris's *McTeague*, which made him famous, was almost ready. Morro Castle grew from the mist, batteries lining the hills like "two long, straight yellow scars." Norris stood in awe of Crane; he called him "the Young Personage" and described him memorably:

> The Young Personage was wearing a pair of duck trousers grimed and fouled with all manner of pitch and grease and oil. His shirt was guiltless of collar or scarf and was unbuttoned at the throat. His hair hung in ragged fringes over his eyes . . . Between his heels he held a bottle of beer against the railing of the boat, and when he drank was royally independent of a glass.

Crane was unkempt, profane, famous, and devoid of fear—everything Norris wished to be.

During the wait, one could glimpse the racism that stained the campaign. Hundreds of Tampa's Cubans flocked to join the *mambisi*; they donned guerrilla uniforms, drilled in public, departed in secret. Yet they were ignored by the military and portrayed by correspondents with amusement or contempt. As the *Chicago Tribune* reporter H. J. Whigham searched for stories in Ybor City, he wrote that the Cubans were "amusing children," but if they were "good specimens of the race," a free Cuba would be "a very dangerous experiment."

Luckily, army brass still treated Cubans as allies. Two weeks before war was declared, Miles sent Lieutenant Andrew S. Rowan to contact Calixto García. Rowan belonged to the army's fledgling Military Information Division and would be the war's most celebrated American spy. He started from Jamaica on April 23, came ashore at night in a remote stretch of the southern coast, crossed the Sierra Maestra with a rebel escort, and approached Bayamo. The Americans simply did not know the status of the Cuban army. Were they stronger in the east under García, or around Havana under Gómez? Except for news that occasionally leaked out through stragglers like Funston, Oriente was a Great Unknown. Americans still thought the rebel strength lay in the west, and most early war plans emphasized landing on that side.

Rowan found the opposite. Conventional wisdom in Cuba today holds that rebels alone would have wrested the country from Spain had the United States provided ample food and arms, but the stalemate was ossified. But things *were* better in Oriente, and by April 17 Governor Blanco had ordered his troops to abandon the eastern interior in anticipation of an invasion. The Spaniards moved out of Bayamo, and on April 29 García moved in.

Oriente seemed a wasteland to Rowan. He saw one house in a hundred miles, and it was burned out—"no evidence of human life" as he rode through untended fields with grass so high "that our horses were hidden." This part of Cuba reminded him of "a tropical garden gone to waste": the Royal Road from Bayamo to Santiago lay in disrepair; telegraph poles leaned at crazy angles; wires snaked across the road. The roadside forts, which resembled "railroad water-tanks," lay in ruins. When Rowan rode into Bayamo on May 1, García met him at his headquarters door, a big, grizzled man but still "a gentleman in appearance and manner." Rowan handed over his papers from Miles, and the old general gave him breakfast and a glass of rum. Miles had given Rowan a list of questions, the most important being the location and strength of his forces. García's answer was heartening. By June, he would have 5,000 men around Santiago, another 2,000 around Holguin, 1,000 at Manzanillo; and 6,000 blocking Guantánamo from the rest of the country. In all, he could block 20,000 Spaniards from aiding Santiago.

Rowan left that night loaded with maps and intelligence. García promised thousands of guerrillas to act as scouts, help with a landing, and keep Spanish forces bottled in their forts. He sent some officers with Rowan to coordinate strategy. The group landed in Key West on May 11 and met soon afterward with Shafter and Miles.

Similar missions reached Gómez in the west, but what they found was dire. Cuban forces there were beyond saving: García's men might be ragged, but Gómez's were starving. The *reconcentrado* strategy had hit them hard: in Matanzas Province alone, 96 percent of farms and 92 percent of sugar mills were destroyed, 94 percent of horses and 97 percent of cattle slaughtered, and not a single chicken remained. Gómez said he could aid invading troops given adequate food and arms, but when his men failed to protect the *Gussie*, the calculus altered. Cuban strength in the east and weakness in the west determined America's invasion.

Trains bearing troops to Tampa crept across the United States, but none would generate the same levels of emotion as the four regiments of black Regulars. Organized shortly after the Civil War, the Twenty-Fourth and Twenty-Fifth infantries, and the Ninth and Tenth cavalries, had been stationed on the Western frontier. For thirty years, the Buffalo Soldiers lived in Montana and the Dakotas, New Mexico and Utah; they fought Native Americans on the Plains and in the Rockies, kept whites out of Indian Territory, put down railroad and mining strikes, and watched one another's backs. They'd saved the storied Seventh Cavalry from Sioux vengeance after the Massacre at Wounded Knee. Every commissioned officer was white, except for a few chaplains; although some white officers resented these assignments, many grew protective of their men. By 1890 the Buffalo Soldiers were a legend: their exploits and steady service during the Indian Wars made them a source of pride for black America. They hoped such exemplary conduct might dilute the "race-hatred" too common in turn-of-the-century America.

But not all were sure of the mission ahead. "The Negro has no reason to fight for Cuba's independence," wrote *The Washington Bee* on March 5, 1898. "He is as much in need of independence as Cuba is." On April 2 the *Omaha Afro American Sentinel* proclaimed that those blacks who wanted to drive out "the cowardly and treacherous Spaniards ought to show equal readiness . . . to kill off some of their drunken, cut-throat neighbors who make a pastime of hanging, shooting, and burning men, women, and children."

African American churches supported the war, at least at this stage. On Sunday, May 1, the Reverend H. H. Proctor of Atlanta's First Congregational Church preached that loyalty to one's country overshadowed all else. Jesus Himself had said "Render unto Caesar those things that are Caesar's," and the same held for black Americans. This was a "national and not a racial war," Proctor said. "If you say this is a white man's war, then you are bound to accept the doctrine that this is a white man's country. If it's a white man's country, then the black man has no place in it, and consequently no rights that a white man is bound to respect."

Some voices were more nuanced, like that of firebrand John Mitchell, editor of *The Richmond Planet*. In 1886, after reporting a lynching in Charlotte County, Virginia, he received through the mail a rope with a note saying that he'd be lynched if he set foot in the county. Such threats "pass by me like the idle wind," he said, echoing Shakespeare, then strapped on two pistols, boarded a train, and walked five miles to the site of the hanging. Knowing that whites read the *Planet*, he liked to provoke them: "Well, the white folks have been killing us in peace, and now they are killing each other in war," he wrote on May 14, 1898. "God bless the white folks!" Regarding enlistment, he wrote, "If we are not presumed to be good enough to exercise the right of franchise, why should we be good enough to enlist in the service of the United States?" But once war was declared, he changed his mind—with a caveat. The "colored brother" should go, but only if commanded by black officers he chose.

The War Department—and many blacks—assumed that African Americans possessed a natural immunity to tropical diseases, so the Buffalo Soldiers were among the first mobilized. They started moving in early March: the Twenty-Fourth Infantry and Ninth Cavalry arrived in Tampa on Saturday, April 30; the Twenty-Fifth Infantry and Tenth Cavalry, the second week of May. The infantry regiments camped at Tampa Heights, near the Scrub, David Fagen's home.

More than four thousand black troops moved into camp, and Buffalo Soldiers and Floridians did not mix well. The newcomers were appalled by the treatment doled out to local blacks; local whites were appalled that these soldiers considered equality possible. Yet this very attitude served as a wondrous vision for those from the Scrub and Ybor City; they mobbed the concerts held by Buffalo Soldier bands, watched in astonishment as they marched, shoulder arms. It was good marketing. The War Department had ordered that all regiments must have three battalions of four companies each, or 750 men per regiment. The enlistment lines must have been long: one observer remembered that white volunteers streaming to Tampa would "rush to the recruiting tents, catch one glimpse of the 'nigger' soldiers, and flee."

The local press turned on black soldiers. The May 5 *Tampa Morning Tribune* reported, "The colored infantry . . . have made themselves very offensive to the people of the city. The men insist upon being treated as white men are treated and the citizens will not make any distinction between the colored troops and the colored civilians." Daily stories of "rackets" by "black ruffians in uniform" spread through the South. When a white barkeeper in Lakeland refused to serve a black soldier, he returned with forty friends; when the owner smashed the men's' glasses after they finished drinking, the soldiers closed down his and neighboring saloons. The "Lakeland riot" ended in gunfire, the accidental death of a white resident, and the arrest of two black cavalrymen. The sight of black military police arresting white soldiers caused an uproar. "It shore doesn't seem right for a nigger on a horse to be herdin' up white folks," a local sheriff told Charles Post. "Any you fellas ever punch them black bastards?"

The historian Willard Gatewood Jr. concluded that the presence of so many armed blacks in Florida "contributed to the final capitulation of the white South to extreme racism." Whatever internal restraints had existed now vanished: Buffalo Soldiers' defiance of local racial control was used "to justify lynchings and other crimes against Negroes." He quoted as evidence the black editors of *The Washington Bee*, *The Savannah Tribune*, and *Iowa State Bystander*. On June 18, nearly two weeks after the Lakeland riot, John Mitchell wrote in *The Richmond Planet*: "Negrophobia is getting as prevalent here as is the yellow fever in Cuba." In such a hothouse, Gatewood lamented, "racist demagogues throughout the South came into their own."

In mid-May, Frederick Funston entered the Pleasure Dome. By then, 23,220 troops saturated Tampa, and Funston wrote Charles Scott that the place was in chaos, but then, his life had been chaotic since leaving New York City. He'd signed with the Kansas City booking agent to give lectures about Cuba, and though reviews were generous, crowds were small. He still suffered from his wounds. He'd been there before, eking out a small existence from his Alaskan exploits. The formula had to change, but how?

As often happened, Fate intervened. In March, Funston lectured at

Topeka's Elks Lodge; afterward, Kansas's Populist governor John W. Leedy sat next to him at dinner and discovered that he was "much more entertaining in conversation than . . . on the platform." In fact, he seemed a natural-born soldier. When war began and Leedy was tasked with forming the state's volunteer corps, he remembered the little guerrilla fighter from the Elks Lodge and sent for him.

Funston was lecturing at Fort Leavenworth when Leedy's summons arrived. He appeared in the state capital's Executive Chambers the next day in "muddy boots" and a "seedy-looking" raincoat. Though Funston agreed to sign on as commander of the Twentieth Kansas Volunteer Infantry, he thought others better qualified. Leedy didn't care: the political wrangling over naming commanders made him so "d—n mad" he wouldn't have appointed "my own brother." Funston took the job and canceled his last nineteen lectures. On May 8 he received his colonel's commission; five days later, the Twentieth Kansas was sworn in. Three days after that, they marched to the ornate Union Pacific Station downtown and boarded a troop train for San Francisco.

Funston did not accompany them, at least not immediately. On May 12 Washington ordered him to assist General Shafter with invasion plans: he was to help produce "a pamphlet containing valuable information concerning Cuba" gained during his days as a *mambi*. It all happened so quickly that he'd not even been issued an officer's uniform or sword. Still, it was his chance to return to Cuba, and he arrived at the Pleasure Dome on May 18.

He was not treated well. Shafter passed him down to his intelligence chief, Lieutenant Colonel Arthur L. Wagner, who fired off questions about Cuban leaders, geography, armies, and tactics, then passed him to Lieutenant Rowan of "Message to García" fame. Rowan distrusted Funston: nothing in him cried "military." He was bereft of uniform, didn't have a sword, and his tales of dragging a Hotchkiss gun to the walls of Spanish forts were unbelievable. When the story came out that Funston had deserted the rebels, he tried to explain, but no one cared.

Around this time, the correspondent Thomas Dawley heard tales of a "stray colonel from the West, whose regiment had been ordered to the Philippines"—a "country, unmilitary-looking chap" who'd gotten his commission through politics. One day Dawley spotted a small, bearded man sitting alone in the lobby, pointedly ignored by army officers. "If an ordinary tramp had been washed and dressed in a cheap suit of store goods, and set down in a luxuriously appointed hotel, he could not have appeared more out of place than did that little man." But when the outcast noticed Dawley's interest, he rose and stuck out his hand. "My name is Funston, and I heard of you in Cuba," he said. By God, Dawley had heard of him, too.

At least he had one friend, but Funston still grew depressed the longer he stayed. On May 2 he received cables that his Twentieth Kansas had arrived in San Francisco; on May 25 three ships carrying 115 officers and 2,386 enlisted men left the Golden Gate for the Philippines. The Kansans didn't go: they still needed training. Funston hoped against hope to catch up with them. On May 26 the calculus changed. On that day, Commodore Winfield Scott Schley's Flying Squadron spotted Cervera's fleet safely harbored at Santiago. With 300,000 residents, this was Cuba's second-largest city, nestled in a protective ring of mountains and foothills, 472 land miles from Havana. The harbor's only access lay down a narrow, mined channel protected from above by another bleak Morro Castle. Cervera had slipped in ten days earlier: though Schley had missed him on a first pass, he realized that if he couldn't get in, neither could Cervera get out.

This was a sterling opportunity: with Cervera's ships bottled up, the army could land. Though defended by ten thousand troops, Santiago was isolated from the rest of the island. If Shafter could take the heights surrounding the city, Sampson could send in minesweepers, followed by his fleet. Cervera's ships would be sitting ducks. The plan required far fewer troops than needed to conquer Havana, and García's guerrillas were in better shape to aid a landing than Gómez's.

Schley's discovery reached Washington that same day. McKinley gathered a war council and approved a plan: U.S. forces would sink the enemy fleet, take Santiago, and march west toward Havana, swallowing Cuba's ports en route while raining stockpiled food on the starving populace. Miles ordered Shafter to "load 25,000 men and all supplies" for a landing at a still-undesignated site, effective immediately.

This was too much for Funston to bear. He'd been left behind by his Kansans and frozen out by Shafter, all for want of proper attire. When Miles returned from Washington shortly after June 1, Funston asked for an assignment, any assignment, just anywhere out of this limbo. Miles scrutinized the little outcast and replied more kindly than anyone else so far. Since you're a colonel with the Twentieth Kansas, Miles counseled, you should go join your men.

Funston saw Dawley soon afterward: the Kansan was disgusted with so much wasted time, but at least a decision had been made. "Perhaps it is the best thing for me, after all," he said. "I'll join my regiment in the Philippines, and perhaps there will be something doing out there."

With these orders from Washington, the slow world of waltzes and hangovers ended. The Quartermaster's Department assembled an invasion fleet of about thirty-five transports, with other tugs, barges, small steamships, and colliers thrown in. From June 1 to 7, Tampa's streets vanished beneath a frenzy of preparation. More than a thousand boxcars had already squeezed into the railyards and sidings; now a horrendous logjam developed as three shifts of stevedores hauled supplies from the railroad cars, humped them to the pier, loaded them aboard, and started again.

Private Post learned from Tampa residents that he'd be leaving. Transports filled the bay, some already docked and taking on stores. Locals knew these were army ships from the "huge, fifteen-foot-high numerals painted on each bow." Post learned how to make a "horse-collar blanket roll" to carry on his back, and he was issued a dog tent and given finger-size .45-caliber cartridges that could "knock down two men, the one it hit and the one who fired it." The 70 grains of black powder in each slug discharged a white cloud of smoke "somewhat the size of a cow." Men overwhelmed the chaplain with baptism requests; Post's friends wrote home.

The Rough Riders arrived in the middle of this, at seven p.m. on June 1 after a four-day journey. Tampa was an "awful confusion," Wood wrote, "no head or tail." He reported in and was billeted with Wheeler's cavalry, near today's Armenia Avenue and Kennedy Boulevard. The press descended, eager to learn how the cowboys and "gentlemen dudes" had fared.

Front and center stood Richard Harding Davis. This week began Davis's fixation with Roosevelt and the Rough Riders. The two had met in

New York when both "were making youthful reputations," wrote Davis's biographer Arthur Lubow. Both were dandies with a genius for self-promotion. Roosevelt privately thought Davis "entirely unintelligent and an everlasting cad," yet he "cultivated journalists as an arborist tends fruit trees," suspecting that the famous reporter could make him a legend. From now until war's end, the two seemed inseparable. Roosevelt granted so much access to Davis for stories that wags called him T.R.'s press agent. And Davis could be useful. On June 6 he escorted Edith Roosevelt and some foreign attachés to a two-mile "demonstration drill" of two thousand cavalrymen. The Rough Riders rode up front, swords flashing, red and white guidons snapping in the breeze. He already knew some of the regiment "swells." "They use my bathroom continuously," he wrote to his brother Charles. He'd return to his room to find a heap of dirty clothes on the floor and someone in the tub. "It's all right don't mind me," a voice would call out. "I'm one of Teddy's 'Brownies.'"

Herman Hoffman Philip had arrived in Tampa early, which meant he spent some comfortable nights in the Pleasure Dome. But when the Rough Riders arrived, he traded this for a tent amid palmettos and withered pines. He was assigned to Bucky O'Neill's Troop A, composed largely of cowboys. As a "swell," he was fair game. He received a coveted Krag-Jørgensen carbine, and soon, two "serious eyed ex-cowboys" visited his tent. He'd gotten that rifle by mistake, one said: it should go to a man from New Mexico, said the other. Philip smiled: he knew cowboy tricks. Maybe so, he replied, but this rifle had been entrusted to him and he didn't plan to relinquish it unless ordered otherwise. He went to O'Neill, who sent him to Wood and T.R., who started laughing. Roosevelt placed his hand on Philip's shoulder and told him to guard that rifle with his life, "even to the extent of taking it to bed with me at night."

Like Private Post, Philip spent his time in detail and drill. By the second day in camp, Wood hosted a visit of "English, Roman, German, Japanese," and other military observers "who said they had heard of the peculiar idea of this regiment and wanted to see us." Few besides Wood were allowed to leave camp; Roosevelt seemed the lone exception. Every day, he picked up the unit's mail at the Port Tampa post office; every evening Wood gave him dispensation to spend the night with Edith at the

Pleasure Dome, despite his loud condemnation of others who slept in such luxury. Some accounts claim that this lasted one night; others, several. In all cases, he vacated the room by four a.m. to be back in time for reveille.

Loading transports ended at eleven a.m. on June 6, even as Davis and Edith Roosevelt watched the cavalry parade. From this exhilarating high, the Rough Riders and others descended to deep lows. With the ships loaded, Shafter knew exactly how much room was left for soldiers—far less, in fact, than he'd estimated. He cut the invasion force from 25,000 to 17,000: they must share space on the ships with 959 horses, 1,336 mules, 112 six-mule wagons, and masses of ammo and guns. All cavalry troops but one must leave their horses behind. Only army Regulars, the Rough Riders, and the Seventy-First New York and Second Massachusetts volunteer regiments would make up this first wave. Siege guns stayed behind, tons of regimental baggage, essential hospital stores. Troops must carry five hundred rounds per man. Shafter alerted the units of their share in the winnowing. For the Rough Riders, this meant room for only eight of their twelve troops; no horses would go save those of the seven officers. All charges would be on foot, like the lowly infantry. On June 6–7 Wood and Roosevelt broke the news: of the 1,060 volunteers who'd boarded the train in Texas, only 560 would go to Cuba. Those left behind burst into tears.

But all was not heartbreak. On June 4, at the last possible minute, David Fagen became a private in Company H of the Twenty-Fourth U.S. Infantry. He lied to do so: he told the recruiting officer Charles Tayman that he was single, when in fact he was still married to Maggie Washington. Marriage made him ineligible, and Maggie never surfaces again. Whether they still lived together is unknown, though she did hold on to the house in the Scrub. He listed his age as twenty-two years, seven months, when in fact he was nineteen. At 5 feet, 10¼ inches, and 140 pounds, he was slightly larger than average, though not "gigantic" as later described. The recruiting officer attested that Fagen could read and write "satisfactorily," when in fact he just made "his mark," an X, since he could not yet sign his name. He was number 52 of the fifty-four men who enlisted in Tampa, plus another eight who reenlisted. His enlistment wed him to the army for three years, a union that effectively ended whatever remained of the one with Maggie.

His two enlistment witnesses were proof of what he could expect. The first, Corporal Anthony A. Morrow, would rise to the rank of regimental sergeant major. But it is the second witness, Corporal John W. Calloway, whose history would be tragically entwined with Fagen's. Calloway was a slight man, standing 5 feet, 7½ inches, weighing 125 pounds. According to army records, he was born on October 26, 1876, in the town of Bristol on the Virginia-Tennessee border. This made him Fagen's elder by three years. He was light-skinned, the grandson of a white Virginia planter and a "mulatto slave." His father had been emancipated; his mother was a freeborn black woman from Maryland. After the Civil War, the couple moved to Boston, where Calloway received a good education and learned the printer's trade. He was a "race man," an advocate of Booker T. Washington's long view that self-improvement and accommodation with whites would eventually unite the races. Like Washington, Calloway believed that education was the key to the future. He'd first enlisted in the Twenty-Fifth Infantry on May 30, 1891, when he was nineteen. He spent his first tour of duty in Montana and in 1892 helped put down a miners' strike in the Coeur d'Alene. He was discharged with an "excellent" character record in November 1893, then reenlisted four months later in Chicago. This time he signed with the Twenty-Fourth at the rank of corporal, and that June and July, he put down railroad strikes in Colorado and New Mexico. By now the army had put his intelligence to good use: in 1897 he was promoted to regimental quartermaster at Fort Douglas outside Salt Lake City, balancing accounts, updating company rolls and returns.

But education did not make a person equal. On September 17, 1897, he was court-martialed for disobedience after accusing a white captain of altering cost estimates and pocketing the difference, a common scam. Blacks who got ahead in the army did *not* accuse white officers of petty corruption. Calloway was busted to private, but he stayed in the army and rose back to corporal. On April 17, 1898, shortly before the Twenty-Fourth left for Tampa, he married Annie Hinton at Fort Douglas. There is no record of divorce, a detail that comes back to haunt him.

It has been assumed that since Fagen enlisted on this late date, he'd still be in training when the Twenty-Fourth shipped out to Cuba on June 8: such reasoning supposes that he left Tampa on June 30 with a second wave of new recruits, thus missing the Battle of San Juan Hill. Yet army records do not support this. In the absence of letters or diaries, the best way to determine an individual's history during this period is through monthly regimental reports, called "morning reports," which list soldiers absent for any reason, be it death, injury, sickness, temporary postings, or training. When the Twenty-Fourth shipped out, their numbers were still low: they'd left Salt Lake City with 540 enlisted men and officers, and only 54 more signed up in Tampa, leaving them far short of the mandated 750-man regimental strength. Although this does not prove Fagen's presence, three men who enlisted with him on June 4 would be recorded as casualties in the attack on "Fort San Juan": Thomas Ledell, Jesse Wilson, and Thomas Swift. Also listed as wounded was "Alexander Morrow," most probably the Corporal Anthony Morrow who'd served as one of Fagen's witnesses.

If Fagen did leave in that first wave, he was lucky. On the night of June 6–7, all hell broke loose in Fort Brooke, Ybor City, and the Scrub. The "Tampa riot" would be one of the worst racial clashes in any army camp during the war, a culmination of all the hatred that had grown between blacks and whites since the Buffalo Soldiers arrived. On that Monday night, black soldiers began fighting whites in a Fort Brooke bar; they tore up the business, took every unbroken bottle of beer or whiskey, then started shooting until the provost marshal arrived. The mayhem rolled to Café Cantante, where Buffalo Soldiers stormed a brothel and reportedly raped the women inside. Soon the melee spread to the Scrub and Ybor City.

At dawn on June 7, the most infamous moment occurred when some drunken white Ohioans snatched up a two-year-old African American boy. One held him up by his feet and spanked him with a shingle as others cheered; he then held the boy at arm's length as others used him for target practice. One bullet pierced the boy's sleeve and grazed his arm. Only then did the soldiers hand the child back to his hysterical mother and move on.

Members of the Twenty-Fourth and Twenty-Fifth who'd witnessed this were not laughing. They raged through the streets, firing pistols, wrecking saloons, mobbing white brothels. By nine a.m. matters were so serious that a battalion of the Second Georgia was called to suppress the riot: "Killing niggers," they said, was their job. "Bring me back a scalp," onlookers cried. Order was restored that afternoon. Though the *Tampa Morning Tribune* called the "riot" nothing more than a string of isolated incidents, several Georgia volunteers and twenty-seven black soldiers were rushed to the hospital at Atlanta's Fort McPherson, all in serious condition. Two black soldiers were found dead; no one was arrested or charged. It was safer to fight in Cuba than to stay home.

On the evening of June 7, Shafter was sipping coffee after dinner when a wire from the White House ordered, "You will sail immediately." Shafter's compliance created a traffic jam: between nine p.m. that night and five p.m. the next day, 16,286 troops rushed down a single stretch of track to find and board assigned transports. The embarkation turned into a huge slow-motion stampede. Regiments snatched trains and rolled down the track without order or plan; those lucky enough to find a ship threw their gear in great tumbling heaps onto the deck or in the holds.

African American soldiers were scattered among six different ships: the *Miami*, *Alamo*, *Comal*, *Concho*, *City of Washington*, and *Leona*. On the *Concho*, Buffalo Soldiers descended to the lowest, darkest deck, where only those near the main hatch could see. Bunks rose four tiers high, built so close that a man could barely squeeze between them. It was like sleeping in a coffin: the lumber was rough, and a six-inch rim surrounded the sleeper and his gear, including his rifle and ammo. The ship had one toilet for 1,256 men.

The black Tenth Cavalry was assigned to the *Leona*, along with the headquarters staff of the Second Cavalry and most of the First Cavalry. Their quartermaster was First Lieutenant John Joseph Pershing, a Missouri boy and West Point graduate, later general of the army during World War I. The Tenth, just like all combat regiments, had been told to secure a ship and board. Otherwise, they'd be left behind. Pershing was pleasantly surprised: the *Leona* was in "relatively good shape," with a "thoroughly disinfected" hold and bunks or hammocks already set up. The problem was food—there wasn't any. They'd received no rations. When Pershing tried to make arrangements, shopkeepers told him it would be bad for business to feed black soldiers.

The most famous story about the mad rush was Roosevelt's. Since their train never arrived, the Rough Riders marched to a different siding and commandeered an empty coal train. When they arrived at port, the transports waited in line to occupy empty berths. The harbormaster told Wood that they'd been assigned to the *Yucatan*, yet she'd also been allotted to the Second Infantry and the Seventy-First New York. They spotted the *Yucatan* anchored midstream: Wood grabbed a small boat and rowed to the ship while Roosevelt "double-quicked" his men to its berth "to hold her against the Second Regulars and the Seventy-First, who had arrived a little too late, being a shade less ready than we were in the manner of individual initiative." When a captain of the Seventy-First said, "That's our ship," Roosevelt grinned and replied, "Well, we seem to have it." He ended the tale with a kicker: "I understand the Seventy-First spent the next two nights on a train."

Nice tale, but questionable. No corroboration exists, even among principals. Charles Post of the Seventy-First rode his flatcar up to "No. 23, the *Vigilancia*, our troopship and transport," to which they'd been assigned—not the *Yucatan*. No confusion or delay exists in his account, no stomping off in a huff, no "two nights [spent] on a train." He leaves the flatcar and forages for breakfast at "Last Chance Village," a line of huts and tents set at right angles to the docks and filled with local black women cooking fried chicken and a bartender serving cold beer. More damning is Wood's diary. The harbormaster tells him to "board and take possession of the 'Yucatan,' which I did." He doesn't row to the middle of the stream, as Roosevelt claimed: instead, the ship is already quayside, and Wood, Roosevelt, and Captain Allyn Capron reach her at the same moment. The Seventy-First does not figure into Wood's account, and Capron is left out of Roosevelt's account entirely.

Why would Roosevelt concoct such a tale? He first told it during testimony before the 1899 Grenville Dodge Commission, then again, with embellishments, in his *Rough Riders*. By then, he'd been elected governor of New York, and his political future looked promising: he called Shafter "criminally incompetent," though the feat of moving sixteen thousand soldiers over one track in eight hours suggests that, in fact, as the sympathetic Roosevelt biographer Edmund Morris concedes, "Shafter did not do too badly." Roosevelt's forte was accusation and insult, delivered with a bon mot and a twinkle. Shafter represented the Old Guard; Roosevelt the new generation. Every self-made myth has a moral, and this one was simple: Roosevelt got things done! Wood never publicly refuted his subordinate's exaggerations, and Capron by then was dead.

And so they boarded in chaos and sat there for the next five days. A rumor surfaced that Spanish raiders had escaped Santiago and lay in wait in Nicholas Channel, a route the U.S. armada would follow. Floating garbage festered at quayside; drinking water turned brackish. Army rations of "fresh beef" proved so repulsive that three out of every four cans were pitched overboard. On June 10 the ships moved from port to midstream, sharks prowling between them. Mules died in the holds.

So began the Splendid War.

Part III

LIBERATORS

All wars are fought twice, the first time on the battle-field, the second time in memory.

—VIET THANH NGUYEN

13

Invaders

For six days, 16,072 men and 815 officers floated midstream. On Tuesday, June 14, they finally set off; one day later, a few eminent Bostonians called a mass meeting in Faneuil Hall, where the colonials had denounced the Boston Massacre and Abolitionists condemned slavery. The dizzying rush of events was troubling: the country had grown feverish with an expansionist dream. Americans sailed to Cuba and the Philippines, shelled Puerto Rico, and would soon engulf Hawaii. The Harvard history professor Charles Norton had already urged young men to ignore McKinley's call for volunteers. The plea that Cuba's freedom could only come through war was a result "either of ignorance or of hypocrisy," he declared.

Hundreds gathered beneath Faneuil's high ceiling. Gamaliel Bradford, a descendant of the Pilgrim governor William Bradford, called the meeting to order: "We are not here to oppose the war." A graver issue loomed: "A war begun in the name of humanity shall not be turned into a war for empire." There seemed little doubt that America would be a world power, but would that power bring "beneficence or malfeasance"? In the name of doing right, would we do wrong?

Even some expansionists had doubts. Though the war was a "necessary act of surgery for the health of civilization," surgery could cause complications, warned Walter Hines Page in the June *Atlantic Monthly*. Had we considered the war's consequences? "Problems that seem likely to follow the war are graver than those that have led up to it, and if it be too late to ask whether we entered into it without sufficient deliberation, it is not too late to make sure of every step that we now take," he wrote. "Our greatest victory will not be over Spain but over ourselves—to show once more that even in its righteous wrath the republic has the virtue of self-restraint."

At nine a.m. on June 14, the rumor of skulking Spanish raiders was disproved: they were U.S. warships seen in the distance, misidentified. The flotilla weighed anchor: some soldiers, "three colored women and a pathetic group of perspiring stevedores" waved goodbye.

"Imagine three great lines of transports with a warship at the head of each line," Wood wrote to his wife, Louise. The ships steamed "800 yards from each other over a sea of indigo blue." It was a motley group: transports, towed barges, a schooner with water, three lighters, one of which sank. White navy vessels herded them on. Military attachés and correspondents—including Davis, Norris, and Remington—rode with Shafter on his "flagship," the *Segurança*; other reporters boarded the *Olivette*, which cast off ten hours later. Norris congratulated himself for boarding with his heroes Davis and Remington, but he found Davis distant, so he chatted with Remington about art and horses. The attachés recalled French maneuvers during which torpedo boats appeared and massacred everyone. The same notion worried Wood, but no one else seemed concerned. Instead, a man might start singing "On the Banks of the Wabash," and soon everyone joined in "from stem to stern," Charles Post observed. "In any moment of silence, one could hear the transport ahead of us singing the same songs we sang." It was like a holiday cruise.

On the second day out, the convoy rendezvoused off the Dry Tortugas with its naval escort, led by the *Indiana*. They formed in three columns, four hundred yards from stern to the bow of the following ship, eight hundred yards from side to side, but the plan fell prey to competing cultures. Captains of merchant ships kept as far as possible from everything else to avoid collision; this kind of close-order drill unnerved them.

By the halfway mark, the convoy stretched thirty to forty miles. North of Cuba it circled in place to let stragglers catch up, then headed southeast along the Old Bahama Channel. The Bahama islands lay to port, Cuba to starboard. Nights were most nerve-racking, but beautiful; the Southern Cross blazed overhead in a pasture of stars, while the convoy's lights reminded *The Washington Star*'s Charles M. Pepper of the lights "of a floating city." There was always the fear that a torpedo boat might run out from a northern port, so some transports extinguished their lights. But Shafter's *Segurança* stayed lit from stem to stern, often with a band playing ragtime.

Dawn showed captains how far they'd strayed. One night the *Leona*, carrying Lieutenant Pershing's Tenth Cavalry, came to a stop due to misread signals. When morning broke, no other ship lay in sight. The isolation was terrifying. Brigadier General Samuel B. M. Young, whose letter to Roosevelt had welcomed war, lost his nerve. He ordered all men to fire their small arms at any Spanish ship, "a precaution that seemed somewhat ludicrous," Pershing recalled.

On they sailed, in groups or alone, on a smooth sea. On June 19 they turned south into the Windward Passage. To starboard lay Guantánamo. "A long blue ridge came over the horizon," wrote Private Post; the mountains, dotted with thatch huts, seemed to slide into the sea. The sight stirred an awakening. To Wood, it symbolized "a new era in our relations with the world." To Roosevelt, it meant Destiny. They crept toward the "nearing future," where "death and hardship," "honor and renown" awaited. "If we failed, we would share the fate of all who fail," he wrote, "but we were sure we would win" and secure the "first great triumph in a mighty world-movement."

For those unblessed by Destiny, the voyage proved an ordeal. When they opened their canned meat, it "had an odor similar to that of a dead human body after being injected with formaldehyde, and it tasted when first cooked like decomposed boric acid," a medical officer testified. One trooper who'd worked as a meat-packer was reminded of "slunk," the tasteless, leathery, nutritionally worthless tissue left over after everything else was rendered into "beef tea." Most of this "embalmed beef" was dumped over the side.

They steered west, and at dawn on June 20 passed Daiquirí, a small village devoted to shipping iron ore, and Siboney, a squalid rail terminus five miles to its west. Charles Post gazed at the little "pinkish-ocher" blockhouses balanced on the ridges; they resembled "tiny forts made for children." Soon Morro Castle loomed above them on its white rock; Sampson's blockading warships rose from the sea. They steamed in a wide curve fifteen miles out from shore. On a beach farther west, a Cuban officer saw the convoy and nearly cried: "No scene could be grander or more thrilling than that moving spectacle after three long years of struggle in the jungle."

June 1898 was the month of invasions. The first occurred on June 7, a week before Fifth Corps sailed from Tampa. On that day, the American cruisers *Marblehead* and *Yankee* entered Guantánamo Bay. A Spanish brigade of 7,086 men and officers held the province, but General Felix Pareja had been ordered to defend cities, not repel invaders. Feeding his men was a major problem. Rebels blocked all roads to the mainland, and their lives depended on cultivation zones circling the cities. When U.S. cruisers shelled the bay, Pareja pulled back but left snipers behind.

Although the press paid what seemed like middling attention to this first landing on Cuban soil, its success or failure held enormous consequence for the entire campaign. No coaling station existed for Sampson's ships, so the navy must either establish one here or make the eight-hundred-mile voyage back to Key West to refuel. On June 10 the First Marine Battalion under Lieutenant Colonel Robert W. Huntington splashed ashore in the lower bay, close to where the U.S. detention center now sits. His force included 24 officers, 633 men, and four 3-inch field guns. They set up camp on a flat ridge overlooking the village of Fisherman's Point, which Huntington had burned for fear of yellow fever. The Spaniards fled so quickly that they left behind two brass 12-pounder field pieces, 300 to 400 boxes of Mauser ammo, provisions, musical instruments, a watch, and "a dozen car-boys of rum." The marines named their new base Camp McCalla, in honor of Captain Bowman McCalla of the *Marblehead*. They raised the American flag; the band played "Hot Time in the Old Town Tonight."

Camp McCalla had problems. White tents sprinkled the plateau with more regard for shade than for defense: the sea rose at their backs while a mountain loomed twelve hundred yards away. Footpaths—little more than green tunnels cut through the jungle—led from the mountain to the edge of the camp; an unknown number of Spaniards watched from these shadows as marines unloaded provisions. They could have attacked at any moment, but had been told to wait until the Americans landed their stores. "They were hungry and wanted food more than dead Yankees," a prisoner later admitted.

That night, Stephen Crane arrived to a scene taken straight from a novel. The fiery light from the still-burning Fisherman's Point turned nearby palms "into enormous crimson feathers." The water resembled "blue steel"; the woods were "somber." He started talking with Assistant Army Surgeon John Blair Gibbs, a thirty-nine-year-old yachtsman from New Brunswick, New Jersey. His father, a cavalry major, had died with Custer at the Little Big Horn. Gibbs was the first private doctor to volunteer, and when Crane walked up, Gibbs said that he looked sick and treated him with quinine. All seemed so peaceful. "We thought it was rather comic," Crane said.

The comedy ended at five a.m. when the enemy finally announced itself with rapid fire. The marines beat them back, but found a sergeant and a private in a forward jungle post killed and apparently mutilated. One man had been shot twenty-one times in the head; the other, fifteen. Their wounds were so extreme it was hard to tell them apart. The Americans had yet to learn that Spanish snipers scratched the tip of their bullets to make the classic dumdum round, which mushroomed on impact for the kind of mutilation produced by a shotgun filled with scrap iron. "The sight made us shiver," Private Frank Keeler said. "Was this Christian warfare?"

A second attack began about three p.m. Many marines were swimming or sunbathing on the beach when firing started; they had no time to grab their clothes or shoes. Huntington ordered them to charge. "This was no fun for naked men," the *Journal* reported, but the Spaniards again disappeared. They merely shifted, for this was the start of what Huntington's executive officer called "100 hours of fighting." That night, snipers came within fifty yards of camp and Crane experienced his first close-up of war. He'd gone to Dr. Gibbs for more quinine when the shooting started, and he "felt the hot hiss of the bullets trying to cut my hair." He'd wanted to see war firsthand, and he'd gotten his wish; someone lay dying seven feet away.

It was Dr. Gibbs. He'd been standing in his tent flap talking with Thomas Steep of *Leslie's*, and he muttered, "Well, I don't want to die in this place" when a bullet plowed through his head. He fell forward, and someone pulled him into the trench. "It took him a long time to die," Crane wrote. His gasps sounded like broken machinery; they went on so long and painfully that Crane said to himself, "I wanted him to die." Day broke and the adjutant hustled past. "Where's the doctor?" Crane yelled. "There's someone wounded over there."

"Just died this minute, sir," the adjutant said. Crane looked over and spotted what looked like a big pile of the dead: "A group of wan-faced, exhausted men had gone to sleep about Gibbs's body so closely . . . that one's eye could not pick the living from the dead until one saw that a certain head had beneath it a great dark pool." Though official histories listed Gibbs's death by enemy fire, McCalla wrote in a June 12–13 letter that he was probably killed "by one of our own men during the [fight] which took place around 1 a.m." But this was not a war where friendly fire was admitted, and McCalla's suspicions ended there.

That morning, Lieutenant Colonel Enrique Thomas and his fifty or sixty *mambisi* visited Huntington. The attacks had come from a Spanish garrison six miles off, its only source of fresh water a place called Cuzco Wells. If the marines and *mambisi* could take it, their tormentors would have to pull back to Guantánamo City. But Cuzco Wells was defended by a blockhouse, which a navy ship would have to shell.

The assault began on Tuesday, June 14, led by marine captain George F. Elliott and accompanied by Crane, who'd been appointed messenger. The Cubans approached along cliffs lining the beach, while marines advanced through an inland valley. "A fight at close range is absorbing as a spectacle," Crane wrote. "No man wants to take his eyes from it until that time comes when he makes up his mind to run away." He watched as Sergeant John H. Quick stood up straight, ignoring bullets, and relayed range and bearing coordinates to gunners aboard the USS *Dolphin* with a blue polka-dot neckerchief tied to a long, crooked stick. He climbed a ridge where navy gunners could see him, and he semaphored the ship, his face "as grave and serene as that of a man writing in his own library. He was the very embodiment of tranquility in occupation. He stood there amid the animal-like babble of the Cubans, the crack of rifles, and the whistling snarl of the bullets, and wig-wagged whatever he had to wig-wag without heeding anything but his business."

The passage is important in two ways: though credited as Crane's best war reporting, it also reveals the prejudice many Americans felt for Cubans. The *Chicago Record*'s Howbert Billman praised the *mambisi* in his account, but Crane's mention of their "animal-like babble" showed that he considered them excitable and unpredictable. They used their rifles like "squirt guns," and the main function of a Cuban lieutenant seemed to be that of waving his machete and yelling "*Fuego! Fuego!*" Buried deep is the detail that Spaniards held a "wholesome dread" of *mambisi*: they were not afraid of Americans, and they pulled back once the Cubans appeared.

The five-hour Battle of Cuzco Wells was the turning point at Guantánamo Bay. Remaining resistance collapsed the next day when U.S. ships steamed up the bay and shelled Caimanera. After that, most Spaniards retreated to Guantánamo City, where they told Pareja they'd been attacked by ten thousand Americans. Camp McCalla would see no more attacks until the marines moved out on August 5.

The battle might be over, but there was no rest for Crane. He returned to the *Three Friends*, his head filled with details that became "Marines Signaling Under Fire at Guantanamo." But his editor, Ernest McCready, wanted "*news*, sent at cable rates. You can save your flub-dub and send it to New York by mail." Newsmen might love Crane as a strange and entertaining companion, but his dismissal of column inches and deadlines frustrated them. The tug steamed to Jamaica to file copy, and Scovel convinced his pal to go on a scouting mission in the hills above Santiago. On June 17 they landed thirteen miles west of the city, planted the *World*'s banner and a Cuban flag on the beach, and began two days of hard climbing up Mount St. Augustiń. Santiago and its harbor lay beneath them in a valley surrounded by hills and mountains; it looked like a soup bowl. Scovel sketched the location of Cervera's ships while Crane lay in the grass. His legs felt like "dough"; his spine burned like a "red hot wire." It had occurred to him that this might make a good place for a TB sanitarium after the war. Maybe he'd come here to heal.

The *World* blasted Crane and Scovel's scouting mission on its front page: "First American Newspaper to Open Headquarters on Cuban Soil Is the

World." The fact that two unarmed reporters could waltz from a beach fifty-three miles west of Guantánamo Bay then up a mountain on a spy mission seemed to say that Americans could do *anything*! The armada off Santiago had grown by now to 48 ships, carrying between them 16,887 soldiers, 2,295 horses and mules, 10 million pounds of rations, plus scattered artillery and Gatling guns. Shafter's aide, Lieutenant John Miley, worried that the pending landing exceeded his boss's grasp: Shafter "did not realize it would take a week to completely disembark the command and supplies," he said.

Other vessels swelled the traffic jam, including the *Sylvia*—the *Journal*'s floating newsroom. Hearst had filled the United Fruit Company ship with a lightweight printing press and an army of newsmen, and he personally planned to cover the war. He brought the star reporter James Creelman and Gottfried Wilhelm "Billy" Bitzer, a "biograph expert" who in time gained fame as D. W. Griffith's cinematographer. At the moment, Bitzer hoped to film live battle scenes. Hearst felt in high spirits, and he spent June 20 entertaining guests—including the teenage chorus girls Millicent and Anita Wilson—while dressed in his commodore's cap and blazer.

At ten a.m. that day, Clara Barton's *State of Texas* weighed anchor and steamed for Cuba. "The screw began to churn the green water into boiling foam astern," George Kennan wrote. Since they sailed alone, unprotected by a convoy, they'd been advised to sail out of sight of land. They rounded Cuba's west point, not the east as had the flotilla, and ran into squalls. Barton confined herself to bed: she felt "perfectly ill, helpless, wet, could not lift my head from the sopping pillow." She took "diladum," probably the opiate Dilaudid, and this seemed to work. Two days later, the sea calmed and they could see the cliffs of the wild Sierra Maestra. "Whoever is hungry we will feed if we can," Barton had told the army's inspector general before leaving, "never forgetting that this was the real object of the war . . ."

The most important meeting on June 20 involved Shafter, Sampson, and Calixto García. The three had never met, and now they could discuss strategy. They'd planned to meet on a ship, but "García's inability to stand the motion of the sea" changed the venue to Aserradero, a small village twelve miles west of Morro Castle. Shafter, Sampson, their staffs, and a

British and German attaché piled into the first two boats; Davis, Remington, Stephen Bonsal of *McClure's*, and Caspar Whitney of *Harper's Weekly* wedged into the third. A line of *mambisi* lined the shore, flanked by a small detachment of horsemen. Mounts were provided to ride up a one-mile trail to García's camp: Shafter's tiny mule nearly disappeared beneath his bulk, but it had a stout heart, assured the officer-in-charge. They rode to a high cliff overlooking the breakers and beyond that could see the silhouettes of transports and ships of war.

The commanders met in an open hut, along with the Cuban general Jesús Rabí, one of the last full-blooded Carib Indians left in Cuba. This was Davis's first chance to observe Cuban troops: the officers were "fine-looking young gentlemen, well, and even smartly uniformed"; the soldiers "ragged and half-starved," but well-disciplined. Five "negro sentries, naked to the waist," guarded the hut; troops of "every shade of skin" and "small laughing boys" crowded outside. American officers and the attachés snapped photos. Inside, the commanders huddled over maps of Santiago. Morro Point housed controls for the channel's electrically detonated mines; across the entrance from that, batteries at Socapa Point defended the bay. Take those two points, Sampson claimed, and his ships could charge down the channel and take Santiago.

The conversation showed how radically U.S. strategy had changed. When McKinley first considered invasion, taking Havana seemed key. But that changed when the Spanish fleet was caged. Take the bay and destroy Cervera's fleet, and Cuba would be strangled, Sampson declared. But Shafter wasn't so sure. Strangulation might take too long. He compared the map with what he'd seen of the southern coast as his ship passed Guantánamo. Three parallel ranges rolled back from the sea: a long bluff rising 200 to 300 feet followed the beach, then foothills and valleys stretched back to the Sierra Maestre. Three V-shaped clefts in the bluff opened into the interior. The Aguadores ravine lay four miles east of Morro Point; six miles east sat the seaside village of Siboney; then, east of that, Daiquirí. A three-mile road connected Daiquirí and Siboney, then the Camino Real ran seven miles northeast from Siboney to Santiago.

This latter seemed the best route, but the War Department said that 7,000 Spaniards waited on the bluffs. Not so, García corrected. There were 900 at most: 600 at Siboney, 300 at Daiquirí. The rest camped back along the Royal Road. If Sampson shelled the coast, García's men under General Demetrio Castillo could clear out survivors. García suggested landing at Daiquirí and as a diversion have Sampson shell Aguadores and the coastal inlet of Cabanas. Shafter agreed.

They posed for photos afterward. One shows García in white linen standing beside Shafter, in army blue. Some *mambisi* in sombreros grin behind them. Davis was impressed by García: "With his beard and mustache of the third empire," he looked "like a Marshall of France." As they planned the attack, Sampson sat on García's right, with Shafter to his left: "It had been a long, hard, and desperate struggle for the white-haired old soldier," Davis wrote, and "he must have thought that at last his reward had come." That may be correct, for García offered to place his forces under Shafter. But Shafter declined, realizing that this made him responsible for their welfare. Still, he donated nine thousand rations and several thousand rounds of ammo as a gesture of goodwill. The meeting would be the war's high point in Cuban-American relations: García would learn the hard way that the Americans had come to supplant, not support, him.

The landing started on Wednesday, June 22, delayed a day due to rough seas. Shafter's order of landing placed Henry Lawton's Second Division first, followed by the independent brigade of Brigadier General John C. Bates. Next came Joe Wheeler's dismounted Cavalry Division, which included the Rough Riders and black Ninth and Tenth cavalries. Then Charles Post with the Seventy-First New York, and finally David Fagen's Twenty-Fourth Infantry. Sampson provided three armed tugs, a dozen armed steam launches, and forty or fifty other boats of various size. After landing at Daiquirí, the troops would follow the coast road to Siboney before heading into the interior.

Daiquirí was barely an indentation in the coast, built by American mining companies to service their inland iron pits. There was no harbor or breakwater, and a strong southern tide broke hard against the coral shore. An iron pier extended into the water, but this had been built for railcars dumping ore into lighters docked beneath them; the pier looked too dangerous to land soldiers. Next to this, a small, slimy wooden pier jutted forty feet into the sea. It was either clamber up the slime or brave the rocky beach. Today a fence cuts the landing zone in half, but the iron dock still remains. A bluff looms over the beach, covered by thick jungle;

at the top, the crumbling blockhouse still stands. "Four hundred resolute men could have prevented the disembarkation at very little cost to themselves," Roosevelt later wrote. But then, as now, the blockhouse and heights were empty. Major General Arsenio Linares, commander of the Spanish Fourth Army Corps, had pulled his men back toward Santiago, abandoning the beaches.

The naval bombardment began at 9:40 a.m. and lasted thirty minutes. Not a single Spanish soldier was lost: the three hundred who'd defended Daiquirí had evacuated at five a.m. At 10:25 a.m. a troop of cavalry charged down the beach, their Cuban flag popping overhead. The forces of General Castillo would greet the Americans when they landed.

Shafter raised the signal to cease firing, and debarking began. The men were weighed down with haversacks, blanket rolls, a hundred rounds of ammunition, and three days' rations; if you fell into the water, you'd sink like a stone. Steam launches towed them forty feet to the slimy pier. Davis watched the rows of little white boats; a man must leap out as a wave pitched him up, then grab hold. The boats heaved up, then "dropped far beneath them like a descending elevator or rose suddenly and threw them on their knees."

The inevitable occurred—two Buffalo Soldiers plunged into the sea. Stephen Crane had made it to the beach when he heard shouts and looked back. "At last it has happened," he wrote: "It is horrible to think of them clasped in the arms of their heavy accoutrements." Lines were flung over and friends reached out, but the two were dragged down. Bucky O'Neill jumped in and tried to bring them up, and above it all a rasping voice screamed "to do this and do that." It did little good: the two died on Cuba's doorstep, "drowned a moment before they could set foot on that island which had been the subject of their soldierly dreams."

Landing was even deadlier for pack animals. The only way to land them was by "throwing them overboard and letting them swim ashore, if they could," Roosevelt said. Only a few landed that first day, mostly officers' horses, and half a dozen drowned, including Roosevelt's Rain-in-the-Face. They'd be led to an open port, and as they gazed down, a whip would crack and they'd leap. Either that or troopers held their heads, pointed them to shore, and pushed. Buglers on the beach played "Charge," "Stables," and other recognizable commands, but many turned around, dazed or hysterical with fear. The whole performance especially upset cavalrymen and spoke of something worse than disorganization. Horses swam in circles or took off for open sea. Others tried to clamber back aboard and got chewed up by propellers: "Some of the horses swam a mile out to sea." After several losses, orders were given to tether three or four horses together and tow them ashore by boat. The slower process proved far less lethal.

Soldiers were met by hundreds of *mambisi* as they staggered ashore. Roosevelt called them "a crew of as utter tatterdemalions as human eyes ever looked upon, armed with every kind of rifle in all stages of dilapidation." They'd be "no use in serious fighting," he said, forgetting exactly who'd fought the Spaniards to a standstill. More than half of the *mambisi* in Oriente Province were black, and Americans took their prejudices ashore. The dislike quickly spread. Once Davis got ashore, he sought out Roosevelt, knowing where to find good copy as a newsman. He sat with the Rough Riders as they cooked their coffee and bacon; as they did, Cuban officers rode through, their camp up the road at Siboney. Their ponies galloped over "the tired bodies of the men with that courtly grace and consideration for Americans which invariably marks the Cuban gentleman."

Six thousand soldiers, nearly half the American force, landed until late at night; those ashore built fires, awaiting orders to go on. The small cove quickly filled with troops; searchlights lit the beach in a ghostly chiaroscuro. The mine shops burned, and in the ruins Crane could see the mine company's "ghostly locomotive." He listened to the Cubans sing "weird, half-savage airs—accompanied by the booming of improvised drums." The soldiers built bonfires with railroad ties to dry their clothes, but this provided scant relief, for now waves of "large, clattering" land crabs charged upon them. "They climbed over everything," remembered one New Yorker. "Some of them, not knowing when to stop, walked right into the flames. They may have been trying to get warm, but roasted themselves instead." They were the size of a halved coconut, red and nearly hollow, which accounted for their rattling sound. You'd be asleep when suddenly they'd be "clinging to one's ears and hands and creeping all over the body."

Shafter had ordered Lawton's men to camp that night in the advance position should the Spaniards decide to counterattack. It never came. At five a.m. the invaders rose, and Crane followed. After lunch, he caught up with the old Indian fighter. The air was hot, dusty, and "sleepy"; bees buzzed around him, and he came upon the tall, graying Lawton lolling with his staff under a tree. He seemed completely at ease: his men were up front, a firefight probably waited around the corner, but in this pleasant tropical copse, the moment was all that mattered. Lawton smiled as if to say "Well, this will be better than chasing Apaches."

The third invasion of these June weeks would be the most peaceful, since one side did not even realize it was at war.

On Saturday, June 4, Captain Henry Glass of the USS *Charleston* stood on the quarterdeck before his officers and crew. They'd just left Honolulu and bore west to Manila; behind the 3,730-ton cruiser sailed three transports carrying the First California and Second Oregon volunteers, five companies of the Fourteenth U.S. Infantry, and a detachment of the First California Field Artillery, a total of 115 officers and 2,386 enlisted men. They were the first wave of General Wesley Merritt's Eighth Army Corps ordered to reinforce Dewey. Things were getting touchy: naval vessels from other nations kept dribbling into Manila Bay. Dewey may have conquered the Spanish fleet, but he didn't "own" Manila until American troops marched in.

Captain Glass ripped open his secret orders, which could only be read at sea. Before joining Dewey, they must first capture the Spanish island of Guam, destroy any enemy forts or ships, and make "prisoners of the governor and other officials and any armed force that may be there." Secretary Long wrote that the operation "should not occupy more than one or two days."

Guam was the largest and most populous of seventeen volcanic islands strung north-south along the 145th meridian; the chain divided the east from the west Pacific and had been discovered by Ferdinand Magellan in March 1521. He called the island chain the "Ladrones," or "thieves," after some Micronesian Chamorros stole a small boat and some scraps of iron. The 1668 Spanish estimate of 50,000 Chamorros had dwindled by 1898 to 10,000 poor natives, mestizos, Spanish soldiers and bureaucrats, whalers and traders, and residents of a leper colony. The island was about 30 miles long, 4 to 8½ miles wide, shaped like the sole of a foot, and covered 225 square miles. It offered little but location: its siting between Hawaii and the Philippines made it a perfect supply depot and coaling station, one of Alfred Mahan's essential ingredients for projecting U.S. power throughout East Asia. McKinley directed the navy to tell Guam's residents that "we come, not as invaders or conquerors, but as friends."

The *Charleston* reached Guam on the morning of June 20, the same day that Shafter, Sampson, and García met at tiny Aserradero and Hearst entertained chorus girls. Through the mist, Captain Glass thought he spotted a target; he alerted his men for battle, but realized it was just a Japanese brigantine gathering coconuts. No other ship lay in the harbor. With nothing to sink, he ordered his men to shell crumbling Fort Santa Cruz. They fired thirteen shells into the fort, but no one fired back. Glass turned his ship toward shore and dropped anchor; soon, a small skiff flying Spanish colors drew near. She did not fly a white flag, but did not seem aggressive.

The skiff carried the port captain, a naval surgeon, a Chamorro padre, and an interpreter. The officers saluted Glass and apologized for not answering his salute: they'd run out of gunpowder months ago. "What salute?" Glass asked. "Those were hostile shots. Our countries are at war." The two Spaniards gawked as Glass told them more bad news: the Spanish fleet at Manila had been destroyed seven weeks earlier, and they were his prisoners. No one knew, they said: no mail had arrived since April 9. Glass paroled the four to go back and tell Governor Juan Marina that they were at war.

The officers returned that afternoon with Marina's reply: Spanish law forbade him from boarding a foreign naval vessel, but he would receive an officer in his headquarters. The next morning, Lieutenant William Braunersreuther came ashore bearing Glass's demand for complete surrender within thirty minutes. Marina returned to his office and twenty-nine minutes later replied, "Being without defenses of any kind and without any means for meeting the situation, I am under the sad necessity of being unable to resist such superior forces and regretfully accede to your demands." U.S. Marines came ashore, assembled the garrison's fifty-four Spaniards and fifty-four Chamorros, and told them they were prisoners.

At 2:45 p.m. on June 21, Glass raised the American flag over the abandoned fortress. A military band played "The Star-Spangled Banner," followed by a twenty-one-gun salute. Although Spanish soldiers remained captive on the *Charleston* until reaching Manila, the native troops were merely disarmed and freed. "They showed great joy at being relieved of their arms," an American officer observed. The fact that they gave away the "buttons and ornaments on their uniforms" convinced Glass that "they were equally glad to be rid of Spanish rule."

Glass left the next day, taking his prisoners and the flag that flew briefly over Santa Cruz. No troops stayed behind. He asked Guam's only American citizen, Francisco Portusach, to "take care of the island" until a real governor arrived. The *Charleston* never came back, wrecked in February 1899 on an uncharted Philippine reef. But Glass holds the distinction of being the first American officer to ever capture an entire foreign colony by himself in a single day.

14

The Royal Road

Cuba's dawn broke suddenly, and with it a chorus of insects and birds. Lawton had been directed to enter Siboney first, followed by Wheeler's cavalry. But "Fighting Joe" didn't see it that way. Since Shafter's orders were addressed to the "senior officer" present, the sixty-one-year-old Wheeler considered himself the most "senior" man there. White-bearded, 5 feet, 5 inches, and 120 pounds, he resembled the frail grandfather of sentimental myth, yet Robert E. Lee had considered J.E.B. Stuart and Wheeler his best cavalry officers, and like Fitzhugh Lee, he missed his secessionist days. When offering Wheeler command of the cavalry, McKinley said that he needed a "high officer" from the South whose selection would say "the old days are gone." As Wheeler's small escort rode past Lawton, he reportedly yelled that he planned to be the first to meet "the Yankees—dammit, I mean the Spaniards!"

Wheeler's group arrived at Siboney at ten a.m. and spotted the Spanish rear guard withdrawing up the Camino Real. Their retreat was so rapid, Lawton later wrote, that it was "impossible to follow up with infantry." Castillo's scouts trailed them to the village of Las Guásimas about two and a half miles northwest and watched them dig in. Wheeler ordered the bulk of his men to move forward; they entered squalid little Siboney that night and barely made camp before the skies opened.

The troops built bonfires after the storm. Roosevelt visited Troop L from Indian Territory and talked with their captain, Allyn Capron; Sergeant Hamilton Fish, one of the socialites, stood beside them. "I caught myself admiring the splendid bodily vigor of Capron and Fish," Roosevelt said. Their "frames seemed of steel . . . in their eyes shone high resolve and fiery desire." He thought that "two better representatives of the American soldier, there were not in the whole army." Even on the eve of battle, Roosevelt lived his boys' adventures.

Around midnight Leonard Wood returned from a strategy session with Generals Young and Wheeler. He told Capron that Troop L would walk point along a ridgetop path paralleling the Royal Road while Young took the main column along the main thoroughfare. The two groups would meet at a herringbone junction forming the enemy's first line of defense—the small village of Las Guásimas, named for a nut tree growing there in clumps. Wood told Capron to get some sleep. "Well," Capron replied, "even if we don't sleep tonight there will be a great many of us who will get a long sleep before tomorrow night."

The comment stopped Wood cold. Soldiers can be a superstitious lot. He hoped it was only that, and not premonition.

Reveille sounded at four a.m. By 5:30 Young sat on a mule and led his men up the Royal Road. It barely deserved that name: rising through steep hills to Santiago, the road had endured a half century of neglect and was better suited for livestock than anything on wheels. The first leg cut through stagnant marsh and was lined by coconut palms. The air stank of decay; mosquitoes swarmed around them.

Fifteen minutes later, Wood started the Rough Riders up the ridge to Young's left. The path narrowed as it ascended and they were soon forced into single file. L Troop took the lead, followed by Wood and the correspondents Edward Marshall and Richard Harding Davis. Roosevelt came next, leading his horse, Little Texas. Bucky O'Neill's A Troop followed Roosevelt, with Hoffman Philip near the front. Stephen Crane slogged farther back. Roosevelt did not cultivate the novelist as he did Davis: he'd known him in New York and considered him trash for haunting the Tenderloin district, home to prostitutes and thieves. Battle order was not a priority. "Goddam it," snapped an army major near Charles Post as he watched them climb. "They haven't got a point out." If anything, Post said, the Rough Riders "only lacked a band at its head to give it a thoroughly festive and inconsequential air."

The Rough Riders ascended five hundred feet, a hard climb for anyone, much less for men used to the saddle. "I staggered along," wrote Hoffman Philip: "The syncopated tinkling of the tin cups which hung from each man's side became, in my exhausted condition, strangely and beautifully reminiscent of the echoing of far-away cow bells." Wood called a halt, and Philip looked back: the sea beyond Siboney was filled with transports disgorging men and supplies. It seemed too peaceful for war.

About fifteen hundred Spaniards waited for them. Las Guásimas was once a bustling place, four and a half miles outside of Santiago, but three years of war had left it a shell. The Camino Real met this jungle path at Las Guásimas, then continued west. Brigadier General Antero Rubin commanded this Spanish rear guard and placed his men in three lines—in the jungle before the ruined village, in some stone breastworks up the road, and past that, in reserve. It was a strong defensive position, but General Linares had been certain the enemy would land at Aguadores between Siboney and Morro Castle and march inland from there. He'd ordered Rubin to fall back to the trenches closer to Santiago on and around San Juan Hill.

It was no secret that the Americans were coming. Young's regulars numbered about 470; they dragged four rattling Hotchkiss guns, and bugle calls kept order. Half a mile to their left and three hundred feet higher, Wood and five hundred Rough Riders struggled through jungle. They'd packed two Gatling guns on the backs of complaining mules. The trail led through thick underbrush bordered with barbed wire. The mercury read 100°F., the air so thick it "made us gasp and sweat," Davis said. Roosevelt would claim that the Rough Riders advanced like "Indians," but if so, they were a loud, inept tribe. The men discussed a cowboy who'd opened a saloon in New Mexico. Crane could hear them talking in the rear: "They wound along this narrow winding path, babbling joyously, arguing, recounting, laughing; making more noise than a train going through a tunnel." He'd already been through battle, and he admitted, "I was frightened almost into convulsions."

This continued for an hour, with short stops for reports by Capron. The captain had placed Hamilton Fish and another soldier at point, with two wary Cubans scouting before them. The *mambisi* had said they should look for the body of a dead *guerrillero*; the enemy was less than five hundred yards past him. "Silence in the ranks!" Wood shouted. The chatter continued. Roosevelt was telling Edward Marshall about a lunch he'd had with his boss Hearst at New York's Astor House when he noticed a strand of barbed wire bordering the path. "My God!" he said. "This wire has been cut today!" The end of the wire was bright, and dew had made it slightly rusty. Even as he said this, the regimental surgeon rode up on a mule. When Roosevelt jumped up to silence him, he "made more noise" than the surgeon, Marshall said. "Then came the first shot."

They'd walked straight into an ambush. The hidden Spaniards had let the two Cuban scouts and Hamilton Fish pass, then fired into L Troop. The two scouts were wounded; Fish was shot through the heart and died immediately. L Troop panicked and fired into their own men. A bullet plowed into Capron near his heart, but he refused to be taken back. "Let me up, I want to see it all," he gasped, and the surgeon propped him up against his knee. Six more soldiers died in this initial ambush, and thirty-four were wounded, many repeatedly. Red-haired Thomas Jefferson Isbell seems the only one not to have been hit in the initial attack: he flattened, lined a Spaniard in his sights, and fired. The man dropped, and so many Mauser rounds rained upon him that he suffered seven wounds. Lieutenant John Thomas of Muskogee took a serious wound to the thigh; the surgeon bound his leg with a tourniquet, and when Davis passed, Thomas yelled, "They've killed my captain! Do you understand?"—then fainted.

The time was 7:30 a.m. Firing swept the line. Men pirouetted and fell as high-speed rounds plowed into them. A bullet sounded like *z-eu* as it approached, then *chug* when it hit. A rumor swept the ranks that Wood was dead; his hated adjutant panicked and fled back to Siboney with the news. But Wood was very much alive, standing in the trail, directing men left or right, as outwardly cool as his nickname "Old Icebox." In fact, he regretted his failure to take out a $100,000 life insurance policy for his family. Hoffman Philip and the rest of Troop A ran up: Corporal George

Doherty asked for a piece of hardtack, and as Philip fished it from his pack, he came face-to-face with Wood. The colonel "gave me a glance of recognition" as, at that instant, "something sped over [Wood's] shoulder and close to my ear with a hiss. I heard a sickening noise immediately back of me as poor Doherty sank to the earth," shot through the head.

The fight was as intense on the Royal Road. Young's men moved faster than Wood's: less than a mile from Las Guásimas, Cuban pickets warned that Spaniards were close, and at about 7:20 a.m. scouts came to a bend where they could see their defenses. It seemed a strong position, nestled on high hills in an old *aguardiente* distillery; earthworks and trenches formed a V pointed toward Siboney. Wheeler rode up and ordered the Hotchkiss guns unlimbered; as it turned out, these started firing at about the same moment the ambush began overhead.

This phase of battle lasted about an hour. Down on the road, cavalrymen were forced to crawl through the growth; on the ridge, Rough Riders could rush forward in a suicidal scrimmage or dart from tree to tree. The heavy growth and their smokeless powder made phantoms of the enemy. Marshall watched as Roosevelt "jumped up and down," his emotions "divided between joy and a tendency to run." Wood had seen this before in those under fire for the first time: he steadied his overexcited subordinate, pointed him to the right, and told him to take a squad down the hill to link up with Young. Roosevelt's panic abated, and he headed off, tripping over his sword as it caught between his legs.

Davis went with him. Rounds zipped overhead. Roosevelt peeked around a palm just as a bullet struck, hurling sawdust and splinters into his ear and eye. The trees opened, and they stared down at Young's men. They could hear Mausers across the valley, but where was the enemy? Davis peered through his binoculars and cried, "There they are, Colonel! Look over there! I can see their hats near that glade!" Roosevelt had studied the same spot, but hadn't seen them; now he ordered his men to concentrate fire. The Spaniards sprang from hiding and ran.

The dense growth prevented them from continuing down the hill, so they returned to the trail at the place where L Troop lay cut to shreds. Davis scooped up a fallen soldier's carbine; all along the trail lay abandoned haversacks and rifles, streaked or matted with blood. "Except for the clatter of the land crabs," he said, "and the whistling of the bullets in the trees, the place was as silent as a grave." He came again upon Lieutenant Thomas, his right leg pierced near the femoral artery, a tourniquet of handkerchiefs and twigs the only thing preventing exsanguination. He'd regained consciousness and raved that he must take revenge for Captain Capron. Another fifty feet and Davis found the captain, dead but still propped against the grieving surgeon. Fifty more yards and he found a big fellow behind a rock, shot between the eyes, chest heaving; he heard for the first time the death rattle Crane had heard at Guantánamo. A man ran up and screamed, "He is my bunkie," then dropped beside him and cried. Davis came upon Hamilton Fish: his open eyes had glazed over, and Davis closed them. He reached the remnants of L Troop, now led by Second Lieutenant Richard Day, the last officer. The Spaniards were pulling back: Davis began "pumping wildly" with his carbine, no longer a correspondent but a soldier.

Marshall had also switched roles. He'd bought smokeless cartridges for his revolver in Tampa, and he fired at the unseen enemy. He'd joined the Rough Riders only the previous day, but "felt that every man who was hit was my personal friend." He watched as Wood rode among them: when a man cursed that he'd been blinded by smoke, Wood snapped, "Stop that swearing—I don't want to hear any cursing today!" Men went down around Marshall like "clods in the grass," and then he heard the dreaded *chug* and found himself lying beside them. "There was no pain, no surprise," he said, but the "tremendous shock so dulled my sensibilities" that he lay "perfectly satisfied and entirely comfortable in the long grass." The battle moved on: some "first-aid men" followed in their wake, calling for wounded. It didn't occur to him to answer. Falling asleep seemed sweet, but he fought this off; three men lugged him into the shade with more wounded. A surgeon examined his wound and said the bullet had shattered his spine, that he'd better write any messages for home: "Be quick!" Marshall interpreted this to mean the end was near.

The time was nine a.m.—the battle was almost over. Wood's and Young's men broke into the open simultaneously, discovering that they'd converged on the village crossroads. This was a dangerous moment for the Rough Riders: when they emerged from cover, they faced a line of trenches filled with Spanish soldiers, while on a ridge to their right lay a blockhouse and more trenches that could catch them in a crossfire. It was the Spaniards' most "impregnable point" at Las Guásimas, wrote Chaplain Theophilus Steward of the Tenth Cavalry, and Wood echoed in his report that "heavy fire" from this ridge "enfiladed our line." The Rough Riders "would have perished" if Wheeler's First and Tenth cavalries had not emerged with their Hotchkiss guns and pounded the enemy. A *Washington Post* reporter confirmed this: "If it had not been for the Negro cavalry, the Rough Riders would have been exterminated." The Spanish troops fired a few more shots, then retreated to their next line of defense up the Royal Road.

About a thousand U.S. troops had driven off fifteen hundred Spaniards. The Rough Riders lost 8 dead and 34 wounded; overall, 16 Americans died in the battle and 52 were wounded. Although early army accounts inflated Spanish losses to 250 dead and wounded, their actual casualties numbered fewer than the Americans: 10 killed and 25 wounded.

Hoffman Philip came up as the last Spaniards left; at his feet lay a dead soldier in light linen "with little blue and white pin stripes." Bucky O'Neill suggested that he cut off two gilded regimental buttons from the man's shoulder straps as souvenirs. Philip gave both to his captain, who smiled and returned one. Vultures already wheeled overhead. "Colonel," O'Neill said to Roosevelt, "isn't it Whitman who says of vultures that 'they pluck the eyes of princes and tear the flesh of kings'?" The exhausted Roosevelt replied he could not recall.

O'Neill's literary aside acknowledged a grim reality. The wounded must be found, the dead buried. Scavengers wouldn't wait. Vultures had already torn out dead Spaniards' eyes; land crabs, "big as rabbits," gathered in silent circles about the fallen. Dead Americans and Spaniards were gathered for burial in separate common graves. The wounded were helped back to Siboney. Charles Post and his Seventy-First New York marched double-time to the front along the Royal Road. "Wheeler's sent for help," wounded soldiers said as they passed. "They got Teddy in an ambush." Some talked; some were silent; one was shot in the stomach; arms were in slings. George Von Kramer, a Manhattan druggist, passed a Rough Rider sitting on a rock; he held his left eye in his left hand. "It had been shot out of its socket, and was hanging on only by the optic nerve." The man fanned himself with his free hand as if this were just another day in the park. When Von Kramer glanced back, the man "had fallen off the rock and was laying on his side."

Edward Marshall snapped from his daze to find Crane and Davis bending over him. "There's a correspondent up there all shot to hell," someone had yelled as Crane made his way up; Marshall had given him work when he was still a starving freelancer. "Hello Marshall," he said. "In hard luck, old man?"

"Yes, I'm done for," Marshall replied. They noticed he couldn't move his legs.

"Nonsense," Crane countered. "You're all right, old boy. What can I do for you?"

File my dispatches, Marshall requested of the younger man. "I don't mean file 'em ahead of your own," he added. "Just file 'em if you find it handy."

Crane decided his friend was doomed: "No man could be so sublime in detail concerning the trade of journalism and not die." Crane and Davis found six soldiers to carry him to a field hospital, then Crane trudged back to file Marshall's stories. For this kindness, he missed the rest of the fight, sent a spare dispatch describing the ambush, and would be fired.

The Spaniards fell back to Santiago's outskirts, their line stretching from the village of El Caney on the American right, through the San Juan Ridge, and down to the seaside village of Aguadores. A string of blockhouses and trenches screened their main defenses, which circled the city. According to the British consul Frederick W. Ramsden, those in the city heard the "cannon and musketry fire" and felt they were doomed: "The officers and others were sitting round without saying a word, and with faces as long and glum as you can imagine." Hunger had already set in, thanks to the American blockade. An egg sold for 15 cents; a biscuit for 20. Over the next week, Shafter would advance from Las Guásimas in small steps, trusting in hunger to weaken the enemy.

Damage control set in. Most early reports agreed that the Rough Riders had blundered into an ambush. Davis's early stories portrayed Las Guásimas as a tale of unheeding cowboys taken by surprise; Burr McIntosh in *Leslie's Weekly* criticized their rash plunge into the jungle, for which there was "no vital end to be gained." The *Collier's* photographer Jimmy Hare believed the result was inevitable, since the Rough Riders suffered from "a superabundance of exhibitionists and egomaniacs." The general consensus was that by ignoring the advice of their Cuban scouts, they'd stumbled into trouble.

Roosevelt would insist that no ambush occurred: they'd planned it that way. "In the first fight we were neither surprised nor ambushed," he wrote to William Tudor on July 19. "We simply drove the enemy from thick cover in a pass, with the loss to be expected from such an operation." He insisted this in his memoirs and in a letter to McKinley. The partnership of Davis and Roosevelt was forged at Las Guásimas, wrote Davis's biographer Arthur Lubow: it was during and after the battle that Roosevelt began to shower Davis with special attention. He urged the Associated Press to cite Davis's courage and offered him a captaincy. The extra attention seemed to work: in his later *Scribner's* piece, Davis claimed that a big difference existed "between blundering into an ambush and setting out with full knowledge that you will find the enemy in ambush" and drive him out—an exact echo of Roosevelt. No such attention was paid to Crane, who, in his seven-sentence dispatch to the *World*, called the ambush "simply a gallant blunder."

As part of this whitewash, Wood and Roosevelt concocted a scapegoat to cover their blunders. Any hint that their sloppy advance had caused the deaths of Capron and Fish could ruin them, and within twenty-four hours both men laid all blame on the Cuban scouts, who'd been wounded, too. The scouts had warned the Rough Riders that the enemy was very close, but Wood and Roosevelt told Stephen Bonsal for his *McClure's* piece that they'd insisted instead that the Spaniards were a half mile away. Thus, the two implied, the scouts were to blame. Yet in a June 26 letter to his brother Charles, Davis admitted the scouts *had* insisted on caution—but no one believed them. "I thought it was a false alarm and none of us believed there were any Spaniards this side of Santiago," he said. Wood and Roosevelt also accused General Castillo of failing to fight beside them, when in fact before the battle, the general had suggested taking five hundred *mambisi* behind the Spaniards and trapping them between the two forces. But once again, Wood paid no attention.

By the third day of the invasion, the Cubans were being excluded from their own war. It started as early as June 20 at Aserradero, when Shafter proposed using them as trench diggers or porters, not soldiers and scouts. "My men are soldiers, not laborers," García snapped, rejecting Shafter's plans. On June 27 García's son Carlos told Shafter that reinforcements from Manzanillo had marched past the city of Bayamo. García wanted to send three thousand men to stop them. But Shafter said no: "Well, let them come and the more there are at Santiago, the more we will take." Five days later, he blamed García for letting them through, accusing him of dereliction just as Wood and Roosevelt had accused Castillo.

It was the thin edge of the wedge that drove Americans and Cubans apart for 120 years. When the Americans landed, they had expected the Caribbean equivalent of George Washington's revolutionary army. Instead, they found poor, mostly black guerrillas, and their surprise turned to contempt. The *mambisi* "regarded every American as a kind of charitable institution," wrote the British correspondent John Black Atkins, "and expected him to disgorge on every occasion." A Cuban would point to an American's shirt or trousers, then point to himself, "meaning that he desired a transfer of property." They were ragged and gaunt, scavenged supplies, and materialized by Yankee cookfires, begging food.

Americans did not know what to think of their new allies: they thought they'd be welcomed as liberators by beauties like Evangelina Cisneros or the "sturdy patriot" portrayed in Junta propaganda. Instead, the cruelty of the rebellion had made them cruel themselves. One soldier quoted the fate of a Cuban cavalryman who'd butchered his horse to feed his starving family; he'd been sentenced to hang. In the week before his execution, he lay on the floor in a barn "with one foot tied to a post and the stinking bones of his dead horse beside him." To Americans, wrote George Kennan, this gulf between reality and romance proved unsettling: "The Cubans disappointed me because I had pictured them to myself as a better dressed and better disciplined body of men, and had not made allowance for the hardships and privations of an insurgent's life." Charles Post found them a "curiosity"; another, "the toughest crowd of people that I ever had the fortune to see." Yet most U.S. soldiers despised them: they were dirty, louse-infested "villains," "mango-bellied degenerates," or "half-breed mongrels."

But most important, Americans despised their new allies because they did not show proper gratitude. The soldiers landed, certain of their role as liberators, only to discover that Cubans did not see them that way. They suspected the avowed intentions of the *norteamericanos*, a wariness echoing Martí's warning about the northern "monster." Antonio Maceo had famously cautioned his troops to expect nothing from Americans: "It is better to rise or fall without help than to contract debts of gratitude with such a powerful neighbor."

Even today, Cuban historians insist that, given aid and time, the *mambisi* could have emerged victorious without the help of U.S. troops. To them, this invasion was less about American beneficence than self-interest, a motive that later became transparent in the Philippines. This moment was a crossroads, and the two symbols of the separate paths were right here: Clara Barton and Leonard Wood. "Clara Barton was a symbol of what good the United States could have done," said Francisca López Civeira, senior professor of history at the University of Havana. She represented the altruism in the American soul. And there was Leonard Wood, soon appointed Cuba's governor, who'd create a commercial subjugation that ended only with Castro's 1959 revolution. Now, three days into the invasion, Wood denounced the Cubans, blaming them for American losses, setting them up for what was to come.

Since Cubans did not show proper gratitude, their "liberators" hated them. Crane saw it early: perhaps the American was at fault for his overweening need to be thanked, he said. The *mambisi*'s stamina impressed him: "He starves and he makes no complaint. We feed him and he expresses no joy." Perhaps this indifference sprang from years of deprivation and war. Yet gratitude, as the historian Louis A. Perez Jr. showed in his 2008 *Cuba in the American Imagination*, is a loaded gun. Its role is central "in the moral calculus of power," and it served as a principal weapon in the colonizer's moral arsenal. In exchange for progress, the "liberated" were expected "to display proper appreciation, most appropriately by way of submission, to their colonial benefactors." Cubans knew this instinctively: "One must not suppose that there was any cheering enthusiasm at the landing of our army here," Crane wired. Instead, they watched the invaders "stoically, almost indifferently," and for that they were despised.

The American soldier "thinks of himself as a disinterested benefactor, and he would like the Cubans to play up to the ideal now and then." Though the attitude was "mighty human," the *mambisi* refused to play that game.

Nothing enrages the godly so much as suspicion of their piety. The reaction "was at times visceral," Perez said. Cubans were a "wretched mongrel lot," shrilled the *New York Post*, "ungrateful to the last degree." As days progressed to weeks, Cubans viewed Americans as a "species of international thieves." Americans saw those they'd come to save as subhuman. "The insurgents are a lot of degenerates, absolutely devoid of honor or gratitude," fumed Samuel B. M. Young. "They are no more capable of self-government than the savages of Africa."

Clara Barton and William Randolph Hearst landed at Siboney on Sunday, June 26: the paragon of American altruism and the avatar of American hubris, breathing the same air. Their paths apparently did not cross: considering her earlier diary entries about Hearst, Barton was probably just as glad. Hearst came ashore with James Creelman and the photographer J. C. Hemment, checked out the *Journal* headquarters, and was stunned by the "wretched and emaciated" condition of the rebels and *pacificos* begging for food. Hearst wanted an interview with García; Creelman, who spoke Spanish, led the way. García and his aides had set up in a neat tile-roofed house at the edge of town. He stood on the veranda as they approached; he was tall and lean, and Hearst had never seen the famous hollow scar above his nose. Well aware of the aid given by the *Journal*, García handed Hearst a battered lone-star Cuban battle flag: "Its colors are faded, but it is the best thing the Cuban Republic can offer its best friend." Hearst was touched; when García shouted "*Viva Cuba Libre*," he joined in.

Hearst next ascended the hill overlooking Siboney. He saw below the "monstrous forms of Sampson's fleet," the masses of soldiers landing on the beach, the "poisonous jungle" over which vultures wheeled. He'd helped create this spectacle, and on the spot he composed three thousand words of purple prose. The first bylined story of correspondent Hearst ran on June 29: "I think the standing of the paper will profit by my being here."

After Las Guásimas, the Royal Road lay clear up to the line of defenses outside Santiago. The invaders must now traverse about five miles of rough country, some covered by jungle. For the next six days, Shafter unloaded his ships, loaded mule trains, and hauled supplies. The road deteriorated as one marched west, turning into a sunken track barely wide enough for one mule-drawn wagon. "The banks of the trail were three or four feet high," Davis wrote, "and when it rained it was converted into a huge gutter, with sides of mud, and with liquid mud a foot deep between them." Right past Las Guásimas lay Sevilla, where Shafter set up headquarters; a mile past that, a hill called El Pozo, or "the well." West lay Santiago; to the north, El Caney, a small village anchoring the northern end of Santiago's defensive line.

It rained from June 24 to June 30. At first it was a delight, washing away the grime of battle. But that quickly changed. The troops' wool uniforms moldered; hardtack dissolved into mush; bacon turned slimy. Tobacco ran out after two days. In their need for a smoke, troops tamped their pipes with dried grass, roots, and manure.

With rain came disease: malaria, dysentery, typhoid, and sporadic cases of what might have been yellow fever. In its early stages, the dreaded "Yellow Jack" resembled malaria, so no one really knew what ran through the camps. A postwar study revealed that 10 to 20 percent of the infantry, and less than 5 percent of the cavalry, suffered from yellow fever, but malaria and a "bilious" fever increased at a steady rate of 60 to 70 percent, so the decimation had just begun. Wheeler fell ill soon after Las Guásimas, as did Samuel Young. Leonard Wood took command of the cavalry, and Roosevelt took charge of the Rough Riders.

Malaria had already filled the hospital tents when the *State of Texas* arrived off Siboney. They'd treated Guantánamo's casualties; now Barton thought they'd anchor here. She sent two workers ashore; in an hour, they came back. Two "hastily extemporized and wholly unequipped hospitals" had already been set up in a pair of abandoned Spanish houses, they said—one filled with Cubans, the other with Americans. No attempt had been made to disinfect either building; the wounded and sick lay on the floor without blankets or pillows. The *State of Texas* had stocked more than enough equipment, and on the night of June 24, the Red Cross broke out its cargo.

The next morning, Dr. A. Monae Lesser, the Red Cross lead physician, landed with five female nurses and a boat of supplies. They trudged to the army hospital and offered their services to "Dr. Winston," the surgeon in charge. "To their great surprise," George Kennan wrote, they were told that any help from the Red Cross "was not desired." This would become a pattern: the *Olivette*'s lead surgeon made it clear "that women, even if they are trained nurses, have no business in an army, and should be snubbed, if not browbeaten, until they learn to keep their place." They walked next door to the Cuban hospital and offered their services there. The *mambisi* were overjoyed: by nightfall, the nurses had cleaned and disinfected the hospital, bathed Cuban patriots, fed them, and put them into clean cot beds. "Our own soldiers, at the same time, were lying, without blankets or pillows, on the floor, in a building which Dr. Winston and his assistants had neither cleaned nor attempted to clean."

It didn't take long for American troops to learn that their care was inferior to that of the despised Cubans. Two days later, on June 29, the chief army surgeon at Siboney overrode Winston and allowed the Red Cross to help. The Army Medical Corps would later seek revenge for such bad publicity. In an official report published in the November 4, 1898, *New York Herald*, Surgeon Major Daniel Appel wrote that there were "a number of surgeons on board the *State of Texas*, and four trained nurses; but although we were working night and day, taking care of our sick and wounded, no assistance was given by them until some days afterward, when our own men were ready to drop from fatigue."

It was becoming apparent that truth would be one of the war's first casualties. If conditions were bad in Siboney, George Kennan wondered what they were like closer to the front. On the same day that the Red Cross graced the Cuban hospital, Kennan and Clara Barton's fixer John Elwell walked up the Royal Road. Dr. Lesser asked to come, too. "Get on your togs," Kennan said, and ten minutes later, Lesser emerged from his stateroom in a black morning suit, white linen shirt, and high starched collar. "Where do you think you are going?" Kennan laughed. "To church?" Lesser complained he didn't have anything else, so Kennan lent him clothes more appropriate for the mud and jungle.

They struggled up the Camino Real. A half mile on, they came to the farthest line of advance, an open field to the right where the long grass was beaten into paths, and at the end of each path lay infantry and cavalry. Beyond this point lay danger, for in the jungle ahead, Spanish sharpshooters had tied themselves onto the trees. One didn't linger in the open; the snipers' smokeless Mausers popped "like a soda-water bottle being opened close to the ear," Crane said. Kennan's group searched down the paths and found a pitiful attempt at a field hospital: two ambulances filled with heatstroke victims sprawled on medical chests, no kettles for boiling water, no hammocks or rubber blankets to keep off the rain. In a camp under some trees, they found Roosevelt, his Rough Riders scattered nearby.

The cowboy regiment was strangely subdued. They'd camped by a clear stream where they washed their bloody uniforms. They had one day's rations left and were learning to fry mangoes. Kennan spotted the mound where they'd buried their dead: they'd planted on it a little cross and piled up small stones. "A curious interval of astonishing politeness and consideration" came to the regiment, said Hoffman Philip, one he attributed to a mute "expression of respect for those who were no longer with us." He'd been drinking coffee when a soldier stumbled over his outstretched legs, and instead of "the usual exchange of disparaging reposts," both said "S'cuse me!" and that was all. Kennan and his companions talked and ate hardtack with Roosevelt and Wood, collected letters to post in the mailbag, and headed back to Siboney.

On the way back, Shafter hove into view in a buckboard, his left foot wrapped in bandages from gout. The heat made him nauseous. His attendants balanced him on a mule, which struggled up El Pozo. At the top, he raised his field glasses.

Ahead stretched a green valley, and the Royal Road snaked through it for about two miles. At the end lay the San Juan Heights and its highest point, San Juan Hill. If they conquered that, they could besiege Santiago and win the Spanish fleet, the ultimate prize. Shafter could make out a long yellow thread of fresh dirt lining the summit, and at the very top a blockhouse resembling a Chinese pagoda. He adjusted the range of the glasses and made out the white sombreros of soldiers and blue coats of officers. Beyond that, Santiago seemed a white smudge.

Between the green valley and the heights stretched an ascending plain. He studied this for a long time. The Royal Road threaded its face, sometimes dipping beneath an embankment, sometimes hidden by chaparral. This was what they'd have to cross: a murderous open field of fire that favored the faceless defenders watching from above.

15

The Heights

The road to Santiago lay over what Sun Tzu called "desperate ground." The ancient general, in *The Art of War*, described the "nine terrains" of battle—some advantageous, others best avoided—but the ground Fifth Corps must cross was that "which can only be saved by fighting without delay." Rufus Shafter studied the hand-drawn map given him by Lieutenant Colonel George Derby, his chief engineer. The road to Santiago ran west through thick forest and up the open plain. The San Juan Heights bisected this route; to Shafter's right and slightly to the front squatted a clump of ranch houses Americans called Kettle Hill. There was no choice but this choice, a frontal assault. The realization did not ease his constant nausea.

He also felt the weight of time. Cuban scouts said that relief from Manzanillo could reach Santiago by July 2–3: they estimated up to 8,000 Spanish troops, though actual numbers were less than half. He wanted to take the city and its 10,000 defenders, but he did not want a siege, recalling the 2,000 British soldiers who'd died of heat and fever 150 years earlier in a similar attack: "If we had attempted to flank them or dig them out by regular parallels to get closer to them, my men would have been sick before it could have been accomplished, and the losses would have been many times greater than they were."

There was one major snag. Two and a half miles north lay the village of El Caney. Reconnaissance by Henry Lawton revealed that it was guarded by six wooden blockhouses and a stone fort that hunched like a Neolithic dolmen atop a high bluff overlooking town. Lawton believed he could take El Caney in two or three hours. If not, six miles of good road connected it to Santiago, which meant that Spanish reinforcements could come up behind them at any time.

Shafter decided to let Lawton take El Caney first as his own greater force advanced through the jungle and artillery pounded the hills. When Shafter did attack, Lawton could hold El Caney and then come down a road to the right, creating a two-pronged attack on Kettle and San Juan hills.

All depended on speed. General Linares's troops were spread around Santiago, not massed directly before the Americans. Lawton's 6,653 men should easily crush General Vara del Rey's 521 defenders at El Caney. The 500 defenders at Kettle and San Juan hills faced 10,000 Americans, a force ratio of sixteen to one, though Shafter thought there were many more. Attacking both points at once sheared a day off the campaign, which could mean everything. Rains might fall in full force; hurricanes could blow from the east; reinforcements could arrive from Manzanilla. Or Yellow Jack could descend like a biblical plague. It was three p.m. on June 30, 1898, and the troops must get into place overnight. What Roosevelt called "my great day" began at dawn.

Lawton's men trudged all night to reach El Caney. One narrow road funneled north through the jungle, so moving artillery and troops proved slow. No attempts at silence appear in accounts; the Spaniards knew they were coming. Near the front rolled the First Artillery's Battery E under fifty-one-year-old Captain Allyn Capron, the father of the slain Rough Rider bearing the same name. Capron had commanded this unit since the December 1890 Massacre at Wounded Knee, and he was better armed then. Battery E had fielded four Hotchkiss guns when the Seventh Cavalry wiped out three hundred Sioux; now he fielded four smaller 3.2-inchers with little penetrating power. He unlimbered 2,300 yards southeast of the village, where the jungle opened to the plain. Accuracy was limited, but since the Spaniards lacked artillery, he anticipated few problems. Still, this war was killing him. He'd passed the lonely grave of his son at Las Guásimas; he'd already contracted the typhoid that would kill him on September 17.

Among the cannons strode several correspondents, including James Creelman, gaily coiffed in a straw hat with a bright ribbon. Frank Norris marched up with some California Regulars. He'd started at five p.m. the previous evening and for five hours had moved ahead in "fits and starts," listening to "the monotonous squash of many boots churning up the mud of the road." The sound of a moving army reminded him of "the noise of the sea." They made camp under order to light no fire, "nor even pipes," and to talk no louder than a whisper. A half hour later, he heard the "long-drawn *centinela alerta* of the enemy's pickets, not a quarter mile away."

Dawn revealed El Caney: "Red roofs," Norris wrote, "a white wall or two, the two towers of the church, a blockhouse of unusual size on a sugar-loaf knoll just outside of town." This blockhouse was El Viso, "the long view," a spiral of stone blocks and loop holes; flapping above it, "a flame-colored tongue of bunting, the flag of Spain." Trenches surrounded El Viso; where goats graze today in bright green clover, defenders had strung a web of barbed wire. The village itself was a maze of rifle pits, barbed wire, five blockhouses, and a church said to be the spot where in 1519 Hernán Cortés offered final prayers before leaving to conquer Mexico. The whole place looked stronger to Norris than what Lawton had painted, and El Viso was the key.

Lawton's guns began firing between 6:15 and 6:30 a.m. He planned the same morning attack he'd used against Indian villages, but this worked only if surprise was complete. And as the army so often did against Native Americans, Lawton underrated his foe. The artillery fired indiscriminately; troops stepped from the trees onto a long naked plain. The advance was a series of sprints from one sparse cover to the next, a pause to steel one's nerve, then do it again. An assault planned to last two hours had by noon dragged to six. By then, the attack on San Juan Heights had already begun.

Shafter watched from El Pozo and despaired. At two p.m. he sent a message urging Lawton to call off the assault and march instead to the Heights, but Lawton ignored him. He was too "hotly engaged" with his troops, he replied. Capron's guns had crept close enough to blow holes in the fort; by three p.m. the troops massed within 150 yards of the fort and charged.

Reporters charged with them. Those defenders left in the trenches fled downhill; those in El Viso didn't have that option. An eyewitness found the interior "floored with dead Spaniards." Abandoning all caution, James Creelman seized the Spanish flag from the flagpole and waved it overhead. Spaniards down in the village resented this: a bullet shattered Creelman's shoulder and left a wound three inches wide. He dropped sideways and passed out, coming to in the grass with the other wounded. His boss knelt over him, scribbling away in his notebook. Mauser bullets tinged around them. "I'm sorry you're hurt," Hearst chattered, his face radiant, "but wasn't it a splendid fight?" The Chief would report the news if Creelman could not. "We must beat every paper in the world!"

Norris entered the fort after Creelman. The dead lay in the trenches, in the pineapple fields descending the slope, crumpled in El Viso's stone spirals. The air brimmed with smells: smoke, gunpowder, a bloating horse, "the strange, acid, salty smell of blood." The first dead Spaniard he encountered sprawled in the bottom of a trench: "He was a young fellow—they were all young fellows, his face the color of wax; one poor, dirty hand hooked like a buzzard's claw; his arm was doubled under him, and—but the rest is not for words. A bullet-wound is one thing, but shrapnel smashes its man, flings him down, and drives and dints him into the dirt."

The Battle of El Caney was nearly over, and the cost was high on both sides. The Spaniards had fought almost to the death: of the 520-man garrison, 150 soldiers were wounded, 120 captured, and 85 killed, including General del Rey, shot three times. The rest straggled back to Santiago or vanished in the hills. American casualties were higher: 81 dead and 360 wounded.

Norris followed the battle into town, hunting for survivors, until victory was declared at five p.m. In a large building off the central square, he and others found forty wounded Spaniards, "no fight left in them." He crossed to a blockhouse and found two Spanish soldiers who "gave themselves up to me, thinking perhaps that I was some sort of officer." He made them walk ahead, "and allowed myself a full breath only when I was once more under the cover of our own rifles." He crept into the mayor's house with James F. J. Archibald of *Leslie's Weekly* and in the dark, silent interior found sprawled the body of a little girl: "I don't believe she was fifteen." She lay on the floor, "her hair across her face like a drift of seaweed." Archibald described her as "a beautiful young girl, dressed richly in a loose gown of light material," but Norris had seen too much horror to romanticize. She was "plain-looking," he said, and "had been stabbed" multiple times. He filled in the rest in a private letter. She had been "raped and then knifed to death just before the beginning of the battle." The assailant was unknown.

Norris stumbled from the house and found others leaving their subterranean holes: "men, women, and little naked pot-bellied children," all half-starved. "Most of them were women trembling on the edge of hysteria," he noted. "Such as were not half crazed were stupefied, gazing slowly about them with unseeing eyes, permitting themselves to be herded like so many sheep." They streamed toward the American lines, where they hoped to find food.

Not all were so lucky. The next day, Hearst encountered Colonel Honoré Laine, the *Journal*'s reporter with the rebels. After the battle, Americans had handed about forty Spanish captives to their Cuban allies. "And what did you do with them?" Hearst asked.

"We cut their heads off, of course," Laine said.

The Battle of San Juan Heights was nearly over when El Caney fell. The famous engagement, portrayed by Frederic Remington as an iconic forward rush of American willpower, did not start well. The San Juan Heights lay 1.6 miles west of El Pozo and rose about 125 feet above the surrounding countryside. Today this landscape has been softened by roads, suburbs, and a kiddie park, but the view facing Shafter was a stark, mile-long ridge running north to south, cloven almost equally in two. The northern segment lay closer, separated from the southern half by an open valley with a small lake and topped by a ranch house with huge kettles used for processing sugarcane, thus Kettle Hill. The long ridge they called San Juan Hill lay directly behind this, and at its southern end the ascent sloped at nearly 45 degrees. This was open country, empty of trees and brush, and at the top sat a typical Spanish blockhouse sometimes called Fort San Juan. Slit trenches girdled this "fort," and along the ridge to the north, the Spaniards had dug additional earthworks and a couple more fortified buildings.

A waist-deep creek called the San Juan River flowed north-south where the jungle ended; its steep, wooded banks were the last cover before entering the plain. The Royal Road cut through the jungle, over the Heights, and on to Santiago; a creek called Río Aguadores wormed beside it and crossed several times. The road seemed the only way through. More than one commander feared that the Spaniards would train their guns on that single point where it opened onto the plain. Brigadier General Adna R. Chaffee, commanding the Third Brigade, suggested cutting several trails through the growth so the force could burst from the trees simultaneously. The Spaniards had indeed turned the opening into a funnel: to the left lay a maze of barbed wire, made fast to tree trunks and hedges. To the right loomed Kettle Hill.

On San Juan Hill, 521 Spanish regulars of the Talavera regiment faced the Americans, as well as volunteers and two Krupp field guns. A second line of 40 men and two cannons lay behind them, and a third of 140 mounted *guerrilleros* nearby. Within the city, General Linares held in reserve 4,352 soldiers, sailors, volunteers, and firemen, but 800 to 1,000 lay in military hospitals. Linares considered the Heights an advance strongpoint, not the main line of defense, and he feared García more than he feared the Americans. He believed the rebel general gathered his *mambisi* east at Aserradero; for this reason, Linares hoped to keep a route open for any Spanish reinforcements and, if need be, a possible withdrawal.

Shafter ordered his troops to camp around El Pozo on the night of June 30: they'd march through the jungle next morning and attack by noon. He planned to direct the action from the hilltop, but the heat flattened him and he retreated to his headquarters. He relied on messengers to bring reports and carry orders, stationing staff officers as his proxies. Three in particular were his eyes and ears: Colonel Edward J. McClernand, who took Shafter's place atop El Pozo and stayed in touch by phone; Chief Engineer George Derby, in charge of a giant Signal Corps observation balloon; and Shafter's aide John Miley, who went ahead through the jungle with the divisions. The patched balloon played a fateful role. Lieutenant Colonel Joseph E. Maxfield commanded the twenty-one-man balloon detail, as well as the auxiliary equipment and tanks of hydrogen gas needed to get it aloft; he reported to Derby, and the two did not see eye to eye. They raised the balloon in the field behind El Pozo, hoping to get a good view of the Heights.

The battle began with an artillery duel. The Second Artillery's four 3.2-inch guns lined up on a hill by El Pozo before dawn. Crane, Davis, Scovel, and others gathered nearby; Wood, Roosevelt, and the Rough Riders watched behind the guns. They began firing at eight a.m. At first it seemed the Spaniards would not answer: "Have they, then, no artillery?" asked a Swedish attaché. The answer came as a peculiar whistle overhead. It exploded, followed by a second and third; shrapnel rained down. A piece hit Roosevelt's wrist and raised "a bump about as big as a hickory nut." The Rough Riders and reporters sprinted down the far side of the hill. The balloon was hauled down. The sketch artist Howard Chandler Christy was trapped in a tree by the battery: he watched a shell explode before a hut that was filled with Cuban guerrillas, tearing the leg off "one poor fellow." A second shell pierced the roof, and Cubans were "blown through the windows and door."

The duel lasted forty-five minutes: the balloon was again hoisted up, away from El Pozo. Derby rode in the basket beside Maxfield, who trained his binoculars on San Juan Hill. Although left out of most histories, a third man rode with them—the telegrapher, Sergeant Thomas C. Boone of Springfield, Massachusetts. Maxfield spotted few Spanish soldiers and could not find the battery. No reinforcements marched from Santiago. Below, the first troops moved west along the Royal Road and were swallowed by jungle. Sergeant Boone's telegraph apparently did not work, so Derby weighted a note for Shafter and dropped it over the side. Maxfield smiled: his balloon was a success, and it was pleasant up there. His woolgathering ended when Derby asked how long it would take to move the balloon halfway down the road; Maxfield thought the idea mad. Mausers had a two-mile range, he said: another half mile closer and bullets would riddle the great sphere. Derby would not be swayed. The balloon was hauled down to treetop level; members of the balloon detail shouldered guide ropes and joined the slow river of troops trudging forward.

Reporters had crawled back up El Pozo: from this height, the advance resembled a parade of toys. The Cubans led off, followed by the Buffalo Soldiers of the Ninth and Tenth cavalries and the Rough Riders. Though Pershing and Roosevelt rode among them, everyone else was afoot; their four Gatling guns came last, dragged by mules. The road was usually about ten feet across, Davis wrote, though it sometimes opened up "as wide as Broadway." Traffic jams were common, but the bordering mud was so "impenetrable" that no wise man considered leaving the road.

The balloon followed the Gatling guns. A British reporter on El Pozo likened it to a glorified kite flown by children: "Two men held it down by a cross bar, and two men walked in front of it holding stays." The rest of the Signal Corps girdled this group, lending support and delivering Derby's messages. Crane watched the balloon skim the treetops: "There it was—huge, fat, yellow, quivering—being dragged straight into a zone of fire that would surely ruin it."

Behind them trudged the infantry, the Seventy-First New York in the lead. Charles Post slogged among them. The march was "halt and move forward; it never changed." Overhead he heard "odd" little sounds, "not quite a click and not quite a whine, and now and again a *buzz* when a Spanish bullet smashed into a tree." Up ahead he heard the *crash-bang!* of American cannons and the mild *plop* of a Spanish shell. "I felt a tenseness in my throat, a dryness that was not a thirst, and little chilly surges in my stomach that no red-flannel bellyband could warm."

The Twenty-Fourth brought up the rear. Two white regiments—the Ninth and Thirteenth—marched with them, all part of the Third Brigade under Colonel Charles Wikoff. Neither Fagen nor Calloway left a written account, but Corporal John R. Conn, also of Company H, wrote a long letter to his sister that was published in the Washington *Evening Star.* He heard American cannons crashing to his left; on the right, gunfire from El Caney. They advanced a mile until the *zip* of small arms grew more distinct; they passed the first wounded—Cubans, who'd been in the lead. A wounded officer lay in a hammock, hit in the groin with a shell fragment; blood dripped from him, slow and steady. He ground his teeth and tried not to groan.

Around eleven a.m. Derby's balloon reached a meadow where a small creek crossed the Royal Road. Its handlers tried to raise it over the trees but in the process blocked the march of everyone behind them. The balloon ascended, slightly higher than the treetops, but caught in the branches and could rise no higher. Even so, Maxfield spotted two new details. First, the Spaniards held San Juan Hill with more troops than earlier thought. Second, a narrow trail branched to the left before this meadow: this offered an alternate route to the San Juan River.

That was all they learned. As Maxfield predicted, the balloon proved too tempting, and soon every Mauser and cannon on the Heights tried to shoot it down. Worse, the Spaniards guessed that the U.S. troops passed beneath it, and the resultant metal rain turned the Royal Road into the world's deadliest highway. Derby looked down and informed the Tenth Cavalry that Spaniards were shooting at them; the Buffalo Soldiers were keenly aware of this, and the epithets hurled back at him "were not very complimentary," Pershing said. Leonard Wood was less charitable: Derby "caused the loss of many lives," he wrote. "It was one of the most ill-judged and idiotic moments I ever witnessed." From his post on El Pozo, Crane concluded that the fire was directed by a lone Spanish officer who walked along the trench rim wearing a panama hat and "gesticulating at times with a walking stick." It was the strangest sight of his life—"that symbol, that quaint figure of Mars." Davis focused on the carnage below: "Our troopers could not retreat, as the trail for two miles behind them was wedged with men. They could not remain where they were, for they were being shot to pieces."

The balloon came down in a heap, pierced in two hundred places. Hydrogen whooshed out, and "we came down with a rush, striking a tree alongside of a creek, throwing us out," Sergeant Boone recalled. Derby and Maxfield leaped free, but Boone was not so lucky. As he fell, an anchor pierced his abdomen; he dangled for "what seemed a lifetime" before falling into the creek "with water up to my shoulders." On the ground, three in the Signal detachment were killed and another four wounded—fully a third of the squad. Someone pulled Boone from the creek; though badly hurt, "owing to the excitement of the time, I did not notice the pain."

In addition to fire from the Heights, hidden sharpshooters sniped as they had at El Caney. While Davis dodged up the road to the front, Crane stayed on El Pozo, preferring a more clinical view. Perhaps no better moment defined each man: Davis, the man of action, guided by gut instinct;

Crane, the falcon's eye floating above. Davis passed a surgeon at work by the stream, "one eye cast aloft at the trees." Every second man seemed wounded or killed; they lay beneath a bush—where "they had crawled with the strange idea it would protect them"—or along the riverbank, "lapping up water with the eagerness of thirsty dogs." It was the first time American troops had encountered "the enlarged lethal zone of the twentieth-century battlefield," wrote the military historian Graham Cosmas, and commanders were amazed by "the absence of cries or groans." The "dull thud of the bullet" was followed by an exclamation of surprise. Then the man died.

Those units in front of the fallen balloon reached the San Juan River between eleven a.m. and noon. The dismounted cavalry began to string out in a long line to the right, along the wooded bank at the foot of Kettle Hill. The units mixed together in the underbrush and tall grass, Buffalo Soldiers of the Tenth Cavalry shoulder to shoulder with Rough Riders. Each officer or soldier highest in rank took charge of the group around him. They all awaited word to charge, but the infantry must deploy to the left, in front of San Juan Hill and beyond; all they could do was lie still and pray. The air above was a haze of bullets; they couldn't return fire because, at this low angle, the Spaniards were well-protected in their trenches. Standing up seemed certain death, but some officers tempted it in the Napoleonic belief that disregard for danger raised men's morale.

To the right, Hoffman Philip's beloved captain Bucky O'Neill strolled before A Troop, a cigarette dangling from his lips. His men begged him to lie flat; a sergeant cried, "Captain, a bullet is sure to hit you." O'Neill plucked out the cigarette, expelled a cloud of smoke, and, according to Roosevelt, said, "Sergeant, the Spanish bullet isn't made that will kill me." As the words passed his lips, a Mauser round took him down. But according to the eyewitness Arthur Tuttle of A Troop, O'Neill had just asked an officer where he thought the gunfire originated. As he turned on his heel, the bullet found him, entering his mouth, exiting the back of his head.

O'Neill's death unleashed pandemonium. "The sound of the bullet was that of a loud slap," Hoffman Philip recalled. He and others dragged O'Neill under a tree, becoming targets themselves. Some were mowed down. "Our stricken captain did not speak," Philip said. "The handsome eyes opened as if in surprise, and he died." An officer rode up and told Philip to tell his commander of O'Neill's death. This means that Roosevelt did not witness it, despite his words otherwise. Philip stepped over troopers "prostrate in the long yellow grass" and found Roosevelt circled by mortality. His orderly, "a brave young Harvard boy," dropped; Roosevelt told his replacement to go back along the trail and "ask whatever general he came across if I could not advance, as my men were being much cut up." The replacement stood, saluted, and pitched forward across Roosevelt's knees, a bullet piercing his throat. Philip passed on his message and ran back, hoping a bullet would not find him, too.

For sixty interminable minutes, the infantry filled in the line before San Juan Hill and farther left, hoping to envelop the Spanish flank and shoot down the length of its trenches. The Sixth and Sixteenth groped through head-high brush until they reached a sunken trail. This made a natural trench, and they fired back, one of the few segments able to do so. Barbed wire lined this trench, and a Cuban rebel cut some gaps with his machete. When the Regulars crawled through the gap and started shooting en masse, it gave them away. The Spaniards fired back: over the next ten minutes, before the Regulars returned to the sunken road, they lost almost one-quarter of the 163 men and officers in this segment.

This left the units deployed to the far left. The fastest way to get there was up the narrow trail discovered by the doomed balloon. The Seventy-First New York trudged along the track, "as narrow as a cowpath," when shrapnel burst overhead. A dozen men fell. Private Post kept going. A "weaving, shuffling mass of men" pressed forward until a soldier would "seem to trip and then sink down, badly hurt or killed." Another gave "a sudden jerk" and crawled "into the jungle growth to get out of the way." This was not how Post had pictured war: men didn't die, arms spread wide, supplicating the gods. Instead, they "just sank down, crumpled and wilted." Flies buzzed and "the little birds chirped overhead," but just ahead a man was shot four times between the knee and thigh, grunted "Je-e-sus," and fell. Post and a friend hauled the poor man to the bushes; they heard their captain and headed that way. A young West Pointer lay dead, and "ants were already crawling" on his eyes. The trail became a green tunnel, the ground slick with mud and blood, sides piled with fallen men. Brigadier General James Kent, commander of the First Division, tried to move them up, but they seemed frozen in place. He dragged them off the trail to make way for the Regulars.

Fear bonds all soldiers, linking them through history. A Prussian officer during the Seven Years' War recalled terrified Russian gunners who hid beneath their cannons and "let themselves be massacred"; a British officer at Waterloo saw men whose "senses seemed to have left them." The *World* later accused the Seventy-First of cowardice, and Roosevelt said that no Rough Rider would sleep in the same grave with "the cowardly dead of the 71st." But collective panic spreads fast when neither flight nor fight seems possible. Good leadership might snap men out of it, but in the Seventy-First, officers panicked just like the rank and file.

As the Seventy-First disintegrated, the Third Brigade moved up, a mix of the Ninth, Thirteenth, and Twenty-Fourth infantries commanded by Colonel Charles Wikoff. The Buffalo Soldiers hustled down the green tunnel; their regimental chaplain had exhorted them, "Quit yourself like men and fight," and they now found themselves hopping over prostrate New Yorkers to reach the same sunken road sheltering the Sixth and Sixteenth. "It was terrible," Corporal Conn told his sister, "just one continual roar of small arms, cannon, and bursting shells." Wikoff ordered the Twenty-Fourth to "move forward 150 yards and lie down," but to do so they must cut through the barbed wire, the most complicated stretch of fence Conn had ever seen: five to nine wires laced and twisted between wooden posts, these pounded into the earth at 2½-to-4-foot intervals. Officers and noncoms may have been targeted, because they all began to fall. The first was Sergeant B. T. Brown, just beyond the riverbank. Then Colonel Wikoff, killed as he formed the line. A lieutenant colonel succeeded him and fell within five minutes; a second lieutenant colonel was given command when a Mauser found him. After that, each man became his own commander.

It was shortly after one p.m. Stephen Bonsal had made it to the front, and time stood still. The lethal landscape seemed imbued with wonder. The blockhouses rose straight up, "wreathed in the gorgeous red clusters" of the royal poinciana, locally called the "flamboyant tree":

> Now and again a gleam of sunlight upon a rifle and the high-crowned guano hat of a Spanish soldier fascinate your gaze. You listen as in

> a dream to the quick, insistent tone of the orders, for the Spaniards are firing in volleys and not at will, and again you rub your eyes and smile incredulously, for the sun is shining peacefully on the heights, and there is not a speck of smoke anywhere to be seen to tell you from whence the firing comes.

The Spanish volleys erupted in such precise unison they seemed delivered "by some quick-firing automaton." The lone metallic click of an American Springfield snapped back in reply.

Until the infantry came up, the Spaniards on the Heights hardly believed they were under fire. But when the Third Brigade arrived and almost two thousand men began firing, they knew they were outnumbered. Earlier, their artillery had run out of shrapnel shells, their most effective defense; now the massed Americans firing from their middle and far left thinned their numbers. At about 1:15 p.m., three of Captain John Parker's four Gatling guns were unlimbered west of the Royal Road and for the next eight minutes cranked torrents of fire straight at the enemy's trenches. The Spaniards fired back en masse, killing one Gatling crewman and wounding another, but their fire grew sporadic. Americans watched as enemy troops ran to the rear.

No one really knows when the charge began, but most place it between 1:15 and 1:30 p.m. Each part of the line felt that it had started the charge. Lieutenant Miley kept sending updates to Shafter, but his messengers got delayed, and he finally ordered the attack himself. On the left, Corporal Conn of the Twenty-Fourth recalled that someone said, "'Let us charge,' and someone sounded 'Let us charge' on a bugle." They rushed forward like a "pack of demons." The military historian Graham Cosmas thinks the middle "initiated what came to be called the charge." If anything, it resembles the synchronous dance of starlings wheeling in flight, or a stampede. "It was as inevitable," wrote Richard Harding Davis "as the rising tide."

In general, the infantry in the middle and left charged straight up San Juan Hill while the cavalry to the right engulfed Kettle Hill, then swerved left to catch the infantry. Units moved at varying speeds, some running ahead, some walking or jogging, stopping now and then to fire. Some paused to regroup or rest, then plunged on. Casualties were heavy at first, but grew lighter as troops reached San Juan's base; to shoot them, Spaniards must lean forward out of their trenches, which made them vulnerable. With that, "the battle was practically won," said Captain J. B. Goe of the Thirteenth. The various units swarmed over the top soon after 1:30 p.m. By then, the fortifications were nearly deserted, save a few Spanish diehards, the wounded, and the dead.

Perspective was everything. Crane watched from El Pozo when someone yelled, "By God, there go our boys up the hill!" He saw "a thin line of black figures" disappear beneath some trees and then start to ascend. Some black dots stopped and no longer moved. "It was the best moment of anybody's life," he said. A British reporter standing beside him cried, "It's impossible. It's plucky, you know! By Gawd, it's plucky! But *they can't do it!* It will simply be a hell of a slaughter with no good coming out of it." Crane felt swept up in the moment's "patriotic insanity," but Davis, who'd returned to El Pozo, felt engulfed by the sheer waste of lives. "It seemed as if someone had made an awful and terrible mistake," he said. Though he would later recast the scene in glory, that's not how he felt at the moment. "You felt that someone had blundered and that these few men were blindly following out some madman's mad order. It was not heroic then, it seemed merely terribly pathetic. The pity of it, the folly of such a sacrifice was what held you."

To Stephen Bonsal, the charge "resembled nothing so much as a great wave sweeping slowly in from the sea." In some places, the wave "grew smaller and thinner, and now and again would subside and seemed to dissolve altogether." His eyes fixed on the Sixth, moving toward the main blockhouse. Sometimes its line moved ahead, leaving behind the "little clump of blue" of the dead and wounded; sometimes he heard a bugler play "to the charge"—with his last breath, he would learn. Above this pulsed the "unceasing 'rup rup' of the . . . almost mechanical musketry fire." The wave thinned to a point; he could count on one hand the men in its vanguard, "and even as you counted they grew fewer." Half a dozen made it, and Bonsal expected to watch them be mowed down, but by then, the Spaniards had retreated, and "in no instance did our line come into closer contact with the retreating Spaniards than from 100 to 150 yards."

When Corporal Conn gained the top, he saw "piles of dead and wounded Spaniards" around him. It seemed "almost impossible that civilized men could so recklessly destroy each other." On the opposite end of the line, Hoffman Philip heard a clamor and saw Roosevelt on his horse, the "only mounted man in sight." Troop A rose around him, and with "yells and cowboy whoops," they all charged up Kettle Hill. One chaplain was shot through the head as he prayed over a dying soldier; he grew delirious, and two men had to hold him down. Buffalo Soldiers of the Ninth and Tenth cavalries got mixed with the Rough Riders. Two lieutenants dropped almost simultaneously: Lieutenant W. H. Smith, shot in the head; Lieutenant W. E. Shipp, hit near the heart. But Lieutenant Pershing survived: his men flowed over and to the left of Kettle Hill, skirted the lake, then held up "as the shells from our own batteries were bursting too close in front of us." This lifted, and "the lines made the last dash and the hill was taken by storm." In the elation that followed, men "threw their arms about each other, and generally behaved wildly quite regardless of rank." Pershing watched as one of his men "gently raised the head of a Spanish lieutenant and gave him the last drop of water from his canteen."

Of the many accounts, only Roosevelt's professes to see everything. He paints himself possessed by an inner berserker, that famous "crowded hour" when "all men who feel any power of joy in battle know what it is like when the wolf races in the heart." At times in *The Rough Riders*, he seems to conquer the Heights alone. He spurs his horse up Kettle Hill, jumps off at a wire fence, turns Little Texas loose, and keeps running. Near the top, two Spaniards emerge from a trench, and his last surviving orderly, the huge Henry Bradshaw, shoots them down. Roosevelt peers across the valley where the infantry charged up San Juan Hill. He wants to be there. He shouts for his men, leaps over a low fence, and runs into the valley separating the hills. After a hundred yards, he looks back: five men have followed, two of them wounded. He runs back and shrieks, "*Are you cowards?*" They hadn't heard his command to charge, they say. General Samuel Sumner arrives, so Roosevelt appeals to a higher power and Sumner orders them on. Roosevelt sprints again to the valley, and several regiments follow. He yells to Bradshaw, "Holy Godfrey, what fun!" Down past the lake, a spent bullet strikes his hand. This is his second minor wound—a first occurred up Kettle Hill as a bullet grazed his elbow. He raises his hand and shouts, "I've got it again, boys, I've got it!" He and

Bradshaw gain the Heights, and two more Spaniards pop up from a trench "not ten yards away" and fire. Roosevelt draws his Colt .45 revolver and fires back, "missing the first and killing the second." The story evolves with time. The man, whom he describes as an officer, "doubled-up" like a "jack-rabbit," but where at first he says he shoots him in the back, he later says he shot him "in the left breast as he turned." He encounters Rough Rider Bob Ferguson, an old family friend, and the two walk through the trenches, stepping over the bodies. "Look at these damn Spanish dead!" Teddy exclaims.

The account beggars belief, for several reasons. We've already encountered Roosevelt's loose commitment to truth in his tale of the SS *Yucatan*, his excuse for the ambush at Las Guásimas, and his criticism of officers spending nights in the Pleasure Dome. His account puts the Rough Riders up front, with him in the lead, while the accounts of Crane and others describe it as a shifting line, with no one person or unit ever up front for long. Roosevelt described the final charge as a triumph for his men, when actually it almost destroyed them—a fact absent in most histories. As they ran up the slope, they found themselves trapped by Spanish fire from all sides. Again the Tenth Cavalry bailed them out, with help from the Ninth. According to a New York correspondent, the Buffalo Soldiers rushed forward firing, leaving their dead and wounded. "Their coolness was superb," he said, "and their courage aroused the admiration of their comrades." Rough Rider Frank Knox, the future secretary of the navy, became separated from his troop and fought with the Tenth during the charge; they were the "bravest men he had ever seen."

Roosevelt also left this from his account, though perhaps it can be forgiven. Memory is fallible when life and death compress around you. Few soldiers adopt the long view in their accounts: their recollections proceed like quick movie cuts, filled with the horrible and the absurd. One's memory seemed dreamlike, said Corporal Conn to his sister, a series of snapshots "disconnected in time and space." Less forgivable were the lies Roosevelt told about the black soldiers who saved him. It didn't start that way. Not long after the battle, he said, "I wish no better men beside me in battle than these colored troops showed themselves to be." By that time, he planned to write of the war, and he added, "I shall have much to say about them."

He did, but not in the way he intimated. When Roosevelt wrote his 1899 *Scribner's* account, he'd read the assertion by *The Washington Post* that at Las Guásimas the "Rough Riders would have been exterminated" if not for the charge of the Tenth Cavalry. That could not stand. Roosevelt would counter that, although the black soldiers were brave, they were "peculiarly dependent upon their white officers." True, some excellent noncoms rose from the ranks, "but this cannot be expected normally, nor is it fair to expect it." White sergeants could carry on a fight by themselves should their officers die or be wounded, but not so with "colored troops": they always needed the steady, guiding hand of a white officer, he said.

Black veterans considered this a slap in the face: the comment even incensed the generally peaceful chaplain Theophilus Steward. Roosevelt's descriptions of black soldiers' "devotion" and "faithfulness" to their white officers "might well fit an affectionate dog." This "undependability" contradicted historical record. For their heroism in Cuba, black Regulars were awarded twenty-six Certificates of Merit and five Congressional Medals of Honor. Sergeant George Berry, a thirty-year veteran of the Tenth, planted his colors and that of the white Third Cavalry on San Juan Hill. In the assault on the left, command often fell to black noncoms. Many observers echoed Richard Harding Davis that "the negro soldiers established themselves as fighting men."

But such writers did not have ulterior motives. Roosevelt identified San Juan Hill as the pinnacle of his "crowded hour": it was the moment that made him a hero and propelled him to the kind of heights he whispered about only to Edith before the war. Thus, the narrative must be burnished constantly. But a counternarrative unfolded too, one centered on the Tenth Cavalry. In the weeks and months following Cuba, the tale that black cavalrymen saved the Rough Riders at Las Guásimas and San Juan Heights became more prominent; even Rough Riders didn't contradict the stories, which only served to bolster them.

Such calumny must be squelched, and by 1899 Roosevelt tried to rewrite history. During the charge up the Heights, none of "the white regulars or Rough Riders showed the slightest sign of weakening, but under the strain the colored infantrymen (who had none of their officers) began to get a little uneasy and to drift to the rear, either helping wounded men, or saying that they wished to find their own regiments." This would not do, Roosevelt said: "I jumped up, and walking a few yards to the rear, drew my revolver, halted the retreating soldiers," and promised to shoot if they continued. "This was the end of the trouble," Roosevelt bragged; the "smoked Yankees . . . flashed their white teeth at one another, as they broke into broad grins," and remained.

Once again, Roosevelt abandoned the truth for something self-serving. Minutes after this allegedly took place, Sergeant Presley Holliday of the Tenth explained to Roosevelt that the Buffalo Soldiers *and* several Rough Riders had been ordered back for rations and entrenching tools. "Everyone who saw the incident knew the Colonel was mistaken," Holliday wrote to *The New York Age* in May 1899. The next day, "the colonel came to the line of the Tenth," said he'd realized his mistake, and apologized. That he now repeated the story uncorrected was "uncalled for and uncharitable." Harry Clay Smith of the black *Cleveland Gazette* said that this proved that Roosevelt was not above magnifying his own deeds at the expense of black veterans. The story would not disappear: when the Reverend William Scott of Woburn, Massachusetts, asked his black congregants, "Does [Roosevelt] tell the truth?" they yelled back, "No; he is a liar!"

Frederic Remington's famous *Charge of the Rough Riders at San Juan Hill* accomplished with visuals what Roosevelt did with words. It captures the moment when Regulars and Rough Riders charge up Kettle Hill. Roosevelt, the only man on a horse, is in the background but placed in a way that draws attention. Close scrutiny reveals a single black soldier, bareheaded, dressed in his regulation blues but obscured by Rough Riders around him. Though placed in the very center of the composition, he is easy to miss. He is almost invisible.

By two p.m. the charge had ended, but not the battle. Americans exchanged an impossible situation in the valley for a perilous one on top: they were strung so thinly along the Spanish entrenchments that a countercharge would have swept them away. The success at San Juan and El Caney had cost Fifth Corps 220 men and officers killed and 1,300 wounded, compared with the Spanish losses of 550 officers and men killed or wounded and another 100 captured. The hard fighting left the Americans shaken, and now the richest nation on earth could provide only three ambulances for the wounded. The Spaniards had retreated to their second line of defense and would keep shooting all afternoon. A suicidal charge by Linares's mounted guerrillas saved a Krupp gun left behind. Three companies of Puerto Ricans and others maintained a steady fire, pushing back any Americans who tried to move forward. Linares himself was severely wounded and lost an arm; members of his staff and other high-ranking officers were wounded or killed. Linares turned over field command to Santiago's military governor, Major General José Toral y Velázquez, who wrote the definitive account of the battle from the Spanish point of view.

With night, they could see Santiago's twinkling lights: it was evident that they were still very far away. One had to keep low, for by the full moon "you could see quite as plainly, and perhaps more distinctly, than by sunlight," Stephen Bonsal said. Joe Wheeler, who'd returned from illness to be appointed second-in-command, believed that with present troop numbers, Santiago's defenses were too strong to storm: even with reinforcements, Americans would lose 3,000 men, he said. Shafter agreed. No American realized how few Spaniards had faced them that day. Shafter estimated the number of defenders at about 12,000. The true number had been around 500.

A day that started with fervor and hope ended in depression and gloom. Those on the front line contemplated the friends wounded and killed: Bucky O'Neill; Allyn Capron; those of the Twenty-Fourth with whom David Fagen had enlisted. A long siege looked likely, and with it many more deaths. A war council called that night by Shafter for his division commanders mentioned retreat, but no one ever owned up to first broaching the idea. In the end, they decided to hold on.

Even the ebullient Roosevelt fell prey to the mood. He blamed Shafter for the impasse, and in his mind, the overweight general would swell larger and larger as the cause of every ill. "General Shafter is a fool and I believe should be shot," he wrote. Never once in all his letters, speeches, and diaries did he ever consider his own role in the misery.

But the reality was inescapable: they'd achieved their military objective, only to find themselves severely compromised, even paralyzed. That night, as his soldiers dug deep, Roosevelt wrote a letter to Henry Cabot Lodge: "We have won so far at a very heavy cost; but—the Spaniards fight very hard, and charging their entrenchments against modern rifles is terrible." One can hear the pause, and the next statement must have broken his heart:

"We are within measurable distance of a terrible military disaster."

16

The Altar of Vanity

Thus began the dreaded siege. The Americans peered over their trenches at the Spaniards, six hundred yards downhill. That night, all movement was back to the field hospital; even now, bullets fell from the sky on surgeons and attendants. The thin line atop the Heights grew thinner as wounds, malaria, and dysentery took a toll: since commanders were loath to winnow their forces, the sick and wounded stayed on the line or picked their way down the hill alone.

So many had died to get here. Eighty-nine out of 490 Rough Riders were killed or wounded that day, a 15 percent casualty rate that Roosevelt boasted was the highest of any unit, "as it should be." He proved poor source material. The Tenth Cavalry had a 17 percent casualty rate; two infantry regiments lost more than a fifth of their men. Three of the fifty-four men with whom David Fagen enlisted in Tampa became casualties: Private Thomas Ledell of Company F, killed; Private Thomas Swift of Company E, wounded; Private Jesse Wilson of Company G, missing in action, presumed dead. That night, Shafter cabled the War Department: "Our casualties will be above 400." By July 3 the true number climbed to 225 dead and 1,384 wounded, almost exactly 10 percent of the 15,065 men in combat that day.

Dawn began with bursting shells. Firing would be heavy all day. July 2 was a costly stalemate: though the Spaniards did not try to retake the

Heights, they killed and wounded another 150 Americans. The exhausted Yankees could do little more than take cover. Around noon Lawton's men marched to the Rough Riders' right; García's Cubans completed a long horseshoe curve that stretched around to the north, further isolating Santiago.

Hoffman Philip's plight resembled that of every soldier. He'd not slept for two days; the rain streamed down; the sun baked him. Since cookfires drew gunfire, you ate cold hardtack and raw bacon. Take off your bush hat for fifteen minutes and black midges of sunstroke danced before your eyes. You sat ten hours in a cramped trench, drank muddy water, and sweated.

Philip's mind wandered. As he watched the navy shell Santiago's forts, he realized that the "martial ardor with which I had volunteered" had vanished. He became convinced that a Mauser bullet would find him as it had George Doherty and Bucky O'Neill. At one p.m. he crawled from his trench, awaited a break in the shooting, then sprinted downhill. He ate and finally slept, but rarely for long. "Every once in a while a shell would drop over among us and get a few of us," the trooper Frank Knox recalled.

Philip watched the dance of death in the field hospital below. A casualty's passage began at the operating tent, where eight to ten surgeons worked twenty-one hours straight, painted in blood. The smell of ether hung sick and sweet; once a man was cut and stitched, bearers took him to a tent for the wounded, but this was overflowing by Friday night, so newcomers were laid in the wet grass outside, still naked from the operating table. Hundreds lay in wait for transport back to Siboney. By midnight Saturday, that number exceeded eight hundred.

That same night, General Shafter felt his blood run cold. The Spaniards were more tenacious than expected, but the real enemy was this island—the disease, biting insects, land crabs, sun, and rain. The longer they stayed, the closer they came to ruin. Shortly before midnight on July 1, he wired Washington: "Had a very heavy engagement today, which lasted from 8 a.m. till sundown." He estimated that casualties would exceed four hundred, most of them wounded, but he received updated casualty figures soon afterward that left him stunned. At two a.m. he sent a second, more ominous wire: "I fear I have underestimated today's casualties. A large and thoroughly equipped hospital ship should be sent here at once to care for the wounded."

He then fell silent for thirty-four hours. Secretary Alger would call this silence "the darkest day of the war." The cabinet could only speculate: How could the army be bogged down a mere five miles from the fleet, or a starving city of forty thousand not be subdued if soldiers commanded the high ground? If the assault stalled, yellow fever would decimate the ranks, Spain would fight on, McKinley would be called incompetent. There seemed to be nothing that Washington could do.

Other commanders had doubts, too. Many junior officers wanted to return to Siboney, an option Shafter believed would destroy the corps' already fragile morale. All during July 2, rumors floated that reinforcements would reach Santiago that night. Shafter threatened to shell Santiago by ten a.m. the next morning unless the Spaniards surrendered, but General José Toral refused. He did, however, ask for a temporary truce to evacuate women and children. Shafter begged Sampson to take the harbor by force but Sampson refused. Should his ships hit mines and sink, they'd all be stranded there.

Thus began a high-stakes game of poker between the obese, aching Shafter and the lean, spectral Toral. Each man overestimated the other's hand. In interviews after surrender, Toral admitted that after his men abandoned the Heights, he had 80 left in the first line of trenches, 400 on the road behind them, and 400 in the hills of El Sueño, farther away. In total, 880 frontline defenders faced thousands of Americans. He believed that July 2 would bring the final assault, and that would be the end: he'd spent 750,000 rounds of ammo during the first attack, and had 1.5 million left, "enough for two more heavy fights." He begged Governor Blanco for help. "I could not defend the city, I could not escape," he later said. "I had no provisions, no clothing, no shoes for my men." Blanco replied, "Do the best you can, don't surrender."

But when the Americans did *not* attack, Toral read Shafter's mind. "The lack of impulsiveness on the U.S.'s part made [me] think they had lost heart." Perhaps time was his ally.

At six p.m. that Saturday, Shafter called together his senior officers—Wheeler, Kent, Lawton, and Bates—to decide on a course of action. Shafter, too weak to sit up, lay on a door freed from its hinges. He'd heard talk that the men were played out: "I have always thought I had the courage to admit an error if I made one, and if we fall back I will take all the blame." Bates, the junior of the four, advised withdrawal: his men held the extreme left, and he feared they might fold if stormed. But Kent, Wheeler, and Lawton advised staying. Shafter decided to hold pat but reassess the situation in twenty-four hours.

It was a waiting game. That night, the Rough Riders deepened their trenches; at daybreak on Sunday, July 3, Hoffman Philip sat at his cramped post and watched thousands of noncombatants leave Santiago along the Royal Road. "These wretched creatures took very little with them," Roosevelt observed. "They came through our lines and for the most part went to El Caney in our rear." When Philip heard the ceasefire signal, he thought it was safe and climbed atop the parapet to watch the refugees. He glanced to his right and realized that Spanish sharpshooters were aiming at him from forty yards away. "I recollect the sound of a harsh command from the officer on duty to get down from there, followed by a sharp pain in the head and a shattering fall into the mud at the bottom of the trench—then a pall of complete unconsciousness."

Firing started again. "This day, the 3rd, we suffered nothing, save having one man wounded by a sharpshooter," Roosevelt said. In fact, the day was momentous: the tide turned, and hundreds of Spaniards died. But Hoffman Philip would miss it. His ordeal had just begun.

The Resurrection of Hoffman Philip may be the grimmest document of the Splendid War: it is certainly the most unknown. Philip would have considered such a claim bombastic in a war that succumbed too often to that sin; instead, he titled his account "A Volunteer of 1898," the unpublished manuscript buried deep in the "Spanish American War Veterans Survey" of the U.S. Army's Military History Institute in Carlisle, Pennsylvania. As far as can be gathered, not even fragments have ever seen light. Philip would go far in life, serving from 1908 to 1910 as U.S. consul general in Ethiopia (then Abyssinia), then from 1917 to 1937 as U.S. ambassador in Colombia, Uruguay, Iran, Norway, and Chile. Though plenty of opportunity existed to publish his memoir, he never did. One does not rat on one's club.

The U.S. dead in Santiago numbered 385 killed in battle and 2,061 from "other causes," usually disease. Such figures imply forces outside man's influence, yet Philip's account suggests something darker: bureaucratic disregard, criminal neglect, mendacity, and a stonehearted vileness that could fit into Francisco Goya's eighty-two etchings titled *The Disasters of War.* Goya's work was designed as an assault upon the conscience; Philip's tale does the same. In both, luck—or fate—determines survival. Misery is common; cruelty, the coin of the realm. For the next two weeks, Philip exists beneath conscious regard. When he does beg for help, few can be bothered.

He regained consciousness on the night of the 3rd, having been out the whole day. Fever consumed him, and he felt too weak to move. He turned his head and realized he'd been carried to the hospital at the base of San Juan Hill. "How I had come there, I did not know." A "sickly moon" pierced the clouds. He grew aware of a clammy weight on his arm. In the dim light, he saw a dead soldier sprawled across him, the realization hitting him like an electric shock, and he jerked free. He sat up and realized that he lay in a "group of 7 or 8 prostrate forms," two shredded and lifeless, "the rest grievously wounded, covered with white bandages."

Although he never describes his injury, circumstances suggest that he'd been grazed in the head by the sharpshooter's bullet, the only wound he could find. George Kennan possibly stepped over him that afternoon. Five surgeons had worked their way through the writhing pile; they examined hundreds of soldiers lined up on the ground while awaiting their turn in surgery. "Some lay on the ground with swollen bellies," Kennan observed, a condition caused by "stricture of the urinary passage and distortion of the bladder caused by a gunshot wound." Some were paralyzed; some delirious; some, like Philip, "in a state of unconsciousness, coma, or collapse, and made no reply or sign of life when I offered them water or bread."

After surgery, most casualties were laid in long rows awaiting transport to Siboney. But Philip had been piled with the dead, and on waking, his only thought was "to get away." One hundred yards off, he spotted the white tents of Joe Wheeler's headquarters. William Astor Chanler, an old friend, was a captain on that staff, and his tent might be among them. Too weak to stand, Philip crawled on his hands and knees and discovered that someone had stolen his "fine Potbury and Lee hobnail boots." At the edge of the camp, he pondered "what I should do." Every tent looked alike; he was too weak to visit every one. He spotted an approaching sentry; maybe he could ask him. But instinct told him to hold up: "For some reason I feared and lay down until he passed." If the sentry noticed, he paid no mind, perhaps thinking he was one more of the dead.

Philip waited twice for the sentry to pass, then crawled down a tent row. He'd just reached the end when a private nearly tripped over him. The man looked like he'd seen a ghost. "Please," Philip croaked, "do you know where Captain Chanler's tent is?"

"Get the hell out of here, you!" the private screamed. Philip thought the man might kick him, so he crawled back to the pile of wounded and dead.

He passed out again. When he regained consciousness, he lay at the bottom of a pile of men being carted in a mule-driven wagon to Siboney. Cries and groans enveloped him. This was the army's torturous second stage of evacuation; Philip didn't remember the ride, but Stephen Bonsal witnessed one such transit and concluded that "many a man now dead would have survived had their journey been made with more suitable transportation." The miles to Siboney rattled over four creeks and spots where the Royal Road had washed out. Ambulances could handle the route: in those, each injured man had his own protected berth, rising tier after tier but designed to prevent overcrowding. But there were only three ambulances, and wagons were not built for such duty. They were built to carry barrels, heavy freight, and cartridge boxes; their beds were worn and ripped into jagged splinters, which pierced a man's flesh, "inflicting uncomfortable and in some cases serious wounds." The wounded had been loaded with care: those who could sit were propped up, those lying flat given plenty of room. Bedding and rubber blankets were tucked around them; upon starting, accommodations "did not seem too horrible." But the wagons drove blindly in the dark, tilting forward and back, side to side. Sometimes they plunged off the road into the stream. Men were shaken around like beans in a jar.

As Bonsal walked back to Siboney, he heard a wagon's slow, creaking approach and with it "a strange, low, moaning sound." As it passed him in the dark, he heard a man cry out, "Stop, stop! For God's sake, let me get out and die in the grass!" Suddenly the moon sailed from behind the trees, and he beheld a nightmare vision "so fantastic and so horrible that at times I have tried to dismiss it altogether from my mind." The wounded whom he'd seen so carefully loaded thirty minutes earlier were now heaped in "indescribable confusion." He couldn't believe his eyes: "There they lay, a squirming, writhing mass of naked, blood-stained, and bandaged limbs."

Luckily, Philip lay unconscious during his journey: the first thing he remembered was that moment the wagon stopped "with a sudden jerk, then silence." Men bearing lanterns and stretchers appeared from the dark; they laid the wounded, one by one, on the ground. Then, one by one, they bore them off into the shadows until he alone was left at this crossroads. "Don't leave me!" he cried. A voice came back through the night with "a tone of obtuse finality: 'You ain't wounded!'" It was the Voice of Judgment: he would be left here, in the dark, alone.

At least the teamster and his mules remained. But when Philip saw the driver unhitch the animals and lead them off, he cried out. "I begged him to tell me where we were and why I had been left on the ground."

"This is the hospital for the wounded," the teamster said. Since Philip bore no visible wounds, the stretcher-bearers would not take him in. And since the driver "had received no orders concerning me," he planned to leave him, too.

In a moment of electric clarity, Philip realized that there were no orders because he'd been piled among the corpses: "I might have been classified with the dead men." A wave of nausea struck. If he stayed here all night, he might join them, and no one would know that for a brief period, he'd been alive. He told the driver he was burning up and didn't know what to do. "There's a fever hospital only a quarter of a mile away," the man answered, but left the rest unspoken. The teamster eyed him, waiting.

Hoffman Philip understood. All during this war, he'd worn a chamois leather money belt next to his skin. He felt around: it was still there! He extracted a $10 gold piece and told the driver it was his if he helped him to the camp. The driver lifted him on a mule and guided it down the road while holding Philip steady. They came to a long line of dog tents in a low, marshy flat; they stopped outside the camp, and the driver refused to go farther. He pulled him from the mule and "[allowed] me to slip down into the wet grass." The gold piece changed hands, and the teamster "went off without a word."

Philip lay outside the camp in a timeless fugue: "I lay there in a sort of trance, too weak to move, even to think." Soon the sun rose, the heat making him desperate. He yelled for help, and a sentry walked up and asked what he wanted. Philip stammered that he might die. The sentry summoned two orderlies who after a while loaded him on a stretcher and passed through rows of tents, unsure where to deposit him. They finally thrust him into a tent with two others and hurried off. He closed his eyes and dropped into troubled dreams.

He woke that afternoon. A neighbor studied him. "Say, Bill," he said, mistaking Philip for someone else, "when did you git it?"

"Get what?"

"Why, the fucking measles, of course!" This was the quarantine tent for measles patients.

Philip screamed and threw himself from the tent. Measles was highly infectious, and thousands died worldwide. This war was like Coney Island's Madhouse: enter a room, and horror jumped out at you. He crawled away, "lay in the cruel sun," and passed out again.

More time passed—it was still day. The same day? He did not know. A doctor saw him while making his rounds: "He asked me some questions, felt my pulse, and looked grave." "*You're very sick*," he said, but the hospital was overcrowded, and the best he could do was place him in the shade of a "fine, big mango tree at the lower end of hospital limits." Philip nodded—at least he would be out of the sun. The doctor led him to the tree, then came back with a blanket and a dose of quinine, which seemed to lower his fever. He also brought a ration card, and with it he could draw some hardtack, unroasted coffee, raw bacon, and quinine each day.

Soon another two patients were brought to the mango tree. The hospital seemed to have expanded its borders with this informal little haven, and for the first time since he'd been shot, Philip felt he might survive. But he started to wonder: the sun and rain penetrated the branches; no one came with their rations. Sentries would pass; the three would cry out, but the sentries walked by.

Late that afternoon, he noticed an officer eyeing him. Philip called out and learned that he was Dr. Arthur Snyder of Georgetown, an old childhood friend. Snyder asked what he could do for him. Some socks would be nice, Philip answered: my feet are cold. Plus, some quinine for all of us under this tree. Snyder advised that it might be best if they stopped depending on the army but instead went to the Red Cross, where they didn't need ration cards or official charts, just voices to ask for aid. By then, Philip was the healthiest of the lot, so he visited a Red Cross storehouse close to the sea. He found provisions, blankets, clean clothing. He found canned meat! He took his treasures back to his delighted little band.

Dr. Snyder watched over him. The next day, an orderly delivered more quinine, said he looked very sick, and arranged to have him taken to a hospital ship where "I could get ice cream and fine care." But when the man walked off, the three realized that this meant they'd be sent home. Philip didn't want this, and neither did his pals, and they decided to return to their units, since they'd heard rumors that the final assault on Santiago would soon begin.

They planned their escape for that night, but they needed shoes. They came to the crossroads where Philip had been dumped and found a discarded heap of shoes and clothes from the dead. He found a pair of army boots, one filled with water and the other slit with a knife over the big toe. Both were turned in, as if the previous owner was pigeon-toed.

The trip up the Royal Road was slow but less torturous than going down. They learned the location of their units and all they'd missed while under the mango tree. They parted ways and wished one another luck. The day was at least July 11, the day the Rough Riders shifted from the siege line to the hills west of El Caney. Philip had been away for nearly two weeks: in that time, the first cases of yellow fever had been detected in Siboney. He'd gotten out just in time.

He found his troop on the road to El Caney, stumbled to the medical unit, and found Rob Church, a medic and friend. Church gawked "like I'd returned from the dead" and said he was damn lucky he hadn't been buried alive in a mass grave. This raises the possibility that some were, an unspoken horror never examined in any history. Church wondered whether Philip hadn't already contracted malaria when shot, which kicked in full-force when he lay with the dead; medical staffs had heard of malaria victims falling into comas so deep they could not be distinguished from the dead. Church took his temperature: it was still high, so he put Philip on a cot and gave him twenty grains of quinine: the dose made "my head feel like the proverbial block of wood." He was reissued arms, a new uniform, and better shoes, then placed on light duty.

Roosevelt hoped that a move to the hills would save his men from fever. But when Philip returned, more than half the Rough Riders were "dead or disabled by wounds and sickness," Roosevelt wrote. Soon afterward, dysentery ripped through the camp, worsening Philip's already weakened condition. Rob Church seems to have appointed himself Philip's personal angel. He dosed him with bismuth and led him into a long tent where beds were lined in rows; as he entered, "the men lying there near me had the semblance of being clothed in black trousers." The trousers flew up as he passed, then settled back—thick swarms of flies covering the men.

Philip turned in horror to Church, who took him to a dog tent. His bunkmate, named Wallace, was in the best of health. In two months, Wallace would die of fever. Only thanks to Church did Philip manage not to follow. The days dragged on. Before going home, he glimpsed himself in a mirror. He looked like a skeleton, like the *reconcentrados* he'd come to save.

The Splendid War of Herman Hoffman Philip was over.

On the day that Hoffman Philip got tossed among corpses, the Spanish admiral Pascual Cervera donned his pressed uniform, sipped the cup of hot chocolate brought by his orderly, and hailed the sun rising over Santiago Bay. He figured he'd be dead by the end of that day. Paintings and photos depict a pudgy, smiling presence who resembles Santa Claus in uniform; a good day for him ended with a Cuban cigar while listening to Spanish Romantic era composers on his gramophone. His career had been a steady rise through the dangerous reefs of Spanish politics, but some of his best memories involved years charting hundreds of islands off the Philippines. Even now, he liked to sit with a map in his stateroom and remember those crystal seas. He stood before the mirror and positioned his flat white sailor's cap precisely. Soon he must tell his men that many would not see the next morning. At least he'd have the honor of dying with them, he'd say.

The admiral had done all in his power to avoid this day. From the first, he'd argued that facing the Americans was suicide. His vessels' hulls were fouled with sea life, drastically cutting their speed. Nearly 85 percent of his ammunition was defective, and his fastest ship, the *Cristóbal Colón*, lacked heavy guns. No ship had the heavy armor plating of the American juggernauts; instead, they were decked and embellished with wood, lovely to look at, firetraps in war. On May 18 they'd slipped into Santiago Bay for coal and repairs, but when Schley blocked the channel, he knew he was doomed. The only question was when.

The fall of the Heights provided the answer. During that attack, Governor Blanco urged him to break from the bay or die trying. Cervera fought back: "I shall never be the one to decree the horrible and useless hecatomb which will be the only possible result of the sortie from here by main force, for I should consider myself responsible before God and history for the lives sacrificed on the altar of vanity, and not in the true defense of the country." He would *not* decree such a futile gesture to pride. It was up to Blanco "to decide whether I am to go out to suicide, dragging along with me those 2,000 sons of Spain."

Blanco took responsibility before daybreak on July 3. "In view of exhausted and serious condition of Santiago," Cervera must "go out immediately," he wired. At sunup, the admiral called his captains to his flagship, the *Infanta Maria Teresa*, for one last council of war. Blanco had ordered a sortie: they must head out as soon as their sailors returned from the siege line lest they lose the element of surprise. The U.S. ships would be aligned in a "great arc," with the *Texas* at the westernmost point. Between it and shore circled Schley's *Brooklyn*, their fastest ship, as well as the armed yacht *Gloucester*, helmed by Lieutenant Commander Richard Wainwright, former exec of the *Maine*. Their only chance lay in springing at the Americans before their boilers were up and they could hit top speed. The *Maria Teresa* would lead, heading straight for the *Brooklyn*; while the American squadron zeroed in on the flagship, the *Vizcaya* would lead the others west to Cienfuegos or Havana, cities not yet besieged.

Cervera's captains clasped hands when their admiral finished. They knew there was one end to this—"death and destruction, from which no power can save us," recalled the flagship's Captain Victor Concas. They denounced the Spanish "statesmen" who'd placed them in this position, and swore that if "anyone of us should survive, he would defend the memory of those who perished in the encounter."

Cervera fired his engines; he sealed a large package containing all official documents and had that delivered to the archbishop of Santiago. The prelate swore under oath to send it back if the admiral survived—or to his relatives if not. They set the breakout for four p.m., but the *Vizcaya*'s crew did not return until late. They'd already ruled out a night escape: the men needed rest, and the great searchlights of the American fleet would shine right in their eyes. Cervera opted for the morning.

Sunday, July 3, dawned with slight fog. Observers in the U.S. blockade had spotted six columns of smoke rising from the harbor the previous afternoon. This probably meant that Spanish boilers had fired up, but when nothing happened, they stood down. No one expected a sortie now. Admiral Sampson sent the battleship *Massachusetts* and tug *Suwanee* to Guantánamo to refuel; he sailed east to Siboney aboard the *New York* for a strategy session with Shafter. Sampson had a bad feeling: "If I leave, I'm sure something will happen," he said, but he passed it off to superstition. Most of the men wore their dress whites for church services. At 9:20 a.m., the *New York* passed out of signal range and Commodore Schley assumed command of the blockade. It had been six Sundays since he'd run his prey into this hole. Schley tipped back his chair on the bridge and said, "This is pretty slow."

Two and a half hours earlier, Captain Concas had taken a small gunboat close to the channel entrance to reconnoiter. The Americans were a little closer than usual, spread in an eight-mile arc, each ship about three miles away. He could not see the *Massachusetts* or *New York*, a good sign. Cervera delivered his final address, read on each ship by its captain. The "solemn moment of fighting" had come: each man must don his full-dress uniform, for there was no more solemn time to wear it "than when a soldier is going to die for his fatherland." All was deathly quiet. "My sons, the enemy is superior to us in strength, but they are not in courage. Hoist the flag and surrender no ship . . . May God receive our souls."

At 9:30 a.m. Spain's ships heaved anchor. They came down the channel one at a time, separated by ten minutes and six hundred yards. The *Maria Teresa* led off, followed by the *Vizcaya*, *Cristóbal Colón*, and *Oquendo*. The torpedo boats *Plutón* and *Furor* brought up the rear. They "came out as gaily as brides to the altar," one U.S. captain observed. Cervera stood in the forward tower by the pilot, Miguel Lopéz. As they emerged from the channel, he said, "Good-by, pilot; go now. Go, and be sure you let them pay you, because you have earned it well."

The next few minutes would present the Americans with a tragic and grand anachronism they'd never see again. Gongs sounded on every ship, bugles blared, watertight doors were secured. Captain Robley Evans of the *Iowa* had just finished breakfast with his son, a naval cadet, when the general alarm for action resounded. His son jumped to his feet: "Papa, the enemy's ships are coming out!" The *Iowa*'s guns were already firing before they reached the bridge. The AP correspondent George Edward Graham stood on the *Brooklyn*'s bridge near Schley and studied the emerging ships through his binoculars: "We saw what probably has not been witnessed since the days of the Armada," he wrote—ships steaming for deadly battle "but dressed as for a regal parade." Each ship spoke defiance, a final quixotic sacrifice to the ghosts of another era, from "their shining black hulls, with huge golden figureheads bearing the crest and coat-of-arms of Spain, to the tops of their masts where fluttered proudly the immense silken flags." The *Maria Teresa* made the right western turn past Diamond Bank when Captain Concas asked Cervera's permission to open fire. He assented, and Concas gave the order; the bugle blew the call for battle and Concas thought that this was the last echo of "four centuries of grandeur." "Poor Spain!" he cried. His "beloved admiral" nodded. Concas interpreted this to mean "he had done all that was possible to avert it." Given the circumstances, it might also be a quiet expression of despair.

On the *Brooklyn*, Schley glanced at his pocket watch: 9:35 a.m. "They will never get home," he told George Graham. He stood on a ledge next to the conning tower, where he could see the action and yell orders to the bridge. The *Maria Teresa* turned toward him even as he asked his navigator, Lieutenant Hodgson, the location of Sampson's flagship. "The *New York* is out of sight," Hodgson said. Schley simply smiled: he did not like the admiral. Now the glory Sampson had always sought would be his. Hodgson yelled the obvious: "Commodore, they are coming right at us!" Schley was transported: "Go right for them!" he replied.

Seven miles east, Captain Frank Chadwick of the *New York* heard distant gunfire. The rumble was followed by "a scurry on deck," then a call to battle stations. By the time Chadwick reached the bridge, the chief quartermaster yelled, "There comes another ship!" Sampson gave the order to turn the ship and steam back to the battle. Gunners stripped off their Sunday best. "For God's sake, get those engines going!" they yelled down the vents to the engine room. "Burn any old damn thing! Get us there!"

What followed would be a lopsided slaughter comparable to Dewey's in Manila Bay. Sampson's intent had always been to sink Cervera's ships in the channel mouth, but that was pointless now. One by one the Spanish ships turned west in an effort to escape; one by one the converging American ships chased them down. Even today, one can drive west along the road threading between the little rocky coves of the southern coast and green bordering bluffs and see the turret guns of the *Oquendo* and *Vizcaya* thrust like rusting monuments above the waves. Hurricanes might roll from the east, knock them loose, and churn the coral sediment filled with the bones of sailors into a new mixture. But they are always there.

The battle did not begin gracefully for the Americans. The ships zeroed in on the *Maria Teresa* as she charged at the *Brooklyn*; they fired at such close quarters that they risked friendly cross fire. By 10:05 a.m. the *Brooklyn* and *Teresa* had closed to six hundred yards: Cervera swung toward Schley as if to ram him, but then broke west with her consorts. The *Brooklyn* might have turned west with her, but in so doing would have exposed her starboard flank to a torpedo or a ramming blow, both fatal. Instead, she circled hard in a move that put her on a parallel course but a little behind. Sampson, even now fuming that Fate placed the battle in his rival's hands, later claimed that Schley ran. This was "silly twaddle," Schley replied.

The maneuver *did* carry the *Brooklyn* across the path of the *Texas*, which went hard astern. The smoke from the big guns hung so heavy that "we might as well have had a blanket tied over our heads," said Captain

John W. Philip. Suddenly a "whiff of breeze" lifted the smoke, and there, "as big as half a dozen Great Easterners," the *Brooklyn* seemed right on top of them. "Back both engines hard!" Philip cried down the tube to his engineers, and "in a twinkling" his ship "was racing against herself." The maneuver saved them, and the *Brooklyn* glided past. The *Texas* stopped dead in the water as the *Teresa* steamed away.

Once the Americans disentangled, the battle became a chase; for a few minutes, it looked like some of Cervera's ships might get away. Most of the Americans had been positioned four or five miles south or east of the channel when the chase started. Even the *Brooklyn*, the closest, was well astern. The *Brooklyn*, *Iowa*, and *Texas* paralleled the Spanish course, but a mile behind them to sea; the *Oregon* and armed yachts followed; the *New York* hurried to catch the vanishing battle. Cervera's squadron also had the advantage of emerging at full steam, while the Americans had only what was necessary to maneuver in a blockade. Columns of black smoke poured from their stacks as stokers shoveled frantically to build up pressure.

Some Spanish ships might have escaped, if not for their wooden decks. This made them lighter than the American ships, but also highly flammable, and the Americans were shooting with every gun. The residents of Santiago could hear the chase fading west; Americans in their siege lines, *mambisi* in the hills. In the course of the battle, not one Spanish ship was vitally wounded in its machinery or hull, but all were set afire. Forward motion fanned the flames; gunners served their guns as decks burned away beneath them.

The *Maria Teresa* was the first to go: witnesses believed she began burning within minutes of leaving the channel. A shell cut an auxiliary steampipe, scalding men to death and causing the ship to lose speed. Another shell burst one of the fire mains, making it impossible to fight the flames. The *Iowa* unleashed a starboard broadside with her 12-inch guns as it passed within 2,600 yards, and Captain Evans was certain "that I saw the shells strike the Spanish ship." Captain Concas was seriously wounded, so Cervera took command. Some ammo stored on deck exploded; the center of the ship became a mass of flames; a great tower of smoke rose from the stern. Cervera realized that his flagship was in real danger of blowing up, so at 10:35 a.m., an hour after emerging, he steered into a small cove called Punta Cabrera, six miles west of Morro Castle, and ran aground. The crew barely had time to leave. Explosions followed in quick succession. Cervera staggered ashore in his trousers and underwear.

The *Oquendo* was next. She'd been the fourth and last battleship to leave the channel; while the *Teresa* received the brunt of fire from closer Americans, the *Oquendo* was pummeled from 2,000 to 5,500 yards by the *Oregon*, *Texas*, *Iowa*, and *Indiana*. Fire blazed fore and aft; the interior was a furnace; one of her guns burst, disintegrating its crew. Captain Joaquín Lazaga steered for a rocky beach two miles west of the *Teresa*; 120 men, about a quarter of the ship's complement, were already dead or wounded, and Lazaga ordered abandon ship. He refused to leave the forecastle as they loaded the wounded into the only two lifeboats left intact. Suddenly he clutched his hands to his chest and fell to the deck, dying in that moment of a heart attack.

The two small torpedo destroyers that came out after the *Oquendo* were overwhelmed by the ships ganging up on the *Oquendo*. A shell landed smack in the *Furor*; smoke and steam rose up, but somehow she limped on. Lieutenant Commander Wainwright on J. P. Morgan's converted yacht *Gloucester* received the signal to go in and finish them; he closed to within six hundred yards and tore them to pieces with his light guns.

The *Plutón* ran on the rocks four miles west of Morro Castle and sank to deck level; the *Furor* lost control and steamed in circles. Someone waved a white rag. When Wainwright sent a lifeboat, his crewmen found a "horrible state of affairs." The ship was burning rapidly, and they took off what survivors they could. They cast off and started back: explosions wracked the sea behind them. The *Furor* flung up her bow and disappeared.

That left two cruisers—the *Vizcaya*, under Captain Antonio Eulate, and the *Cristóbal Colón*. The *Vizcaya* was slower, her hull so badly fouled that she could not make speed. The *Colón* sped ahead and fired twice at the *Iowa*, the first shell striking starboard a few feet above the waterline forward of the bridge, the second tearing a jagged hole forward of the first. The *Iowa* pulled out of the race, leaving the *Vizcaya* to the *Brooklyn*, *Oregon*, and *Texas*, finally back from her forced stop. The *Brooklyn* closed to 950 yards, and a duel ensued. A shell pierced one of the *Brooklyn*'s gun compartments, sheared a steel stanchion, wrecked a staircase, then exploded, injuring one. A second shell ripped through the forecastle, decapitating Yeoman George Ellis, who stood feet away from Schley calling off ranges to gun crews. "There was that low, moaning sound like a lost soul that a shell makes," wrote George Graham. "Then we saw Ellis's body waver and fall headless to the deck, while men wiped from their faces and clothes the brain that had just given us necessary information." Two crewmen picked up his body to heave overboard: in battle, mutilated corpses received such treatment so as not to demoralize the living. "Don't throw that body overboard," Schley yelled. "Take it below, and we'll give it a Christian burial." Twenty-five-year-old Ellis of Brooklyn would be the only American sea death this day.

Plenty of sailors died on the *Vizcaya*. American gunners landed repeated hits to her upper works; she shuddered every time. Fires broke out; water poured into the engineering compartment; their last gun was out of action. Captain Eulate made a last-ditch effort to ram the *Brooklyn*, but Schley veered off. Another steam pipe burst. A bow torpedo exploded in its tube, breaking open the entire bow like a jagged flower. Eulate was losing blood from wounds to his shoulders and head; he staggered to sick bay, had his wounds dressed, staggered back to the bridge, and convened the surviving officers. Was there anything more they could do "in the defense of our country and honor," he asked. *No*, they replied. It was just after 11 a.m., and Eulate turned his ship inshore toward a sandbar off Aserradero, close to García's headquarters. Just as she touched bottom, two tremendous explosions shook her to pieces. The men of the *Texas* cheered. "Don't cheer, boys!" Captain John Philip shouted. "The poor devils are dying!"

It became a rescue operation. The wounded *Iowa* could never catch the *Colón*, so Captain Evans cut his speed to save the *Vizcaya*'s crew. Many survivors stood in water up to their armpits; others swam to shore when, according to Evans, a dozen or more *mambisi* came to the water's edge and picked them off with their rifles. Other reporters concurred, including the AP reporter Chappie Goode aboard the approaching *New York*: he saw puffs of smoke from bushes alongshore, and a quartermaster beside him yelled, "Those Cubans are shooting them Spaniards!" But Cuban sources denied it then and deny it today, citing as evidence Cervera's report of the battle, in which he thanked Cubans and Americans alike for their conduct toward his shipwrecked sailors. Evans could see through his glasses that sharks, "made ravenous by the blood of the wounded," streamed into the cove and attacked the men. Captain Eulate was brought beside the *Iowa* in a boat and hoisted up in a chair; he was "covered with blood from three wounds," and a bloody handkerchief wrapped his head. When the chair settled, Eulate raised up, "unbuckled his sword belt, kissed the haft of his sword," and presented it to Evans as a mark of surrender. Evans gave it back, and his men cheered. Evans led the wounded captain to his cabin, and as they reached the companionway, Eulate turned and said, "Adios, *Vizcaya*!" As if on signal, the ship's forward magazine exploded, creating a smoke cloud visible for fifteen miles.

That left the *Colón*. As her consorts fell wounded, she forged on, "running like a greyhound for safety," John Philips said. For two hours, the *Brooklyn* and *Oregon* gave chase as the *Texas* huffed behind. This was a test of engines, not guns, and the "grim and silent" pursuit sped over a glassy sea. Yet the U.S. ships were newer and more powerful, and by 12:30 p.m. the *Colón* lay within range of the *Oregon*'s 13-inch guns. A roar erupted from its front turret; a fountain of water sprang directly astern the *Colón*. Given its position ahead and to the side, only one of the *Colón*'s smaller 6-inch guns could fire back. Soon, the *Oregon*'s shells geysered the sea before her bow. This was checkmate: all that could pass now was slaughter. Between 1:00 and 1:15 p.m., the *Colón* fired one shot leeward, struck her colors, and ran aground in the estuary of the Rio Tarquino, fifty miles west of Santiago.

The Battle of Santiago Bay was over. American losses totaled one dead and three wounded, all aboard the *Brooklyn*, hit more than thirty times. Out of 2,227 men, the Spanish sustained 323 officers and sailors killed, and another 151 wounded. The Americans took 1,813 prisoners; about 120 sailors made it back to Spanish lines. As the *Gloucester* searched for survivors, Wainwright spotted Cervera among his men onshore. "When I saw that gallant gentleman in his wringing wet underclothes, I felt as if I were a culprit," he said. He took him to the *Iowa*, where the crew swarmed over the turrets and superstructure. As Cervera stepped on deck, marines presented arms, and officers uncovered their heads. "And as the distinguished officer, who had lost more in one hour than any other man lost in modern times, stepped onto the quarterdeck," said Captain Evans, his crew "broke into cheers." At first Cervera didn't understand, but then the truth dawned. For a full minute, he stood in silence and bowed his head.

17

The Fear

Independence Day dawned with a surprise. At noon that Monday, Admiral Sampson's telegram announcing "his" victory arrived in Washington: "The fleet under my command offers the nation as a Fourth of July present the whole of Cervera's fleet. It attempted to escape at 9:30 this morning. At 2 the last ship, the *Cristóbal Colón*, had run ashore 75 miles west of Santiago and hauled down her colors." He'd been so far back in the pack that he got times and distances wrong, not that it mattered. Though the Battle of Santiago Bay was over, what Roosevelt called "the battle of the captains" began. When Winfield Schley reported the victory to Sampson, stony silence greeted him: "It is to be regretted that no word of congratulations, so much valued by men and officers on such occasions, issued from the flagship," Schley wrote. The Sampson-Schley controversy over division of laurels obsessed the nation, embittered officers, and revealed the navy's dirty laundry in ways that might otherwise have stayed hidden.

In time, Schley endeared himself by saying the "victory seems big enough for all of us." Yet that victory hinted at real problems, the worst of which was the navy's poor hit ratio. Of 9,433 shells fired during the battle, investigators found evidence of 122 strikes. Even if that number doubled, navy shooting was abysmal. The U.S. won, not because of accurate marksmanship, but because the shells that *did* hit started fires on the enemy's wood decking. U.S. losses were tiny because Spanish marksmanship was so bad.

On July 4, crowds gathered in Santiago, Havana, and smaller cities to hear Governor Blanco's mournful wire. "Fortune," he wrote, "does not always favor the brave." Cervera's squadron "has just performed the greatest of deeds of heroism," but succumbed to a force "three times as large." Though a hard blow, "it would be unworthy of Spanish hearts to despair." Spain's newspapers called for a new government; rumors of riots spread. Within a week, the Crown declared martial law: it censored the press and limited the rights of all citizens.

In Washington, the news arrived "like splendid sunlight bursting through low-hanging clouds." The chief executive once compared to a cream-filled pastry was now knighted the "war president." That day, he asked Sampson to convey to his fleet "the grateful thanks and appreciation of the nation." Ambassador Hay in London wired McKinley his fulsome praise: "We have never in all our history had the standing in the world we have now, and this, I am sure, is greatly due to the unfailing dignity, firmness, and wisdom you have shown in every emergency of the past year."

The victories of July 1 and 3 marked a shift in national thinking. On July 3, before victory, Governor William O. Bradley of Kentucky worried that the war would turn Americans into "an aggressive and war-waging people." He predicted that "the acquisition of one piece of territory begets a desire for another, and in the end an effort to take by force that which justly belongs to others will lead to the loss of all we have." But success makes believers of everyone. With Sampson's wire, papers coast-to-coast hailed our new grandeur. The recent victories proved that God was on our side, McKinley declared. The Reverend J. F. Carson of Brooklyn's Central Presbyterian Church compared our conquests to Joshua's: if God's plan required us to plant the Stars and Stripes in "Spain itself, America will do it." Another pastor claimed that the victories proved "Anglo-Saxons now hold the perfect type of divinity." *The Chicago Times-Herald* thundered that "the United States owes it to civilization" to spread across the world.

On July 4 Shafter gazed down on Santiago. The original reason to attack had been to capture the fleet: take that, and nothing could stop the army and navy as they rolled west, swallowing cities and storehouses, feeding the hungry, finally surrounding Havana, the ultimate prize. Now Santiago was steeped in uncertainty. If Shafter bypassed the city entirely, he left an enemy army of thousands at his rear. He could attack and throw his men into slaughter or lay siege and expose them to hurricane season and annihilation by disease.

Sickness was already there. On July 4 Stephen Bonsal rode to the trenches, expecting festivities. Instead, soldiers crawled from their "noisome" trenches, "their cheeks hollow and sunken, their skin dry and cracking like parchment." A virulent form of "Cuban malarial fever" called *calenture* ravaged the ranks; dysentery was rampant owing to a dearth of clean water.

Correspondents succumbed, too. Harry Scovel was too weak to leave his hammock; when his wife, Frances, found him in a hut with two colleagues, she decided to care for them rather than sail to Jamaica as planned. The only *World* reporter healthy enough to work was Francis Nichols, whose stories pulled no punches about army medical care. All medicines were scarce; quinine pills sold for several dollars apiece; ambulances languished in ships' holds. Why? These were questions "men have asked as they died out in the cactus under the blazing sun," he wrote. "Someone has blundered and blundered badly."

Two days earlier, Clara Barton counted "one hundred to two hundred men" in Siboney's hospital camp, and that number grew. Red Cross nurses staffed the tents, and Janet Jennings told of "going on duty for 24 hours, caring for 40 patients" at a time. Nurses cooked gruel and a stewed-prune-and-apple concoction called "Red Cross cider." Barton was in the thick of it, clad in her calico skirt and white apron, working sixteen to eighteen hours daily, changing bandages, pressing ice to fevered foreheads as she had in the Civil War: "It did not seem to be me, and still I seemed to know how to do it." She'd thought those days were over. How naïve she'd been.

That night in Siboney, she was handed a note from George Kennan. By Shafter's order, she was to seize empty wagons and bring medical stores to the main field hospital. The next morning, she and her staff commandeered an army wagon, emptied the bales of hay meant for pack animals, and filled the bed with food and supplies. It took four hours to travel the Royal Road; they heard the receding booms of Cervera's ruin and came upon a vast, grassy field strewn with hundreds of men awaiting transport. Many were naked, and "as we passed, we drew our hats over our eyes, turning away as much as possible for the delicacy of the poor fellows." Some younger nurses started to cry. Horror fills her memoirs: What gain had the last thirty years brought to mankind? All they could do was bend beside these men, dress their wounds, give them comfort, bring a cup of gruel. Many had not eaten in four days.

This was the day that Spanish sailors died in the hundreds, the day Hoffman Philip woke among the dead. July 3, 1898, may have been the war's costliest day. On this morning, Shafter threatened to shell Santiago, but the British consul Frederick Ramsden and others begged for more time. "We explained to [the army] what a frightful act they were about to commit," Ramsden said: twenty thousand women and children would be driven into a barren land, while the Spanish Army would endure. El Caney and two other small villages were chosen for refuge, "but of course there was no food." Shafter granted a delay to noon of July 5, then indefinitely. The first refugees left on the morning of the third, before the naval battle, passing close to Hoffman Philip and his fellow Rough Riders. Near midnight on July 4, the navy shelled the harbor mouth when searchlights picked out one last ship, the 3,000-ton cruiser *Reina Mercedes*, left behind to be scuttled in the harbor mouth; she was hit at least five times and partially sunk before failing to plug the channel. Some nervous residents panicked and ran.

The final exodus began on the morning of July 5. When Santiago's remaining residents fled, Consul Ramsden went with them, followed by consuls and expatriates of Germany, Austria-Hungary, Italy, Belgium, Colombia, Argentina, Venezuela, Mexico, and Portugal. The consul and citizens of France had left two days earlier. Santiago was a ghost town: all houses were closed; no lights shone. Only soldiers remained. The journey to El Caney took three and a half hours: "The scene was terrible; people flocking out, sick carried in chairs," Ramsden said, "children getting lost by the way." The entrance to town reeked from the half-buried corpses of horses and men. At journey's end, they found three hundred houses—and no food.

El Caney became the face of the Splendid War. Its population of a thousand swelled twenty times; within a week, this climbed another ten thousand. No food existed but hardtack and mangoes, which dropped from the trees. "The place is one big pigsty," Ramsden wrote. "Soon there must be a frightful epidemic, with the people bathing and washing dirty clothes in the river, from which the drinking water is obtained." Only the daily rain swept the filth away. In one room, Ramsden found fifty refugees, one dying of fever, another with diarrhea, a woman screaming in childbirth. He gathered thirty British citizens in the public square so they wouldn't starve alone.

Major Henry Allen was appointed military governor, backed by the Thirteenth Infantry. The town was built around a plaza: a grove of trees ran down its middle, connecting a church at one end with public buildings on the other. Allen set up in the church, and in the attached chapel the Red Cross distributed food. Every day, they brought hard biscuits, but there were never enough: on an average day, they had 5,000 rations for 30,000 mouths, but they were so understaffed they could feed only 1,200. When the Red Cross brought condensed milk for mothers and children, "there was almost a fight as for life to get some of it." Theft became so serious that Allen assigned eight men per shift to guard supplies. One night they caught three starving *mambisi* stealing biscuits: he sent them off "with the promise that they would be shot if they returned."

The church served as hospital, too; the altar, an operating table presided over by the veteran army surgeon "Dr. Bangs." On July 5, when Crane and Frank Norris rode to El Caney, Crane became mesmerized by the blood-soaked surgeon. A line of fifty-two Spanish prisoners lay or sat in the chancel under the statue of Our Lady of Sorrows, awaiting their turn. A patient, "naked save for a breech-clout," was laid on the altar; something "small and silvery flashed in the surgeon's hand"; though a "merciful sponge" soaked in chloroform was pressed to his nose and mouth, he writhed and moaned. Between patients, Bangs shook Crane's hand, changing the scalpel from his right to his left and "giving me a wet palm." Bangs had a glass eye and would pop it from its socket to polish on his pants leg; he was stout, with a "very red face and a voice like the exhaust of a locomotive," Norris said. Though Crane later portrayed him as an indomitable force, Bangs was very sick; he would die from yellow fever within the week.

When Norris arrived, he'd encountered a "seething mass" from which rose a "persistent, raucous, piercing wail: 'Comida! Comida!'" ("Food! Food!"). He'd reached into his saddlebags for hardtack and "in an instant my horse was literally lifted from his feet, and hands, hands, hands, outstretched, lean, white, black and brown, small and large, a thicket of hands grew instantly from the crowd." He pushed forward and escaped inside the chapel walls.

Now it was seven p.m., time for hardtack and gruel: the crowd knew the schedule, and their cry changed. "It was no longer deep-toned," Norris wrote, but "shrill and piping." The Red Cross hoped to feed children first: Norris peered over the terrace and saw three thousand children pressing against the gates, "half of them naked, the other half ragged beyond words." They were "packed as sand is packed," one frantic organism "swaying forward and back, and from side to side, without knowing why." El Caney changed his view of humanity—first the little girl raped and stabbed, now this mindless mass driven by "the little rat that nipped and gnawed at their stomachs." They seemed a pavement of faces, "crushed together cheek to cheek, upturned, pinched and agonized." "*Let in twenty children*," Bangs shouted, but when they opened the gate, twenty turned to thirty, one hundred, a thousand. They muttered under their breath, "*Comida! Comida!*"

Sickness rode starvation's heels. Henry Allen didn't notice until July 12: he called it "acclimatizing fever," a nice euphemism—grow used to the climate and you'll be fine. He wrote his wife that it would pass in two to five days. Yet by July 16 his men were worse, and he showed symptoms, too. He accompanied them to the hospital in the stone fort, requisitioned an ambulance to Siboney. By July 18 he could no longer manage the thousands; by July 20 his writing deteriorated to a scrawl. "This has been the longest day and the most uncomfortable that I have ever passed" was all he could write. The ambulance had still not come.

When Leonard Wood visited on July 8, he was appalled. "Never saw such a horde of refugees crowded together in great masses." Yellow fever had been reported at Siboney, "and plenty of it. Also reported at Caney." The specter they'd dreaded was here. The first case was reported on July 6; three more in Siboney on July 9. On July 13 the official count was 150.

"Yellow Jack," named for the quarantine flag, was the army's great fear. It was the Black Death of its day, a plague of unknown origin that had been in the Americas since the 1600s, breaking out in periodic urban epidemics that claimed tens of thousands. It began with severe aches, headache, and fever, and at this stage resembled *calenture*, which meant that severe *calenture* was often misdiagnosed as yellow fever. Its final act fueled the fear—an eruption of black blood and stomach lining that covered everyone near.

Though rarely mentioned in war histories, a "disease panic" set in. Malaria and tuberculosis killed just as many people, yet the yellow fever epidemics of 1793, 1878, 1888, and the 1890s had spread with no known reason, and there seemed no place to hide. Many soldiers fighting in Santiago had been children during the terrible 1878 epidemic that raged through the Mississippi and Ohio valleys. George Kennan believed that yellow fever and *calenture* would kill them all. "In less than a fortnight," he wrote, "there were thousands of cases, and nearly one half of the army was unfit for active service, if not completely disabled." But one did not write about this: to do so meant being called "unpatriotic, disloyal, and even seditious." Do so, and the army revoked your press credentials. And so, at first, silence reigned.

Clara Barton had survived Savannah's 1888 epidemic, so she knew what lay ahead. General Shafter might be in surrender talks with his opposite, but "the main talk of the camp was now 'yellow fever.'" On the night of July 7, Barton took an army wagon back to Siboney, but when she arrived, all relief ships were at sea. Where could she sleep? The postmaster, Eben Brewer, offered his little home for the night, but a premonition filled her with "terrible dread." Brewer bragged that he'd never found a climate that suited him better, but Barton thought he looked ill. Again he offered his large, cheerless room: one army cot, a table, and a burning candle stuck by a glob of wax to the wood. She lay on the cot, but "it was impossible for me to stay," for "something constantly warned me to leave." Something deadly was in that room. She jumped up and stood in the door, where she "looked out upon the night and darkness and waited for the gray of morning." When dawn broke, she walked to the beach, awaiting transport to safety.

"I might as well say here," she wrote, "as I will not refer to it again, that six days after, when I returned, they told me that" the postmaster had died of yellow fever:

> I had occupied his cot and he had gone to heaven. I wondered who it was that so continually warned me that night to keep away from that room, away from the cot, away from all connected with it, when I had not the slightest suspicion of anything wrong. "Yellow fever" was then not talked of. Did some one [*sic*] tell me? I do not know, but something told me.

This had been a sign. No safe place existed. Her fear grew.

Forced inaction maddened everyone. Private Post watched from the siege line as "the sickness struck deeper" among his fellow New Yorkers and, with it, despair. He could not remember a "single dirty story told during that period": nothing was funny now. "We were silent, and listened," as if suffering brought with it some higher meaning, if only they could hear. Men walked about, "their eyes glazed with fever," then died. Ed Kroupa, "a quiet, steady man," died in his sleep; they realized this only when his feet, sticking from the tent, did not move. "Laughing, joking," Tom O'Brian took sick and "two days later he was dead."

Sergeant Henry Dobson of the D.C. Volunteers found himself wishing for Tampa again. Yes, South Florida had been a "bum place," but Santiago was far worse. Every night, the sky opened: once "I bathed in 2 inches of water all night," he wrote his mother. Much of his time was spent tracking down the dead. One day he took six men to the sunken road. "Two boys of the 6th infantry had been killed there," he wrote, "and had simply been covered with earth as they had fallen. The rain had washed the earth away, and the buzzards were starting their work. We finished the uncovering and dug two Christian graves and put them in."

On July 2 or 3 Barton was tending her stores at El Pozo when a "rough figure in brown khaki" stopped before her. She'd never met Roosevelt, but knew him by reputation. He told her he had sick men in his regiment who refused to leave, and he wanted to buy some "delicacies" for them. She couldn't sell them, she answered: "We can't sell hospital supplies."

"Then how can I get them?"

"Just ask for them, Colonel." She grinned. He filled a heavy sack and trudged away.

If anything, Roosevelt's star seemed on the rise. He wrote to Henry Cabot Lodge almost daily, his letters filled with gossip, praise for his men, and criticism of Shafter for hesitating to attack Santiago. On July 5 he fumed, "Not since the campaign of Crassus against the Parthians has there been so criminally incompetent a General as Shafter." Lodge calmed him with praise: "You are one of the most popular persons in the war and deserve to be," he soothed. "I hear talk all the time about your being run for Governor and Congressman." Lodge lobbied McKinley to promote him to general, but the president demurred.

During the long weeks between July 3 and July 17, Shafter refined his strategy. By focusing on this period, one sees that history has been unjust. While one mostly remembers Roosevelt's complaints, less attention is paid to what the aide John Miley called Shafter's "remarkable series of negotiations" with Linares's replacement, Toral. Save for brief spates of gunfire on July 10–11, the actual fighting was over. Though Roosevelt and others wished to attack, Shafter held back from what he considered needless slaughter and instead waged a war of words. He maintained a constant threat of navy shelling while allowing the El Caney evacuation. Toral offered to abandon the city if his men could march to the interior; Shafter refused, wanting nothing less than total surrender. The fall of the fleet strengthened his hand; that, and a grim picture painted by a Spanish deserter. Food was scarce in Santiago, officers abusive, fresh water cut off when Lawton captured the city's main pumping station. At night, empty houses were looted. By late June, fifteen to twenty soldiers were dying from fever each day.

In Washington, neither McKinley nor his cabinet had any idea of Shafter's plans. First those gloomy casualty estimates, then ruminations about withdrawing. Now there was talk of letting the enemy march off scot-free. Like many, Shafter had the habit of thinking out loud before reaching a conclusion, in this case thinking by telegraph wire. But Washington saw these as concrete plans of action, and rumors of yellow fever roiled them further. They dispatched Shafter's boss, Nelson Miles, with the reinforcements Shafter had requested long ago. Though Miles was not sent to replace the commander, he did have an agenda: if the new troops could land to the west and circle the city, the final assault could begin.

Miles arrived after a naval bombardment on July 10 that damaged fifty-nine houses but hurt no one. As he conferred with Shafter, his adjutant, Lieutenant Colonel Marion P. Maus, embarked on an impromptu inspection tour. His discoveries troubled him. In Las Guásimas, he found along the road "the graves of the men who had fallen and the graveyard smell of human bones could be strongly detected." In every camp, he found "a good deal of sickness" and short ration supply; the men were hungry, and sickness was widespread. Like everyone else, he worried that this could turn into yellow fever, and then they'd all be doomed.

To his surprise, Miles endorsed Shafter's game. On July 12 Shafter asked Toral to parlay in the shade of a great ceiba tree halfway between the lines. Ceibas have a mystical significance in Cuba: their roots are said to plunge to the earth's core, and a promise made beneath its branches cannot be undone. They met the next day. On the American side sat Miles, Maus, Shafter, his aide Miley, Wheeler, and Lawton. Toral and his staff were equally represented. Toral struck Maus as a "tall, fine looking man, very fair but pale from the effects of fever and dysentery." He spoke at great length, saying that although Governor Blanco authorized him to talk, he could not surrender without Spain's approval. "That is all very well," Shafter replied, but he was fed up with their delays. They had until five a.m. the next day before his ships fired again. Toral shrugged. He would fight to the end: "You would gain practically nothing, and we both would suffer a terrible loss, for my men can fight." That's true, they are tough, Shafter answered, a surprisingly nuanced concession to Spanish pride from the gruff old man.

Hearing that, Wheeler suddenly grasped what was going on. There were undercurrents at play. Toral hoped to preserve his honor, but more than that,

> it was evident to me, from his preoccupied look and manner, that General Torel [*sic*] had constantly looming before him in his mind's eye the events which would follow when he once more stood upon Spanish soil with his conquered troops. It was explained to me by one of the Spanish commissioners that, as general commanding the Spanish forces, he would be held accountable for the surrender; and that he would probably, even though he had received the consent of his Government to capitulate, have to answer for same before a court-martial at Madrid.

Toral repeated that he needed more time: "It can do you no harm; it will not weaken your position; it will not strengthen me." All he wanted was "to save the honor of the Spanish Army," he said. Miles and Shafter walked off and spoke; they'd had the same realization as Wheeler's. They extended the deadline until noon of the fourteenth, then stretched that by another day.

On Friday, July 15, Spanish honor and Toral's head were saved by creative means. Santiago would surrender in two days if American ships shelled the city first, but at such a safe height that no damage or injury occurred. With this, Toral could truthfully say that he'd surrendered under fire. Also, the word "surrender" must not be used: *rendición* would be supplanted with the less pejorative *capitulación*. Shelling would continue until all Spanish troops turned in their guns—which would then return to Spain with the soldiers.

That night, the air shook convincingly and harmlessly above Santiago. The next day, Shafter cabled Miles: "They surrender!" One day later, on July 17, Santiago "capitulated."

During those days, sickness touched everywhere. On July 6 it felled Stephen Crane. That day, he rode to El Pozo to watch a prisoner exchange. The American side involved the return of Lieutenant Richmond Hobson and the crew of the disabled *Merrimac*, which on June 3 had been scuttled in the main channel in a failed attempt to block the harbor. In the process, Hobson became a national hero, though Crane considered him a glory hound. On the ride back, Crane and Davis argued, as they often did. The two had developed a friendly rivalry that was not always friendly. The public needed heroes, Davis said: one mustn't blame Hobson for the hand that Fate dealt him. Crane barely heard. He'd been sick since the Battle of San Juan Hill: according to some, he'd lived entirely on alcohol, and this night he raved: "All I could remember was pickles. Pickles at any price! Pickles!!" When he heard two men on stretchers discuss the death of an anonymous private, he grew enraged by the fuss made over celebrities like Hobson and Hamilton Fish while everyone ignored the "unknowns." His "veins burned and boiled." The next morning, Rea and Scovel dragged him to the hospital and a doctor diagnosed yellow fever.

On July 8 Rea put Crane on the *City of Washington*, bound for Old Port Comfort in Virginia's Hampton Roads. The ship's doctor was terrified of Yellow Jack and refused to let anyone near him, even for food. "Isolate yourself," he screamed. "I don't give a goddamn where you go, but when you get there, stay there, sir." Crane wandered aft to the flagstaff and stretched out "on a little rug" where he stayed for four or five days, shunned by all, lost in visions of ice-cream sodas. When the ship docked, he still breathed. A doctor said he didn't have yellow fever after all, just a bad case of malaria, and let him recuperate in the nearby Chamberlain Hotel.

Crane may have been saved by the sea voyage. Monday, July 11, would be dubbed "The Night It Rained." Clara Barton called it "one of the most fearful storms I have ever seen": "The thunder shook the ground, the lightning blazed like fire" and lit up the distant mountains. Casualties lined up on the ground lay in five or six inches of water, while the trenches flowed like creeks. As a result, those with even low-grade fevers saw their temperatures soar. When Barton drove her wagon to Siboney on the afternoon of the eleventh, she came upon the ruins of mass panic. Every building had been "utterly burned," either gone entirely or still smoldering. The infectious "miasma" thought to cause Yellow Jack was believed to be cleansed by fire alone. So many were dying that gravediggers couldn't keep up, so the army cremated the bodies. But the rains had doused the fires, leaving half-burned bodies atop the pyres.

The number of real and imagined yellow fever cases diagnosed in Siboney from July 9 to 11 leapt from 3 to 116, yet evidence suggests a different cause. For example, of the twenty-two nurses who died during this period, most were listed as succumbing to yellow fever, yet time would pin their deaths to typhoid. If anything, the misdiagnosis fueled mass panic, evidenced by Siboney's smoldering remains. The air was thick and blue with smoke; when Barton pulled up, doctors and attendants "ran about the grounds smutted and bareheaded like children." Anyone suspected of having Yellow Jack was immediately rushed by rail to a "fever hospital" a mile and a half away, with only thirty minutes' warning. Siboney's Cuban residents had been driven from their houses "into caves in the cliffs." She gazed at the ruins and wrote, "General observation would go far toward convincing a very ordinary mind that everybody had gone crazy."

But not even Barton was immune to the fear. She held her panic in check until boarding the *State of Texas*, where she learned that Dr. Lesser and his wife, Bettina, had been diagnosed with Yellow Jack and sent to the fever hospital. Several nurses, too. The panic now hit close to home. On July 12, she dithered over whether to isolate the ship completely or keep sending out supplies. But when, on July 13, the number of "confirmed" cases jumped from 116 to 150, that tipped the scales. Early on the morning of July 14, a letter delivered from a "W. Woods"—most probably a doctor in the First Division Hospital—said "we are now nearly surrounded by yellow fever." He implored her to "remove" her ship so she, too, would not die.

George Kennan returned to the *State of Texas* during this period. These days, he spent most of his time at the front writing stories for *Outlook*, but he also sent requests to Miss B. On either the 13th or 14th, he found her banning several stewardesses and nurses from the ship, including Katherine White, the nurse reporting for *The Chicago Record*. They'd be put ashore "with no place to sleep and no blankets," since all had been burned. Kennan lost his temper: "I spoke my mind saying that I thought it was barbarous and I thought it wasn't a fair thing to virtually abandon our own people ashore." His objections seemed to have effect: though we don't know about the stewardesses, Katherine White was still aboard on July 19. But Barton took offense: "She said she had never been accused of barbarity before [and] accused me of reading her a lecture without previously consulting with her privately." Barton claimed that she'd quarantined the ship under orders from Shafter and Leonard Wood, but when Kennan asked to see those orders, she would or could not produce them. Dr. Gardner, the ship's main physician, had "panic in his bones," while "Miss B. has shown fear of it from the beginning." Panic spread through the ship as Kennan watched: his quarters were burned out; he was forced to sleep on deck, his equipment piled around him. When she passed by him, he wrote, "Miss B doesn't speak to me."

None of this would ever be revealed. Kennan never broaches the subject in his *Campaigning in Cuba*; Barton omits all mention in her books, letters, and journals. The only place it appears is in Kennan's overlooked diaries. When the Red Cross is needed most, Barton floats offshore. Kennan is unable to leave until July 19. The hospital ship cruised between Siboney and Santiago, viewing the wrecks of the Spanish fleet. "Miss Barton has been so afraid of yellow fever that she has forbidden communication with the shore," wrote an outraged Kennan: thus, he misses historic events on land. "When we arrived her orders were issued that no one could go ashore and return to the ship. If anyone went, he or she had to stay ashore."

One nurse left voluntarily. Janet Jennings was fifty-six, tall and slender, with light gray eyes, an "eager, kindly, resolute face," and dark hair streaked with gray. Like Katherine White, she was a correspondent who served as a Red Cross nurse to skirt the army ban on frontline "lady journalists." Unlike White, she was not affiliated with any paper. She was not a "trained nurse" like Clara Maass, but in the crisis no one cared. She worked in Siboney's hospitals and had time to write one report for *The Chicago Times-Herald* on the lack of medical supplies. Then Shafter ordered the worst wounded and sick taken back to the States to make way for new casualties. To do this, he drafted the troop transports floating idly off the coast and by fiat turned them into "mercy ships." One was the *Seneca*.

Charles Post had ridden to war in the *Seneca*: he called it a "puny, coastwise tin can" with no ventilation and "one large kettle" for meals. Now it was tasked with carrying one hundred sick and wounded back to New York, and Jennings was caught in the mad rush to transfer men aboard.

She first took a boatful of sick to the *Seneca* on July 13. To her surprise, no other nurses were aboard. She *did* discover Thomas Baird and William Hicks, two young "contract doctors" who said no nurses had been assigned to them. She volunteered on the spot, and on the 14th rowed to the *State of Texas* to tell Barton her plans. This was the day Miss B began throwing people off the ship, and whether Jennings was aware of this is never said. Barton cut her loose with her blessings: Jennings had time to grab her luggage, a large sack of food, and some medical stores. She rowed back to the *Seneca* an hour before it weighed anchor.

Once they set sail, Jennings took stock of their supplies. To her horror, there was next to nothing: a few rolls of bandages, some plasters and disinfectants, some quinine. No medicines, antiseptics, or thermometers; one or two scissors, and forceps for operations. The drinking water was murky, and only enough for two days. There were more passengers than bunks, so those who could move sprawled topside. One other woman sailed with her, but she couldn't move. Frances Scovel had doctored the *World* correspondents until she fell to *calenture*, and would be bedridden the entire voyage. The captain was drunk, the crew surly and threatening, the air foul. The *Seneca*'s one hope for saving its passengers was a short voyage.

But the ship hit strong winds. Slow progress meant more death, and the only pain medicine was whiskey. Once a day, Jennings toured the ship, doling out shots, but that didn't help those suffering from gunshot and shrapnel, whose wounds had grown infected. One twenty-eight-year-old sergeant had been shot through both lungs; his wounds ran with pus, and she could not hold her emotions back when telling Dr. Baird. But he could not help, and he "almost wept" from frustration. Soon he, too, fell sick, leaving Jennings and Dr. Hicks to carry on.

The six-day voyage of the *Seneca* must have seemed endless, like that of Coleridge's Ancient Mariner. To Frances Scovel, Jennings seemed everywhere. She checked pulses, fed the weak, moved a raving patient up top, propped up a gunshot victim so he could breathe. She never once removed her clothes or lay down for eight hours of sleep. "She almost worked herself to death," one private said. "Her endurance was wonderful," chimed another man. Only later did she admit that she kept it up by downing shots of the same whiskey she doled out to the men.

The ship reached Norfolk on July 18, and though doctors took off the worst cases, quarantine officials refused debarkation to everyone else for fear of yellow fever. So the *Seneca* limped on to New York, dropping anchor on July 20 at 10:20 a.m. Officials counted nearly one hundred invalids packed in the airless holds. *The New York Times* asked whether the Army Medical Corps "meant to kill off our sick and wounded soldiers by shipping them from point to point on unfit transports, without physicians, without medical supplies, and with nothing but beans."

New York's health officials had been warned that the ship carried fourteen suspected yellow fever cases, six very probable, and when they arrived, they were quarantined on Swinburne Island. Other sick and wounded went to Bellevue Hospital, while passengers, crew, and the reporters who interviewed them spent the night in quarantine at Hoffman Island, including Jennings. By now, survivors had bragged of their savior, and newspapers dubbed her "The Angel of the *Seneca*." As Jennings left the quarantine boat on the morning of July 22, she "was at once singled out by the crowd," reported the *New York Evening Post*: "She was assisted to the pier, a hundred willing hands being stretched to do this little service for her. She smiled and walked towards the street, bowing right and left; the men bared their heads as she passed by."

She'd said she would not talk until relieved of her Red Cross duties that afternoon; then, good to her word, she talked to reporters in her room at the St. Denis Hotel. "The blame for the whole confused state of affairs belongs in Siboney," she said. "The poor fellows, sick and wounded, were put between decks in cattle pens, there is no other name for their quarters, and the awful trip began." Pulitzer's *World* headlined "Someone Blundered—Wounded Suffer" on July 25. Countless other papers followed.

Stories of a second "horror ship" surfaced almost immediately. Henry Allen had the bad luck to be aboard the *Concho*, which left Siboney on July 25. An ambulance finally picked him up at El Caney and took him to the fever hospital; for two weeks, he suffered chills and delirium, only to develop an abscess on his face, which grew infected. The *Concho* seemed well-stocked: it had lain off Siboney since July 1 and should have had time to take on ice and rations. Engineers installed a distiller, so there should be fresh water. But when Siboney's lead surgeon shunted a last-minute 176 patients onto the ship, the staff was overwhelmed. By the first day out, most patients had dysentery. Six ounces of creolin, a coal-tar distillate, was the only antiseptic available; the only medicines quinine, brandy, and home remedies. Ice was gone within a day; water in the storage tanks stank; all food had turned rancid. One man later said he wished he'd stayed in Siboney: "I'd rather they'd left me where they found me, under the chaparral of the San Juan slope; I'd have died, but I wouldn't have had to suffer so much."

One consequence was the quick spread of typhoid. By July 28–29, four men had died. Somehow, Henry Allen survived and was sent to an army hospital; on August 23 he wrote a long letter to his wife, Jennie: "When

I stand up, my legs shake considerably." Jennie took him home to Narragansett on August 27; she nursed him back to health in time for him to observe one of the greatest U.S. atrocities in any of its many foreign wars.

The sagas of the *Seneca* and *Concho* reached all the way to Washington, and on August 2 Janet Jennings spoke with McKinley. On September 8 the president authorized the formation of a group called the Dodge Commission and ordered it to investigate "every aspect of the Army's administration" of the war. The repercussions of the "horror ships" had just begun.

As doctors and nurses drowned in a tide of the sick, the army turned to "Immunes." Common wisdom held that African Americans were immune to tropical disease: many blacks believed it, too. Booker T. Washington wrote Long that Cuba's climate would be "peculiar and danger[o]us to the unaclimated [*sic*] white man. The Negro race in the South is accustomed to this climate." Ten all-black "Immune" regiments were proposed, then whittled to four, but by the time of the crisis, not a single regiment had arrived. None would until August 15.

But the seed had been planted. On July 15 Shafter penned an order assigning sick men to fever camps and asked for at least five hundred volunteers to care for them. Eight white regiments turned down his request. By four p.m. the order had reached the far left end of the siege line, where David Fagen's Twenty-Fourth Infantry kept watch. By then, Private Fagen had been in the army for forty-two days. The war had been hard on him. The Twenty-Fourth had lost 104 officers and men in the attack on San Juan Hill and subsequent siege. In El Pozo's big medical tents lay two officers and sixty-seven enlisted men from his Company H, all battle casualties. In the days since taking the Heights, black regiments had been ordered to dig trenches for whites: they'd finish one and start another. One soldier wrote, "Now we are almost naked, no medicine, not much to eat, hot water to drink, sleeping on the bare ground and no papers of any kind." Anything seemed better.

In the early hours of July 16, the Twenty-Fourth was ordered to march back to Siboney. They trudged "through places so dense and dark they were compelled to clasp hands to find their way." They sang the hymn

"How Firm a Foundation," as much to keep together as to boost morale. Sometime between 3:00 and 3:30 a.m., they collapsed on the hill overlooking Siboney. As his men slept, Major A. C. Markley walked down the hill alone. He found Dr. Louis La Garde, surgeon major of the fever camp, and learned of his assignment. There were thirteen hundred men in this camp, La Garde said: some died every hour for lack of proper care. Markley's heart sank: here was one more slap in the face for his brave soldiers. Now they were being told to serve as attendants for the doomed, and for many it would be their own death sentence.

Markley climbed the hill. He drew the men up and explained the urgent need for help down below. He also explained the danger of yellow fever, since by then he apparently did not believe the common "wisdom" that blacks were naturally immune. If anyone wished to volunteer as a nurse, he could step forward. The whole regiment did so. Markley picked sixty-five of them, including Captain A. A. Augur, Fagen, and fourteen others from Company H. Others volunteered for burial details, to cook, pitch tents, clean out filth, police the camp, and do other chores.

Fagen packed his gear and went down the hill. Men were dying in rows of white tents; any building once built on this spot had been burned, the tents pitched on the ashes. The camp had been raised in a stagnant green swamp that swarmed with mosquitoes. At the moment, it was believed that fever spread through human contact; it would be two more years before it was proved to spread through the bite of the infected *Aedes aegypti* mosquito. Fagen and his friends cared for the sick, carried them out when they died, burned their clothing, scrubbed the place with chloride. Within forty-eight hours, forty-two of this first group came down with either yellow fever or *calenture*. Markley spoke again, and replacements came down the hill.

It is uncertain when Fagen fell to the fever. Though army medical records state that he was diagnosed with "malarial remittent fever" on August 22 and remained in treatment four days, the Twenty-Fourth's "morning reports" indicate that he was placed on sick call in July. John Calloway was also admitted for treatment on August 21–22, so record-keeping was probably more a matter of catch-up than accuracy. The Twenty-Fourth had dwindled to the point where soldiers were shuffled between companies: Fagen was moved from Company H to Company I, now consisting of five sergeants, six corporals, a wagoner, Fagen, and one other private. Fagen and Calloway were released on August 25, the day the death camp closed. They'd been at the camp forty days. The next day, the last patients moved twelve miles by rail and were carried aboard the hospital ship *Neuces*. Fewer than half of the Twenty-Fourth could walk unaided. White soldiers cheered as they limped by.

Of the 456 men of the Twenty-Fourth who marched to Siboney on July 16, a mere 24 escaped sickness. Only 9 officers and 198 men could march to the train when it was time to ship out, and the actual number of those who died in camp is unknown. Though regimental returns recorded 17 Buffalo Soldiers and their officers dying in the camp, Stephen Bonsal would write that Captain Charles Dodge and 35 privates remained behind in graves that have long since disappeared.

18

"We Are Not Savages"

Americans amazed and confounded Calixto García. He'd come to admire them as individuals: they were adept and inventive, brave in a crisis, willing to lay down their lives for an ideal. He'd liked his little artilleryman Frederick Funston, and still wondered if he'd made it from Cuba alive. Yet Americans in positions of power seemed another matter entirely. He knew that General Shafter depended on his men to encircle Santiago, yet little evidence suggests that the American commander kept García apprised of his plans. Did the Americans anticipate a frontal assault? Shafter did not say. If this did happen, García expected to be included: "It is a question of honor for us to assist to it and I can spare fifteen or twenty hundred of my men with that object, as I have now in camp over five thousand," he wrote on July 12. Shafter did not reply. On July 13, when Shafter, Miles, and Toral hammered out terms under the ceiba tree, García heard of it only later, secondhand. Shafter knew that he was "sore," but did not seem to care. On July 15, as Shafter arranged a token bombardment to save Spanish honor, he merely sent a note to García, saying "all our trouble is nearing its end."

García's main U.S. contact at the moment was Brigadier General William Ludlow, who'd commanded Lawton's First Brigade at El Caney. He spent a lot of time with Ludlow at Aserradero, listening to tales of the Yellowstone Valley and of saving George Custer from a grizzly bear. Ludlow often coughed, and García worried that, like Funston, he was close to death. He'd be correct: Ludlow would succumb in June 1901 to pulmonary tuberculosis contracted during the Santiago campaign. Unlike Shafter, Ludlow valued his Cuban allies, and on July 15 he thanked them for the "immense amount of work" they'd performed "with almost no applause whatever." He thanked García "personally and not officially," adding, "I have been more closely in touch with your forces and have had better occasion to observe their work and the value of their cooperation than perhaps any other." As if he knew what was coming—and felt powerless to intervene.

García appreciated such gestures. As a group, the Americans lacked empathy. He knew they considered his men savages and feared they would slaughter the residents of Santiago—their own people! He'd seen such blindness in José Martí, who'd lived in New York too long. Martí claimed to distrust Americans, but in the end he was like them, trusting only himself. Americans even disparaged the *reconcentrados* they'd come to save as being too needy. By Saturday, July 16, he'd learned that Santiago would be surrendered the next morning—but that Shafter had neglected to tell the people who called it home. He rode with his escort into Las Cuabitas, west of El Caney, looking like "an old warrior of the time of Napoleon," wrote U.S. sergeant John J. Turner. As refugees thronged him, he said they could go home again. "*Viva Cuba Libre!*" they cried. "The sick felt cured, the old felt young," Turner observed.

García protested to Shafter when he learned that he'd been excluded from the surrender. But he was not alone. Correspondents were excluded: when they asked *when* they could enter, Shafter answered "god-damned never"—while he was in charge. Most went in anyway. Even the navy was snubbed. There was such a stink that on the 17th Shafter finally sent out invitations. Yet by the time Sampson and Captain Chadwick received theirs, it was too late to attend.

When García received his late invitation, he learned that all other *mambisi* were excluded. He rode to the city, and at the first army outpost was stopped by a Rough Rider. Edwin Emerson Jr. had written for *Leslie's Weekly* until July 10, when Roosevelt swore him in. His presence at the roadblock that morning was his first day of active duty; he'd been told to keep Cubans out and apparently did not know that García was the sole exception. Emerson stepped forward, drew a derringer from his boot, and told the general he'd have to turn around. García returned to camp, convinced finally that American vows of *Cuba Libre* were empty air.

At 9:30 a.m. Generals Toral and Shafter met midway between their lines and rode into Santiago. The path was strewn with dead horses draped with saddles and bridles; vultures had scratched open shallow graves. The "odor was horrible in the extreme," wrote the reporter James F. J. Archibald, who had together with Frank Norris discovered the murdered girl. Toral was surrendering to Shafter 11,500 soldiers in Santiago, 7,000 in Guantánamo, 3,500 in San Luis, and another 1,500 within a thirty-mile radius. "I was simply thunderstruck that, of their own free will, they would give me 12,000 men that were absolutely beyond my reach," Shafter said. What would he do with them all? They zigzagged through a maze of barbed wire, sandbags, and trenches; defenders had walled off roads with paving stones and loopholed houses for rifle fire. The city was much as it is today: a crowded grid of streets little wider than one oxcart, all cloistered beneath overhanging eaves. Joe Wheeler realized what a "hard task" it would have been to take this "city by storm."

The ceremony took hours: Spanish and American soldiers marched past the Governor's Palace, saluted, shook hands. Thousands crowded the central square. Rough Riders gave Roosevelt three cheers. When the U.S. flag rose, the six-mile semicircle of soldiers watching from the hills stood and cheered. Some Spanish cavalrymen shared two casks of rum with the Buffalo Soldiers who were camped nearby. When the English correspondent George Clarke Musgrave heard Cubans cry "*Viva los Americanos*," it seemed gracious and sad. A Cuban officer commented that by being excluded, "we feel as the patriots under Washington would have felt had the allied armies captured New York, and the French prohibited the entry of the Americans and their flag."

"The war was over," wrote Charles Post, who watched from the hills. "Now we could go home. And what a dinner we would order." Unfortunately, Post was jumping the gun. Though it *felt* like the war had ended, in truth the only thing finished was the Santiago campaign. War with Spain was still officially declared, and it would be another ten days before Spain sued for peace. The future was hazy.

For many, these were moot points. The British consul Frederick Ramsden watched soldiers preen and salute, "but [I] went off home with a strong fever, and I feel bad." Quinine didn't help. His exposure and labors at El Caney had finally caught up. By August 10 he was dead.

One incident at the ceremony became well-known. As the Stars and Stripes rose over the Palace, Scovel shinnied up a tree until his head and shoulders peeked over the roofline. Shafter's aide Miley noticed. "There's a man here on the roof, and he won't get down," he said. "Then throw him down," Shafter snapped. By then, Scovel had dropped to the ground. After the ceremony, Scovel tried to explain that he hadn't meant trouble, but according to witnesses, Shafter yelled, "You son of a bitch. You and all your tribe are goddamned nuisances." Scovel admitted that he should have walked away, but instead he protested: "You shouldn't use such language to me, sir." Shafter turned and swung, though he later called it a "flamboyant gesture of dismissal." The blow hit Scovel in the face, and he staggered back. Without thinking, he yelled, "You!! A Major General of the United States Army! You ought to be ashamed of yourself," and swung back. Guards pounced on Scovel from all sides. "Let no one see that man," Shafter exploded. "Let no one speak to him." Scovel was thrown into a "moss-grown calabozo" whisked to Siboney the next morning, and chucked aboard the next ship to New York.

García would have been amused if he'd not been past the balm of comedy. He would never believe his exclusion had been a mistake; rather, it was an intentional act certifying his fears of Americans. He moved his men into the interior to join Gómez, where a debate started within Cuban ranks. Would the Americans renege upon their promise of freedom? The angriest urged Gómez to continue the war—but now against *Americanos.*

García would not go that far. Since cooperation was impossible, he resigned rather than submit to Shafter's authority. He wrote one last letter, reminding Shafter of his own nation's history. "I have been until now, one of your most faithful subordinates," he wrote, "honoring myself in carrying out your most faithful instructions as far as my powers have allowed me to do it." Yet he had not been honored with "a single word" about negotiations or "with a kind word" of invitation to the surrender ceremony. Instead, he learned that "you have left in power in Santiago the same Spanish authorities that for three years I have fought as enemies of the independence of Cuba." Was this the action of an honorable man representing a great nation?

> A rumor, too absurd to be believed, General, ascribes the reason of your measure and of the orders forbidding my army to enter Santiago for fear of massacres and revenge against the Spaniards. Allow me, sir, to protest against even the shadow of such an idea. We are not savages ignoring the rules of civilized warfare. We are a poor, ragged army as ragged and poor as was the army of your forefathers in their noble war for the independence, but like the heroes of Saratoga and Yorktown, we respect our cause too deeply to disgrace it with barbarism and cowardice.

It is one of the most famous Cuban documents of the Splendid War, taught in Cuban schools, coloring through the decades ideas of their neighbor's honor. Humiliation is a harsh pill to forget and forgive. Cuban teachers "taught us that history was black and white, and about the United States all was black, black, black," said Maria Isabel Colón, a Cuban émigré to the United States who in the 1980s attended public school in García's birthplace of Holguin. "We learned that Cuba was already winning the war" when the United States "blew up the *Maine*" to enter on its own terms. In 1959, when Fidel Castro toppled Fulgencio Batista, he invoked García's letter, saying that no foreign army would exclude him from a Cuban city; when he emerged from the Sierra Maestre, he first entered Santiago, not Havana. This "was the answer to 1898," said Alejandro Ferro, eighty-seven, who'd fought beside Castro and in 2008 still felt the rage.

Even Shafter sensed the implications: when he heard of García's decision, he realized that his slight could create "complications of a grave character." The "trouble with General García," he groused, "was that he expected to be placed in command of this place." He'd told García that questions of Cuban independence were not his to decide, yet the incident brought the growing estrangement into relief. In the month after surrender, Americans grew convinced that Cubans were an ungrateful rabble, and their earlier scorn evolved into calls for action. "A dual government can't exist here," Shafter told Washington. If both sides claimed sovereignty, let there be war.

As always, Gómez decided the future. He received García's resignation with sadness, but let him go. García was loved by the ranks, and many wanted to continue the fight. But Gómez knew that would be suicide. "Thinking that the Americans intend to annex Cuba is an insult to the great nation freed by Washington," he declared. He advised against war, and for this, Cuban nationalists later took him to task: his decision marginalized the Cuban army, leading to its disbanding at the moment power was still up for grabs.

Nationalists had good reason to be scared. Even then, portents of Cuba's future appeared in U.S. newspapers: "New Cuba More Attractive Than Yukon Gold Fields," *The New York Times* announced in late July. Growing coffee was a Cuban gold mine; "the richest deposits of iron ore in the world" lay near Santiago; thirteen million acres of untouched primeval forest filled with "mahogany, cedar, logwood, redwood, ebony, lignum vitae," and ironwood begged to be harvested. Streetcar conductors, machinists, and carpenters could reinvent themselves as "rich planters, street car magnates and influential citizens in the eastern end of Cuba." Though thoughts of economic takeover tortured Gómez, he no longer had much of an army left to fight with—and even fewer resources to feed those who remained.

Gómez retreated to his headquarters in Las Villas Province to brood. One question haunted him. On May 4, before America landed, Governor Blanco had sent a note that infuriated him at the time. "We Spaniards and Cubans find ourselves facing a foreign people of different race, of a naturally absorbent tendency, and with intentions not only to deprive Spain of her flag over the Cuban soil, but also to exterminate the Cuban people, due to its having Spanish blood." They should stand together and "repel the invader," Blanco entreated. Perhaps by doing so, they could heal their own wounds.

"I wonder how you dare write me again," Gómez replied. Years of subjugation could not be forgiven. There were good nations and bad nations: the United States was an example of the first, Spain of the second. "I don't see the danger of an extermination by the United States," he ended. "If it be so, history will judge."

Perhaps history was judging him now. Perhaps he'd made a colossal mistake and invited in the Monster against which Martí had always warned. He was a literate man—he should have seen. What if Cervantes was right, and the true Voice of God was Irony?

On the clear blue morning of Monday, July 25, 1898, Private Charles Sandburg and 3,313 other volunteers invaded Puerto Rico.

It seemed to Charlie that he'd never leave Camp Alger alive. On June 21 sickness so ravaged the Sixth Illinois that only twenty-five soldiers reported for duty. He spent that day on sick call, fighting the "trots, those vaults, [the] shitie [*sic*] reruns." A winnowing begins: of 283 Illinois soldiers to die in the war, disease kills 279. For two hours each day, Charlie walked guard duty and wondered "why I had enlisted." But sometimes he saw "midnights of stars" and recalled a similar transcendence when riding the rails.

On June 30 they heard that they'd depart that afternoon—only to learn it was a false alarm. A madness arose that he'd not see again until years later, when he covered Chicago's race riots and witnessed the terrifying power of the mob. After the letdown, disappointed officers issued blanks and decreed "sham battles" between the Sixth Illinois, Eighth Ohio, and Sixth Massachusetts, apparently deeming it a way to blow off steam. The Eighth Ohio "seemed to lose their heads completely" and started an actual fight with the Sixth Massachusetts, seriously wounding "a number of men." Several attackers surrounded Harry Reed of the Sixth: he threw up his hands and cried "For God's sake, don't shoot!" but they fired into his face, tearing away an ear and blinding one eye. A few miles away, the Second Tennessee attacked the Third Missouri and First Rhode Island, shooting and wounding two men.

On July 1 Sandburg had heard about the fall of the San Juan Heights and feared the war was over. Where did you spend the war? girls back home would ask. In a pesthole called Camp Alger, he'd say. One week later, they boarded a troop train for Charleston, South Carolina, and on July 11 boarded the *Lanta Rita*, a lucky break since Companies D and M had been left behind. Seven hundred of them crammed into the converted cattle boat; there were no life preservers, and the food was "something awful." Captain McGirr ordered cooks to make a daily pan of bacon, hardtack, and kitchen scraps for his Saint Bernard; the men were so hungry they intercepted the repast and "ate it hungrily themselves." It later came out that the cooks so hated the dog, they "spit in this slop, and trampled upon it, yet the men were permitted to eat it" anyway.

The *Rita* arrived in Santiago Bay on the night of July 14–15, but they could not debark for fear of yellow fever. They left for Guantánamo Bay on the seventeenth and reached there that night, but again could not leave. They waited three days until, at three p.m. on July 21, they finally sailed.

But where? The rumor was "Porto Rico." Claimed for Spain in 1493 during his second New World voyage, Columbus originally named it San Juan in honor of Saint John the Baptist; a few years later, it was renamed "Porto Rico," or "rich seaport." The new colony measured 100 miles long, 50 to 60 miles wide, and was "as square as a dry-goods box," one chronicler said. By 1815 Yankee traders discovered its commercial promise: an 1897 consular report said that the year's coffee yield was 26,655 tons, sugar 54,205 tons, and tobacco 1,039 tons. Immense herds of cattle wandered the island; cotton grew in its valleys, rice on its hills. As war's end approached, the kind of independence promised Cubans by the Teller Amendment was never an option. Puerto Rico was a peaceful, very Spanish possession, with a strategic position in the Caribbean and promise as a cash cow.

According to the best intelligence, Spain kept 8,233 Regular troops on the island, plus 9,107 volunteers. Two thousand Regulars who'd fought in Cuba were armed with Mausers and concentrated in four areas: most near San Juan, but also west in Mayagüez, south in Ponce, and in Caguas on the central plain. Puerto Rico's 1898 population numbered between eight and nine hundred thousand: one hundred thousand were Spanish, the rest native-born.

In early May, the Bureau of Military Information sent Lieutenant Henry H. Whitney of the Fourth Artillery to learn more. He'd already performed a similar spy mission by carrying a secret message to Gómez, but now newspapers published details of his mission, and Spanish authorities boarded his ship when it landed. By then, he was stoking coal in the engine room and covered in black dust; they missed him, and he landed elsewhere. A later investigation concluded that the leak could only have come from the office of the garrulous War Secretary Alger. Whitney confirmed the troop count, and more. Volunteers were poorly trained; there was almost no artillery; a hundred small, antiquated vessels comprised the "navy." A well-maintained macadam road ran from Ponce in the south and north to San Juan, straight through the central mountains.

Miles intended to divide his forces, then scour the countryside of Spanish troops as his columns converged on San Juan. He originally said he'd land thirty miles east of the capital at Point Fajardo, but he remembered the leaks plaguing Whitney and changed his plans once safely out to sea. He couldn't tell the secretary that he didn't trust him; he merely said, "Circumstances were such that I deemed it advisable." His wire said, "Spaniards surprised," but Alger was, too.

Sandburg's convoy sailed east from Guantánamo for four days, running at night without lights, hugging the north coast of Haiti and Dominica. Late on July 24, they sighted Puerto Rico and continued toward San Juan while daylight lasted, but then they doused their lights, turned about, and, except for one well-lit decoy in the north, nine transports and four warships steamed south down the Mona Passage, an artery of tricky currents connecting the Atlantic to the Caribbean Sea. Miles rode aboard the *Yale*. "We could never see his ship," wrote Sandburg, "but we could read his mind." In the early hours of Monday, July 25, they rounded the island's southwest point and steamed twenty-four miles east to enter the unsuspecting Bahia de Guánica.

The town of Guánica was much as it is today—a small port facing south onto a horseshoe-shaped bay, surrounded by sugarcane. A channel cuts between two buttes, then halfway in grows too shallow for deep-drafted vessels. Blockhouses, a wharf, and a granary lay on the east bank, mangroves on the west. Straight ahead, a little pier butted onto the main street: today it sports a small plaque and a slab of white coral commemorating the landing. The road led north for one mile into sugarcane: alleys branched off, lined with huts made of palm leaves.

As Miles said, the defenders were surprised. At six a.m. the *Gloucester* entered the bay and fired her 3-pound gun at the blockhouse. The small garrison of troops ran to a brush-covered prominence at wharf's end. A small force of twenty-eight bluejackets rowed to the blockhouse and hauled down the Spanish flag. The defenders fired from the brush, but after the marines set up their Colt machine gun, the Battle of Guánica ended quickly. Those defenders who'd not been killed or wounded by modern technology fled to nearby Yauco.

The Sixth Massachusetts stepped ashore first, followed by the Sixth Illinois. Sandburg heard shooting down the main street and saw white puffs of smoke as skirmishers retreated. One American was shot through the thigh. Sandburg climbed down the rope ladder, rowed his lighter until it hit bottom, walked hip-deep through seagrass, then marched up the street past coconut palms. He'd been assigned to kitchen detail, and he rowed back for pork and beans. He delivered these to the cook, then rowed back again to fetch Captain McGirr's well-fed dog.

He might joke later about his war, but that night in the sugarcane was no laughing matter. Shots rang in the hills; "most of us expected to go into battle, to shoot and be shot," he wrote. It was a false alarm: outposts mistook wandering mules for the enemy. The *pop-pop-pop* of gunfire lasted until sunrise, the Sixth Illinois shooting at anything, even phantoms.

The real battle that night was with mosquitoes. They were "large, ravenous, pitiless," so big that "one could kill a dog, two could kill a man." Days were spent slapping his hands and face; sleep was impossible if the least patch of skin was exposed. One morning his eye was swollen shut from bites. He later saw a man with two eyes shut; a third with his whole face swollen.

Company C stayed in Guánica from July 25 to July 30 while other units moved ahead to take the little farming village of Yauco. Guánicans had fled to the hills on the morning of the invasion, but filtered back to find "considerable marauding," mostly by the Sixth Massachusetts. Spain had carpeted the island with flyers depicting Americans as rapists and killers, and looting wasn't a way to make friends. On July 27 Brigadier General J. C. Gilmore issued General Field Order No. 3 prohibiting looting and "wanton violence" against civilians: either could merit the death penalty. But on the whole, each side respected the other. Puerto Ricans handed Sandburg coconuts, which he found "rich," and native cigarettes, deemed "elegant." He found the senoritas beautiful: "Lady, I love you ever and ever," he fantasized.

Sandburg invaded a land untouched by war and ruin. The only recent serious uprising against Spanish rule had occurred thirty years earlier, the September 23, 1868, separatist revolt commonly known as *Grito de Lares*, which inspired Cuba's Ten Years' War. Separatist sentiment went underground after that, surfacing only occasionally. Gratitude was more common here. "It's a wonderful sight how the natives respect us," wrote

Private Joe Bohn of the Sixth Massachusetts. Private Karl S. Herrmann summed up the country in a line soldiers took to heart: "Life for both sexes and all grades in Puerto Rico is a rose, a kiss, and a cigarette; song, laughter, and mañana."

Press coverage of the invasion was a pale shadow of that in Santiago. Richard Harding Davis said that for the first three days, only two correspondents traveled with the army, and he was one of them; there were never more than ten at any time. Sandburg never mentions encountering a correspondent, while in Cuba soldiers couldn't help but trip over one. There were several reasons, not least of which was the fact that many were as sick as the soldiers. Miles's strategy of marching and encirclement never held much appeal for American editors, who still considered the potential capture of Havana the ultimate story. Finally, the fever raging in Cuba and the return of the "horror ships" turned into bigger stories than originally imagined.

Company C left Guánica on Saturday, July 30, heading east on a road little wider than a wagon track. They started with ninety-eight men, each dressed in heavy blue-wool pants and thick canvas leggings, loaded down with rifle and ammo, tent-half, and gear. Blankets soon lined the road. They marched six miles to Yauco; on Sunday they moved to a mill town named Guanilla and on Monday to Ponce, a total of sixteen miles. They forded "twenty little rivers," endured daily downpours and the tropical sun. Sunstroke, heat prostration, and fever winnowed their ranks; Sandburg passed one fellow "on the ground raving about the heat." When they pitched camp outside Ponce, they'd dwindled to 82 or 83, a 15 percent drop from when they'd begun.

But there were consolations. As they passed haciendas, old women carried out huge jars of "cool, sweet water" for their canteens. Crowds yelled "*Porto Rican Americanos*," and no place embraced the Americans as wildly as Ponce, the island's largest city. On Wednesday, July 27, before Sandburg left Guánica, the *Annapolis*, *Dixie*, and *Wasp* steamed into port, about two miles south of downtown. The *Wasp* arrived first, and found a huge crowd gathered for the landing. Miles sent Ensign Rowland Curtin and four sailors under a flag of truce; the *Ponceños* mobbed him and forced gifts on every man. The 350 Spanish soldiers in the garrison wished to retreat, or join the party, but their commander refused. Yet when he saw the *Wasp*'s guns pointing at him, he asked that his troops be allowed to hand over their arms and retire into the hills. Miles agreed.

Miles wasn't surprised by this reception. One reason he'd invaded the south was the knowledge that historical resistance against Spain had been higher around Ponce than elsewhere on the island; though decades past, people still remembered. The city's 38,000-plus populace lived off a vast export trade; the business of America was business, and that should make them rich. Self-interest, in any language, was as American as apple pie.

At ten a.m. on July 28, Miles issued a historic proclamation in Spanish to justify the invasion. We are not savages, Miles said. Instead, we've come to "bring you the fostering arm of a nation of free people":

> It is not our purpose to interfere with any existing laws and customs that are wholesome and beneficial to your people so long as they conform to the rules of military administration, of order and justice. This is not a war of devastation, but one to give all within the control of its military and naval forces the advantages and blessings of enlightened civilization.

As the first official statement of American policy, Miles's proclamation has been parsed endlessly and compared with Dewey's promises to Aguinaldo or Shafter's to García. In each case, the vows seem similar—in exchange for your help in defeating a common enemy, the United States will not treat you as a fief, but will accept you as an equal. According to the Puerto Rican historian Luis González Vales, the pledge was really "an astute example of psychological warfare." Since neither Miles, Dewey, nor Shafter had the power to make promises, the U.S. was not bound by what they said. The distance between promise and fact rang through the years.

Nowhere is this more apparent than in Ponce: one day after Miles's glowing statement, a second proclamation spelled out the new reality by declaring martial law. Commanders would ensure that Puerto Ricans obeyed U.S. authority, "the power of the military occupant being absolute and supreme." If Puerto Ricans obeyed, their property and laws would be respected; if not, judgment lay with the military. Taxes were paid to the army; private property could be seized; compensation was paid at a value deemed fair by U.S. courts. The promises of freedom were one thing, the realities of conquest another.

Miles landed shortly after releasing the first declaration. Davis believed it was Mayor Félix Matos Bernier's fourth surrender in four days: first to Ensign Curtin, next to three stray officers, third to the captain of the *Dixie*, and now to Miles. The troops formed into ranks and marched into town. Music played in the streets; red, white, and blue streamers hung from every balcony. "The people welcomed the American forces as liberators and friends," wrote the bilingual *Nueva Era*. When Miles visited City Hall and stepped onto the balcony, a band played "Lo, the Conquering Hero Comes."

Stephen Crane rose from his sickbed to cover Ponce's surrender. Fired by the *World* for his kindness to his wounded rival Edward Marshall, he returned to Hearst's *Journal* out of revenge. On their first night in town, Crane and Davis found each other at an inn near the central square. Both were amazed by how quickly these towns surrendered: one to a lost officer, another to a teamster who'd come to steal ponies. Crane said it was so easy that even a reporter could conquer a town, so Davis picked the village of Juana Díaz, nearly eight miles east of American lines. They'd go together the next morning, but Davis overslept and Crane set out alone.

What exactly happened is anyone's guess. In Davis's story, "How Stephen Crane Took Juana Díaz," the novelist, clad in a khaki suit, arrived in town before the American troops, and the mayor gave him the keys to the town jail. Crane divided spectators and released inmates into "good fellows" and "suspects," then, with the former, painted the town. Yet the press historian Joyce Milton does not believe this version: the prank seemed too "arrogant and mean-spirited" for Crane. The novelist's account was much different: he and a fellow reporter sauntered down the road, stopping before a store where thirty locals stood outside. "We drew up and looked at them," he wrote. "They looked at us. Not a word was said." Crane interpreted this silence as a hypocritical "straddle" until more Americans arrived and everyone became friends. For once, his empathy failed him: caught between foes, the locals' best chance of survival lay in biding their time.

Ponce belonged to America when Sandburg arrived. His company marched through the city center on August 1 and camped in a field north of town. Yet sickness was catching up: Corporal C. O. Johnson and Private Rollo Hopkins collapsed; Homer Spillman fell out near Yauco to reappear in a hospital with typhoid. Captain McGirr fainted, then vomited when they arrived in camp; his dog Smuggler had been unable to keep up, and arrived later on an army wagon.

But for those who could walk, Ponce beckoned. Sandburg visited that night for a shopping spree: he "partook of [a] large variety of pastry and confectionary," ate supper in a coffeehouse, and exchanged currency at the rate of $3.50 Spanish for every $2 American. Others ranged through town buying new shoes. Shopkeepers, who'd thought their stores would be looted, suddenly realized they'd entered an unheralded age of prosperity. As soldiers "spent with a recklessness never before witnessed on the island," the merchants concluded that every soldier must be a "full-fledged millionaire."

But all good things must end: the men would soon be on the march into the northern mountains. Their days filled up with target practice, bayonet drill, skirmish drill, all of them unaware that on July 26, the day after they landed in Guánica, Spain had sued for peace in Washington. On July 30 the State Department outlined terms, which included Spain's relinquishing all claims in Cuba and ceding Puerto Rico, Guam, and the Philippines to the United States. McKinley sent these terms to Spain on August 1; on August 2 Spain accepted all except giving up the Philippines. Thus ended a global empire spanning four centuries and worth billions in silver and gold. All that remained were the Philippines, some small islands in Oceania, and the arid lands of the Spanish Sahara.

That same day, McKinley called for an end to all combat in Cuba and Puerto Rico. The Sixth Illinois heard none of this. They didn't know that fighting was officially over, or that on August 7 the first shipload of soldiers left Siboney for quarantine and home. All they heard were plans for Miles's four conquering "prongs," each starting in different parts of the island to converge on the capital city. Sandburg's "prong," led by General Guy Henry, would march through the mountains to Adjuntas and Utuado, continue north to the coast, then hover like Death six miles outside of San Juan.

The Sixth Illinois and Sixth Massachusetts began their march at nine a.m. on Tuesday, August 9. Before them lay a chain of low mountains strung east to west that split the island in two. These hills didn't feel low to the marchers: disease had taken its toll. Ninety-nine Galesburg-area boys had started with Company C when they left Guánica eleven days earlier; now thirty-five of that original group remained, most felled by typhoid. The company was padded by stragglers from companies in even worse shape. They followed the Río Grande Arecibo north into the cordillera, a route replaced today by Highway 10. They carried the same equipment as earlier, but the August heat blazed upon them and the first eight miles was all uphill. They passed deserted coffee plantations; curious hummingbirds flitted before their faces; kingfishers dove into the river like spears.

They camped that night on three small "shelves" running parallel to the road. The clay slope descended steeply to a four-hundred-foot drop; there was no room for tents, so they made shelters from ponchos and banana leaves. At midnight a shriek woke everyone. One of the bulls hauling wagons had stomped on a sleeper; as the panic spread, some men fell into the ravine, which, luckily, was twenty feet deep at that point, not four hundred. The human avalanche took Captain McGirr and others over the side with it; one poor lad was pulled out with a broken leg.

It took all morning to get disentangled, so they did not start until two p.m. A heavy rain fell for two hours, accompanied by a howling wind. Each man monitored his footsteps lest he slip and sail into the empty air.

They reached Adjuntas on Thursday, August 11, at about 5:30 p.m., pitching their tents on a gentle slope outside of town. Adjuntas nestled in a bowl between high mountains: in the 1960s copper would be discovered, but in 1898 it was a small hub of about 2,320 people, surrounded by jungle and farms. The men planted their tents in rows, wrung out their blankets, washed their clothes. Adjuntas was free of mosquitoes; roosters crowed; frogs trilled. *Tik-tik, tik-tik. Co-keet, co-keet!* Sandburg watched clouds rise from the mountains like steam.

They stayed until Tuesday, August 16, and marched north to Utuado in a day, following the river to some of the highest elevations and richest land in Puerto Rico. Conical upthrusts called *maipongo* towered above them; the red-blossomed *flor de muerto* blazed through the shadows. In 1898 Utuado was Puerto Rico's largest producer of coffee, a crop so valued throughout the Caribbean that residents called it *oro negro*, or "black gold." Sandburg would sit in one of Utuado's coffee shops and marvel that he'd never tasted coffee so good. A grand theater and casino invited newcomers to lose their pay. Yet the United States would make sugar the new crop of importance, not coffee. Sandburg's visit heralded the change.

It was in Utuado that Company C finally learned that Spain and the United States had signed a preliminary "Protocol of Peace" five days earlier, ending all fighting and leaving the fate of the Philippines until later. The two nations would meet in Paris sometime in October to hash out details. Company C's vacation was over: they left Utuado on August 26, passed Adjuntas on August 28, and camped outside Ponce late that evening. On September 7 they boarded the transport *Manitoba* for the voyage home.

What had it been for? As they awaited transport, they spent the night in a building once used for drying coffee; each man nestled into a coffin-size bin rich with its smell. At least they were alive. By August 13 half of the island lay in American hands and U.S. forces had easily defeated every Spanish force they encountered. Yet by that date, four thousand Spanish troops still waited for them in the north, and if not for the Protocol, it would have been Company C's job to flush them out, followed by the long siege of San Juan. Their losses could have exceeded those at Santiago. Instead, U.S. casualties in Puerto Rico totaled nine men killed or mortally wounded and forty-six less severely injured.

But they were not unscathed. The costs were insidious and lingering. All but six had lost weight: Andy Tanning lost 12 pounds; Wiz Brown, 16. Sandburg dropped 22, from 152 in April to 130. They looked gaunt, with a "slightly yellow tint on the hands and faces"; by late August, three hundred cases of typhoid fever raged through the Sixth Illinois alone. When soldier correspondents from Galesburg were told to record their experiences, they were too sick to write more than a line. "I will excuse myself for today," wrote Gus Williams. "Too sick to answer at length," wrote Archie McCall. There were no combat deaths in the Sixth Massachusetts, but one year later, twenty-four had died.

How did this make sense? As Sandburg awaited transport, he realized it didn't—unless viewed cynically. Their march through the cities, up the hills and down, had been nothing but a show of force, while he and his friends were the expendable fodder of empire. And these cheering islanders, dreaming of American freedoms and riches, would soon learn that conquest and liberation might look similar, but they were not the same.

A kernel grew in Sandburg that something had gone wrong. He'd been part of a business that veered from its stated purpose. As that suspicion took root, it made him furious. Pasted on the flyleaf of the pocket dictionary he'd carried with him were lines from Shakespeare's *Measure for Measure*:

The miserable have
No other medicine, but only hope.

He, like the others who'd signed up, had thought they were bringing hope.

He now suspected that he'd brought something else entirely.

19

Coming Home

The war was over. In sixteen weeks, from war's declaration on April 25 to the August 12 Peace Protocol, we'd seized an empire. We had our own colonies and our own "natives." Our new dominions might be small, but they were spread across the world. Puerto Rico was ours, Hawaii, Guam; soon, the Philippines. Cuba, at least temporarily: we'd made a pledge ensuring her independence, but who could tell what the future might bring?

"*What ought we to do?*" This month, future President Thomas Woodrow Wilson wrote a memo to himself titled with those words. "A brief season of war has deeply changed our thought and has altered, it may be permanently, the conditions of our national life." We'd gone to war out of "human indignation and pity," but the real issue now was America's future. "The question is now, which nation shall possess the world?" scribbled the forty-two-year-old Princeton professor. "It is not simply a matter of expediency . . . It is a question also of moral obligation. What *ought* we to do?"

The answer was obvious to Charles Post, still outside Santiago: Get us out of here! On July 26, 630 new fever cases sprang up among American troops; the next day, another 822 cases were recorded. The total sick list stood at 4,122, of which 3,193 were diagnosed as fever. That day, a mere 542 men reported for duty. The entire corps slid into a "wretched condition": men entertained the "darkest forebodings."

And people kept dying. Each morning after reveille, Post would hear rifle volleys from burial details in the hills, then the simple notes of the bugle: "Taps, those slow, steady, and plaintiff notes that mark the end of a day or the end of a soldier's life." Each day, more died: Joe Howard and John Dinan, in separate hospitals; Johnny Shaw, in his dog tent; Fred Engels, on a mercy ship. "The volleys became more frequent and one bugle followed another throughout the day." They followed one another "as if they were but echoes among the hills."

The Buffalo Soldiers fared no better. David Fagen and Sergeant Calloway still labored in the fever camp as more of their friends fell out on sick call. Lieutenant Pershing's Tenth Cavalry was so weak they could barely drag into their new camp five miles back from the siege line. Nearly 75 percent of the Tenth was ill or convalescing; Pershing had chills every day, "followed by a raging fever." The Ninth Volunteers, the first black "Immune" unit scheduled as replacements, arrived on August 20 and stayed until April 1899. They mustered in at New Orleans with 46 officers and 984 men; by the time they left, they'd lost one officer and 73 men.

On July 25 McKinley finally heard of the troops' condition. His realization gathered slowly, through casualty reports and two officers with the Eighth Ohio, the unit of the president's nephews. Shafter ordered camps moved every few days to higher ground, on Surgeon General Sternberg's theory that fever was "impossible" above a certain elevation. But fever rates intensified. The 3,370 men on sick call on July 27 jumped to 4,290 on August 2. Moving ever higher was impossible, given the decrepit state of the railroad and the men.

On August 3 Shafter strengthened his hand. History disparages the corpulent general, largely due to Roosevelt, but now he used the outspoken Rough Rider as his pawn. On that morning, he called a meeting of all commanders and medical officers in his new Santiago headquarters. He invited Roosevelt, too. This surprised the Rough Rider: he was well aware that Shafter knew of his criticism, as well as the flood of correspondence urging the Hero of San Juan to run as New York's next governor. One misstep, and this rising tide could recede.

Shafter started the meeting by polling his doctors, who advised immediate evacuation. He next administered a dose of reality: Washington hesitated to bring them back, fearing they'd infect the nation. They preferred that the troops stay put until disease-free. Pleas to recuperate in New England brought protests; the South howled in terror if even a few convalescents returned. Sick troops might even contaminate the ships and make the entire Caribbean fleet unusable. The patriotic hordes who'd wanted this war had now abandoned them.

The officers themselves had contributed to this situation. Until Shafter's gloomy August 2 report, commanders had given little hint that their men were near collapse. Though Roosevelt later wrote that his Rough Riders lay in their dog tents too sick to move, he'd insisted until late July that they were ready for action. "We earnestly hope you will send us . . . to Porto Rico," he wrote to Alger on July 23. Such unrealistic reports led Washington to believe that all was well.

One bright spot existed. On July 28 Sternberg suggested establishing a quarantine camp in the United States, and Alger selected five thousand acres at Montauk Point on the eastern tip of Long Island. Well-watered and breezy, it was so remote that troops could debark without passing through any port cities. The War Department envisioned a moderate-size camp, and construction was just starting. On August 1 Shafter suggested sending some cavalry there as a test; if they remained fever-free, others could follow.

Shafter now turned to his commanders, saying that the War Department failed to understand the seriousness of their situation. They must force Washington's hand. A document might do it, signed by all the generals, expressing their unanimous decision "that the army should be sent home at once," recalled Brigadier General Adna Chaffee of the Third Brigade. With such a document, "we strengthened General Shafter's hand."

This "round-robin letter" became a major, if manufactured, scandal. In time, largely due to his memoirs, Roosevelt was credited with the scheme, but this was not true. Most early histories of the war used as their sole source of this incident Roosevelt's *The Rough Riders*, dictated soon after his November 8, 1898, governor's election and published the next year. Already there was talk of future presidential or vice-presidential hopes; as the biographer Edmund Morris pointed out, on the first page of the manuscript "he proudly repeated the words *I*, *my*, *me*." So many later histories built on this account that it became accepted fact, refined by Roosevelt's 1913 *Autobiography*. Yet, as he had earlier in his tales of the

Yucatan and his charge up San Juan Hill, Roosevelt manipulated facts to his own ends.

In fact, the idea of a group letter had been coalescing for days. "Had the withdrawal begun immediately after surrender took place, two-thirds of this army might be today in the United States without the slightest danger to itself or our own people," Chaffee wrote in his diary. "It provoked me last week to see transport after transport leave the bay with hardly a soul on board besides the crew. All should have been loaded with troops." Instead, "we believe that more than half this army will never see America."

As Chaffee implies, the generals had talked about such an escape at least a week before this August 3 meeting. Talk must have been common enough to drift to the lower ranks, for on July 31 Roosevelt wrote to Lodge: "I am determined that my skirts shall be clean of this particular form of murder, and so I have written the enclosed letter"—apparently a rough draft of the letter he later claimed to write at the instigation of others. Thus, Roosevelt's allegedly spontaneous missive was sketched out at least four days earlier.

Some confusion ensued after Shafter asked for the "round-robin letter." Who would write it? Roosevelt claimed that the officers hesitated, as "their entire future career might be sacrificed" for standing up against the War Department. "So I wrote the letter," he said, "reading over the rough draft to the various generals and adopting their corrections." Yet, according to his July 31 note to Lodge, he'd *already* written that letter, and so had come prepared. To ensure that the reader recognizes the episode's true hero, Roosevelt includes it verbatim as Appendix C and specifies that "after Colonel Roosevelt had taken the initiative," the letter was penned. Instead, all clues point to the fact that Shafter had already hatched the plan.

Roosevelt's memory improved in his 1913 *Autobiography*. In this, Shafter told Roosevelt that since he intended to return to civilian life, he could take risks "which the regular army men could not afford to take." Roosevelt was safe because "the hostility of the War Department would not make any difference to me." Shafter had thought it out as if it were a chess game, and Roosevelt finally understood why he'd been invited. It must have been humbling: Shafter used Teddy's grandstanding for his own purposes, essentially daring him to "put your money where your mouth is," and Roosevelt could not refuse.

Shafter had outmaneuvered Roosevelt just as he'd outbluffed Toral. *The Rough Riders* indicates that Roosevelt wrote the final draft alone, but again this was not true. He took several correspondents into the room with him, including the *Philadelphia Press* reporter Ralph Paine. For once, Roosevelt seemed unsure how to proceed. "What do you boys think of it?" he asked, which suggests that he pulled from his pocket the rough draft sent to Lodge. "Have you any changes to suggest?" Roosevelt also wondered how the letter would affect *him*, Paine said: "How will the American people take it? Will it alarm them and send the mothers worrying?" The reporters ease his qualms: he hands them the final draft for inspection and returns to Shafter.

Meanwhile, the generals had written their own version and signed it in "round-robin" fashion, thus the name. Wood penned this second letter: it was similar to Roosevelt's in content, if not style. Wood's was more direct, and began with a group decision: "We, the undersigned General officers . . . are of the unanimous opinion that . . . this army must be moved at once, or it will perish as an army. It can be safely moved now. Persons responsible for preventing such a move will be responsible for the unnecessary loss of many thousands of lives."

Roosevelt's florid letter was twice as long: "To keep us here . . . will simply involve the destruction of thousands," he wrote, adding that about fifteen hundred cases of malarial fever had already struck Fifth Corps. "The whole command is so weakened and shattered as to be ripe for dying like rotten sheep." But six weeks of rest "would make us all as fit as fighting-cocks" and ready for combat again. "I write only because I can not see our men . . . go to destruction without striving so far as lies in me to avert a doom as fearful as it is unnecessary and undeserved."

Wood had handed his letter to Shafter, as had the chief surgeons, who drafted their own version. But when Roosevelt tried to give *his* letter to Shafter, the commander waved it away, saying, "I don't want to take it"—Roosevelt quoted him in his *Autobiography*—"Do whatever you wish with it." When Roosevelt again thrust his letter at Shafter, the general "shoved it toward the correspondent of the Associated Press." This is interesting: Shafter was willing to take responsibility for every version but

T.R.'s. When the AP reporter "took hold of it," Roosevelt said, "I released my hold."

Everyone left the room. As the AP reporter wired Wood's and Roosevelt's letters to the States, Shafter composed a long cable to Washington detailing the disorganization of Fifth Corps. He admitted for the first time that 75 percent of his troops were sick and his command was "an army of convalescents." Further change of camp was impossible because the men were too broken to march; though a full-scale yellow fever epidemic had not yet hit, one would arrive if they stayed longer. "In my opinion," Shafter concluded, "there is but one course to take and that is to immediately transport the Fifth Corps" to the United States. If not done, the "death-rate will be appalling." If not done quickly, "I believe there will be few [soldiers] to move."

Shafter's plan to scare Washington into action worked: that same afternoon, Alger authorized him to send to Montauk Point every soldier he could spare. On August 4–5, Alger also gave him control of all ships in the harbor and directed those in other ports to steam to Cuba.

The next morning, McKinley saw Wood's and Roosevelt's letters side by side on the front page of his paper. The president "became very much excited and indignant," Alger said. Since the administration had kept secret early reports of Fifth Corps's condition, the headlines revealed to the public the first details of their heroes' health. That day, McKinley announced that the soldiers would be coming home: the conjunction of this order with the round-robin letters convinced the public that the president had left the boys to die until the press, and Roosevelt, saved them.

As a result, fatal decisions were made. The administration panicked. If McKinley had waited a week to send Fifth Corps to Montauk Point, tents, hospitals, and medical aid would have been ready. Instead, soldiers were greeted by an empty beach and rolling hills.

The first troop ship left Santiago on August 7. Others quickly followed.

What would we do with Santiago now that it was ours? The army had dreaded that question. Though the Spanish government still existed in Havana, Santiago was our responsibility now. The prospects were daunting. Every day, troops watched hundreds of vultures circling overhead.

Sometimes the breeze blew from the city and carried the stink of rot out to sea. Suddenly the United States was faced with a humanitarian crisis greater than anything in its history. The emergency centered in Santiago would expand into the province and then throughout the island. The crisis evolved into America's first experiment with nation-building, one Cubans never forgave.

Responsibility for Santiago fell to Leonard Wood. On July 18 he rode through its narrow streets; at every turn, skeletal, "ghastly-looking" figures dragged themselves into patches of shade. Rotting animal carcasses were piled in heaps; human excrement clogged open sewers; hundreds of dead lay unburied. In the military hospital's central courtyard, the main well was choked with slime a foot thick, which floated through human and animal skeletons. The task ahead was hydra-headed: bury the dead, heal the sick, feed the hungry, clean the city.

On that same day, Clara Barton's *State of Texas* pulled into Santiago harbor, escorted through the mines by the navy. She assembled her nurses on the bow to sing "America" and "Praise God from Whom All Blessings Flow." Even George Kennan was touched: "The crowd, upon hearing and seeing Clara's arrival song, got on their knees and praised God." Rich and poor crowded the dock, a hundred spyglasses trained on the small figure in black. As if knowing what waited, Kennan paints her heroically: "the bravest of the brave, always going where suffering humanity most needed her." A small, modest bust was later set on a plinth near her landing site: in a nation where few American memorials remain, Clara Barton's simple statue still stands.

For Cuban historians, July 18, 1898, marks a symbolic crossroads in Cuban-American relations. "What were Americans' intentions?" asked Professor Francisca López Civeira, the dean of Cuban historians. "Clara Barton was a symbol of what good the United States could have done": she offered help without strings. And there was Leonard Wood, who at first seemed a stabilizing force, but whose actions progressively proved that Cuba was not for Cubans. "The common people wanted the U.S. to leave after the war was over," Civeira said. But Wood failed to report this, saying rather that "influential Cubans wanted the Americans to stay."

Right then, the starving must be fed. Starting at six p.m. that Monday, the Red Cross discharged 1,200 tons of stores, the remainder of the

1,400 tons brought to the war. This was piled on the wharf and in nearby warehouses. Unloading was complete by six p.m. on Thursday, July 21: the Red Cross hired 125 Cuban stevedores and paid them in food, but soldiers were also marched from the hills, including Charles Post and his fellow New Yorkers. They ate steak, broiled over a fire made from the emptied packing crates; "tomatoes, softly thickened with flour and a dash of salt and sugar"; Lyonnaise potatoes, "boiled that afternoon"; coffee, port wine, and peach pie with cheese. "Amazing as it may seem," Post gushed, "the Red Cross thought of everything." At first the organization managed the soup kitchen, serving bread, meat, and milk to ten thousand hungry people per day, but soon the army took over, adding eighteen to twenty thousand rations to the total and serving canned meat, hardtack, sugar, and rice from morning to night in endless food lines. Soldiers pushed back the starving, trying to keep order. "These were strange and very unusual sights for an American," Wood wrote, "and very unpleasant ones."

The Red Cross brought more than food: it would bring 65 doctors and 129 nurses, including Annie Wheeler, "Fighting Joe's" thirty-year-old daughter. She'd come to nurse her father and older brother when she'd heard they were ill; when she healed them, Barton took her into the Red Cross and gave her charge of a newly opened hospital in Santiago. Charles Post was smitten when she stepped off the ship: "I have never forgotten the picture she made in that brilliant tropical morning against the background of the hungry city." She wore a light straw sailor hat with a black ribbon, a crisp shirtwaist with full sleeves, and a soft, ankle-length skirt of pearl gray. "She was utterly lovely." Many men fell in love, and one sent her roses. "These are beautiful," she said. "I shall give of each to some of my boys; not the officers, though I am detailed to them, but to the privates—the regulars—for they have no friends near."

Wheeler stepped into a battle for resources between the Red Cross and the army. When she took over the hospital, she encountered "trouble with Miss Brooks," a nurse on Sternberg's staff, Barton said. The problem was settled with Miss Brooks's discharge. If this was a solitary case, it could be written off as a personality clash, but other conflicts appear in her writing. "Army stealing all it can" of their stores, Barton writes on August 2, and on August 9 complains that the Army Medical Corps had "stolen an entire shipment and don't know how to get out of the consequences."

Barton wants to distribute her stores to Matanzas, Sagua, Cardenas, and other starving cities, but the army demands that it all stay in Santiago.

On July 21 Shafter made Leonard Wood the military governor of Santiago: with that, the Red Cross's influence and Cuban memory of the occupation begins to change. Wood proclaimed martial law: "I am hustling things about rather lively," he wrote to his wife, "Lou." In some ways, this was necessary: by now, the death rate had topped two hundred a day. Many houses contained decomposed bodies; Wood required homeowners to notify authorities or face thirty days in jail. He assigned the former New York City supervisor of street cleaning, Major George Barbour, to the task, giving him a thousand civilians and every horse and wagon in town for the job. There were too many corpses for burial, so Barbour's department hauled them to the city's edge, piled them eighty-high between layers of dry grass, and poured gallons of kerosene over the pyres. Each day, black columns of sick, sweet smoke rose in monstrous pillars. "It was the only thing to be done," Wood wrote, "for the dead threatened the living and a plague was at hand."

Wood brooked no dissent. When kerosene ran low, city merchants hiked the price to one Spanish dollar per gallon. Wood gathered them in his old Palace office and growled, "We have come to Cuba at your call to relieve your distress, and you are repaying our efforts by trying to make money out of us. I call such conduct murder." The cost fell to its previous level, but not without protest. "I don't understand you Americans," Santiagans complained. "You are proud of your liberty and right to do as you please, yet here you walk into my house and tell me that I must clean my yard and sidewalk and how I must do it. Why, the Spaniards never would dare to do such a thing." Such complaints were ignored. Barbour broke down doors and horsewhipped citizens who violated regulations. In defense, Wood pointed to the fact that the death rate plunged within a month from 200 a day to 37.

If this were all, Cubans would no longer consider Wood a symbol of U.S. arrogance. Yet he initiated a more lasting change. During this period, he opened Santiago to large American corporate interests, a pattern he'd repeat across the rest of the country. By August 15 the first and perhaps most important had arrived: the New York–based North American Trust Company, with capital of $1 billion and cash reserves exceeding $200 million. As Wood traveled through the province, he realized it would be off-limits to U.S. investment unless a railroad linked it to the rest of the island. The North American Trust was apparently a test run. To be fair, a railroad linking Santiago to the rest of Cuba could be a boon to the regional economy. But the means used to build it skirted laws protecting Cuban interests, and even then Wood envisioned Cuba as an extension of American business. If the Teller Amendment outlawed political annexation, a similar state might be achieved through commercial means.

During this autumn, one notes a change of attitude toward what had been considered the "better class" of Cuban. Before, Americans primarily found fault with *mambisi*; now they found fault with *all* Cubans. "Cuba for Cubans" did not sit well with American decision-makers. "A dual government can't exist here," Shafter wrote on August 16: "We have got to have full sway of the Cubans." At one point, he snapped, "Why those people are no more fit for self-government than gunpowder is for hell."

U.S. officials began to claim that a long-term presence might be necessary. "When the time comes we shall withdraw and leave them to work out their own destiny," *The New York Times* wrote in an editorial reflecting Washington's thinking: "If that time never comes we shall continue to control the island, and ultimately, in all probability, it would be annexed by the United States." Self-government required maturity, and Cubans must grow into the mastery that defines adulthood. Cubans had suddenly been relegated to a never-ending "political childhood," the main metaphor to validate imperialism since the sixteenth century. Authority, wielded by the adult, expected obedience from the child—and those Cubans howling for freedom were ungrateful children. After all, Wood said, "We are dealing with a race that has been steadily going down for a hundred years. We have got to infuse new life [into them]."

Suddenly Americans saw themselves as they would through the rest of the twentieth century and into the twenty-first: "a righteous people," said the historian Louis Pérez Jr., "given to the service of righteous purpose." They'd swing from shock to rage when someone claimed otherwise. Although they'd shared the same goals and beliefs as Cuban and Filipino revolutionaries, they now fell prey to the very human unwillingness to concede power once it was granted.

As a result, they found themselves in the same spot as the prewar

Spaniards: while they held the cities, guerrillas controlled the countryside. Realizing this, Secretary Alger created on August 12 the Department of Santiago: it covered the entire province, and he placed Henry Lawton in charge. In a practical sense, Wood ran the city while Lawton tackled the province. On August 16, Lawton cabled Washington: What should he do with the Cuban army? They maintained their ranks, were "threatening in their attitude," and kept the "inhabitants stirred up and panicky by threats and acts of violence." Washington responded: interference in the exercise of American power would not be tolerated.

But how exactly, Lawton fired back, should he handle such disrespect? Start a new war with old allies? Washington didn't say.

Life in the interior was worse than in the city: after five years of war, the country was a place of starvation and bones. On August 1 Clara Barton visited General Shafter, ostensibly to offer ten tons of ice to army hospitals. She never wrote about the meeting, but immediately afterward sent the Red Cross doctor Charles R. Gill into the interior with two Cuban doctors, a guide, an escort, and two Cuban officers returning to Calixto García. A member of Shafter's staff—the "Christian General" Oliver Otis Howard—asked Gill to find García and make amends.

The group rode west on the battle-scarred road to Manzanillo. They entered a burned hamlet and found "the skull of some poor woman lying in the middle of the road." They stopped in the village of Concepción to distribute food and medicine to a "motley, ragged, cadaverous, and hungry-eyed crowd." In every place, they found Cuban soldiers suffering from unhealed wounds. In Palma Soriano, they left supplies with the mayor, a former loyalist *guerrillero* "thoroughly hated by all the Cubans," who'd been set in place by unheeding Americans. It was "one of those blunders which our dear Government is frequently making," Gill remarked, "in a land in which it understands neither the language nor the people." They learned that García was ninety miles north, besieging Spanish holdouts in Holguin. The two Cuban officers left to find their general; they took Howard's message, but Gill doubted it would do any good. He headed back, leaving food and medicine at every stop, passing through a land of skeletal men and women, children with bloated bellies, "climactic fever," and typhoid. They guarded the horses at night lest they be stolen and eaten. When he asked one "pale, sad-faced" woman, "How do you do?" she answered "*Pasando lo que Dios quiere*" ("Passing through that which God wishes").

Gill could not rest easy after his journey. "The war has intensified [suffering]," he told Miss B upon return. Whatever might be the war's ultimate goal, "thousands of innocent lives must yet be lost before adequate relief can reach them."

Henry Lawton no doubt read Gill's report and despaired. He'd neither sought the governor's post nor wanted it, but the War Department expected the impossible from him. With peace, he'd hoped to retire as a brigadier general with a good pension. One probable reason Alger named him to the post was the common knowledge that Lawton could empathize with the conquered and the poor. While relocating the Northern Cheyenne in 1873, he'd made sure that all had shelter. "He was a good man, always kind to the Indians," one former enemy said, and for that they called him "Tall White Man." He drank one night with Lieutenant Henry Flipper, the first African American graduate of West Point, and Flipper wrote of his "great admiration" for Lawton, who'd helped ease his way. "Lawton, you will have your troubles," Shafter said, "but if any man can run this institution, you can."

The press called him "The Hero of El Caney," but he did not feel like a hero. Conflicts rose between Cubans and remaining Spaniards: he replaced abusive Spaniard police with Cubans; by summer's end, he'd formed a Cuban mounted patrol. He reopened bars and taverns and removed insurgent flags from public buildings. Between Lawton and his old friend Leonard Wood, the city, if not the province, came under control.

Yet the job took a toll. In July, he contracted malaria and dysentery, which he tried to hide from all but the closest few. Sickness brought out his grim streak. "Growing steadily stronger," he wrote to Shafter on September 2, but "very lonesome." Yellow fever drove his staff "daft with fear." On September 6 he wrote to his old friend George Albee, "I don't drink, haven't time or inclination." Same with women: "I have been so run down and worn down that I have not had a 'hard on' since I left the U.S. So don't worry, I won't disgrace myself."

But he was already headed that way. The historian Brian Linn wrote that for all his good points, Lawton could be a "self-pitying alcoholic." More than that, he was subject to extreme mood swings. He probably suffered from what now is called bipolar disorder but in that era was labeled manic-depressive psychosis—what Churchill, another soldier, called his "slough of despond" or "black dog." Churchill worked feverishly to stamp it out; Lawton drank, hard, and his behavior completely changed. The man of whom soldiers said "a better officer never lived" became violent and tyrannical, going off on binges.

This happened soon after his letter to Albee. On some unspecified date, he plunged into a weeklong drunk, assaulting several citizens, nearly destroying a city tavern in a brawl. A reporter for the New York *Evening Sun* witnessed the fight, and rather than file a story, he contacted his editor, William MacKay Laffan. It was definitely another era. Rather than running a story, Laffan informed McKinley of the episode, thus averting a scandal. In early October, the War Department brought Lawton home under pretense of medical leave and placed him on probation. Leonard Wood was made military governor of both Santiago and the surrounding province.

Lawton was not the only "hero" to be chewed up and spit out by Cuba. By mid-August, it ground down Clara Barton. On August 7 she made one last mercy trip, this time to San Luis, visited days earlier by Dr. Gill. A "very polite French gentleman," Mssr. Rosseau, opened his warehouse for supplies that could feed seventeen thousand in the city and country. She returned to Santiago in the rain, one of the last of the original band on the *State of Texas* when it first sailed. Of the twenty who'd landed in Siboney, "eleven had been sickened, been nursed and gone home, and one had gone to heaven." One by one they fell away. "Dr. and Mrs. Gardner," the "Lessers and all their nurses," and now George Kennan—all were fading, "unable to regain strength in the climate . . . and so on, one after another, quietly down and out . . . and still we are pushing on."

Kennan ate dinner with her one last time when she returned to the *State of Texas.* They'd made up: she admitted the fever scare had been overblown, "for scare it was," and he apologized for his harsh words. They both knew change was coming to the Red Cross after the war ended, and Kennan would be a proponent for that change; yet never to the end of her life would Kennan publicly utter one disparaging word about Miss B. He did not look good: malaria hit him hard, first a chill followed by headache, then fever that spiked at 104°F. If he stayed in Cuba any longer, he'd be a "yellow-fever suspect" and sent to certain death at Siboney's fever camp: to avoid this, a Red Cross doctor insisted he return to the United States. He was booked for a New York–bound steamer on August 12 and would recover in his cabin in Nova Scotia for the rest of the year.

He was one of the last reporters left: most others had gone home with the soldiers. All, like Kennan, suffered recurring bouts of *calenture* for the next few years. Richard Harding Davis returned to New York after leaving Puerto Rico; Crane stayed in Havana to write "color pieces"; Scovel steamed to New York after his one-night Shafter-ordered prison stay.

Norris was on his way to Puerto Rico when the war ended, so he rerouted to Manhattan. "I need a rest very badly and a bit of change for a while and a good opportunity to forget a good many things I had to see during the war," he told a friend. From a distance now, "the whole business seems nothing but a hideous blur of mud and blood":

> There is precious little glory in war, if the Santiago campaign is a sample, and when you try to recall the campaign, it's only the horrors that come to you, the horrors and hardships and nothing of the finer side . . . I have seen men who were shot in the throat stretched out in the sun at the Division hospital who had been forty-eight hours without water, food, sleep, shelter, or medical attention. I have seen a woman of seventy trying to carry on her back another of ninety-two, and at Caney I was the first to discover . . . the body of a little girl . . . I want to get these out of my mind and the fever out of my blood . . .

Some never recovered: weakened by war and malaria, they'd die soon and die young. Crane went first, carried away by consumption in a Black Forest spa on June 5, 1900. Norris died next, of peritonitis from a ruptured appendix on October 25, 1902. And then Harry Scovel, from *calenture* and an abscessed liver, dying beneath a surgeon's knife on February 12, 1905.

Their publishers had learned by then that the Splendid War wasn't all it seemed cracked up to be. The cost of a fleet of tugs and never-ending cables had wiped out Pulitzer's profits; dealers neglected to cut orders between battles, and the *World* was swamped with returns. Hearst had similar problems: his fleet of ships, army of correspondents, and barrage of extras cost him so dearly that his accountants ordered him to cut staff when the boys came home.

Hearst also suffered from postpartum blues. He believed he'd given birth to the war, but he felt unappreciated. "Anybody can have Cuba that wants it," he told James Creelman, who was recovering in his Ohio home. To his mother he moaned, "I guess I'm a failure. I made the mistake of my life in not raising a cowboy regiment I had in mind before Roosevelt raised his. I really believe I brought on the war but I failed to score in the war." Though he'd praised Roosevelt during the fighting, he turned on him when he ran for governor, perhaps due to envy.

Though the papers themselves were often manipulative, Clara Barton missed individual newsmen. True, they were unruly and reckless, but they wrote the truth as they saw it and did not hide a knife behind their back while acting like your friend. Barton knew she faced an insurrection back home. The *reconcentrado* effort and war relief had nearly emptied Red Cross coffers, which ignited old criticisms. Why did she insist on being in the field when she could concentrate on fundraising? Some said that she was too old to lead, that the Red Cross had become a cult of personality, or that she mismanaged funds. A new spirit was rising, a corporate ethos of "managerialism" that elevated the organization over the individual, driven by a new corps of male "efficiency experts" said to better reflect the values of the Progressive Era. But internal documents later showed that this was nothing more than a power grab. Even now, the thirty-eight-year-old Washington socialite who embraced the new ethos and forced Barton out had entered the scene: Mabel T. Boardman was close to William Howard Taft, and by 1902 would lead a crusade filled with personal smears. Barton was "an adventuress from the beginning and a clever one," she'd say: she made insinuations about Barton's sexual life, including an accusation that she'd given birth to three "mulattos" by a secret lover. Such malice suggests that Boardman envied Barton's worldwide fame—something she coveted but would never have, even when she replaced Miss B as board chair. Yet the campaign had its effect: in 1904 the eighty-three-year-old Barton would resign her presidency in the organization that she'd founded and nursed for more than twenty years.

Barton was tired; her friends were gone; the war and venality around it had changed too many things. Sometime during this period, she fell in the ship and hurt her right eye; both eyes were swollen, and she feared that flies had poisoned her. She hoped for one more mercy drop in Havana, but this was blocked by bureaucracy. The army wanted her last remaining stores. "If any one tells you that we have been badly treated" by the military, she told her sister-in-law Harriet, "do not believe him," but in fact the War Department was so relentless that she finally gave in. "I will make no more suggestions," she wired Washington on August 18:

> Have stood here eight months with burden of this work to detriment of body and mind endeavoring to do my duty. Confess my judgment is inferior. Had arranged to ship small lots supplies to Matanas—Sagua—Cardenas—Caibarian with Cobb by steamer here twentieth to meet immediate needs. Have countermanded orders. Will await your directions. We have thirty thousand dollars at your disposal.

Two days later, she and her "little band" transferred to an old steamer lent by McKinley. On the bright Sunday morning of August 21, 1898, Clara Barton sailed home.

At seven a.m. on Sunday, August 7, the first detachments of men scheduled to return to the United States marched to Santiago's wharves or piled onto flatcars for the four-mile journey by rail. No attempt was made to maintain order: tents were left standing, clothes piled in heaps, bedding left behind. These were the signs of a panicked retreat, not victory: "Most of the boys," recalled a *Boston Herald* reporter, "were so weak that they could hardly drag one foot after another and had to be helped along by their comrades." He watched their officers beg food from Clara Barton, who still unloaded stores from the *State of Texas*; he stumbled upon Roosevelt, who "looked ill." The Rough Riders boarded the *Miami* with Joe Wheeler and a Third Cavalry squadron: they slipped up the channel past deserted shore batteries, past the hulk of Lieutenant Hobson's *Merrimac* and the silent walls of Morro Castle, into open sea. They passed in the harbor a small island quarantining two hundred yellow fever patients watched over by three nurses; a quarter of them and one nurse never left the island, all buried in the "death island's" tiny graveyard. The *Miami* turned east and steamed past Siboney and Daiquirí where, forty-seven days earlier, the Conquering Army had landed. They plowed north through the Windward Passage for the eight-day journey to Long Island, quarantine, and home.

Next morning, Charles Post and the Seventy-First New York boarded the *Grande Duchesse*, a Ward Line steamer. There were no pillows or mattresses for their bunks, but any place lacking land crabs and giant spiders seemed sheer luxury. "It smelled clean too!" he exulted. The crew stared at the gaunt wretches limping aboard. "You fellers ain't et much!" one sailor occasioned. They cast off—and bobbed in the bay for three days. At night, they watched sharks cut figure eights that "left brilliant phosphorescent arcs"; by day, the men lined up for sick call. One morning the door of the forward latrine was blocked by a dead man; his yellow hand stretched out as if, in that final instant, he'd reached for the balm that could save him. His bony fingers curled like spider legs. No one bothered to move him: when Post returned that evening, someone had pushed his body beneath the washstand so that it "no longer interfered with the door."

The same day that Post boarded, the first of ten ships owned by the Transatlantic Company of Spain arrived to take the Spanish prisoners home. The United States provided all passage costs, rations, and medical supplies; it regarded the ships as neutral agents, giving them safe conduct over the sea. On August 10 this first ship set sail with 1,038 officers and men; from then until August 18, the ships carried 22,864 refugees, including priests, officers' families, and hospital nuns. Some returned to Cuba when faced with the economic depression back in Spain. One would be the twenty-two-year-old Galician cavalryman Ángel Castro y Argiz, who returned in 1905 to become a successful rancher. He hated Americans, and passed that hatred down to his son Fidel.

Not all felt that way. After surrender, Spanish and American troops mixed in mutual admiration for one another and mutual contempt for Cubans. Americans beatified Spain's Twenty-Ninth Battalion, which resisted them at El Caney against impossible odds. The Spaniards—those defilers of innocent maidens in the months before invasion—were now heroes, and Admiral Cervera's visit to a Portsmouth, New Hampshire, prison camp filled with his sailors was treated like a victory tour. A collection was started to buy him a home in Florida. Finally, there was the widely circulated letter by Spanish private López de Castillo to the "soldiers of the American Army," bidding farewell on behalf of his 11,000 comrades before sailing home:

> You fought us as men, face to face, and with great courage, as before stated—a quality we had not met with during the three years we have carried on this war against this people without a religion, without morals, without conscience, and of doubtful origin, who could not confront the enemy, but shot their noble victims from ambush and then immediately fled . . . With this high sentiment of appreciation, from us all, there remains but to express our farewell, and with the greatest sincerity we wish you all happiness and health in this land, which will no longer belong to our dear Spain, but will be yours. You have conquered it by force and watered it with your blood, as your conscience called for under the demands of civilization and humanity; but the descendants of the Congos and Guineas, mingled with the blood of unscrupulous Spaniards and of traitors and adventurers—these people are not able to exercise or enjoy their liberty.

General José Toral could not expect such generosity back home. When Governor Blanco wired that he must not surrender Santiago, he knew then "the immensity of my misfortune." His men had not eaten properly in forty days and were "nothing but electrified corpses." What could he do? When an American translator consoled, "I don't think the nation can blame you," Toral fought back tears. The young man did not understand what awaited Spanish commanders: Toral, Cervera, Montojo, all would face court-martial, scorn, and ruin for centuries of blasted Spanish pride. That day, he said, "I know I am morally ruined, dead as a soldier, discredited in the eyes of the army, and to my name will always accompany as a shadow the surrender of Santiago, the destruction of the Spanish fleet, the loss of Cuba." Yet the mystery of that defeat intrigued him. It seemed astounding that a nation as young as the United States "and formed by the mixture of so many races" should win: it was a given in Spain that only the purest racial strains could prevail in wars of survival. Yet this war had disproved the accepted wisdom. "I have said to my officers, there is a great deal to learn from these people." Pride had blinded Spain for too long: "We Spaniards have often said that you had no history and no tradition," and yet, "if my government does not punish me too severely and I live to do it . . . I will come" to the United States for "three or four years . . . to get acquainted with your country."

"We did not know how to comprehend" the modern world, editorialized *El Fomento de Trabajo Nacional*, "and until recently we have not seen it clearly." If one dreamed of empire, one could not rule from the center. One's colonies must be partners, not slaves. Commerce must bind them, and government must be "suitable to the temperament and to the interests of each colony." One lesson came from the defeat—a lesson other empire builders should heed: "We have practiced the opposite . . . and from there the spirit of rebellion awakens."

The departure of Fifth Corps from Cuba stretched through August 7–25. Approximately twenty thousand soldiers, half suffering disease, crowded daily into steamers bound for Montauk Point, now called Camp Wikoff after the Third Brigade colonel who'd been killed at the base of San Juan Hill. Only the severely ill and yellow fever "suspects" stayed behind, bemoaning their fear that they'd been left to die in a strange land. In fact, specially equipped hospital ships would take them home before month's end. The regiments left wagons, tents, ammo, and heavy equipment; the Immune volunteers of the permanent occupation arrived as replacements, and the ships that brought them joined the evacuation flotilla. On August 25 Shafter and his staff sailed for home.

As feared, Camp Wikoff was still under construction when on August 15 the first ship arrived: the *Miami* unloaded Joe Wheeler and the Rough Riders into a camp without facilities. Supplies were still being rushed up; the men endured days of short rations, while the sick could go untreated for days. Emaciated soldiers lay on the bare ground as workmen hammered and sawed around them.

One thing not lacking was manpower. On August 8 the War Department ordered those 3,500 cavalrymen left behind in Florida to move to Camp Wikoff; they might even escape a typhoid outbreak by helping with the construction. When Joe Wheeler stepped off the *Miami*, he put them all to work. As Fifth Corps's second-in-command, he made free use of his authority until Shafter arrived. Wheeler purchased tons of food, hired extra doctors and nurses, built a bakery and a laundry. He laid out "company streets" lined with floor-boarded tents, pumped running water to every regiment. Private relief agencies established diet kitchens and recreation tents; tons of donated food, liquor, and other articles made Camp Wikoff more livable.

Roosevelt stepped off the *Miami* to face a mob of reporters. He showed off the pistol he'd used to kill his Spaniard, saying that although he was ready to conquer Havana, the Peace Protocol denied such fun. He bucked to see his family, but was thwarted by the five-day quarantine; instead, Edith was smuggled to his tent by a young officer. Within two days, Roosevelt wired New York's Republican Party about running for governor, and on August 21 he met with Senator Thomas Platt at Manhattan's Fifth Avenue Hotel. Though Platt had doubts about the young upstart, Roosevelt's popularity was off the charts because of the war. A few days later, the colonel returned to Camp Wikoff to muster out his men. They were true Americans, he said: on September 15 the Rough Riders disbanded. "*All things pass away*," he told the reporter Jacob Riis as they lay outside his tent and a meteor streaked overheard. "But they were beautiful days."

The colonel might claim to be the picture of health, but of the 21,000 soldiers passing through Montauk Point, fully half suffered from disease, Charles Post among them. On August 24 Secretary Alger toured the camp, clad "in frock coat and silk hat," trailed by his retinue. He'd walk from tent to tent and ask, "How are you, men?" One soldier might say everything was fine; another would counter that all was rotten. Word rippled ahead that Alger wanted the truth, and Post's pals chose him to speak for them. Suddenly the secretary appeared inside the tent flap. Someone cried "Attention!" Those who could rose by their beds.

"How are you, men?" Alger's voice seemed pleasant enough, his tone unimposing. Post saluted, breathed deeply, and dove in: "Mr. Secretary, I am speaking for this tent and many other tents. We are dying here without attention, without rations or medicines. Five men were picked up yesterday, dead." One holds one's breath with Post as he spins his account: he is aware of the men behind him, of others pressing against the tent outside, listening. "Every effort has been made to make this place nice for your inspection. And it's a lie."

Silence descended: camp staff standing two paces behind Alger stiffened. One was probably the surgeon in charge, and Post wondered if they could shoot a sick man at dawn. If he were smart, he'd shut up, but the gates had opened: "You have been lied to in this inspection, Mr. Secretary." They were not getting their medicines; friends tried to send food, but could not get through. "We will die if we are kept here."

"There, there, my man," Alger answered mildly. "We'll fix everything." He passed to other tents: "How are you, men?"

Yet gumption can pay dividends. After an interval, Post got a pass to the Roosevelt Hospital in Manhattan, accompanied by a Red Cross worker. Nurses in their white uniforms stared: he was the first man they'd seen back from San Juan Hill. The next morning, experts on tropical diseases stopped at his bed. They took blood samples, checked his temperature every hour, dumped him in a bathtub with a twenty-pound block of ice, gave him an ounce of alcohol to drink, and poured icy slush on his head. He was one of the 4 percent treated with opium, and he soon conversed with a "smooth white cockatoo perched at the foot of my bed who said the wittiest things." The nurses later told him he was usually delirious, though whether from fever or opium, no one knew. Since no one understood the exact cause of his malady, they finally settled on "Compound-Enteric-Typhoid-Malaria." It had a nice ring.

He stayed in the hospital for three weeks, each day measured by ice-water baths, a meal of some milk and egg-white concoction, his fever's ebb and flow. Then one day he got solid food; on another, they taught him to walk again. "And then, one day, I was well." He would learn that the Seventy-First mustered out on November 15, but he spent that day in his hospital bed. Fifteen men had died in battle, sixty-seven were wounded, three died in accidents, one committed suicide. And seventy-seven perished from disease. "I was lucky," Post said laconically. "I had survived."

Not all were lucky.

On August 27 Sergeant Henry Dobson debarked at Point Montauk, so weak that a doctor was summoned: he misjudged Dobson's condition as malaria. When his mother arrived, his temperature had soared to 103.4°F. As with Charles Post, Dobson's condition was too serious for Wikoff:

instead, doctors sent more than a thousand of the most dangerously ill—like Dobson and Post—to hospitals in New York, Boston, Philadelphia, Providence, and other cities. On September 7 they sent Dobson to Brooklyn's St. Peter's Hospital, a malaria clinic, but on the way, he cried out "Attention, company," and called roll. Doctors ordered his mother from his bedside, but she refused; when they ordered her out again, she transferred Henry to Long Island College Hospital, where he was finally diagnosed with typhoid. By now, he was near death, and she wired her husband, also a doctor. By the time he arrived, his son's temperature had seesawed from 102 to 105.

On Sunday, September 11, his reserves gave out. At 9:15 a.m. he started to moan. "My mother began to moan just before her death," his father recalled, and his hair stood on end. Henry would draw a breath, hold it, breathe out. At 9:30 his face screwed up as if in pain, and then he grew calm. At that very moment, the nearby Presbyterian church rang its Sunday bells:

> I thought my heart would break as I looked at the dear boy I loved so well, and for a minute I did not know but I was going too. I could not breathe, I was in a convulsion which alarmed all about me, but it passed away, and I am still here, though longing to be with him. Mama, dear mama, sat at his feet while I was trying to [help] him, and for two hours she prayed for the life of her boy. It was enough to melt a stone, but her prayers fell on deaf ears, and he was taken. I cannot see any providence or justice in it now, may be [*sic*] I will sometime, but why one so fair and true as he should be taken when he could be of so much good, and those saved who are a curse to the world and always will be, I cannot say.

They buried him in grave 5835A in Arlington Cemetery, near their home. Four other members of the Ordway Rifles who'd fought with him were buried nearby; a sixth was interred farther away. "Others will soon be there," Dr. Dobson added, "for death is after them."

Shafter docked at Montauk Point on September 1; the *Nueces* carrying David Fagen, John Calloway, and others of the Twenty-Fourth arrived the next day. Fagen and Calloway had been recovering from the fever's miserable first stage when they left Siboney; then the second, often toxic, phase began. Both waited it out in camp, though according to the chaplain, Calloway "suffered near to death with the disease." A group of black women from Brooklyn brought a decorated regimental flag stand and a home-cooked dinner with four hundred berry pies. The Twenty-Fourth stayed until September 23: by then, the Regular Infantry had been ordered back to their prewar posts. They boarded a steamer to Weehawken, New Jersey, then a train to Fort Douglas, Utah.

Camp Wikoff had become a ghost town. In late August and early September, the volunteer regiments headed back to their home states, where they were mustered out. By September 23 only seven Regular Army regiments were still at Wikoff, and like the Twenty-Fourth, they slowly threaded back to their old garrisons. On October 2 Shafter formally disbanded Fifth Corps, and twenty-five days later, the last unit, a volunteer Signal company, departed.

The dunes of Montauk were empty. From first to last, 21,000 men had passed through the camp, and Secretary Alger claimed that only 126 men died—a creditable record, he said. Later statistics showed that 257 soldiers actually died in Wikoff, most from disease. Official records claimed that from April to September, when the army's strength numbered 274,717, only 345 men died in action. Those who died of "noncombatant causes" like disease came to 2,565.

A later breakdown was more sobering. From August 13 to September 13, 1898, 44 ships moved 22,221 troops to Montauk Point: of those, 3,252 were sick, and 87 died on the journey. According to Wheeler's report, tents and hospitals were built to accommodate 3,000 to 4,000 sick, but that in no way illustrates the full extent of the problem. "While only 3,252 were reported sick when the ships landed," he wrote, "the great bulk of troops that were at Santiago were by no means well, and many of them, fully 5,000 to 6,000, developed sickness after their arrival."

The true numbers would be staggering and can only be parsed by careful attention. When the army spoke of 345 killed in action during the Cuban campaign, 243 died in the Battle of San Juan Hill itself, while the rest were killed in other engagements. Another 1,345 were wounded. Yet 514 soldiers died of disease around Santiago, 87 died on their way home, and 257 died at Camp Wikoff, totaling 1,107 "battle dead," not 345.

According to J. A. Hilliard, the national historian for the United

Spanish War Veterans, even these numbers were deceptive, as they accounted only for the Regular Army. Of the 10,668 officers and 220,213 men enlisting in the volunteers in 1898, 4,544 would be discharged for disability—usually disease. Another 18,554 were discharged before final muster-out: they would be cared for or die elsewhere, unrecorded by army statisticians, usually at home.

On September 21, 1898, Private Charles August Sandburg came home. The Sixth Illinois's return to civilian life was not as long or torturous as that of Charles Post, Fagen, or Dobson, simply because yellow fever and malaria had not decimated those sent to Puerto Rico in the same way it had in Cuba. On September 7 they boarded the steamer *Manitoba* in Ponce, debarked in Weehawken on September 15, and played tourist in New York for a day. Sandburg ate a loaf of bread and drank a quart of milk: "I had been an animal and was now a human being." The next morning, he boarded the express to Illinois and unloaded that afternoon at Camp Lincoln in Springfield. They camped in quarantine until their muster-out papers arrived. Their belongings were steamed for two or three hours in an immense cast-iron boiler, their trunks and luggage disinfected and crammed by the hundreds into a small troop train.

When they stepped off the CB&Q special in Galesburg that Wednesday afternoon, it was obvious to all that they'd not returned unscathed. The local paper reported that a huge throng watched as "those who were too weak to walk were tenderly helped out"; others were carried out on stretchers, and even "Capt. T. L. McGirr was among the sick." No one from Company C had been killed or wounded in battle, but disease was rampant: 279 of the 283 Illinois boys who died in the war were killed by dysentery, malaria, and typhoid. The other four died in accidents. Almost every soldier in Company C had lost weight: Charlie lost forty pounds. He saw his mother, brothers, and sisters in the crowd, laughing and waving their arms. The parade led by the marine band snaked through downtown, including eight lame soldiers in carriages who sat up straight and waved.

The men complained about Captain McGirr even before coming home. On Saturday and Sunday, September 17–18, a petition circulated through Company C demanding that he not be allowed to lead the homecoming parade, nor give a speech thanking the crowd. Let Lieutenant Byloff lead instead. This was signed by all but three men and sent to the Army and Navy League of Knox County. They charged the captain with favoritism and undue severity: "When they went to McGirr in Puerto Rico to lodge their complaints of rotten food, etc., McGirr treated them like beasts, turning them away with curses." Then there was McGirr's dog. When they stepped off the train, they griped about Smuggler, and the story ran the next day. One volunteer said that as he rode in the hospital wagon to Ponce, Smuggler trotted alongside. McGirr ordered the man out to make room for his dog. "I should have shot the dog as soon as McGirr left," the private said. Life in town would be hard for McGirr after that, and in 1899 he led the Forty-Fifth Illinois Volunteers to the Philippines, where he stayed until a few years before his death, in 1926.

For Charlie, it was too early to mull over the significance of the war. He was just glad to be home. He showed his father his discharge papers, and August beamed over the line that his son had been "a good soldier, service honest and faithful." He framed and hung it in the front room. Charlie had been paid $103.73 on muster-out, and he gave half to his dad. August had aged: he walked more slowly, was thinner, and "the hump of muscle on the right shoulder stood out more." Charlie's younger brother asked what was next—after all, he'd been a hobo and a soldier so far. One of his comrades, a student at nearby Lombard College, convinced Charlie to enroll. "Maybe I'll go to college," he said. "Jesus, that'll be something!" his brother replied.

But first he must rest. Charles Sandburg was tired. That first night, he went home with his sister Mary who lived outside town in nearby Dahinda, where she taught country school. She put him in a bedroom with a four-poster feather bed. He climbed on the mattress, laid his head on the pillows, and sank into the feathers. He tossed for half an hour, then stretched on the rag carpet beside the bed. He fell asleep in thirty seconds, as if one must never grow too comfortable in case the call came to march. As if, in this new America he'd helped shape, one always lived in a state of war.

Part IV

THE AMERICAN CENTURY

How do I know what the howling hyena wants?
I ask the hyena inside me.

—"UNTITLED," CARL SANDBURG

20

The Other War

Memory has not been kind to what is known in the United States as the Philippine-American War. Today, few Americans know the details, and few memorials remain. It produced no great works of American literature or film. It made a national hero of Frederick Funston and a demon of David Fagen, but both have been forgotten. It led Mark Twain to despair about the changing nature of his nation's soul. Where the Cuban campaign lasted a few weeks, that in the Philippines slogged from 1899 to 1902, by some accounts to 1906, by others to 1913. Scholars believe that some twenty thousand Filipino soldiers died in battle, while up to one million civilians succumbed to disease, starvation, genocidal madness, and American cruelties that became known worldwide.

For Emilio Aguinaldo, the betrayal of hope started even as Cuba's invaders gathered in Tampa on May 19, 1898.

The bad faith began on the afternoon he'd finally come home to Manila from Hong Kong aboard the USS *McCullough*. It had been two and a half weeks since Commodore Dewey annihilated Spain's fleet; warships from all nations had gathered as the revenue cutter dropped anchor by Dewey's flagship in Manila Bay. The capital city rose before him; the Luneta where Rizal had died. The commodore's launch separated from the *Olympia* and puttered near.

Aguinaldo would always return to this moment when analyzing his legacy. He'd live many years, wondering how he survived, but the defining moment was now—the outset of what he first imagined was a love affair with America, but later saw as betrayal. As he, Goyo del Pilar, and his personal secretary José Leyba stepped onto the *Olympia*'s deck, the Presence Himself descended, sheathed in white raiments. Rear Admiral George Dewey smiled and stuck out his hand.

Aguinaldo would later portray this episode as a "double cross," but that might be too harsh. Fighting in Cuba had not started; McKinley did not know what to do with the Spanish defeat in Manila Bay. But others had made up their minds. The newly designated "U.S. Army, 8th Corps" was placed under Major General Wesley Merritt, the second-highest-ranking U.S. officer after Nelson Miles; Merritt wrote from San Francisco that the work ahead meant conquering a territory "inhabited by 14,000,000 people, the majority of whom will regard us with the intense hatred born of race and religion." Henry Cabot Lodge told Roosevelt, "Unless I am utterly and profoundly mistaken the administration is now fully committed to the large policy that we both desire." On May 24, five days after the handshake, Secretary Long would warn Dewey "not to have political alliances with the insurgents or any faction in the islands that would incur liability to maintain their cause in the future."

Dewey led his guests into his private quarters and "was effusive with hospitality and cordiality," Aguinaldo recalled. He asked the commodore whether he'd really sent through Consul Pratt a wire recognizing Philippine independence. Yes, he had, Dewey said: the United States had come "to protect the natives and free them from the yoke of Spain." He assured Aguinaldo that he "must have no doubt concerning the recognition of Philippine independence on the part of the United States." Filipinos and Americans "should act toward one another as friends and allies." He then switched gears: Could Aguinaldo convince his people to rise and overwhelm the Spaniards? Aguinaldo smiled. Events would speak for themselves, he said.

"Well, now—" The commodore beamed, his greatest hopes confirmed. "We have got our forces at the arsenal at Cavite; go ashore and start your army." He gave Aguinaldo sixty-two Mausers seized from Spanish warships, plus thousands of rounds of ammo. He promised to send a steamer to pick up those arms purchased by Consul Wildman.

Dewey later testified that he never suggested that Philippine independence would follow cooperation with the United States, never considered Aguinaldo an ally, though he "did make use of him and the natives to assist me in the operations against the Spaniards." When one senator asked, "You did want a man there who could organize and arouse the people?" the irritated commodore snapped, "I didn't want anybody. I would like to say now that Aguinaldo and his people were forced upon me by Consul Pratt and Consul Wildman"—thus shifting blame.

Aguinaldo and his aides slept that night aboard the flagship and next morning asked for more assurances. He admitted to Dewey that some of his people feared that the U.S. might not recognize rebel authority; if so, the two might be enemies. Dewey scoffed—their independence was assured. Aguinaldo pressed: Could this alliance be sealed in writing? The old seaman smiled: "The word of an American," he allegedly said, "was more positive, more irrevocable, than a written agreement." Aguinaldo let the matter drop. As they walked back to the launch, Dewey made two final requests: Create a Philippine national flag, but don't unveil it until Spain's defeat. And don't take Manila before U.S. troops arrive.

Thus ended the first meetings. With time, both men remembered them differently. When considering "the word of a Malay adventurer against the word of an American admiral and gentleman," wrote the *Hartford Courant* in a typical analysis, "we believe George Dewey." The commodore never wrote down a word, while Aguinaldo insists that he took detailed notes. "In the archives of the government in Washington and in almost all the history books on the Philippine-American War," Aguinaldo flatly claimed, "it is of record that both [*sic*] Dewey, Pratt, and Wildman completely denied having made every promise that they had made to me."

Aguinaldo landed at the Cavite Arsenal that day. News of his return tore through the provinces: volunteers flooded the arsenal; native militiamen deserted their Spanish units and came over with twelve thousand rifles. He moved with his wife, Hilaria, and infant son into the former residence of Admiral Montojo. Recruits formed into units, drilled in little groups, cleaned thousands of weapons, turned into an army. On May 24, 1898, as tent cities rose in Tampa, Aguinaldo announced a temporary dictatorship that would stay in effect until a constitutional convention later that year. It was the first of that summer's flood of proclamations, most in Spanish or Tagalog, which Leyba passed on to Dewey. They all seemed overlong to the commodore, and he sent them without comment or apparent perusal to Washington.

Despite his gruff show of confidence, Dewey played a dangerous game. Though he'd annihilated the Spanish fleet, he did not control very much—Manila Bay, and the former Spanish navy yard and arsenal at the northern tip of Cavite. Everything else belonged to Spain. When Dewey first urged Aguinaldo to create a rebel army, no one in Washington seemed to take the plea seriously. Yet without manpower, America's control of the interior was a pipe dream.

Washington hoped to rectify this. When McKinley asked how many men he needed to hold Manila and the islands, Dewey said about 5,000; by the end of May, McKinley ordered General Merritt to take 20,000. But what did McKinley want done with them? As early as May 15, Merritt wrote, "I do not yet know whether it is your desire to subdue and hold all of the Spanish territory on the islands, or merely to seize and hold the capital." On May 18 Merritt prodded: "The force ordered at this time is not expected to carry on a war to conquer an extensive territory." One day later, as Aguinaldo met for the first time with Dewey, McKinley answered that the army's job was to drive out the Spanish and give "order and security to the islands while in the possession of the United States."

But what did that mean? Should Merritt kill Spaniards and *insurrectos*, too? It was a delicate balance. Though Merritt might be military governor with "absolute and supreme" power, McKinley wanted the populace to believe that "our occupation will be as free from severity as possible." When America demanded taking the entire archipelago from Spain, no one seemed to consider that Filipinos might want their freedom and be willing to fight for it, too.

It's hard to see how the United States could have been so blind. On May 28, a battle around an armored train resulted in three hundred Spanish soldiers being captured or killed. That same day, twelve thousand Filipinos took Spain's last stronghold in Cavite. Against Dewey's wishes, Aguinaldo's men unfurled the new national flag. During this period, José Leyba dined with Dewey's staff and told them of a major offensive scheduled for May 31: they'd charge up the isthmus connecting Cavite to the main island, surround Manila, and swing north to swallow the central and northern provinces. Dewey's aides privately called this nonsense. On the scheduled day, a typhoon blew from the sea, delaying the advance by twenty-four hours, but on June 1, according to the Jesuit chronicler Father Miguel Masó, "from noon till night, one hears the loud roar of cannons and rapid firing" from the isthmus town of Zapote. Later that day, the Spanish line broke: General García Peña surrendered 900 infantrymen, 80 artillerymen, and all weapons.

The panicked streamed into Manila. On June 6 Aguinaldo offered Governor-General Augustín a chance for an honorable surrender; when Augustín refused, Aguinaldo decided to let the defenders starve. On June 13 he issued the Philippine Declaration of Independence, penned by Rizal's distant cousin Ambrosio Bautista; the Manila attorney read it from the balcony of Aguinaldo's family home in Kawit. Based on the American model of 1776, it listed a long line of grievances against Spain stretching back to 1521, conferred upon Aguinaldo "all the powers necessary to enable him to discharge the duties of Government," and affirmed Philippine freedom "under the protection of the mighty and humane" United States. Though invited, the commodore said that this was the fleet's "mail day" and he was thus too busy to attend. Aguinaldo sent a Spanish copy to the *Olympia*, but Dewey later said he failed to read it and had mailed it to Washington. "I never dreamed that they wanted independence," he later claimed.

On June 23 Aguinaldo's dictatorship was replaced by a revolutionary government; as promised, he declared himself its first president, or *El Presidente*. By then, he'd moved his headquarters nearly three miles from Kawit to Bacoor, more centrally located and within sight of the old city of Manila; he handed field command to the duelist Antonio Luna and lieutenants like Goyo and Artemio Ricarte. By June 30 nearly every province in Luzon was in revolt. By the middle of July, "Aguinaldo had all of the Spanish forts and positions around Manila captured, the Spaniards driven into the outer defenses of the city, his coils drawn tightly," wrote Private Jesse George, one of the first American soldiers to arrive. By August 6 Aguinaldo's men held nine thousand Spanish prisoners and ruled the provinces of Cavite, Batangas, Mindoro, Tayabas, Laguna, Morong,

Bulacan, Bataan, Pampanga, Nueva Ecija, Tarlac, Pangasinan, La Union, Infanta, Zambales, and the towns around Manila. By the time McKinley signed the August 12 Peace Protocol with Spain, Aguinaldo ruled most of Luzon.

During this period, U.S. troops shipped out of San Francisco. On May 25 the first expedition, under Brigadier General Thomas M. Anderson, left with 115 officers and 2,386 enlistees on three transports. On June 15 the second expeditionary force under Brigadier General Francis V. Greene sailed with 3,500 troops. On June 27–29, the third expeditionary force under General Arthur MacArthur left on six ships with 4,650 men. Merritt came with MacArthur: by then, his forces totaled 10,651 soldiers. It took twenty days to sail the 7,689 miles (or 6,681 nautical miles) from San Francisco to Manila, but since the flotillas restocked in Hawaii, the average transit lengthened to five weeks. Thus, the first U.S. troops did not arrive in Manila until late June, and Merritt's complete army would not assemble until late July.

Only with the army's arrival did Washington fully realize its dilemma. But there'd been hints. With each new success, Aguinaldo's former deference to Dewey transformed. He'd stand very erect, black hair pompadoured, fingering his sword. He joked about Spain's $25,000 bounty for his capture or death. Dewey told Washington that his protégé had gotten a "big head."

Then there was Manila itself. Lieutenant Aime Ernest Motsch was squadron leader aboard the *Bruix*, the only French warship present: the city's encirclement stretched through a summer so hot, he wrote, that "the earth seems to shimmer, and even the skies and the sea are enveloped in a burning mist." He watched as corpses of twenty-year-old Spanish conscripts were laid in rows before cremation: "What have these poor Galicians, Andalusians and lively Sevillians done to be disfigured and bloodied?" he wondered. The bodies decayed quickly, "their eyes half-closed, covered with flies, their mouths hideously open in an attempt to emit a last cry."

One big reason for America's blindness could be the lack of press coverage. During this period of Aguinaldo's most phenomenal success, all American eyes were fixed on Santiago Bay. Cuba lay ninety miles south of Key West and was flooded with newsmen; the Philippines lay thousands of miles to the west, and fewer than thirty correspondents would ever land. The only American reporters present at this point were the three who sailed with Dewey; for that first month, all news from Manila was their exclusive domain. By late May 1898, the *Journal* sent a fourth. But once the Cuban campaign started, the press turned away; even the fact that rebels declared the Philippines a free republic seemed irrelevant to U.S. editors. A brief story on Aguinaldo's plan to declare independence was buried on page 8 of the June 7, 1898, *San Francisco Chronicle.* Though the *Herald*'s Joseph Stickney attended the June 13 reading of the Philippine Declaration of Independence and snapped a photo of about a hundred *ilustrados* milling in frock coats and top hats, he did not seem to grasp the significance. The press historian Charles H. Brown described it well: "It was as if an audience watching a play had had its attention distracted from the stage for a few moments by a loud noise and a flash of light in the rear of the theater." Then it turned back to the main stage.

The Philippines were simply terra incognita for most Americans. Army maps indicated that some seven thousand islands formed the archipelago, but only a thousand were inhabited. Part of the ignorance involved communications: a cable sent from Manila to Washington, D.C., took forty-nine minutes top speed, and on the average, American papers ran dispatches five days after they were wired. In fact, most stories from the Philippines during that summer read like something from *National Geographic.* The July 1898 *Literary Digest* tried to dispel a notion that "Malays are wild men." *The American Monthly Review of Reviews* offered backhanded praise: "However lacking in intelligence the natives of the Philippines generally may be, they could not in truth be characterized as savages." They were "as industrious as the Chinese and Japanese," less "criminally disposed," and their homes were havens of "orderly children, respected parents, women subject but not oppressed, men ruling but not despotic." They were a "simple, orderly people," who should be "very happy under the enlightened rule of a European power."

For one brief moment during these months, Dewey seemed to glimpse the future. Though he'd ignored the Philippine Declaration of Independence, he'd been struck by a "constitutional program" drafted by the thirty-four-year-old polio victim Apolinario Mabini. That summer, Mabini shaped Aguinaldo's greater ambitions: his studies of the French and American revolutions had convinced him that a government's first duty was to "interpret faithfully the popular will." To do this, Mabini proposed creating a national legislature, cabinet, and supreme court once the war ended. The plan envisioned democratic institutions unique for Asia: national elections and freedom of speech, religion, and the press were guaranteed. Women could vote, attend schools at all levels, and hold some public offices. Except for such wartime offenses as "military insubordination in the face of the enemy," capital punishment would end. At this early stage, Aguinaldo adopted most of Mabini's plan; after all, *El Presidente*'s intent was to prove to the world that Filipinos were not savages: "We are quite capable of governing for ourselves our unfortunate country," Aguinaldo said, and would do so in the Western liberal model.

Dewey seemed impressed. He told Washington, "In my opinion, these people are superior in intelligence and more capable of self-government than the natives of Cuba, and I am familiar with both races." He later added, "Further intercourse with them has confirmed me in this position." Their combat success bolstered that opinion.

Yet by the first week of August 1898, that same success worried McKinley. As U.S. troops arrived, he finally realized that by solely focusing on Cuba, big problems had evolved. On August 1 Aguinaldo told Oscar Williams that as more troops arrived, his people were questioning U.S. intentions. Annexation was *not* wanted, only independence, he said. Though he, personally, trusted the United States, not everyone did. "I pray," he ended, "that you entreat the Government at Washington to recognize the revolutionary government of the Filipinos."

The meaning was clear: Emilio Aguinaldo and his new Republic planned to stay.

Many Philippine historians today believe that this was Aguinaldo's moment—and the fact that he missed it, his greatest failure. In June and July, Dewey stayed in Manila Bay. The U.S. Army had not yet arrived in force; Spanish defenders were starved and eviscerated. Yet Don Emilio hesitated, playing Hamlet when, with a single dramatic act, the capital and country could be his. "Why, why, *why* did he delay?" cries the historian Nick Joaquin. Taking Manila "could have startled us into a nation, as that action of Dewey on Manila Bay had electrified the country into a world power. For that moment in our history Aguinaldo was our history."

This is a remarkable statement, depicting history as a string of missed chances. Can a nation's fate boil down to "either/or"? Was his hesitation a failure of character, bourgeois prudence, or native timidity shaped by centuries of subjugation? In 1961, as he neared the end of his life, Aguinaldo told an interviewer that Dewey begged him not to attack Manila until U.S. troops arrived: *begged*, as if this appeal touched his heart and vanity. The request suggests that Dewey feared that his protégé *did* intend to take Manila. Within a month, that momentum stalled.

Many throughout the world assumed that Aguinaldo would take Manila; his American cheerleaders certainly thought so. On June 10 Spencer Pratt wrote, "All is coming to pass as I had hoped and predicted," adding that he'd soon have "the pleasure of congratulating you upon the capture of Manila." On June 11 Pratt wrote, "You and you alone were equal to the occasion." Aguinaldo's revolt became the symbol of world revolution, and fighters joined from China, Japan, Malaysia, and Great Britain, along with even some deserters from Spain. On June 28 Rounsevelle Wildman wrote, "Now, insomuch as the Spanish want more bloodshed in the Philippines, I trust you will let them have a taste of real war. Do not be so tender with them, handle them as they would treat you. I suppose you have taken Manila by this time. I hope so."

By late June 1898, Aguinaldo had circled the swollen city in a fourteen-mile loop, with a mere six kilometers separating his men from the Old City wall. In response, Spanish defenders built an inner loop of trenches, embankments, and fourteen small blockhouses. Only the seaward approach yawned open, and Dewey's fleet blocked this, sweeping the waterfront nightly with spotlights. Filipinos sealed off the Pasig River should any Spaniards try escaping that way. On June 27 rebels captured the single pump station supplying water to Manila; the governor begged in the name of Heaven to allow in a trickle of water, but Aguinaldo politely declined.

Though most Americans paid scant attention to Aguinaldo's success, the State Department seemed terrified. They could not touch Dewey for any promises made, but they could scapegoat one of their own. On June 20 Washington ordered Spencer Pratt to "avoid unauthorized negotiations with the Philippine insurgents," and Pratt replied that he'd left the matter to Dewey and acted as a go-between. Five days later, the State Department told Pratt that "it was pleased to learn that you did not make political pledges to Aguinaldo."

Pratt sighed in relief, but not for long. Around the same period, a cable arrived in Washington quoting an earlier story in the June 9, 1898, Singapore *Straits Times.* This described the gratitude of Singapore's Filipinos for what Pratt had done for their country. On June 8 some twenty-five to thirty people showed up outside the American consulate with their musical instruments to give Pratt a *harana*, or serenade. It was the Philippine way of saying thanks, and Pratt was touched. He grew effusive: they should all be proud of Aguinaldo's accomplishments, he said, and very soon they'd prove "themselves fit for self-government." He reiterated his small part in their success: "When, six weeks ago, I learned that General Aguinaldo had arrived incognito in Singapore, I immediately sought him out." He smiled, adding, "The rest you know."

The State Department was not happy: the story caused them "a feeling of disquietude as to whether some of your act may not have borne a significance and produced an impression which this government would feel compelled to regret." Pratt's address to the serenaders could make them believe that America's ultimate goal was "the independence of the Philippines." He'd acted *ultra vires*, making statements the U.S. was unwilling to honor, and soon afterward Pratt was "quietly separated" from the Singapore consular service. Undeterred, he asked Aguinaldo to make him his first U.S. ambassador.

Throughout July, pressure mounted on Aguinaldo to take Manila. Shiploads of American soldiers arrived two weeks apart, unloading at Cavite's arsenal, the only dry land under U.S. control. He could see the flotillas from his headquarters at Bacoor. The first expeditionary force arrived on July 1; the second on July 17; the third on July 25. While General Anderson's first expedition unloaded at the arsenal, Greene's second camped in a narrow peanut field south of Manila, "sufficiently large to accommodate seven or eight thousand men." "Camp Dewey" was indeed a fortunate find. Before its discovery, all approaches to the city were blocked off. Now they'd found a back door, and only a few blockhouses and barricades stood in the way.

By midsummer, the rumor mill assumed that Aguinaldo would be betrayed. The London *Times* predicted that America would annex the Philippines or sell it to someone else, possibly Great Britain. On reading this, Aguinaldo exploded. Surely, he queried McKinley, this was "a diplomatic trick invented by the friends of Spain." McKinley did not respond. On July 6 the Jesuit diarist Miguel Masó noted that America had assembled a "syndicate" tasked with cornering the Philippine market in sugar and hemp, a suspicion that would become true enough with time. On July14 Masó wrote that Aguinaldo's move from Cavite to Bacoor was to escape Yankee vigilance, and that the Americans "had already singled out the man to assassinate him."

One explanation for Aguinaldo's inaction was that he feared the great powers. They could divide up the archipelago as they were doing with China, and only the United States stood in their way. Evidence of this grew daily in Manila Bay. On June 17 Dewey wired that five German, three British, one French, and one Japanese warship floated outside Manila and more were rumored en route. This buildup may explain Dewey's disregard of his protégé's success, for as many as fifteen foreign ships had dropped anchor around him. All knew what was at stake. Manila was the key to the Far East, and as early as July 25, Rounsevelle Wildman described for Aguinaldo a nightmare scenario: "The latest Telegraphic Dispatches assert that all the great powers of Europe (except Great Britain) have arrived at an agreement that the Philippines cannot become a part of the United States, but will be divided up among themselves as has been the case with China. Should this prove to be true, you will have a greater battle on your hands than you have already had, and it will require all the power of the United States and Great Britain to keep your Islands intact, and to hold you as the first man in them."

No such conspiracy existed, but Wildman's note reflected a greater truth: the great powers would march in should America leave—Germany, especially. The German empire included northeastern New Guinea and some Solomon Islands, and in 1885 it had considered occupying the Sulu Archipelago in the southern Philippines. The kaiser had anticipated Dewey's destruction by Montojo, and when that didn't happen, he told the German secretary of state Prince Bernhard von Bülow that he expected *some* compensation, though in what form is never made clear.

Aguinaldo knew nothing of this intrigue. Neither did Dewey. But the Germans irritated the commodore. They were high-handed. Their fleet was uncomfortably large, and one study painted it as 20 percent stronger than Dewey's. The Germans refused to respect his blockade: they communicated openly with the Spaniards and menaced Filipinos in Subic Bay. The breaking point came on July 9, when a German ship broke the blockade but refused to be boarded. The next day, Dewey asked Vice Admiral Otto von Diederichs's personal envoy, "Does His Excellency know that it is my force and not his that is blocking the port?"

The German officer conceded the point.

"And is he aware that he has no rights here except such as I choose to allow him, and does he realize he cannot communicate with that city except by my permission?"

The German officer shrugged.

"Do you want war with us?"

This got the envoy's attention. "Certainly not," he said.

"Well, it looks like it," Dewey snapped, "and you are very near it, and you can have it, sir, as soon as you like." The envoy retreated. "Your admiral seems to be in earnest," he told a U.S. officer, who replied, "Yes, and you can be certain he means every word he says."

There were several eyewitness accounts, all ending with Dewey's threat of war. Dewey had no more right to threaten war than to promise independence, yet the incident showed that he *would* speak his mind as circumstances dictated, and the consequences were as far-reaching. The "Manila Incident," as it was called, was picked up by the world press, all depicting Germans as the aggressors. It became the standard American view of events, creating an image of Yanks and Brits standing together against the kaiser. German ships backed off, though as one final insult, von Diederichs slipped Governor Augustín out of the city in his flagship when he left Manila Bay.

During this period, Philippine and American forces interacted warmly. Though two skirmishes occurred, the prevailing sentiment was illustrated when rebel leaders invited U.S. Army and Navy officers to a feast in Cavite. During postprandial speeches, the Filipinos said they wished to be annexed by the U.S., not conquered. An American officer rose and said that they "had not come to make them slaves, but to make them free men." The Filipinos rose as one; Felipe Buencamino, Aguinaldo's future secretary of state, raised his goblet and cried, "We wish to be baptized in that sentiment." Then he and every rebel officer poured wine over their heads.

All changed on July 25 when the third expeditionary force arrived. On that day, Wesley Merritt took command, becoming Shafter's analogue. The younger Merritt had accompanied Grant at Appomattox and fought with Custer in the Indian Wars, but now, at sixty-two, he'd grown stout and prickly. Lieutenant Motsch said he had "a massive head, a double chin, a heavy moustache over thick fleshy lips," and made "no effort to be pleasant." In fact, Merritt told everyone that American supremacy "must be absolute" and was the first of many frontier-trained officers to call Filipinos "Indians." According to McKinley's orders, he was not to treat with Filipinos, recognize them as a government, or promise anything. Americans would rule Manila alone.

Before Merritt's arrival, Dewey had tried to arrange a peaceful surrender, using the Belgian consul Édouard André as a go-between. André would write down a statement from Augustín, take it to Dewey, and write down his reply. On July 23 Augustín tacitly admitted the hopelessness of their cause. By now, seventy thousand people crowded the Old City: they slept in the streets, and disease spread exponentially. But since he'd allowed negotiations, he'd succumbed to "defeatism," and command of the city passed to his second, General Fermín Jáudenes. As in Santiago, Spanish honor demanded some show of resistance; as in Santiago, Spain would never surrender to "savages."

Dewey was in the middle of this dance when, on July 28, Merritt attended his first meeting. A phony fight had been planned that would save Spanish honor, but Merritt objected: he itched for the real thing. Nevertheless, he was overruled. When André asked him about his relations with Aguinaldo once he controlled Manila, he replied, "Aguinaldo is just the same to me as a boy in the street."

Rains delayed the phony attack until August 13 at nine a.m. Dewey agreed to lob a few shells at the decrepit Fort San Antonio Abad at the south end of town. His *Olympia* would then run up the international code flags for surrender, and Spaniards would raise the white flag. Both sides would sign a truce, and Americans could march unmolested into Manila.

The showmanship would end that afternoon "without loss of life," Merritt said.

But glitches occurred. One of Dewey's captains failed to tell his gunners of the ruse: when he gave a false range ensuring that no one would be hurt, they thought he'd made a mistake and adjusted their sights accordingly. They scored several direct hits on Spanish troops before their skipper frantically called a ceasefire. The charade was harder to manage on land. In one zone, Colorado volunteers found a blockhouse empty and saw a white flag fluttering atop the Old City, all according to plan. But in a second zone, rebels assumed that the U.S. attack was real. They joined in as Spaniards retreated, took the observatory, and hung the Philippine flag from its high window. Spaniards fired back, and the rebels returned fire. When firing ceased, four thousand Filipinos had parts of the Paco and Malate districts, cutting Manila in two. When Americans surrounded their positions to keep them from taking more, rebels screamed back that this was their capital and they did not plan to leave.

The dead included six Americans, forty-nine Spaniards, and an unknown number of Filipinos. Dewey blamed Merritt for rushing in "too soon." Too late, Aguinaldo discovered how thoroughly he'd been fooled. His protests were all ignored. The ruse had succeeded: Americans were inside the city, looking out, while for the most part rebels were outside looking in. And for those Filipino and European residents still trapped in Manila, a reign of terror began.

21

The Republic of Self-Restraint

An uneasy truce filled the rest of the year. Filipinos watched troop and passenger ships disgorge soldiers and the prostitutes, swindlers, and gamblers that shadowed empire. The Escolta became an open-air honky-tonk: "doxies" from Shanghai, Tokyo, Hong Kong, and San Francisco walked the streets in transparent bodices and red slippers. The number of bars quadrupled in two weeks, a "twenty-to-one" ratio compared with Manila under Spain.

"The people have reason to believe that the United States is a nation of drunkards," lamented Chaplain Cephas Bateman. Private Howard Middleton of the Fourteenth had never seen such drinking: "the moans, shouts, and songs" of those possessed by the anisette-flavored, opiate-laced *vino blanco* or *beno* formed the background. *Beno* drove Americans mad: it was not rare to see a trooper crash down the street, "hurling off a pack of Filipino citizens and soldiers who were trying to apprehend him." Private John Bowe of the Thirteenth Minnesota watched a man mix *beno* with Cyrus Noble whiskey, run amok, then tell the captain and the major, "I respect you, but G-d-you, I can whip you both." They gagged and bound him, then threw him into the brig.

For Americans, Manila was alluring, disturbing, and incomprehensible. Even street signs made no sense. The first contact with Filipinos was often commercial, the haggles for food, liquor, transport, or sex in the pidgin English called "bamboo." Refugees crowded the streets; garbage piled up; narrow lanes ran with sewage. The worst was the never-ending rain. This was monsoon season, and few Americans had experienced downpours of such force and constancy. William Oliver Trafton of the Thirty-Third Texas watched it rain "20 days without slack; there was nothing to do but lay around in camp, and if one wanted to fight, go to it, it was something to do." A casual brutality developed as the months dragged by. Trafton lined up once for dinner when the man standing beside him glanced at someone near the kitchen and said,

> "Watch me uncouple that certain fellow." He had nothing at all against him, but he walked out of line and hit him in the back of the neck and dragged him to a pile of ashes which had been took from the stove and buried his head in them. He almost choked him to death in those ashes. This fellow yelled for help, but we were going to dinner and had no time for him.

It didn't take long to target residents instead. The assignment of Filipinos to subhuman status occurred even faster than with the *mambisi*. Soldiers first called them "niggers," which evolved to "yo yo" and finally "gugu." Filipinos were deemed filthy, lazy, diseased, and treacherous, which meant they deserved whatever came their way. Shouting matches, knife fights, and even shoot-outs erupted daily between Americans and Filipinos. Civilians were coldcocked with beer bottles; street vendors robbed; store owners stiffed in a practice called "bulldogging." Houses were looted, women assaulted or raped at gunpoint; even native policemen were threatened. According to William Thaddeus Sexton, between 1898 and 1902, more than 350 officers and soldiers would be convicted by court-martial for offenses involving cruelty to natives, but these were just the few even charged. Sentries shot Filipinos for the least reason: a boy for stealing a banana, a man for "looking suspicious." It was common practice to knock down a native with a rifle butt for "seeming disrespectful."

Not every American acted this way. Soldiers repaired roads and reopened schools, set up clinics, vaccinated children for smallpox; some attended concerts and dances, admiring locals' grace and hospitality. Yet resentment grew, and one black soldier wrote that he didn't think war would have broken out if the occupiers had treated residents "as people." Instead, they applied "home treatment" and "cursed them as damned niggers, steal from them and banish them, rob them on the street of their small change, take from the fruit vendors whatever suited their fancy, and kick the poor unfortunate if he complained."

Manila's Europeans called these soldiers an "unruly mob." By day, they "are on their best behavior and pay for all their purchases," wrote French lieutenant Motsch, but at night "they rid themselves of their inhibitions, drink excessively, and, when quite drunk on whisky," kill at the slightest provocation. No woman was safe, wrote the London barrister Richard Brinsley Sheridan, who witnessed sentries strip Filipino women on the street "on the pretense that they concealed arms." One day Sheridan's wife awaited him in their carriage when a sentry passed and in an odd attempt at flirtation fumbled with his loaded rifle. The gun went off, "the bullet only just missing my wife's head." Flirting ended quickly: "Well, I guess there's something wrong with the lock of my gun," the soldier blurted. Sheridan rushed out to find his wife convinced she'd almost been killed. "Thus," wrote Brigadier General Anderson, "it happened that the common people, from at first hailing us as deliverers, got to regarding us as enemies."

On August 15 Merritt proclaimed himself governor of the Philippines. Yet while he controlled Manila, Aguinaldo ruled the rest of Luzon and the Visayas, the sprawling island groups in the southern Sibuyan Sea. Aguinaldo's reach irked Merritt: he itched to charge forth and take it, but in the lull, some normalcy returned: banks, shops, and newspapers reopened; clattering electric trams restarted. The undersea cable linking Manila to Hong Kong was restored. McKinley wired his congratulations and appointed General Arthur MacArthur as the city's provost marshal and put General Greene in charge of customs and finances. Other officers took over the port, courts, schools, and public works. When Merritt asked Aguinaldo to move his troops from the suburbs, their numbers just multiplied. A stalemate locked into place that would stay until Spain and the United States reached some permanent peace—whenever that might be.

Just as Americans dubbed them "gugus," Filipinos created stereotypes, too. An American thought he was superior. His unblinking eyes resembled those of fish: one looked away, saddened by his lack of shame.

His nose was so large and bony that his voice resembled that of a hornbill. His shameless stares at women led to a common exchange: "Why did the Americans come to help us?" The answer: "To get our women."

Thus, small clashes intensified. Though Merritt allowed insurgents to enter the Old City, American sentries delighted in searching officers before their own men. In return, rebels taunted their rivals. On August 24 two "drunken Americans" were killed in Cavite during a fight; in another incident, one man was killed and three wounded. Aguinaldo apologized, but told Cavite's governor, "Give up your life before abandoning that place." On September 9, six hundred Americans tried to push rebels back in San Lazaro but failed. Aguinaldo ordered his captains to fire the next time.

Though Aguinaldo's words seemed conciliatory, his actions show that he readied for war. The betrayal at Manila had taught him a hard lesson. He sent troops throughout Luzon on the theory that the more territory he held, the stronger his hand. An August 29 report by Merritt's intelligence chief conceded twenty provinces north and south of Manila to Aguinaldo—in essence, all of Luzon. Aguinaldo's gains bolstered his claim that *his* was the true nationalist army, not the invading Americans.

Though arms were still Aguinaldo's great weakness, large shipments did get through from Hong Kong and Shanghai. Weapons crates were unloaded at Dagupan, the major port of northern Ilocos Province, then shipped south on the railroad. Other shipments landed in remote Batangas, far from American eyes. Arms and ammo were listed in invoices as tobacco products to confuse spies: "cigarettes" meant ammo; "cigars," rifles; "Havanas," rapid-fire guns. One wire read like a smoke shop: "Havanas, 2; cigarettes of same kind, 3502; cigars, 492; cigarettes of same kind, 500,000." Remington rifles were "chopped," while Mausers were "straight cut."

The second leg of Aguinaldo's strategy was "civilizational," as proclaimed by the Republic's newspaper *La Independencia.* By 1898 imperialists saw the world split between civilization and barbarism. Those who believed in America's superiority also believed it a duty to save heathens from themselves. McKinley asserted that American control over any people "is always for the sake of humanity and the advancement of civilization," and he used as an example the conquest of Native Americans.

Imperialists called them "wards": since wards were not adults, they'd be fit for self-government only after time and education ended their "political childhood"—the same argument used on Cubans but without the supposed protections of the Teller Amendment. Overseas expansion and westward expansion were philosophically identical, supplying a New Frontier for the old one Frederick Jackson Turner mourned.

The Indian metaphor allowed all. In January 1899 the Chicago political scientist Henry Judson argued that "uncivilized nations" occupied "the same status precisely as our own Indian." They were, "in fact, 'Indians'—and the fourteenth amendment does not make citizens of Indians." A Western writer claimed in the March 16, 1899, *Nation* that since Filipinos were no better than Indians, the average Westerner held "no scruples in allowing a denial of rights to such cattle." Another writer insisted in the May 13, 1899, *Harper's Weekly* that "Indians" was the proper ethnographic label for most Filipinos. Roosevelt agreed: "The reasoning which justifies our making war against Sitting Bull also justifies" making war on Filipinos. Two years later, the newly sworn President Roosevelt called Filipinos "savages," "wild and ignorant," and "Sioux."

Aguinaldo could sense the coming storm. The army believed that 20,000 to 40,000 rebels surrounded Manila, but only half were armed and fewer could aim. He moved his headquarters from Bacoor to Malolos, twenty-five to thirty miles northeast of Manila, where the Dagupan railway ran through town. When he made the move, he rode around Manila rather than cut through it, a route that would have placed him in American hands.

He rode into Malolos in a carriage drawn by four white horses. In the central plaza loomed a cathedral draped with Spanish trappings. Aguinaldo lived in an adjoining convent; out front he posted six soldiers and two spear-wielding natives, and he hung the flag of the Republic over the door. He brought with him his cabinet: Apolinario Mabini to serve as secretary of state; Antonio Luna as secretary of war and editor of *La Independencia*. The creation of a formal government, replete with a constitution and elected assembly, was the manifestation of his "civilizational" policy: with this in place, Americans could not call them uneducated savages unable to govern.

Aguinaldo had launched this campaign before the betrayal in Manila.

Six days earlier, on August 7, he appointed Felipe Agoncillo as minister plenipotentiary, able to negotiate treaties: "Tell [the Americans] that they cannot do with the Philippines as they please, because many misfortunes may happen both to us and to them if we do not come to an agreement as to our foreign relations." Three days later, he ordered Agoncillo to Washington to speak with McKinley, taking José "Sixto" Lopez as his secretary. Agoncillo was the Junta's most cosmopolitan member: Rounsevelle Wildman said he could be "the head of the State Department of any civilized country in the world." His job was nearly impossible: to convince McKinley to grant him a seat at the approaching Treaty of Paris so the Philippine Republic would have a voice in its future. On September 9 Agoncillo and Lopez boarded the steamer *China* in Hong Kong for the twenty-day voyage to San Francisco.

As the two sailed east, Aguinaldo began Part Two of his "civilizing project." Starting on September 15 and lasting nearly a month, he convened ninety-five Filipino intellectuals and *ilustrados* to hammer out a federal government, elected assembly, and constitution. The latter would be what scholars called "the first democratic constitution ever promulgated in the whole of Asia." The Malolos Congress began with Aguinaldo reading softly from a short address that echoed the Monroe Doctrine—America for Americans, the Philippines for Filipinos. Delegates wore cutaway coats and top hats, looking nothing like the natives seen in travelogues. Although facts are hard to separate from myth, the accomplishments were breathtaking: within the Republic's first hundred days, delegates planned free compulsory education; a system of secondary schools; a military academy headed by Luna; a new army, also under Luna; a new tax and fiscal system; an official government organ, *El Heraldo de la Revolución*; a reformed currency; a diplomatic corps under Mabini; and various departments—of justice, courts, sanitation, finance, and so on. Several Europeans attended, including the U.S. minister to Siam John Barrett, who recorded his impressions in the July 1899 *Review of Reviews*: this was no mummer's play in fancy dress, he said, but serious business in which delegates "showed a knowledge of debate and parliamentary law" and the executive was filled with "bright men who seemed to understand their respective positions." The historian Leon Wolff would say, "Today few doubt they would have governed the islands adequately," and that the agenda seemed supported by every adult Filipino "who had even the foggiest notion of what was taking place." In less time than Cubans, or even Americans one century earlier, Filipinos had proved they could "self-govern" their new nation.

What exactly did the new constitution establish? This is hotly debated today. The U.S. Philippine Commission would later say that because the Malolos Constitution established a bill of rights, representative government, and separation of church and state, the "political ideal of the Filipinos coincides with the political practice and tradition of the American," a statement that implies that American democracy is a natural state—the organic endpoint for those seeking freedom. Aguinaldo's and America's constitutions embodied "precisely the [same] principles," the commissioners said. Thus, the Malolos Constitution could have been an attempt to assure Americans that the new Philippine Republic was able to govern itself—and do so firmly in the American mode.

Yet there were differences. Though the Malolos Constitution protected against government abuse, this was a common trait in many nineteenth-century European constitutions, not just America's. Though its articles of property rights were similar, it omitted the right against self-incrimination and the protection against arbitrary search and seizure, among others. The constitutional scholar Lance D. Collins, in a 2020 revisionist essay, wrote that this omission suggests that the U.S. Constitution was not the sole model, as the commissioners claimed, but one of several. In fact, parts of the Malolos Constitution were copied word for word from Spain's 1812 Constitution, when it won back independence from France after a bloody guerrilla war. Both defined sovereignty not so much in terms of physical boundaries, but as "residing exclusively in the hearts of the people." Though emulative of America's "We the people," the line was Mabini's, reflecting the same Romantic sense of *nationhood* espoused by Martí and Rizal.

Seen in this light, the Malolos Constitution was a chameleon, able to be what the moment demanded. When Felipe Agoncillo finally argued the case for Philippine independence before McKinley, he linked the U.S. and Malolos constitutions in the same breath, neglecting to mention those sections copied directly from the 1812 canon of the conquered Spaniards. It was not even the product of a unified body. Where Mabini and fellow liberals sought universal suffrage and agrarian reform, the conservative *ilustrados* forming the majority of the congress limited suffrage to the landed gentry and discarded many of Mabini's egalitarian ideals. Though Aguinaldo sympathized with Mabini, the *ilustrados* gave his new government the kind of cultured patina Western powers might accept. And so, according to the historian Teodoro Agoncillo, many of Mabini's ideas were overruled. Deep divisions pervaded the body that released the Malolos Constitution to the world.

In fact, Mabini and his allies didn't even want a wartime constitution, and had proposed to Aguinaldo a temporary military dictatorship like that during the earlier war against Spain. The young Republic needed a unified front, they said. To them, the Malolos Constitution was an imperfect working document, not a final draft, moving toward something that was neither American nor Spanish nor European, searching instead for something more exclusively Asian and Filipino. In this way, Collins suggests, it was closer in intent to the *pronunciamientos* used throughout nineteenth-century Latin America to test the waters for a coup d'état. *Pronunciamientos* were a "temporary framework for revolutionary guidance," never considered permanent. Fine details could be hammered out once freedom was won.

If Aguinaldo's house lay in disorder, McKinley's did not. On September 16, 1898, McKinley hosted a farewell dinner for the five peace commissioners before they sailed to Paris. They included former Secretary of State William R. Day; Senator Cushman K. Davis of Minnesota, chairman of the Foreign Relations Committee; Senator William P. Frye of Maine; Senator George Gray of Delaware; and Whitelaw Reid, editor of the *New York Tribune*. Davis, Frye, and Reid were expansionists; all but Gray were Republican. McKinley's instructions focused on the path ahead: keep Cuba independent, but under American guidance; Puerto Rico, Guam, and other pinpricks became possessions. Finally, Dewey's triumph brought "obligations," and America expected "the cession in full right and sovereignty of the island of Luzon," where at least half of the Philippines' 7.6 million people lived.

McKinley wanted the treaty in time for the congressional session of January 1899. As he had in Cuba, he got on his knees and prayed. What should he do with the Philippines? Then one night, a well-organized answer came from above:

> (1) that we could not give [the Philippines] back to Spain—that would be cowardly and dishonorable; (2) that we could not turn them over to France or Germany—our commercial rivals in the Orient—that would be bad business and discreditable; (3) that we could not leave them to themselves—they were unfit for self-government—and they would soon have anarchy and misrule over there worse than Spain's was; and (4) that there was nothing left for us to do but to take them all, to educate the Filipinos, and uplift and civilize and Christianize them, and by God's grace do the very best we could by them, as our fellow-men for whom Christ also died.

Then he went to bed, "slept soundly," and the next morning contacted the War Department's chief mapmaker to tell him "to put the Philippines on the map of the United States."

As Felipe Agoncillo crossed the China Sea, he did not know that his puny if polished voice must contend with McKinley's God. The *China* picked up passengers in Manila and sailed east. He sat in his cabin, refining points he'd make to the American president: the Philippines, he'd say, deserved sovereignty. After leaving Manila, he discovered among his co-passengers Generals Francis V. Greene and Wesley Merritt. Agoncillo could understand Greene's presence: he'd been recalled to meet with the president before heading to Paris. But Merritt?

Agoncillo did not know that Merritt had asked to go home. He hated the Philippines and was angry that McKinley had not let him conquer it all. He'd served as military governor a mere two weeks, from August 14 to 30, and spent most of that time on a ship awaiting his replacement, the sixty-one-year-old Major General Elwell Stephen Otis. Agoncillo tried to talk to Merritt, but the old Indian fighter would not talk to *any* Filipino, much less one whose demeanor challenged the notion that all gugus were savages. But Greene proved a different animal. Like Merritt, he did not think Filipinos ready to govern. Unlike Merritt, he gave Agoncillo an ear.

Over several meetings, Agoncillo advanced arguments he'd use on

McKinley. How could Filipinos not be ready for independence when they had trod the same path as Americans a century earlier? Hadn't the United States given the Republic recognition when its navy and diplomats dealt with Aguinaldo? Since the Philippine Army had so thoroughly overwhelmed Spain that she no longer "owned" anything outside Manila, the Crown could not cede territory it did not have. Greene was impressed and would try to set up a meeting with McKinley in Washington, he said.

The *China* anchored off San Francisco on Thursday, September 22. A large crowd turned out to ogle the representative of the "uncivilized" Philippines. Magazine stories still claimed that Filipinos had not advanced far up the evolutionary ladder: some had just come down from the trees and still had tails. Instead, a "dapper-looking little fellow" in a top hat, suit, and tails stepped off the gangplank, better dressed than anyone else there. He was "quick-witted," said the *San Francisco Bulletin*, "well-educated," said the *Boston Evening Transcript*, and courteous and likable, which surpassed all comprehension. The two improbable diplomats overnighted at the Palace Hotel, then caught a morning train for the slow journey to Washington, D.C.

As the U.S. geared up in the Philippines, one question seemed paramount. How well could she wage a protracted foreign war?

One need only look to Cuba for answers. By then, it was clear that the Splendid War would have been a disaster if Spain had not folded. Shafter said as much: "At Santiago, we had to deal with things as they were—not as they should be." Republicans had annexed the war as theirs, but what should have been a triumph in the months before midterm elections had disintegrated into demands for investigations into the army's handling of the war. For the party in power, this could spell disaster at the polls. On September 8, 1898, McKinley created a commission of "distinguished soldiers and civilians" to investigate every aspect of the War Department's stewardship of the Cuban campaign. The former Union general Grenville Dodge was appointed chairman: if Dodge could shepherd the transcontinental railroad into existence, he might improve the U.S. military. In late September, his work began.

For four months, the Dodge Commission examined every aspect of the army's record: they interviewed Secretary Alger, all senior bureau chiefs, lesser officers, medical personnel, charity workers, and enlisted men; pursued information in Chicago, Detroit, Harrisburg, Cincinnati, Philadelphia, New York, and Tampa. They heard nearly five hundred witnesses, one of whom was the nurse Janet Jennings of the *Seneca*. She testified that the only thing that kept the men going was the doctor's whiskey: "I took it myself," she said. "I had never before, but I did every day several times, as I am quite sure I could not have kept up." Few reputations survived those "wintry days of censure": one was Lieutenant Hobson, hero of the *Merrimac*, "who had the good luck to be of junior rank"; one was Commodore Dewey, who was out of reach; one was Roosevelt, to whom nothing stuck. McKinley stage-managed it well enough that Republicans eked past the November elections with as little damage as possible. A scandal seemed contained.

At least until on December 21, when Nelson Miles testified about defective rations. He singled out "embalmed" beef as "one of the serious causes of so much sickness and distress," and wondered whether the tins contained deadly preservatives. Criminal speculators could bid for government contracts with no oversight; the army had rushed contracts with Chicago's "big three" meat-packers—Morris & Co., Swift & Co., and Armour & Co.—and the meat they supplied was so poorly preserved and chemically adulterated that it caused an unrecorded number of illnesses and deaths from food poisoning and dysentery. It was "unfit for swine."

In the end, blame focused on War Secretary Alger. Fairly or not, he stepped down, replaced by the New York attorney Elihu Root, known for his quick mind, political loyalty, and "quick and murderous" smile. "I know nothing about war, I know nothing about the army," Root protested, but McKinley didn't care. The president "has got to have a lawyer to direct the government of these Spanish islands, and you are the lawyer he wants," Root was told.

Cuba lay in ruins: Was there any reason to suppose the Philippines would be different? In many ways, the two prizes were similar. Cuba might have won her thirty-year struggle against Spain, but the cost in lives and property was enormous. Nearly two generations of Cubans had died or were ruined; thousands were destitute. When Fitzhugh Lee rode through the interior after the armistice, he compared some places in Cuba to "an ash pile, in others the dreary desert." Total dead hovered at three hundred thousand, most of them *reconcentrados.*

Over everything lay the truth of disease. America's conquest had created conditions that sent the death rate soaring. "Story of Horrors Hourly Grows Worse," Hearst's *Journal* screamed. Less publicized was the army's call for "contract nurses" as typhoid raged. A total of 1,563 women were hired, with a maximum 1,158 serving at any time. They'd serve in the States, Cuba, Puerto Rico, the Philippines, the hospital ship *Relief,* and even in Honolulu. Typhoid struck 140 of them, and 13 died in 1898 alone.

Clara Maass, like most, did not have much time to settle her affairs. On September 28, 1898, she received a telegram from the surgeon general to start immediately once her contract arrived. It came the next day. She'd earn $30 a month as a member of the Army Nurse Corps. She boarded a train for the three-day ride to Jacksonville's Camp Cuba Libre; on October 3 she stepped off, paid a porter $1 to transfer her luggage, paid another dollar for cab fare, and reported at the Second Army Division's field hospital, which was filled with wounded and sick soldiers from Cuba.

It was a far cry from the German Hospital. Hundreds lay in bed from malaria, dysentery, and typhoid. Maass worked all day to ease their torment, then collapsed on her army cot each night in a tent she shared with three Pennsylvanians. On her time off, she hung signs on the canvas front: "Camp Cuba Libre" and "Potato Patch Tent." She teased soldiers from the Sixth Missouri assigned to guard them from other too-friendly Americans.

In November, she transferred to the Seventh Corps hospital in Savannah, a thousand-bed facility for occupation forces from throughout the Caribbean; in late December, she received orders for Santiago. She arrived in early January 1899 to the same vistas seen by Roosevelt and David Fagen: the Sierra Maestra, Morro Castle asleep on its rock, the half-sunk *Merrimac* by the harbor channel. Bodies were gone from the streets; daily deaths had fallen from 200 to 37. In some places, Wood's men still dumped kerosene on cobblestones and set whole streets afire to burn away filth. New businesses had sprung up: the "Chicago Restaurant," "Arizona Saloon," "United States Hotel."

Maass was assigned to San Luis, which had become a major supply depot. She heard the names of three bacteriologists—Juan Guiteras, Aristides

Agramonte, and William C. Gorgas, all graduates of U.S. medical schools. They drew blood from yellow fever patients and peered through their microscopes to track down the source of the scourge. In another two years, their lives would be fatally linked: now, she may only have heard of the Cubans, Agramonte and Guiteras, but Gorgas, an Alabamian, came to know and respect her. The field hospital was a conglomeration of large tents housing fifty cots per side, with a passage down the middle. Nearly every bed was filled. Patients begged not to die in Cuba. Outside, beggars whispered "*Me comida.*"

She stayed less than a month, until her contract expired. On January 21 she was honorably discharged and sent home. She returned to East Orange and moved in with her mother, but grew fidgety and hoped to rejoin. She watched for news of the Philippines, where all believed the next war would come.

Felipe Agoncillo arrived in a city geared for war. San Francisco overflowed with soldiers, most headed to the Philippines. Officers dined in swank restaurants like Marchand's and Tait's; commanders accepted dinner invitations to the palaces of railroad and mining barons on Nob Hill. Men in blue tunics flowed through the four-story pile of stores on Montgomery Street called the "Monkey Block." They loaded into ships belching coal smoke, sought out whores in the brawling streets south of Mission, drifted in protective herds through Chinatown. Most hailed from Western states and territories like Nebraska and Oklahoma. They'd jammed into Pullman coaches dragged through god-awful high mountains and debarked in a city leveled so often by fire that a rising phoenix was emblazoned on its municipal seal. They camped in and around the Presidio, the old Spanish fort whose occupants once hunted and killed local Miwok Indians.

Frederick Funston arrived on June 16 to take charge of his Kansans. He'd spent the journey reading a book on military tactics, with a brief stopover in Iola to see family. "What do you know about military tactics, Fred?" his father asked, and Funston admitted, "Not much, but I am halfway through the book and by the time I reach San Francisco, I will have mastered it." The Twentieth Kansas was in sorry shape: many volunteers did not have uniforms or boots, and they still wore overalls. Many had never seen a body of water bigger than a lake; one had never seen a lemon, and he planned "to send it back to the folks." They all were "blonds, chiefly, with brown skins and light hair," wrote the *Kansas City Star.* "Their eyes have a far-away look, as of men who remember the grasshopper, the army-worm, and other things that make living tough in Kansas." They pitched their tents in Camp Merritt, a low, wet field outside the Presidio gates, and by the time Funston arrived, two had already died: Orville Knight of pneumonia and the KU pharmacy graduate Albert Fargus of spinal meningitis. Soon, Private Pepper of Company I would die of "quick consumption," and Captain William McAllister of pneumonia following a bout of measles. The latter disease landed three more men in the hospital. A belief sprang up that they would either die in San Francisco or miss the war entirely.

Frustration touched everything. Funston's Kansans were so pathetically trained that they'd be one of the last units to leave for Manila. Every morning, he tried to hammer his men into shape with target practice and close-order drills, but they called him a martinet and a "Cuban deserter" and turned into a "coyote pack yelping at my heels." The frustration rubbed off on Funston, too. On July 4 the army staged a grand review through downtown, a chained eagle carried before them. "I did not consider it a very fine symbol of liberty," said Corporal Henry Ruppenthal of Company M. Funston's horse had injured its leg, so he drew as replacement a nervous beast that bucked at every loud noise. Funston spotted several ruffians up ahead, harassing troops with lit firecrackers as they marched past. Horses were a special target, and one of them tried to toss a "cannon" under Funston's spooked animal. "Right then and there, murder came into my heart," he wrote, "and I made a hard and conscious effort to kill him." Like all mounted officers, he held his saber unsheathed; he cut at the "hooligan," who jumped back, the blade missing his throat by six inches. "I deeply regretted my failure," Funston said.

Funston and his Kansans were still camped at the Presidio when Agoncillo arrived. There is no indication that the diplomat traveled that far north to observe the soldiers bound for his country. He didn't have time. He stepped into a mob of reporters all wanting interviews, so he took them to his stateroom at the Palace Hotel. As reporters fired off questions, "I endeavored with some reticence not to disclose the object of my mission to them." He wired Aguinaldo: "On that very day, the newspapers reported that we are not a savage people, and possess a civilization comparable to any other."

"The political representative is the political image," noted the Welsh cultural critic Raymond Williams. In that respect, Agoncillo's mission succeeded: his "optics" proved that Filipinos were not savages. Yet the nuances of race did not disappear. Almost every newspaper fixated on his small stature, "a phenotypical criterion of American racialism," noted the Philippine scholar Oscar Campomanes: he was a "little fellow," according to the *San Francisco Examiner*; "small, alert, and dark," to the *Chicago Tribune*; "small in stature," but "alert and dark as the darkest American Indian," to the *Chicago Evening Post*. Agoncillo proved a troubling vision for Americans: he projected more culture and intelligence than many rubes on his route, symbolizing a nation with a right to be represented at the Paris peace talks and on the world stage.

These talks were nine days away, slated to open on October 1. He could not linger. On September 23 Sixto Lopez and he boarded the Overland Express for Washington, D.C. They reached Chicago early on September 26 and took a carriage to Lincoln Park, where Agoncillo stood before a bronze statue of Abraham Lincoln for about fifteen minutes and bared his head. They ate breakfast with General Greene, also taking the same train. As the train pulled off, Agoncillo told reporters that he was "delighted with America": it was "the land that we have looked up to for many years, and the one in whose footsteps we have tried to follow."

They arrived in Washington on September 27 and moved into a four-room suite at the Arlington Hotel. McKinley and his cabinet discussed him that morning. His presence "embarrassed" the president, revealed the *Chicago Tribune*: McKinley "would be much better satisfied if they had remained in the Philippines." He agreed to meet Agoncillo, but "only as a private citizen of the Philippines," the president said.

Agoncillo and Lopez walked to the White House at 10:15 a.m. on Saturday, October 1. Both were formally dressed in light-striped trousers, frock coats, silk hats, vests, patent leather shoes, and carried canes. It was a beautiful autumn day, and the accompanying presence of General Greene set them at ease. But the air turned chilly inside. They were directed to a public waiting area, then ushered before McKinley in the Cabinet Room.

Second Assistant Secretary of State Alvey A. Adee offered to translate, but Lopez did the honors, though at times his words lagged. McKinley stared at the diplomat and asked him to state his case. Agoncillo pressed the arguments he'd made to Greene: the harsh history of Spanish rule; the promises made by Dewey, diplomats, and American officers; the Malolos Constitution and its American model; the natural imperatives of liberty. The president remained silent. Agoncillo finished up, and after a pause, McKinley asked if he had anything else to add.

Could he be represented on the American peace commission to Paris? he asked.

McKinley thought not.

Could he be heard by the commissioners?

McKinley thought it impractical, considering his inability to speak English, and suggested instead a written memorandum. He promised to give it due consideration. They were ushered outside, where someone asked Agoncillo for his autograph. "*Hasta mañana*," he replied, his nerves finally catching up, as he hurried away.

Agoncillo delivered the document to the White House three days later; as promised, it laid out a ten-point argument for Philippine sovereignty. Is it right that the Philippine people be denied a voice in the process "which will affect their destiny in history," he asks in point 5. Do not Filipino pleas embody the same "principles of liberty, justice, and right" expressed in the "sacred Declaration of Independence," he adds in point 8. The document is never acknowledged.

Four days later, on October 8. Agoncillo and Lopez sail to Paris. Before sailing, he wires Aguinaldo. "Try to strengthen yourself during the crisis," he warns. "All towns should be captured. Prepare all that is necessary." He lands in Paris and asks repeatedly to speak before the commissioners. They refuse every time. He is, to them, invisible.

A strange imperial finality unfolds as these last years of the old century hasten to their end. Perhaps it started on July 7, 1898, when the United States finally annexed Hawaii after attempts and debate stretching back to the 1850s. But war finally tipped the balance, and McKinley called Hawaii an imperative naval base and coaling station in the conflict with

Spain. Most of the islands' forty thousand natives stayed at home in protest during the August 12 annexation ceremony; many of those who ventured out wore the Hawaiian flag pinned to their breast with the words "*Kuu Hae Aloha*," "my beloved flag." American ownership spread across the Pacific after that: in addition to events in the Philippines, in 1899 and 1900 the United States would annex half of Samoa and uninhabited Wake Island.

McKinley seemed set in his course by two late-breaking factors. One was Greene's Philippines report, delivered at the same time as Agoncillo's: despite his courtesy to the diplomat, Greene stayed committed to U.S. control. Only full annexation would bring peace and prosperity to the archipelago, he emphasized. McKinley could not separate protection and possession: one could not "protect" territories without total control.

McKinley's second deciding factor was a swing he took through the Midwest soon after Agoncillo's departure. He had not traveled west of the Mississippi since his inauguration; now, from October 11 to 25, he made whistle-stops in Iowa, St. Louis, Omaha, and Chicago. The Republican faithful turned out in thousands. There was much talk of "Dewey," "justice," and the "courage of destiny"; the Cuban war had brought new markets, he said. Even as he spoke, the United States took formal possession of Puerto Rico on October 18, and Major General John Brooke was made its first military governor. This growing benevolent empire had been "planned and designed by the Master of men," and as McKinley toured the Midwest, he could finally see how "the currents of destiny flow through the hearts of the people." We'd gone to war "not because we wanted to, but because humanity demanded it," and now "we must accept no settlement that will not take into account the interests of humanity." He basked in applause: to him, the voice of the people was the same as the Voice of God.

As had happened before, popular winds set his course. By tour's end, he wired the commissioners in Paris to insist upon annexation of the Philippines, which could be claimed by right of conquest—even if American forces only held Manila and parts of Cavite. On October 31 the delegates announced for the first time their demand for complete cession of the archipelago. Their Spanish opposites declared their "amazement" at the magnitude of this demand.

Not all Americans liked the idea. On October 17 the Anti-Imperialist League adopted its official platform during its Chicago annual meeting: "We hold that the policy known as imperialism is hostile to liberty and tends toward militarism, an evil from which it has been our glory to be free," wrote founding member Carl Schurz, the former senator from Missouri, newsman, and ambassador to Spain, and a leading figure in the reform politics of the day. "We hold, with Abraham Lincoln, that 'no man is good enough to govern another man without that man's consent.'" With this declaration, the battle lines were drawn. After victory in Cuba, most Americans seemed aligned with expansionists; the Anti-Imperialists' power lay not in numbers, but in influence and caliber. Prominent members included William James, Harvard president Charles William Eliot, Samuel Gompers, Massachusetts senator George Frisbie Hoar, Boston political reformer Moorfield Storey, steel magnate Andrew Carnegie, and most famously, Mark Twain. The backlash was swift, though not yet full-throated. Roosevelt would be among the first to accuse league members of treason: "They are little better than traitors," he told Lodge on January 26, 1899.

To such drumbeats, Funston fell in love. In September or early October, he attended a Sunday gathering at the Belvedere, the estate of a San Francisco banker whom he'd met in college. While there, his eyes lit upon a dark-haired "stunner in looks" who stood three inches taller than he and played the violin. Eda Blankart was the twenty-four-year-old daughter of an Oakland businessman. She's "well-read and musical, a great Kipling girl," he told Charles Scott, and politically "a Presbyterian." He wooed her for three weeks, and on October 25 they married in a small ceremony in her Oakland home. Two days later, Funston and two battalions of the Twentieth Kansas boarded the USS *Indiana* for Manila. On November 8 Eda Blankart Funston and the remaining Kansans boarded the USS *Newport* and sailed for her "bantam colonel."

Agoncillo and Lopez haunted Paris in their increasingly futile mission. By November, Agoncillo wired the Junta to speed up arms purchases. "Independence will not be granted us," he warned. Others made the same conclusion. On October 18, a full month before Agoncillo's cable, Rounsevelle Wildman had written to McKinley's secretary John Addison

Porter to offer his services as a go-between with Aguinaldo: "The way matters are going on now, it seems to me we may drift into a miserable war that would be as unnecessary as it would disastrous." Porter brushed him off: "The people are pleased with the progress both domestic and international which has been made by the United States during the past two years."

When the U.S. demanded the entire archipelago, Spain seemed ready to break off talks entirely. But on November 23 the commissioners added a sweetener: instead of demanding the islands, they would *buy* them for $20 million and allow Spain free commercial access for ten years. Under these terms, both sides relinquished all future claims. This was America's final offer; Spain had one week to reply.

It was the best deal Spain had gotten, and on November 25 Juan Manuel Sánchez, the Spanish minister of state and duke of Almodóvar, told his commissioners to sign the treaty and take the money. "Further resistance will be useless," he said. Spain revealed her decision three days later. The scene was "dignified and mournful," Commissioner Whitelaw Reid told McKinley. "They looked and no doubt felt as if they were at the funeral of some dear one in the family."

Both sides haggled over minor points for twelve more days, but at 8:45 p.m. on Saturday, December 10, the final draft of the Treaty of Paris was signed. Its terms adhered largely to those of the August 12 Peace Protocol and McKinley's instructions. The president got everything he wanted: the Philippines, Guam, Puerto Rico; a free hand in Cuba, as well as throughout the Caribbean. The $20 million came straight from the growing U.S. Treasury, no debt assumed. The treaty still needed Senate ratification, but no one anticipated problems.

"We have beaten Spain in a military conflict, but we are submitting to be conquered by her in the field of ideas and policies," the Yale sociologist William Graham Sumner wrote one month later in *The Yale Law Journal.* Imperialism and expansionism were simply "the old philosophies of national prosperity which have brought Spain to where she is now." They were new names for a "national vanity and national cupidity" as old as the seven deadly sins. "They are delusions, and they will lead us to ruin unless we are hard-headed enough to resist them." But few nations ever are. Many feared that the United States had come to a crossroads where the "glittering allurements" of power and riches had turned better men's heads.

The treaty would be the apex of McKinley's career—one that set the United States on a course for the next two centuries and defined her place in the world. It is hard to fathom McKinley's swing from one end of the imperial spectrum to the other in less than a year. Yet he always viewed events through a veil of virtue that didn't quite reflect reality. National honor, economic profit, altruism, racism, and evangelical zeal—all fused together in the neat package he called Duty. "And so it came to pass," he'd tell his secretary, "that in a few short months, we have become a world power." He was happy but pensive, calmer than John Porter had lately seen him. "And I know," he continued, "sitting here in this chair, with what added respect the nations of the world now deal with the United States, and it is vastly different from the conditions I found when I was inaugurated." Our wisdom and power could not be denied. On December 21 the president issued a policy bathed in that spirit, one so blindly self-righteous that Filipinos responded with equal parts ridicule and anger. "It shall be the earnest and paramount aim of the military administration to win the confidence, respect and affection of the inhabitants of the Philippines by assuring them in every possible way that full measure of individual rights which is the heritage of free people, and by proving to them that the mission of the United States is one of benevolent assimilation"—a "high mission" designed for the archipelago's "greatest good."

Agoncillo returned to the U.S. two days after the signing, nothing left in Paris to fight for. A faint hope existed that the Senate might not ratify the treaty in February 1899. On January 30 he filed a nine-part "Memorial to the Senate," laying out why the treaty was not binding on Filipinos: Spain had no right to sell the islands because, "except [for] minor garrison posts," it no longer owned or controlled anything in the archipelago. Lopez and he turned their attentions to the Anti-Imperialists, who became their strongest U.S. allies.

Aguinaldo wrote years later that the Treaty of Paris hit him like a bomb. In Malolos, delegates cursed the day they'd heard of America. Mabini urged a declaration of war; Luna vowed to drown the islands in blood. Conservatives urged moderation, a stance Aguinaldo supported in hopes that the U.S. Senate would not ratify. At the same time, he smuggled more guns.

Yet the rifts opened by the treaty were so great that Aguinaldo seemed to receive a searing vision of the Philippine Republic destroyed from within. His very presence made this so. On December 25 he wrote a letter to his people that played upon his name. *Aguinaldo* in Tagalog means "Christmas box," and this letter was a Christmas surprise. He began by reviewing their gains: the army had formed rapidly and destroyed the Spaniards; congress had been in session for three months and adopted a constitution. Nevertheless, he must be truthful: a crisis was coming, one too great for him. Their new nation needed a man of greater strength and better education, an abler, older, wiser man who could lead them through the difficulties ahead. His burdens were too great to bear. "It is true, as the song says, there is no island without snakes, big and little, but I should hope that our Philippines might be spared the serpents, or at least the large ones," he said. He was not cut out to succeed in the "political vices" they'd learned from Spain. Release him from the presidency, he begged. Give him his own "Christmas box." Let him resign in favor of a man more suited to guide them forward.

The letter was never circulated, the speech never delivered. When Mabini and his allies discovered Aguinaldo's note, they convinced him to put it away. Aguinaldo was the ideal of thousands. True or not, they feared that if the letter was released, the coming war with America might be aborted. They convinced him to stay the course, and both nations paid.

One last transition occurred that could serve as a lesson for those convinced of the kindness of liberators. On December 11 Calixto García died, at age fifty-nine. He'd headed negotiations with the White House for relief of Cuban veterans. But Washington winters were harsh, and he caught pneumonia in early December. A few days later, he succumbed in his room at the Raleigh Hotel. Conspiracy theories rose then and even now that he'd been poisoned, but most Cuban historians believe he was just worn out after decades of war. Old injuries had finally caught up. Negotiations stopped; the commissioners went home.

García was buried temporarily in Arlington National Cemetery, then his casket transported aboard the USS *Nashville* for final interment in Havana's huge Colón Cemetery. By then, General Brooke had shifted from Puerto Rico's governor to Cuba's and had repeated the same insults Shafter had made. In military tradition, an old soldier's comrades are afforded top honors in a funeral procession and placed at the front of the line. Brooke put them in the rear. Later American accounts call it a mistake, but considering what happened in Santiago, one cannot be sure. There were protests, but nothing changed. García's comrades withdrew from the ceremony. The old soldier, who'd done as much as anyone for *Cuba Libre*, was buried alone.

22

"My Principles Are Yours"

Eda Funston hated the roaches. Manila's "baking heat" was bad enough: between nine a.m. and four p.m., all one could do was lounge inside the shadowed house "in the most negligee of garments," but after five, one could stroll outside. "The stories of scorpions are false," she said, and she'd come to adore the "dear harmless little lizards" that crawled on the walls and ate bugs. But the cockroaches were "simply enormous": they flew at one's face, and the first night she saw one, "I thought it was a mouse." When the truth dawned on her, "I felt awfully crawly."

Funston caught sight of Manila on the night of November 30. Eda arrived on December 5. "The City lay stretched out before me," she wrote. "The bright tin roofs . . . the monotony . . . broken only now and then by a church dome or tower, reflecting the rays of the sun." Their first rental house overlooking the Luneta had "the most beautiful view imaginable," but this was too far from the regiment, and they moved to a larger house stuffed with the Funstons, Major Frank Whitman, and two Chinese servants. "We made a very merry, happy family," Eda said.

This new life took some adjustment. Manila was dirtier than Oakland: people urinated in the streets and spat everywhere. The neighborhood stank of "night soil." Water came from the Marikina and Pasig rivers, which meant it must be boiled. Assuming it even got there. The

Funstons lived at the far end of the city pumps, so when water came from their pipes, it was a trickle.

Still, Eda could stroll down the Escolta and enter banks from all over the world: the Hong Kong and Shanghai Banking Corporation; the Chartered Bank of India, Australia, and China. The Manila-Dagupan Railway ran daily, starting from Manila at 6:05 a.m. and ending 120 miles north at Dagupan at 2:08 p.m., with five stops between. There were even beer ads: "Amidst the roar of battle, the boys all thought of Schlitz Beer."

This illusion of normalcy stopped at the edge of town. It seemed only a matter of time before war would come. "Almost without exception," one major reported, soldiers and officers "refer to the natives in their presence as 'niggers,' and natives are beginning to understand what the word 'nigger' means." Homes were searched without warrant; natives hissed threats in Tagalog. Fights at checkpoints and street corners were common. "We have to kill one or two every night," Private William Christner wrote to his father. One day Funston came upon a South Dakota sentry who lay wounded, with a bolo slash to his face; his assailant lay nearby, his head blown off at close range. The soldier claimed that the Filipino attacked without warning, so no charges were preferred. "As great a rover as I have been in my life," Funston told his mother, "I am now farther away from home than I have ever been before."

Relations were in tatters by Christmas 1898, and most blamed the U.S. commander. When the French journalist Henri Turot met Elwell Otis in 1899, the general was a portly, somewhat comical figure with muttonchop whiskers and a shrill voice. He'd graduated from Harvard Law School, fought Confederates and Native Americans, and founded the army staff college at Fort Leavenworth. But none of this had prepared him for the Philippines. The men dubbed him "Grandma Otis"; MacArthur thought of an upended locomotive, "its wheels revolving at full speed" but going nowhere. Otis rarely ventured from the Malacañang Palace, basing his opinions about the rebels upon those of a few conservative *ilustrados.* James Blount, a U.S. district judge who wrote a blistering account of the period, described Otis's "unswerving devotion to the desk in time of war"; many historians believe that his complete misjudgment of the revolution caused a similar blindness in Washington.

Otis could have benefited from the kind of fact-finding tour taken in October and November by navy paymaster W. B. Wilcox and Cadet L. R. Sargent. As they rode through provinces north of Manila, they encountered civil governments working to repair the damage left from the war with Spain. They found the equivalent of a state National Guard, observed working courts, and grew convinced of the natives' "capacity for self-government." Filipinos desired "the protection of the United States at sea, but fear any interference on land." They wanted to govern their own nation, and if war came, "the Philippine Government has an organized force in every province we visited."

Though Dewey said that the report proved the natives' "capacity for self-government," Otis disagreed. On the whole, he believed most of them "robbers" whose only real desire was to drive "Americans into the sea." When he complained that the masses "do not trust us," he could not understand why. By mid-December, without evidence, he wired McKinley: "Insurgents favorable to American annexation."

Few greater misreadings of an opponent's intentions exist in American history. Otis's mischaracterizations led to decrees guaranteed to prod Filipinos into war. The first was McKinley's December 21 "Benevolent Assimilation" announcement, filled with statements about the new sovereign's right to determine Filipinos' "private rights and relations." Dissidents would be handled "with firmness"; natives could hold local office as long as they took an oath of allegiance accepting American "supremacy." Even Otis saw problems with this and eliminated some of the more nettling statements while inserting new ones that expanded native officials' powers beyond that dictated by the president. On January 4, 1899, he released his modified policy, but his gambit failed. Filipinos ridiculed the idea that assimilation could be "benevolent," and within twenty-four hours, every poster was torn down.

"Benevolent Assimilation" proved to be such a debacle that it is mocked in the Philippines to this day. One day after Otis released his revision, Aguinaldo derided America's assumed sovereignty, and on January 8, 1899, he released "*Otro Manifiesto del Sr. Presidente del Gobierno Revolucionario*," a review of America's betrayal and broken promises. All "friendly relations with the army of the United States" were finished, he said. What irony, he jeered, for America to call itself the "champion of oppressed nations." Instead, it belonged to the "oppressors of nations and the tormentors of mankind." If the U.S. Army attempted to take permanent possession of Manila, "upon their heads be all the blood which may be shed."

The statement in a nutshell outlined America's original sin, said Oscar V. Campomanes, professor of American and Philippine history at the Ateneo de Manila University in Quezon City. "Aguinaldo did not write as himself, but as a symbol of all the insurgents," a kind of hive mind. "The Filipinos, and the Cubans too, reacted with a bitterness when they finally realized the gap between America's ideals and her practice. It is a lingering bitterness that remains today . . . the kind of bitterness one sees in a jilted lover" that turns into hatred. "And the U.S. never gets it," Campomanes added. America "makes the same mistake again and again."

The least spark could light a war. In the third week of January, a Chinese resident kicked at a Spaniard's dog, but his wooden shoe flew off and struck a passing Filipino instead. A fight started; doors banged shut. Guns emerged. "There was not a man, woman, or child who was not aware that his neighbor was fleeing from some dreadful, unknown monster," a reporter wrote: the frenzy ballooned into a stampede. Thirty to forty thousand residents fled Manila, clogging the roads outside the city for twenty-five miles.

On January 20, 1899, the Philippine Congress gave Aguinaldo permission to declare war whenever he felt necessary. He stalled, probably awaiting guns. On January 25, one of Rounsevelle Wildman's spies wrote that, from July 1898 to January 1899, 100,000 Mausers had been smuggled from Macao to the east coast of Luzon. Even now, 15,000 rifles were being smuggled from Hong Kong aboard the Norwegian steamer *Oslo*. Gathering such information was dangerous: Wildman's spy concluded that "one of my men has disappeared."

By the end of January, Aguinaldo's army numbered roughly 80,000, most in Luzon but also spread through Mindanao, Panay, Leyte, Samar, and the smaller islands. Between 21,000 and 30,000 men surrounded Manila, but only half had guns. Fewer still knew how to aim and shoot: they failed to grasp the purpose of the rear sight, and never learned the trigger squeeze, so they fired high. By January 16 Aguinaldo issued his "rules of war," which borrowed heavily from the Geneva Convention. Even at this stage, he anticipates guerrilla war: he urges commanders to drill soldiers in the "irregular position, in which one is hidden" and avoids "direct conflict with the enemy." A fifth column, called the *Sandatahan*, was ordered to "dress as a woman and take care that the sentinel is not able to discharge his piece"; slash "right and left with bolos"; and store boiling water and "rags soaked in coal oil" on roofs to rain upon Americans.

Though Funston tried to downplay his worries, Eda said "Now, do be careful" every time "Fritzie" left on his rounds. "Do you want me to hide behind a stump?" he'd say, laughing: after all these years, it was strange to have someone fret over him. And there was plenty to worry about, not from Filipinos alone. On December 8 smallpox appeared in camp; by January 18, eleven in the Twentieth had died and twenty-six were stricken. The incidence rate averaged about ten to fifteen men per company. Malaria was common, and 25 percent of the Manila command would soon be on sick call with venereal disease. It was so bad that Private Ruppenthal hoped the U.S. would abandon the Philippines. "I can't see what we want with the [islands]," he wrote to his family in Russell, Kansas. "The idea of admitting the Filipinos and Chinese here to United States citizenship is revolting."

Funston's greatest worry was his six-hundred-yard front. The Twentieth Kansas anchored the extreme left flank: it lay in the city's north, where salt ponds, marshes, and swamp ran into Manila Bay. His line extended right to the Manila-Dagupan Railway, whose tracks divided the Twentieth Kansas from the Third Artillery. Funston always tried to keep seventy men on duty, a challenge with so many on sick call. The Filipino line was a hundred yards away. His line looped to the east, where the First Nebraska Volunteers faced rebels at a lonely curve called Santa Mesa. At that point, the San Juan Bridge connected the two sides. Funston had seen this spot on his rounds and pegged it for trouble. He was glad his men weren't posted there.

On the warm, moonless night of Saturday, February 4, 1899, Privates William W. Grayson and Orville Miller of the First Nebraska began a routine patrol along Santa Mesa's perimeter. They were nervous: two nights earlier, Filipino patrols had entered neutral territory between the lines;

they'd occupied a six-hut village called Santal, plopped where the road split between Manila and the Marikina pumping station. The San Juan River looped at this point, creating a small pocket open to the north; Filipinos held the high ground, as well as blockhouses 6 and 7. The two sides were separated by a hundred yards. Santal was said to be deserted, but sentries did report five hundred Filipinos somewhere near. An advance post of Americans lay where three roads met—one from each blockhouse plus the road linking Manila and Santal. A little before dusk, natives would dip into a blockhouse, jeer at Americans, then leave for their lines. Small patrols were sent to the San Juan Bridge every thirty minutes. At 7:30 orders came down: "No armed insurgents to enter the town or its vicinity." Two commands would be given to halt; after a third, Nebraskans could shoot to kill.

Grayson and Miller set out shortly before eight p.m. Grayson would be interviewed hundreds of times about what happened, so his version is best known. A lean youth of twenty-three who'd tended horses in the small town of Beatrice, he'd always craved adventure and had volunteered on May 1, 1898. From June to July, he was assigned to Camp Dewey outside Manila, but "exhaustion" confined him to camp from September 28 to October 16. His year of service would bring him pain *and* fame: in May 1899 he'd be confined to Bed 8 of Manila's First Reserve Hospital for "fatigue caused by heat and serious dysentery." After discharge, he suffered severe cramps, ulcers, and vomiting, none of these experienced before the war.

Several histories place what happened that night on the San Juan Bridge, but surveys and local papers placed it between blockhouse 7 and Santal. If so, Grayson and Miller had strayed outside American lines. Both were sweaty and eaten by mosquitoes; Grayson felt sick and scared. As he advanced, he heard low whistles and saw a red lantern flash in blockhouse 7. According to a Philippine inquiry, Corporal Anastacio Félix and two privates had camped in the blockhouse and were standing in the door when an American passed. Suddenly he turned and fired. "In spite of this, our own people did not reply," wrote a Commander Serapio on February 5: it was only when other Americans began shooting that they fired back and withdrew. No mention of casualties is made in Filipino reports or letters.

Grayson's account was more dramatic, and it changed with each telling. In most versions, he'd pulled ahead of Miller—and, in some, a third, unidentified soldier. A shadow appeared in a door about twenty feet away—probably Corporal Félix and his men. "Halt!" Grayson shouted as he raised and cocked his Springfield. "*Halto!*" the shadow echoed "mockingly." Grayson repeated his challenge; the shadow mimicked him again. Grayson fired once, and two or three more shadows appeared in the door. He retreated, blazing away.

The first American report, written by Second Lieutenant Burt D. Wheedon of Company C, First Nebraska, supports Grayson's tale, but does not mention Filipino dead. Yet on August 5, 1899, Grayson told a San Francisco paper that when the Filipino shouted *Halto!*, "I thought the best thing to do was to shoot him. He dropped. If I didn't kill him I guess he died of fright." Miller also fired, and "dropped one." Grayson spotted a second man sprinting left: "Well! I think I got my second Filipino right there." The two retreated back to the pickets; as Grayson took cover, he shouted, "Line up, fellows, the 'niggers' are in here all through these yards." They all fell back to some large water pipes and stayed undercover until dawn.

Grayson mustered out on August 23, 1899, and two months later married twenty-year-old Clara Peters, whom he'd met before the war. By now, "hero" was permanently etched to his name. In a newspaper piece about his wedding, he expanded his tale: "It was simply a case of killing that Filipino before he killed me." More important, he revealed for the first time his panicked flight through the brush and the Pasig River: "There was no time to spare, and I let him have it. I could hear low talking on all sides, and the next thing I did was to get back underwater. On the way back I lost my hat and had my coat torn off in the brush. I never expected to get back to the guard lines . . . that I was surrounded." He'd lost his hat "somewhere near where I killed my rebel, and I found it there the next day."

A possible alternative truth is revealed by the unfolding inconsistency. On the night of February 4, William Grayson had drifted past his lines and saw shadows in a blockhouse door. He spooked, fired, and in a panic fled to his lines. He ran through the brush, losing his hat and coat, and jumped into the river, diving underwater to escape an imagined fusillade. Since he could not admit panic, which was seen as cowardice, he told of shooting one rebel, then a second, under insurmountable odds. The ever-changing story was never questioned. Instead, Grayson was cited in 1906 for bravery.

Scarcely had Grayson and Miller fired at phantoms than shooting began on the left, zippering through the Colorado, South Dakota, and Pennsylvania volunteers before reaching the Twentieth Kansas at the end of the line. In the city, an orderly rushed into an arena where hundreds of soldiers and civilians attended a circus; he screamed that war had started, and clowns and soldiers burst into the street. The Spanish and foreign population rushed to their homes, barred the doors, and extinguished the lights. A lieutenant colonel driving to rejoin his regiment was attacked by a boy with a sword. The boy hit him once with the blunt edge, and when he renewed the attack, "it took three shots from the Colonel's revolver to silence him."

The firing reached the Kansans by ten p.m. Eda and Funston had spent a quiet night reading; she'd come to bed, and he was about to dim the light when Major Wilder Metcalf, Funston's second-in-command, pounded on their door. "Come out here, Colonel!" he cried. "The ball has begun!" Funston threw on some clothes: "Fred got a little excited in his hurry to dress," Eda wrote, "and I flew around helping him." Funston and Metcalf leaned out a window and heard the faint rattle of Mausers. "Did you ever hear that racket before?" Metcalf asked, and Funston nodded: there was no mistaking the sound. "They have commenced," he told Eda, and then he and Metcalf rushed to join their men.

Grayson had fired in panic thirty-four hours before the U.S. Senate was scheduled to ratify the Treaty of Paris. By then, Secretary Alger said that the Filipinos had fired first, while Anti-Imperialists blamed the U.S. Army. Most newspaper reports blamed Filipinos. "The first blow was struck by the enemy," McKinley claimed in the Senate chamber on the Monday following Grayson's shot. "They assailed our sovereignty, and there will be no useless parley, no pause, until the insurrection is suppressed and American authority acknowledged and established." The treaty debate lasted until late: Republicans generally favored it, as did many Democrats, while opponents feared its ratification would change the very nature of our nation. "This treaty will make us a vulgar, commonplace empire," cried Senator George Hoar, "controlling subject races and vassal states, in which one class must forever rule and the other classes must forever obey." But in the end, the zeal for expansion ruled the day: the Senate voted 57 to 27, just over the two-thirds majority required. McKinley signed it that day.

Grayson's bullets also ended the mission of Felipe Agoncillo. He'd spent all of January seeking a meeting with U.S. officials, asking three times to meet with the secretary of state, who'd ignored him three times. The sudden hostilities made him an enemy agent, and he could be arrested. On February 5–6 he boarded a train for Montreal, thinking he'd be safe in Canada, but he quickly learned that American "patriots" had dogged his steps and meant to assassinate him. Like Aguinaldo, his romance with America had ended. He booked a ship to Halifax, Nova Scotia, and from there to Europe, hoping to drum up support on the Continent and even in the Vatican. But as his steamer neared Scotland, it was caught in a storm and capsized. He climbed aboard a lifeboat with nothing but the clothes on his back and a small satchel of diplomatic documents. The lifeboat, named *Liberator*, reached London on March 9.

So it began. America called what followed the "Philippine Insurrection," a name that attempted to strip the Philippine Republic of legitimacy. In the same breath, Aguinaldo's army would be called rebels or insurgents, never soldiers—and later *ladrones*, Spanish for bandits or thieves. To Philippine nationalists, America had begun a war of conquest against a young republic no less legitimate than the one founded by American rebels a century earlier.

Such wars were necessary, claimed Rudyard Kipling, Britain's voice of empire. On February 4, 1899, his "The White Man's Burden: The United States and the Philippine Islands" ran in *The Times* of London. It was printed the next day in *The New York Sun*, then in *McClure's Magazine*. There's no misreading this poem. Empire was the moral burden of the white race, which was divinely chosen to civilize a barbarous world. Kipling intended it as an American spine-stiffener; its language, he said, was "biblical." The seven-stanza octet starts with a call to arms:

Take up the White Man's burden—
Send forth the best ye breed—
Go bind your sons to exile
To serve your captives' need;
To wait in heavy harness
On fluttered folk and wild—
Your new-caught, sullen peoples,
Half devil and half child.

The "new-caught" peoples, of course, were the "sullen" Filipinos. Kipling invited America to shoulder with Great Britain the great universal mission of spreading God's Christian Empire, thus proposing the détente that would in time become the "Special Relationship." The poem also became an instant object of satire: there would be a "Brown Man's Burden," "Black Man's Burden," "Real White Man's Burden," and "Poor Man's Burden" in 1899–1902 alone. But the average American liked it well enough, and would read hundreds of reprints across the nation.

By then, each side already saw the other in the poet's racialized terms. John F. Bass of *Harper's Weekly* thought that Americans and Filipinos differed "so absolutely in mind, body, and soul" that they "could not live together under the then existing conditions." Aguinaldo's troops saw U.S. troops as "rough and tyrannical"; Americans saw Filipinos as "tricky and dishonest." Bass considered Filipinos the most "unlovable people" he'd ever met, but realized that by ignoring their wish for independence, America had turned a negotiable situation into one where "we have fallen heir to the hatred" Filipinos long felt for Spain. This was a "race war" now, he said. Where compromise might have been possible, "Now we must crush them."

Willie Grayson's shot unleashed America. At four a.m. on February 5, Dewey's ships came to life with devastating accuracy. Lieutenant John Twiggs Myers of the USS *Charleston* watched an 8-inch shell land on a rebel headquarters, "and when the smoke cleared, the house had disappeared." These shells weighed 250 pounds apiece and traveled at 2,000 feet per second; reports later mentioned forty bodies where one shell exploded. Land-based artillery further battered the Filipinos: they'd never imagined such annihilation, and they fled, leaving their dead and wounded piled in trenches. Once the order to advance rang out at eight a.m., U.S. volunteers charged with a "Jawhawk cheer" or "Montana yell," only to confront the navy's slaughter. They then overran their objectives in pursuit of the enemy. Funston's Kansans rushed north along the coast so fast that shells from the USS *Concord* fell around them. Nebraskans, South Dakotans, and Coloradans swept across the river, stormed the San Juan Bridge, and chased natives into the hills.

The fighting south of Manila was just as intense, but units there maintained closer order. Rice fields stretched before them for hundreds of yards, seeming as "flat as a billiard table," wrote Percy McDonnell for *Scribner's*. Across this unprotected stretch, soldiers from California, Washington, Idaho, and the Fourth Cavalry rushed up in ten- to fifteen-yard sprints, dropped flat to fire, then ran forward again. The Californians captured an ammunition dump in Santa Ana, then raced to San Pedro Makati, another two miles on. The Fourth Cavalry moved so fast that they crossed the Pasig River ahead of the retreating natives and took the only boats available. Idaho and Washington regiments caught up, trapped the enemy midstream, and cut them down in cross fire. "From there the fun was fast and furious" as dead Filipinos stacked up "thicker than buffalo chips," wrote Lieutenant Frederick Sladen, Otis's young aide. Some Western troops wrote to their parents that "picking off niggers in the water" was "more fun than a turkey shoot."

Fighting broke out in Cavite, where Regulars guarded the old Spanish arsenal. Dewey gave the Filipinos until nine a.m. to surrender; they burned the town behind them as they retreated, and Americans rushed in to stop firebugs. Private Burr Ellis ran into a house where he found a Filipino "down on his knees fanning a fire." So "I pulled my old Long Tom to my shoulder and left him to burn with the fire." As he took his knife, "another jumped out of the window and ran, and I brought him to the ground like a jack-rabbit." He added, "I had lots of fun that morning."

The towns around Manila burned as Americans spread from the center. In Tondo, Paco, and Santa Ana, churches became rubble and thatch houses turned to ashes. Squads of troops stalked the streets, destroying buildings to flush out snipers. To one Englishman, the Yanks seemed possessed by a "mad fury": he watched as "houses were ransacked, women raped, jewels taken and villages burned under the pretext of searching for hidden arms." In Pandacan, when soldiers chanced upon some "bewildered women carrying their smallpox-stricken children," they ripped them from their embrace "and threw them in the flames." A letter in *The North American Review* gloried: "I tell you that this war is great and I love it, as long as I am not killed in it . . . Destroy, burn, kill—It's beautiful! As soon as your blood is heated up, nothing stops you; you become enraged and destroy as much as you can."

As he gazed at the bodies, a British resident told an officer that this was not war, but "simple massacre and murderous butchery." Vague rumors of American atrocities filtered out: "Very few prisoners were taken," said Lieutenant Myers of the *Charleston*. "We hear some of the regiments got out of hand and spared only the few women who had not gone to the interior." He blamed it on the Filipinos' provocations: now their "day of reckoning" had come.

American casualties for February 4–5 numbered 59 killed and 278 wounded. A true count of Philippine dead is still unknown. The army's official report numbered 4,000, but that was guesswork, and it later came out that field commanders exaggerated the slain. The weekly *Independent* of New York estimated native dead at 5,000; General Otis wrote that his men buried 750 on the field but thought their casualties might be 3,000. The historian Leon Wolff gives a conservative guess "that casualties went against the insurgents four or five to one," thus putting the dead at about 1,400. Whatever the metric, the bloodiest day of the entire bloody conflict ended by midafternoon; it was clear that the Filipinos had taken a serious beating. If this was the standard, a "short sharp war of subjugation" would end before the summer rains began.

That first day stunned Aguinaldo. At his behest, two prominent *ilustrados* approached Otis under a white flag. He offered a truce and peace talks, but Otis wasn't interested. "The fighting, having once begun, must go on to the grim end," he said. This was the whole point: plans existed to attack the Filipinos in force the moment an incident occurred. "Yes, we had a prearranged plan," MacArthur later testified: soon after Grayson's first shot, "I simply wired all commanders to carry out our prearranged plan." This involved taking the waterworks eight miles east and the rebel headquarters at Malolos, which might end the war.

Late that day, Aguinaldo addressed the losses. Great conflict spawned great suffering; his people had "not yet recovered from past losses and are not in the condition to endure others." But which was worse—death or slavery? He knew "how bitter is slavery," but their losses must be viewed in context: "Our independence has been watered by the generous blood of our martyrs." The mass slaughter of February 5, 1899, filled the same grave as that of José Rizal, the martyrs before him, and even Bernardo Carpio. "Be not discouraged," he said: this was a long holy war.

Aguinaldo did not despair alone. That night, José Alejandrino was rushing from Malolos when he came upon Antonio Luna. "Our enemies are too strong!" Luna wailed. Alejandrino had never seen him like this: Luna's brash confidence was gone, his contempt for all who considered peace faded. The soldiers he'd exhorted had all collapsed, and for this brief moment, Luna's nerve collapsed, too. Few chiefs had been at their posts when the shooting started; most, like Luna, were attending a conference north in Pampanga. Like Alejandrino, he'd rushed back to behold the ruins. News from the south was even worse: General Thomas Anderson's First Corps had pushed forward for *four miles*, wiping out the brigade of General Pio del Pilar, staining the Pasig River with their blood. *Sandatahan* infiltrators had accomplished little: they lit small portions of the city and sniped at firefighters. More than fifty Filipinos were killed, but few Americans.

A chill gripped Aguinaldo's inner circle. The first day of fighting demonstrated how one-sided this war might be. Arms were part of the calculus: a third of their troops lacked rifles and fought with spears, bows and arrows, or stones. Experience also played a part. Most U.S. officers were veterans of the Civil and Indian wars, while Philippine generals were young and untested.

But the typical Philippine fighter did have unseen advantages. He was usually a peasant, or *tao*, short in stature, dark-skinned, usually barefoot; observers claimed that a deep-seated toughness, forged by centuries of Spanish abuse, often lay concealed by what one Englishman called an "inbred courtesy." In time, this toughness would translate into a different kind of warfare. The evolving *insurrecto* could subsist on a handful of boiled rice eaten off a plantain leaf, occasionally topped by a bit of fish or fowl. He lived off the land, carrying his water bottle with him, but no tents, blankets, or haversacks. Since he did not depend on a supply train, Americans could not keep up with him. He could ambush a U.S. patrol, hide his weapon, and melt into a supportive populace providing food, shelter, and information. One boy remembered how women in the marketplace wrote U.S. troop movements into the mango and guava prices slipped to guerrillas. When sentries drew near, children "accidentally" tossed balls into huts as warning.

But it would take months for these advantages to dawn on the Filipinos. For the rest of spring 1899, Aguinaldo and his generals adhered to Western tactics, which meant endless retreats and high losses. They wanted so much to be a Western democracy that they were willing to die that way. The war's first phase mirrored that costly first day. By the end of February, U.S. forces pushed outside the ring of Manila; by mid-March, they took the town of Caloocan, three miles north. Far to the south, General Marcus Miller took Iloilo and the Visayan islands of Cebu and Negros; soon Americans invaded the southernmost Sulu Archipelago. But Aguinaldo's Republic was always the prime target, and Otis's forces sped through Luzon. One division under General Thomas Anderson headed south from Manila. A second under Arthur MacArthur headed north.

By all markers, this war should end as quickly as Cuba's Splendid War. Yet it dragged on. This would have seemed impossible after that first day of slaughter and the steady advances of spring. Why? The Philippine War would be "one of the least understood phases of our history," lamented the historian Richard O'Connor, "one of those obscure episodes swept under the rug, for the best of psychological reasons, and forgotten."

It is easier to forget than to question how such a war transforms nations and men. Maybe violence is liberating: old norms no longer apply, encouraging a change to something deeper and stranger. Nations honor such actors by their exploits, but by so doing absorb what's unleashed into their national DNA. Shape-shifting played out on both sides, but nowhere more publicly and famously than in Frederick Funston.

On February 8 MacArthur's First Brigade marched north to Malolos along the Manila-Dagupan Railway. The Kansas and Montana units moved forward in waves, one unit rushing ahead to a line of trees while the other covered them from behind irrigation dikes that bordered rice fields. Kansans quickly gained a reputation for reckless charges: "There goes Kansas," observed MacArthur, "and all Hell can't stop her." Otis complained that Funston could not control his men. Indeed, Funston began proposing to MacArthur the same suicidal schemes he'd run past Gómez. On the first night of war, he begged the general to let him take a platoon across the lines in search of Aguinaldo. MacArthur's reply was like the Cuban's: "If anyone can do it, you can, but I cannot spare the men."

MacArthur's first big target was Caloocan. The coastal town, sitting at the southern edge of the vast farming country called the Central Plains, housed the railway's shops and roundhouse. Seizing transportation is a tactical concern, and Antonio Luna waited with four thousand men to stop the onslaught. The Kansans poured through the small bordering town of Maypaja: when the battle ended, said an officer, "not one stone remains on top of another."

The attack on Caloocan began at three p.m. on Friday, February 10, with a massive bombardment of Luna's trenches by the army and Dewey's big guns. This ended an hour later, and three quick cannon blasts signaled a walking advance by twenty-six companies. The correspondent John Bass accompanied some Montanans: At first "the bullets were few and far between," but as they "came thicker and thicker," a soldier fell next to him, "sinking in a limp heap." Then a lieutenant colonel slumped to the earth, shot through the lung. The soldiers charged into town, firing as they ran. The smell of powder and smoke seemed to excite them: they burned the town to flush out *insurrectos*, stepped over trenches heaped with the dead, passed white-clad bodies strewn on the roads "like great disfigured dolls thrown away by some petulant child." When a handful of defenders holed up in the Catholic church, Funston ordered his bugler to sound a charge, and those Filipinos who weren't killed ran north to the far bank of the Tullahan River. Once again, Funston lost control of his men: they chased the enemy despite orders, so Funston hopped on his pony and caught up with them half a mile north of town. He was yelling that the enemy was too far off to give or take wounds when a Mauser round plowed through his pony. His men started laughing, but at last regained their senses.

Funston led them back. They ate and slept in the churchyard as "great gothic spires of flame" shot up around them. Bass rode through town with his face covered. "Homeless dogs ran howling through the streets. Motherless broods of chickens peeped hopelessly." Doctors wandered the dark, calling out for the wounded. "Caloocan was supposed to contain seventeen thousand inhabitants," wrote Captain David Elliott of Company G: "Now Caloocan contains not one living native." Only the railroad shops, houses of its English owners, and the "battered walls of the great church and dismal prison alone remain," he observed. "War is worse than hell." In nineteen days, Elliott would be dead, "shot through the stomach with a brass covered Remington ball."

Captain Elliott was not the only Kansan to grasp the enormity of their actions. Filipinos "will never surrender until their whole race is exterminated," wrote Ellis G. Davis of Company A. "They are fighting for a good cause, and the Americans should be the last of all nations to transgress upon such rights." Private Theodore Conley wrote, "There is not a feature of the whole miserable business that a patriotic American citizen . . . can look upon with complacency, much less pride." This war reversed history, placing America in the role of Great Britain in 1776, making the war "a crime against human liberty as well as against Christianity and civilization." He added, "Honest to God, I feel sorry for these people."

Funston was proud of his men, but a change had come over him. In Caloocan, he was involved in one of the war's earliest controversies, just five or six days after fighting began. From the start, the War Department had permitted Otis free rein in censorship, possible because he controlled the only cable from Manila. But he could not control what the soldiers wrote home. Within six weeks of Grayson's opening shot, battlefield letters were reprinted in American newspapers. The unvarnished accounts were as diverse as the soldiers: some were horrified by what they'd seen or done; others, like a private from Utah, extolled the "fun" of hunting "Goo Goos." But brutality in the heat of battle and the cold-blooded execution of captives are two different things: such charges arose in units throughout the war, but the very first on record was a letter from Private Charles

Brenner of Minneapolis, Kansas, assigned to the Twentieth's Company I. They'd taken four prisoners, lined them up, and asked Captain William H. Bishop of Company M what to do with them. "There occurred the hardest sight I ever saw," Brenner wrote. Bishop looked at his men and replied, "'You know orders,' and four natives fell dead."

The accusation might have been forgotten if not for later corroboration. Arthur Minkler wrote that the insurgents jumped from cover and ran, but never got far: "I suppose you are not interested in the way we do the job. We do not take prisoners. At least the Twentieth Kansas does not." Corporal Robert D. Maxwell of Company A explained the reasoning: "Sometimes we stopped to make sure a native was dead and not lying down to escape injury," he wrote. "Some of them would fall as though dead and, after we had passed, would climb a tree and shoot every soldier that passed that way. Even the wounded would rise up and shoot after we passed. This led to an order to take no prisoners, but to shoot all."

The most damning accusation came from First Lieutenant John F. Hall, a platoon leader. In letters home, protests to Kansas officials, and a detailed letter reprinted in Hearst's *San Francisco Examiner*, Hall said that on February 9 Funston "ordered no prisoners to be taken." According to Hall, Funston's friend and subordinate Wilder Metcalf was the worst offender. After crossing the first line of enemy trenches, even before entering Caloocan, "Major Metcalf shot and had shot" several Filipino prisoners. One unarmed prisoner brought to Metcalf suddenly realized he was about to die:

> The prisoner dropped . . . upon his knees, grabbed Metcalf by the calves of his legs with both hands and pleaded for Christian mercy. Metcalf tore himself away from the prisoner, stepped back and a little to the left and with his own pistol shot the prisoner in the right side of the neck, the bullet ranging down toward his left breast. The little brown Tagalo pitched forward dead, and obeying Metcalf's orders, other prisoners were shot at that time and place.

Hall accused Funston of complicity. On February 11 the colonel asked Metcalf, "I understand that you take no prisoners?" to which Metcalf gave his "tacit" consent. "I did not deny it," he later said. On March 23

Funston broached the issue again. It was the day before the Twentieth Kansas attacked Malolos, and during a regimental officers' meeting

> Colonel Funston said, with a grin, "Don't kill any more prisoners than you have to," or words to that effect. The manner in which he gave this order led all the officers I talked with to the belief that it was a matter of very little concern to Colonel Funston how many prisoners were butchered.

Funston's supporters and the Kansas historian Thomas Crouch would say that there was "no substance in [these] accounts." They blamed lingering resentment over favoritism. But the accusations that began with Private Brenner and rose up the ranks would split the Twentieth Kansas into pro- and anti-Funston factions, a fracture that worsened with time. Those in the pro-Funston camp benefited: by March 29 Metcalf was promoted from major to colonel; by May 9 Bishop was promoted to major. Despite the fact that Hall's letter ran in papers across the United States, including several in Kansas, Metcalf and Funston denied all accusations. Because the army never preferred charges, both claimed they were the victims of slanders and lies.

No charges *were* preferred, but not because the army thought the men innocent. On July 13, 1899, five months after Brenner's first letter, Otis revealed to the War Department that he'd first considered court-martialing Brenner for his allegations, but then "doubted the wisdom" of this, "as it would give the insurgent authorities a knowledge of what was taking place, and they would assert positively that our troops practiced inhumanities." Thus, Otis's first instinct was to punish the messenger. In time, the army's judge advocate general determined that Private Brenner's accusations probably did have merit, but "considerations of public policy, sufficiently grave to silence every other demand, require that no further action be taken." In other words, a cover-up was in the best interests of the army.

What happened? This was the young idealist who returned from the Cuban Revolution without a shred of evidence that he'd violated a single article of war; the same Freddie Funston whose lifelong friends called him the "soul of modesty." For the first time in this conflict, we see the

José Martí, architect of *Cuba Libre* (Courtesy of the Library of Congress)

José Rizal, inspiration for the Philippine Revolution (Courtesy of the Library of Congress)

Maximo Gómez, commander of all Cuban rebels during their 1895–1898 War of Independence from Spain (Courtesy of the Library of Congress)

Calixto García, veteran Cuban general and Frederick Funston's former commander, who most closely worked with U.S. forces during the Santiago campaign (Courtesy of the Library of Congress)

Valeriano Weyler, governor-general behind Spain's deadly *reconcentrado* policy (Courtesy of the Library of Congress)

Fitzhugh Lee, U.S. consul general to Havana during events leading to the Spanish-American War (Courtesy of the Library of Congress)

Frederick Funston, shown in the uniform of the U.S. 20th Kansas Volunteer Infantry; he served as a volunteer artillery officer under Gómez and García from 1896 to 1898 (Courtesy of the National Archives, NAID 100310713)

THE JOURNALISTS

Joseph Pulitzer, Hungarian American publisher of the *St. Louis Post-Dispatch* and the *New York World* (Courtesy of the Library of Congress)

William Randolph Hearst, publisher of the *New York Journal*, whose fierce rivalry with Pulitzer gave birth to "yellow journalism" (Courtesy of the Library of Congress)

The American novelist Stephen Crane was already famous for *The Red Badge of Courage* when he wrote for various newspapers during the Cuban and Puerto Rican campaigns (Courtesy of the Library of Congress)

Richard Harding Davis, renowned war correspondent who focused almost exclusively on Theodore Roosevelt and the Rough Riders during the Santiago campaign (Courtesy of the Library of Congress)

Frank Norris, famous author of *McTeague* and *The Octopus*, was still an unknown when he covered the Santiago campaign (Courtesy of the Library of Congress)

THE EXPANSIONISTS

William McKinley, twenty-fifth president of the United States, who reluctantly declared war on Spain after the explosion on the USS *Maine* (Courtesy of the Library of Congress)

Henry Cabot Lodge, U.S. senator from Massachusetts and strong proponent of war with Spain (Courtesy of the Library of Congress)

Theodore Roosevelt, wearing the uniform he designed for his appointment as colonel in the Rough Riders (Courtesy of the Library of Congress)

REMEMBER THE *MAINE*!

Broadside view of the USS *Maine*, showing the extensive gun placements fore and aft (Courtesy of the Library of Congress)

Wreckage of the *Maine* in Havana Harbor, the morning after the explosion on February 15, 1898 (Courtesy of the National Archives, NAID 512929)

THE VOLUNTEERS

Clara Maass, German American "trained nurse" who served in Cuba and the Philippines and volunteered to be a test subject in the National Board of Health Yellow Fever Commission's experiments in Camp Lazear in Havana (Courtesy of Clara Maass Medical Center)

One of the best-known American poets of the twentieth century, Carl Sandburg (right) joined the Sixth Illinois Volunteers with his friends. He is shown washing his clothes in a stream in Puerto Rico (Courtesy of CARL 00001 Carl Sandburg Papers, National Park Service, Carl Sandburg Home National Historic Site, Flat Rock, NC 28731)

First Sergeant Henry A. Dobson of Company D, First D.C. Volunteers. During training, Dobson contracted typhoid, the leading cause of death during the Cuban campaign (Courtesy of University of South Florida, Florida Studies Center: "Henry A. Dobson Photographs," Image 2)

One of the "swells" in the Rough Riders, Herman Hoffman Philip survived the U.S. Army's medical care in Cuba to become an American ambassador and career foreign service officer (Courtesy of the Library of Congress)

U.S. Navy rear admiral William T. Sampson, commander of the North Atlantic Squadron, which blockaded Santiago Bay (Courtesy of the Library of Congress)

Clara Barton, founder of the American Red Cross, who spearheaded the relief effort for Cuban *reconcentrados* (Courtesy of the Library of Congress)

Studio card of a Buffalo Soldier with the U.S. Army. This would have been David Fagen's uniform when he joined the Twenty-Fourth U.S. Infantry in Tampa (Courtesy of the Library of Congress)

Major General William Rufus Shafter, commander of the U.S. Army's Fifth Corps at Santiago (Courtesy of the Library of Congress)

Henry Plant's Tampa Bay Hotel, known to the journalist George Kennan as the "Pleasure Dome" (Courtesy of the Library of Congress)

Southwestern view of Morro Castle, guarding the entrance to Santiago harbor (Courtesy of the National Archives, NAID 329585245)

The stone fort known as El Viso overlooking El Caney (Courtesy of the Library of Congress)

Street scene at El Caney (Courtesy of the Library of Congress)

A view through the long grass of the ascent up San Juan Hill (Courtesy of the Library of Congress)

Soldiers of the U.S. Sixth Infantry and their mascot, under fire at the base of San Juan Hill (Courtesy of the Library of Congress)

Frederic Remington's *Charge of the Rough Riders at San Juan Hill.* The Buffalo Soldier in the center of the painting can barely be seen (Courtesy of the Library of Congress)

Teddy Roosevelt and his Rough Riders posing atop San Juan Hill (Courtesy of the Library of Congress)

The American trenches outside Santiago (Courtesy of the Library of Congress)

Commodore George Dewey, commander of the U.S. Asiatic Squadron during the Battle of Manila Bay (Courtesy of the Library of Congress)

Emilio Aguinaldo, first president of the Philippine Republic, photographed shortly after his capture by Frederick Funston (Courtesy of the National Archives, NAID 329584516)

Antonio Luna, commanding general of the Philippine Revolutionary Army and the Republic's first secretary of war (Courtesy of the National Archives, NAID 405225966)

General Henry Ware Lawton, in his trademark white pith helmet (Courtesy of the Library of Congress)

U.S. Army brigadier general Arthur MacArthur. As the Philippines' third military governor, he declared martial law in December 1900 (Courtesy of the National Archives, NAID 405220171)

A group of U.S. soldiers administering the "water cure" to a Filipino prisoner (Courtesy of the National Archives, NAID 329578714)

Jacob H. Smith, U.S. Army general who ordered sweeping retaliation on the island of Samar after the Balangiga Massacre on September 28, 1901 (Courtesy of the Library of Congress)

William Howard Taft, first civilian governor of the Philippines and twenty-seventh president of the United States (Courtesy of the Library of Congress)

William Howard Taft and family friend Mabel Boardman, who ousted Clara Barton from the executive board of the American Red Cross after a vicious smear campaign (Courtesy of the Library of Congress)

consequence of the phrase "words matter." By legitimizing the execution of prisoners, Funston legitimizes other atrocities. By covering up the actions of Bishop, Metcalf, and Funston, Otis and the War Department legitimize murder in the name of public policy. When the letters of Private Brenner and other witnesses go public, many Americans support Funston, thus normalizing the use of murder and torture in U.S. foreign policy.

It began with a choice, which Funston justified as payment in kind. In addition to the *insurrecto* practice of playing dead, an unsubstantiated rumor was accepted as truth by at least March 23: "The Filipinos have about the same traits as the American Indians, when it comes to prisoners," wrote Henry Ruppenthal. "Two California boys, a Utah surgeon and three Twenty-second Infantry men were captured and disemboweled—heart, etc. cut out, and in other ways mutilated." He was proud of the fact that Kansans "have made more 'good Filipinos' than any other regiment in the field." The *insurrectos* were an "illiterate, semi-savage people," Funston later told *Harper's Weekly*. They deserved what they got, since they were "waging war, not against tyranny, but against Anglo-Saxon order and decency."

Some wondered about that decency. One day while awaiting an order to charge, Private W. R. Smith studied his fellow Kansans and realized that "the majority of the men of this army [were] strange." It was as if they'd all abandoned God: "Never in my life before have I heard so many blasphemous expressions and vain oaths uttered with the least provocation." Perhaps the army just recruited "ruffians." There'd been plenty of grousing in Cuba, but one does not encounter any such passages addressing a shaken faith in the American character.

Private Smith was not alone. Others feared that something had changed. Captain Frederick S. Wild had fought the Sioux in 1890–91 and was cited for bravery in El Caney: now the thirty-five-year-old company commander with the Thirteenth U.S. Infantry could not believe the quality of his men. They were a "scrub lot," he told his parents: "They don't seem to be as good men as those we had in Cuba." Two or three times during that April, he found sentinels drunk or asleep, "the gravest offense at a time like this." Punishment could be death, but instead they were court-martialed or discharged, and the taint only spread. By May 27 he'd court-martialed four men and put five more up on charges.

One lieutenant slept through night battles, explaining that "night is the time to sleep, and I want to go to bed at the proper time," which for him was 7:30 p.m. New recruits were hopeless: "They eat green fruits, drink everything wet, impure water included, get sick (one of mine died the other night), contract loathsome diseases, think they know everything and are the devil's own to discipline." By April 20, 33 percent of Wild's men were on sick call. He'd be criticized for needlessly exposing himself in battle, but many officers like him "get to that point," as if they no longer cared.

Sometimes simple humanity forced one's attention. On June 2 Henry Ruppenthal came upon a rebel shot through the groin; the man raised his hand and moaned "*Spero*" ("Spare me"). As Ruppenthal examined the man's wound, he realized this was a Spaniard who'd switched sides. The man knew he would die, and he murmured, "God, my poor mother." Where is she? Ruppenthal asked. "*En Toledo, España*," the man said. He fumbled in his tunic, drew out a leather packet, and asked Ruppenthal to send it to Senora Jarez y Cordova at 126 Calle de Rey, Toledo. He agreed. The dying soldier grabbed his hand: "*Muchas gracias, caballero.*" He smiled and died, and Ruppenthal turned away. The soldier was buried in a trench with 137 others.

But one cannot escape the impression that war "liberated" a surprising number of U.S. soldiers. Funston is the most chronicled: we watch him become increasingly reckless, outrageous, and aggressive. Before, he usually kept it in check. Now, as the Twentieth drives north, the Kansans divide roughly into those who perform their duty but are appalled by the destruction and those who find it "fun." Funston admired his First Brigade commander, Brigadier General Lloyd Wheaton, because "he seemed to enjoy fighting for its own sake," a sentiment Funston shared. Fighting in war involves killing, and research has shown that once it begins, "men became increasingly brutalized," wrote Christopher Browning in his study of German bakers and shopkeepers who became Nazi exterminators. "As in combat, the horrors of the initial encounter became routine." The ethicist Ervin Staub relates how the initial distress of a helicopter door gunner in Vietnam disappeared as he became accustomed to killing: "Flying over a group of civilians in a helicopter, he was ordered to fire at them, an order he did not obey":

> The helicopter circled over the area and again he was ordered to fire, which again he did not do. The officer in charge then threatened him with court-martial, which led him to fire the next time around. He vomited, felt profoundly distressed. The veteran reported that in a fairly short time firing at civilians became like an experience at a target-shooting gallery, and he began to enjoy it.

"You get used to it," war veterans say.

MacArthur's Second Division lingered in Caloocan until March 24, then advanced north on Malolos. Funston's Twentieth led. They steamrolled across a plain crossed by creeks, streams, and rivers, pushing Luna's men back through the farming towns of Tulijan, Malinta, Polis, Bigoa, and Guiginto, the carnage in each spot like that in Caloocan. This week ended with 539 American casualties, an advance so swift, men dropped from exhaustion, Funston included. At one point, he'd not slept in two days, so he rolled up in some leaves. The regiment lost track of him, thinking he was dead. Finally, a soldier spied a thatch of red hair sticking out from some debris, and since "this was the way bodies are prepared for burial in that part of the world," the man feared the worst. "Colonel, are you dead or alive?" he asked. "Neither, I'm sleeping," Funston grumbled.

On March 31 the Kansans entered Malolos, but it was empty: Aguinaldo had backed fifty kilometers north to San Isidro. The Americans followed, and on April 24 came to the banks of the Rio Chico, where they were blocked by a partially collapsed steel bridge. Heavy enemy fire came from the opposite side. Funston took ten men to the bridge and edged fifty yards out on the smashed girders. When they could go no farther, they dropped and swam the rest of the way. They made it across, unarmed and barefoot. Fortunately, the rebels had retreated.

The next day, MacArthur and Wheaton stopped on the south bank of the Rio Grande de la Pampanga. Across the river lay four thousand rebels under Luna, waiting in trenches and backed by a lethal Maxim gun. Scouts determined that the only good option was for a small unit to cross under artillery fire. They tried on the night of April 26, but barking dogs gave them away.

The next morning, Funston took 120 Kansans to a narrow part of the river several hundred yards from the bridge. As 100 American sharpshooters and division artillery aimed at the trenches, Privates William Trembley and Edward White from Company B scurried to the river carrying a long coil of rope, and they dove in. The Rio Grande was stronger and wider than any other Americans had faced, but the two were good swimmers, and they came ashore in a blind spot beneath Luna's fortifications. They tied the rope and tugged; two more soldiers started to pull themselves across in a leaky dugout, but this capsized.

Funston was in trouble: with MacArthur and Wheaton as audience, all he'd accomplished was to strand two men. If they died, "I would be damned in my home state all the rest of my life, and held up to scorn by all the corner-store tacticians in the country." Nothing was worse than the disparagement he'd faced in college and the Pleasure Dome. He took seven men with him on a raft and ordered the remaining Kansans to cross in stages. They dashed to the trenches, only to find them filled with dead and wounded. When the Maxim gun had been flanked, the crew abandoned the gun.

Luna counterattacked the next day: two Kansans standing beside Funston were shot in the head. Soon he, too, was wounded: "I felt a most terrific blow to my left hand, in which I was holding a pair of field glasses." He didn't know he'd been shot until a lieutenant steered him to the field hospital. "Blood was splattering all over, and I had no desire to look at the offending hand." He looked away and asked the corpsman, "Is there anything left of it?"

"Clean shot," the corpsman said. MacArthur looked in on him and grinned: "Well, Funston, you got it at last. I'm glad it is no worse." He was sent back to Manila and on the train received a wire that MacArthur and Wheaton had recommended him for promotion to brigadier general of volunteers. No one could laugh at him now. "I was extremely grateful," he wrote, "and nearly forgot the throbbing of my hand."

Eda was waiting. A carriage brought him back, "and never, never shall I forget that moment," she wrote. "After I had satisfied myself that I really had him again safe and alive, I was ready to hear something of what he had to relate." He handed over proof of his promotion, which paid $5,500 annually. "Impossible to describe my delight," she said. Sometime later, he, Trembley, and White were each awarded the Congressional Medal of

Honor. In the May 20 *Harper's Weekly*, William White compared his pal's exploit to that of Roosevelt on San Juan Hill. Roosevelt took notice: here, it seemed, was an ally in an uncertain war.

In June, Funston returned to the front, but this part of his war was nearly over. He succeeded Wheaton as commander of the First Brigade of MacArthur's Second Division, and Wilder Metcalf, who'd been sent back for a wound to his foot, was promoted to colonel. This promotion, perhaps more than anything, reanimated old hatreds. Yet monsoon season had arrived. The roads turned to soup. MacArthur reported that "the sun, field rations, physical exertion and abnormal exhaustion from almost constant exposure to fire action" made further advance impossible until after the rains. Conquest would not come as quickly as they'd hoped. The Twentieth lay forty miles north of Manila and would go no farther.

It was worse than MacArthur let on. The soldiers suspected "that someone had blundered," James Blount said. Many who'd volunteered for Cuba "to save the Cubans" had not intended "to kill Filipinos for also wanting to be free." Acid letters drifted home: "The boys are sick of fighting these heathens," wrote Private Tom Crandall of the First Nebraska. "Their patriotism is wearing off. We all want to come home very bad." Sergeant Arthur Vickers, another Nebraskan, echoed, "I am not afraid, and I am always ready to do my duty, but I would like someone to tell me what we are fighting for."

The patriotic sheen back home was also wearing thin. There were still avid supporters, like *The Salt Lake Tribune*: "The struggle must continue til the misguided creatures there shall have their eyes bathed in enough blood to cause their vision to be cleared." But opposition surfaced, too. "Otis Has Seriously Blundered," headlined *The San Francisco Call*. Otis's proclamations that the rebellion was on the brink of collapse had proved untrue. "Our troops have pushed the unavailing butchery of war with uncomplaining endurance and dash," continued the *Call*, "yet the barefooted enemy, remembering his hut burned and his paddy field destroyed, lurks in the jungle and fights."

In late June, the Kansans were ordered to Manila in anticipation of transport home. They'd be garrisoned outside of town through August, and they watched as Regulars arrived to replace them. This included David Fagen's Twenty-Fourth Infantry. On June 24, the same day that four ships carrying Buffalo Soldiers sailed from San Francisco, the Kansans boarded a train for Manila. In the past year and a half, the Twentieth had lost 35 men to disease, 14 of them in the earlier smallpox epidemic. Three officers and 30 enlisted men died in battle; 10 officers and 129 enlisted men were wounded.

On July 15 another Funston profile ran in *Harper's Weekly*. Although he said he was not an expansionist, he believed in the army's purpose and was willing to stay until the rebellion died. The U.S. should "rawhide those bullet-headed Asians til they yell for mercy," he said.

Teddy Roosevelt likes what he reads. On July 22 he writes the first of many letters to Funston, telling him that he hopes to see him "rise high in politics." To this end, he should make good use of his prominence when he comes home. He's been following Funston's adventures and sees real similarity in "style" and "principles" between Funston and himself. He thinks McKinley will be in a good position to win a second term in 1900, and hopes to work closely with the president to prevent the election of Bryan, "which would mean the abandonment of our destiny abroad and treachery to all traditions of honor at home." He invites Funston to visit him in New York: such a journey might be profitable for them both. After all, he adds, "My principles are yours."

On September 20, Funston and his Kansans board the transport *Tartar* and leave for home the next day. The war is far from over. But "Fightin' Fred" has done well.

23

The Far Side of the World

On January 19, 1899, Henry Ware Lawton packed his wife, son, and three daughters into the USS *Grant* for the fifty-five-day voyage to Manila. With him came two regiments of the new Fourth Army Corps. Though the Philippine War had not yet started, McKinley had convinced him that Elwell Otis would soon retire and leave him the helm. At the very least, Lawton could expect an independent field command.

The gods had smiled on him. His drinking binge in Cuba would have killed most careers, but the public considered Lawton America's closest equivalent to Britain's Lord Kitchener. McKinley concurred, though he still read him the riot act during his autumn 1898 trip through the Midwest. McKinley got him alone for a temperance lecture, and Lawton took the pledge. He swore never again to allow "a drop of alcoholic stimulant to pass his lips." McKinley believed him, and Lawton kept his vow. But he didn't have that long left anyway.

Like Stephen Crane, Henry Dobson, and thousands of others in Cuba, the Splendid War would shorten Lawton's days. He believed he'd contracted tuberculosis while there and "had not many years left to him," he told a friend. "I am not sure I shall come back alive. It looks as if I was to die of consumption or be shot, and I believe I would rather be shot." Colleagues believed he had a death wish; they'd watch as he sat erect on his black horse during "a beautiful battle," pith helmet pipeclayed to a glistening white, yellow raincoat the brightest thing for miles. But those who fought with him against the Apaches said he was just as reckless then.

Lawton stepped off the *Grant* on March 10, 1899, to a month-old war. Despite McKinley's assurances, Otis did not plan to step down. Lawton was obviously an unwelcome addition. The old Indian fighter realized that Otis's strategy was built on hope and little else: secure the capital, generate goodwill through public works, throw his 21,000 volunteers and Regulars at Aguinaldo's 30,000 homegrown fighters. Such odds were too long for success, and pressure was already mounting to bring home the volunteers. This war would last longer than the one in Cuba—but how long, no one knew.

On March 17 Otis placed Lawton in charge of the First Division, relieving Thomas Anderson. Lawton took the field in early April, driving south with fifteen hundred men and artillery against Santa Cruz on Laguna Bay, the same area razed by Wheaton a month earlier. He took his eleven-year-old son, Marley, with him. Dressed in a miniature army uniform, the boy followed his dad everywhere: when bullets struck near his feet, Lawton gloated, "Why, sir, he would make a first-class soldier right now! Did you see him under fire?" Correspondents loved him, and comparisons between Otis and Lawton soon appeared in print. When Lawton captured Santa Cruz on April 10 and advanced on two other towns, the campaign opened his eyes. He predicted it would take 100,000 soldiers to pacify these islands, a close estimate to the actual 125,000. He established garrisons to hold his gains, but on April 16 Otis ordered him back with *all* soldiers, and *insurrectos* reoccupied every town.

This was Otis's infuriating constant that baffled everyone. Whenever Americans gained ground, Otis ordered them back. Two weeks after taking and losing Santa Cruz, Otis ordered Lawton to support MacArthur in the north; the Filipinos had so effectively hamstrung "Mac's" supply lines that his advance on San Fernando was halted. Lawton drove his men as hard as he had against the Apaches, covering 120 miles in twenty days, traveling light, capturing town after town. On May 17 he took San Isidro, Aguinaldo's latest capital; he stuck so close to "Aggie's" heels that he begged Otis to let him press on. Instead, Otis withdrew Lawton to Manila, and the harried Aguinaldo reentered San Isidro for a well-deserved rest.

This was madness, Lawton cried. He stormed into Otis's sanctuary claiming that the war would drag on forever. Give him two regiments and a free hand, and within sixty days he'd bring Aguinaldo back, dead or alive. According to an officer present, Otis laughed in scorn. Army tradition demanded Lawton's quiet acceptance; instead, he spoke to the press, criticizing Otis's complacency. The rift became big news: some politicians called Lawton insubordinate, while others demanded Otis's dismissal. Lawton seemed surprised by the flap, and he backed off; the eruption settled, at least briefly, but Lawton neither forgot nor forgave.

Journalists had been uncovering disquieting hints of Otis's lies all spring; now Lawton urged those he knew and trusted to circumvent army censors and print the "truth" of the war. Otis's daily drumbeat of victory had grown unreal: they'd been to the front and could separate fantasy from truth; they'd talked to Filipinos about the rebellion, and they knew that its popular support was broader than Otis let on. Otis's strategy bewildered everyone: Lawton was not the only commander called back after taking a town. Time and again Otis reported to the War Department that the war would end soon; he reported Filipino losses "in the ratio of twenty to one," wrote Albert Robinson of the *New York Evening Post*, when in fact "the twenty is guesswork" invented to support his illusions.

The worst lies to newsmen were those Otis used to create "an ultra-optimistic view that is not shared by the general officers in the field," falsehoods abetted by the War Department, since it allowed his censorship policy. Soon after Lawton's confrontation with Otis, John Bass wrote a scathing four-thousand-word piece for *Harper's Weekly* that he slipped past censors on a ship to Hong Kong. "Why is it that the American outlook is blacker now than it has been since the beginning of the war?" he mused in the June 1899 article. Otis never visited front lines, accurate maps did not exist, army management was unwieldy, and "the whole population of the islands" sympathized with the rebels. Bass painted the war as a huge, unheeding beast lumbering blind through the countryside: "The sooner the people of the United States find out that the people of the Philippines do not wish to be governed by us, the better."

On June 30, an even more damaging white paper penned by the AP's Robert M. Collins landed on Otis's desk: it contained details never before revealed, quoting Bass and several other reporters. Bass and a colleague had said that "they had personally seen our soldiers bayoneting the wounded." A story that rebels in Dasmariñas cut the ears off two American corpses had, in fact, been in retaliation for the same practice by Americans. Where Otis reported that 7.5 percent of American soldiers were ill, army surgeons put that number closer to 20 percent. They'd refrained from making this public because they did not wish to cause "sensations." But matters had gotten out of hand.

Otis read the report, dragged Collins, Bass, and two other reporters into his office, and started screaming at them. "Gentlemen, you have served an extraordinary paper on me," he railed. "You accuse me of falsehood," which in itself "constitutes a conspiracy against the Government." He threatened to throw them "off the island," but they knew the threats were hollow. After the meeting, they smuggled their statement and Otis's response through the same underground route Bass had used earlier; soon, even the nation's most pro-imperialist publications ran some version of the tale.

Journalists weren't alone in harrying the beleaguered general. In March, Protestant missionaries appeared, itching to "save" natives in unpacified regions. That same month, a presidential commission arrived to "adjust differences" between Filipinos and Americans. McKinley named as its chairman Jacob Gould Schurman, president of Cornell University, and also appointed the zoologist Dean Worcester, who considered himself an expert on race, and Charles Denby, the former U.S. envoy to China. When the "Schurman Commission" broached the idea of eventually eliminating the military government, Otis insisted that the three be recalled. When their April 4 report recommended giving Filipinos a small measure of self-government, Otis blasted the notion. Later that month, Schurman recommended suing for peace. By then, Otis knew this conflict would be long and painful in more ways than one.

If the war worried Americans, the rebels despaired. Apolinario Mabini admitted that outright victory was impossible: perhaps the only option was the Cuban kind—fighting a guerrilla war until exhaustion set in and some kind of peace could be brokered. But with each new defeat, Antonio Luna's wrath mounted. He'd fly into such rages that even friends questioned his sanity. He'd slap officers, even generals; threaten to kill others or throw them in jail. When his brother José, a doctor, interceded for an Englishman jailed on a minor offense, he snapped, "If you utter one word I will throw you in the same place he is."

By May, Luna's rages terrified his men. Though Philippine popular culture today has turned him into a martyr after the release of the bloody hit movie *Heneral Luna*, historians believe he could have become a tyrant and demagogue. He virtually handed Malolos to the Americans when he left the front to scold a subordinate for courting a woman he also desired. His men called him "General Article One," since death was his preferred punishment for every offense, no matter how trivial. He executed a Chinese man without trial; seized a whip and drove away women and children crowding a train. Mabini was shocked that such an educated man could so easily overstep his authority. "It would be better if he was replaced," he finally told Aguinaldo.

If character is destiny, Luna's rages foretold his end. Though the Philippine Army swore allegiance to Aguinaldo and, by extension, Luna, this was in fact a factional, not *national*, army, based upon clan. A Tagalog soldier devoted to Aguinaldo would not feel the same loyalty for an Ilocano like Luna. During the battle of La Loma Church, Luna ordered the Kawit Company under Pedro Janolino into the fight, but Janolino declared that he only took orders from Aguinaldo. When the counterattack failed, Luna accused Janolino of cowardice and disarmed the entire company. Within a week, Aguinaldo rearmed them all.

On May 7 Aguinaldo reorganized his cabinet, keeping Luna as director of war but naming *ilustrado* Pedro Paterno as chairman and Felipe Buencamino as secretary of state. The fact that Buencamino's conservative version of the constitution had supplanted Mabini's was finally too much, and the man called Aguinaldo's "Dark Chamber" resigned in disgust. "Such men are not intended for great things," Mabini said in parting. "They are barely useful in themselves." Aguinaldo sadly accepted Mabini's resignation, but he needed Paterno's and Buencamino's wealth to fund the war. The new cabinet became a warring body, divided between Luna's followers, who sought independence at all costs, and wealthy conservatives seeking peace.

The inevitable occurred on May 25 in Cabanatuan, the newest seat of government. When Paterno and Buencamino suggested forming a "peace commission" to explore Jacob Schurman's peace feelers, Luna grew petty and accused Buencamino's son Joaquin of cowardice during a lost battle. Buencamino reminded Luna that he'd also fled in similar circumstances. Luna slapped Buencamino and pushed him to the floor, then accused the cabinet of plotting to surrender. He ordered his men to charge the entire body with treason and cast them into exile.

Aguinaldo was present during the blowup: he'd heard of Luna's rages, but this was apparently the first time he'd witnessed one firsthand. As always, he played peacekeeper. He promised Luna an investigation, then released the ministers once Luna departed. Subsequent actions show that the incident unsettled him. Whom could he trust? Though Aguinaldo, like Mabini, admired Luna's intelligence, he'd not supported his Little Republic in 1896 and had even informed against Rizal, though probably under torture. Even Mabini warned that Luna's flaws spelled ruin. After the slap, Aguinaldo grew aloof around Luna; he wrote letters describing the "grave danger" around him, but did not give details. Rumors ran rampant of a coup.

On Saturday, June 3, Aguinaldo received a wire from Luna seeking a personal meeting in Cabanatuan. Its purpose is still a mystery: perhaps he meant to discuss the American offer, perhaps to dissolve the cabinet. Nobody knows. But Aguinaldo responded in alarm. The next morning, he rode to San Isidro without answering, and there found a loyal force of three thousand under Gregorio del Pilar. The future Philippine president Manuel L. Quezon recalled that Aguinaldo donned his dress uniform, reviewed the troops, and ordered every officer to "swear that we would fight on his side against all enemies." It was the first time the young Quezon ever laid eyes on *El Presidente*. "I asked him if he was celebrating some happy event, and he just smiled and said nothing." The next day, Aguinaldo weeded Luna's men from the officer corps.

Aguinaldo may not have answered Luna's telegram, but *someone* did. On June 4, the day Aguinaldo rode to San Isidro, Luna received his own wire, purportedly sent by the president, asking him to meet in his residence in Cabanatuan. On June 5 Luna left with aides Francisco Roman and Eduardo Rosca. They arrived at 1:30 p.m. Aguinaldo lived in a convent off the main square, guarded by soldiers of the Kawit Company, the same unit Luna had disgraced earlier. Luna left his aides, marched into the convent, and confronted an officer he'd belittled days earlier. In the most detailed account, Luna roared, "Weren't you and these soldiers the ones I disarmed in Calumpit for cowardice?" The captain replied, "The same, my general."

"Well, well—I'll soon fix you," Luna snapped, and stomped upstairs to find Aguinaldo.

But *El Presidente* was not there. Instead, he found Felipe Buencamino, whom he'd slapped at the cabinet meeting. "Where is Aguinaldo?" Luna cried. "San Isidro," Buencamino said. The two started shouting, when a rifle went off downstairs. Luna rushed down the steps and at the bottom found Captain Pedro Janolino, the commander he'd excoriated at La Loma Church. "Idiot, fool!" Luna screamed. "You do not know how to handle a rifle!"

This was the last straw. "I was frightened and immediately hit him in the head with my dagger," Janolino would claim in 1929. This released a feeding frenzy: other Kawit soldiers rushed in and hacked, stabbed, and shot the hated Luna. "No one ordered us to kill General Luna," Janolino confessed. "I assume the whole responsibility for the sad happening."

But Luna wasn't dead, and he managed to flee outside. His final moments are remembered today in a scene echoing Sam Peckinpah's *The Wild Bunch*: he draws his pistol, staggers forward, and screams "Cowards! Traitors! Assassins!" The movie *Heneral Luna* portrays it as a bloody ballet in which Luna seems nearly indestructible. His aides rush to save him: Colonel Roman is mowed down; Captain Rosca is shot in the thigh and escapes by crawling into the church. When the smoke clears, Luna lay dead, bleeding from more than forty wounds.

Now Buencamino takes charge. He searches Luna's body and grabs the telegram that could implicate Aguinaldo in his murder; he asks whether any Kawit men are hurt and sees their dawning fear. "We will take care of you," he says. Suddenly Aguinaldo's mother, nicknamed Kapitana Teneng, opens an upper window and leans over the balustrade. She'd heard the shooting and saw Luna fall. She screams at the soldiers in Tagalog, but two versions exist. The most generous is "*Ano ba ang ginagawa ninyo sa general? Kawawa naman, huag ninyong patayin!*" ("Why did you kill the General? Didn't you recognize him? You are all bad men!").

The less generous: "*Ano ba, nagalaw pa iyan*?" ("Well, does he still move?").

Buencamino was good to his word. No punishment befell the assassins; Luna's officers and supporters were decimated, jailed, or slain. Luna's brother Juan, a famous artist, died on December 7 from what many suspect was poisoning. José Alejandrino, an early Aguinaldo ally who'd drifted into Luna's camp, fled north to the safety of his brother's unit and survived. An investigation concluded that Luna died in a "military collision," caused because "ambition was stronger in him than gratitude." Even the sympathetic Mabini concluded that Luna had aspired too high: "If he had got what he wanted, there would have been a division that would have annihilated us." Nevertheless, Aguinaldo paid. People coupled Luna's death with Bonifacio's—and blame haunted him for the rest of his days.

When Otis heard the news, he could have shortened the war. Peace feelers were out; monsoons had bogged operations. The climate had ravaged 30 percent of Otis's force, and the surgeon general called the "weakened hearts and quickened pulses" of his troops a condition "akin to typhoid fever." A window had opened to shorten the war with a little diplomacy, but Otis stuck to his oath to grind down the enemy; as a result, he ground up his men.

The rain fell in sheets when David Fagen landed in Manila. He'd never seen such rain. From June through October, seventy inches fell on Luzon, as much as had fallen on California in the past seven years. Fagen's convoy docked on July 25, and for the next three weeks, several typhoons blew through. The railroad washed out; bridges collapsed; rice paddies surrounding the city became a glimmering lake. Manila's narrow streets became Venetian canals.

It had been a long journey for Fagen. The fever had come close to killing him. On September 26, 1898, after three weeks' recuperation, the Twenty-Fourth left Montauk Point for its former post at Fort Douglas, Utah, outside Salt Lake City. Private Fagen and Sergeant Calloway rode among them. They no doubt knew each other by then: both had been diagnosed with yellow fever on August 25, had left Cuba together on the quarantine ship, and passed from remission to the second phase. More than forty men of the Twenty-Fourth survived this toxic period, though some were left disabled. Fagen still felt weak as the train trundled through the Midwest and over the Rocky Mountains. They were met in Salt Lake City by a parade and a regimental band.

Fagen put his time at Fort Douglas to good use. He apparently attended the post school where Calloway taught. This had been established for soldiers with limited education; attendance was encouraged, and army records show that he learned to sign his name. He also developed skill as a gambler: according to *The Salt Lake Herald*, he became a fixture in "the gambling resorts on Commercial Street, where he was known as a jovial, reckless player with a penchant for stud poker and an exhaustless fund of luck." He was good enough that W. D. Robinson, the fort's "colored milkman," considered Fagen a good risk: "It was like coining money to lend Fagin [*sic*] a few dollars" for a game stake. "In five minutes he'd give me back twice as much as I let him have." Fagen's biographer, Michael Morey, said that although a $200 win in stud poker was not that unusual, the sum rarely lasted through payday. Still, regular success in high-stakes face-offs like stud makes a name for a gambler, for good and for bad.

The story appeared in October 1900, after Fagen's name hit *The New York Times*, and it is telling for what it gets right and gets wrong. A halftone print shows a confident young man, clean-shaven, with a broad forehead, thick brows, and short hair parted down the middle; he wears a starched collar, tie, coat, and vest, probably bought with his winnings, as a private's monthly pay was only $13. Old hands of the Twenty-Fourth, like gray-haired "Sergeant Williams," picked through their memories and got facts wrong. "He was just naturally too lazy and had too much book learning in his head," Williams claimed. "He had been through the university of Nashville [presumably Fisk] and when he joined the regiment here he wanted to be giving orders and didn't like to take them." Williams's memory went beyond flawed, but Fagen *did* champ at army discipline: during this first stay in Fort Douglas, he was fined $2 in summary court, with added fatigue duty. Army records do not describe the nature of his infraction, just the fine.

In mid-January 1899 the War Department thinned ranks, offering more than five hundred men who'd joined to fight in Cuba an early discharge. On January 28 Fagen took the offer. "The gain is a pecuniary one," *The Salt Lake Tribune* explained, since each soldier received $75 in travel pay. Fagen received a "good" rating on his discharge papers and boarded the train for home.

He stepped off in Tampa on February 6, 1899, two days after the start of the Philippine War. Nothing remained for him at home. His father, Sam, had died while he was away. Although there is no record of divorce, Maggie Washington lived with another man under her maiden name at 813 Harrison Street, where Fagen had lived with her. He had siblings in town, but other than that, what could Tampa offer? He'd seen the world outside South Florida, had adventures, nearly died. Three days later, on February 9, he showed up at Fort McPherson outside Atlanta and reenlisted in the Twenty-Fourth, apparently requesting assignment with Company I, the unit he'd served with at the fever camp in Siboney. He signed his name in shaky letters, but not an X; passed the physical; had his character reentered as "good." The next morning, he boarded the train for Fort D. A. Russell outside Cheyenne, Wyoming. The army was his family now.

Events probably influenced him. Hope that Buffalo Soldiers' heroism in Cuba might ease racial tensions had been replaced by violence so extreme that some feared the dawn of a "racial calamity." On July 3, 1898—two days after the charge up San Juan Hill—*The Richmond Planet* listed a dozen Southern lynchings that had occurred since war was declared. On August 27 Joseph Williams had been lynched in Scotland Neck, North Carolina, for being "impudent" to a white man. On November 10, two thousand armed whites overthrew the biracial city government of Wilmington, North Carolina; burned down the black-owned Wilmington *Daily Record*; and killed as many as sixty black citizens. On November 24 black and white volunteers turned on one another at Camp Shipp in Anniston, Alabama, leaving one man dead and others seriously injured. "By putting guns in the hands of negroes as soldiers and making them peers of white men," fumed State Senator John T. Morgan, "race conditions have been greatly aggravated."

Fagen's train reached Cheyenne in mid-February 1899. The city of fourteen thousand was socked in by that winter's third blizzard. Fort Russell lay three miles away, connected by rail. Officers' quarters sat on two sides of the frozen parade ground, enlisted barracks on the other two. Fagen reported to Sergeant George D. Powell, with whom he'd served in Siboney. Company I's first lieutenant was James Alfred Moss, who'd led two companies of the Twenty-Fifth at El Caney.

Moss will play a consequential role in Fagen's future. He'd graduated number 3,616 in West Point's class of 1894—the "goat," or very last, who traditionally got the last choice of assignments. He'd hopped a train to Fort Missoula, Montana, the youngest second lieutenant in the Twenty-Fifth Infantry. Many new officers resented commanding blacks, but Moss seemed to thrive: he created a well-publicized "bicycle corps" and pedaled nineteen hundred miles to St. Louis with a journalist, a surgeon, and eight Buffalo Soldiers on donated Spalding bicycles. For his initiative, he was promoted to first lieutenant and transferred in September 1898 to Company I of the Twenty-Fourth Infantry.

Fagen received his first punishment at Fort Russell within two months of Moss's arrival. This may have been a general crackdown surrounding a "whiskey ranch" brawl involving Company I. According to the *San Francisco Chronicle*, the free-for-all "with knives and razors" ended with Corporal George Greenhow dead and Sergeant Walter Barnes severely injured. Fagen was not named, but he'd worked with both men in the fever camp and his troubles had started soon afterward. On March 25 he was fined $1 for an unlisted offense, the start of Fagen's deteriorating relations with white officers, Moss in particular.

Fagen stayed out of trouble until summer. During that time, Sergeant Calloway reached the end of his five-year enlistment; he'd risen to the level of regimental clerk and had applied to the U.S. Customs Service. The regiment's adjutant, First Lieutenant Joseph Leitch, wrote a glowing recommendation, but begged him to re-up and offered a promotion to battalion sergeant major, as high as a black soldier could rise. When Calloway reenlisted on March 7, he was recorded as "married"; a year later, in the census of June 1, 1900, he is "single." Whether the contradiction is a clerical error or dissimulation, it will affect his fate almost as harshly as Fagen's punishments do his. For now, his prospects look good.

As winter turned to spring, small detachments of the Twenty-Fourth were sent across the nation on odd jobs: one group went to Alaska, another to Alcatraz Island. On May 2, Moss led 25 men—16 from Company I, including Fagen—to ride more than 140 miles of trails through Sequoia and General Grant national parks to curtail illegal logging, hunting, and cattle and sheep grazing. Many were still "nearly broken down from the effects of Cuban fever," and the army hoped that fresh air would do them good. For three weeks, they rode back trails: on June 7 in Halstead Meadow, Moss and Fagen argued, and Moss fined the private $5, nearly a third of his monthly pay. It was Fagen's most serious offense to date, possibly the real beginning of his downfall.

On June 20 Moss got word to rush to San Francisco: they were off to the Philippines! They arrived two days later, but not in time to join the four hundred men of the Third Battalion aboard the *Zealandia*. Three days later, Moss and his men boarded the *Sheridan* with fifteen hundred whites. The next afternoon, the four-ship convoy sailed off to war.

By now, signs of old racial hatreds had intensified. Though black Regulars realized that Cuba had not improved their lot, they were less inclined to take abuse than earlier. As the Twenty-Fourth awaited transport, a white soldier slashed Private George Patterson for objecting to a racial slur. Private Stephen Patterson, also of the Twenty-Fourth, expressed the growing discontent at the white soldier's trial: "We did our duty in Cuba, and we don't think we should be insulted because we are black."

By the summer of 1899, black opposition to "McKinley imperialism" had grown heated. On August 7 the editor Julius Taylor of Salt Lake City's *Broad-Ax* wrote, "Any black man who enlists to fight the Filipinos is perfectly satisfied with the abuse heaped upon him in this country." The *Washington Bee* editor Calvin Chase asked on September 9, "Will Darkey Fight Darkey?" and quoted a War Department official who said that if brought "face to face with their colored Filipino cousins," black soldiers might hesitate to fight them. It boiled down to fairness, Chase said: "If the Negro understands the Filipinos are fighting for liberty and independence, ten chances to one they would take sides with them."

Proximity did not help race relations. According to a September 1899 *Oregonian* report, "fighting broke out between black and white soldiers on transport ships carrying them to the Philippines." On July 14, three weeks after setting out, Moss fined Fagen $2. For the first time, Fagen requested transfer to another company. The request was denied. The *Sheridan* arrived in Honolulu, and on July 23 Corporal James Boyd deserted;

the ship went on without him. The *City of Para* left San Francisco a few days after the *Sheridan* with a larger contingent of the Twenty-Fourth and Twenty-Fifth, including Sergeant Calloway. Once again, whites outnumbered blacks: among them was John Clifford Brown of the U.S. Army Corps of Engineers. Brown came from the wealthiest family of Portland, Maine, and graduated from the Massachusetts Institute of Technology; of all soldiers, he'd seem sympathetic to African Americans, but on August 10, upon arriving in Manila, he wrote, "The niggers left, and very glad we were to have them go." In fact, "we hated the colored men on the ship." He believed that blacks "do not seem to think like white men." His opinion hardened: nearly one year later, he wrote, "I am rapidly acquiring a very poor opinion of the race and should heartily support any attempt to disenfranchise them, or to limit their suffrage."

What was the source of such anger? No one really knows the *why*s, but its appearance in the Philippines seemed immediate: the ferocious racial hatred toward both American blacks and Filipinos was almost simultaneous, and it soon merged. One private wrote that "the white man's prejudice followed the Negro to the Philippines, ten thousand miles from where it originated." Buffalo Soldiers learned that whites of all classes—from privates to generals' wives—held black soldiers and Filipinos in equal contempt, calling both "niggers" and "black devils." When the Twenty-Fifth relieved some "Western volunteers," one white soldier cried, "Hello, nig! Didn't know you'd come. What do you think you're going to do over here?" The response is telling: "The big negro unbent himself, as a smile went along the car windows, and with an expression on his face as though the effort was about to be too much for him, replied: 'Well, I doan know, but I ruther reckon we're sent over huh to take up de White Man's Burden!'"

Given such enmity, it's not surprising that Filipinos and Buffalo Soldiers became friends. When blacks first arrived in Manila, natives viewed them with awe and fear. They saw them as Negritos, the black tribes of the northern mountains. But as fear turned to friendship, they nicknamed them "*Negritos Americanos*," reasoning that they were "very much like ourselves, only larger." Military authorities observed that in towns "garrisoned by colored troops the natives seemed to harbor little or no enmity to the soldiers," while soldiers "seem contented with their lot and are not perpetually pining for home." But rather than see the advantage, this fact worried the officers, who feared that blacks might hold more sympathy for the Filipino cause than policy allowed. The *Harper's Weekly* reporter Stephen Bonsal, assigned to follow the soldiers, wrote, "While the white soldiers, unfortunately, got on badly with the natives, the black soldiers got on much too well." The future U.S. president William Howard Taft, who would become the Philippines' first civil governor, lamented that black troops fraternized "too well with the native women."

The *Sheridan* deposited Moss and his troops in Manila on July 25. They marched through the rain to their outpost a mile and a half northeast on the Balic-Balic Road. The front was close: local uprisings were rumored, and guard details doubled. Still, this was a fascinating world. In town, Fagen could get a haircut from a Chinese barber, buy stuffed bats from crowded shops, and eat steamed grasshoppers for a penny. He posed for a photo portrait, sitting in a Renaissance Revival armchair, gazing to the left, one leg draped over the other. His expression is serious: anything can be read into it, or nothing.

On August 11 the rest of the Twenty-Fourth and units of the Twenty-Fifth arrived aboard the *City of Para*; by month's end, 2,100 Buffalo Soldiers had arrived. Some took the train north to the furthest line of advance; others, like Fagen and Company I, stayed longer. On August 28 Moss took charge of the company when its commander stepped down for health reasons. On September 11 he docked Fagen $10, almost a month's pay, for an undescribed infraction: with that came time in the guardhouse, kitchen duty, or digging latrines. On September 22 Moss fined Fagen another $5, meaning he'd gone a full month without pay, and then some.

Fagen again requested a transfer; again, it was denied. He felt trapped, but bided his time.

Fred Funston's Kansans came home to a reception none ever imagined. The *Tartar* left Manila Bay on September 3 and sailed through San Francisco's Golden Gate on October 10. Funston and Wilder Metcalf met California's governor and received the Kansas delegation; the Twentieth Kansas marched from Market Street to the Presidio, where over the next two and a half weeks they'd be demobilized. On October 28 they went through the "last act," the ceremony converting them back to Kansas militiamen.

During this month, Funston realized that he'd become a popular hero. He was good copy, willing to sprinkle his comments with "fine, old-fashioned anger-purging profanity." This new public persona supplanted the old Frederick Funston: he was a person of consequence, free with his opinions. In some ways, it had started on the archipelago: his portrait had graced the May 20 cover of *Harper's Weekly*, and in the July 15 issue, he said that he wanted America to stay in the Philippines. Back home, he got more ink. In the *San Francisco Call*, he said that the Filipino only understood force: "I believe they should be ruled with an iron hand, whether they like it or not." And all this talk of war crimes?

> This was the most humane war against a half-civilized people that the world had ever seen. The stories of brutality on the part of volunteers were sent out by correspondents whom no one knew either in Manila or on the firing line. As for the soldiers who tell such tales, they are simply liars.

Such coverage brought notice, including by Roosevelt. In July he'd aligned their "principles." Now, on October 17, he said, "All Hail! And a thousand congratulations." Roosevelt's sights were already set on the White House, but McKinley was too popular and the election was only eighteen months away. Instead, he told Lodge, the best path was either to wait for the 1904 presidential nomination or take a turn as McKinley's running mate in 1900. Roosevelt's note showed that he considered Funston part of that future: he asked him again to visit the Governor's Mansion in Albany and bring "our good friend White of the Emporia Gazette."

Others also focused on the returning hero. On October 21 the War Department asked Funston to extend active duty as a brigadier general commanding a new batch of volunteers. He'd been chosen by McKinley and the new war secretary, Elihu Root: if he agreed, he must return to Luzon immediately.

This was a hard choice: there'd been talk of his running for Kansas governor or U.S. senator. A "Funston Club" had formed. But McKinley's offer was a sure bet, and Eda had found the life of a general's wife congenial. On October 27 he wired back his acceptance and asked for ten days, leave to visit his parents. The War Department confirmed his appointment and the leave. On October 29 the Kansans and Funston boarded two Union Pacific trains and headed home.

With celebrity came controversy. During a speech at Stanford University, Funston called the archipelago's Dominicans so "bitterly hated" that if the United States expelled them, "the insurrection would fall to pieces." San Francisco's archbishop called Funston an anti-Catholic bigot. Old stories about executing prisoners surfaced and refused to go away. Condemnations increased when the Twentieth mustered out: in early 1900, Funston's critics formally asked the army to charge him with violating the Articles of War.

But for the moment, the return of the Kansans overshadowed all. The Twentieth arrived in Topeka on November 2, 1899. The streets were decked in bunting and lined with cheering fans. A woman thrust her baby into a Pullman window for Eda to kiss; suddenly, dozens of babies filled the window. A parade wound two miles to the capitol building, and more celebrations packed the next six days. On November 4 Funston and Eda returned to Iola, and the *Daily Register* estimated that ten thousand people waited at the train station. Funston pulled no punches in siding with the expansionists. The U.S. was not waging "a war of oppression against a people fighting for their liberty," he said, but "crushing an insurrection in a part of the United States"—a new twist in an increasingly spiteful debate. Like nine-tenths of his men, he believed that the war was as just as any the U.S. had "ever engaged in or will ever engage in." Filipinos were not fighting for freedom, but acting "at the dictation of scalawag politicians." The war would be over in six months if America sent in sixty thousand troops. The crowd roared.

On November 8 Funston received orders to return to San Francisco. He said goodbye to family and friends, reaching the Presidio on November 19. He arranged to leave Eda with her parents in Oakland: Luzon had been hard on her health, and she needed a rest. On November 23 he told Roosevelt that he could not come to visit: "You know the War Department requested me to return to the Philippines." But he promised not to forget their mutual future. "I am going to quit the service as soon as the fighting is over and then I am going to come to Albany and we will talk things over," he said. The next day, he boarded the USS *Indiana* and sailed back to war.

These autumn months of Funston's apotheosis would be devastating for Fagen and the Twenty-Fourth. On August 21 a disaster unfolded that affected them for the rest of the year. At six a.m. members of Company F marched to the Marikina River, where the regiment halted. The night before, they'd heard shots on the opposite side, so their captain wanted to send scouts. Yet constant rain had swollen the river, and the only way across was by bamboo raft hitched together with the rattan straps Filipinos used to build everything. Sergeant Sanford M. Thomas of Company H saw twelve to sixteen men climb aboard, far too many for a flimsy raft pushed by poles. They made it halfway across when there was a crash, and the raft began to spin. The men onshore watched helplessly as their friends plunged one by one into the raging water, screaming for help as they washed away. Eleven men drowned: nine from Company F; John E. Poole from Company H, who jumped in to save another; one man from the hospital corps. Only two or three men survived. "One who witnessed it can never forget it," Thomas said.

The effects appeared in company records almost immediately, as though group despair set in. Two men died of unspecified illness on September 18 and 25: though unrelated to the accident, it seemed part of a widespread debilitation. Two men deserted, one as early as August 15, a second on September 1. On September 13, three were dishonorably discharged and given tickets back home. During this period, Fagen was fined twice, on September 11 and 22. The Buffalo Soldiers prided themselves on being tough, so such a mass breakdown was highly unusual. Fagen's growing woes with Moss did not occur in a vacuum.

Over the summer, Otis devised a three-pronged plan that he hoped would end the war. MacArthur would lead a division north from Angeles, driving Aguinaldo before him up the Central Plain. Lloyd Wheaton would sail with two thousand men up the west coast and land behind Aguinaldo at the Lingayan Gulf, closing off his escape route to the mountains. The third arm operated under Lawton. He'd take the First Brigade, which included the Twenty-Fourth, northeast up the Rio Grande de Pampanga. This route was most difficult: while MacArthur headed north by railroad and Wheaton by sea, Lawton followed cart tracks that were often impassable. On paper, Aguinaldo would be trapped between three armies: he could surrender or be annihilated. It was the same basic plan the army had used twenty-one years earlier against the Sioux and Cheyenne at the Little Bighorn River. Now, as then, everything depended on coordination and speed.

On September 28 Fagen's Third Battalion boarded the train to San Fernando, once an agricultural hub of 3,000 souls but now burned and reduced to 1,500. Company I made camp in town, and October proved worse than September. Three men drowned, one died of disease; one man in Company K deserted, two got dishonorably discharged, two committed suicide. Fagen was punished and fined twice, but he was one of many, including Eugene Young, fined $7, and William Watson, fined $10 and given fifteen days' hard labor.

On October 1 a typhoon roared across the island, flattening thousands of huts, killing more than three hundred mules. In these gray weeks, suicides increased, not limited to Buffalo Soldiers. Private Frank Johnson of the white Twenty-Second shot himself while on night-guard duty; he tried to make it seem an ambush, but the bullet traveled from his mouth to the rear of his cranium and the coroner ruled it suicide. Two back-to-back suicides in the Twenty-Fourth seem less planned. The MIT graduate John Clifford Brown witnessed one: "While I was sitting here writing the colored infantry was drilling in extended order across the river," he wrote on October 3. "After the drill one of the men came down and jumped in the river drowning himself. They have just got his body. One did the same thing Sunday. I guess they have been driven hard."

Suddenly the Twenty-Fourth became the focus of every local defeat and failure, and Fagen seems targeted as a main offender. One day after the typhoon, he stood before Moss for an unspecified offense; the rain beat down outside. Within two days, Captain James E. Brett would depart for the United States, leaving command of Company I's 114 black soldiers to Moss and his second lieutenant, Charles E. Hay Jr., the twenty-four-year-old son of Secretary of State John Hay. Moss could have eased up and tried to salvage a good soldier, but instead he ordered Fagen to forfeit another

$15 in pay and spend thirty more days at hard labor. But the sentence had to wait: in this first phase of Otis's "Great Roundup," units massed for the push north, and this included Fagen and Calloway.

On Tuesday, October 10, General Samuel Young led the first contingent of Lawton's three-thousand-man force east from San Fernando. Rain turned the roads to gumbo, and wagons bogged down. They tried rafting on the Rio Grande de Pampanga, but rocks and white water made this equally daunting. The first village they reached was Arayat, set at the foot of an extinct volcano of the same name. Mount Arayat rose 3,366 feet; the god Sinukuan lived at the top and gazed down on the Central Plain. Control of the Plain meant winning or losing the war.

The Twenty-Fourth plodded through knee-deep mud past Arayat to Cabiao; on October 19 they mauled nine hundred enemy fighters from San Isidro; another ten days and they reached Cabanatuan, Aguinaldo's newest HQ. Their lines stretched perilously thin. The roads might be severed at any moment by washed-out bridges; when engineers built new ones, the rivers washed them away. By the end of October, Lawton placed his men on half rations. The Twenty-Fourth was strung along the route, so Fagen's exact location is unknown. But on October 16, seventeen men from the Twenty-Fourth were ordered to guard the ferries near Arayat, and on this day, Moss again fined Fagen, this time for $6. The period for rapprochement had passed: his biographer Morey surmises that "Fagen was either incapable of escaping the wrath of his superiors or, more likely, determinably unrepentant."

During the advance, scouts discovered broadsides addressed in broken English to "The Twenty-Fourth Infantry (colored) our brother regiment." They were nailed to trees outside garrison towns. Others appeared mysteriously in camp; sometimes troops found tied bundles awaiting distribution. "To the Colored American Soldiers," they read:

> It is without honor nor profit that you are spilling your costly blood.
>
> Your masters have thrown you to the most iniquitous fight with double purpose. In order to be you the instrument of their ambition. Soon make the extinction of you race.
>
> Your friends the Filipinos give you this good warning.
>
> You must consider your situation and your history. And take

> charge that the blood of your brothers Samuel Hose and Gray proclaim vengeance.

The author was assumed to be Aguinaldo: whoever the author was, he did know current events. In 1899 Edward Gray was lynched in Louisiana; on April 22, 1899, Samuel Hose was chained to a pine tree outside Newnan, Georgia, and a fire lit beneath him as two thousand people cheered. This seemed common knowledge: William Simms of Muncie, Indiana, was shocked when a young Filipino boy asked him, "Why don't you fight these people in America who burn Negroes, that make a beast of you?"

On November 1 Fagen, Calloway, and three companies of the Twenty-Fourth arrived in San Isidro and set up permanent quarters. A small farming town near the southern edge of Nueva Ecija Province, San Isidro served as a hub for supplies coming upriver from Manila. Fagen and his comrades manned outposts, guarded launches, escorted supply trains. They patrolled San Isidro's graveled streets, bought souvenirs from thatched stalls in the central square. They interacted with locals and sometimes made friends. This month was less lethal than October, but two men died of disease on November 19 and 21, and sickness left 226 absent from duty. "The rain fell incessantly and in torrents," wrote one officer, "until the entire valley was one vast marsh." On the day they arrived, Private Clem Bonaparte of Company K was swept from a launch, his body discovered downriver.

San Isidro also crawled with spies, most of them connected with an underground *beno* supplier. Colonel Lyman W. V. Kennon ordered a proprietor arrested and his liquor destroyed. But it was too late, at least for Fagen: a young woman linked to both the dealers and the *insurrectos* caught his eye. According to an April 16, 1902, story in the *St. Louis Post-Dispatch*, David Fagen fell in love. On the morning of Saturday, November 25, three companies of the Twenty-Fourth were scheduled to cross the river and head north, but Fagen had decided not to go. That previous night, after a "protracted vino debauch," the twenty-one-year-old Fagen made his plans.

"Love for a native Filipino woman was the cause of Fagin's [*sic*] desertion," claimed the *Post-Dispatch*: "She held out promises to him of advancement in the insurgent forces if he would desert"—a tempting offer compared with a future ruled by Lieutenant Moss. Fagen's biographer Morey wrote that his desertion was a "conscious political act" designed to "make war on white Americans." It may have turned into that, but at the time it was more likely that he was fed up and tired. The army, for which he'd charged up San Juan Hill and volunteered at the fever camp, had turned its back on him. Betrayal is a strong motivator, and his resentment grew. He'd been given a way out: In his mind, what other choice was there?

The rain ceased before dawn. The sky cleared. The bugler blew reveille, and Company I woke to a rare cloudless day. The Twenty-Fourth formed in the square before the walls of the convent: by then, Fagen had stuffed as many revolvers into a gunnysack as could fit and had slipped to the edge of town. A Filipino officer named Delfin Esquivel sat astride a pony, waiting for him. Esquivel held the reins of a second horse, already saddled. The young black American appeared with his bulging gunnysack, and Esquivel handed him the reins. There was no turning back. That morning, David Fagen became a wraith, a legend, and one of the two most hunted men in the Philippine-American War.

24

Pursued

As Fagen made his choice, Aguinaldo ran. Every day, Otis's pinchers drew tighter. On November 7 Lloyd Wheaton's 2,500 men landed at San Fabian on the Lingayen Gulf while Samuel Young captured the main rebel supply train. The next day, MacArthur moved against the Republic's last capital at Tarlac, but the rains bogged him down. By the time his men captured Tarlac, on November 12, Aguinaldo had slipped twenty-six miles north to Bayambang.

On November 13 Aguinaldo called a council of war. MacArthur lay 26 miles south, Wheaton 20 miles north, Young 25 miles northeast and closing. Aguinaldo's only escape lay through a narrow corridor between Wheaton and Young. He ordered his men to switch from easily battered battalions to small mobile units that could launch lightning raids and disappear. From this moment forward, the Philippine Army would fight without fronts. They were now guerrillas, *insurrectos*, *amigos*, blending in with the local populace, indistinguishable. He disbanded the Army of Liberation and told soldiers to go home and prepare for the long insurgency ahead.

This "amigo war" reflected a changed political perception. Aguinaldo hoped that a war of attrition would change America's mind: that as more men died and more money vanished, the public would lose patience. Perhaps the U.S. Congress would balk during December debates, or voters would dump McKinley as president the next year. Cuba had proved that Americans were fickle.

Aguinaldo left by rail. His departure marked the first of many tragedies: his infant daughter, Flora, died of fever while still in Bayambang, and Aguinaldo could not linger at the graveside. He detrained in the dead of night at coastal Calasiao, where he met fifteen hundred Ilocoans led by the twenty-two-year-old Manuel Tinio, a Chinese mestizo born to one of the richest families of Nueva Ecija. Tinio had accompanied Aguinaldo in exile and fought Wheaton at San Jacinto, withdrawing only when Gatling guns killed 134 of his men. But Tinio's ferocity had slowed Wheaton's advance, making possible the escape corridor north toward the mountains.

Yet this was also the territory of those who'd revered Antonia Luna—and the Lunestas wanted revenge. All during this period, Aguinaldo's group would be attacked by unknown fighters wielding bolos. One group was probably the Guardia de Honor, a messianic cult led by "God Almighty." There were mounted Macabebe Scouts, who hated the Republic and all Tagalogs. There were silent killers who struck without warning and disappeared. At dawn on November 14 in the town of Santa Barbara, Aguinaldo joined the Byronic Gregorio del Pilar. Goyo knew this vengeful country; if anyone could get them through this minefield, he could.

They fled twelve miles northeast for tiny Pozorrubio, nestled at the foot of towering mountains. They split into two groups. Goyo led the advance group, which included Aguinaldo, his sister, wife Hilaria, various aides and families, and 250 soldiers. Manuel Tinio led the larger and slower rear guard: this included Aguinaldo's mother and four-year-old son, Miguel, nearly a thousand men, and Luna's nemesis Felipe Buencamino. Pedro Paterno, Aguinaldo's other senior deputy, had already defected, taking with him 90,000 pesos in insurgent funds.

They set off in the rain, but the rear guard fell behind. Aguinaldo reached Pozorrubio late on November 14, but between Manaog and San Manuel, the Third Cavalry overtook the rear, capturing everyone but Tinio and a few men. Wheaton was so close that he could take Pozorrubio easily, yet he'd barely moved since the fight at San Jacinto. Young's cavalry told him that *El Presidente* was within his grasp. A little further and this damnable war would end.

But Wheaton still lingered. The moment spawns controversy. According to William Sexton, Otis's overcautiousness warped Wheaton's former drive. Had Wheaton shown "even a modicum of initiative, Aguinaldo undoubtedly would have been captured," but there had already been several false "Aggie" sightings, and Otis's orders were confusing. He did not move until November 15, and by then Aguinaldo had slipped past. Even so, Young's mud-spattered cavalry almost caught him: they'd pressed on but too late learned they'd been tricked by their guide, an Aguinaldo loyalist who led them in the wrong direction.

Aguinaldo's breather did not last long. At nine a.m. on November 15, "we received the news that the Americans were at the entrance to the town," wrote Simeon Villa, a former ophthalmologist who now accompanied Aguinaldo as his chief of staff and medical officer. The nearby sounds of battle announced Young's men. A thirty-hour deluge of rain concealed Aguinaldo's escape but chilled everyone to the bone. Hilaria Aguinaldo fainted; they built a bamboo hut to warm her, stopped and rested, pressed on. Tinio and his last troops materialized through the gray curtain—they struck a zigzag course back to the coast at Aringay. The rain did not stop: their clothes were drenched, their teeth chattering. By November 16 they'd climbed to five hundred feet: "It seemed that we were at a great altitude and pretty close to the sky." At eight p.m. they paused on a mountain peak at Rancheria Famy, where they took shelter and built a fire. "We ate badly cooked goat's meat, slept in the goat's pen, with the horse's blankets for mats," Villa recorded. Capture might come at any moment, but they were too exhausted to continue, and they slept for the first time since fleeing Pozorrubio. Goyo kept with him his leather briefcase containing a girl's love letter and a lock of her hair. "Brothers," he exhorted his men, "what do you prefer—to die fighting or to die running away like cowards?" One man replied, "We want to die fighting." But the Americans did not catch up, and they pressed on.

They fled north for two weeks, through the provinces of Pangasinan, La Union, Ilocos Sur. They traveled by night, the Americans close behind. "Our vision grows dim," Villa wrote; "our legs and knees are already weak and tremulous, our breathing laborious and our thirst immense." In Naguilian, Aguinaldo was met by "a great crowd of people" and a municipal band; for two days, they gathered strength, then at midnight on November 19 crept off after hearing that pursuers were two or three hours behind. They stuck to the coast along the national road until reaching Candon. The gunboat *Samar* cruised the same coast and spotted Villa; it lobbed shells until he hid in the *cogon*, or high weeds. The pursuit slowed: Young's men were breaking down. Wheaton refused to continue; most Macabebes would go no farther. But Aguinaldo's route was blocked by an abrupt wall of mountains, and on November 22 he turned east through the famous tiered rice paddies, on through the town of Concepcion, higher. Their goal was a steep pass into the mountainous heart, a gateway that opened 4,500 feet straight up along a narrow winding trail. On November 23 they crossed *el Paso de Tirad.*

They'd entered an unknown world. The cloud-capped Cordillera Central fills nearly all of Northern Luzon. Mount Pulag is its highest peak, 9,606 feet above sea level; the range stretches 8,700 square miles and covers a sixth of Luzon. Viewed from above, it resembles a vast green, turbulent sea. The mountains were feared by those who lived in them; even Spaniards, who stopped at nothing for conquest, stayed away. Aboriginal tribes collectively called the Igorot practiced ritual headhunting; though the practice has stopped, tribal wars still break out over water or hunting rights, quarrels going back centuries. To the rest of Luzon, Emilio Aguinaldo was the "invincible liberator of the Philippines." In these mountains, he was just another intruder.

Even today, what happened at the Tirad Pass is seen as a central moment in Philippine identity. It's transformed beyond fact into legend, like Martí's suicidal charge or Roosevelt's sprint up San Juan Hill. As the little group filed up the trail, Goyo jumped from his horse onto a huge boulder and studied the land. He liked what he saw. "The Americans could never take this pass," he said, "and if they do, it will be over my dead body." He ordered sixty men to stay behind, build stone barricades across the twisting footpath, and dig parallel rows of trenches into the rocky slope. He put three men in each trench, then followed Aguinaldo down the opposite slope to the village of Angaki (today called Quirino). Tirad Pass would be impregnable, he said.

They rested there a week, and on November 30 Aguinaldo's party rode three hours southeast to the larger village of Cervantes. Yet Goyo felt uneasy. That night, he heard a heavy thud, as if a saddle had fallen. A check revealed nothing: all saddles in place, horses serene. But he could not sleep, and at dawn he told *El Presidente* that he must rejoin his men. Aguinaldo begged his favorite to stay; they'd left more than enough officers behind to defend the pass, but Goyo insisted. As he mounted up, Aguinaldo noticed that a tuft of his horse's mane had twisted up, considered bad luck for riders. Worse, the horse twisted and wheeled, another bad omen. But no one could convince Goyo to stay. At least take his famous white horse Rosello, Aguinaldo said. Del Pilar paused: this, he could do. He rode off shortly after dawn, as stylish as ever, clad in his new khaki uniform, silver spurs, and gleaming shoulder belt. His white steed could be spotted from far away.

Goyo and his escort returned to Angaki shortly after midday. They rested, then at dusk saw a guard at Tirad's highest point, "nervously waving a red flag, a signal that the enemy had been sighted," wrote del Pilar's aide-de-camp Vicente Enriquez. They rushed up and spent the night near the summit. That night, Goyo wrote, "I have a terrible premonition that the enemy will defeat me and my valiant men, but I die fighting for my beloved country." Such a fate, in this setting, made this "the most glorious moment of my life." It was his last entry.

The Americans were climbing after them. Young's men had pursued Aguinaldo to Candon, where the trail had grown cold. During the week that *El Presidente* rested, riders ranged the coast, offering bribes. On November 30 the villager Januario Galut revealed that Aguinaldo had climbed the Tirad Pass and was believed to be in Cervantes. Young guessed that he planned to link on the Abra River with the Tinio Brigade, the last Filipino unit of any real size. Young assigned three hundred men from the Thirty-Third Infantry and fifty Texas sharpshooters to the pursuit. At their head he placed Major Peyton C. March, the tall, athletic son of a Pennsylvania English professor. On December 1 March's squadron entered Concepcion. They climbed the zigzag trail the next morning at dawn.

They'd ascended three hundred feet when Goyo's Mausers drove them into the dirt. March ordered a second company to attack, but they were driven back, too. At this point, Januario Galut proved invaluable. He knew an alternate route: it meant backtracking to the trailhead, crossing a deep gorge, and sneaking up a hill above and to the left of the defenders. March sent ten sharpshooters and a lieutenant; simultaneously, he ordered Troop H up a peak overlooking the pass. Those Americans still pinned down settled in; sometimes they poked up a hat to keep the insurgents occupied. Goyo's men rolled boulders on them to conserve ammo. Clouds rolled in, disguising shapes, muffling sounds; a rumor started that a force under Aguinaldo was rushing to catch them from behind. Three lost their nerve and rushed the barricades: two were killed, one seriously wounded. Company H worked its way up, men hauling one another by rifles, web belts, ropes made from knotted blankets. March ran up and down the trail, urging patience, reassuring his men.

Goyo grew impatient, too. He sent his aide to survey defenses. The captains told Enriquez they'd limited firing to "very close range" to save ammo. Enriquez joined a squad near the summit, where he had a better view: the Americans below rested under cover, "their rifles piled in stacks." Their position seemed impenetrable: "We all agreed that we had the upper hand." Del Pilar joined them and took command: firing rose and fell. He ordered his men to stop and stepped onto a promontory to study the enemy below.

Five hours had passed; the midday sun burned down. Shortly before noon, Company H emerged on the high peak above Goyo's position; at almost the same moment, sharpshooters reached the hill behind the defenders. As Company H fired from the heights, March ordered his hunkered battalion to rush the barricades. The Filipinos fell back, only to be picked off by the waiting Texans. It ended quickly: of the sixty Filipinos guarding the trail, fifty-one died, including Goyo. Yet the rearguard action gave Aguinaldo those precious hours to flee.

The Battle of Tirad Pass remains the most legendary battle of the Philippine War: the "Filipino Thermopylae," Goyo's Last Stand. Ironically, the myth sprang not from rebels, but from two accompanying journalists: John T. McCutcheon of *The Chicago Record* and Richard Henry Little of the *Chicago Tribune*. Little's article, the more quoted one, veers furthest from fact: he watched down below in Lingay as Pilar sat atop his white horse at the first entrenchment, scolding and praising his men, "cursing, appealing to their love of their native land." As the firing grew hot, he fell back to the second line: soon "every man around him was down," and only then "did he turn his white horse and ride slowly up the winding trail." As he did,

> we, who were below, saw an American squirm his way out to the top of a flat rock and take deliberate aim at the figure on the white horse. We held our breath, not knowing whether to pray that the sharpshooter would shoot straight or miss. Then came the spiteful crack of the Krag rifle and the man on horseback rolled to the ground.

March's troops poured over the barricades and found Pilar dead. They stripped him of everything, Little said: his diary and letters, pants, shoes, silver spurs, uniform buttons, handkerchief with "Dolores Hosea" crocheted in a corner, "a golden locket containing a curl of a woman's hair." This is the moment enshrined by a statue at Tirad Pass that overlooks the valley and the steep path below. Del Pilar's horse rears up as Goyo slumps forward, mortally wounded.

Yet Little's account is contradicted in almost every detail by the few rebel survivors. According to Enriquez, they'd rushed to the upper trenches when the final act began. "Our soldiers, pointing with their hands, warned Del Pilar that the enemy was almost on top of us," yet nothing could be seen "save an irregular movement in cogon grass." As Goyo stood for a better look, a bullet hit him: "The general covered his face with both hands, falling backward and dying instantly." Enriquez's account is corroborated by that of Adjutant Telesforo Carrasco, who warned del Pilar that the Americans aimed exclusively at him. He should stay down. Instead, Goyo grabbed a carbine and rose: "At that moment he was hit by a bullet in the neck that caused instant death." The soldiers jumped up, ready to flee, but Carrasco pointed his rifle and cried, "I will blow the skull off the brains of the first to run." Neither witness mentions a white horse; both attribute del Pilar's death to lack of caution. Enriquez dragged the body to the next line of trenches: he tried to go farther, but the enemy was rushing up, and he pulled from Goyo's finger a diamond ring that he would give to another commander. He sprinted upslope to dense trees and hid there with the bugler and two others. Three others escaped through the pass and made their way to Cervantes to warn Aguinaldo. Carrasco was taken prisoner, but he managed to escape. By five p.m. he too reached Cervantes. "What happened?" Aguinaldo asked.

"General Del Pilar is dead."

There was no time to mourn. Aguinaldo plunged into the Cordillera, March and his men five hours behind. The fugitives passed through the hamlets of Bagnen, Sagada, Bontoc, and Amburayan; on December 7 they climbed the summit of Mount Polis, 6,216 feet above sea level. As they stared from that peak, the mountains seemed "without end." They learned that Tinio's force had surrendered on the day Goyo died. News of other surrenders followed. "At every step we found the mountains getting higher and the cold more chilling," Simeon Villa wrote. "Our skin had become dead to feeling and our lips drawn and purple from cold."

There came a point where neither pursued nor pursuers could go on. Aguinaldo's band lived on rice, salt, and spring water; March's men were shoeless and sick, worn down by short rations and hard climbs. On December 21 Aguinaldo sent a messenger back down the trail, asking to surrender the women. March promised their safe conduct to Manila. They included Aguinaldo's wife and sisters, who said they'd rather suffer here in the mountains than live under Americans. Yet Hilaria's fainting spells had grown worse, and all had grown lean. At times they could barely stand. Aguinaldo still bore the guilt of his daughter's death; sacrifice defined revolution, he'd preached, yet death weighed on him. The women rode off with a soldier escort the next morning, further winnowing Aguinaldo's forces. "The sun is beclouded," Villa wrote. "It is a sad day for us." Their departure bespoke "the abyss of death" that had pared them from 2,000 to fewer than 150.

As promised, March received his captives and turned around. They rode over the same route: down the mountains, through Cervantes, over Tirad Pass, past del Pilar's grave. By now, Goyo had been buried. One day after the battle, Enriquez and his fellows had emerged from hiding. They came upon their general's corpse, stripped to his underwear. Enriquez spotted "a wound in the cheek that I supposed was what killed him." They wanted to bury him but did not have tools, and they feared the Americans might return, so they "put him in a ditch and covered him with stones and dry leaves." Later, some Igorots placed him under a large stone. Sometime after that, American lieutenant Dennis Quinlan buried the remains with honors in the same spot and inscribed a headstone with the words "An Officer and a Gentleman."

Now March and his group rode past the grave. As they approached, one captive woman, reportedly of the "highest official rank," turned to Enriquez's younger brother José. "When we reach the site where the general died, stop and tell me," she whispered, "and don't move even if they kill us." The Igorot guide pointed to the stone; the reporter John McCutcheon watched as several captives rode past the fresh gravel and bared their heads. Enriquez called the woman one of Goyo's many *amantes*: she knelt by the stone and prayed. "We were at the height of 4,500 feet," the young lieutenant recalled, "and it seemed we could touch heaven with our prayers."

McCutcheon turned to Major General Venancio Concepcion, a captive who one day would be named president of the Philippine National Bank. "Isn't the revolution all over?" he asked. After all, here lay their hero. Their president had fled into the mountains. On November 23 MacArthur had wired Otis: "The so-called Filipino Republic is destroyed."

Hearing this, Concepcion shook his head and sighed: "Ah, you think it is, but it isn't." McCutcheon always remembered the words, which assumed the force of prophecy: "You now have disrupted the army and scattered it far and wide. You have some of the leaders in prison and your troops occupy the whole northern country. But how many rifles have you captured?" he asked.

The war had entered a new phase: "On February 4, 1899, we had an army of 22,000 men with rifles," Concepcion continued. "We have received many more arms since then. The Americans have not captured 3,000 of these arms. The rest are hidden. We have our commanders in the very districts occupied by your troops. The muster rolls are being kept up although the army is now in white clothes and is peaceably working at their homes. When Aguinaldo left Tarlac he advised his men to return to their homes, hide their rifles, and at a later time be prepared to answer a call to arms."

Concepcion gazed at McCutcheon, his expression sad. "When you've the arms, then, and only then, will the Revolution be over." He glanced at Goyo's grave and rode down the trail.

No, the war was not over. Aguinaldo had slipped the noose; many capable generals remained. After Aguinaldo, the man for whom Americans lusted most was Apolinario Mabini.

After his ouster from Aguinaldo's cabinet, "the Sublime Paralytic" settled for a time in the small town of Rosales in Pangasinan Province, close to the National Road. There he wrote letter after letter, article after article, seeking to prove the American occupation illegal. By November, he knew the Republic was a lost cause. But that didn't make it right, and he poured out manifestos extolling freedom. To Otis, Mabini's writing inspired the rebels to fight. Aguinaldo was "only a figure head, but Mabini was the brains and directing power behind him."

By mid-November, supporters brought Mabini a few miles south by hammock and bullcart to Cuyapo, a town of about sixteen thousand that had been a revolutionary stronghold since the first revolution. A rat's nest of small, overlapping *barangays*, it was a fugitive's dream. He hid in the house of a man named Zacarias Flores, across the street from a store that sold *basi*, a potent home brew made from sugarcane; it was run by the father of twelve-year-old Damian Pascual.

The Americans entered Cuyapo on Saturday, November 18, soon after Aguinaldo abandoned nearby Pozorrubio. As the Yankees passed, Pascual caught his father glancing at a house across the street. Why are the Americans here, he asked, and his father told him to stay indoors "or the Americans will eat you." But Pascual was perceptive and soon saw two men sneak into the house. They left a few minutes later, as if trying to avoid observation. "Did you see that?" his father asked. "I think they have brought Mabini a message." He then told his son about the hunted man. "If the *Americanos* capture him, the revolution is lost. We must do our part—we must never tell the *Americanos* that Mabini is hiding" in the house across the road.

Aguinaldo's "Dark Chamber" was, in fact, putting finishing touches on an article that would, outside the Philippines, become his strongest case against the invasion: "A Filipino Appeal to the People of the United States" would be published in the January 1900 *North American Review*. The timing suggests that the two men Pascual saw may have smuggled away the finished article. Mabini's "Appeal" challenged the U.S. contention that Aguinaldo started the war: "If the Filipinos had wished hostilities," he wrote, "they would have begun immediately after the capitulation of Manila." He listed the areas Aguinaldo had controlled, saying that the Republic hoped to parlay with a country it believed would "not sink to the level of the theocratic Government of Spain." They'd miscalculated. But that did not mean they were wrong. Time would show who was right: "The Filipino people are animated by our unalterable faith in the justice of their cause, and they know that if the American people will not grant them justice, there is a Providence which punishes the crimes of nations as well as of individuals."

His article slipped through the net just in time. Aside from the U.S. soldiers, Pascual noted strangers loitering around the store. His father thought they were spies. One day an American sergeant walked in and asked about the coffee-brown liquid being sold. *Basi* wine, his father said. The sergeant ordered a glass, then a second and third. The next day, he returned with others. As they got drunk, he noticed them staring at the buildings outside.

On December 10 the sergeant returned, this time dropping all pretenses. "Hey boy," he snapped, "Mabini *aqui*?" Pascual realized that the sergeant had been tipped off. He pointed at the house across the street, grabbed Pascual by the arm, shook him, and said again, "Mabini *aqui*?" Pascual remembered his father's admonition not to betray Mabini, but his look must have given him away. Suddenly the sergeant shouted out, and a squad of American soldiers with fixed bayonets entered the store. The sergeant held Pascual close to his body as they crossed the street: he realized he was being used as a human shield. They found the front door bolted, so they climbed a ladder to a second-floor kitchen and found two shotguns. They turned right and entered a small room where a pale man with somber eyes sat in an easy chair. Pascual had seen him before: the look in his eyes was resigned, even relieved, as if he'd known this day was inevitable. Mabini gazed into the boy's face and asked if he'd betrayed him: Pascual shook his head and tried to explain. "Mabini seemed to have been satisfied with my explanation," Pascual said years later.

What happened next surprised the boy. Mabini was carried out with a full military escort, and as the group passed down the street, people cheered "*Mabuhay si Mabini!*" ("Long live Mabini!"). The captive bowed his head as if to thank them. Oddly enough, the soldiers joined the cheers, as if they "wanted to show the people that they, too, were friends of the Filipino hero." But the crowd made no attempt at a rescue.

Mabini was taken to Manila and imprisoned in Fort Santiago, the last abode of José Rizal. He continued to write essays from his cell. One month later, his "Appeal" appeared in the *North American Review* and lit a fire under the moribund Anti-Imperialists.

Otis raged. The war was *over*, he screamed: the United States had *won*! The claim that Filipinos could be governed by Aguinaldo or the insurgency "can no longer be made under any fiction," he wired on November 24, one day after Aguinaldo threaded the Tirad Pass. Philippine troops operated not as armies but in small bands, "acting as banditti, or dispersed and playing the role of 'amigos,' with arms concealed." Aguinaldo himself was "a fugitive and an outlaw."

Henry Lawton wasn't sure. Filipino forces had already started to regroup even as Aguinaldo disappeared. The enemy exhibited a surprising resiliency; a new kind of war was starting. He'd feared all along that it might swing this way. If the United States had started on a different footing, with a government devoted to fairness, Filipinos would be "a peaceable, thrifty happy people," he told the *Boston Review*. Instead, "we were not able to give them a chance to sample our government before hostilities opened," and now, he said, "what we want is to stop this accursed war." All they want "is a little justice."

On December 16 Lawton returned to his family before launching an offensive to retake San Mateo on the Marikina River, eighteen miles northeast of Manila. The stronghold linked rebels in Luzon's north and south. Two nights later, his wife, Mary, and he hosted a dinner in their grand Spanish mansion. Among the guests was the *Harper's Weekly* correspondent William Dinwiddie, whom Lawton trusted. During the meal, he admitted that he could not decide whether the war was ending or just truly beginning, but despite Otis's claims, he said, "They have not surrendered." He mused on future plans: maybe he'd be an observer in South Africa's Boer War. "No, you will not, dear," his wife interrupted. "You're going home with me to Southern California to raise oranges."

Lawton, Dinwiddie, and their escort left Manila at nine p.m., riding all night through a monsoon. They arrived the next morning on the outskirts of San Mateo, dismounting on a bluff overlooking the battlefield. San Mateo lay between a high mountain and the Rio Marikina: though usually a broad, shallow stream, the rains had turned it into a flood. Rebel trenches were dug on the wide sandbar forming the opposite bank; beyond that, low buildings. They'd have to ford the river to take the town, but must first descend a floodplain broken into rice paddies.

Opposing Lawton were five hundred men under General Licerio Geronimo, a native San Matean appointed by Luna. Like many Lunestas, Geronimo's fortunes had suffered after his general's death. Many of his horses were dying; his men were barefoot and in rags. Bread was scarce, so they lived off bananas and *carabao.* But Geronimo had a secret weapon—the last seven or eight members of the famous "Luna Sharpshooters," also known as the *Tiradores de la Muerte* ("Marksmen of Death"). Each wore a distinct dark blue uniform; each boasted prowess with his bolt-action Mauser. Luna had always believed that better marksmanship could make the war so costly for Americans that it would turn the tide. These were the Philippine Army Special Forces: where most *insurrectos* tended to aim high and miss, the *Tiradores* aimed true.

Lawton's men crossed the plain and got within three hundred yards of the river before the Filipinos spotted them. He formed his troops up behind a paddy dike and directed them in place as more arrived. The battle began at eight a.m. The *Tiradores* spotted him immediately: he was hard to miss, a towering figure in his long yellow raincoat and white pith helmet that he'd worn since Cuba. They soon got his range: bullets clipped the grass nearby, and officers warned him to take cover. Suddenly Lieutenant Ethelbert D. Breckinridge wheeled and fell, shot through the groin. Breckinridge, son of the army's inspector general, had been with Lawton since El Caney: that seemed to waken Lawton to danger, and he said, "I am afraid this isn't a good place for a general." He helped carry Breckinridge to the field hospital and headed back. Again, his officers begged him to be careful, but he answered, "I must see what is going on in the firing line."

Bonifacio Mariano watched the big man in yellow return. Little is known of Mariano: as a *Tiradore*, he would possess keen sight and cool nerves. It didn't take a genius to know that the big man was important: he strode twenty paces over the rice, stopping to survey the battle, and younger officers swarmed around him like bees. Two ran toward him now. Mariano lined the big man in his sights, took a deep breath, let it out slowly, and fired.

Lawton swatted at his chest as if he'd been stung by an insect, and he turned pale. The two aides rushed up. One cried, "What is the matter, General?" Lawton clenched his teeth and said either, "Jesus Christ! I've been shot," or "I am shot through the lungs." Blood poured from his mouth, and he fell into their arms. Mariano's bullet had pierced his tubercular lungs and sliced through an artery; in some versions, the insurgents cheered. Lawton's men sat him in a clump of bushes; it was 9:30 a.m., and he was dead. They covered his face with his pith helmet. An hour later, American cheers rose over the last volleys as the *insurrectos* fled San Mateo. The Medal of Honor winner who'd never suffered so much as a scratch during forty years of conflict would be the only fatality in what historians now deem a small punitive expedition of limited significance.

Thousands lined Lawton's funeral procession in Manila; navy ships fired their guns as the USS *Thomas* carried his body from Manila Bay. At Nagasaki, four Russian cruisers and a German man-of-war dipped their colors; the big gun at Alcatraz Island fired first as the *Thomas* entered San Francisco Bay. Thirty thousand mourners lined the funeral cortège. "There was no music, all moving by in dead silence," wrote George Hamlin Fitch for *Harper's Weekly*. Lawton's burial in Arlington Cemetery on February 9, 1900, was attended by McKinley, his cabinet, Supreme Court justices, hundreds of government officials, every senior army and navy officer in town, and thousands of ordinary citizens. McKinley eulogized him as a great warrior, others as a proponent of the enlightened "conquer and relinquish" approach to imperialism. "How long, oh Lord, how long must our noble sons be slain in this far off slaughter pen of the Orient?" wrote one Arizona newspaper. An editorial cartoon showed Uncle Sam grieving at Lawton's grave, and underneath it the caption "He Deserved to Die in a Better Cause!"

And what of the man who shot him? This is Bonifacio Mariano's moment in the spotlight, but he disappears. There had been rumors that Aguinaldo had put a bounty on Lawton's life, that prominent Filipinos had raised more than $50,000 in a day. But this was too much to pay one man: "The reward was lowered to $20,000, then $15,000." The rest was "placed in a fund for the purpose of rewarding others who might in the future be fortunate enough to rid their country of hated American leaders." It is doubtful that Mariano got any money at all, as the brief article describing the reward got Mariano's name and unit wrong.

Thus ended the first year of the Philippine War. The colonial excursion that was supposed to end as quickly as that in Cuba resulted instead in the needless death of a likable, flawed, and very brave man. Over it all hovered the question: Where was the revolution's living symbol?

Exiled to the Wasteland.

The Wastes hold special meaning in myth. The cursed land can only be saved by the King. But the King is wounded—an injury that's mortal, moral, or both—and he must journey through the Wastes to find the cure. Only by healing himself can he save his devastated land.

Mountainous wastes hold a singular place in the myths of religions and nations, often one and the same. They are sacred places, closer to Heaven and therefore to God. One can see farther and more clearly, leaving behind all earthly distractions. Jesus defeated the Devil in himself on Mount Tabor and for that was revealed as the Son of God. The Prophet Muhammad received his first revelation on Mount Hira. Andrés Bonifacio reminded his Katipuneros that somewhere in these caves of Mount Tapusi, Bernardo Carpio would rise and set them free. Emilio Aguinaldo wandered the Cordillera Central, and when he emerged, the land would be healed.

To the rest of the world, Aguinaldo's fate was a mystery; he existed to the north outside space and time. But to *El Presidente* and his companions, their daily reality was a bitter one. They ate vegetable roots and unripened guavas; sometimes they went without food for four to five days. They clawed up steep mountains and slid down the other side. Sometimes they enjoyed days or weeks of rest, but even then they were not safe, for their hosts wanted their heads.

Lowlanders living at the fringe of the Cordillera called the mountain tribes Igorots, but they avoided the interior and knew only those natives who came out to trade. In fact, the term encompassed three separate cultures—the Kalingas, Bontocs, and Ifugaos. Others, gathered in *rancherias* of up to a thousand residents, went by other names. These villages always seemed at war: one inhabitant visiting another might be killed. Each village was distinct, but all had commonalities. They'd perfected the system of terraced farming, where they grew rice and the native sweet potatoes called *camotes*; these terraces were similar to those Aguinaldo had passed when he turned east. Men and women went naked or wore tiny loincloths, adorning themselves with earrings and necklaces of copper wire, animal teeth, and pottery shards. They were extensively tattooed. The few Spanish missions to pierce the range rarely made converts: most Igorots were animists, worshipping snakes, trees, and mountain spirits, and Simeon Villa believed they held a "deep hatred for Christians." They greased their long hair with hog fat and carried murderous lances and poison-tipped arrows. According to Villa, they all hunted human heads.

Villa and Aguinaldo witnessed the *Kanao*, or "head-dance," firsthand. The sight chilled and worried them. They came down from the summit of Mount Pulas on December 7 and that night entered the *rancheria* of Banane; they stayed until December 21, the day they decided to send the women back to Peyton March, then pressed on. The *Kanao* may have hurried this decision.

The dance and feast, which took six days, occurred when a warrior cut the head, hands, and feet from an enemy. The *insurrectos* watched as a line of fifty Igorots—each wearing a feathered headdress and carrying a spear—swayed in time as they carried the head on a long pole. They took it to the house of their chief, dancing for a long time around the head before entering. Inside, they sat for a feast: they used the victim's severed hands and feet to scrub their faces. The body itself was buried on the third day of festivities, the head and extremities on the sixth. They'd wait until decomposition was complete, then dig up the skull and display it as a trophy.

Aguinaldo quickly realized that they were in a precarious position. Despite what seemed an uneasy truce, the Igorot of Banane were "only waiting for the opportunity to cut off our heads," Villa wrote; they'd proved as much when they ambushed a Filipino patrol, wounding four rebels and taking three guns. With that in mind, the group left Banane on December 21 and plunged deeper into the mountains. Early on December 28, *El Presidente* rose to answer the call of nature when he spotted a tribesman, spear poised. He cried out, his soldiers grabbed their guns, and the panicked Igorot "let himself fall into the mountain precipices." In the confusion, other tribesmen stole a gun. They'd be attacked three times during the next two days; at one point, lances rained from every direction as Aguinaldo's men roasted an injured horse to stave off starvation. The attacks grew more brazen, but somehow none of Aguinaldo's men were wounded or killed.

The terrain also seemed determined to kill them. They turned east, escaping for a moment all pursuers; they'd climb one barren peak and behold an even higher one beyond. Extreme heat, hunger, and thirst combined into "nauseating sickness"; "excessive perspiration is wasting our energies"; men wept in pain as they crawled. They wanted to stop but could not, fearing they would never move again. They kept crawling east, deciding that if they encountered another American column, they'd attack in one final, glorious charge.

But for once Fate was kind. One month and three days after the heartbreak of Tirad Pass, they emerged and saw spread before them the vast, fertile Cagayan Valley. They'd crossed three provinces, scaled the highest mountain chain in Luzon, and now stood at the eastern flank of the Cordillera. They formed into a ragged column and sang as they marched down the mountain; every part of them hurt, but for once they ignored it as "we were filled with enthusiasm." Night came and Aguinaldo sent out messengers to the village of Oscaris, down the valley by the Magat River. Village elders answered back that they'd find no enemies here. On the clear morning of Monday, January 8, 1900, Emilio Aguinaldo emerged from the wastes as a hero.

The King had returned.

25

The American Century

By 1900 the United States had by accident become a world power. In just a hundred years, her population had skyrocketed from 5 million inhabitants in 13 states to 76 million in 45, sprawling three thousand miles across a continent linked by five railroad empires. By 1900 she was churning out ten million tons of steel a year, more than any other nation. Moving pictures were a reality; cities were being electrified. Anything seemed possible.

Although the twentieth century would not be officially called the "American Century" until the publisher Henry Luce coined the phrase in a February 17, 1941, *Life* magazine editorial, every ingredient was present in 1900. The old frontier was a thing of the past. A New Frontier beckoned: that frontier was the world.

Was 1900 the last year of the old century or the first year of the new? The Old Guard—William McKinley, Queen Victoria, Pope Leo XIII—were convinced that the twentieth century was still a year away. But to America's young, that millisecond separating December 31, 1899, from January 1, 1900, was called "crossing the divide." The act of "crossing" seemed mystical. "No one considered 1900 just another year," wrote the historian Judy Crichton. People trusted that New Year's Day 1900 would be pivotal in man's history.

The young wanted to be involved. On February 6, 1899, two days after the Philippine War began, Clara Maass reapplied as a contract nurse. By September 22 there'd been no word, so she directed all letters to Dr. Anita Newcomb McGee: "You will think I am the bother of your life but really I do not want to trouble you and will try not to very much." She wanted to serve in the Philippines and would pay her train fare to Chicago if the army paid the remainder to San Francisco. "I would like so much to go and hope I may go soon."

At midnight on November 20, 1899, a knock came at her door. A Western Union messenger handed over a telegram dated two days earlier: the surgeon general had assigned her to serve with the Eighth Army Corps in the Philippines, for $50 a month. She must proceed to the army transport *Logan*, docked in New York Harbor, which sailed in two hours. She scooped up some personal items, kissed her mother, and crashed out the door; she grabbed the train to Hoboken, caught the Hudson River ferry, and hailed a hansom cab. It pulled up as the last visitor walked down the gangplank. She handed over her orders, and the *Logan*'s whistle blew.

The voyage took six weeks and two days. The *Logan* was a converted cattle ship, and the nurses joked that the cows probably had more room. Their wooden bunks were thirty-six inches wide, stacked four high; the aisles between them were so narrow that they scheduled dressing by lot. A soldier was posted outside with a rifle across his knees: closely mixing men and women was still believed to be the fast track to Hell. They debarked in Manila on Friday, January 5, and Maass was assigned to the city's First Reserve Hospital. The wards were like those in Florida, long rows of beds filled with men felled by malaria and typhoid.

Otis's Great Roundup had ended by the time Maass stepped ashore. One month later, on February 4, 1900, the war's first anniversary passed without celebration. During Maass's transit, the year of conventional warfare sputtered to an end: some enemy commanders surrendered; Americans occupied every major city and town in Luzon, plus the major ports of the Visayas and Mindanao, second in size only to Luzon. Yet the war was entering a deadlier phase. Filipinos no longer fought U.S. troops directly; instead, they aimed to bleed them until they went home. By February 4, U.S. field reports showed that as enemy surrenders tapered off, ambushes, raids, and assassinations escalated. The army responded by burning villages and destroying crops and livestock even as they built roads, bridges, and more than a thousand schools—a carrot-and-stick strategy that the correspondent John Bass dubbed "a harsh and philanthropic war."

The infrastructure of this new resistance was almost ready by the one-year anniversary. In each town and village, Katipunan cells revived. They funneled funds to guerrillas, reported on troop movements, and conducted espionage. In some places, native priests participated. They revived the *Sandatahan*, its primary job to assassinate collaborators, called *Americanistas*. A *Sandatahan* cell in Ilocos Sur killed thirty *Americanistas* around Vigan, spiriting them at night to a beach where a grave had been dug. The victim knelt by his grave, was hacked to death, his body burned. The assassins returned to their ordinary lives.

During this period, a cautionary tale circulated through the ranks that assumed the force of Gospel. Pampangan guerrillas were said to have captured three Americans on a chicken-stealing raid in November 1899; they took them to their camp on Mount Arayat where, for six weeks, they endured starvation and mock executions. In January, as U.S. troops neared the camp, guerrillas cut the throat of an imprisoned *Americanista* and slashed the Americans with their bolos. One soldier died; two survived to tell of their ordeal. Similar tales surfaced elsewhere: three troopers on Panay had their throats cut on a priest's orders; in Leyte, rebels beheaded an American. Although U.S. captives reported humane treatment, each new rumor became God's Truth. Troops lived in terror of capture. Preemptive revenge was not far behind.

Clara Maass could see the toll. Fear and sickness haunted her wards; malaria, cholera, beriberi, dysentery, diarrhea, intestinal parasites, venereal disease, and skin maladies were everywhere. The great killer seemed to be typhoid, but opinions varied. The surgeon Joseph A. Guthrie swore that the land itself was deadly: "the air, water, soil, the whole earth and its sundry encumbrances" reeked of germs. Soldiers suffered "Philippinitis," an amalgam of everything. Otis's weekly report for January 8–10, 1900, was grim: during the week of Maass's arrival, thirty-four soldiers died. Among these, five were killed in action, six had drowned, seven died of typhoid fever, four of malaria, four to dysentery, and one committed suicide.

In February, Clara caught dengue fever. Caused by a cousin of the yellow fever microbe and spread by the same mosquito, dengue, though rarely fatal, was so miserable that she wished she were dead. Many called it "breakbone fever" after the agony in the muscles and swollen joints, but the throbbing pain in her eyes and hideous headaches were as bad. She held on as long as possible, but on March 24 she asked for an annulment of her contract due to health reasons. She sailed aboard the USS *Sherman* on April 1, recuperated in San Francisco from April 30 to May 5, and returned home on May 13. She hadn't lasted three months in Manila.

Charlie Sandburg's American Century began in the summer of 1899. That May, four army buddies brought news: Congressman George W. Prince of the Tenth District had offered a West Point appointment to someone from Company C, and Sandburg's old commanders chose him. Though he never mentioned a promotion to corporal, he must have done something right, for in June he packed off to West Point and for three weeks crammed for entrance exams. Douglas MacArthur and Ulysses Grant III studied for the same test; unlike them, Sandburg had never completed high school. On June 3, 1899, word came on a typed half sheet of paper that he'd failed the tests for arithmetic and grammar. He went home, embarrassed and disappointed.

But he did have a fallback plan. After muster-out, his buddy George Longbrake suggested that he attend Lombard College with him. A small Universalist school in town, Lombard offered a free year's tuition to two veterans, and one had died of fever soon after returning home. This was Charlie's chance. Two colleges existed in Galesburg: the more prestigious Knox, and the newer, smaller Lombard, with 175 students and 19 faculty. Universalist schools boasted of religious and intellectual freedom, which appealed to him. He entered Lombard's preparatory school to earn his high school diploma, then threw himself into literature and the humanities, got a job as call man for the Galesburg Fire Department, slept in the Prairie Street station, and took classes during the day. As a student, he searched for that same nebulous something he'd sought as a soldier and a hobo. At age twenty, he was older than most freshmen, and classmates dubbed him "the Terrible Swede."

Educators of the era believed that college could create a new middle class. Only 2 percent of the population then attended college, and attrition was high. Still, "working men's colleges" like New York's City College and Lombard claimed to take working-class children and help them rise above their circumstances. By exposing them to the Great Ideas, professors hoped to transform their manners, tastes, language, ways of thinking, and even aspirations—and through them transform America. Sandburg's professors called him a textbook example: he entered Lombard a "rough-featured," "proletariat" youngster, and left a cultivated gentleman. During this period, he decided to be a writer, and since one must look the part, "for a year or two I took to wearing a black tie known as an Ascot, with long drooping ends," like Oscar Wilde.

Sandburg's first year at Lombard was the first year of the Philippine War. His army experience informed his views. Nine days after the war started, he considered the roots of evil as he read Robert Louis Stevenson's 1886 *The Strange Case of Dr. Jekyll and Mr. Hyde.* "In every person there is both good and evil," he wrote; he searched himself for "Jekyll and Hyde streaks" and found "several Hyde streaks that it wouldn't do to write about." Perhaps it was best not to look too closely, for doing so had doomed Henry Jekyll, and "the oftener you yield, the easier you give way in the future." He read Thomas Carlyle's account of a man who slit his throat while shaving, when "it came over him that life would be damned monotonous shaving every morning as long as he lived," and he remembered the neighbor boy on Pearl Street who'd hung himself in a similar spasm of despair. The life of individuals, as of nations, was a current of "endless unrest," where the thinnest interface separated dark thought from dark deed.

No better instrument existed to fight darkness than the mind. During this time, Sandburg fell under the wing of Philip Green Wright, a lean, spare poet, mathematician, and economist who'd soon teach at Harvard. Wright saw something in the former hobo and soldier, and he printed Sandburg's first published poems on his basement press. From Wright Sandburg learned of British social critics, Karl Marx, Thorstein Veblen's *The Theory of the Leisure Class*, and Jacob Riis's *How the Other Half Lives.* Socialism most intrigued him, though "socialist" meant many things. The most utopian was the Arts and Crafts movement, which held that the root cause of all social ills was the dehumanization of workers and work. Transform mindless work into art, and the artist's imagination could be an instrument for social change. Art held back Hyde's darkness, a stance Sandburg would never abandon. Later he promised the love of his life, Lilian Steichen, that they'd work together as artists to "help usher in the New Civilization."

Though most Americans balk at such radical chic, one socialist mantra became gospel—the idea of the "average man." The "average man does the work of the world," Sandburg wrote in an essay for Wright: the Average Man's "heroism [was] as profound and undemonstrative as the ocean during a gray rain." Yet the Average Man was ignored, and because of that, Sandburg feared, America would never be a "really great civilization."

Nineteen hundred was an election year, and the Average Man wanted change. The news brimmed with confrontations between workers and "trusts" such as Standard Oil, Anaconda Copper, and United States Steel. Frank Norris's *McTeague*, the tale of a "simple man" brutalized by greed, was published after Norris returned from Cuba; he worked now on *The Octopus*, his name for the railroad trusts that caused the death and suffering of California ranchers. The new "middle class" backed women's suffrage, a minimum wage, and work and health standards. "Progressives" like Sandburg believed in the perfectability of man. That February, when McKinley announced his bid for reelection, he addressed the spirit of reform, proposing legislation to restrain the trusts and prevent their abuses. Once more, his opponent was William Jennings Bryan, who waged a campaign of anger against banks, trusts, the gold standard, and the new imperialism. McKinley boiled his message down to *prosperity*, America's magic word.

Our new possessions should be workshops for change—and nowhere more than in Cuba. From January to December 1899, McKinley placed the island under the military governorship of General John Brooke, the sixty-one-year-old career soldier who'd been one of Miles's brigade commanders in Puerto Rico. On December 20, 1899, Leonard Wood succeeded Brooke and would stay there until May 1902. The occupation had three goals: maintain political stability, rebuild the economy as a way to attract U.S. investment, and keep Cuba within America's "sphere of influence." A 1916 biography of McKinley called Cuba's progress in 1899 "a marvel of recuperation and reorganization," and most Americans seemed to agree.

On the surface, Cuba seemed a progressive's dream. Roads, bridges, and rails were rebuilt; ports improved. To end starvation, the War Department supplied 5.5 million rations at the cost of $1.4 million, mostly paid by the Cuban treasury. The 48,000 remaining *mambisi* disbanded: the U.S. paid them $75 for their guns and equipment at a cost of $2,540,750, and offered posts in a new Rural Guard. Two million dollars was routed to sanitation in Santiago and Havana to beat back yellow fever. From December 1899 to June 1900, public school enrollment jumped from 36,306 to 143,120, and $4.5 million was appropriated to turn old Spanish barracks into new schoolhouses. In summer 1900, Harvard brought 1,281 Cuban teachers to Cambridge for an education workshop. They returned home "full of new ideas and of zeal."

Yet scratch that surface and underneath glistened a sophisticated moneymaking machine. McKinley's instructions looked simple: prepare Cuba for republican government; set up courts and schools; leave the island as soon as possible. This last proved challenging. How could one keep a tether on Cuba once the occupation ended? By economic control.

Wood had already experimented with this in Santiago in the fall of 1898 by allowing the New York–based North American Trust Company to buy up Cuban property and build a railroad. The time was ripe for similar moves. Almost one-third of Cuba's sugar plantations had burned: in Matanzas Province, once its sugar hub, the number of mills dropped from 434 in 1894 to 62 in 1898. Throughout Cuba, 207 mills still operated, down from 1,100 in 1894. Thousands of small farms, cattle ranches, and coffee and tobacco plantations vanished; about two-thirds of Cuba's wealth had been consumed by the three-year war. Those whose homes and farms had survived faced creditors and taxmen, and pawnshops dotted the land.

When Cuban businesses appealed for low-interest loans to survive, Brooke and Wood rejected their pleas. Loans and charities encouraged dependence, they said. As a result, nearly four thousand Cuban farm owners defaulted annually between 1898 and 1900: prices fell so steeply that land sold for one-tenth to one-twentieth of its value. Thousands of Americans flooded Cuba: in the days after the Peace Protocol, Stephen Crane watched ships disgorge into Havana "cattle men, gamblers, speculators and drummers," all searching for deals. The Ever-Faithful Isle had become the land of the quick buck for everyone but the Cubans. Speculators were everywhere.

Many U.S. historians have traditionally seen Wood as a nation builder, but Cuban historians do not see him in such glowing terms. According to Professor Francisca López Civeira and others, Brooke may have started the process, but Wood engineered and refined the conditions that gave U.S. corporations a nearly blanket ownership of the island that lasted until the 1959 Cuban Revolution. The memory stirs bitter resentment today. After taking the reins, Wood used the Cuban treasury to fund a public relations campaign encouraging U.S. investment in tobacco and sugar while lobbying Congress to lower tariffs. Before 1899, almost every tobacco company on the island was Cuban- or Spanish-owned. By May 1902 North American companies controlled more than 50 percent of cigar and cigarette production and more than 90 percent of the export trade. The United Fruit Company of Boston invested $20 million in sugar; its rival, the Cuban American Sugar Company, built the *centrale* "Chaparra," which became the world's largest sugar estate. *Centrales* could grind up to two thousand tons of sugarcane a day, driving out small family farms. Wood granted more than 218 mining concessions to U.S. companies, which soon owned more than 80 percent of the country's ore exports. Cuba might seem independent, but controls had been set allowing the U.S. to dominate its economy and government for the next sixty years.

Control was not simple. Three separate pieces of legislation, passed to appease Anti-Imperialists, limited foreign investment on the scale envisioned by Wood. Two passed before the war: the Joint Resolution of 1898 stated that by right Cubans were a free people; the Teller Amendment further declared that the U.S. could not annex Cuba as a result of the war. After conquest, the Foraker Act prohibited the U.S. military government from granting concessions to U.S. companies. Wood found economic ways around this, but in Puerto Rico, such machinations were unnecessary. The United States owned the island and could do with it what it wanted. That meant decades of sugar extraction at the price of poverty and disease.

Americans see what they want, and in the Caribbean they saw America as a force of good. But one year after invading the Philippines, neither the war's progress nor our own moral compass seemed certain. From Otis's seat, the focus was Luzon. Everywhere else was an afterthought. In 1899 Mindanao and the port of Jolo in the extreme southwest received a few companies; in January 1900 McKinley insisted that the islands of Samar and Leyte be garrisoned to take control of the hemp trade. A few thousand troops should suffice, Otis said.

To Americans and *insurrectos* alike, Luzon was the prize. Its natural and economic riches were more diverse; it was home to the capital city and half the population. Sugar, coffee, tobacco, and abaca, the source of hemp, were the chief exports, valued at $34 million in 1899. From Luzon sprang the strongest resistance, and at one time, four out of every five American soldiers were posted there. One officer posted in the Visayas summed up the dominant thinking: "Hold the insurgents in check in the outer islands, and crush the rebellion on [Luzon]." After that, the rebellion "will cease of itself."

Otis placed MacArthur in charge of the Department of Northern Luzon, home to nearly two million Filipinos and twenty-five thousand American soldiers for most of the war. And in this command, the U.S. assigned top priority to the heavily populated and fertile Central Luzon valley. Whoever controlled this breadbasket controlled the nation.

Funston returned to Manila on Christmas Day 1899 and reported to Otis the next day. Otis insisted that the war was won and the natives must accept Americans as their rightful overseers. He handed Funston to MacArthur, who put his favorite Kansan in charge of the Third Brigade: 2,400 men stationed in Nueva Ecija and parts of Pangasinan and Pampanga. Two battalions of the Twenty-Fourth and some Thirty-Fourth Volunteers garrisoned towns in the north; towns in the south were manned by the Twenty-Second, the Thirty-Fourth, Troop G of the Fourth Cavalry, and Macabebe Scouts. Funston also assembled a squad of cowboys and former Rough Riders called Headquarters Scouts who numbered no more than twenty at any time. He used them as an early Special Forces and a personal escort on his "hikes."

Such "flying squads" gained favor throughout Northern Luzon that year: they were quick and mobile, and they took the law in their own hands. In Abra Province to the north, the twenty-three-year-old Texas cowboy William Oliver Trafton belonged to the "Mosquito Fleet" attached to the Thirty-Third Volunteers: "Mosquito" because they were mounted on small, eight-hundred-pound native ponies; "Fleet" because they operated alone, like naval units far from home. They treated sorties like Indian warfare: start before dawn, reach the enemy as they slept, "charge into the village like Comanches, whooping and yelling." They rarely discriminated between guilty and innocent: "I recall one incident when we ran into a village, we killed most everyone who ran out" except for "one poor fellow" who lay still, "groaning awful" from his wounds. "Trafton," his commander yelled, "go finish that fellow and stop that fuss." Before Trafton could obey, a comrade nestled his rifle barrel against the man's head "and pulled the trigger."

Funston's first "hike" commenced on December 27: he left the train at Calumpit and rode for two days with his adjutant, Captain E. V. Smith, and his aide and first cousin, Lieutenant Burton J. Mitchell. They rode native ponies, carried Krags and service revolvers, and rode off alone to his new headquarters, San Isidro. "I thought the insurrection could not last many months longer," he said. Today this portion of the Central Valley boasts vast expanses of rice farming, but at the time it was a mixed region of forests, savannah, swamps, lakes, and farmland—a still-wild district that from 1900 to 1940 would be transformed when 200,000 hectares were cleared for rice paddies. The three rode past farmers working in their fields; along waterways lined with buri palms and bamboo; through forests where the peasant farmer, or *tao*, gathered firewood, fished, and hunted game. To the east, he could see the blue Sierra Madres, which ran the full length of Nueva Ecija and grew thick with hardwoods like kapok and yellow narra. Nothing happened on this trip, but Funston could see that it was a land perfect for hiding *insurrectos.*

Funston settled into his new headquarters on New Year's Day. San Isidro had once been Aguinaldo's capital; his house was now Funston's, a planter's home called Sideco House, overlooking the central square. Servants buffed teak floors and washed laundry; the wicker furniture lent an elegant air. Eda would like it there. MacArthur had divided Northern Luzon into four operational districts, and Sideco House would be the Fourth District headquarters for the rest of the war. The Rio Pampanga bordered the north city; the "better class" of San Isidro's 9,800 residents lived near him on the square. If he looked southeast, he could see a jutting finger of the eastern mountains where guerrillas hid out; turn around, he could see miles of open country sprinkled with farms and little villages. He was part of something bigger than himself and no longer needed to seek meaning. He'd found his place, and his defense of it would be ruthless.

Funston's first two months were quiet, but not because of anything he did. Pantaleon García, Central Luzon's rebel commander, suffered from lingering illness; he suspended attacks until his guerrillas reorganized. On January 9 he granted autonomy to each provincial *jefe*: in Nueva Ecija, this was Pablo Padilla; in Pangasinan, Luna's protégé José Alejandrino. When the bedridden García was captured in April, Alejandrino took over.

Yet "quiet" did not mean "safe" during the first months of the American Century. Control extended as far as the range of a Krag. No U.S. citizen could leave a city or village without military escort, a fact Otis tried to suppress. Newcomers discovered that the "minor police actions" described in his reports meant constant scouting parties, nerve-racking engagements, tense garrison duty in hundreds of isolated villages, and ambushes at any place and time. By early 1900, about 150 Americans had been captured or gone missing; two disappeared on December 28 as Funston rode to San Isidro, one just a few miles away. That day, four Buffalo Soldiers with the Twenty-Fourth escorted a Signal Corps sergeant who was headed north from tiny Santa Rosa to the town of Talavera. They were scheduled to pass through Aliaga, manned by 110 black soldiers of James Moss's Company I.

They never made it that far. Somewhere between Santa Rosa and Aliaga, about fifty guerrillas fired from the bush, killing Private Jesse Jones. The sergeant and two privates escaped, but rebels captured Privates John Quarles and Edward Sanders and led them to the mountains Funston saw from his window. From there they were taken to Colonel Padilla's camp deep in the foothills east of Peñaranda, where they were shocked to see a familiar face.

Nothing had been heard of David Fagen since he deserted; it was assumed he'd gone east to join Padilla, and this supported that claim. The first mention of Fagen in official reports appeared on March 20, 1900, by Major Joe Wheeler Jr., "Fightin' Joe's" son. "Three American Negroes are with Padilla," he wrote, "one named Davis [*sic*] is a traitor. Others are prisoners." The guerrillas initially called Fagen "David," and two later reports by Wheeler referred to the "Afro-American traitor named David."

The guerrillas held Quarles and Sanders hostage for six months, treating them well; they later said that Fagen tried to persuade them to switch sides. Though they refused, no harm befell them.

Later reports reconstructed Fagen's movements after his desertion. The simplest route was to ride twelve miles east through forests and rice fields until reaching Padilla's main camp in Papaya's Sierra Madre foothills, a region Americans had not penetrated. One 1902 article in the *St. Louis Post-Dispatch* claimed that Padilla had "commissioned him a second lieutenant and gave him a separate command," but later reports corrected that he'd begun as a drill instructor teaching guerrillas to shoot straight and only later assumed command. His troops called him "General," a detail American papers reported as fact; the guerrillas also called him a "giant," since most only stood up to his shoulders. He may have been active around San Isidro even before revealing himself to Sanders and Quarles: *The Manila Freedom* claimed that Fagen "delighted in harassing his old company and regiment, [and] often sent insulting messages to the officers." The Twenty-Fourth was posted in tiny villages strung north to the foothills, and Company I, Fagen's old unit, garrisoned the northern town of San Jose. For the first three months of 1900, his old nemesis James Moss led them. *The New York Herald* and *The Washington Post* claimed that Fagen played cat and mouse with Moss during this time. During one ambush, "a tall negro" rose from the bushes, bowed, waved his hat, and yelled, "We're off for the day, boys! Ammunition gone! No use peppering away at me like that. You can't hit me! I bear a charmed life!" With another bow, the "tall negro" dropped into the bushes and disappeared.

Buffalo Soldiers recognized their tormentor, and news that Fagen led the rebels spread quickly. A second party went out with orders to "Bring him back, dead or alive." Soon after this, Fagen's "love letters" to Moss, or *billets-doux* as he called them, appeared in obvious spots outside the garrisons. Though we can't be certain that he wrote all of them, they did show an insider's knowledge of Moss and army operations. "Have decided to make you my valet," one read. "Need a good valet so will get you before long." Another materialized: "Wanted—a private in my company to command like you commanded me. Moss please apply." Then a third: "Got to be someday soon now. Be careful."

In March, Moss was promoted to regimental commissary and sent north to Pangasinan, a job that took him from the field. Second Lieutenant Charles Hay Jr. took command of Company I. The love letters ended, yet Moss's disdain for black soldiers increased. When a soldier complained that an officer called him a "nigger" and struck him "with a six-shooter," Moss dismissed the charge as "malicious prevarication." When asked about the large number of soldiers thrown into the brig and tried by general court-martial—the same practice that led to Fagen's desertion—Moss replied that the Twenty-Fourth contained "a large number of scoundrels."

At first the army did not reveal Fagen's provocations. They saw him not just as a rogue, but rather as a harbinger. From 1898 to 1902, volunteers and Regulars in the Philippines totaled 126,468, and about 5,000 were African American. As the war entered its second year, racism had grown. As in the Jim Crow South, blacks were barred from "white only" barbershops, restaurants, even brothels. They endured verbal abuse: "Hello, nigger" and "All coons look alike to me" were common greetings. Sometimes the slurs preceded violence. The October 4, 1899, *Manila Times* reported that a soldier from the Twenty-Fifth was told "I don't like a nigger nohow" right before an "intoxicated white soldier proceeded to beat him with a cane." The May 11, 1900, *Manila Times* reported that discharged Sergeant F. E. Green of the Twenty-Fifth was nearly killed when "several intoxicated members of Company I, 20th Infantry," chased him into a hotel dining room and "picked up chairs, water decanters, and everything movable" with which to beat him. The attack continued until the arrival of the sergeant of the guard.

Unlike Fagen, most black soldiers did not desert, but army brass merely had to scan the African American press to glimpse discontent. "I feel sorry for these people and all that have come under the control of the United States," wrote Sergeant Patrick Mason of the Twenty-Fourth in a November 17, 1899, letter to *The Cleveland Gazette*: the first thing Filipinos hear in the morning "is the 'nigger' and the last thing at night is the 'nigger,'" he said. "You have no idea the way these people are treated by the Americans here." Another soldier with the Twenty-Fifth wrote in the February 3, 1900, *Richmond Planet* that he understood why Aguinaldo preferred to fight to the bitter end: *El Presidente* "takes it for granted that just as the colored people are treated in the United States that his people would be dealt with accordingly . . . Their defeat would bring upon them a role far more bitter in its effect than the Spanish regime."

Some white soldiers lamented what they saw. Colonel Cornelius Gardener, an 1869 West Point graduate who'd served in both Cuba and the West, commanded the Thirtieth Infantry in Southern Luzon. He feared the long-term consequences of this war. "The Filipinos are not ignorant," he wrote on February 21, 1900, to Michigan's reform-minded governor Hazen S. Pingree. "They have read history. Many read English fluently. They have heard of our race antipathy to any person of dark skin. They have read of our treatment for 100 years of our Indians. They read of how we burn and torture niggers in the South; how a nigger has in the South no right which a white man is bound to respect. You can't blame them when they predict that there will be a similar fate" waiting if conquered by U.S. troops.

By 1900 African American papers that once called fighting patriotic now deemed it otherwise. As early as June 6, 1899, the Chicago *Broad-Ax* wished that "every soldier in the Philippines who uses the term 'nigger' . . . be cured of his fiendish malady by a Filipino bullet buried in the heart of such a wretch." Do not sign up, begged the February 1, 1900, Helena *Reporter*: "Any Negro soldier that will cross the ocean to help subjugate the Filipinos is a fool or a villain, more fool, however, than villain, we trust. May every one of them get ball-stung is our sincere prayer."

At this early stage, the army seemed to hope that Fagen would be killed in battle, or fade away. Instead, he became the symbol they feared. "The desertions from the negro regiments were large," wrote Steven Bonsal, "much larger, I believe, than from the white organizations; and these desertions were invariably of a different character. The white man deserted because he was lazy and idle and found service life irksome." But blacks "deserted in scores and for the purpose of joining the insurgents, and many of them, like the celebrated Fagan [*sic*], became leaders and fought the white troops or their former comrades with zeal and ability."

This was perhaps the most famous statement of a black soldier's plight to come from the war. Yet Bonsal got it wrong. "Scores" did not desert, black or white. Since such "facts" had to come from army sources, they reflected army fears. Records suggest that only 15 of the roughly 125,000

American soldiers deserted between 1899 and 1902; Filipino anecdotes suggest many more. Although the army made a habit of lying, there were no hard numbers. Of the fifteen listed in U.S. records, nine came from black regiments—six in an unexplained rush in 1901 from the Ninth Cavalry. This left six white deserters, at least three of whom joined the *insurrectos*.

Thus, actual desertions were low and had no real effect. But the fear of black desertions en masse was very real. The cause lay in what Bonsal called "the tenderest of ties." While "white soldiers, unfortunately, got on badly with the natives, the black soldiers got on much too well." Black soldiers did get along better than whites because, one Buffalo Soldier said, "they do not push them off the streets, spit at them, [or] call them damn 'niggers.'" The journalist James A. LeRoy recalled hearing a lieutenant brag that he walked "up and down the streets of a Cavite town shooting water buckets out of the hands of startled natives" in order to "keep the gugus in a proper frame of mind." By 1901 many officers feared "that the negro soldiers were in closer sympathy with the aims of the native population than they were with those of their white leaders and the policy of the United States."

Love and lust lay at the heart of this fear. White and black soldiers alike had relations with Filipino women, and though the army officially restricted such behavior, the greater weight of enforcement fell upon blacks. While soldiers of both races lived with *queridas*, or Filipino mistresses, whites seemed to take such arrangements less seriously: "A white American never marries a Filipino woman, but a great many of them live with Filipino women in Manila, and in the provinces," noted the black journalist T. Thomas Fortune. "When they are ready to leave for the United States, they do so without regard to their obligation to Filipino women and children." Black soldiers lived with Filipinas, sired children, and got married. Chaplain George W. Prioleau of the Ninth Cavalry noted that black troopers spent their pay on the "women and children they were obligated to support." After the war, an estimated one thousand black soldiers stayed in the Philippines or brought their new families back home. The army rarely focused on the positive affects of amity, just on the dangers to loyalty. It was no coincidence that the first reports of Fagen's desertion emphasized the role of a native temptress.

During this period, Sergeant Major Calloway questioned the morality of the war. This was not a righteous crusade like Cuba; there, whites and blacks charged together up San Juan Hill and died together in the fever camp. But what seemed like the dawn of new race relations had disappeared. He'd watched Fagen—whose recruitment papers he signed *twice*—go from patriot to turncoat, pushed by an officer who delighted in petty punishment. Now he watched the guardhouse fill with similar young men. In a year and a half, the "whites have begun to establish their diabolical race hatred in all its home rancor in Manila," he wrote on November 16, 1899, one day after Fagen skipped. He'd sent these words to *The Richmond Planet* with his name unwisely attached, an act of quiet protest that would have consequences.

How, he wondered, did Filipinos view black versus white soldiers? To find out, he questioned three natives: Tardolica Santos, a physician; Antonio Consunji, a wealthy planter; and an unnamed third. The anonymous respondent told Calloway that before black soldiers arrived, whites warned them "of your brutal natures, your cannibal tendencies—how you would rape our senoritas, etc." But they soon learned that "between you and him, we look upon you as the angel and him as the devil." Dr. Santos observed that whites seemed to "connect race hatred with duty." Consunji shuddered: "What we are resisting is effacement" designed to eradicate "Filipinos." The only natives left after the war would be those molded into "white Americans."

These revelations troubled Calloway. He'd experienced racial solidarity with Filipinos, but had sworn a loyalty oath to the U.S. Army, which called them the enemy. It made him lonely. Early in 1900, he stayed in Santa Rosa, where he met a young Filipina named Mamerta de la Rosa, known as "Nene." They wrote and visited, and soon fell in love.

In early February, Calloway was assigned to escort prisoners to Manila. Even then, Fagen ranged the Talavera road and posted his "love letters," but Calloway's detail went unmolested. On the way back, he stopped in San Fernando to visit Consunji and his son Tomas, with whom he'd worked in the provost marshal's office. Tomas spoke fluent English and had served the army as a translator. Calloway considered him a friend. The Consunjis invited Calloway for dinner, and they talked about the course of the war. Calloway admitted his misgivings: This war was unjust, but what could be done? He placed hope in the gradualist approach of Booker T. Washington: mass education might end such prejudice, given time.

A few days later, Calloway wrote to the younger Consunji: "I am constantly haunted by the feeling of how wrong morally we Americans are in the present affair with you":

> Would to God it lay in my power to rectify the committed error and compensate the Filipino people for the wrong done! But what power have I? If I could muster every youth of the race under my hand I would say to them be not discouraged. The day will come when you will be accorded your rights. The moral sensibilities of all Americans [are] not yet dead.

He dated the letter February 5, sent it off, and forgot about it; Consunji stuck it away in his house and forgot about it, too. In April, Nene de la Rosa moved to San Jose to be with her soldier, and they set up house. For the moment, no one seemed to care.

The war raged on with new and brutal virulence. Aguinaldo's holiday in the plains of Nueva Vizcaya came to an end; amid the feasts, horse races, and concerts, there were also spies, and the Americans closed in. On February 7 he read long-delayed reports from his commanders and the Junta, and from a spy in the capital who mentioned "the frenzied conditions of the Manila people, who were ready to drink the enemy's blood." He signed some decrees in the name of the Honorable President, or "H.P."; learned that his wife, mother, son, and sister were safe in Manila; pardoned a deserter who was about to be executed. "Hurrah for the honorable president!" his men cried. But the idyll did not last. On February 14 he distributed three quarts of rice to each man in his escort; the next morning, they plunged back into the mountain nightmare, where Igorots concealed bamboo stakes in roads and three of his men were wounded, where within two days they were lost. Aguinaldo despaired, "What shall we do?" They go on, through rain, cold, starvation, and endless mountains, through small leechlike parasites called "limatiks" that attached to his face and his men's bodies and sucked their blood. Finally, atop a mountain, he cried, "What a costly thing is liberty! How we are suffering!" and his men whooped like madmen, which perhaps they were. "Hurrah for independence!" they cried.

They go on. By February 29, 1900, mountains surround them; by March 2 they learn that three guides who'd helped them have been killed, heads and feet taken, hearts consumed. March 22 is Aguinaldo's thirty-first birthday, and they stop in the town of Lubuagan for a feast of "stew a la Mauser" and "roast beef a la bayonet." Of the hundreds of thousands who once flocked to him, only 107 remain. He learns that the Igorots send back news of his whereabouts to pursuing Americans, who are four days behind. "How these people do love us," Villa says.

Spring arrives, and Aguinaldo orders his generals to combine forces to bring Nueva Ecija to its knees. They must harass them without pity and impress upon locals the need for loyalty—if need be, by fear. The March 17 *Manila Times* reports that eight women carrying bananas to sell to Americans in Peñaranda are beheaded, their bodies left beside the road. In Papaya, guerrillas murder a Spanish farm manager, his wife, and five children. One group called *El Gapang*, or "the crawler," abducts collaborators, wraps them in an American flag, and buries them alive. A Filipino cook for William Trafton's Mosquito Fleet is discovered one morning in the kitchen "all in one pile—his head, feet and arms were cut off and piled on top of him with some kind of a note on him stating what caused his health to fail."

March 1900 marks a turning point, when tales of U.S. atrocities are no longer surprising or rare. Reports flow from throughout Northern Luzon. In Ilocos Sur, Private Milton Nixon wrote that a Third Cavalry trooper fell into guerrilla hands; his body sported thirty-three bolo cuts, eighteen rifle wounds, gold fillings ripped from his teeth, and a tattoo of a woman on his arm skinned away. A few weeks later, the cavalry captured a guerrilla captain wearing a gold watch chain made from his fillings: "What happened to this captain is not recorded," writes Nixon, "but he was not turned over to the prison authorities." On April 22 Nixon writes that when native priests refuse to salute the flag, "the butt of a gun applied to them showed that the U.S. and not the pope in Rome is supreme on these islands." On May 6 they wound the guerrilla chief Ysabello Abia, who'd allegedly decapitated a Candon police officer with his three-foot, double-edged sword. His capture presents a problem: guerrillas will try to set him free. Nixon was in charge of prisoners when he watched his lieutenant speak to his sergeant. "Abia was being carried in a litter just ahead of me," he wrote. "When I saw the sergeant drop back along the line working his gun bolt, I knew what would happen, and so did Abia, as I saw him cross himself. The sergeant fired as he came abreast of Abia and instantly killed him."

Summary hanging becomes the order of the day. William Trafton's Mosquito Fleet hangs *amigos* suspected of aiding Aguinaldo: "We would take some hombre out and give him a good hanging, hang him until he was dead or ceased to move, and then take him down and pour water on him until he came to and repeat the remedy." But information obtained this way was not always reliable. The victim "would send us into a death trap": if he were leading them through brush, he'd "duck and be gone" just as the ambush began.

Funston was in the vanguard. From March 23 to 27, he rode to the mountains southeast of San Isidro with his Headquarters Scouts to flush out guerrillas. On the first day, they captured a lone rebel who promised to lead them to his band if they freed him. Funston agreed. That night, they crept down a twenty-foot-wide canyon that had perpendicular walls; ahead they spied a fire with two sentries, and Funston realized they'd located the main camp. They crept within thirty yards and started firing, killing the sentries; others fired back and disappeared into the predawn. In ten seconds of firing, the Americans had killed two insurgents and captured twelve rifles with eight hundred rounds of ammo; two of Funston's men were seriously wounded. As promised, he let the informant go.

It was on the way back, in the early hours of March 27, that Funston would again be accused of executing prisoners. Even then, the year-old accusations of misconduct against Funston and Wilder Metcalf were winding their way through army investigators and being reported in the *San Francisco Examiner* and Kansas papers. Now it happened again. As Funston rode back to his base, a bloody Macabebe ran up, crying, "My companions!" They'd been captured and tortured in a nearby village: Funston ordered his men to charge in the direction indicated by the Macabebe. They plowed into the barrio, killed three guerrillas, and found two officers hacking captured "Macs" with their bolos.

Scout Jack Ganzhorn told what happened next. Raised in Tombstone, Arizona, amid tales of Wyatt Earp, Ganzhorn idolized Funston; the scout's 1940 memoir *I've Killed Men* is one of the main sources describing the struggle between the Little Guy and David Fagen. Now Funston asked, "Doesn't this come under General Order No. 100 of 1863?"—a Civil War manual of warfare allowing the immediate execution of captives caught in the act of killing prisoners. "If it don't," came the answer, "nothing ever did." Funston ordered his men to rig a gallows and called out villagers to watch: "Quickly these two brutal savages were strung up on the limb of a mango tree, the only appropriate penalty for their crime."

When Funston reported his actions, Otis upheld him, but both he and Ganzhorn omitted salient details. Although Macabebes were exceptional at ferreting out *amigos*, their methods were as "savage" as their prey's. Hatred existed between rebels and Macabebes every bit as vengeful as that between *mambisi* and the loyalist *guerrilleros*, whom Funston despised. But in Cuba, U.S. soldiers had not participated. On March 23 near Malolos, a captain with the Fourth reported: "I found the natives every where [*sic*] terror stricken at the approach of the Macabebes, the natives charge these troops with indiscriminate slaughter of inoffensive citizens, the rape of women and [the] burning of barrios without cause or provocation." Macabebe Scouts were known to hang victims upside down from trees and threaten to rape their wives; suspend them by their toes before lighting a fire beneath them; shoot victims' legs so blood oozed out while hanging from a tree. On the same day of Funston's action, a group of Macabebes captured 130 alleged guerrillas and killed all of them during what a witness called an attempted escape.

The importance of Funston's action is that he may have been the first U.S. field commander to invoke General Order 100 in his own defense. Conceived by the early political scientist Frances Lieber and signed by Abraham Lincoln, Order 100 contained 10 sections and 157 provisions that tried to detail every contingency faced by an occupying army. Until March, the manual had not been quoted or enforced, but as American casualties mounted, one heard the magic formula invoked more often. The fact that Otis supported Funston in this closely watched case seemed to resonate. By late 1900 soldiers increasingly enforced their own interpretations: crop and property destruction increased, alleged spies were killed more frequently without trial. One official noted that by year's end, 14,640 Filipinos had been killed and 3,297 wounded, a five-to-one kill ratio that reversed statistics from the Civil and Boer wars. When Edward Atkinson, president of the Anti-Imperialist League, mentioned this, MacArthur replied, "It arises from the fact that our soldiers are trained in what we call 'fire discipline'; that is, target practice. In other words, they know how to shoot." By then, informal lethality had become a "new and more stringent policy," allowing Order 100 executions with little oversight, if any.

Americans employed various torture techniques to extract information, from simple beatings to a "rope cure" similar to the Spanish *garrote.* The most notorious was the "water cure." The Anti-Imperialist League mentioned it first in 1899, but as soldiers' letters described torture, the "water cure" became the most publicized method, so common that it turned into code for all forms of atrocity. At first the Macabebes administered the age-old method they called *timbain*, but their American allies caught on. In May 1900 A. F. Miller of the Thirty-Second Volunteers described it to his hometown *Omaha World-Herald*: "Now, this is the way we give them the water cure," he said. "Lay them on their backs, a man standing on each hand and each foot, then put a round stick in the mouth and pour a pail of water in the mouth and nose, and if they don't give up, pour in another pail. They swell up like toads. I'll tell you it is a terrible torture." Four or five gallons of water could be poured down a throat using a syringe, bamboo stick, or canteen, or simply by placing a man under a faucet. In one case, salt water was used; in another, the prisoner's jaws were held open by a brass cartridge, which he crushed flat between his teeth. Private Edward H. Beal of the Thirty-Fifth Volunteers said he helped give the water cure to "12 or 15 natives"; their provost marshal "inflicted this torture on a 10-year-old Filipino boy whose father was a paymaster in the native army." Edward E. Brown, also of the Thirty-Fifth, wrote on April 29, 1900, that they'd captured eighty-nine soldiers in a fight and "gave the prisoners the agua [water cure]," presumably all eighty-nine. Once the "body becomes an object frightful to contemplate," the water was squeezed out by kneeling on the victim's stomach or, in one case, "a good hevy [*sic*] man jumped on his stomach sending a gush of water from his mouth into the air as high as six feet."

The process was repeated until the rebel or suspected *amigo* talked or died. He almost always talked. Such violence could be a civilizing agent, wrote Chief Judge Advocate Stephen Groesbeck in his 1901 report examining whether the Philippine War was a lawless one. "I believe the water cure, as practiced by the American Army in the Philippines, to be the most humane method of obtaining information from prisoners that is known to modern warfare."

26

The Will of the People

With each new outrage, it was hard not to think that evil had befallen the Philippines. The realization that American boys would rob, rape, torture, and kill those they'd sworn to civilize mocked the image of World Redeemer. One gets the sense that Americans had not yet grasped the war's magnitude: army censorship hid the fact that during that first year alone, the war cost $50 million and a thousand American lives.

For the moment, the public saw atrocities as anomalies. As justification took shape, theories of "degeneration" rationalized the sins. The more Americans were exposed to "Asiatic" cruelty, the more "Asiatic" they became. The theory's most vocal proponent was Acting Assistant Surgeon Henry C. Rowland, who'd served two tours of duty in the Philippines. In his "Fighting Life in the Philippines," published in the July 1902 *McClure's*, he sends soldiers Tom, Dick, and Harry to Luzon, where they watch the degeneration of their friends. A sergeant is "seized with acute dementia" and fires on his fellows; a corporal beats a Filipino with no "discoverable cause"; a third attempts "the murder of a native." All human feeling fades. They decide that the only true route to peace lay in "an inundation of human blood."

If even half the reported atrocities proved true, something had gone seriously wrong. McKinley again found himself in Storm Central. Elections were eleven months away; in that time, he must move the islands away from war. The only hope lay in successful transition to civilian rule. In mid-January, the Schurman Commission released its plan: A colonial governor appointed by McKinley sat at the top; an advisory committee composed of Americans and natives reported to him. A legislative assembly, partly appointed and partly elected, would choose provincial governors. McKinley hoped this system would be "sufficiently elastic" that, in time, full government could be turned over to Filipinos. He created a second Philippine Commission to guide the transition, and he knew who he wanted to lead it.

U.S. circuit court judge William Howard Taft of Cincinnati personified turn-of-the-century America, said the historian Stanley Karnow: "He was ambitious, optimistic, diligent, and above all, big—from his bejowled face and elephantine torso to the boisterous laugh that erupted beneath his extravagant blond mustache." Philippine historians still chuckle at photos of the 325-pound Taft perched atop a *carabao*, since no native pony could carry his bulk. Industrious rather than brilliant, he would climb from assistant city prosecutor, at age twenty-three, to president of the United States after Roosevelt, at fifty-one—and after that, to chief justice of the Supreme Court, his great dream. He'd made few enemies, attributed by biographers to his good nature. Yet the jovial front concealed complexities. Roosevelt, when they were friends, warbled "One loves him at first sight"; Roosevelt, years later when they clashed, called him "one of the best haters" he knew.

The first hint of Taft's future arrived by telegram from McKinley: "I would like to see you in Washington on important business within the next few days." His heart sank when he found War Secretary Root and Navy Secretary Long flanking the president. "Judge," said McKinley, "I'd like to have you go to the Philippines."

Taft knew nothing about the archipelago, and he said so. The president shrugged. Few in his administration did; they learned on the job. Taft was not adventurous, he feared the climate, but more than anything else, he feared that the assignment would derail his judicial ambitions. McKinley jumped at that opening: "Well, all I can say to you is that if you give up the judicial office at my request you shall not suffer. If I last and the opportunity comes, I shall appoint you."

On February 6 McKinley announced Taft's acceptance. Two days later,

The New York Times approved: "No nomination . . . made by the President has been received with more general approval." On April 17 "Judge Taft" and the other members of the Second Philippine Commission sailed from San Francisco on the transport *Hancock*. Helen Taft and their three children followed later: to her surprise, they'd stay in the Philippines for four years.

Change was certain. On April 3 Elwell Otis asked Washington to relieve him of duty. McKinley granted his request on May 5, relieved that he would not have to fire the man. To the end, "Grandma" Otis insisted that he'd won the war. Left unsaid was the scope and success of resistance. Soldiers entered sick leave in overwhelming numbers every day. Rifles and ammo disappeared. On April 9 in Laguna and Cavite, guerrillas captured seventeen army wagons loaded with gold: those wagons in Laguna held $5,000 apiece; in Cavite, $2,000 in gold and ammo. Telegraph lines were cut: in Ilocos Norte, wires were snipped twenty-three times in six weeks; patrols disappeared into the bush to fix them and fought for their lives. This was not war as Otis understood it: no tactics and front lines, just endless rain and spreading inhumanity among his own men.

Otis was not alone in misinterpreting the age. An unquenchable anger had spread across the globe: the Philippine War was one of three colonial conflicts then burning. All were similar: lightning raids and torture rather than grand battles. Early that year, Great Britain sent 180,000 soldiers to suppress the South African Dutch settlers known as Boers. Britain's scorched-earth policy rivaled that of Valeriano Weyler: civilians were herded into concentration camps, where thousands died. In China, the nationalists known as Boxers went on a killing spree, determined to rid their country of opium, missionaries, and great powers. In June, even as Taft landed in Manila, McKinley ordered five hundred soldiers from the Philippines to join the multinational force, leeching men from every garrison in the archipelago. Those left could barely hang on.

Faster communication and transport linked the world. But rather than create Utopia, it spread rage. Even the meaning of "anarchy" changed. During this period, a new, violent strain of anarchism seized the imagination, and assassinations committed by its adherents claimed the lives of President Sadi Carnot of France, Prime Minister Antonio Cánovas of Spain, Empress Elisabeth of Austria-Hungary, and King Umberto of Italy.

In April, an attempt was made on the Prince of Wales by a sixteen-year-old boy claiming to avenge the "thousands slaughtered in South Africa." On November 18, 1900, a "deranged woman" threw an axe at the kaiser and the Prince of Saxe-Meiningen as they rode in a carriage through London. She missed. The anarchist writer Emma Goldman gave lectures advocating the assassination of all rulers. Leon Czolgosz, the jittery son of Polish immigrants, attended one and felt reborn.

The man who replaced Elwell Otis harbored few illusions about the world's brutality. Arthur MacArthur was a child of his day. To the surprise of all, he'd be even more controversial than his predecessor. At age fifty-five, the Medal of Honor winner had developed a girth and a fastidious fashion sense; even so, quipped Stanley Karnow, his pince-nez glasses gave him the air of a greengrocer. Those who'd fought under him in the first stage of the war believed him a military genius; since he was generous with promotions and decorations, the loyalty of junior officers like Funston was unwavering. But to those outside this charmed circle, he was sanctimonious and self-absorbed. In one note to McKinley, the general warned that Filipinos stuck together like glue: "The adhesive principle comes from ethnological homogeneity, which induces men to respond for a time to the appeals of consanguineous leadership." In other words, natives liked Aguinaldo because he was one of them. In another message, he charged that natives had been "maddened by rhetorical sophistry," a great moment of irony that MacArthur apparently missed.

Yet Lawton's death made MacArthur the senior officer in the Philippines, so Washington was stuck with his foibles. He *did* fit McKinley's goals. His commitment to a big American presence in Asia was absolute, and he would tell a 1902 Senate subcommittee that—like Cuba in the Caribbean—the archipelago's "strategic position is unexcelled." Its "commanding" location between China, Japan, and India protected American interests "with the very least output of physical power." Our acquisition of the Philippines was a boon for the "Aryan race": to doubt our presence there was to doubt the future of all "Americanism."

The man who moved into the white mansion in Malacañang Park knew he'd inherited a lopsided war. To give generals better control, MacArthur handed his old command to Lloyd Wheaton and divided the north into six districts: Funston took over the Fourth District in Nueva Ecija.

Sometimes Otis's Benevolence *did* seem to make gains. Several towns had created municipal governments in the U.S. model; city services that crumbled in the war's first year restarted; roads, bridges, schools, and markets were being rebuilt. Yet casualties and engagements sometimes surpassed 1899's numbers, and conditions in the countryside deteriorated daily. Fighting sprang up everywhere: a five-day siege in Samar; a garrison in Mindanao attacked by a thousand rebels; frequent attacks in Bataan, Nueva Ecija, and Leyte; Ilocos Norte in full bloody rebellion. Every day, panicked officers wired that without help, they'd be overrun.

Though MacArthur said he neither liked nor disliked Filipinos, America had assumed sovereignty and they'd best get used to it. If acceptance took ten years of "bayonet treatment," so be it. When he'd captured Malolos in March 1899, he thought that "Aguinaldo's troops represented only a fiction" and that most Filipinos welcomed America. Now he'd changed his mind. "I have been reluctantly compelled to believe that the Filipinos are loyal to Aguinaldo and the government which he represents," he admitted. Victory must be total, and the best way to achieve this was by capturing or killing *El Presidente*. Alive, he'd be "a white elephant upon the hands of the Administration." Dead, "the situation in the islands would be materially simplified."

Though MacArthur believed Benevolence programs nonsensical, he did not ditch all of them. He championed leniency for prisoners in hopes that guerrillas would act the same. On June 21, 1900, he declared a ninety-day amnesty and a thirty-peso payment for every rifle turned in: the results were "meager," with only 5,022 surrenders, none of them from senior leaders. In some places, *insurrecto* "shadow governments" seemed more efficient at collecting taxes and keeping records than official bodies established by Americans. This was the summer he sent two regiments to fight the Boxers; the summer the War Department began sending reminders that in one year all volunteer units would demobilize, halving his forces. Taft diminished his power further.

By summer's end, MacArthur was so constantly short-tempered that his staff feared he'd contracted a disease. This bitterness had real-world consequences. His treatment of enemy soldiers and suspected collaborators would be as harsh as anything in U.S. history. One can see the change by at least August 31. That day, he cabled Washington: "Week by week, situation shows little improvement; month by month, progress slow." Recently captured papers had revealed Aguinaldo's hope that continued resistance might affect the U.S. presidential election, cause enough blood and grief that McKinley might lose, replaced by a more sympathetic Democratic administration. "Captured papers contain convincing evidence that insurgent leaders are making strenuous efforts to hold together until after election," he said.

His predictions immediately came true. In September, guerrillas launched concerted attacks on U.S. patrols and garrisons and in less than a week inflicted two of the worst U.S. defeats thus far in the war. On September 13, in far-flung Marinduque Island, Captain Devereaux Shields of the Twenty-Ninth led fifty-one soldiers into ambush, and all surrendered. Four days later, in the same place, 130 Americans charged guerrillas, and a third were wounded or killed.

Later that month, MacArthur told McKinley that popular support for the rebels ran high: fear "as the only motive is hardly sufficient to account for the united and apparently spontaneous acts of several millions of people," he said. He followed this up on October 1 by questioning McKinley's assumption that Filipinos were eager to bend a knee. Maybe they cooperated in civic works, as U.S. funds built roads and increased trade, but these same villages supplied guerrillas with shelter, recruits, money, and food. Across the United States, newspapers reconsidered what the *Springfield Republican* called the "horrible mire in which we have now been floundering."

To MacArthur, the only solution was total war. The balmy days of Benevolence must end: from now on, it was Us versus Them. For the next two months, field reports indicated that soldiers increasingly enacted General Order 100. Since nothing had happened to Funston, what could happen to them? In November, Lloyd Wheaton sentenced a guerrilla to hang for three "murders." When MacArthur commuted that sentence to imprisonment, Wheaton charged the man with three more murders, found him guilty, and hung him anyway. To deny support to the guerrillas, Samuel Young proposed concentrating the population in controlled zones—Weyler's solution. He suggested the summary execution of any "Asiatic" violating his oath of allegiance and the arrest of anyone "deemed prejudicial" to America's goals.

The new brutality in the field shaped policy at the top. On December 19 MacArthur told generals to expect a "new and more stringent policy," and the next day, he issued the harshest interpretation of General Order 100 in American history. Written in English, Spanish, and Tagalog and printed in bold type, it ran every second day in *The Manila Times* and other papers and stated that, by continuing to fight, guerrillas violated the laws of civilized warfare and were thus subject to "extreme punishments." Benevolence was a thing of the past. Not only were insurgents criminals, but so was anyone supporting them. MacArthur's proclamation allowed the seizure and destruction of property, the exile of citizens, reprisals for assassinations, and summary executions of fighters not in uniform. "Whatever action is necessary," MacArthur wrote, "the more drastic the application the better." Filipinos from insurgents to loyalists read this as blanket permission for outrage. Cooperate or else—and even then, no one was safe.

Nearly two years after McKinley promised liberty and benevolence, MacArthur promised a "war without limits" or moral boundaries.

Taft arrived in Manila on June 3, at the beginning of MacArthur's dark change. McKinley's instructions were clear: Taft's commission would set up American-style governments throughout the islands and oversee a transfer of power from the military to a civilian governor-general. McKinley even set a timetable: on September 1, 1900, Taft's commission would assume the functions of a legislative body, with the power to raise taxes, allot funds, fix tariffs, set up courts, and enact laws. When helping Elihu Root draft the instructions, Taft carved for himself the role of chief executive—a role MacArthur did not want to relinquish. Yet Taft held a trump card: every dollar allotted to the Philippines, even from the War Department, must first funnel through his commission. MacArthur's power would be cut to nothing.

So MacArthur, like the guerrillas he fought, waged a war of attrition. It started on the day Taft arrived. When the *Hancock* docked, MacArthur did not meet it, but sent the judge advocate general and a few silent Filipinos and army officers. The next day, Taft and the commissioners went to Malacañang Palace for a reception that Helen Taft later dubbed "so cold that Mr. Taft said he almost stopped perspiring." MacArthur said their very existence was "humiliating to him personally": they weren't needed, and he could discharge their duties himself. MacArthur gave them offices in a crumbling part of the palace, rarely deigned to meet with Taft, and conducted business through formal letters. Their relations never improved.

MacArthur was not Taft's only problem. When he'd said on arriving that the U.S. held the Philippines for Filipinos, the American press in Manila turned on him. As in Cuba, throngs of speculators had streamed to the country; they secured title to land that Taft meant to sell to natives, and the army protected them. An American firm bought a large newspaper ad showing Taft's photo and the caption "This is the cause of our leaving the Philippines." Coverage emphasized Taft's "naiveté": "It's a shame to spoil his illusion that folks the world over are just like the folks he knew out in Ohio." When during a speech Taft called the Filipino "our little brown brother," soldiers pointed out that these "brothers" killed Americans in the jungles, mutilated their corpses, and sometimes buried them alive. The Filipino "may be a brother of Big Bill Taft," went one soldiers' song, "but he ain't no brother of mine!"

Commissioners sheltered within their bubble of work, at least until their families arrived. Despite army objections, the commission assumed responsibility for civil government on July 20, and twenty-three formerly hostile provinces were turned over to its charge. It reorganized agriculture, mining, health, police and courts, banking and currency, and education in the American model; for better or worse, the twentieth-century Anglicization of the Philippines began here. Taft kept for himself areas like the civil service, the disposition of public land, and the troublesome friars. Monks descended on Taft as quickly as they'd descended on the generals, demanding restoration of their power and property, while Filipinos cried "*Muerte a los frailes!*" Though there was no question of giving power back, Taft respected private property. In time, Washington bought all church land from the Vatican: Taft took title to 410,000 acres for $7,239,000 and sold it back to Filipinos in installment payments mortgaged over several years.

Right away, commissioners began a tour of all provinces not closed to them by war. Taft's August 21 report to McKinley was optimistic. He said that most of the country had been pacified and that most Filipinos believed the United States held their best interests at heart. Taft's view of the war was the opposite of MacArthur's: instead of a nationalist conflict supported by a people at arms, Taft saw it confined to specific regions and waged exclusively by Tagalogs.

Without a doubt, Taft saw only what he wanted, but then so did MacArthur. Officials often embark on fact-finding missions with preconceived notions; even before landing, Taft maintained that Aguinaldo and his followers were "desperate men" who "overawed" their followers, and nothing encountered on this tour could convince him otherwise. The people with whom he talked were the same small group of *ilustrados* who'd influenced Otis: they held their people in contempt, and when Taft wrote that the "vast mass" of natives were too "superstitious and ignorant" to qualify for autonomy, he was parroting their words.

If anything, Taft's report to McKinley was wishful thinking, and in important ways it duplicated Otis's sunny missives. A *New York Herald* report released that same month painted a more complex picture. Guerrilla commanders operated in every province in the archipelago, even those controlled by Taft. Guerrilla cells awaited Aguinaldo's call. The *Herald* made clear that the war wasn't ending soon. Yet Taft's report served a purpose: in this election year, McKinley could quote it as proof that he'd soon win the war. On schedule, the commission assumed civic power on September 1, leaving the army nothing but management of the war. MacArthur's power was "cut down to almost nothing," Taft triumphantly told a friend.

The infighting between MacArthur and Taft meant little to the rebel or dogface stuck in the countryside. They knew a quick end to the war was not likely. In 1899, one American was killed for every four or five wounded; by 1900 that changed to one U.S. soldier killed for every two wounded. *Insurrectos* had grown more efficient, and, like the *mambisi*, owned this style of war.

During this period, home folks began noticing what the war did to their loved ones. On April 1 Sergeant Charles E. Barnes of the Twenty-Seventh sailed home on the USS *Sherman*, the same ship with the dengue-stricken Clara Maass aboard. Barnes had been ten months in the field; the bank accountant's life he'd once thought boring now resembled paradise. The army had offered him $750 to reenlist, but he turned it down. With him on the *Sherman* were thirty soldiers who'd been driven mad: "Insanity is said to be a common affliction among the soldiers," he told the *Roanoke Times*, "caused by sunstroke and by drinking the native 'beno'!" Many "of those same soldiers who have assisted in murdering innocent women and little children are now being brought home raving maniacs," claimed the May 5, 1900, Chicago *Broad-Ax*: "Gen. Otis has recently ordered one thousand pair of handcuffs to be used in handcuffing the large number of demented soldiers and bringing them back to the country. The General says in his report, that 'from May 1898, one thousand men have been bereft of their reason and almost one hundred so far have taken their own lives.'"

Sometimes the land drove men mad. When Cornelius Gardener marched his Thirtieth Infantry into Southern Luzon on January 4, 1900, they occupied towns in Laguna, Tayabas, and Batangas provinces. His force was considerable: three infantry regiments, nine cavalry troops, and six mountain guns. Rebels melted before them, yet within a week every road had become lethal, and his men were limited to half rations of hardtack, bacon, and coffee. By February 21, four officers resigned. "They can't stand the isolation," he said. It took a month between food shipments, four months to get letters from home. One could not wander a quarter mile from town without risking an ambush; twenty-four-hour pickets and night patrols were essential for keeping guerrillas at bay. Six men had already been killed and twelve wounded; eight men were taken prisoner when 150 insurgents attacked a wagon train guarded by forty of his men. He knew they were held captive in mountains a hundred miles to the south, but he could not spare men to rescue them.

During this period, Gardener discovered that his men looted the homes of natives. One whole company was involved, and he doubted he could stop them: impose restrictions in one place and crimes popped up elsewhere. The men resented his interference: "He is entirely in sympathy with these people," complained his cavalry major, Matthew Steele. "He is a sort of a communist anyway." When Gardener stopped his men from taking food from natives passing through the lines, Steele snapped that it might go to the insurgents. "If we can't win this war without starving women and children," Gardener snapped back, "we had better quit."

Despair often turned to hatred. On January 31 Captain Frederick Wild of the Thirteenth took command of the Pozorrubio region, gateway to the Central Cordillera. The appointment made him "sole arbiter and king of over 9,000 people." Rain fell in buckets and never stopped; ants swarmed in billions, from the "tiniest little bit of a thing" to "a giant Hercules of an ant about three quarters of an inch long." Dogs roamed in snarling packs, roving the bush in search of rebel and American carrion. Wild declared "our wretched policy of humanitarianism and philanthropy" a failure, as over the next five months he deposed nine town officials for treason and conspiracy, killed half a dozen guerrillas in a night fight, filled his guardhouse with prisoners, fired a schoolmaster, and destroyed "gallons and gallons" of *beno*.

By May 7 he openly admitted that "these natives make me sick. They are dirty, ignorant, immoral, and unprogressive" and spent all their free time gambling at cockfights, an activity he tried to extinguish but which would destroy him instead. Filipinos returned the hate: "They smile in one's face and tell you they love you" until the next ambush, and they "think that the murder of a soldier is a fine thing." The town priest was the worst: Wild believed the "little sanctimonious skunk" was involved in the murder of a first sergeant and stirred people against new American schools. A soldier was killed or wounded every other day; Wild tried to fight disease by tackling the slops and waste residents threw under their houses, but they "think Americans are crazy because we are always improving and cleaning our surroundings."

Wild wondered why he came. His men were falling apart, and he watched as several fell into alcoholism: "A few days ago I went over to the quarters to inspect my men and found at least twenty-five" drunk on *beno*. How could he throw so many in jail and still maintain security? Not one man reenlisted: "They are so glad to get away, to go home, to be relieved of the task of being always on the alert." Could he blame them? "I am all alone here, and isn't it lonely?" Something in him is changing. He fears he'll never return to the man he once was.

If such madness changed men, could it alter a nation's "soul"? The genesis of national character lay at the heart of Martí's and Rizal's writing about the Cuban or Filipino soul. But what about the "American"? One traditional definition included the fact that we were neither England nor Europe, which meant a deep aversion to "empire." A moral strain of anti-imperialism had persisted in national consciousness since the Revolutionary War: the phrase "American exceptionalism" meant we were the exception in a corrupt, greedy world. Yet McKinley's transformation of the United States into a global power recast the definition of "exceptionalism": where American identity once stood against European "decadence," it now opposed the "uncivilized."

In our case, that meant Filipinos, just as the great powers targeted Africans and Asians.

Had we become a nation where ideals no longer mattered and might alone prevailed? The prominent historian Charles Francis Adams Jr. feared as much: "We have one by one abandoned our distinctive American tenets, and accepted in their place the old-time European tenets and policies, which we supposed the world, actuated largely by our example, was about forever to discard." The fear tripled the ranks of the Anti-Imperialist League, from 25,000 in 1898 to 75,000 in this election year. By 1900 the league boasted chapters in most major cities; its roster read like "a combination of the *Social Register* and *Who's Who in America*," wrote the historian Stuart Creighton Miller. Early membership was a mash-up, drawing old abolitionists, Republican Mugwumps, Populists, reformers, labor organizers, businessmen, Democrats, and even unreformed Confederates. Yet McKinley's reelection brought focus, and by 1900 most Anti-Imperialists agreed that the president had betrayed America's founding principles. The new opposition included former Presidents Cleveland and Harrison, industrialist Andrew Carnegie, labor leader Samuel Gompers, House Speaker Thomas B. Reed and Senator George Hoar, college presidents, academics, educators, social reformers, and clergymen. Prominent writers joined: Edgar Lee Masters, Edwin Arlington Robinson, Ambrose Bierce, Lincoln Steffens, and William Dean Howells. All might oppose McKinley for separate reasons, but all agreed that the United States had no business subjugating other people.

Three league voices grew especially prominent, each concerned about America's soul. W.E.B. Du Bois, working on his 1903 *The Souls of Black*

Folk, saw the Philippine War as a passion play in which America's history of greed and oppression slammed against traditional ideals. In a 1900 speech, he framed the war within our racial history, stating that capitalism fueled racism's spread. The oppression of Filipinos and American blacks sprang from the profit motive. William James, Du Bois's professor at Harvard, called the war the end of American individualism: by denying Filipinos their independence, the United States was "crushing out the sacredest thing in this great human world—the attempt of a people long enslaved to . . . be free to follow its internal destinies according to its own ideals." Allowing this gave birth to a spiritual corrosion as permanent as Dr. Jekyll's metamorphosis to Mr. Hyde.

The third voice became the one imperialists most feared. By mid-1900, Mark Twain had made enough money in his global lecture tour to pay off creditors; he summered north of London before returning home. The man who called himself "the American" cast himself onstage as a rude, taboo-breaking, white-suited court jester for the buttoned-down Victorian age. His fourteen-month journey took him first to America and Canada, then west across the Pacific Ocean before returning to Europe and England. Before 1899, Twain was "an ardent imperialist": the war with Spain was the "worthiest" war ever fought, and he'd favored the annexation of Hawaii. "I wanted the American eagle to go screaming into the Pacific," he told *The New York Herald*. "Why not spread its wings over the Philippines, I asked myself?"

But as he sailed west, he did not like what he saw. In *Following the Equator*, he described his growing "hatred and condemnation of imperialism of all stripes": he'd become more aware of such European imperialists as Cecil Rhodes, who expanded the British Empire in Africa, and Leopold II, king of the Belgians, whose quest for rubber in the Congo Free State led to the death, torture, and maiming of thousands. Twain began to think of the Chinese Boxer as a patriot: "He loves his country better than he does the countries of other people," and wished him success in his doomed revolt. Though he'd not yet spoken of the Philippines, he would make clear in time that he was not pleased with his country's transformation.

Twain's vision of America was one of nostalgic innocence, resting on an image of clean hands. America's were "the only hands guiltless of the sordid plunder of any helpless people's stolen liberties," he wrote, though he knew that such "innocence" was a construct, considering the near extermination of Native Americans and the legacy of slavery. "The very ink with which history is written is merely fluid prejudice," he admitted. Yet he also knew that this image held public sway. The religious underpinnings of American thought had created the sense that if America erred, at least its intentions were honorable. To lose this sense would send America adrift.

Though Twain's fame was at its peak, he felt adrift, too. His daughter Susy had died in 1896, and his wife, Olivia, had begun the slide that ended in her death in 1904. His boyhood dreams had not been realized, he wrote in the January 1900 *McClure's*, "for Age is upon us, with the indignity of its infirmities, and Death beckons!" He feared that his life had taken a wrong fork, and for all his fame, something had gone wrong. In the twilight of his life, there would be few chances to redeem himself. He needed a great cause.

Redemption matters in an unjust world. Anti-Imperialists saw this war as a contest between good and evil, and the coming election as America's last chance for redemption. In June, the Republican Convention in Philadelphia nominated McKinley for a second term, with Roosevelt as vice president; Garret Hobart, McKinley's first vice president, had died in office in 1899. In July, Democratic delegates in Kansas City nominated William Jennings Bryan for president and Adlai E. Stevenson for vice president. It was the election of 1896 redux. The Democratic platform called McKinley's imperialism the "burning" and "paramount" issue. While Republicans accused Democrats of causing American deaths through war opposition, Democrats accused Republicans of trampling the Constitution and waging the dirtiest war in American history. McKinley emphasized continued prosperity and the "full dinner pail." Bryan pounded trusts, plutocracy, and special privilege. Republicans spread the rumor that Democrats conspired with Aguinaldo. Anti-Imperialists dug up more U.S. atrocities.

McKinley's only other serious rival had self-immolated two months before the Republican Convention. Ever since Dewey's return to the States, the press wondered whether he'd be a nominee. On April 4 he called a *World* reporter to his house: "If the American people want me for this high office, I shall be only too willing to serve them," he said. Either party could nominate him: after all, "the office of President is not such a very difficult one to fill, his duties being mainly to execute the laws of Congress." The surprised scribe asked him about his platform. "I think I have said enough at this time, and possibly too much," the commodore said.

The mockery following this odd moment sank Dewey's hopes. A typical response is reflected in Roosevelt's April 9 letter to Leonard Wood. "What an extraordinary business this of poor Dewey is!" he howled, adding, "Mrs. Dewey has just cordially announced that she would like to have me as Vice President." He'd graciously turned her down.

Roosevelt told Wood and others that the vice presidency was "about the last office that I would care to fill." He'd rather be appointed secretary of war or governor-general of the Philippines. "I have been pretty successful as Governor," he told Lodge, "but in the Vice-Presidency I could do nothing," and he did not want to be a "figurehead." Yet, by the time of the convention, Roosevelt changed his mind: "Our nation, glorious in youth and strength, looks into the future with eager eyes and rejoices as a strong man to run a race," he roared to delegates. And no one stumped harder: he made 673 whistle-stops, taking a squad of Rough Riders as bodyguards. When hired "muckers" in Cripple Creek, Colorado, stoned him with granite, a wedge of his men saved him. Elsewhere, one of his Rough Riders shot a Populist newspaper editor for daring to criticize "mah Colonel." The editor lived.

Not long into summer, Bryan revived his Populist plank of "free silver," meant to replace the gold standard. The campaign instantly changed. Anti-Imperialists like Charles Francis Adams, George Hoar, and Andrew Carnegie saw economic chaos as a greater threat and switched to McKinley. A large number of "Gold Democrats" concluded that the U.S. must first set its own financial house in order. After that, there'd be time to devote to the Philippines.

As summer ended and Election Day neared, the problem for many was choosing the lesser of two evils: the "platitudinous" McKinley, or the "rattle-brained" Bryan. "What a choice for a patriotic American!" groaned Grover Cleveland, who planned to go duck hunting on Election Day. His former agriculture secretary Julius Morton wrote back, "I am going to shut my eyes, hold my nose, vote, go home and disinfect myself." *The Nation* suggested that the McKinley campaign adopt a new slogan: "The Nation's Choice—of Evils."

For more than a year, Aguinaldo promised far-flung guerrillas that the election would pivot their struggle. In village and town, he penned coded messages admonishing commanders to stockpile supplies and add recruits, and his strategy showed results: in the first seven months of 1900, American deaths totaled 995, an average of 4.7 deaths daily. Bryan's nomination was "a ray of hope," and though Aguinaldo overestimated the Democrat's chances, thousands listened. All that summer, people in the countryside held mass gatherings celebrating national independence and, according to one poster hanging in the town of Tarlac, "The American People Who Sympathize with the Filipino Nation." He fired off manifestos to foreign sympathizers and issued General Order 202, commanding his men to "give such hard knocks to the Americans that they will . . . set in motion the fall of the Imperialist party, which is trying to enslave us."

Yet the American belief that McKinley's Benevolence had caught fire was just as delusional. Peyton March was shocked by the July turnout for local elections in Bangued, the capital of Abra Province. Out of 13,000 residents, only 26 registered to vote, and of them, 21 cast ballots. American-style government in Northern Luzon "is more or less a farce," March said.

Guerrillas doubled down, attacking soldiers throughout the Philippines. On September 13 rebels under Colonel Maximo Abad ambushed a sixty-man patrol of the Twenty-Ninth at Pulang Lupa on the island of Marinduque: every man was killed, wounded, or captured. Four days later, 200 guerrillas under General Juan Cailles attacked 130 Americans less than fifty miles from Manila: 21 Americans were killed, 23 wounded. In "pacified" Ilocos Sur, insurgents cornered an American patrol in a canyon, killed a lieutenant and 4 soldiers, and wounded 14. As a result, Secretary Root ordered MacArthur to delete the word "ambush" from all future cables.

The war acquired new life, with no apparent end. From May 1900 to June 1901, army reports chronicled 1,026 strangely similar battles that began and ended in an instant and filled 734 typed pages. During this "chaotic" period, 245 Americans died, 490 were wounded, and 118 captured, an unprecedented toll. Insurgents, as always, fared worse: 3,854 killed, 1,193 wounded, and 6,572 captured. Yet lopsided statistics brought little comfort to those doing the fighting, for, as in later wars emphasizing "body counts," numbers did not translate into victory. A June 1 report in *The Manila Freedom* described a night attack at San Miguel, twenty miles from Funston's headquarters: "The rebels seemed to be everywhere, yelling and shouting." Five Americans died in hand-to-hand combat; another seven were wounded. If so many rebels had died off, how could they keep coming?

During these dangerous days, Funston and Fagen came to know each other well. For both, the face of the enemy became personal. Their relationship began on May 29, 1900, when a seven-man patrol under Captain Charles Roberts was captured by *insurrectos* under Colonel Simón Tecson, whose guerrilla stronghold sat atop verdant Mount Corona. Funston could see the peak from his window, and he assembled a 1,300-man rescue party to free Roberts and his men. Jack Ganzhorn and the Headquarters Scouts rode among the saviors. At daybreak, they found the rebels at the foot of the mountain and charged, but Tecson retreated uphill to prepared positions and fired down on Funston's men. A bullet pierced Ganzhorn's canteen, soaking his leg; he glanced down, sure that he was covered with blood, then looked up and saw Funston grinning at him. That same moment, a bullet struck the ground before Funston's face, spraying dirt into his eyes. Before Funston could regain sight, the guerrillas melted into the trees.

Seven weeks later, the *Davenport Weekly Leader* quoted a letter from an American captive saying that the insurgents who'd fired at Funston were led by "a deserter from the Twenty-Fourth Infantry." This was the first reference to Fagen of any sort in the American or Manila press, though he still remained unidentified. Funston returned to San Isidro after the skirmish for more ammo, then rode back with his scouts and forty-one men of the Twenty-First under Captain George J. Godfrey, a small, handsome man sporting a "big, pointy mustache" who'd survived the worst of El Caney. Again, the guerrillas faded back; again, Funston followed—up the mountain for four miles, the rebels always just ahead.

Funston emerged from the forest into a large glade; he rode into the open, when suddenly the rebels fired from the trees to their left, only seventy yards away.

Funston was stunned. He tended to be reckless, but he assumed that the Filipinos were such bad shots that they "let fly as soon as our point came in sight," and even then, they couldn't hit anything. "But this outfit," he discovered, "was better handled." They'd dug a "splendid deep trench" from which 50 to 100 men poured out deadly fire. Captain Godfrey fell ten yards from Funston, shot through the heart; seconds later, a Private Etheridge fell beside him. The firing continued for thirty minutes until the rebels again "vanished into the depths of the forest."

During the battle, Funston and Ganzhorn spotted one or more "American horses" back in the trees. Neither mentioned this in his account, but a story running two years later in the April 16, 1902, *St. Louis Post-Dispatch* revealed that these "better handled" rebels had been Fagen's. During the fight, Americans watched "the gigantic figure of Fagin [*sic*] [rise] from behind the trenches, and, standing, take deliberate aim at Capt. Godfrey, and fire." Fagen's biographer Michael Morey believes Funston was the source; one week later, a second account appeared, this time in Funston's hometown *Iola Register.* In this article, Fagen offered to "fight it out": they'd "meet between the two forces" like medieval knights in the field of honor. Funston did not accept, but he would have seen this as an insult. Soon "every commander in his brigade received orders that Fagin [*sic*] was to be killed or captured at any cost."

Thus began the contest portrayed in the press as a clash of titans. Funston limped home, but Fagen was not finished. Two days later, on June 5, two detachments of the Thirty-Fifth Volunteers who still searched for Captain Roberts entered the highlands around Mount Balubad. Guerrillas pinned them down; one soldier died, and ten were wounded. During the fight they heard "an American shouting and taunting the troops from above"; no other American fought with Tecson at this moment but Fagen. General Frederick Dent Grant, son of Ulysses and commander of the Fifth District, assembled another 1,300-man force to overrun the stronghold, but by the time they struck on June 10, Tecson, Fagen, and their men were long gone.

Fagen had led his men north into Funston's territory. Resistance in

Nueva Ecija had stuttered after the capture of García and Padilla, so thirty-eight-year-old General Urbano Lacuna was sent north from Bulacan with two hundred men to reignite the war. Fagen must have joined Lacuna almost immediately, and would report primarily to the well-respected general for the rest of the war. On the night of June 10, Lacuna's third-in-command, Major Tomas Tagunton, attacked San Isidro; the hour-long assault left several residents dead and some Americans wounded. This was Lacuna's calling card: firing into a garrison at night, fraying defenders' nerves. Soon afterward, bounty posters signed by "Major Fagan" were found in the area offering a 2,000-peso reward for Funston's death. Four days later, Joe Wheeler Jr. wired Manila that Lacuna, Tagunton, and the "Afro-American traitor called David" planned to attack his sixty-man garrison at Papaya with four hundred "armed bandits." That night, Funston and his Headquarters Scouts found Lacuna's men and drove them back, killing twenty-two and wounding thirteen.

Wheeler's cable for the first time showed the importance Americans attached to Fagen's capture or killing. Army records between July 1900 and March 1901 list nine firefights that mention Fagen by name. Few strayed far from San Isidro, a weird, sparsely populated region where the Rio Grande de Pampanga flowed southwest into the huge Candaba Swamp and the lone peak of Mount Arayat glowered down. It was the very image of the "boondocks," the most lasting slang to come from the war: drawn from the Tagalog *bundok*, for "mountain" or remote area, it came to be associated with a distant, bewildering unknown. Funston could not stand unknowns: he favored quick spurts of action followed by quicker success, yet with each encounter Fagen emerged victorious, then disappeared. As Fagen eluded capture, the American press portrayed him as a "gigantic Negro," "the most daring and bloodthirsty of the Filipino Generals." With each new success, guerrilla recruitment shot up. He'd become Robin Hood.

The weather did not help Funston's temper. Monsoon season began in earnest soon after Lacuna's defeat; while the rain confined Funston to his garrison, guerrillas attacked their immobilized foes. On July 4 Tecson and Lacuna combined forces to attack Gapan, Peñaranda, and the small barrio of Manicling with 700 to 800 men. All three posts held out. On July 16 Funston marched from San Isidro to wreak vengeance with his own 800-man column, but Lacuna escaped. Funston pursued him into the mountains and searched without luck for days. He'd grown disgusted and petty: when a private took a villager's chicken, he made the man broil it up, then ate it in front of him. Fagen was far away—in the southern mountains with Tecson's guerrillas, pursued by Major Wheeler. Jack Ganzhorn was assigned to the chase, thanks to his knowledge of the steep, rocky trails. On July 22 he guided a column commanded by Captain George Gibson up a deep ravine near Mount Corona, where Roberts and his men were still being held. A steep, crescent-shaped hill loomed to their right, a ravine dropped to the left, and on the other side towered a rocky cliff. At 2:30 p.m. a soldier spotted a rebel standing atop the hill and fired; hidden insurgents began shooting, and there was nowhere to hide.

As Ganzhorn watched, men would be hit and then roll down the mountain; all one could do was grab clumps of grass and climb. A man to Ganzhorn's right screamed and fell into the ravine; when Ganzhorn glanced up, Fagen stood twenty yards from the top, "grinning and mocking us, still wearing parts of the uniform he had disgraced." His friend Albert Fryberger took aim, but Fagen fired first and Ganzhorn could hear the bullet rip into Fryberger's right shoulder. "For God's sake, Ganzie," he cried, "kill that black devil!" But before Ganzhorn could drag out his six-shooter, Fagen fired again. "Blood and brains from a terrible hole in poor Fryberger's head splattered into my eyes," Ganzhorn wrote forty years later. He watched the limp body slide into the ravine. "Sobbing for breath, crazy mad, I wiped the warm sticky mess from my face," but when he looked up, Fagen was gone. Men continued to fall. A soldier crouching between Ganzhorn and Captain Gibson flopped onto his side. "Come on, soldiers," Gibson cried, leaping up. "Give that black devil the hell that's coming to him!" A bullet struck him under the eye, plowed through his face and shoulder, and came out the small of his back. He flung up his arms and pitched down the hill.

The Americans had again marched into ambush; the firing ended only when some finally reached the crest and could shoot down into the rebels in their rifle pits across the canyon. Then they vanished, leaving several Americans seriously wounded and Gibson and Fryberger slain. In his report, Lieutenant David Stone, who took over from Gibson, wrote that the "firing of the Insurgents was low and accurate throughout the engagement." He believed they were spared greater casualties because their khaki blouses and trousers blended into the dry grass around them. "I could not see my own men lying or kneeling in the grass fifty yards from me."

It was a humiliating defeat, and they were lucky that more were not killed. They staggered back to base two nights later, carrying their dead and wounded. Fagen was not mentioned in the release, but everyone knew who'd taught the guerrillas how to shoot. In time, he'd be blamed for almost every devastating firefight, even the one that killed Henry Lawton. On page 4 of Stone's report, he mentions that "David Fagan [*sic*], a renegade, deserted from the Twenty-Fourth U.S. Infantry . . . was plainly seen and shot at by members of Co. 'F' but they were not fortunate enough to hit him." This was kept from the press, and Fagen's first mention in American papers would be an oblique reference in the July 24 *Davenport Weekly Leader* of Funston's failed sortie to save Roberts.

The secrecy did not deceive Funston's men. "During the long, sad trip back to San Isidro, the bitterness of our loss seemed greater because we knew it was largely due" to Fagen, Ganzhorn wrote. The "grinning" black villain, "leering" from above: "Every man in that fight prayed for a chance to kill the traitor." So would every white soldier in Funston's command.

Thus began the first of two great dramas that symbolized this war. Funston has been portrayed as a lone wolf out for glory, but in truth he drew energy from those around him and could feel the hatred for Fagen in his men. Their defeat would have been bad enough if Fagen were white, but he was *black*, and his ability to outwit them disproved their perceived superiority. Fagen seems to have transferred his original hatred from James Moss to the Kansan. Though he'd be portrayed as a renegade black only satisfied with the extermination of whites, those white Americans who became his captives were in fact treated with reserved affability.

On the day after Fryberger's death, Funston assembled three companies of the Twenty-Second and three Macabebe squadrons to scour the trails around Mount Corona and Mount Balubad. When they didn't find Fagen, they burned villages and cornfields. This was a new phase of warfare, reported in the July 26 *New York World*: After a comrade's death, Americans burned indiscriminately and killed "right and left natives who are only suspects." Where such actions previously had been labeled individual infractions, they were now a general, if unofficial, policy. As more villagers refused to cooperate, they'd be "strung up by their thumbs, or nooses put around their necks and . . . partly strangled" to compel information. The *World* conceded that few Americans would believe such reports: no matter how detailed the facts, "people would refuse to believe that such barbarities take place under our flag."

Funston's quarry was right under his nose, hiding in the forests along the San Miguel Road. On August 1 the young Signal Corps lieutenant Frederick W. Alstaetter was leading a three-man survey group seven miles south of San Isidro. Alstaetter had only been in the islands for ten weeks, all but the last five days in Manila; now he was assigned to map the road from the capital to San Isidro. He'd heard the tales of American captives whose noses and ears were lopped off, the gaping wounds covered in salt; of soldiers buried alive. Before they rode out, he read the account of how a lieutenant and his sergeant were staked naked over anthills. He was glad his party was accompanied by eleven men from the Fourth Cavalry, but on this day most had pulled ahead. They plodded through the crushing heat, the road surrounded by swamps and rice fields.

Gunfire erupted at 12:30 p.m. from both sides. The four engineers grabbed their Krags from their mounts and plunged into a rice paddy. Private Tischler was killed immediately, shot through the abdomen. The horses fled. The men carried 120 rounds apiece, but after three hours were down to their last shells. Private Brewer was shot in the arm, Private Newman in both arms. The end was near: Alstaetter's men threw their revolvers and gun belts into the swamp so the rebels would not get them, and he contemplated saving the last bullet for himself. But that was "the easy way out," he'd say. When the guerrilla commander sent forward a white flag and promise of good treatment, provided instant surrender, Alstaetter knew he had no choice.

They were taken before an American black man who was as muddy as they were. "Fagen led the attacking party," Alstaetter later said. Over his objections, "my watch and class ring were taken from me, and the negro took charge of them." Fagen ordered a burial party for the unfortunate

Tischler and had his men round up the horses. As Alstaetter watched, the deserter issued orders in Tagalog, seeming to have an easy control of his men. He realized that Fagen led 350 to 400 rebels, who "made a great deal of" him, and when they reached camp, Lacuna seemed pleased. He sent the two wounded men back to San Isidro with a note promising to treat the lieutenant well. Fagen and his band left, and Alstaetter would not see him for another three and a half months. Four days later, *The New York Times* reported Alstaetter's capture. Once again, Fagen was not named.

Funston found these victories intolerable. He wired General Wheaton that he planned a sweep between San Isidro and San Miguel with two thousand men. But the weather did not cooperate, and on September 1 a massive storm flooded San Isidro's streets, flattened huts, obliterated a hospital. Roads linking villages were impassable; the tangled woods surrounding each village turned swampy and bright green. Vengeance turned inward, and Funston's spies uncovered fourteen prominent *amigo* collaborators in San Isidro; he threw them into prison on charges of aiding the enemy and sent out his men when possible, burning crops and huts in night raids. The use of torture escalated. Private Edward H. Beal of the Thirty-Fifth Volunteers described the fate of one captive major: "They put him on the rack till I thought he'd die but they could not get him to talk," so they left him in a deserted hut. "He was too far gone" to live, Beal said. Another time they tied six suspects in a crouch and sank them in a creek. A man would stand on each suspect "until they could tell from the bubbles that the captive had enough," then let him take a breath "and down he'd go again."

But nothing worked. Lacuna commanded 8 to 12 companies, each of 10 to 50 men, each assigned to a different segment of Nueva Ecija. They hid in the woods and maintained contact through patrols; they never fought Americans "from the front," but "never let [them] pass unmolested." Twenty or more officers supplied troops, gathered intelligence, and collected taxes; those town leaders who did not pay might receive a fatal visit at night. They manned roadside checkpoints; fired into garrisons at night; returned prisoners, something the Americans rarely did. On August 14 Simón Tecson paroled the last enlisted men who'd been captured with Alstaetter and brought them down the mountain: of the original survey group, only Alstaetter remained captive.

Though spies told Funston of Fagen's camps, he'd vanish when Americans arrived. On August 16 Lacuna, "an American Negro Insurrecto," and one hundred guerrillas were said to rest in the village of Pajo, south near the border of Bulacan Province. The next day, a wire from Joe Wheeler Jr. increased these numbers to four hundred, saying they'd "seized four women in Gapan accused of being spies for the Americans." One was "given to David," a salacious detail Wheeler saved for last. On August 28 Funston heard that fourteen to seventeen prisoners were in or near the large camp, more captives than had ever been revealed in American cables. If this was true, rebels were capturing Americans right and left, but the army hid that information. Funston's men swept south toward the camp but got lost in the Candaba Swamp. They wounded and captured Lacuna's second-in-command, but little else. All others disappeared, including Fagen.

Like a ghost, the "Negro Insurrecto" appeared when he chose. On September 6 General José Alejandrino promoted him to captain, an elevation Lacuna seconded ten days later. His name was just beginning to gain wider attention: a brief report in the September 9 *Manila Freedom* ran the next day in the *Pittsburgh Daily Post* and several other U.S. papers: "David Fagin [*sic*], a deserter from the Twenty-Fourth Infantry, is heading a band of Filipinos in Nueva Ecija. This band is very active in raiding the quartermasters' wagons and in robbing peaceful natives." It was the first time his name made the American papers.

On the morning of September 13, Sergeant Walter L. Washington of the Twenty-Fourth set out from the beleaguered garrison at Manicling to San Isidro. He led an eight-man detachment protecting a mule wagon; they were to pick up rations, as well as a second wagon of provisions, and return that afternoon. Washington and Fagen may once have been friends: they'd probably charged together up San Juan Hill, where Washington was wounded; they definitely served together in the Siboney fever camp and reenlisted in February 1899, though not on the same day. But where Fagen ran afoul of Lieutenant Moss and deserted, Washington rose from corporal to first sergeant, a twenty-seven-year-old respected noncom standing 6 feet, 2 inches.

Washington's detachment made it safely to San Isidro and turned around, picking up two additional teamsters and Corpsman Patrick

Shea—twelve men in all. Fagen's 150-man force awaited their return. The battle did not last long. Washington was wounded and last seen firing at the enemy. Six of his men escaped, four of them wounded. Hours later, three of these staggered into Manicling; a search party found a fourth the next day. Rebels tracked down the last two and killed them. Four men were captured, including Corpsman Shea. One loaded wagon was led to Lacuna in San Leonardo. Fagen set the second wagon alight, presumably to lure a rescue party.

Rescuers weren't long in coming, including Lieutenant Richard Day and sixteen of Funston's scouts, who would later narrate events to Jack Ganzhorn. As they rode straight at the column of smoke, a guerrilla volley killed two horses. The rebels pushed the rescuers back to the Rio Peñaranda. "Captain Fagan's [*sic*] done got yuh white boys now," the hated deserter allegedly jeered. "Less'n you all surrender, my little gugus is gonna chop on you with their meat cutters!"

Lieutenant Day leaped up and cried, "Go to hell, you black scum!" Two riders dragged him down. "A million of you yellow-bellied rats couldn't whip Funston's Scouts!" But they had, repeatedly, and only night and reinforcements saved them. As before, Fagen melted away.

Ganzhorn's account must be taken with a grain of salt: he conflates details from the Mount Corona attack, at which he was present, with this incident, at which he was not. Yet in so doing, he turns Fagen into a mythic force threatening white civilization, and his inclusion of Fagen's dialect-laden taunts made it clear that the feared American race war had come to the Philippines. Day's angry response has a ring of truth, especially since "Hartzell and Bates" drag him back down. The next day, General Wheaton chastises Funston: the area around Manicling is so dangerous that "small detachments unable to resist one hundred guerrillas must not be sent on the road," he warns, adding that this matter "has been the subject of instructions heretofore."

Three days later, on September 16, guerrillas attacked Manicling again, but this time with little effect. That same day, Sergeant Washington's body was found in the high grass by the burned-out wagon; weather, wounds, and insects had taken effect, and he could be identified only by his blue army blouse and the sergeant's stripes on his sleeves. Soon afterward, the bodies of two other soldiers killed in the ambush were found in the empty ration wagon abandoned outside Gapan. Few Americans now ventured outside their strongholds. Funston was ordered to send one large supply shipment to the beleaguered defenders of Manicling, and after that, few entered the area. Lacuna and Fagen had free run of the land.

The scenario in Nueva Ecija was a common one: American and Filipino commanders came to know one another by name and act, and for them the war was personal. Yet no other duel became as famous as the one between Fagen and Funston. Fagen became almost supernatural: the leering "black devil" who moves like a ghost, immune to capture, danger, or shell. His path resembles that of the revolutionary "Winchester Negro" of the Gulf Coast, and Fagen no doubt saw the similarities. Though most white pursuers were probably unaware of these vigilante tales, they did respond to a deeper chord. Fagen echoed a basic tenet of the frontier myth: when he entered the wilderness, it entered him. Like the legendary "White Indian" of the American West, David Fagen had "gone native."

One problem existed with tales of the "black devil": Fagen could be kind to Americans, black or white, who became his prisoner. Since these accounts came out gradually, they did not balance out Fagen's early demonization. A May 5, 1901, *Manila Freedom* article reflects the general consensus: "Unhappy was the fate of any American prisoners who fell into Fagan's [*sic*] hands. He was shot, and tried afterwards."

Not so, said one former captive nine days later in the same paper. Private George W. Jackson was captured by Fagen during the same ambush that killed Sergeant Washington. He'd been assigned to Company I, Fagen's old unit, and if the deserter's rumored hatred for it had been real, Jackson would have been the first to know. Instead, Fagen protected old comrades from guerrillas, some of whom were happy to abuse them: Thomas Brown told of an officer who had him dragged into the bush and flogged. By the end of 1900, most would be released or exchanged for Filipino prisoners and, like Jackson, be recuperating in Manila hospitals when the *Manila Freedom* article ran. "I will say that there are (or have been very recently) patriots in every hospital in Manila who were captured by or been in Fagen's custody as prisoners and each one of them claims that Fagan [*sic*] treated them all right and would not let the natives hurt them," Jackson said on May 15, 1901. Private Michael Morgan of the Ninth and Corpsman Patrick Shea also said that Fagen treated them "the very best he could under the circumstances."

And then there was the famous Lieutenant Alstaetter, held on Mount Corona. After his release, Alstaetter gave a string of interviews that provided a glimpse of the fugitive. On September 15 the lieutenant wrote his five sisters that although he'd been a prisoner for a month and a half, he still experienced "the most kindly treatment from his captors." He stayed in a little hut guarded by several troops who said that if he tried to escape, he'd get lost in the jungle and die of hunger, or be shot during the attempt. Yet he grew bored of his "gilded cage," so filled his pockets with hardtack and plunged into the brush. Thirty hours later, he was found, hungry and thirsty but no worse for wear.

As Funston and Lacuna worked on a prisoner exchange, Fagen returned to Mount Corona from late November 1900 "until four days before I was exchanged," Alstaetter said. During that time, he saw Fagen continuously. "We slept side by side together in a little hut and ate out of the same dish; usually small amounts of rice and some dried fish." He found Fagen amusing and came to think of him as "a typical Southern negro with no education and ignorant, but he possessed good common sense." Fagen showed the lieutenant his captain's commission and said that since both were officers, "we are equals; we amount to something." To his credit, the young Ohioan did not find this offensive, emphasizing that Fagen treated him "very kindly."

A vast tragic gulf separated whites and blacks in 1900s America, but something like friendship developed, and during those days, Fagen opened up to him. "He feared capture by the American soldiers," Alstaetter recalled, "and imagined the whole army was after him. He would proclaim that the Filipinos were sure to be victorious and that the American soldiers were about to give up. He did this to buoy up his own courage and that of the Filipinos. His influence over the natives was wonderful." They both laughed that his men called him "General." But then Fagen would grow pensive and state "that he would never be taken alive." He once commented, "The American Army wants me bad. They won't get me."

He was not imagining things. Every soldier in the Fourth District, from Funston to the lowliest white private, dreamed of catching the "notorious renegade." The February 26, 1901, *Manila Times* declared, "Next to Aguinaldo there is no man whom [American authorities] are so anxious to capture"; they also reported that Fagen had been spotted around Manila, the first of many false sightings. Funston's hometown *Iola Daily Register* later wrote that it was a matter of faith "that the regiment that killed or captured [Fagen] would stand high with the commanding officer." And he didn't expect mercy if captured alive: José Alejandrino later wrote that Fagen often woke at night from a recurring nightmare of being seized by a white mob.

By mid-November, Lacuna's second-in-command had recovered sufficiently from his wounds to be traded. Funston offered to exchange him for Alstaetter, and Lacuna agreed. On November 16 Fagen walked the lieutenant to the edge of Gapan and set him free. Before he left, Alstaetter asked for his West Point class ring and Fagen said "he had loaned it to a friend," probably a lie. The lieutenant walked across fields and down a road, accompanied by a native porter. The garrison had not expected him, and rejoiced when he appeared.

Summer and fall 1900 were not good days to be a black soldier in the Philippines. On May 11, in the dining room of a Manila hotel, twenty drunken white soldiers with the Twentieth tried to beat to death a recently discharged black sergeant. Summer race riots in New Orleans, New York City, and Raleigh, North Carolina, filled the news. On September 29 General John C. Bates told *The Manila Times*, "I believe the Filipinos are naturally more intelligent than our colored people," adding, "The Filipinos resent being treated as inferiors. They object to being called offensive names and to being knocked about"—which implied that American blacks didn't mind. On September 30 a Private Snyder of the Twenty-Second wrote home to Nebraska that 150 black deserters had killed 75 white soldiers in a pitched battle, and the hometown paper printed the letter. A War Department investigation determined that no such incident occurred.

It was only natural that Funston entered the debate, considering his elusive quarry. On October 11, after Fagen captured several men from Company I detailed to telegraph repairs, Funston wired, "It is impossible to arrive at any other conclusion than that the negro soldier here will not fight unless led by white officers." This, after several men were killed in hand-to-hand combat, and Private George Jackson was recommended for the Medal of Honor in the battle that saw the death of Sergeant Washington. Contrary to evidence, Funston insisted that black Regulars "go to pieces as soon as attacked," echoing Roosevelt on San Juan Hill.

During this period, black captives were more likely to be killed or injured by white rescuers than by their captors. There seemed a tendency to conflate all African Americans with Fagen or other deserters. On September 10 a spy reported that "three American negroes, armed" were seen riding with Lacuna on "three American horses." Since no defections of black soldiers had been recorded in Northern Luzon during this period, the men had either gone unreported or been taken prisoner. On October 14 spies said that two of the black Regulars captured with Private Jackson were being held in the swamps. When rescuers rode up, they killed Private James Benjamin, assuming he'd deserted. The others dealt "severely" with Thomas Brown, thinking he was Fagen until discovering otherwise.

No African Americans suffered more than the men in Fagen's old regiment. They were hunted by their old bunkmate and assailed by their commander. As John Calloway had written to *The Richmond Planet*, "We black men are so much between the 'Devil and the deep blue sea' on the Philippine question": in little more than a year, it had grown worse. Morale plummeted even lower than when Fagen defected, and company records show increasing numbers of soldiers in confinement, punished for minor offenses and for "going bamboo." Reenlistment rates dropped below 20 percent. Troops felt maligned by their officers all the way up the line.

At the top sat Funston, who tormented black soldiers as his inability to catch Fagen continued. A story told by one of his white officers speaks volumes. A sentry had intercepted a letter from Fagen to a former messmate: "Come and join us," it said. Funston brought the man in, hoping he possessed "sufficiently strong stuff" to lay a trap, but he realized that he was "one of the superstitious ones, who could face bullets, but would never do this for a secret mission of danger." Funston toyed with the man, never cracking a smile while his officers "convulsed with mirth," some leaving "to keep from spoiling the fun." Funston commanded, "You have to obey orders if you are a soldier. Now I am going to order you to go out with this letter and get Fagan [*sic*] . . . The Negro seemed, all at once, to crumple up at the knees. He slid to the floor in front of one of the staff officers. Tears streamed down his cheeks and his voice choked as he sobbed his plea: 'Please, Marsa Captain, please jest tell the Gen'l t-t-that I ain't that kind o' a soljer.' "

With Thomas Brown's "rescue," the secret the army had labored to hide finally broke free. In the October 16 *Manila Times*, Brown repeatedly mentioned Fagen, saying that his guerrillas called him "General Fagan." Fame is a matter of timing. On October 26 Fagen and seventy-five rebels waylaid the steam launch *Stonie* as it chugged up the Rio Grande de Pampanga towing a barge of supplies. Fagen's men fired from the east bank until the captain pulled over; they robbed the passengers, took the supplies, and melted away. *The Manila Times* ran the story two days later. This and Brown's account led to the famous front-page headline in the October 29, 1900, *New York Times*: "American Deserter a Filipino General":

> Fagin [*sic*], who holds the rank of General among the insurgents, has sworn special enmity to his former company. Of the twenty men he captured a month ago several have returned. One was killed in a fight, his body being mutilated. Fagin sends messages to his former comrades threatening them with violence if they become his prisoners.

Much of this was wrong, not that it mattered. The army that feared mass desertions by black soldiers now feared Fagen's influence even more, and it cracked down. Anyone whose path had crossed Fagen's became a target. Lives were ruined.

Sergeant Major John Calloway was among the first. He'd signed Fagen's reenlistment papers, served with him in Cuba and Nueva Ecija, and wrote signed letters home protesting the plight of Filipinos. On the same day as the *Times*'s front-page story, the army's provost marshal in San Fernando, Captain Arthur Williams, accused the merchant Antonio Consunji of aiding rebels after taking the oath of allegiance, considered treason under martial law. Calloway had made the mistake of mentioning his son Tomas in his letter about army racism that ran in the December 30, 1899, *Richmond Planet*. Did the army read these missives? Enough correspondents to the black press signed their letters "Anonymous" to suggest a fear of surveillance among the men.

When investigators searched Consunji's home in October, they found Calloway's earlier letter to Tomas: in it, he'd admitted to feeling guilt because of "how wrong morally we Americans are" in waging this war. Captain Williams sent the letter to Calloway's commander, sixty-three-year-old Colonel Henry B. Freeman, a stickler for the rules: "The writer is, to say the least, very indiscreet," the provost marshal said.

Colonel Freeman had tried to destroy Calloway once that year, but failed. Six months earlier, in April, Calloway's lover, Mamerta de la Rosa, had joined him in his new station at San Jose; she moved into his house, and at first they carried on a discreet affair. It became less discreet on July 12, when they loudly quarreled; by then, she was four months pregnant. This came to the attention of the adjutant, First Lieutenant C. H. Miller. "A native woman here lives openly with [Calloway] in the same house," Miller reported, "but it is well known to every one that they are not married." Such living arrangements were common in the army, and many white officers lived openly with a *querida*. Army Surgeon Wilfrid Turnbull noted that "each trooper had a woman, and the 1st sgts had two." The adjutant's letter was filed, and no action was taken.

By October, times had changed. Though Calloway married Mamerta, the army's stance toward fraternization had hardened. Filipino women were thought the enemy's most effective recruiters: sex formed a bond stronger than any army oath, and Freeman wouldn't allow it on his watch. He discovered a glitch in Calloway's records: although his March 7, 1899, reenlistment papers said he was married, the June 1900 census said he was not. Freeman charged Calloway with bigamy, but the sergeant major was acquitted "on account of lack of technical proof."

Later that same month, Provost Marshal Williams forwarded Calloway's letter. This was stronger ammo, and Freeman rushed Consunji's letter to Wheaton. "Sergeant Major Calloway is one of those half-baked mulattoes whose education has fostered his self-conceit to an advanced degree," he wrote, revealing the source of his hatred. Not only was Calloway a bigamist, but "he is likely to step into the Philippino [*sic*] ranks should a favourable opportunity occur."

This was a palpable fear. If, as Stephen Bonsal wrote, "Negro soldiers were in closer sympathy with the aims" of natives than "with those of their white leaders," the Eighth Army might find itself saddled with a frightening number of David Fagens. Calloway's letter to an accused rebel sympathizer seemed to manifest that fear. Freeman recommended that Calloway be sent to Manila "for safe-keeping, until he can be discharged without honor and deported." Wheaton passed the report to MacArthur, adding that Calloway might "desert to the assassins infesting this Department if he has the opportunity." On November 22, 1900, MacArthur agreed. Two days later, Wheaton had Calloway arrested and sent to Manila's Bilibid Prison.

Calloway's downfall was swift and sure. On December 11 he wrote that his only guilt was to feel pity for the centuries of suffering the Filipinos had endured. "I too was a member of an oppressed race." He felt "a cord of sympathy" for another "colored race" whose human rights were being trampled. An "Inspector General Willis" visited Calloway in his cell, and after several interviews concluded that he was "a bright man, with an adroit mind, a very good command of language, and a marked skill in evading a question and misconstruing words." Though Calloway insisted that his letter was "nothing more than a friendly, sympathetic missive," Willis saw it differently. If the letter expressed sympathy, it was "with the Filipino insurrection." He recommended deportation under restraint and a dishonorable discharge.

And so it was done. Calloway fought back, citing his meritorious service, filing letters of support from white officers, to no avail. On December 15, 1900, MacArthur signed papers busting him down to private; he was locked in the hold of the USS *Sherman* bound for San Francisco—where, in February 1901, he'd be discharged without honor or hearing. MacArthur wrote the War Department: "It is very apparent that [Calloway] is disloyal and should he remain in these islands, he would undoubtedly commit some act of open treason and perhaps join the insurrection out and out. One man of the 24th Infantry by the name of David Fagin [*sic*] has already done so and as a leader among the insurrectos is giving great trouble by directing guerrilla raids."

Like David Fagen, all black soldiers revealed their guilt by the color of their skin.

At ten p.m. on Monday, October 15, the luxury liner *Minnehaha* docked in New York after a week's transit from England. The gangplank descended. Newsmen swarmed.

Mark Twain had come home. In a few minutes, he appeared at the top, clad in his trademark bow tie and white linen suit, an unkempt corona of white hair framing his face, the white walrus mustache plastered upon a bemused grin. He'd been a newsman himself and understood such frenzies. It was better, and safer, to stay above it when possible. Some shouted questions concerning remarks he'd made about the Philippine War before sailing.

There was no denying it. On October 5 he'd told a *World* reporter that he thought the war "a quagmire"; better to rule the islands "according to Filipino ideals." He'd thought the Cuban campaign had been a worthy effort, the only war in history he'd ever considered necessary, but the advent of the Philippine Insurrection made him uneasy, and by 1900 he felt alarmed. "I have tried hard, and yet I cannot for the life of me comprehend how we got into that mess," he said. "Perhaps we could have avoided it—perhaps it was inevitable that we should come to be fighting the natives of those islands—but I cannot understand it, and have never been able to get to the bottom of the origin of our antagonism to the natives. I thought we should act as their protector—not try to get them under our heel."

Now, standing atop the gangplank, it was time to defend his words. "You've been quoted here as an anti-imperialist!" a man with the *Chicago Tribune* shouted. "Well, I am," he replied.

One can imagine the scene. The old humorist would cock his head slightly, as he did when pressed for impromptu brilliance onstage. "A year ago I wasn't," he admitted. "I thought it would be a great thing to give a whole lot of freedom to the Filipinos. But I guess now that it's better to let them give it to themselves."

"Then you're a Bryan man?"

"I guess not," he said. "I'm rather inclined toward McKinley, even if he is an imperialist. But don't ask political questions," he pleaded, for he'd just returned and still felt uninformed.

With these words, Twain edged into the Great Debate, giving a string of interviews that added new zeal to doubts about America's future. When he'd read the Treaty of Paris, he continued that night, he'd suddenly realized that America had gone to the Philippines "to conquer, not to redeem." So yes, maybe he *was* an Anti-Imperialist: "I am opposed to having the eagle put its talons on any other land."

Twain would change direction by Election Day, refusing to endorse either candidate and dropping his tepid support for McKinley. That could not save William Jennings Bryan. Roosevelt stormed cross-country calling Anti-Imperialists traitors. *All* Americans voting for Bryan were traitors. At least one paper compared them to David Fagen. "It is obvious to every candid mind that this fellow Fagin [*sic*] is doing openly and with arms in his hands on the field precisely what Bryan is doing with voice and pen, if not in a more substantial way, to this country," wrote the Rochester, New York, *Democrat and Chronicle*. Fagen was "simply campaigning for Bryan in the Philippines instead of in the United States."

Though poll results are hard to interpret, most historians believe that prosperity, along with McKinley's "full dinner pail," trumped moral questions. Bryan's threat to replace the gold standard with "free silver" scared too many supporters away, Twain included. He stayed home on Election Day, paralyzed by the same dilemma that froze Grover Cleveland and Andrew Carnegie. "Bryan was all wrong on the money question, so I didn't vote for him," Twain told New York's Century Club. But news from the Philippines caused "a strong aversion to sending our bright boys out there to fight with a disgraced musket under a polluted flag, so I didn't vote for the other fellow." When several club members rose in protest, Twain did not respond. But later he wrote, "The standard of honor is shrinking pretty fast everywhere."

McKinley won by about 861,000 votes: he received 7,219,525 ballots; Bryan, 6,358,727. Though it was the Republicans' greatest numerical victory since 1872, it was also the most expensive presidential election up to that point: one report put the cost at $5 million, or more than $176 million in 2022 dollars. On the whole, voters stayed away. Although the national population on November 6, 1900, had increased by five million since 1896, only 65,000 more votes were cast. McKinley called it a vindication of his policies, and specifically a mandate for imperialism.

Election Day in San Isidro was dreary. The suspense depressed Funston, so he wrote Roosevelt to wish him luck and say he believed that the resistance only continued in hopes that Bryan would win. "What an awful shame it would be to give up and go home like a whipped cur, leaving the thousands of natives who have befriended us to be butchered by the cruel and bloodthirsty [rebels]," he said. On December 24 Roosevelt answered: "Thank heaven, the country did not vote on the Bedlamite and traitor side. I felt as though this canvas was a repetition of that of 1864. Now I do hope we can settle matters in the Philippines in one shape or other."

The news of McKinley's victory hit insurgents like "a boxer who receives a crushing blow over the heart," wrote Leon Wolff: they staggered, and from this point the insurrection gradually lost power. Yet the administration had hoped for such a dramatic collapse, and by year's end, MacArthur was forced to give Washington a bitter dose of reality. "Expectations, based on results of election, have not been realized," he wired Adjutant General H. C. Corbin: "Process of pacification . . . still very slow."

The fact that McKinley's reelection did not end the fighting seemed to startle America. It certainly startled MacArthur and Taft. It was time to crack down, and on December 20 MacArthur officially declared martial law. The war must stop, by any means.

It was during this period that John Calloway was shipped to San Francisco. Between December 20 and February 1, 1901, six hundred suspected collaborators were arrested in Manila, hundreds more in the provinces, and seventy-nine captives were executed. The Philippine press was muzzled, and those that fought back were shut down: *La Patria*, *La Democracia*, and *La Alborada* in Manila; *La Opinion* in Iloilo; *Nuevo Dia* so heavily censored it appeared with blank pages. In mid-January 1901 MacArthur arrested Mabini for allegedly writing to guerrillas; he was deported to Guam along with forty-eight other prominent Filipinos and eleven unlucky servants. They left Manila aboard the *Rosencrans* on Wednesday, January 16, 1901. Americans "segregate us, like lepers, from social contact with our fellow men," he told his brother.

But word did not reach Fagen that the war should end. A longing to catch and string him up consumed Funston's command; every chance rumor sent troops pouring in the dead of night to his newest supposed location. On October 2, forty men of the Twenty-Second swooped upon the barrio of San Pablo, where Lacuna, Fagen, and a hundred guerrillas were said to be. They barged into the village after twenty minutes of fighting and found Fagen's raincoat and a tin cup etched with his name. They also found a cache of Lacuna's papers that would later prove invaluable. But no Fagen. Over the next days, Fagen is seen in multiple barrios, and on October 10 Captain C. C. Crittenden of the Twenty-Second comes close: this night seems to be the one in which Fagen tarried in a village on the banks of the Rio Chico de Pampanga. "Fagen was very fond of carousals and drinking," José Alejandrino wrote, and after finding a guitar, he and others "began to drink and serenade the women of the place." Just before dawn, a guerrilla shook Fagen awake. "He was certain that he heard footsteps and the voices of American soldiers." They heard voices again. Fagen leaped out the window into their midst; the Americans could not fire for fear of hitting their own. Fagen had no such compunctions: he shot his way out and escaped into the trees.

In November 1900 Eda Funston arrived from Oakland, accompanied by her younger sister, Magdalene Blankart, and two other officers' wives. Jack Ganzhorn was dazzled when they appeared. "They were the only white women I had seen since leaving the United States," and although he'd encountered "beautiful women among the Spanish and native Filipinos, I was getting lonesome for my own kind." Somehow their appearance in "this land of sudden death" made him think of his own pioneer mother "and how she must have felt during those fear-ridden days under the Apache menace." That night, the threat came home. Fagen sent taunting notes to Funston; he could be heard yelling Funston's name outside town. In a letter to her family, Eda described a night when Fagen was rumored to attack at half past midnight and Freddie set out extra watchmen: "We went to bed with some of our clothes on and waited. At about twelve there were three shots fired by one of the sentries in the outpost, but that was all."

An officer's wife was expected to stay calm, but worry got to her. One night, as the scouts prepared to depart, "Mrs. Funston followed the General out of headquarters and stepped to where I sat on my horse," Ganzhorn wrote. She whispered to him, "You'll take care of my General for me, won't you?" Ganzhorn "swallowed hard" and saluted her. "Not only I, Mrs. Funston," he answered. "Every man of the Scouts will always side him, till we've busted the last shell."

But on December 5 Ganzhorn nearly broke his word. As they rode into the village of Rio Chico, Fagen waited. The Americans had 70 riders; the guerrillas about 100. Funston's men dismounted and charged through the village until emerging on the other side. The guerrillas waited on the far riverbank, and for the first time, Funston saw his nemesis: "I got a fairly good look at the notorious Fagen at a distance of about a hundred yards, but unfortunately had already emptied my carbine." But Fagen still had ammo, and he aimed. A Sergeant Schwartz stood ten feet away and was hit in the face "with a sickening plunk." Ganzhorn watched in horror as Schwartz clapped his hands to his face and "saw the blood spurt out between his fingers." He whirled and "fell face down between two rows of sweet potatoes." Ganzhorn turned him over, thinking his eyes would be shot out, but the high-powered Mauser round had "passed clear through his head" and in time, "Sergeant Schwartz got completely well." Yet the placement in his memoirs showed that Ganzhorn realized the same thing could have happened to Funston.

The "black renegade's" continued survival reflected upon Funston's reputation as a soldier and a man. His own men would never say so, but Eda and Magdalene would say it, at least in jest. That Christmas Day, the women threw a dinner party for the officers, complete with "manufactured" souvenirs and prepared "dainties." Eda had a brainstorm: knowing her husband's obsession with his tormentor, "what, then, could he wish more than the capture of Fagan [*sic*] for a Christmas present," she wrote in *The Iola Register*: "From black cloth we made a doll with black darning cotton for hair, dressed it as a soldier and, with a rope suggestively tied around its neck we presented the deserter, with all becoming formality, to the general for his Christmas gift." Fred was "delighted with the 'capture,'" she said.

Her sister Magdalene wrote a "jingle":

By Jimminy Christmas, Fred
What's this I see?

Poor old Fagen
Hanged to a tree?
How did it happen
This is queer
Tell us about it
We're dying to hear.

They all thought it a grand joke. "After the laughter subsided," they filed to the dining room for shrimp salad, deviled ham sandwiches, candy, salted almonds, and other delicacies.

27

Winners and Martyrs

Every war has winners. The price of victory in lives and matériel can resemble defeat, but individuals can and do emerge from war with untouchable auras. William McKinley seemed one such winner, transforming the brief Cuban campaign into an American Empire. His second inauguration, on March 4, 1901, was apparent proof: the American people had spoken. Yet the real winner would be the "man of destiny" standing behind him on that blustery day. The war elevated Roosevelt to fame, adventure, a governorship, the vice presidency, soon the presidency, and eventually the Nobel Peace Prize. "How particularly gratifying . . . it all came out," Samuel B. M. Young burbled in a letter, "and rosier than our enthusiasms had pictured it."

Would there be a comparable winner in the Philippine War? At first it seemed to be Dewey, but his presidential episode punctured that image. Not one commanding general emerged untainted. The American soldier, deemed a hero at San Juan Hill, was now a butcher and torturer; Buffalo Soldiers, hailed for their sacrifice at Siboney, were now deserters or enemy sympathizers.

If one person seemed this war's "winner," it would be the "Little Guy." Funston had won the Medal of Honor, been promoted to brigadier general, and commanded the Fourth District in Central Luzon. Articles were written of him, poems published, songs composed. Roosevelt wanted him to run for office after the war. Allegations of war crimes rolled off him like oil.

One contributor to this fame was a new medium. In 1899 the film studio of Thomas Alva Edison had produced a series of films on the Philippine War. Although these reenactments appear crude today, they were quite popular then. The experiment that started with the Kinetograph version of San Juan Hill had been renamed "wargraphs" by 1899; Edison made six in his West Orange, New Jersey, studio, all depicting the war's early days. Five were released in June 1899, and in each, the Kansans charge the enemy and always win. The sixth and longest was released three months later, on September 23, 1899. Titled *Col. Funston Swimming the Bagbag River*, it runs 1,000 feet, as compared to the 75-foot June films. It starts at a riverbank where Funston undresses for a swim. On the opposite shore, Filipino soldiers peep from bushes and shoot; Funston swims across as a raft of Kansans also crosses. Funston reaches shore and dons his uniform. Filipinos retreat. The U.S. flag is unfurled, and Filipinos flee. Funston rides a white horse; his soldiers march from right to left. Americans conquer territory.

Strange as it sounds, this was better film coverage than that afforded the Rough Riders. The film made Funston a star, but stars can quickly fade. He was still a volunteer, and in April the War Department planned to replace all volunteer units with Regulars. When the Twentieth Kansas mustered out in September 1899, Eda and he had talked about this possibility. What sort of career suited a war hero? He fantasized becoming a college professor or a businessman. For every fantasy, Eda gave the same answer: an officer's billet was more dependable.

He must somehow rise in the Regulars. But how? Catching Fagen might do it, but all attempts failed. The irony was that Funston enjoyed greater success at this moment than during his entire year of fighting. In early 1901 he captured 150 rifles, as many as during the previous four months. Colonel Teodoro Sandico's men dispersed; Major Tomas Taguntun was killed on the Malimba River; guerrillas surrendered. In February and March, Funston's and Grant's men in the Fourth and Fifth districts pushed deep into the mountains, burning villages, confiscating supplies. On February 25 Grant wired, "Almost no rice has gone to the mountains and the insurgents cannot live in the mountains during the coming rainy season. All rice belonging to the insurgents has either been captured or destroyed."

None of this mattered outside Luzon, where Aguinaldo and Fagen's continued freedom was the litmus test of the army's competence, or lack thereof. The front page of the February 26 *Manila Times* announced that the "daring" renegade had come to town: "Fagan [*sic*] the renegade has added another chapter to his notorious career and apparently is as daring as he is unscrupulous. Sunday he visited one of his old haunts in Manila, and was identified; but during the interval between his identification and his attempted capture, he gave his pursuers the slip."

This had become a public relations war, with American officials ultrasensitive to all criticism, no matter how minor. The flap over "A. Ross" is a good example: an obscure junior cashier in the Manila branch of the Hong Kong and Shanghai Bank, he'd written home to the *South Australian Register* describing American misbehavior. *The Manila Times* demanded an apology, diplomats demanded justice, and the bank transferred Ross to another country. Even statistics were flash points: the total deaths in Manila from January 1900 to January 1901 came to 10,343, compared with 7,161 in larger Hong Kong. Public health officials feared disease, but censors squelched all discussion of cause. Instead, officials blamed the tropical clime.

Censorship might work in the islands, but not back home. During this period, Mark Twain emerged as the premier Anti-Imperialist. His iconoclasm on the *Minnehaha* had been news, but many figured this was just Twain being Twain. But on December 12, when introducing Winston Churchill at the Waldorf-Astoria Hotel, he showed his colors. Churchill was touring the United States to lecture about his exploits in the Boer War. Some Anti-Imperialists boycotted the event, but Twain agreed to be toastmaster. He revealed for the first time a pattern he would refine: compliment the honoree, tell a witty story, and pounce when the audience felt at ease. This night began with a rambling salute to the shared values of the United States and Great Britain, some satirical observations, and then he plunged the dagger: "I think that England sinned when she got herself into a war in South Africa which she could have avoided, just as we have sinned in getting into a similar war in the Philippines." Nervous laughter rippled around the banquet table; Churchill smiled uneasily. "Mr. Churchill by his father is an Englishman, by his mother he is an American, no doubt a blend that makes the perfect man. England and America, we are kin. And now we are also kin in sin, there is nothing more to be desired. The harmony is perfect—like Mr. Churchill himself, whom I now have the honor to present to you."

Churchill did not rise to Twain's bait. He'd brought criticism upon himself five years earlier when remarking about his small part in the Cuban revolution. Although an imperialist, he chose not to go toe-to-toe with "the American," and he stuck to his South African experiences. He'd noticed strong Anti-Imperialist views in the audience, not just in Twain. "There is a strong pro-Boer feeling," he wrote to his mother, "particularly in New York."

Twain followed this up in *The Minneapolis Journal* on December 29 with the brief but caustic "Salutation Speech from the Nineteenth Century to the Twentieth, Taken Down in Shorthand by Mark Twain," one of several imagined salutations by famous men: "I bring you the stately matron named Christendom, returning bedraggled, besmirched, and dishonored, from pirate raids in Kiachow, Manchuria, South Africa, and the Philippines, with her soul full of meanness, her pocket full of boodle, and her mouth full of pious hypocrisies."

Twain's new, fierce focus gave him new literary life. The Anti-Imperialist League, broken after Bryan's defeat, discovered in his eviscerating voice a reason to live. When the New York league asked Twain to be vice president, he accepted: though he'd be "a useless because nonlaboring" vice president, he'd also be "prodigiously endowed with sympathy for the cause."

Twain would hold the post until his death, in 1910. Encouraged by his "salutation speech," he wrote "To the Person Sitting in Darkness," published in the February 1901 *North American Review*. Like the salutation, this attacked the world's "civilizing powers": Britain in South Africa, the great powers in China, "the Blessings-of-Civilization Trust" doling out "Glass Beads and Theology, and Maxim Guns and Hymn Books." He regretted the "bad mistake" America made in the Philippines. If the game had been played "according to the American rules," Dewey would have sailed off after destroying the Spanish fleet, leaving Filipinos "to set up the form of government they might prefer."

But this did not happen. America had strayed so far from her ideals that the Person Sitting in Darkness might think, "There must be two Americas: one that sets the captive free, and one that takes a once-captive's new freedom away from him, and picks a quarrel with him with nothing to found it on; then kills him to get his land." Perhaps this was too crude; facts must be reshuffled and history re-explained. In the end, all would be well. The Blessings-of-Civilization Trust would bestow the magic symbols that healed all ills: the Liberator's Sword, the Slave's Broken Chains. To these would be added a new flag for the Philippines—the U.S. flag, but "with the white stripes painted black and the stars replaced by the skull and cross-bones."

Despite its length, "To a Person Sitting in Darkness" was reprinted in scores of papers and magazines; in hundreds more as excerpts; and in 125,000 pamphlets distributed by the league. Almost daily, a newspaper ran an editorial: Twain, gushed the February 3, 1901, *Springfield Daily Republic*, had not only become the country's leading Anti-Imperialist, but "the most dreaded critic of the sacrosanct person in the White House." Andrew Carnegie called Twain's piece the "New Gospel of Saint Mark." For 1901–1902, he was the league's highest-profile star: he gave speeches and interviews, wrote letters and pamphlets, worked on satires of the "damned human race," and toasted the unwary. Late that year, he opened a dinner at the Lotos, his favorite New York club. Roosevelt was present, an opportunity he couldn't turn down: the nation's premier imperialist and its most zealous anti-imperialist, together, and Twain had the floor. He started with a story about how a "reverend gentleman" accused him of treason for his attacks on the Philippine War—exactly as Roosevelt had targeted Democrats, something Twain left unsaid. "If I had my just deserts I would not be a guest here," the reverend added, though "I should be a guest somewhere else maybe, or be dangling from a lamp-post somewhere."

What was the nature of patriotism, Twain asked, turning toward Roosevelt and the crowd. Was it that point where we stood by the flag and stopped thinking "about whether the nation was right or wrong?" Was it treason to disagree? What was the true flag: Was it the one we'd grown up with, or the new one, where skulls and crossbones replaced the stars?

Twain didn't stop the war crimes, but some patriotic cant had the wind knocked from its sails. Even Roosevelt's enthusiasm flagged. He confided to the New York attorney Frederic Coudert that although it was our duty to civilize the Philippines, he wondered whether we were "fortunate or unfortunate in having to hold them." It was a remarkable admission, one he would never state publicly: we must never again assimilate a land whose people were capable of self-government unless they wanted it—"and not necessarily even then." Colonies meant profit and power, but the obligations were many and wearing—and profits went to the already rich and powerful few.

One martial fantasy rarely changes: seize the leader, and all is won. Fagen might be Funston's obsession, but Emilio Aguinaldo was the army's. His "capture had been the one great consummation most devoutly wished," wrote James Blount: while Aguinaldo lived, Filipinos believed "that pro-American tendencies were treason . . . possibly for years to come." And thus, said Blount, "each and every one of General MacArthur's 70,000 men was, and had been since 1899, on the *qui vive* to make his own personal fortunes secure for life, and gain lasting military distinction, by taking any sort of chances to capture Aguinaldo."

Yet ever since his December 1899 disappearance, no American knew his location. That didn't stop the rumors. In January 1900 Funston had heard he'd taken refuge near the border of Nueva Vizcaya and Nueva Ecija; he galloped north with his scouts and found nothing. Private Milton Nixon of the Thirty-Third Volunteers reported on June 13, 1900, that they'd killed him in a mountain village named Sagada: "An important looking man was shot off a white horse just as the Filipinos were escaping." Manila papers declared it "very probable" that he was dead. The mountain tribesmen who tried so often to kill him finally deemed him a "supernatural man," wrote Simeon Villa: "He flies through the air, and . . . ordinarily stays with the thunder."

Aguinaldo stayed in the Cagayan Valley until American troops groped too close on May 22, 1900. He followed the Cagayan River south into Isabela Province where, again, he was greeted as a saint: the townspeople of Enrile and Tuguegarao threw a ball that lasted more than eleven hours. That spring, he renewed contact with his commanders, sending coded instructions, assuring the faithful that he lived. In the first week of June, his group stumbled upon some empty huts outside Naguilian, which they christened *Tierra Virgen.* They stayed two months and twenty-one days. Aguinaldo had contracted malaria, bronchitis, and stomach problems during his odyssey, but now he could recuperate: he sent raiding parties to U.S. outposts, sent couriers to his generals. Newspapers came with the mail: he no doubt read about the other hunted man, David Fagen, but for all their fame, there would never be documentation or even rumors to suggest contact between the two. He exhorted his people to endure; wrote Mabini to sue for peace if America offered freedom. He learned that his son, whom he'd thought dead of smallpox, was alive and well.

But on August 26 he heard that U.S. cavalrymen had entered a nearby village and planned to attack *Tierra Virgen.* After a session of torture, a wounded rebel agreed to lead them to Aguinaldo. It was time to flee. He left behind nearly fifty soldiers and headed east with sixteen sharpshooters, Simeon Villa, Dr. Santiago Barcelona, and two other officers. They crept at night through the Isabella plain, ghosting past two mounted search parties; they entered the Sierra Madres on September 1 and traveled north along rivers and ridges. On Friday, September 6, they entered Palanan, an isolated town of crumbling huts, three hours west of the Pacific Ocean.

Their new home lay on a level plain bisected by a wide river; a jungle path led into the mountains behind them. Villagers knew only that some nationalist soldiers sought residence; in return, they'd rebuild the crumbling town. Residents greeted the newcomers with food and drink and in another three days threw a party. They'd originally lived close to the coast, but fled here for fear of invaders; they preferred these primitive conditions to submission "to the foreign yoke," they said. Aguinaldo felt safe. The nearest town, Casiguran, lay ninety miles south; the closest U.S garrison lay another sixty-nine miles southwest at Baler. The road here from town was long and difficult, and spies could spot anyone drawing near. The only other trail wound through the mountains to the coast; this, too, was manned by sentries. They all adopted false names: Dr. Barcelona was introduced as their chief, "Capt. Santos Baltasar"; Aguinaldo was his secretary, "Lt. Esteban"; Simeon Villa was "Senor Alvaro," a sergeant and hospital steward. They rebuilt the town in two weeks, and on September 19 heard that a steamer with arms and ammo had anchored to the east. They hiked to the beach and swam for the first time in the Pacific Ocean.

For the next six months, a comforting regularity ruled their lives. Couriers came and went laden with orders and letters; balls were thrown; soldiers drilled and watched the trails. It became apparent that the Americans had heard rumors of Aguinaldo but could never pinpoint his location: soldiers marched from Casiguran or Ambatuan but always turned back. If anything, Aguinaldo needed reinforcements, and on January 15, 1901, he sent Private Cecilio Segismundo south with twenty letters for his generals in Central Luzon. Send four hundred men, he said. He trusted Segismundo: he'd served the Spaniards as a native policeman, but he'd joined the Katipunan and became Major Nazario Alhambra's messenger at the start of the war. Simeon Villa drafted a pass directing *presidentes* of the towns Segismundo would visit to render him aid. His party included a sergeant and four privates; his southern route headed inland over the Sierra Madres into Nuvea Ecija.

But Segismundo's mission fell apart quickly. In the plains outside Baler, he ran into an ambush that killed two of his party. The rest fled, but he continued, starving and alone. He climbed through a mountain pass into northeast Nueva Ecija and the hill town of Pantabangan. He begged the local mayor for help, presuming fealty. But this was one of the few mayors loyal to the invaders, and he coaxed the weakened courier to give in. How long must you starve? he said. Late on the night of February 9, 1901, he took Segismundo to the garrison manned by a company of the Twenty-Fourth and handed Aguinaldo's letters to its commander, Lieutenant J. D. Taylor. The lieutenant took one look, wired Funston, and two days later took his captive to San Isidro.

Funston could not believe his luck. The dispatches were written in code, so he deciphered them with Lazaro Segovia, a former Spanish secret service officer turned *insurrecto* who then surrendered to the Americans. Segovia could read Spanish, English, Tagalog, and a smattering of Malay: Aguinaldo's cipher transformed every dispatch into jumbled nonsense, but one Malay word furnished the key. It took three hours to translate the dispatches after that, and then "we rested, smoked a cigarette, and took a drink." Each dispatch was signed by "Pastor" or "Colon Magdalo," two known pseudonyms of Aguinaldo's: one to Lacuna ordered him to hunt down all bandits in his province and punish them "severely"; another asked whether his followers despaired after "Emperor" McKinley's reelection. One was especially intriguing—a dispatch ordering his cousin, General Baldomero Aguinaldo, to replace José Alejandrino as Central Luzon's commander and to send him four hundred men whom he could deploy through Isabela Province and the Cagayan Valley. No document revealed Aguinaldo's hideout, but the one to his cousin revealed that Segismundo knew the location and could lead reinforcements there.

Funston interrogated the luckless courier, "by exactly what means, history does not reveal," wrote Edwin Wildman. There are hints: though Funston wrote in his memoirs that Segismundo talked after enjoying a good meal, he admitted privately that he resorted to more "forceful means." Near the end of his life, when all other combatants had died, Aguinaldo wrote in *A Second Look at America* that Segismundo said he'd been waterboarded twice and had finally broken down. He admitted that *El Presidente* hid in Palanan, an isolated mountain village on Luzon's rugged northeast coast, surrounded by a few loyal officers and guards.

That night, Funston couldn't sleep, and at four a.m. he jumped out of bed. What if he went after Aguinaldo himself? If he succeeded, his army future might be assured. Everything hinged on Aguinaldo's call for four hundred reinforcements sent in small groups. He recalled that when he'd raided Lacuna's camp in October, he'd found the general's correspondence and a large quantity of official stationery sporting the letterhead *Brigada Lacuna.* He'd wondered how to use the stationary ever since. What if they forged Lacuna's signature on it and used it to catch Aguinaldo? It was the kind of swashbuckling exploit he'd suggested to Calixto García years earlier, but always as a suicidal charge. This would be different. The plan taking shape in his early-morning mind must be clever—not one of his stronger points, he realized.

He roused Segismundo. Could he land a secret force on the coast and march to Palanan? No, it would be seen: the courier described the failed

American probe months earlier. *Any* steamer landing within a hundred miles would be spotted by Aguinaldo's spies.

So Funston planned an inside job. They'd go as the soldiers Aguinaldo requested, and to do that Funston picked eighty-one Macabebe Scouts who spoke Tagalog. They'd wear peasant garb like insurgents and would carry captured rebel Mausers. Though army officers would still lead, they'd be disguised as prisoners: in addition to Funston and aide Burton Mitchell, they'd include Captain Henry Newton from Manila, who knew the northern coast, and the tall, gangling Hazzard brothers—Captain Russell and Lieutenant Oliver—who'd organized the Macabebes. Finally, they'd need rebel officers known to Aguinaldo: Hilario Tal Placido, who'd been captured in May; Lieutenant Gregorio Cadhit, who'd surrendered with Joaquin Natividad; and former lieutenant Dionisio Bató. All had taken the oath of allegiance, which now would be tested. Segismundo would go, as well as Segovia, who'd assume the role of commander.

When Funston outlined his part in the plot, Segovia blurted, "The devil, General, this is rather strong." Funston grinned: "Not at all. It is very easy. You know Aguinaldo?" He did, and he did not think *El Presidente* knew of his surrender, as at that time, he'd been on the run. Funston sent his plan to Manila, and on February 16 met with MacArthur and Wheaton. While the former believed the scheme might succeed, Wheaton did not. Nevertheless, both gave it their seal of approval. Funston returned to San Isidro to polish final details.

A plan like this must be held in strict confidence if the plotters hoped to survive. Yet word leaked out. Funston's scheme seemed an open secret in San Isidro, and the leak may have come from his own household. On the day Funston returned from Manila, Magdalene Blankart described in a letter to her mother the plan to catch "Aggis." Success would be "a feather in Fred's cap," she crowed. On February 26 Eda wrote that "Fred expects to go on his trip to the other side of the Island in about a week." In the prison, the recently captured Major Crisanto de la Fuente warned Aguinaldo on a piece of cigarette paper:

> My dear Presidente:
>
> I have definite information that Colonel Hilario Tal Placido and that officer Lazaro Segovia have met with the American army, and

> there is a rumor, which is true, that these officers will go to your place, accompanied by soldiers.

He smuggled the note to a confederate with instructions to pass it to Aguinaldo, then passed a copy to another *amigo*. Despite Funston's sloppiness, neither note reached Palanan.

On March 6, Funston's party boarded the gunship *Vicksburg* for Manila. That afternoon, he visited Malacañang Palace for one last conference with MacArthur. "Funston," he said, "this is a desperate undertaking. I fear I shall never see you again." He also had bad news: he'd received orders a few days earlier to send Funston home. Like all volunteers, he was to be mustered out, but MacArthur had delayed the departure by saying he was needed for "special duty." The news hit Funston hard. He'd always known of the recall, "but this, coming at the time that it did, filled my heart with bitterness." It was the same treatment he'd received in Tampa, "and nothing but a feeling of the loyalty that I owed to my division and department commanders made me willing to go on with the apparently thankless and all but hopeless task."

The *Vicksburg* steamed south from Manila Bay, rounded Batangas Province, and continued east through the San Bernardino Strait linking the Pacific Ocean to the Sibuyan Sea. On March 7 Funston revealed full details to the group, and the three former rebels were "thunderstruck": they'd already been branded traitors, yet now Funston planned to use them for the most traitorous act imaginable! Funston reminded them that since they'd taken the oath, they could participate or die: "If they were faithful they would be well-rewarded, if not, there would be but one penalty and that would be inflicted, if it was the last thing done." For the next few days, Funston and his officers drilled the actors in their roles. The *Vicksburg* was still chugging north when, on March 9, Eda wrote to her family, "Fred has gone on his expedition by now."

On the moonless night of March 14, they entered the choppy Casiguran Bay. They'd planned to beach aboard some *lantsas*, but all sank in the rough seas. They piled into the *Vicksburg*'s boats and prayed that the gunship could sail from sight before dawn. While boarding, one Macabebe dropped a bolo on his foot and was taken to the infirmary. Another was so terrified that he burrowed belowdecks in some netting and did not emerge until the party was gone. It rained all night, drenching their clothes and rations. Yet the sailors steering the boats landed successfully. If all went as planned, they'd meet again on March 25 off the coast of Palanan. If Funston and his men weren't there, the *Vicksburg* must "land a force and march to the town to ascertain if possible what had become of us"—an admission that they were probably dead.

The men had to march 110 miles through enemy territory. Funston and the Americans wore the blue tunics and khaki leggings of enlisted men; they each carried a towel, comb, and change of socks in a half-rolled blanket. The Macabebes exchanged their Krags for captured Mausers and wore peasant clothes. Like rebels, each carried a day's portion of rice. They wended along the coast and at noon discovered some fishermen beached at a creek mouth; Segovia wrote a letter to Casiguran's *presidente*, claiming to be a detachment sent north by Urbano Lacuna to meet the "Dictator": "I beg of you to have sufficient food ready as my soldiers are greatly fatigued, having marched for the last fifteen days over mountains." As the fishermen cut across the bay with their note, they continued along the beach. At about four p.m. a lone guide appeared to bring them in.

"We entered the town in great style," Funston said. Casiguran consisted of about a hundred thatch huts surrounded on three sides by groves and farmland; they were led to an old Spanish church, where Segovia and his men were welcomed as heroes and the village band belted out a tune. The Americans were stared at with cold curiosity: they were the first the villagers had ever seen. They rested two days, during which time they sent two forged letters on Lacuna's letterhead to Aguinaldo. One, purportedly from Lacuna, said that by order of Baldomero Aguinaldo he was sending these eighty men under the command of Segovia, Tal Placido, and Segismundo. The second, purportedly by Tal Placido, recounted how his men had encountered a small American survey party, killed two, and wounded three, who escaped. But they captured five, whom they now brought in. Destitute villagers pulled together three days' rations for the seven-day march to Palanan; the vice mayor worried about their chances and drafted twelve villagers to serve as their bearers and guides.

They left at six a.m. on Sunday, March 17. The rain fell daily; they hugged the beach, forced to eat snails, the occasional octopus stranded in tidal pools, and limpets and small fish steamed with donated cracked corn. It was "a revolting mess," Funston said. By the fifth day, they were going without food and reeling from side to side, half-dazed. This "madcap adventure" seemed doomed: Funston regretted that he "had led all these men to such a finish."

But at five p.m. a distant miracle took form. A lone figure had been approaching, though Funston could not trust his eyes. Segovia went forward, and as Funston watched, the man handed over a letter. Segovia limped back and muttered, "It is all right. We have them." The letter, from Simeon Villa to "Lieutenant-Colonel Hilario Tal Placido," advised him not to bring the prisoners to Palanan, as they might recognize the "Dictator." Instead, they must remain eight miles back at Dinundungan, a crossroads with two huts even then being built by an old Tagalog and some younger Negritos. They arrived after dark, "and again we lay down supperless to bed."

Time was running out: the *Vicksburg* would arrive in three days, and by then they must get in and out of Palanan with Aguinaldo. That night, they talked in whispers. Tal Placido wrote a note saying that they'd like to resume their march in the morning, as instructed, but as his men "had not had so much as a grain of rice to eat in the last twenty-four hours," all were too weak to go on. Aguinaldo felt generous: that day, March 22, was his thirty-second birthday, and Palanan was in "gala dress." Arches had been built; festivities included "horse races, dancing, serenades, and amateur theatricals," and now the arrival was the icing. Aguinaldo ordered enough rice to feed 110 starving pilgrims and had it sent down to them.

The rice arrived at 8:30 a.m. and drove their hunger away. Yet an unquiet irony dawned on Funston: the very man he planned to kill or capture had just saved his life. He'd also deceived Casiguran's vice mayor, who'd collected rations that his poor villagers could barely afford. Of all the sins of which Funston had been accused— using the water cure, hanging insurgents, condoning the execution of prisoners—this breach of hospitality would earn him the most loathing back home. Funston's exploit has entered textbooks of international law as a classic "ruse de guerre," and is not considered illegal today. At the time, though, even he called it "dirty."

But with the rice came complications: Aguinaldo was also sending eleven of his personal guard to watch the prisoners in Dinundungan as Tal Placido and the "reinforcements" moved on to Palanan. Again, the party hatched a scheme. The Macabebes would head up the trail early in the morning; an hour later, they'd send back another false, forged message telling their jailer to send the prisoners up, too. When the message arrived, the old Tagalog groused "that he did not see why they had put him to so much trouble if they didn't intend to use the shelters." He let them go up, with two Macabebes left behind to guard the crossroads.

Despite breakfast, Funston and his fellows were so weak that they could barely limp up the trail. Funston had no conception of time: "I had to lie down flat on the ground every few hundred yards to get a rest," he said. Suddenly a Macabebe sergeant burst from the bushes, motioned for silence, and pointed off-trail. They'd just crouched in a stand of bamboo when Aguinaldo's guard walked past, chatting gaily, unaware of the Americans. The guard had come upon Segovia's party minutes earlier, but as he chatted with them about the hard journey, he signaled the sergeant to sprint back and warn Funston.

Aguinaldo waited on his veranda, and at two p.m. spotted Tal Placido crossing the Palanan River. At that point, it was deep and a hundred yards wide; the only way across was by the village's single boat, which held eight men. Tal Placido and Segovia crossed first, telling the others to come up quickly. They'd assemble on the opposite bank and march to the village plaza. Aguinaldo stood outside to greet them with Dr. Barcelona, Simeon Villa, and four others; about twenty of his guard were lined up to greet their guests. Tal Placido and Segovia saluted Aguinaldo, and they mounted the stairs together. Aguinaldo said he'd provided their tired men with food and barracks; he praised them for their "gallantry to have brought me five prisoners."

"Many thanks, my President," Segovia said. "You know that we are ready for everything necessary against the Americans." The nation would reward them, Aguinaldo replied.

Twenty minutes had passed. The Macabebes under Dionisio Bató and Gregorio Cadhit had crossed the river and formed opposite Aguinaldo's honor guard in the square. Segovia descended the stairs and stood at the head of his company; he'd made sure that morning that their rifles were loaded, and they stood at "order arms." Segovia looked up and could see Aguinaldo and his officers outlined in the second-story windows. Tal Placido stood behind Aguinaldo. Segovia raised his sword as if for one final cheer, but instead shouted "*Now*, Macabebes!" The impostors raised their rifles, aimed at the honor guard lined before them, and fired.

The surprise was complete. Two guardsmen died instantly, while the rest bolted. The Macabebes fired in all directions—a riot of gunfire from which even the villagers ran. At first Aguinaldo thought his men were celebrating: he leaned out the window and shouted, "Stop that foolishness! Don't waste your ammunition." But then the "reinforcements" aimed at him. He realized "that the newcomers were enemies," stepped back from the window, and searched for a means of escape. In Tal Placido's account, he'd dropped to the floor when shots first rang out, then jumped up and grabbed Aguinaldo from behind. He was a big man, rather fat, a bulk that would stop anyone. In other accounts, Tal Placido started firing in panic. One of Aguinaldo's bodyguards was hit three times and fell. Other officers jumped from a back window, including Major Nasario Alhambra, commander of Aguinaldo's guard.

The accounts of Dr. Barcelona and Lazaro Segovia are less self-aggrandizing. In these, Segovia and a sergeant ran upstairs together; as Simeon Villa struggled to free his revolver, Segovia shot him through the wrist. Villa turned to flee, and Segovia fired again, the bullet passing from his back to his chest, just above his heart. Aguinaldo drew his revolver, but Barcelona clasped him in his arms and cried, "Don't sacrifice yourself. The country needs your life." Segovia announced, "We are not insurgents, we are Americans. We have taken you by surprise. Surrender unconditionally without offering the slightest resistance. If not, you will be killed." Barcelona answered, "Yes, sir, we surrender," and pulled a white handkerchief from his pocket. "This is the flag of peace," he said.

The shooting was over when Funston arrived. He'd paddled across the Palanan "in frantic haste" while his Macabebes dragged the slain to its banks and threw them in, "to be devoured by the crocodiles which abound there," Bató said. Segovia ran downstairs as Funston limped up, "his face aglow with exultation," clothing spattered with blood. "It is all right," he cried in Spanish. "We have him." Funston climbed the stairs and introduced himself to the man the entire U.S. Army had tried to trap for two years. But Aguinaldo seemed dazed: "Is this not some joke?" he asked. Funston assured him it was not, "though, as a matter of fact, it was a pretty bad one for him." He suddenly sympathized with his captive, something he rarely did with Filipinos: Aguinaldo's "bearing was dignified, and in this moment of his fall there was nothing of the craven." He was "far and away the best Filipino I ever was brought in contact with," Funston later said. They dressed Villa's wounds and searched for insurgent records. Outside, the Macabebes threw their arms around any American who dared venture near.

They rejoiced, yet the *Vicksburg* was not due for another day. Funston placed Aguinaldo, Villa, and Barcelona under guard. At one point, Aguinaldo said it had been Lacuna's forged signature that fooled him. Funston detailed the plot, and Aguinaldo blurted, "What can't you Americans do?" He even wrote Funston a note, "congratulating me on the outcome of the perilous expedition." As vulnerable as Funston was to criticism, he was equally touched by praise. His heart went out to the man: "The pleasantest relations were soon established between captors and captured," he said.

Yet Aguinaldo still tried to escape. According to Villa, the three captives were tended by a Macabebe who'd been assigned as their orderly. Aguinaldo softly urged the man: Change your mind. Think of the future of your country. His persuasive powers were well-documented, especially with peasants: if the Macabebes wished, the Americans "need not be killed but merely captured and imprisoned." Incredibly, the man's heart was touched, like Funston's. He whispered back that he was willing to free him, but only if other Macabebes agreed. The next day, he murmured that he'd convinced "half," but still needed a majority. This never happened, and Aguinaldo's slim hope of a countercoup failed.

Funston never realized how close he'd come to failure. The next morning, on March 25, the party left for Palanan Bay and the *Vicksburg*. Along with the three rebel officers, they took one of Aguinaldo's wounded guards. They reached the beach by noon and spotted a wisp of smoke out at sea. They'd packed a bedsheet from Palanan, and as the gunship drew near, they wigwagged "We have him. Send boats for all." The reply was quick: "Well done."

One last attempt to save Aguinaldo took shape outside Palanan. During the night, Major Alhambra collected those soldiers he could find; another five hundred peasants from surrounding villages had also come up, distressed by the news. Alhambra was still weak from his head wound but apparently running on adrenaline: he feared for Aguinaldo's safety, thought Funston still lingered in Palanan, and told the crowd that they outnumbered the Americans. "Are you ready to die," he cried, "to fight until the last moment?" The assembled cried out: "*Kill the invaders!*"

They rushed to Palanan, passing through the long *cogon* "like mountain people running after wild beasts." Alhambra led, possessed of a fury he thought magical, as if he wore "an amulet and did not care for the shadow of death; his pants were rolled up to the knees and his feet were covered with mud." The mob shouted "Long live the Philippines!" They divided into groups, rushed the police station and convent, ready to free *El Presidente.*

But he was not there. Not a single American or Macabebe remained. Someone said the party had left for the coast, so they followed, screaming Aguinaldo's name. But when they reached the beach, all they saw was the *Vicksburg*'s diminishing smoke on the horizon.

With that, weakness finally consumed Alhambra. His eyes grew red; he felt faint; he sat on a tree root and shook his head. He placed his right hand on his sweat-dotted forehead.

"Forgiveness for the treacherous countrymen," he said, his voice trembling. The mob around him grew quiet, "and a silence, born of hurt and disappointment, reigned."

The *Vicksburg* sailed for three days in a voyage best called subdued. Aguinaldo and his officers were given the captain's quarters and treated like guests of honor. A certain regret comes across, as if even Funston realized that something fragile was broken. "The whole affair was not clean," Funston later told José Alejandrino, who wrote in his memoirs that Funston "asked me about my opinion and I answered him that if I had resorted to a similar ruse against the Americans, I would have been hanged for being a forger . . . My answer drew from him a frank and loud laughter." The guilt-ridden Segismundo admitted that he'd endured the water cure twice before revealing the Palanan hideout. Aguinaldo stayed quiet: what others interpreted as silence was in fact a storm of emotions that ranged from anger to distress to numbness, as if this were a "bad dream from which I would surely waken." Then despair overwhelmed him. The dream of freedom was over. "I had failed my people and my Motherland."

Into this emotional havoc walked Lazaro Segovia. Of those aboard the *Vicksburg*, Segovia spoke longest and most thoroughly about what Aguinaldo might expect in Manila. Would the Americans shoot him or send him to Guam like Mabini? They only shoot criminals, Segovia replied. Concerning Guam, he did not know. A feeling existed that Aguinaldo, if captured alive, stood in the way of Americanization. One solution was exile.

To circumvent this, Segovia seems the first to suggest the wisdom of calling for an end to the war. I am just a prisoner now, Aguinaldo often said in disgust: I can have no effect on those still fighting. Segovia disagreed: "You know only too well . . . that should you speak to [the people] in the name of the country, it would create a great impression. You know the strong hold you have upon the people." What, Aguinaldo asked, was the people's will? Segovia shrugged: *El Presidente* divined their soul better than anyone alive.

The *Vicksburg* anchored in Manila Bay at two a.m. on March 28; four hours later, Aguinaldo, Funston, and some officers boarded the ship's launch and steamed up the Pasig River to Malacañang Palace. Aguinaldo was left in a room under heavy guard while Funston went to find his commander. It was barely daybreak, and MacArthur was still in his dressing gown; he shook Funston's hand, "looked at me in a quizzical way, but did not ask a question," Funston wrote. There had been many wild-goose chases in this war, and MacArthur probably thought this was another. Funston finally told his commander, "Well, I have brought you Don Emilio."

MacArthur's mouth dropped: "Where is he?"

"Right in this house."

MacArthur stuttered, "Wait until I get some clothes on."

Almost immediately MacArthur ordered Funston to stay quiet: the War Department had imposed a blackout, especially on anything Aguinaldo might say about "earlier claims or promises by American officers." There was also the matter of Funston himself: he was thought a glory hound. If he'd lost his life, many would have said "I told you so." Adjutant General Henry Corbin considered him "a boss scout—that's all." On

March 29 a *San Francisco Call* correspondent wrote that the department's general reaction was "Anybody but Funston!"

But the cat was out of the bag. Funston's staff was as publicity-starved as their boss, and they leaked details before the mission ended. On the day the *Vicksburg* retrieved the party, the *Boston Herald* ran a front-page story proclaiming "Funston's Plan to Capture Aguinaldo by Ruse." The *Call* had run the story the previous day, before it was known whether Funston still lived. Most editors waited until March 28–29, after Washington acknowledged the capture. Then the news blared from coast to coast: "Funston, The Captor," roared *The Baltimore Sun*; "Kansans Wild with Joy," led *The New York Times*. Funston's mother stood in her kitchen and said, "I never lost faith in Fred's lucky star." Jayhawkers cried out, "Funston for governor!"

Some coverage grew strange: Hearst's March 28 *Evening Journal* ran the banner headline "Funston's Nerve Took Wily Filipinos Off Their Guard" and focused on physiognomy. "Funston's Typical American Eyes" stare straight ahead beneath the headline, and placed beside it in equal size and type, "Aguinaldo's Remarkable Eyes" glance to the side. Funston's eyes are those of "a woman when he is not stirred up," claims the writer, but "they are deep set, and the softness changes to sternness when he has a difficult job on hand. He is a man absolutely without fear." Aguinaldo's "most remarkable" eyes are "almost of hypnotic power and at times savage. They are coal black and piercing. He has the power to control men with them." Thus, Aguinaldo looks to the side, as his "savage" gaze would be too much for the average reader to withstand.

Not all were enamored, focusing on the means by which the capture occurred. *Life* magazine jeered at Funston's "treachery," while others called his ruse "a violation of the accepted laws of war." The McKinley administration felt worried enough to call in Theodore Woolsey, Yale's expert in international law. Writing in *Outlook*, Woolsey argued that Funston's gambit existed "well within the traditional 'ruses of war.'" Legal or not, it left a bad taste, and the *London Saturday Review* made it emblematic of the entire war:

> There have been more wicked wars than this . . . but never a more shabby war. It is nearly three years since the Americans, having gone

> to war with Spain for the liberties of Cuba, decided that it was their manifest destiny to deprive the Filipinos of their liberty. For some time the Americans quite honestly believed that they were doing a rather noble, self-denying thing; but the cant phrases of three years ago are worn threadbare . . . [Aguinaldo's capture] was effected by a piece of sharp practice thoroughly in keeping with the rest of the war. Of all the curious mixture of sentiments, noble and ignoble, out of which the war with the Filipinos sprang, only the element of hypocrisy seems to have retained its original vigour.

But on the whole, Funston was the hero of the hour. His glory rivaled Dewey's. McKinley urged the reluctant War Department to grant Funston a Regular commission as a brigadier general, the army's youngest at the time and the fulfillment of Eda's dreams. "Well, Funston," MacArthur said, "they do not seem to have thought much in Washington of your performance. I am afraid you have got into trouble." He then handed him the cable with his appointment. All other volunteer officers in the capture got Regular commissions, too, while the Filipinos were given "appropriate rewards in various sums." Not surprisingly, Funston received a second Medal of Honor.

On March 30 Roosevelt congratulated Funston, praising a career "filled with feats of cool courage, iron endurance and gallant daring." He mentions this, he says, because there is no "danger of your head being turned, as poor, gallant Dewey's head was turned," and urges him to stay in the army. As America's reach and influence spread, "we may find ourselves pitted against a big military power where we shall need to develop fighting material at the very onset, and then I am one of many millions who would look with confidence to what you would do." When that day arrived, "I shall hope to be serving under or alongside of you." After all, he thinks he could raise "a brigade of three or four such regiments as I commanded before Santiago."

Wreathed in triumph, Funston returned to San Isidro. Much work remained: Generals Lacuna, Alejandrino, Tinio, and Aguinaldo's cousin Baldomero still ranged through Nueva Ecija. Fagen posted his "love letters." On April 2 Eda's sister wrote home that Fred's promotion meant a longer stay in the Philippines, "but nothing could be better," since Fred was "no business man and now as long as he does his duty he will have plenty and Eda won't have any worry." Funston had given her Aguinaldo's inkstand: "Isn't that great? It is an American ink stand but then Aggie used it." Nevertheless, daily life "rolls along just as before, we eat, sleep, and read all day long."

One question remained: What would the U.S. do with Aguinaldo? Some imperialist editors howled for his death: "It is impossible to forget even now that he directed the burning of Manila and the assassination of all Americans, without distinction of sex," clamored *The Philadelphia Press.* Even Dewey called for executing the man he once called "my good friend, Don Emilio." But cooler heads, including War Secretary Root, knew that Aguinaldo's detention might be a way to end the war. Execution meant martyrdom, the same mistake Spain made with José Rizal. Assimilation was a different matter.

For the next three weeks, Aguinaldo was kept under close guard at Malacañang Palace, but assigned sumptuous quarters and a secretary. His family came to stay. MacArthur, other Americans, and prominent *ilustrados* spoke to him, extolling the prosperity and bright future waiting for him if this war ended. The alternative meant ruin. He'd been captured alive, so he could tell his people to stop fighting—and his people listened to him. Yet for those three weeks, he held his tongue.

On April 19 Aguinaldo made his decision. A few days earlier, he'd asked for an English tutor; his wife and children pressured him to take the oath, since anything less meant exile. That Friday, he swore allegiance to the United States and signed his Proclamation of Formal Surrender. He told his followers to lay down their arms. So many bright hopes had been ground down by a greater force; so many friends and colleagues had died. "There has been enough blood, enough tears, enough desolation," he said, eloquent to the end. "I cannot refuse to heed the voice of a people longing for peace." He put down his pen and retired to his mansion in Kawit, where the Little Republic had begun. For the rest of his life, he wore a black bow tie, in mourning for his country's lost dream.

It would be MacArthur's last triumph. On June 20 Elihu Root relieved him of command. He'd wrangled with Taft for power too long, and Taft had won. Root appointed Adna Chaffee in his place: Chaffee might be a hero for leading U.S. forces against Chinese Boxers, but that would not save him if he threw up obstacles to civilian rule. "We have had a long, hard year with General MacArthur," Taft commented drily. Even MacArthur seemed ready to end the drama: he told subordinates he couldn't stand the strain much longer, and he felt humiliated.

On July 4, 1901, Taft moved into the palace. Arthur MacArthur sailed home.

Nature abhors an empire. Some conquerors knew this instinctively. In 480 BCE, Xerxes I of Persia scourged the sea with three hundred lashes and branded it with hot irons after a storm destroyed his pontoon bridges across the Dardanelles, his invasion route into Greece during the Second Persian War. According to Herodotus, he ordered his men to lash the waters with chains and shout, "You bitter water, your lord lays on this punishment because you have wronged him without a cause, having suffered no evil at his hands."

In the tropics, conquerors strove against an invisible foe. Death seemed part of the land. The isolation of quinine tamed malaria's worst ravages, so that by 1900, yellow fever drew more attention: it was more lethal, threatening to kill America's Caribbean ambitions. Politicians and industrialists had long dreamed of cutting an ocean-linking canal through the Isthmus of Panama, but the French attempt of 1881–88 was abandoned after so many workers died. One of the most terrifying things was that no one knew its cause. "To trap yellow fever is like trying to trap fear," one doctor said. "The murderous Unseen Fiend continues to prance lightly before and around us," a second mourned. Yellow fever is a virus, carried by the *Aedes aegypti* mosquito, then called *Culex quinquefasciatus*; other mosquitoes were later discovered as carriers, able to pass the virus down generations in its eggs. It is believed today that *A. aegypti* originated in West Africa and came to the New World aboard slave ships, the revenge of the enslaved.

And so the United States declared "war" against yellow fever in the same way that Xerxes declared war against the sea. Leonard Wood had established his sanitation protocol as a way to stamp it out; he forbade anyone from uttering the name, insisting that it be called "pernicious malaria" instead. "Fear can kill," he said. "People aren't nearly as afraid of malaria." But rebranding did not help, and by 1900 death rates in occupied Cuba skyrocketed.

U.S. Army Surgeon General George Sternberg vowed to beat the enemy. A near-fatal bout in Pensacola, Florida, began his lifelong obsession with the disease. In 1879, after fever scourged the Mississippi Valley and left more than sixteen thousand dead, the National Board of Health established its first Yellow Fever Commission, tasked with studying the disease in Cuba; the board appointed Sternberg and the Cuban bacteriologists Carlos Finlay and Juan Guitéras. All three would chase Yellow Jack for the next twenty-five years. In 1893 Grover Cleveland promoted Sternberg to surgeon general, and in 1898 Sternberg shifted the frontier doctor Walter Reed from his typhoid investigations to isolating the cause and origin of yellow fever.

Clara Maass had observed these first stages when, in January 1899, she served outside Santiago at Camp San Luis. There she met Juan Guitéras, the Cuban bacteriologist Aristides Agramonte, and Dr. William C. Gorgas, whom nurses called "Dr. Gorgeous." These three ran the tests, while Finlay and Sternberg served as administrators. Though called a boon for Cubans, the real purpose was to save Americans. Often fatal in adults, the disease could cause such mild symptoms in children that it sometimes went unnoticed and could create lifelong immunity. Thus, in Cuba, where yellow fever was endemic, the disease was of little concern; those who survived a childhood infection were immune. Enteritis, meningitis, malaria, and pneumonia took more Cuban lives than yellow fever; tuberculosis was a leading cause of death, killing more people each year in Havana than yellow fever did island-wide. Cuban doctors begged the commission to dedicate at least a fraction of their funds to TB, but Americans ignored their pleas until 1902. The campaign against yellow fever would not take a back seat to anything: its eradication should prove to the world that Americans were indeed "civilizers," and U.S. conquests could be justified on humanitarian grounds.

Two theories prevailed about its source, or "vector." The older one was environmental: an unknown "miasma" carried the disease, a logical theory since yellow fever seemed most virulent in low, swampy areas. Americans favored this view: during the army's panic at San Juan Hill, soldiers moved into the mountains in the hope that this would slow contagion.

It seemed spread by "fomites," an inanimate object contaminated with whatever caused yellow fever. Thus, contact with a "fomite" spread the disease. Sternberg and Gorgas adhered to this theory: since poor sanitation lay at its heart, cleanliness should end the scourge.

The Cubans, especially Carlos Finlay, believed that yellow fever was spread through a mosquito bite. As early as 1879, Finlay had noticed in microscopic studies what looked like pinpricks in victims' skin and had theorized that something injected the fever into people's blood. In December 1880 he began studying two prevalent species of mosquito in Havana: the long-legged *Zanendo*, and the smaller *Culex*, or *A. aegypti*, which lived and bred around humans. Using mosquitoes that had been contaminated from biting yellow fever victims, he ran live tests on Spanish Army volunteers; on August 14, 1881, he presented a report at the Academy of Sciences titled "The Mosquito Hypothetically Considered as the Agent of Transmission of Yellow Fever." By June 1900 he'd inoculated 102 volunteers. The majority caught the fever; forty-one had no other attacks for six years afterward, suggesting some immunity.

Though Finlay's work was accepted in Europe, the American commission still scoffed. That soon changed. Despite the fact that Sternberg and Reed believed in fomites, others were losing faith. The dissenters were *not* American: James Carroll was British, and had brought with him two of the newest, most powerful German microscopes. Allied with him were Agramonte and Jesse Lazear, Cubans trained in U.S. schools. On August 1, 1900, they visited Carlos Finlay in his Havana home. Finlay was elated: he detailed his theories, handed over articles and experimental notes, and gave them a porcelain dish containing *A. aegypti* eggs. From August 11 to 25, nine attempts were made to infect human volunteers, but none succeeded. The mosquitoes seemed picky: they didn't want to bite where too much hair was present, and they preferred to feed at dusk or dawn. By now, Carroll had grown frustrated, and he allowed himself to be bitten by an infected mosquito: "If there's anything to the mosquito theory, I should get a good dose," he said. Four days later, he grew so sick that he nearly died. Jesse Lazear was already convinced, but on September 13 he was bitten by a stray mosquito and died twelve days later, leaving behind a wife and two children. His death shook them all, even Leonard Wood, who wrote to Lazear's widow in Baltimore, saying that her husband "gave up his life for science." He petitioned the War Department for a pension, writing, "His widow, I understand, is left with little or no means."

Lazear's death changed everything. Sternberg still thought the mosquito theory specious, but when Reed visited Havana, his doubts were swept away. On October 23, he presented the commission's findings at the annual meeting of the American Public Health Association, held in Indianapolis; his paper was a paradigm shift, and the dialogue changed. Even William Gorgas, Havana's chief sanitary officer and a proponent of the fomite theory, began to doubt old certainties: his men had turned Havana "spotless" with the street broom, incinerator, and disinfectant spray, and for the first six months, disease rates dropped so low that only six cases were reported. But with the autumn, hospitals filled. Perhaps the cure lay in eradicating mosquitoes and their breeding places. The two theories must be put to bed. An experimental camp to test volunteers in controlled environments must be built, but insiders doubted that Sternberg would requisition funds. Wood gave $10,000 for start-up and promised another $10,000 as needed.

Clara Maass had recuperated in East Orange with her mother and younger sister Sophia during these months of debate and study; she'd come home on May 13, and by now, the worst of her dengue fever had disappeared. Sometimes she'd visit friends in the German Hospital, and one day she announced that she was engaged "to a certain businessman in New York." They pressed her for details, but she just grinned and called him "My Captain." On Sunday, October 14, 1900, she received a cryptic wire: "Come at once," signed "Gorgas, Chief Sanitary Officer." Some inquiries revealed that she'd work as a civilian nurse in Havana's Sanitary Department, which meant she'd be employed by the occupation and paid from Cuban funds. That was all she knew. What about her wedding to "My Captain"? That could wait until she returned, she said.

Cuba had changed since January 1899. Leonard Wood ruled with an iron hand. The country was "orderly," he told McKinley on April 12, 1900: more than 2,600 schools had been built, and 130,000 children enrolled. The prisons were overhauled, and prisoners eligible for release or pardon were let go. Unrepentant *mambisi* who refused to accept U.S. authority were called "bandits" and hunted down: a notice in *The Havana Post* offered $500 in gold "for the bandit Lino Lima, dead or alive."

Tourist photos available for purchase showed three bandits hanging in a public square. The first elections for mayor, treasurer, and city attorney were held on June 16, 1900, in 110 municipalities; the second election for thirty-one delegates to a Constitutional Assembly was held on September 15. Balloting was limited to literate Cubans over twenty-one who owned property worth more than $250; only members of the dissolved Liberation Army were exempt from that rule.

Maass reported to Las Animas Hospital, then on Havana's outskirts. It sprawled atop a hill of the same name for twelve to fifteen acres; she thought it the prettiest hospital she'd ever seen. White stucco wards with red-tile roofs seemed laced together by green shrubs and flowering trees. But the real work took place a short carriage ride west at the experimental camp dubbed Camp Lazear. Two frame buildings were being built eighty yards apart, each mosquito-proofed with two thicknesses of walls and doors lined with cotton batting to plug the smallest cracks. The first building was for fomite tests: three nonimmune volunteers would stay for twenty days in a 14-by-20-foot room filled with the most horribly soiled bedding imaginable. Yellow fever victims had vomited on the sheets; a coal oil stove kept the temperature at a hellish 95°F. The second building was nicer, but comfort came with a price. It had two sanitized rooms, with ocean breezes blowing through window screens. In one room, doctors turned loose mosquitoes infected with yellow fever: one volunteer entered the room, and it was sealed.

Live tests are controversial and highly regulated today, but not so much then. Commissioners planned to use American and Spanish volunteers who had not contracted the disease in childhood. Two Americans, supervised by Walter Reed, would go first, followed by six recent Spanish immigrants supervised by Aristides Agramonte. All were told of the risks; all were paid $100 apiece, a real temptation at a time when American soldiers averaged $15 a month and Cuban residents even less: $100 USD then was worth slightly less than $3,423 in 2022 dollars.

The first volunteers entered the fomite building on November 30. The stench was so bad that men unpacking the infected bedding ran out to get a breath, and one vomited. But volunteers stayed inside for twenty days without infection and were healthy when they emerged. On December 21 the first tests began in the mosquito building. The two rooms were screened apart: three cots were placed in the smaller room, one in the larger. Three young men who'd been quarantined for thirty-two days entered the small sterile room. At noon, fifteen infected mosquitoes were released in the larger room, and a clerk named John J. Moran entered clad in a nightshirt and flung himself onto the bed. He lay there for thirty minutes as mosquitoes bit his hands and face seven times. He entered again at 4:30 p.m., stayed for fifteen minutes, and was bitten five times. He would repeat the exposure the next day, for a total of fifteen bites over two days. Fever struck three days later, at eleven a.m. on Christmas Day: Moran was rushed to the hospital with a severe case, but he survived. As more volunteers were bitten and grew sick, the mosquito theory gained credence.

"My assistants and I have at last been permitted to lift the impenetrable veil," Reed wrote to his wife, Emilie, on January 1, 1901. Soon after, Gorgas gave a short sermon in Las Animas's small Episcopal chapel. The early Christians called those who risked their lives in the care of others the *Parabolani*, or "Gamblers": they carried messages to prisoners, cared for the sick, lived among lepers. When the plague hit Carthage in AD 252, the Christian bishop Cyprian asked them to bury the dead and comfort the bereaved. The city would have been wiped out if not for the Gamblers, Cyprian wrote. "As for me," Gorgas said, "I hope I can go on pouring out my life for others until the very end." The world needed Gamblers: he only hoped that "we may be employed to correct some of the faults that we have made down here."

Clara Maass apparently replayed the sermon in her mind that winter and spring. Fomite trials were discontinued; mosquito trials were held on March 7, March 25, May 15, May 16, and May 27. Thirty soldiers and civilians participated, and twenty-two contracted yellow fever; six people newly arrived from Spain volunteered, and two of them died. By June 1901 the protocol changed so that volunteers were bitten by *A. aegypti* mosquitoes that fed on hospital fever patients: this way, researchers had a better idea of the virulence.

The sickness winnowed all of them, even the indomitable Leonard Wood. That summer, he grew so sick from "pernicious malaria" that he sailed to New York to recuperate. That June, Maass made up her mind to volunteer, the only woman to do so. Except for three letters home, she never comments, but the fact that Doctors Gorgas and Guitéras had known her since San Luis and asked her to come back suggests that they may have tried to talk her out of her decision. Since she would not budge, they supervised her trials. On June 4 Guitéras unstoppered a test tube containing an infected mosquito: they'd named her Vergera, because she'd bitten the dying patient Santiago Vergera. Guitéras upended the tube and pressed it to Clara's arm. When the mosquito flew to the top, Guitéras gave it a soft tap and Vergera hovered over her skin. Clara watched as it landed, barely a tickle. Vergera penetrated her flesh with its hair-thin proboscis; it would feed five times.

That night, Clara wrote the first letter to her mother. "I will soon send you $100," she said. "It will pay immediate debts and enable Sophia to come to Cuba. I can get her a position as a nurse here at $50 a month. She can take my place Mother, for—now don't be surprised—I am soon to be married."

Three days later, on June 7, she felt the first symptoms. At eleven a.m. she asked to go back to her room and wrote to her mother again: "Don't worry, Mother, if you hear that I have yellow fever. Now is a good time of the year to catch it if one has to. Most of the cases are mild, and then I should be immune and not afraid of the disease anymore." She sealed and stamped the letter and dropped it in the mail. Then she returned to her room and crashed into bed.

Hers turned into a mild case, and within a week, she was back on the wards. She'd been spared, but Guitéras told her the case had been *so* mild he did not think she was immune. On August 14 Maass volunteered again, this time to feed mosquitoes "loaded" with the virus, hoping that her earlier bout bestowed immunity. She bared her arm and was bitten twice. On August 18 at six a.m., she woke trembling. She reached for her thermometer and watch; her teeth chattered so badly she thought she'd bite through the glass, and she recorded her pulse as 80 beats a minute. She crawled under the wool army blanket but was soon too hot; she recorded her temperature as 100 and her pulse as 90. By noon, she ached all over and was moved to the yellow fever ward. Two hours later, her temperature climbed to 102 and her pulse to 115.

She wrote her mother while she still could. "Good-BYE, Mother," she started. "Don't worry. God will care for me in the yellow fever hospital the same as if I were at home. I will send you nearly all I can, so be good to yourself and the two little ones. You know I am the man of the family now, but do pray for me." At ten p.m. Gorgas visited: her condition had abated slightly, but this meant only that she had entered the more deceptive Phase 2.

Monday, August 19, starts well. Her temperature is normal, her pulse down to 80. But by noon, her temperature has climbed again to 100 and her body feels as if she's been beaten. She cries out for water and tosses in bed. That night, she is so exhausted that she sleeps well.

This reprieve does not last. On August 20 her temperature climbs to 102 at noon, 104 by six p.m. She can't bear the weight of the blankets and throws them off; her gums are swollen; jaundice is recorded as her liver floods her blood and skin with bile. She rarely sleeps, and when she does, she cries out from nightmares. Gorgas writes to her sister Sophia: "Miss Maass has yellow fever." Her temperature soars, averaging 103.

For the next few days, Clara's treatment follows a standard regimen. She lies flat, placed on an "absolute diet" of no food whatsoever, water, and cracked ice; she is prescribed an analgesic for headache and muscle pains, given mustard plasters for stomach pains. If she passes less than 500 cc of urine in twenty-four hours, she is given a saltwater enema; if her temperature remains above 103, she is sponged every two hours with cold water. This means constant bedside attention and the regular recording of temperature, pulse, and urine; she would have been part of such treatment for other patients, and in her lucid moments, she knows what is being done for her and why. Gorgas believed that the regimen could be a lifesaver: he would write that the method saved 12 to 15 more lives per 100 at Las Animas than at any other Havana hospital.

By the morning of Saturday, August 24, Clara complains to Gorgas that her stomach feels as small and hard as a billiard ball. He wires her mother, "Miss Maass worse," and she has vomited. "Fly wings," reads her chart, the sinister black specks presaging black vomit. Gorgas stands by her bed all day: her nose bleeds profusely, her eyeballs and skin are deep yellow, hiccups wring her small frame. He dabs at the blood pouring from her nose and mouth, and by evening it gets worse. He has seen this before and knows what awaits. Brave little Miss Maass has gambled and lost. Between 6:00 and 6:30 p.m., he sends for Dr. Guitéras to come immediately.

He barely arrives when a strange gurgling rises within her. She doubles up, then stiffens; she arches up, and a geyser of vile black liquid shoots from her mouth, spraying both doctors and the attending nurse, all of whom instinctively cover their nose and mouth and look away. Her eyes bulge; there is still understanding in them; her limp body sinks back in the bed. Gorgas reaches forward to wipe up the vomit when her body shoots up and black vomit sprays everywhere. Horror and pity overwhelm both doctors as her body jerks like a puppet; the vomit never stops, spraying everything. She tears at her throat, unable to breathe; she stares at Gorgas, aware that there is no hope, a stare Gorgas will always carry with him. Then she heaves once more and falls back, her body quivering with the last reflexive tremors, air sighing from her lungs.

"Miss Maass died twenty fourth six thirty," Gorgas wires to her mother and sister.

Sophia Maass was already there. She'd arrived in Havana slightly before her sister's death, but according to the *World*'s Havana reporter, "No word of greeting passed." With Clara's death, live tests ended. Within twenty-four hours of her death, she was placed in a lead coffin and interred in Havana's Colón Cemetery, close to the dead of the *Maine*. Sophia gathered her sister's few belongings and returned to East Orange to mourn.

On Monday, August 26, 1901, *The New York Times* ran the story of Clara Maass's death on the front page, complete with pictures and an editorial, which was unusual. The mysteries of self-sacrifice supplanted Philippine bloodshed and world politics, at least for two days. "The ethics of the Cuban experiments would seem to depend a good deal upon the motives actuating the victims," the *Times* led, somewhat uncomfortably:

> In the case of Miss Maass, the young nurse who died on Saturday, it would seem to have been the very highest which could inspire a self-sacrificing woman to put her life in peril. She not only was willing to incur risk of infection if thereby she might assist in establishing a scientific hypothesis of first importance in the etiology of yellow fever, but she desired to make herself immune, to the end that her usefulness in her chosen vocation might be increased and her

> opportunities of service to those suffering from the disease enlarged beyond what should be possible in one liable to contract the disease. No soldier in the late war placed his life in peril for better reasons than those which prompted this faithful nurse to risk hers. Facing death on the battlefield does not call for the highest kind of courage. Thousands who would have rushed up San Juan Hill with a shout would turn pale at the thought of facing less imminent danger in the quiet of the clinic, as the subjects of an experiment like that of a bite from an infected insect that might, or might not, be capable of imparting the disease he is supposed to carry.

Martyrdom "for the sake of truth" was perhaps the noblest of human endeavors, concluded the *Times*, yet its ranks were filled with "unmarked and forgotten graves."

No war in American history has been more "loaded" with the symbols and rhetoric of martyrdom than the Spanish and Philippine wars and the long rebellions defining them. Every participating nation was locked in a deadly tarantella that romanticized butchery in the name of sovereignty and empire. Sociologists have said that martyrs rarely appear alone but materialize in groups, drawing straight from a vein of collective identity. They see themselves as "liberators," ridding mankind of some shackle. Those who died were dubbed "martyrs" as easily as the evening news proclaims today's newest "hero." Spain had its Eloy Gonzalo; Cuba, Antonio Maceo, Calixto García, and José Martí. The Philippines anointed Gregorio del Pilar and José Rizal; there is debate whether Antonio Luna and Andrés Bonifacio deserve the honorific, while Emilio Aguinaldo insisted to the day of his death that he was a martyr to the cause. Among Americans, the 266 crew members who died aboard the *Maine* were called martyrs, as was Henry Lawton and now Clara Maass. Society assigns the homage, not the dying themselves: though they may not have chosen death, they chose to place themselves in its vicinity. That makes the *Maine*'s dead the most problematic, since their deaths probably resulted from accident, but Americans and the yellow press interpreted them otherwise. A martyr's death is not his to own. The details differ, but one thing links all: they are the doomed offspring of nations at war with themselves.

One last "martyrdom" awaits three weeks after Maass's death, unexpected, unprepared.

But not unforeseen. A year earlier, on August 3, 1900, McKinley's currency comptroller Charles Dawes received a letter from Mark Hanna; in it, the Ohio senator had inserted a statement from an unnamed detective "relative to a plot to assassinate the President." The detective described an organization located in Paterson, New Jersey, that he called the "Grotto of Socialists," whose goal was to "rid the earth of a number of its rulers." Although no such "grotto" has ever surfaced except in the detective's notes, Paterson *was* known as a hub of anarchist groups centered around the Italian silk weavers' trade, the most famous of which was Gruppo L'Era Nuovar ("The New Era Group"). In order of lethal dispatch, the "Grotto" listed Empress Eugenie of Austria; Umberto I, the king of Italy; the Prince of Wales or Queen Victoria; President McKinley; and, lastly, the kaiser. Empress Elisabeth of Austria-Hungary and the Italian king had, by then, already been killed; in April 1900 an unsuccessful attempt was made in Brussels on the Prince of Wales. According to the detective, Gaetano Bresci, the silk weaver who'd killed King Umberto, had been part of the Paterson Grotto; he'd been the second person selected by lot after the first failed his assignment and was killed by fellow members "by the rules of the Grotto." A second drawing was held, and "the slip falling to Breschi [*sic*], he kept his oath," the detective affirmed.

Charles Dawes was concerned; Mark Hanna, too. The president was not. "Appreciating that the President and his best friends do not feel apprehensive for his safety," the detective felt prompted to write "by what he *knows* to be *true*." A year later, McKinley was still unconcerned. On September 5, 1901, he opened the Pan-American Exposition in Buffalo with a speech in which he extolled the virtues of subduing foreign lands so that they must trade with us, a new way to sell "our increasing supplies." This was the upside of empire: "Our capacity to produce has increased so enormously, and our products have so multiplied, that the problem of more markets requires our urgent and immediate action." Empire's captive consumers comprised one lucky solution. The audience roared its approval. Afterward, McKinley toured the attractions. His secretary, George Cortelyou, remembered the president's appearance the next day at the Temple of Music, where he would shake the hands of those standing in line to meet him. The vision troubled Cortelyou, given the violence directed at heads of state and the detective's report from the previous year. He canceled the event, but McKinley had it reinstated. Cortelyou begged him to reconsider. "Why should I?" the president answered. "No one would wish to hurt me."

At four p.m. on Friday, September 6, McKinley appeared at the head of the receiving line, punctual as always for these meet and greets with his people. He once said that he'd learned to shake fifty hands per minute with a two-handed technique that moved a line right by. An organist played Bach while patriotic bunting draped behind him on the stage. A small girl led by her father came first; she asked for the red carnation he always wore in his lapel as a good luck charm, and he gave it to her. A short, dark man with a mustache came next and smiled. Third in line stood a slender, clean-shaven young man in a black suit, his right hand wrapped in a handkerchief, as if injured. In it, he held a short-barreled, .32-caliber Iver Johnson revolver.

McKinley's biographer Margaret Leech wrote that the details of Leon Czolgosz's life were "bleak and scanty." Now twenty-eight, he was the fourth child of Polish immigrants: his mother had died in childbirth; his father worked as a farm laborer until he could save up enough to buy a small shop in Cleveland. Czolgosz had worked in a wire mill in 1898, then suffered a nervous breakdown and moved back to the family farm. He grew withdrawn and irritable and in 1901 felt impatient to move away. That spring, he attended a lecture by the anarchist leader Emma Goldman, who advocated the assassination of national rulers everywhere. "She set me on fire," he later said of the woman whom the *Chicago Daily News* dubbed "The High Priestess of Anarchy." Her words "went right through me, and when I left the lecture I made up my mind that I would have to do something heroic for the cause I loved." He vowed to become an anarchist, but when he tried to contact Goldman or join anarchist groups in Chicago and Cleveland, they turned him away. They thought him untrustworthy, his revolutionary talk unfocused, his thinking confused. No records indicate that he ever contacted the lethal Grotto of Socialists that so worried Charles Dawes and George Cortelyou. Czolgosz drifted, and by September 1901 he ended up in West Seneca, New York, a trolley ride away from downtown Buffalo.

By most accounts, Czolgosz did not entertain an assassination attempt until he read of the president's reception at the Temple of Music. According to a friend, the self-professed anarchist despised the "outrages committed by the American government in the Philippine Islands." Gaetano Bresci's words after killing the king of Italy resounded with him: "It was time for the common people to take history into their own hands." He shadowed the president in Buffalo, attended his trade speech at the Esplanade, studied his schedule in the papers. He queued up early at the Temple of Music. At 4:07 p.m., when the president reached for his unbandaged left hand, Czolgosz pressed the revolver in his right to McKinley's chest and fired.

McKinley gasped; he stepped up on his toes, then back. A silence fell over the hall. Czolgosz fired again, this second bullet entering just below the navel, and McKinley reeled backward into the arms of Detective John Geary. "Am I shot?" he asked. Geary unbuttoned McKinley's vest and saw blood. "I fear you are, Mr. President," he said.

A Secret Service agent pushed Czolgosz to the ground; a black waiter named James Parker leaped upon him; another Secret Service agent ripped away the gun. A scrum of police beat Czolgosz until he lay bleeding. "Let no one hurt him," groaned McKinley, raising his bloody right hand as Czolgosz was dragged away. "He could not have known." Cortelyou bent close, and McKinley whispered, "My wife—be careful, Cortelyou, how you tell her—oh, be careful."

At first it seemed he would rally: the first bullet had only grazed his ribs, but the second entered his abdomen and could not be found. This grew infected, and by Wednesday, September 11, unseen gangrene had spread in his stomach, which doctors diagnosed as indigestion. Then his pancreas shut down. By six p.m. on Friday, doctors abandoned hope; press telegraphs clacked that McKinley was dying. He emerged from a stupor and said, "It is useless, gentlemen. I think we ought to have a prayer." He asked for Ida, and Cortelyou led her into the room. "Good-bye—good-bye, all," he muttered. Ida held his hand and kissed his lips. "I want to go with you," she whispered. "We are all going, my dear," he said, and slipped into a coma.

Death was pronounced at 2:15 a.m. on Saturday, September 14.

The hunt for scapegoats began. People could not believe that Czolgosz acted alone. Hundreds of anarchists and sympathizers in Chicago, Cleveland, Detroit, and other industrial cities were questioned, some arrested and detained. Emma Goldman was tracked to Chicago and arrested; she was released after two weeks and went into seclusion. Not a single accomplice was ever charged, so public wrath turned on anyone who'd criticized McKinley. There had been many. Hearst became Villain Number One. During the spring, his *Journal* had run an editorial sympathetic to political murder: "If bad institutions and bad men can be got rid of only by killing," it posited, "then the killing must be done." Death threats flooded his paper; for fear of a bomb, he refused to open packages addressed in his name. Hearst's name was dirt, wrote *The New Yorker* on September 26. "He will always remain the degraded, unclean thing that he is."

Czolgosz died a month and a half after McKinley. Though his lawyers argued for innocence by reason of insanity, he refused to testify in his own defense and was sentenced to execution in New York's relatively new electric chair. On Tuesday, October 29, he was led into the death chamber and strapped in; he stared at the witness-box and declared, "I killed the President because he was the enemy of the good people—the good working people. I am not sorry for my crime." The switch was thrown, the connection made. Afterward, his body was consumed so totally by sulfuric acid that nothing remained but sludge.

McKinley's martyrdom began on the day of his death. There was panic on Wall Street: "A cold wind of change seemed to blow with McKinley's passing," one biographer said. His was the third presidential murder in thirty-six years: What sort of society spawned such violence? Black-columned newspapers ran paeans to "Our Martyred President"; commemorative coins struck with "Little Mack, Our Martyred President" embossed on the obverse; commemorative sepia paperweights appeared with "Martyred President" beneath the sphinxlike photo. Books flooded the stands: *Life of William McKinley, Our Martyred President*, by Samuel Fallows; *The Authentic Life of William McKinley*, by Charles Morris; *The Illustrious Life of William McKinley*, by Murat Halstead. A stereograph slide of "William McKinley, the martyred President, grand in Public and Private, heroic in Life and Death," could be viewed in glorious three dimensions. The Edison Studio's *The Martyred Presidents*, directed by Edwin S. Porter, was released within days. "We predict for this picture a remarkable success," claimed the Edison Catalog. The film's guaranteed effect upon the audience was one of "mingled sorrow and sublimity." In all of this, what McKinley actually died *for* was never quite defined.

In Cuba and the Philippines, nations conceived by the words of two poet-martyrs, few people mourned.

28

"Between Them and Us Is a Chasm"

Theodore Roosevelt took the oath of office on the afternoon after McKinley died. With a few words, he became the nation's twenty-sixth president; at forty-two, he was its youngest. He entered the house of mourning and raised his right hand: "In this hour of deep and terrible national bereavement, I wish to state that it shall be my aim to continue absolutely unbroken the policy of President McKinley for the peace and prosperity and honor of our beloved country." One day later, he told reporters, "I am President, and shall act in every word and deed precisely as if I and not McKinley had been candidate for whom the electors cast the vote for President." The news invoked apathy in Manila: not "half a hundred" Filipinos had heard of the man who now controlled their lives.

How would Roosevelt govern the Philippines? He'd wanted these islands, had called them Asia's gate, but beyond some broad strokes, he had no idea what to do. Thus, he'd consult friends and experts more than he would about Cuba. He ran ideas past Henry Cabot Lodge and War Secretary Root, who said that most Filipinos were "but little advanced from pure savagery." He listened to Funston, who on September 2, 1901, wrote that all Filipinos were thieves best ruled with an iron hand.

He did not listen to Filipinos: little exists in his papers that was authored or inspired by them. The only letter from a native before Roosevelt's presidency came from Agoncillo's secretary Sixto Lopez, dated

August 13, 1900. He mentions a recent speech in which Roosevelt called Filipinos the "precise analogues" of Boxers and Apaches and challenges him: "You come to our country, you call us 'Dear General Aguinaldo'; you ask, accept, and profit by, our aid in the defeat of your enemy. You deliver Spanish prisoners over to our charge . . . When your enemy has been defeated, you turn upon us, shoot us down by the thousands, and when our resistance is greater than you anticipated you declare that we are the 'precise analogues' of Boxers and Apaches." Was this "the conduct of a gentleman and soldier?" The comment struck home: in March 1902 Roosevelt told Root that he had "absolutely no sympathy with Sixto Lopez" and refused to dine with him. Lopez was soon watched by government detectives.

Above all, Roosevelt listened to Taft, whom he valued for his "stability and serenity." At cabinet meetings, he'd say "Don't you think so, Will?" as a way "of getting what he regarded as the most convincing buttressing of his own opinions." Yet Taft had no more clear vision of the Philippines now as governor than when he'd first arrived. On June 30, 1900, he told the U.S. Supreme Court justice John M. Harlan that, as a group, Filipinos were "the greatest liars it has been my fortune to meet"; they needed "fifty or a hundred years before they shall even realize what Anglo-Saxon liberty is." Fourteen months later, this hadn't changed. Despite shows of warmth, he doubted they'd ever qualify for independence. If so, it would take "a generation," maybe longer, owing to the many character defects that could "only be cured by careful tutelage."

Since Taft didn't give credence to U.S. atrocities, neither did Roosevelt. Instead, Taft created a mirror world: "There never was a war conducted, whether against inferior races or not, in which there was more compassion and more restraint and more generosity" than in the Philippines, he told the Senate on February 4, 1902. Atrocities were a fact of life: though the war's immediate results might be terrible, its long-term gains were immense—an ancient rationale. "Robbery, slaughter and plunder they falsely name empire," said the historian Tacitus of the Romans: "They make a desert and call it peace." Roosevelt and Taft were well aware of American offenses: a May 5, 1902, letter by Root listed the names of more than 350 soldiers court-martialed for offenses against Filipinos. The response was to heap praise: Root told West Point's 1902 graduating class that those criticizing the army were unpatriotic and ungrateful.

One thing was clear to Roosevelt: the U.S. was a world power, and the Philippines were a part of that power. As the nation amassed empire, the "common defense" became the protection of all American interests, where before it more narrowly meant the protection of frontier settlements. Maintaining the common defense now meant military intervention in the affairs of other nations, some as close as Mexico, others as far as China and Russia. The idea of "distance" had changed. As the world "shrank," new buffers were needed. In 1904–1905, Roosevelt's Corollary to the Monroe Doctrine turned the entire Western Hemisphere into defensible space. Our Pacific possessions became a new line in the sand.

Roosevelt hoped he'd inherited a war that was winding down. In the weeks and months following Aguinaldo's capture, a growing number of insurgents in Northern and Central Luzon laid down their arms. Aguinaldo's appeal eliminated the stigma of treason; in quick succession, Generals José Alejandrino, Manuel Tinio, Teodoro Sandico, and others surrendered. Aguinaldo's cousins Baldomero and Pedro joined Emilio in Manila. On March 29 General Licerio Geronimo surrendered in the same town where his sharpshooters had killed Henry Lawton. But it was the May 19, 1901, surrender of Urbano Lacuna that seemed to signal the end of resistance, at least in Northern Luzon. "The surrender was a very impressive sight," wrote Corporal George Anthony of the Twenty-Second as rebels marched to San Isidro. *Insurrectos* in their tattered clothes "filed into town in columns of twos"; children and wives "circled about these fathers and brothers for the first time in two years." Funston read the Oath of Allegiance. "We had a gay time of it," Magdalene Blankart wrote to her mother. By early June, she'd head home.

From June to September, four thousand rebels surrendered in Luzon, and for the moment, the U.S. seemed almost forgiving: the Filipinos "had a right, of course, to make war upon us," one editor wrote, but "no right to wage it according to the rule of uncivilized people." It was time to "forgive and forget," remembering that "Filipinos were much like children, requiring to be petted and pampered, else they became stubborn and rebellious." But not all agreed. Funston felt uneasy. "Things out here are going a bit queerly just now," he told Roosevelt on September 2. "It is a difficult situation to analyze":

> Large portions of the Islands are perfectly quiet, while in some places the Devil is to pay. I wish we would throw off our mask of benevolent assimilation and rot of that kind, and rule these damned turbulent rebels with an iron hand . . . They do not need self government and cannot appreciate it. They need control, relentless enforcement of law, and a certain amount of education for the younger generation. In them is our only hope for the future. The present generation needs the gallows more than the ballot box.

Funston echoed a popular theme. In the McKinley-Taft model of conquest, Filipinos would be assimilated by transforming minds. The real target was the next generation. One month before Funston's letter, a former cattle boat rechristened the *Thomas* steamed into Manila Bay. Crowding its decks were 540 young Americans, most recent college graduates. The men were dressed in blazers and straw boaters, the women in flowing skirts and large flowery hats; they carried tennis rackets, guitars, cameras, and binoculars, but were not on vacation. When in 1901 McKinley directed the U.S. Civil Service Commission to hire 1,000 teachers, nearly 8,000 applied. They became known as the "Thomasites," after the first wave on this ship, and by the end of 1901, they'd fanned out across the archipelago to set up schools. Precursors of Peace Corps volunteers, they'd keep coming until 1933, imbued with a sense of destiny. "We are not merely teachers," wrote young Philinda Rand from the island of Negros. "We are social assets and emissaries of good will."

The enterprise rang with apostolic zeal. The *Thomas*'s 1901 log proclaimed: "Our nation has found herself confronted with a great problem dealing with a people who neither know nor understand the underlying principles of our civilization, yet who, for our mutual happiness and liberty, must be brought into accord with us. Between them and us is a chasm which must be bridged by a common knowledge and sympathy; fellowship must be made possible." Education was that bridge; it would Americanize Filipinos, cementing their loyalty by teaching them to speak and write in English, the tongue of the "civilized" world. English would pluck them from darkness. Language was identity: the next generation would no longer say *Ang Ingles Ay Ang Tongue ng Ina Mo*, but "English is your Mother Tongue."

This was blatant social engineering, though the phrase was not yet coined. In fact, the United States and Canada were engaged in a similar social experiment with a similar conquered race at exactly the same time. From 1879 to 1902, the U.S. Bureau of Indian Affairs built twenty-five "Indian boarding schools" in fifteen states and territories, their stated aim to remove Native American children from their parents, teach them English, break tribal bonds, and assimilate them into white society. The very first—the Carlisle Indian Industrial School in Carlisle, Pennsylvania—put children in uniform and forced them to live by military protocol; its founder, Civil War veteran Captain Richard Henry Pratt, said in an 1892 speech, "A great general has said that the only good Indian is a dead one. In a sense, I agree with the sentiment, but only in this: that all the Indian there is in the race should be dead. Kill the Indian in him and save the man." Private and religious schools followed quickly. On the whole, the schools produced a dismal record of shame, intimidation, disease, and death, which has yet to be fully told. No one knows how many Native American children died from sickness or abuse; in Carlisle, 186 children from 50 tribes are buried in unmarked graves, their bodies stacked one above the other for lack of room.

To be fair, the Thomasite body count did not approach that of the Indian schools. Children lived at home and were not ripped from their known lives. Yet Thomasites taught such a revision of Philippine history that hundreds of thousands of twentieth-century students knew nothing about Aguinaldo's Little Republic or the war that raged from 1899 to 1902. In time, Philippine, not American, teachers indoctrinated the nation: Americans trained Filipino educators, whose numbers swelled. In 1905 there were 1,074 American teachers and 3,414 Filipino; by 1925 American teachers numbered 353 and Filipino, 25,241. By 1940, 97 Americans remained.

The Thomasites washed away Philippine history. Their prime text was David Barrows's 1905 *A History of the Philippines*: since Barrows served from 1903 to 1909 as the occupation's director of education, "his textbook is universally tied to the American colonial project," claims the historian Reynaldo Ileto. The story is one of Progress, which only began when America arrived. A race can only progress if it has a history, but not any history will do: "The white, or European, race is above all others, the great historical race," Barrows wrote, because it was the first to evolve from the medieval to the modern age. Memories were reshaped: the war was no longer America's violent suppression of independence, but "a misguided, even stupid, rejection of a gift of further enlightenment" by Aguinaldo. Researchers in the 1960s and 1970s who interviewed Philippine War veterans found that recollection of the torture and interrogations they'd survived were attributed to Japanese invaders of the 1940s. Violence performed by the U.S. Army, proved in documents, had been replaced in their minds by the equally violent acts of the Japanese.

Amnesia sank into the family. Ileto had no inkling that his grandfather Francisco Yleto had been a citizen of the republic, accused as a spy by Americans, and thrown into jail. His own father, Rafael—a West Point graduate who'd fought the Japanese and rose by 1970 to commanding general of the Philippine Army—did not know. Ileto only discovered the truth in the mid-1970s when he found a letter by his grandfather stored in captured insurgent records in the U.S. National Archives. The American empire had created a false narrative, said Ileto, one "that induced a forgetting of the war."

Suppression came with a price. Like Clara Maass, Thomasites threw themselves into the cause; like Maass, they died. Complete numbers are unknown, but of the 540 original shipmates, at least 27 were dead within two years. "Mr. Collins drowned in rough seas," eulogized the U.S. chargé d'affaires Michael Malinowski in August 2001: Mr. Guernsey died of diphtheria; Mr. Jamizon and Mr. Badger of cholera; Mr. Allen of smallpox. In 1901 Price W. Cooper, a young teacher from Auburn, West Virginia, started teaching in Ilocos Province for $1,200 a year. Smallpox killed him on April 7, 1903. A friend visited him in the "Pest House": "Dead wagons, hearses of all kinds and descriptions are forever coming and going, all is death," he wrote. "The smoke out of the crematory chimney tells you that someone died homeless and friendless, no one claiming the remains."

As Thomasites became the youthful face of Benevolence, malaise swept through army ranks like cancer. Talk of the low quality of recruits grew so widespread that the Philippine *Argonaut* felt compelled to defend them. The current crop of soldiers was "well up to average at home," the editor claimed: "They are not Sunday superintendents or lay preachers, and wings are not sprouting from their shoulders," but they did their job. Yet the rot could ruin a man's career. By 1901 Captain Frederick Wild despised Filipinos and hated his men. All natives wanted to do was "have cockfights and gamble," he said, yet when he tried to close the cockpits, he received complaints, and when two of his men were stabbed to death at a cockpit, friends burned it down in revenge. Headquarters insisted that he punish the soldiers but he refused, sympathizing with their action. But, since several officers had already defied orders from the commission, Taft made an example of Wild. Despite his long career and Cuban bravery, he was court-martialed for disobeying orders and sent back home.

Though combat might be ending in the north, killing continued on both sides. Armed Filipino bands roamed unchecked; Americans took delight in killing natives. In summer 1901, five Filipinos entered the home of a man named Ragudo, tied up his family of five, and set them all ablaze. In Cavite, rebel colonel Esteban San Juan captured two privates with Company H of the 4th, tied them to a tree, and garroted them. The American teamster Henry Cline rode his bicycle outside Parañaque until coming upon "four small native boys gathering grass," the *Atlanta Constitution* said. "With no other apparent motive than natural depravity, he proceeded to shoot these boys with his revolver, wounding three and killing the fourth."

On May 2, 1901, George A. Raymond of the elite Brigade Cavalry Scouts was discharged from his unit in Angeles with an "excellent" character rating and a service record "Honest and Faithful." He was paid $57.83 by the paymaster, spent four days in Manila, returned to Angeles, and went on a crime spree. From May 7 to 9, he robbed the ex-soldier Henry Bohn of his pay and killed him; robbed the resident José de Jesus of two saddles, a bridle, and three horses; and raped sixteen-year-old Roberta Rivera in nearby Amsic barrio. He'd dreamed of leading a band of discharged Americans who'd rob and kill Filipinos as they rode south, but at this early stage he acted alone. His arrest and trial were covered in most Philippine papers.

MacArthur's successor Adna Chaffee saw the rot as metaphor. The dour cavalryman did not share the optimism of Otis, MacArthur, McKinley, or even Roosevelt, who admired him. This war was not over, he'd say; it wasn't even winding down. Benevolence was a flabby creed, made flesh by Taft's sweat-stained corpulence, but Chaffee wisely kept mum. Still, he believed the archipelago a "volcano," ready to erupt at any time. Only the army stood between civilian government and total collapse. This war would not end by wishing it away.

In Chaffee's mind, the looming apocalypse could only be checked by greater violence. To prove his point, he ordered the execution of three hundred Filipinos and six American criminals, including the murderous scout George Raymond. Though Raymond's hanging received little notice in the States, Manila papers reported that ten thousand Filipinos attended on September 27, 1901, in Barrio Talimundua, Angeles. Funston watched as Raymond mounted the gallows, turned to the parish priest, and asked to be baptized Catholic. Padre Vicente grabbed a basin and poured holy water over Raymond's head. "*Dimas, ego te baptizo*," he said, christening him after Dimas, the thief crucified with Christ who begged forgiveness. Raymond thanked the priest and bade him goodbye. The black hood came down; the trapdoor opened; his "lifeless body slightly swung under the gallows floor." Funston did not mention the conversion in his memoirs: "Despicable criminal though he was, [Raymond] had the good taste not to lower the prestige of his race in the way he met death, and, defiant to the last, went to his doom with sullen courage."

One day after Raymond's hanging, events unfolded in southern Samar that shook American complacency. When one reads of the late stages of the Philippine War, two events stand out: the massacre of forty-eight U.S. soldiers at the small town of Balangiga, and the ensuing reprisals by Brigadier General Jacob H. Smith that forever christened the island "bloody Samar."

The Philippines' third-largest island, Samar was the first land sighted by Magellan as he drew near in March 1521. The San Juanico Strait separates it from Leyte by 1.2 miles; the two islands comprise the Eastern Visayas. Samar was a primeval place, its interior a mélange of mountains, jungles, and swamps pierced by rivers and streams. Its 1896 population numbered 244,781, spread between 40 *pueblos* mostly set along the coasts.

Samar already possessed a bloody reputation before war arrived. The main source was a millennial sect called Dios-Dios, whose adherents believed they were the children of God. Caucasians were "sharp-nosed children of the devil"; Filipinos not of their sect must be converted or killed. Those who faced them in battle called them fearless: dressed in red and twirling huge bolos, they attacked in suicidal waves—like "breakers dashing against the rocks," recalled an American who survived one such charge.

The Philippine conflict came to Samar on New Year's Eve 1899, in the form of General Vicente Lukbán y Rilles, scion of a rich Chinese mestizo family from Luzon. Lukbán did not look like a guerrilla: he was a fortyish, pudgy Tagalog attorney, yet historians have judged that of all Aguinaldo's generals, he "may have been the most talented." He arrived in Samar's capital city of Catbalogan backed by one hundred riflemen and Aguinaldo's order naming him chief of the Eastern Visayas; he met little resistance and had a year to prepare. He set up arsenals and training camps, raised an army of a few thousand, and collected taxes. He married a local woman and grew familiar with local customs. His headquarters in the mountains above Catbalogan was guarded by snares, mantraps of poison-dipped stakes, and deadly trip wires; his alliance with Dios-Dios was cemented by confiscating church property and executing Spanish friars.

Everyone wanted Samar. The island produced the world's finest hemp, necessary for making rope and known locally as abaca. American farmers and seamen depended on it, and McKinley wanted control. Yet two British firms had monopolized Samar's trade for nearly fifty years: Warner, Barnes & Company and Smith, Bell & Company, who bought hemp from native middlemen throughout the island and then shipped it from the ports of Catbalogan and Calbayog. Even Lukbán's arrival didn't diminish the trade. The United States schemed to wrest the monopoly from the British, much as she'd wrested Cuban sugar from Spain, but as of yet no one knew how.

The "Hemp Scheme" began as early as July 31, 1899: Major Henry O. Heistand, a McKinley crony assigned to the Adjutant General's Office, proposed forming a company to control hemp exports and tried to interest the War Department and the attorney general. Otis seemed intrigued: on August 29, 1899, he wired Washington that Samar was "one of the islands which contains large quantities of hemp," and suggested entering the trade once it was occupied. In fact, hemp was in such short supply by late 1899 that Elihu Root ordered U.S. soldiers to seize Samar's ports, and in early 1900 he placed in charge of both islands General William A. Kobbé, whose mandate included securing the hemp trade.

American warships arrived off Catbalogan on the morning of January 27, 1900. An American colonel demanded Lukbán's surrender, and Lukbán suggested that he leave. The navy gave him two hours to surrender before shelling the city; during that time, Lukbán, his army, and the city's residents took to the hills over the town. As Americans landed, Filipinos watched, a scenario repeated throughout Samar. For the next four months, both forces launched sorties: dozens of Americans were killed each month; Dios-Dios spies killed sympathizers. One notable punishment was turbaning a sympathizer's head in a kerosene-soaked U.S. flag, then setting it afire. From March 1900 to spring 1901, Lukbán's forces attacked far-flung American garrisons with mounting force. On April 15, 1900, hundreds attacked the northern town of Catubig; a four-day siege left eighteen Americans and untold Filipinos dead. Similar attacks followed throughout the island, including a second in Catubig. By June 1901, seven U.S. infantry companies were spread across Samar, all helpless beyond their barricades. Eleven coastal towns were burnt husks; every bridge lay in ruins. When Chaffee replaced MacArthur, most U.S. officers considered Samar the hottest spot in the war.

This had to end. On May 13, 1901, in one of his last acts as commander, MacArthur handed control of Samar and Leyte to Brigadier General Robert P. Hughes, a thin, mercurial inspector general who'd fought rebels on the island of Panay since 1899. By March 1901 he'd nearly wiped them out, and his strategy in Samar would be identical: use wide-ranging sweeps for the scorched-earth destruction of natives' food, fields, livestock, and homes. On June 13 Hughes ordered all Samar ports blockaded, and he built supply camps in the main river valleys from which to fan through the interior. His men struck everywhere: a patrol in a twenty-mile strip up the Oras River "burned houses by the hundreds"; the garrison of Laguna destroyed 145 houses and 5,025 bushels of rice. On August 13 a First Infantry unit in the northern half of the island wounded Lukbán, captured his family, and discovered most of his papers. As soldiers burned out crops, Samarenes migrated to "protected zones," much like Weyler's *reconcentrado* camps. And as in Cuba, these became breeding grounds for starvation and disease. In May 1901 the population of Calbayog grew by 5,000. Elsewhere, the population soared from 6,000 to 20,000 in ninety days.

Yet Hughes found Samar harder to subdue than Panay. As patrols threaded through head-high grass, hidden bolomen cut them down. Samar soon resembled Northern Luzon: besieged towns, ambushed patrols, decimated supply trains. On June 19 a twenty-six-man patrol under Lieutenant Edward E. Downes became symbolic of the effort. The patrol left Guivan in Samar's southeastern tip to cut a trail up the peninsula, but ran out of food and water and marauded farms and homes. On June 23 noncoms suggested that they return to the coast, but Downes persisted. That afternoon, bolomen charged from the forest, killing two soldiers, wounding two. Downes, fifteen yards ahead, was stabbed through the heart and groin. "Well, I guess I am killed," he said to the soldier cradling him, and he died. Survivors abandoned their dead; they straggled into Guivan three days later, barely alive.

Hughes wrote that he'd best "do some cleaning up down there." One effective tool in Panay had been his acting judge advocate Edwin F. Glenn, a forty-four-year-old West Point graduate and lawyer whom the historian Brian Linn called an "eager practitioner" of the water cure. Glenn would ride into villages with the mounted Gordon's scouts, torture local officials in his search for arms and insurgents, then burn down the town. Now Hughes brought him to Samar.

One of the judge advocate's first acts was to study the Lukbán documents confiscated in the August 13 raid. He noticed that middlemen for the British hemp firms paid a portion of their earnings to insurgents as the cost of doing business, a common "protection racket" worldwide. Lukbán's records included the middlemen's names, as well as those of the principal brokers, J. H. Gibson and G. W. Brown of Warner, Barnes, the largest firm, and "Mr. Easton" of Smith, Bell. It is probable that their names were listed because they were the chief officers. Nevertheless, Hughes called this solid evidence of guilt, using it as a wedge to destroy the British monopoly.

On September 10, 1901, Glenn issued preliminary orders that both firms must leave Samar for "aiding and abetting" rebels; from September 14 to 17, Glenn's men entered their Calbayog and Catbalogan offices and demanded names and details of every middleman. On September 15 the British consul in Manila confronted Chaffee, who said he would not interfere. The consul sailed to Samar and on September 18 found J. H. Gibson and his assistant under house arrest; in Calbayog, he discovered that the army refused to let agents wire the London Home Office. The next day, a Reuters news dispatch titled "Englishmen expelled from the Philippines" ran in the London *Times*. On September 21 a passenger aboard the cargo ship *Lotus* told Gibson that his middlemen had been tortured. The man was afraid to say more.

Amid tales of torture, takeover, and scorched earth, seventy-four men of Company C, Ninth Infantry, splashed unopposed onto Samar's south coast on August 1, 1901. The little town of Balangiga sat on the east bank of a river of the same name; it boasted 200 huts, a central square with a large stone church, convent, and town hall, and 3,000 residents spread between the town and surrounding fields. Mayor Pedro Abayan had written Chaffee for protection from "Moro pirates," though if Army Intelligence had done its homework, they'd have learned that pirate raids had disappeared. In late May, as word spread that Americans might land, Abayan wrote a letter to Lukbán pledging "a deceptive policy with [Americans] doing whatever they may like, and when a favorable opportunity arises, the people will strategically rise against them." Abayan's letter was included in Lukbán's seized papers, but Glenn's operatives missed it. When the mayor greeted Captain Thomas W. Connell at the beach, he studied his seventy-one soldiers carrying Krag-Jørgensen rifles. The three officers wore Colt .45s, just revived from the Indian Wars as the only thing able to stop a religious fanatic at close range. Villagers cheered. One soldier quipped, "Boys, we're in guguland for sure now!"

Veteran fighters who'd fought in Cuba and Northern Luzon, Company C had just returned from the Boxer Rebellion, where they'd stormed

Peking. Captain Connell, a twenty-eight-year-old West Pointer, was backed by Lieutenant Edward A. Bumpus, a Harvard graduate, and the company surgeon, Major Richard S. Griswold. In their six weeks in Balangiga, the men did not report any contact with rebels, and Bumpus's letters showed growing confidence. On August 28 he wrote that while on patrol "we keep constantly on the alert with bayonets fixed, magazines loaded." Nine days later, they'd scouted a wide radius and had yet to encounter "any *ladrones* with bolo or gun." The surgeon played chess with Valeriano Abanador, the police chief; Bumpus squared off against Father Donato Guimbaolibot, who lived in the convent, too. "The *padre* and I generally break even," Bumpus said. Chief Abanador tutored soldiers in the Philippine art of *eskrima*, or stick fighting, and a romance began between Sergeant Frank Betron and Casiana Nacionales, a lay prayer leader who lived across the square.

It seemed idyllic, but climate and isolation took a toll. Though combat-hardened, many of the young soldiers had never been far from home. As mail delivery diminished, their isolation grew; increasing numbers indulged in *tubâ*, a white coconut wine known for insomnia and hangovers. On August 20 a Private McGilligan died of dysentery and was buried in town. Three days later, Private William Denton "deserted while crazed with *tubâ*," Bumpus wrote: he ran into the forest and "probably died in the woods." But Captain Connell wasn't convinced. Though Denton's shoes were found near shore across the river, Connell suspected that he'd defected to the rebels, a suspicion later confirmed. In a December 23, 1935, interview, the district rebel commander Eugenio Daza said that Denton "fought with us for the cause of the Revolution against his very countrymen." More men went mad. On September 4 a soldier committed suicide by shooting himself with his Krag. Soon afterward, Private F. Schechterle tried to shoot a fellow soldier, then ran howling toward the jungle. Three men caught and held him until Surgeon Griswold ordered them to roll him tightly in a canvas pup tent; he sat at the edge of a hospital bed, laughing to himself, convinced he was home in New York for Christmas. On September 25 Bumpus took Schechterle to regional headquarters in Basey in an outrigger canoe. It turned out that Schechterle's madness saved him.

According to rebel sergeant Pedro Duran Sr., the Americans were initially so well-liked that Mayor Abayan's betrayal seemed threatened through simple goodwill. But relations soured as morale deteriorated. One week after arriving, Connell announced at Sunday mass that all men eighteen and older must pay a 20-centavo tax for upkeep of the town. Soldiers began taking pigs, chickens, and cattle without payment; like Frederick Wild, Connell complained to the *padre* about the raucous Sunday cockfights. Like Wild, he was met with a shrug. The captain's threat to ban the women's midriff-baring *couture* was also ignored. The best he could do was forbid his men when it came to attending cockfights and fraternizing with local females.

As the soldiers' *tubâ* intake increased, so did rumors of *kalamadya*, or "defilement," an improper sexual advance that could be anything from simple innuendo to rough horseplay. This is qualitatively different from *lugos*, the local word for rape, though historians later mixed the details. And one could lead to the other if fueled by sufficient alcohol. On September 8 a sixty-five-year-old woman reported to Connell that she had been raped days earlier by a man matching William Denton's description. But he'd been missing since August 23, and Connell dismissed her. Soon three young girls said they'd been abused, and as proof lifted their skirts to reveal bruises. Connell, a devout Irish Catholic, was mortified. He ordered the company into formation and led the girls past them, asking them to identify their attackers. They could not, so he marched them past the sentries with the same result. On Saturday, September 21, when two soldiers reportedly harassed a girl tending a *tubâ* shop, her brothers rushed in and pummeled them. Connell issued orders that even touching a native woman would be considered the same as rape.

The breaking point for the villagers came on Sunday, September 22. Two weeks earlier, Lieutenant Colonel Roger Foote had come to Balangiga and told Connell to clean up the town: dispose of garbage under the huts; cut down trees and brush that limited the lines of sight of night patrols. Connell hadn't seemed worried about this earlier, but one day later, he issued orders for cleanup details. Some garbage was burned over the next two weeks, but the order to cut down vegetation put the mayor in a real quandary. Clearing the land meant destroying those patches of sweet potatoes and banana trees used to feed the rebels; obeying American orders meant placing village officials in danger. So Connell's orders were ignored. After dusk that Sunday, Connell called a meeting in the square; when villagers arrived, they saw two conical Sibley tents, each able to hold sixteen men. Connell ordered his men to round up the 143 men present and make them his prisoners. They'd remain so until the town was clean. Rebel sergeant Pedro Duran, caught in the roundup, asked how long they'd be captives. Connell snapped, "Until New Year."

It turned into a standoff. Though Connell didn't feed his captives, he allowed relatives to bring meals. On Tuesday he ordered a house-to-house search for every bladed weapon or farm tool. Seven sacks were collected, and during the search, more women were allegedly manhandled. On Wednesday he ordered the mayor to cut down all banana trees and destroy all rice stores, presumably to keep them from rebel hands. This was finally too much: since the vice mayor alone remained free, he was sent to the rebels' Captain Daza. Town elders agreed that an attack was the only way to save themselves from these mad Americans.

So what started as friendship ended in hate, the history of America's Philippine adventure encapsulated in one small village. Though later American accounts called the "Balangiga Massacre" unprovoked, locals painted a village backed against a wall. Preparations played out under the nose of Connell and his men. Daza timed the attack for the morning of Saturday, September 28: since a cockfight was planned, villagers would flood the square. Daza chose breakfast time, when the Yankees stacked their rifles to eat and only a few sentries were armed. From September 24 to 26, Daza visited surrounding barrios: he told villagers to assemble on the night of September 27 at a place called Canara, about a kilometer northwest of town. Bring bolos, daggers, and clubs. Balangiga's women were sent off: in their stead, fighters would enter the square in women's dress, hiding weapons beneath their skirts. Others were smuggled inside coffins. Father Guimbaolibot opted to leave for Leyte; attackers divided into units of seventy men. When church bells rang, Police Chief Abanador would give the signal. About five hundred men lay concealed in the forest, awaiting the peal of bells.

Fierce chess opponents develop strong friendships, and it has been suggested that Guimbaolibot urged Bumpus to take a well-deserved break from town. But Fate played games with him. On September 25 he sailed north to Basey with the insane Private Schechterle and spent the next day playing chess with Captain Edwin V. Bookmiller, Company G's commander. He collected mail and caught up on current events: it was the first he'd heard of McKinley's assassination. He returned on September 27 with the mail and the sad news. Connell ordered the flag to half-staff and told his men to sew black-crepe mourning bands on their sleeves. This did not sit well: the men wanted to read their letters. As they sewed, they ate *carabao* meat and drank *tubâ*. It was the company's dire secret: years later, when Private Adolph Gamlin's granddaughter asked him why survivors were not awarded the Medal of Honor, he said, "They did not deserve it, for they were all drunk the night before."

Reveille sounded, as always, at 6:30 a.m. on Saturday, September 28. The men rolled out of bed, lined up, and sat for breakfast at an outdoor kitchen a hundred feet from their quarters, rifles stacked nearby. As they read mail and ate at the long mess table, they did not notice native workmen milling near the police chief and in the square, nor the guerrillas dressed as religious adherents slip through church doors. Only an American sergeant and two privates were armed.

The police chief was the first to act. He approached Private Gamlin, grabbed his rifle, and smashed it into the side of his head. "*Atalee, mga Balangignon!*" he yelled ("Attack, men of Balangiga!"). Gamlin dropped to the ground, stunned. The bell ringer in the belfry heard the yell and rang the bells. Fighters ripped off their disguises, brandished their weapons, and charged their assigned targets. They fanned through the mess hall and kitchen, main barracks, and two smaller barracks; those in the church poured into the convent after the three American officers.

The slaughter was merciless and quick. Connell leaped from his second-story window in his pajamas and was hacked to death by bolomen. Surgeon Griswold was stabbed to death in his room; Bumpus, who had a pile of mail in his lap, never rose from his chair. In the kitchen, soldiers were overwhelmed: one of the first victims was the company's first sergeant, his skull cloven by an axe. Another man's head fell into his breakfast plate. Most were butchered before they could stand; the cook threw boiling water at his assailants; others fought back with picks, chairs, and pots and pans. Most of the thirty-six who survived the first attack gathered around the lovestruck Sergeant Betron, who assumed command. A few had grabbed guns, and Betron figured their best chance of escape lay by sea. They fought their way to the beach, with them Private Gamlin, who staggered after the mob after being poleaxed by Chief Abanador. Five outrigger canoes lay at the edge of the surf; they placed the wounded inside and were about to cast off when a soldier spotted the Stars and Stripes still fluttering over the plaza. Private Claude Wingo and three others ran back and hauled it down; Wingo and one other returned. They paddled into heavy seas.

Their troubles were just starting. Heavy surf tossed one boat back onto the beach: all but two men were killed, and they ran to the jungle. On September 29, two boats reached Basey after twenty hours at sea; a fourth reached Leyte around five a.m. The final boat beat north until heading ashore; natives following behind them swarmed from the trees. Only two soldiers paddled away, picked up at sea the next day. Nine who'd escaped either died of their wounds in the boats or were killed. Those who fled to the jungle, including Private Wingo, were never seen again.

Survivor's tales emphasized the macabre, as if Nature itself turned against them. Private George E. Meyer, the company musician, recalled the escape as a mad haze. The sea splashed on their wounds, causing "excruciating agony." The wind headed against them; stars disappeared. Searchers' fires lined the shore; the "hideous sound of the conch shells" signaled their sighting. "Grimly we paddled on." A school of sharks stalked the boats, drawn by blood. "Their presence was revealed now by a shark fin above the water, now by the flash of a great white belly." Only one soldier could speak coherently when they landed in Basey. Years later, a survivor wrote, "I often live over again that dreadful morning of slaughter, and wake up screaming."

In all, 48 of Company C's 74 men died, either at Balangiga, during the escape, or in the hospital. It was the largest slaughter of U.S. soldiers in one encounter of the entire war. Another 22 were wounded, and only 4 emerged unscathed. Numbers of Filipino casualties varied: American survivors claimed to have killed 150 to 300, but decades later, Eugenio Daza listed 22 wounded and 28 slain, including Mayor Abayan and Police Chief Abanador. The Americans left behind 100 Krag rifles, 25,000 rounds of ammo, and chests of equipment and medicine. Lukbán praised the Balangigans and wrote that the victory was a sign of God's justice. People seemed to listen: 10 Americans were killed and 6 wounded in a similar attack at Gandara.

Captain Bookmiller boarded the *Pittsburgh* the next morning with fifty-three volunteers and some survivors. The ship's cannon and machine gun scattered the few natives firing at them from shore. Soldiers, bayonets fixed, charged into town. What they found beggared the imagination. Their comrades had been mutilated in ways never seen, as if the villagers had succumbed to an imaginative frenzy. Connell's head had been severed and set afire; a sergeant was upended in a water barrel, feet missing. Others were slit open and stuffed with jam and molasses to draw ants. Even the company dog was killed, its eyes gouged out, replaced with stones.

Bookmiller had interrupted a funeral for villagers killed in the attack: their bodies were laid in trenches but not yet covered, and twenty Filipinos were dragged from hiding. Bookmiller had them replace the dead Filipinos with mutilated Americans; he ordered them covered with dirt and shots fired in salute, then stacked the native dead like cordwood, doused them with kerosene, and set the pyre afire. He handed the gravediggers to survivors, who led them to the woods. Shots rang out. He turned to his men. Burn the town, he said. Pull down the ruins. Leave only ash and rubble. He turned his pocket Bible to the Old Testament, where the prophet Hosea foretold doom upon Israel for its impious ways.

"They have sown the wind, and they shall reap the whirlwind," Bookmiller read out as, around him, flames consumed all.

29

"The Better You Will Please Me"

No single event in the Philippine War shocked Americans more profoundly than the Balangiga Massacre or questioned more vividly their nation's civilizing role. It was, headlines claimed, the greatest U.S. military disaster since the Little Bighorn. "It was a disaster so ghastly in its details, so undreamed of under the conditions of almost universal peace which had been established, that it created absolute panic," wrote Helen Taft. "Men began to go about their everyday occupations in Manila carrying pistols conspicuously displayed, and half the people one met could talk of nothing else but their conviction that the whole archipelago was a smouldering [*sic*] volcano and that we were all liable to be murdered in our beds any night."

Most blame fell on her husband. *The San Francisco Call* warned that America must learn that "conquered people" rarely remain conquered long. The debate over military versus civilian control returned with renewed rancor: Balangiga "made the Army officers more certain than ever that the Islands should have remained under military control indefinitely," Helen Taft wrote. "I cannot deny that, at the time, their arguments seemed to have some foundation."

No one agreed more than Adna Chaffee. Before Balangiga, he'd reined in his contempt for civilian control. After the news broke, he held a rare press conference: "The whole Philippine people are now engaged in making war in a manner not in accordance with the recognized laws of war," the same point made by MacArthur before declaring martial law. The army was "not to blame for Balangiga"; the blame lay with Taft's "soft mollycoddling of treacherous natives." But those days were over: "The situation calls for shot, shells, and bayonets," and to that end, Chaffee appointed sixty-two-year-old Brigadier General Jacob Hurd Smith to regain control.

Chaffee's dictates came from the top: Roosevelt ordered him to take the "most stern measures to pacify Samar." He would not risk his new presidency over endless war. Chaffee created the four-thousand-strong "6th Separate Brigade" and ordered Smith to instill a "wholesale fear" of the army throughout Samar.

According to the historian Brian Linn, Smith's appointment was "one of the gravest blunders of the entire war." A cranky little Kentuckian with a wrinkled linen uniform, his troops called him "Hell-Roaring Jake" for his booming voice in battle. He'd survived the Civil War; the Indian Wars; an inquiry into black-market schemes that increased his fortune from $4,000 to $40,000 in three years; several bankruptcies and debtor lawsuits; and two courts-martial for insubordination, plus a third for operating an illegal saloon. In 1886 he was ordered dismissed, but friends had persuaded President Cleveland to issue a reprimand. His luck changed on San Juan Hill when a spent Spanish bullet struck him in the chest; the bullet did little damage, and he refused to leave his men. Praise led to a promotion to brevet lieutenant colonel. By October 1899 he'd become a full colonel, given command of the Seventeenth Infantry; by fall 1900 he ruled Tarlac, Pangasinan, and Zambales provinces as military governor.

Like Frederick Funston, Smith's real problem was his temper; like Funston, his language is how history remembers him. When he told a subordinate to make "the interior of Samar a howling wilderness," he uttered the war's most famous words. Even Smith realized that at times he went too far: when his wife warned, "General, you talk too much and are too outspoken in your intentions," he asked the journalist Stephen Bonsal "to come to my defense when abused by the papers in the States for my apparent harshness." It did little good. His inveterate tongue convinced many that he was insane. Henry Allen, reborn from El Caney as Taft's chief of the new Philippine Constabulary, bluntly called him "loco."

Chaffee, his greatest advocate, feared putting him near reporters, in the likely chance he'd "act like an unbalanced lunatic."

What would be called the "Rape of Samar" began in Balangiga. The first wave of vengeance was assigned to four companies of the First Marine Brigade, bolstered by multiple navy gunboats and launches. Placed in command was the twenty-two-year veteran Major Littleton Waller Tazewell Waller, who'd fought in Egypt, Cuba, and the Boxer Rebellion, and whose severe drinking saw him relieved for ten days. Contemporaries thought him ruthless and swaggering, yet able to endure endless misery in the field. The southern one-fifth of Samar, an area of some six hundred square miles, fell under his command. On October 24 he stepped off the collier *Zafiro* with Jake Smith to find Balangiga still under siege. Earlier that morning, two navy vessels had shelled enemy trenches outside of town. The group picked its way past burned buildings to the plaza, where they discovered that wild hogs had dug up and strewn the corpses of Company C. Smith ordered a fence built around the graves, then flew into a rage. Castigation was not enough, he told Waller: the major must kill all persons in this district capable of bearing arms.

Waller was stunned. It seemed "that these people were born with bolos in their hands," he later testified at his own court-martial. "Even children carried bolos. Were they to be killed, too?" There must be no doubt. "I would like to know the limit of age."

Ages ten years and older, Smith spelled out. "I wish you to kill and burn," then added, "The more you kill and the more you burn, the better you will please me."

How does one interpret such a command? "We are not making war on women and children," the appalled Waller told an aide. Nevertheless, he drew up orders. The marines' mission was to stem the flow of all food to the interior; they must starve, capture, and kill guerrillas and their enablers, and any Filipino males who did not surrender by the next day, the 25th, would be "regarded and treated as enemies." Never go unarmed, he warned his men, even during meals or in the latrine. Expect no quarter and give none. Always remember Balangiga.

Yet executing ten-year-olds seemed beyond the pale. Even Funston did not endorse killing children. Balangiga changed that: one can make the case that this is the pivotal moment, not only in the war itself but in the American way of making war. Jake Smith's statement echoed Phil Sheridan's call for total annihilation of the enemy in the Civil and Indian wars. The easy success of the Splendid War transformed America into a martial society, and Smith's template appears over the next two centuries in conflicts in which an entrenched enemy, of a different race, turns to guerrilla tactics; it informs "police actions" in the many "Banana Republics," Vietnam, Afghanistan, and Iraq's Abu Ghraib. The Philippine War was the first time Sheridan's dictates spread beyond America, during our premier attempt to "civilize the world." There is no great difference between Smith's command to Waller and Captain Ernest Medina's nearly identical March 16, 1968, briefing before the My Lai Massacre. "Our job is to go in rapidly, and to neutralize everything," he allegedly told Charlie Company. "To kill everything." After Balangiga, the American public accepted the fatal logic of "pacification": it becomes a "necessity" lodged inside American memory that refuses to disappear.

Starting on October 31, Waller's marines ranged through "Subdistrict South Samar." They began by burning San Antonio, a hub of rice smuggling, then the village of Gibasey because an official entered Basey without permission. Four days later, marines on the gunboat *Villalobos* destroyed two coastal villages on the way to Balangiga. Once there, a patrol entered a hut occupied by two women and an old man; when they found some relics from C Company, they killed all three. On October 28, seventy-five marines stormed ashore in southernmost Guivan and burned it down. On November 5 a patrol scouted up the Cadacan River; by November 10 they'd burned 255 houses, destroyed a ton of hemp and half ton of rice, killed 13 *carabao*, scuttled 30 fishing boats, captured 18 guerrillas, and killed 39. Waller's reports do not give ages.

Destruction continued as Smith released directives: "Short severe wars are the most humane in the end," one stated; every native should be "treated as an enemy until he has conclusively shown that he is a friend." The most famous was his edict to turn Samar into a "howling wilderness"; once this was made public, his nickname changed to "Howling Wilderness Smith." One marine wrote home that platoons were "hiking all the time killing all we came across." Captain David D. Porter later testified that although marines were only supposed to "kill and burn" *insurrectos*, it was "understood that everybody in Samar was an *insurrecto*."

In the weeks after Balangiga, navy and marine patrols burned hundreds of buildings in the north and south, slaughtered thousands of cattle, destroyed untold tons of rice and hemp, and killed anything that moved. Neither Chaffee's reports nor Philippine Insurgent Records go into detail, but the general impression was one of extermination; an April 21, 1902, AP dispatch estimated that what happened in Samar comprised "the most widespread killing of Filipino civilians in the entire period of the war." Smith's orders were "to shoot, not to capture," claimed the October 26, 1901, *Manila Times*.

Scorched-earth seemed the only policy. Andrew Pohlman of the First Infantry recalled discovering a herd of one hundred *caribao* north of the town of Borongan and killing them all. Soldiers cut their ropes and drove them into a large clearing: "Our first volley hit many of the animals in vital parts, and they fell instantly." Others ran at "a staggering trot," came to a halt, bled out, and "sank gradually and steadily to the ground." Lieutenant Yates Stirling Jr., commanding the gunboat *Paragua*, was told by Hughes to use plenty of "black paint" on the villages. "Black paint was fire," Stirling said. "He was telling me that he wanted all the native towns burned down." They steamed up the Gandara River to a tranquil valley of well-tended fields and picturesque hamlets: "Every house from two miles from either bank was destroyed by us. We killed their livestock: cattle, pigs, chickens, and their valuable work animals, the carabaos." He observed in his men "a diabolical satisfaction of seeing things that men had toiled to construct being consumed by flames in a few short minutes." As he steamed off, the valley crackled behind him. "I guess the human species must love to destroy."

No woman was safe. Private Pohlman and a friend watched in shame as a "young and very beautiful" Filipina was raped by their comrades: "Her tears and entreaties that she did not wish to give birth to a white child were to no avail, and my friend and I turned away." When they'd dared to interfere earlier, "[we] nearly lost our lives." Any rescue attempt "would be quickly stopped by bullets from unseen men behind us in brush or by the butts of the rifles of some of the crowd." Even officers participated. In Catbalogan, a lieutenant raped a woman in the same room where she cared for her child; he threatened to have her husband, a prisoner in the guardhouse, shot the next morning if she did not give in.

Up to this point, the military had characterized torture and cruelty as "individual eruptions," but what happened in Samar was an officially condoned system of violence employed for terror. All was permissible. Between October 1901 and January 1902, Hughes's intelligence chief Edwin Glenn and his naval escort ranged up and down the narrow strait separating Leyte from Samar. They confiscated boats essential for Leytan fishermen's livelihood and towed them back to Samar, refusing to release them even when Leyte's governor, Joseph H. Grant, complained. Worse, Glenn kidnapped civilians and whisked them to Samar for interrogation and torture. Three of these were priests, including Balangiga's Donato Guimbaolibot, suspected of aiding the massacre. They joined two other priests held in the convent of Calbiga. Glenn and his men tortured all five for nearly four months, and Father Bartolome Picson died. When Governor Grant confronted Hughes about the kidnappings and deaths, the general answered that Glenn's "work was thorough, and had a widely spread effect."

From September 28 to October 9, Glenn used war as a pretense for the final expulsion of the British hemp firms. On October 6 his men cross-examined Agent J. H. Gibson in Calbayog and demanded the records of all native middlemen since January 1900. Two native office staff were taken off Samar and probably tortured. On October 9 Gibson received orders to close his offices and leave Samar within four days. Even then, he refused to believe rumors that the Americans were subjecting his buyers to the water cure and the "rope cure," where a water-soaked rope passed around the body from armpits to knees would tighten and squeeze as it dried. Such "fiendish practices were impossible," he said. But when witnesses corroborated the story, he wired the British consul and on October 13 left for Manila.

Glenn repeated his actions in Catbalogan: he charged into the office of Agent G. W. Brown, demanded his books, tortured his staff, and ordered the company out of Samar by October 11. When Brown confronted an American doctor who'd tended to the tortured men, the doctor confessed that "for the first time in his life he was ashamed to call himself an American."

In Catbalogan, Glenn also committed fraud. While perusing Brown's books, he discovered that the firm owed the buyer Cecilio Sison $14,000 for hemp he'd bought in their name. He visited Brown's office holding three unpaid drafts and "asked me to cancel [the drafts] and give him one in his own favour," which he then cashed in a bank in Manila. When the British consul told Chaffee of Glenn's "legal extortion," this, too, was ignored.

As McKinley had wished, America wrenched hemp from Great Britain under a legal guise. British firms were not allowed back until May 24, 1902. By then, inventories had vanished and buyers had scattered. During this period, the U.S. set up its own hemp empire, first administered by the army, then run by the "Hemp Trust," authorized by Congress in the Philippine Tariff Act of March 8, 1902. Two British agents were barred from ever returning, including J. H. Gibson, who'd told London papers about the torture: he was henceforth "undesirable and objectionable in Samar," Chaffee declared.

By this point, Smith realized that conquest would be easier if his forces on the east and west coasts could work as one. Communication was the key: it was only thirty-five land miles from the eastern posts to his western headquarters at Basey, but ninety-three miles by the southern sea route and road. He'd long wanted telegraph wires to stretch that thirty-five miles, and on November 19 Waller volunteered. He'd "belt" the southern end of the island, he said, starting at the coastal port of Lanang and heading west by the river of the same name. Reliable trails into the interior did not exist, so the only route across seemed by water. With this apparently logical choice, Waller began the process that revealed to the world the almost unbelievable story of the U.S. military in Samar.

From the first, Waller's choice had problems. This was monsoon season, and officers who knew the country warned Waller that the swollen river was unnavigable. If he waited for good weather, the transit would take five days. If not, he'd be forced into the mountains. One patrol did in fact emerge from this area right before he left: they seconded that no trail existed and warned that "the hardships of mountain climbing" might kill them all. This was a fairly large expedition: six officers (including captains David Porter and Hiram Bearss), fifty marines, two Philippine Scouts, and thirty-three native porters. One of the marines was Sergeant John Henry Quick, the former signalman about whom Crane had written at Guantánamo Bay. Waller also took only four days' rations. Other officers begged him to take more food, but Waller reasoned that four days of transit at nine miles a day was child's play.

Waller plunged into the interior on December 28 without telling anyone of his route or itinerary. They started by boat, but by the first river town, they'd already portaged around several impassable rapids. Past that, the trail disappeared. They cut a path through the jungle, always keeping the river close: according to an unpublished account by Captain Bearss, it roared like an enemy "bemoaning its inability to reach up" and drown them all. Sometimes they *had* to cross, and that proved deadly: two porters slipped on the rocks and "went over the falls."

After two days, they'd hiked only twelve miles. By December 30 they were lost. Waller reduced their rations, and halved that again on the thirty-first. On New Year's Day, no food remained.

Since they could not survive the river, Waller ordered them to climb the bordering mountains. These rose as diagonal "hogbacks" that must be ascended one after the other. They'd entered a land so "wild and barren" that even "beasts shunned the place and not a monkey or parrot" cried out that could sate their "terrible hunger," wrote Private Joseph H. Hawkins, who'd joined the marines the previous year. Raised in Wardensville, West Virginia, Hawkins was no stranger to wild country, and he sensed quickly the hell they'd entered. His "Diary of Samar" would never be published, and sits in the archives of the U.S. Marine Corps History Division in Quantico, Virginia. Yet, like Hoffman Philip's "A Volunteer of 1898," it chronicles a nightmare so much worse than anything narrated in later histories that one can see why it was forgotten and filed away.

The climb started with small irritations, which turned debilitating. One constant pain was their "pack"—a blanket roll wrapping their kit, this encased in a rubber poncho slung over one shoulder. The uneven weight chafed without mercy. Since porters' packs were strapped to their back and shoulders, weight was more evenly distributed—which meant they did not suffer so. By the second day, the marines' envy turned to hatred, which grew with the pain. Cuts and sores festered; leeches fastened on. Blood loss and infection weakened them. By January 1–2, wrote Bearss, they struggled on, because "there was nothing left to do."

Friday, January 3, 1902, would be the turning point. They'd gone for seventy-two hours without the "slightest vestige of food," Hawkins claimed: their feet were "raw, covered with sores, and horribly swollen" from leech bites and the constant rain. Most were ill. Waller finally admitted that many could not continue, so he proposed pushing west toward Basey with a lieutenant and thirteen soldiers in the best condition, then send back a relief party at the first chance. He left Captain Porter in charge of the invalids, with instructions to follow when they could.

One day after leaving, Waller discovered a clearing that was bursting with bananas, sweet potatoes, and coconut palms. In its center stood a shack with five natives, two of whom knew the road to Basey. Waller's ravenous men fell on the food. During the feast, Hiram Bearss and a corporal suddenly appeared, carrying a message from Captain Porter: his men were so desperate that they planned to retrace their steps back to Lanang. Waller sent a message by one of the five men in the hut that this paradise lay only one day away. But the message never reached Porter: the native returned two days later, citing *insurrectos* so thick in the jungle that he feared he would be killed. Waller's rejuvenated party continued west, and on January 6 staggered into Basey. Some of his men wept, he wrote, while "others laughed hysterically." He plunged back into the bush with relief, but nine days later returned empty-handed, close to death from fever.

Meanwhile, Captain Porter tried to retrace the eastern route back to Lanang. He took with him Sergeant Quick, six marines in middling condition, and six porters, but along the way four of the marines announced that they could not continue. He left them in a jungle potato patch and pressed on, reaching Lanang on January 11 with all six porters, Sergeant Quick, and two marines. A relief party formed up, but rains delayed their departure for three days. Miraculously, they found those abandoned in the potato patch and carried them to Lanang.

That left the thirty-three weakest marines under First Lieutenant Alexander Williams Jr. and Second Lieutenant A. C. Lyles, a group that included Private Joseph Hawkins. Soon after Captain Porter left on January 4, they tried to follow but were too weak and would not try again for five days. During that time, they seem to have gone mad. According to the official account, Williams and his men grew convinced that the porters lived off a hidden cache of food and planned to kill them. Instead, Hawkins wrote, the marines plotted the porters' demise.

On January 7, after three days in camp, "the hungry, famished, half insane Marines cast suspicious eyes on the native *cargadores*," Hawkins wrote: they debated "in their minds why one of the native bearers should not be sacrificed as an extreme measure to appease their hunger and save their lives." He rationalizes that such things had happened before, such as when Arctic shipwreck survivors, "thousands of miles away from food, [have] drawn lots to see which should be killed that his companions might live." And yet, he says, "nothing of the sort has yet occurred in the Philippines," where soldiers were always close enough to base "that they might have marched to safety in two or three days." The condemnation is unspoken: they'd been abandoned by their officers, by the Corps, and by God.

Of all the marines' personal accounts, that of Hawkins is the only one to mention "survival cannibalism"—and it takes a while for him to even utter the word. For this alone it might be disputed, yet rationalizations so thread the account that a sense of guilt cannot be ignored. He describes what sailors called "the custom of the sea," the drawing of lots so one died to save others, but not even that pretense of fairness occurred in Samar. Lots were not drawn, and the Filipinos were butchered by armed marines. He dances around the act, but returns to that moment when "insane thoughts of cannibalism and murder had entered their minds," and reproduces as evidence the February 1, 1902, notes of the "Manila Times correspondent at Tacloban, Leyte Island, P.I." who writes: "Cannibalism and murder were the revolting crimes against nature, which for two days and nights seem to be the sole escape from maddening hunger and ultimate starvation which the poor, emaciated marines suffered, as no one can imagine the sufferings." The army apparently censors the story, hoping it goes no further. Yet the marines do feast on *something* from January 7 to 9, 1902, for Lieutenant Williams admits in his account that when they set out on the ninth, they'd bolstered their strength on the meat of two slaughtered hogs—this, in a part of the jungle "shunned" by beasts and birds. Hawkins fails to mention such convenient provender, allegedly captured and killed by men too weak to move.

On the ninth, Williams ordered his 33 men and 13 remaining porters back to Lanang. All could not go. Joseph Baroni, a twenty-six-year-old private from Bangor, Maine, was too "sick to move and he is left behind," Williams says. From this point on, "my recollection of time and events is very hazy": by day, "we stumbled painfully forward"; by night, they "lay in a stupor, tormented by the most vivid dreams of food and comfort." Each object weighed a ton. They dumped 29 rifles and 3,000 rounds of ammo, and Hawkins presumed it ended up in enemy hands. Weakness returned, and they "could not crawl, or, in most cases, move." Private Timothy Murray of Athlone, Ireland, was the second to give up, knowing full well that stopping meant suicide. In the end, ten of Williams's men refused to move farther and were never found again.

That left twenty-three marines, starved and half-mad. And now, Williams says, the porters mutinied. The Americans were convinced that they'd hidden food from them, and Williams told three porters to gather firewood, ostensibly to boil taro root. They refused. When Williams tried to force them, a fight erupted: he was bitten and lightly stabbed with a bolo, he claimed. According to Hawkins, the lieutenant tried to fire his revolver, but was so weak "there was not strenght [*sic*] enough in his trigger finger to discharge the weapon." One porter wrenched it away and aimed at Williams, but "the devil was [too] ignorant of the mechanism" to shoot. A Sergeant McCaffrey staggers up and raises his rifle, but cannot work the bolt. The three men plunge into the jungle with the revolver and wisely never return.

Ten porters remain, still carrying rifles and gear. If they were treacherous, why did they stay? This is an important point, one that is never raised. Hawkins's account must now be considered: if cannibalism had occurred earlier, the three "mutineers" may have seen Williams's order to build a fire as prelude to another cannibal feast. If so, fighting back and running away made perfect sense. Those who stay will wish they'd run, too.

It is now January 18, and rescuers from Lanang have struggled upriver for four days. At 9:30 a.m. they hear shots. They paddle upstream and find ten marines sprawled in the sand, all "delirious with fevers," all "without shoes, shirts, or trousers enough to cover their privates," said the officer-in-charge. The men point inland—the others are there! They hack for a mile and find Alex Williams and his party "on the verge of starvation and death," the ten constant porters still with them. The rescuers carry them to the boats and the party reaches Lanang before nightfall.

On the morning of January 20, the gunboat *Arayat* docked at Tacloban in Leyte, carrying the surviving marines. All were rushed to the hospital, but two died of injuries and weakness within a few days. Some were in such a "state of imbecility" that Hawkins guessed they'd "not be fit for active duty again." Infection from leech bites caused agonized itching: some required amputation of arms and lower limbs. Others "will lose their eyes, their faces being covered over by a cancerous eruption." A few of them might eventually return to duty, but for the absolute worst, "only death" could end their suffering.

Also aboard the *Arayat* rode the ten porters. Although their loyalty had helped save the survivors, they found no gratitude in Lanang. Instead, they were accused of "treachery," on the grounds that they did not intercede to save Alex Williams from their comrades. Cannibalism was never mentioned, and only peeked forth in Hawkins's diary, the notes of the unnamed reporter, and the ravings of survivors tied to their hospital beds. The porters were clapped in irons belowdecks for the journey to Tacloban.

Waller still recuperated in Basey and had not heard of his men's ordeal nor that ten had been left to die. On the afternoon of the twentieth, Sergeant Quick escorted the porters across the San Juanico Strait, where he found the feverish Waller wrapped in bandages. Because Quick had escaped the jungle with Captain Porter, he had no firsthand knowledge of the alleged attack on Alex Williams; nevertheless, he accused the Filipinos of treachery, saying that Porter recommended execution. As for his own opinion, Quick stated, "I would shoot them all down like mad dogs."

Revenge had actually started the previous day. When Waller's temperature reached 105°F, the camp surgeon deemed him unfit for command. Authority fell to his adjutant, Lieutenant John Horace Arthur Day. A man denounced as a spy by Basey's mayor had confessed under torture. As a warning to villagers, Day shot him in the street and left his body in the sun. Now Waller faced the ten porters. No one seemed to know the whole story: some said that twenty marines had died; the survivor George Davis accused three porters of hiding potatoes, while of the other seven he said, "They were all thieves, sir, that I know of, and they were all worth hanging." Waller ordered them executed without trial, then collapsed back into his sickbed.

With this delirious act, what had been hidden became infamous: Waller's decree released Samar's tale to the world. The adjutant's squad led the men to the square, stood each on a barrel, and fired. Residents were told they must die "because they had been disloyal and tried to murder Americans": one cannot help wonder whether it was also to hide the rumors of cannibalism. Two days later, on January 22, Waller's fever broke, and he wired an explanation to Jake Smith: "It became necessary to expend eleven prisoners," he explained: since eleven Americans had died on the march, eleven Filipinos died to balance the scales. Three months later, he would write a longer report in which he claimed that he would not have acted differently: "It seemed, to the best of my judgment, the thing to do at the time."

Among the many U.S. narratives, one thread prevailed: carnage was never blamed on Americans. Widespread attacks upon women were never included in official reports; nor were prisoners stuffed into suffocating tents or rampant drunkenness among the men of Company C. No tales of cannibalism emerged, or of Major Glenn's extortion of British hemp dealers. These would only trickle out, often over decades—through Philippine sources, family tales, buried archives. Jake Smith's orders to kill everyone over age ten would not emerge until court testimony.

The path to revelation began on January 23, 1902—three days after the porters' executions. After the number of complaints about Jake Smith's "pacification" could no longer be ignored, Chaffee materialized in Tacloban for an inspection. Protests came from General Grant in Leyte, from that island's merchants and residents, even from "Big Bill" Taft. Chaffee had made a serious mistake when he'd publicly blamed Taft for Balangiga, and on October 8 Roosevelt cabled, "I'm deeply chagrined, to use the mildest possible term, over the trouble between you and Taft." Kiss and make up, he warned: "I wish you to see him personally, and spare no effort to secure prompt and friendly agreement in regard to the differences between you." Roosevelt didn't need to spell out what would happen if Chaffee failed to comply.

Now tongues were wagging about executions, so Chaffee hurried to Tacloban. Howling Jake Smith picked him up at the dock. On the ride back to headquarters, Chaffee blurted, "Smith, have you been having any promiscuous killing on Samar for fun?"

The question took Smith by surprise. He'd later testify that he'd not yet heard of the executions. "No sir," he said.

"Well, I understand that at Basey they have been killing some people over there."

He'd look into it, Smith said.

Treachery became the common excuse for U.S. war crimes. Waller's men acted as they did due to the porters' "treachery." The massacre at Balangiga succeeded because of the "treachery" of town officials. Other military disasters occurred from the planning of "treacherous" army deserters, headlines claimed, and with this, previously unreported desertions began to materialize. During a February 8 battle near Lokilokon, the deserter John Winfrey, who'd been commissioned a second lieutenant by Lukbán, was killed with eight of his men. On February 25 the wounded deserter William Dunston was captured in a battle outside Cagayan. Even the British were deemed treacherous: army reports said they smuggled guns and food to guerrillas, and the army judge advocate banned more British citizens from Samar.

No other American conflict has been so suffused with accounts of betrayal; themes of treachery weave through the Cuban and Philippine wars. García and his *mambisi* were betrayed in Santiago; Aguinaldo claimed that every promise made by Dewey and the consuls dissolved into betrayal and lies. Americans called broken promises a preemptive strike, since everyone knew that "savages" would not honor manly vows. Blacks were duplicitous by nature, as shown by the well-publicized desertion of six Buffalo Soldiers from the Ninth Cavalry in Albay Province in February and March 1901. Filipinos were duplicitous, as shown by their "amigo war." Democrats and Anti-Imperialists were traitors for publishing proof of American atrocities. The law states the case against a traitor with simple logic: "If a state gives a citizen protection it has a claim to his allegiance," wrote Rebecca West in her study of treason. But, she added, "if he gives it his allegiance, it is bound to give him protection." The black press asked what protection these soldiers could expect from lynch mobs back home.

In this war of symbols, the greatest failure was the continued survival of David Fagen. By the fall of 1901, he was blamed for almost every American setback, from Lawton's death to Balangiga. His freedom spoke volumes about America's impotence as a colonizer. The civilizing impulse is absolute: control must look total, but the outlaw thumbs his nose. Fagen's life had gone full circle: he'd evolved from the "Winchester Negro" of adolescence to the lone desperado opposing Empire.

Despite many far-flung "sightings," no verified records suggest that Fagen strayed far from Nueva Ecija. The spring 1901 collapse of the rebellion had been his undoing; Lacuna's May 1, 1901, surrender forced him to flee. Though Northern Luzon was now generally quiet, it was not good enough for Fagen to fade away. His role in District Four's resistance had been central; records show that he led virtually every successful conflict against U.S. forces under Frederick Funston during that period. Interviews with Fagen's former captives claimed that he was neither the monster nor the illiterate savage Funston painted him to be. Yet surrender was not an option: "Whatever he had been before," Funston wrote, "he was now a bandit, pure and simple, and entitled to just the same treatment as a mad dog." No mercy could be expected. He must vanish to survive.

Old comrades were sad to see him go. As it became obvious that further resistance was impossible, "I really felt sorry in having to leave Fagan [*sic*]," wrote General José Alejandrino. In the short time he'd known the "negro giant," Alejandrino developed a closeness that "could only be expected from a brother or son." As the youthful general grew weak from fever, Fagen "was very affectionate and helpful to me, going to the extent of carrying me in his arms or on his shoulders when" crossing rivers or ascending steep grades. The enigmatic American intrigued him: "His most outstanding characteristic was his mortal hatred of the American whites," yet his kind treatment of Lieutenant Alstaetter proved otherwise. When Alejandrino set off to surrender, he said, "I left him some twelve rifles for his defense." The young general never saw him again.

Even before this last act, the strain showed. By 1901 Fagen was living in camp with a woman described as his common-law wife, perhaps the same lover who'd coaxed him away from San Isidro two years earlier. "One morning this woman presented herself to me crying and showing me one cheek bitten off and saying that Fagan [*sic*] had done it," Alejandrino recalled. He sent for the American "giant" and asked what had happened. "I was only dreaming," Fagen said. In his dream, he'd finally been cornered and "not having the intention to be caught alive, he resisted as much as he could with punches, kickings and bitings." He woke to screams and found that "his fury against the enemy in his mind had been rained on his woman companion."

Alejandrino surrendered to Funston at Arayat on April 29, 1901. When he said that Fagen and two other deserters "wished to know if they would be able to leave the islands if they surrendered," Funston refused, adding, "You cannot surrender yourself without first delivering Fagan [*sic*]." Otherwise, he'd be jailed. Alejandrino stood his ground: "The surrender of Fagan [*sic*] is an infamy which I cannot commit because I know that if you get to catch him in your hands, you would be capable of bathing him in petroleum and burning him alive."

Funston just stared. "Then you will remain a prisoner," he said. Alejandrino guessed the general wanted to hang him, too, so out of caution he invoked the name of Arthur MacArthur, with whom he'd once negotiated. But Funston was not moved: "You're under arrest," he snapped, and that night, Alejandrino was kept under guard. The next morning, orders arrived from Manila to release Alejandrino and allow him to arrange his commander's surrender.

When Lacuna surrendered on May 16, 1901, he, too, tried to bargain for Fagen's life. Funston's response was predictable. "This man could not be received as a prisoner of war," he said. "If he surrendered it would be with the understanding that he would be tried by court-martial, in which event his execution would be a practical certainty." Lacuna bowed to the inevitable: three days later, all of his men, save Fagen, marched into San Isidro, laid down their arms, and took the oath of allegiance to their new colonial masters.

Fagen left the guerrilla camp sometime in May with his wife and another *insurrecto*. Events suggest that the three headed north, where the forest was thick and game plentiful. The army hunted him throughout that summer. A May 14 *Manila Freedom* story said he'd been caught in San Fernando and placed in "double-irons," but a *Manila Times* report two days later denied this, saying he was now in charge of a "robber band." On June 24 the soldier of fortune J. W. McMeeken, who went by "Filipino Bill," advertised in the *Manila Times* that for $1,000 in gold, he and three army scouts would "deliver one Fagan [*sic*], now in the mountains of Nueva Ecija." McMeeken promised to capture him in two months; if not, "No capture, no pay." Though nothing more was heard of "Bill," the ad suggests a new strategy: Funston gained Wheaton's authorization for a $600 bounty for "Fagen, dead or alive." Wanted posters in Spanish and Tagalog went up in towns throughout Nueva Ecija.

But Funston had no more luck than "Filipino Bill." Fagen dropped from sight: suddenly, he was everywhere. An August 16–17 *San Francisco Chronicle* story claimed that he'd boarded a troopship under a false name, debarked in Los Angeles, and was arrested for stealing a bicycle. It turned out that a young thief had used the name "Fagen" to honor his hero. *The Manila Times* sent a reporter to interview men from Fagen's old company. One officer heard that he'd fled south to Batangas; another that he'd been shot and his right arm paralyzed. One said he lived in the Nueva Ecijan jungles east of Santa Rosa. One officer called him a "good-for-nothing whelp"; enlisted men didn't blame him for "clearing out." One sergeant mused, "I certainly condemn the course he has taken and the bad repute brought upon the regiment, but the public doesn't know all that an enlisted man has to put up with or they would not be so quick to judge."

The Balangiga Massacre drove Fagen from the news. But not for long. Most credible rumors still put him in Nueva Ecija, and sometime in early November, Corporal William Watson of the Twenty-Fourth hiked into the mountains with nineteen privates from Company I. Watson and Fagen went way back: in October 1899 the two had served time together in San Fernando's guardhouse. One year later, Watson became Fagen's prisoner for two months. Watson pressed his old comrade closely, but in the end Fagen got away.

Nevertheless, Watson's hunt pinpointed this region as Fagen's hideaway. On December 5 a deer hunter walked into Bongabon, a sugar sack slung over one shoulder, rifle in his hand. Anastacio Bartolomé was well-known in these mountains, and behind him trailed five young men, carrying between them more sacks and rifles. Bongabon was a ten-hut village crouched in the Sierra Madre foothills; the army had seen fit to garrison it with only one sergeant, a platoon of Philippine Scouts, and their commander, Lieutenant R. C. Corliss from Denver. Bartolomé had a good sense of theater: he stopped before Corliss and without a word reached into his sacks and pulled out items one by one—a U.S. Army Colt .38 revolver and leather holster; a pair of saddlebags; a well-worn army-issue blue shirt; a pair of field glasses and gauntlets; a vest and shoulder straps worn by insurgents; and two photos. Bartolomé waited a beat, then drew from the last sack the "slightly decomposed head of a Negro." It belonged, he said, to David Fagen.

Corliss wired San Fernando, then sat Bartolomé down for a deposition. He'd not gone hunting for Fagen, he claimed: his party had crossed east over the mountains to hunt, fish, and "buy 'bejucos' from the Negritos" who lived in that region. They set up camp at a lonely place called Dingalan Cove on the east coast, where the Umiray River runs into the sea. On the night of November 30, they had cooked a dinner of fish and sweet potatoes, when Fagen walked into camp with his wife and two armed Negritos. Bartolomé knew Fagen: he'd served as one of Lacuna's scouts, and he knew about the $600 reward. Bartolomé invited the visitors to share their meal and spend the night, but said he made plans.

At about ten a.m., Bartolomé was cooking breakfast when on a prearranged signal the six "turned on Fagen and his men with bolos," Corliss wrote. The two wounded Negritos escaped into the jungle. Fagen's wife ran into the ocean and drowned. "Fagan [*sic*] was mortally wounded and ran about 100 yards and dropped dead." Bartolomé's party cut off Fagen's head, buried his body, gathered his effects, and began the five-day trek west to Bongabon.

Bartolomé produced other items: "a worn photograph of Urbano Lacuna, his officer's commissions (in the Philippine Army), and a West Point ring he had confiscated from the POW Lieutenant Alstaetter." The army told Corliss to make "a complete and satisfactory investigation of the evidence," including "any marks about the head and especially the teeth." Corliss replied that the severed head, though "partly decomposed," had the following features: "Complexion, dark;—Hair, curly;—Teeth, good and regular; nose, large and flat;—forehead, receding;—ears, set close to the head. Features seemed to correspond with the photograph brought in, presumably Fagans [*sic*]." The army sent Corliss's description to officers who'd known Fagen, including James Moss. Now a captain and the Twenty-Fourth's adjutant, Fagen's former commander sent back an "Information Slip" describing him as "a rowdy soldier and a 'bad man'" prone to "slang and profanity." Moss seemed ready to close the books on Fagen, as did Captain E. B. Gose, Company I's new commander. On December 13 Gose wired that his survey of the men "who knew Fagan [*sic*] well" concluded that the deserter's teeth were, indeed, "even, small and white," and "his head was small—he (wore) a 6 7/8 hat, came to a point on top, flat behind," apparently similar to the one Bartolomé brought in.

But this contradicted the written record. Fagen's recruitment form described him as a solid fellow: 5 feet, 10 inches, 183 pounds, with a "curved scar ¼ inch on chin." His photo from Manila and sketches in *The Salt Lake Herald* do not depict a small-headed, small-statured man. Descriptions of Bartolomé's severed evidence never mention a quarter-inch scar on the chin. The head *was* the size of an Aeta adult, one of the Igorot tribesmen in the area with whom Fagen traveled. Several officers offered alternate explanations: that Bartolomé found Fagen's camp, stole the gear and other evidence, and later added the head of some luckless Aeta. Or that Fagen colluded with Bartolomé, turning over Alstaetter's ring and other possessions as "proof" of his death, thus hoping to end further pursuit. The latter made more sense: Bartolomé could reap the bounty while Fagen lived the rest of his life unhunted. The doubters had some pull: the file on Fagen's "death" is titled "the supposed killing of David Fagen." And though Wheaton told Corliss to pay Bartolomé for the retrieved weapons, no record exists that the army ever paid the $600 bounty—this in a war where the quartermaster recorded every penny.

But the objections were buried by an army that by now had a well-established record of bending reality to suit its needs. It suited the army that Fagen was dead. Captain Gose's conclusion was wired to Lloyd Wheaton in Manila; Wheaton forwarded this to Adna Chaffee; Chaffee sent the file to the adjutant general in Washington, D.C. Fagen's effects were auctioned for $4; Alstaetter's ring was given to Funston, who planned to pass it to the owner when he returned home after the new year. On December 7, 1901, the *Manila Freedom* and *Manila Times* announced Fagen's death on the front page: "Fagan [*sic*] has been reported killed time and time again," led the *Freedom*'s account, but this time, they promised, it was true.

Papers across the United States followed suit. Even America's black press believed Fagen dead. One of the most eloquent obituaries ran in the December 14, 1901, Indianapolis *Freeman*. "Fagen was a traitor, and died a traitor's death," wrote the editor George Knox: "but he was a man, no doubt, prompted by honest motives to help a weaker side, and one to which he felt allied by ties that bind. Fagen, perhaps, did not appreciate the magnitude of the crime of aiding the enemy to shoot down his flag. He saw, it may be, the weak, the strong, he chose, and the world knows the rest."

Only one Philippine newspaper questioned Fagen's death, and this would be ignored. On December 7—the day of the Manila *Times*'s and *Freedom*'s breathless headlines—the city's third English-language paper, the *Manila American*, mocked army claims. "Fagan [*sic*] is dead—maybe," it said. "He has been killed again. The fact that he has been killed twelve times in the last ten months makes no difference. He goes on being killed with a regularity that is surprising." The bold headline professed doubt: "Officers Take No Steps" to prove Fagen's death, it claimed:

> The commanding officer at Bongabong [*sic*] is so positive that the man who brought in the head of an American negro actually slayed Fagan [*sic*] that he threw him in the guardhouse as a reward, and right away began an investigation to learn how many American negro soldiers have failed to answer roll call lately.
>
> The truth of the matter is that the military authorities do not take a bit of stock in the story told by the native who brought in the head, but are inclined to believe that the head was sent in by Fagan [*sic*] himself.

"The whole story is decidedly fishy," the paper concluded, predicting that in the near future, "the public may hope to be regaled with the details of Fagan's [*sic*] death again." In the United States, only one paper ran the *American* article. The January 19, 1902, *Leavenworth Times* buried it deep in the paper, just like another Fagen sighting later that year.

David Fagen was more convenient as a dead man. The war had become the very antithesis of all America professed to stand for, and it was easier to forget or pretend. This was Jack Ganzhorn's reaction: as Funston's watchdog awaited transport home in Manila, news of Fagen's "death" filled the air. He remembered those who'd died trying to kill the deserter: Captain Godfrey; his pal Albert Fryberger, "begging me with his last breath to kill Fagan [*sic*]." Rage and its justifications no longer mattered. Ganzhorn was drained: "I couldn't get any satisfaction out of just knowing Fagan [*sic*] was dead. I kept thinking of Fryberger, calling to me. All of a sudden I wanted to get to hell out of there. I hated the damned country. Never wanted to see it again."

30

War by Any Name

Jack Ganzhorn was not alone. The American people were tired. The war had dragged on too long. By the fall of 1901, the number of provinces under civil control had steadily increased, yet historians believe that Balangiga had "panicked Chaffee into authorizing the most extreme measures" against what resistance remained. The first wave of panic brought Jake Smith to Samar; the second wave involved Luzon's far southern Batangas Province, where, Chaffee said, all Filipinos "without a doubt . . . are intensely hostile." His reprisals created a holocaust surpassing Samar's, which brought the United States full circle. Now, like the Spaniards, they were annihilators.

Chaffee chose J. Franklin Bell to clean up Batangas. Almost forty-six, Bell had risen in three years from cavalry captain to brigadier general: he'd served as intelligence officer, provost marshal, and Northwest Luzon's "director of pacification," and he'd received the Medal of Honor for a September 1899 charge into gunfire. Bell's first permanent posting after West Point had been to the Seventh Cavalry, which in 1878 still reeled from the Custer debacle. Like many Indian fighters, he compared Filipinos to Native Americans, and in his mind, the latter were superior. After sending Bell to Batangas, Chaffee told a reporter, "If you should hear of a few Filipinos more or less being put out of the way, don't grow too sentimental over it."

Though Bell is best known in the United States for Batangas, he is better known in the Philippines for his late August 1900 correspondence with Apolinario Mabini. MacArthur had not yet exiled Mabini to Guam, and Bell pressed him to accept American rule and urge an end to the war. Mabini refused. Bell's letters offered Philippine historians a glimpse into U.S. attitudes about justice and power. War could be justified, Bell said, only if a combatant might win; if not, humanity demanded that they "surrender and accept the result, although it may be painful to its feelings." To Bell, the path to civilization meant acceptance of U.S. sovereignty: "The Filipino people can only show their fitness in this matter by laying down their arms."

Mabini mocked this argument, which assumed that the United States was "just and humanitarian" because its army was more powerful. "Not even the most ignorant Filipinos would believe" such reasoning, he said. No one deplored the "guerrilla and ambush system" more than the Republic, but they'd been "forced to adapt" when the balance of power left no other choice. Were Filipinos expected to stop "defending their homes and their freedoms against an invasion" just because they were the weaker party? Civilization was defined by resistance to submission, not surrender. Resistance, Mabini said, was the true mark of a civilized people.

Five months later, MacArthur exiled Mabini to Guam.

Now Bell applied the same principle to Batangas, Tayabas, Cavite, and Laguna—the four Tagalog provinces south of Manila where the First Philippine Republic had been born. While still in Palanan, Aguinaldo designated the veteran officer Miguel Malvar as his successor; with Aguinaldo's capture, Malvar assumed supreme command of the Republic's five thousand remaining fighters. He christened them the Army of Liberation and deployed them throughout Batangas, his native province, where the 1899 population numbered 312,192. By the summer of 1901, his men no longer fought as organized units, but hid their weapons, took refuge in towns and barrios, collected taxes, and ruled through assassination. Bell's predecessor, Brigadier General Samuel S. Sumner, concluded that war there could not be won except by "harsh and stringent" measures that promised widespread suffering, an extremity he deemed "inhumane and unwise." Like Aguinaldo, Malvar hoped the Americans would tire of guerrilla war. He promised rewards for those aiding the revolution, regardless of class, and for the first time promoted the revolution as a class struggle. They would fight for a decade if necessary. "Perseverance, perseverance, and always perseverance, without fear of sacrifice," he preached. "Let us continue, as the will of the people has always been more powerful than the most powerful armies."

On November 19, 1901, Chaffee ordered Bell to begin the measures Sumner rejected. His new Third Separate Brigade comprised 7,600 soldiers and Philippine Scouts, operating in Batangas, Cavite, and Laguna provinces, plus two large islands to the south that encompassed the provinces of Marinduque and Mindoro. Chaffee encouraged Taft to turn the area over to the military, and Taft agreed. He already considered Bell one of the archipelago's best generals, and like Chaffee, he had grown weary of Malvar. He told Elihu Root that the generals preceding Bell were "incompetent"; the entire country wanted the war over, he said.

Bell took formal command on November 30. From December 1 to January 23, 1902, he issued "circulars" outlining the coming campaign, based on his reading of General Order 100. He informed officers that Filipinos could not be swayed by "kindness and benevolence alone." Only "physical force" would do. He believed that fighting continued because Batangans supported Malvar, not the idea of a "peasant's war." "Neutrality" no longer had meaning: one must identify guerrillas; those lacking proper zeal were enemies. Punishment began with fines and rose in stages through property destruction, imprisonment, exile, and execution.

Bell's campaign started in Batangas and Laguna, then spread to every part of his domain. The first phase began on December 13: he issued orders to relocate the populace to *zonas*, the same *reconcentrado* policy as Weyler's. Anyone found outside the *zonas* was an insurgent and would be shot on sight, regardless of gender or age. Everyone must live in these "zones of peace," and curfew was set for eight p.m. Filipinos seen on the street after that would be shot; if any U.S. soldiers were killed, a native would be chosen by lot and executed. If guerrillas cut telegraph wires in the *zonas*, all nearby huts were burned. The first *zonas* were established in eastern Batangas, and all surrounding inhabitants must move in with food and possessions by December 26. After that, outside areas were deemed enemy territory. All property found there could be destroyed; all people would be arrested, and if they tried to escape, they would be killed.

In the space of twenty days, 100,000 Filipinos, or one-third of the provincial population, poured into designated zones. Food ran out, replaced by disease: 54,000 Batangans died. Bell disavowed responsibility: "The innocent must suffer for the sake of speedily ending the war," he said, a view endorsed by Chaffee. Yet when the first death rates were compiled in January 1902, Chaffee realized he'd unleashed an apocalypse. The public outcry against "Weylerism" was not that long ago, but rather than end Bell's pogrom, he strove to destroy evidence. In a January 10, 1902, missive to Army Adjutant General Henry Corbin, Chaffee asked that his letter notifying War Secretary Root of Bell's results be destroyed. He wanted no evidence of "what may be considered in the United States as harsh measures or treatment."

As thousands died in the *zonas*, Bell started the second phase. Like Weyler, he reasoned that guerrillas could never be beaten without destroying their food. On January 1, 1902, approximately 1,800 soldiers spread out in a designated area and destroyed everything in their path. They burned 500 tons of rice, killed hundreds of hogs and chickens, 800 head of cattle, 680 horses, and 200 *carabao*, and burned more than 6,000 houses. Another wave of soldiers bulldozed a neighboring zone. Sector by sector, Bell's men laid waste in a well-planned campaign of devastation, the catchphrase "Remember Balangiga!" on their lips. "I will burn everything that stands," Bell said, "and kill everything that lives in Batangas to have peace." His men took those words to heart. A correspondent called one such march "relentless": U.S. soldiers killed "men, women, children, prisoners and captives, active insurgents and suspected people, from lads of ten and up." Every Filipino, he wrote, was considered "little better than a dog." It was "not civilized warfare," but "we are not dealing with a civilized people. The only thing they know is force, violence and brutality, and we give it to them." He watched soldiers round up peasants, stand them on a bridge, and shoot them "one by one, to drop into the water below and float down as an example to those who found their bullet-riddled corpses." A congressman who toured the area said that the troops raked the sectors so thoroughly that "there isn't anybody there to rebel." Americans "took no prisoners [and] kept no records"; they simply "swept the country, and wherever or however they could get hold of a Filipino, they killed him."

Though U.S. troops kept detailed records of livestock slaughtered and rice burned, no accounting was kept of natives killed. Veiled orders to take no prisoners were issued as "Take this fellow and hunt chickens," or "This man should be removed." Yet names and specifics did leak out: Basilio Martinez, "shot dead because he did not confess what he was obliged to confess"; three other men who died after torture; eight women raped. Because Bell's main targets were the wealthy and educated, they were impressed into work gangs, tortured, killed. The family of Agoncillo's secretary Sixto Lopez became some of the first victims.

After Agoncillo returned to Hong Kong following his failed mission, Lopez and his sister Clemencia stayed behind—first in London, then, in October 1900, back to Boston as a guest of the Anti-Imperialist League. From 1900 to 1901, the two were shadowed by government agents but never arrested, probably due to this patronage. Sixto became *the* U.S. voice of the Philippines: his writings were published from New York to San Francisco and collected in Anti-Imperialist pamphlets; he spoke for Filipino rights onstage. His December 20, 1900, "Christmas Letter to the President of the People of the United States" was read by thousands: "In this great land, wherein we enjoyed the blessings of liberty and abundance, there are those who would shrink from the mere idea of killing a fellow being, yet who, under the influence of martial glory, do not realize that thousands of brave men and equally brave women are being slain, by sword and starvation, in a conflict which can only result in death to one people and withered laurels to the other." This was the Season of Peace. Must the carnage continue?

His grace period ended in the spring of 1902, when he tried to testify before the Senate: he was detained, presented with a loyalty oath, and deported when he refused to sign. The Louisville *Courier-Journal* called Lopez's banishment one more example of government "silence and suppression." The *Springfield Republican* said this was not the "atmosphere" of the America we once knew: "It is the atmosphere of Prussia, Poland, of Siberia and Turkestan." Sixto returned to Hong Kong and proposed negotiating Malvar's surrender for a promise of eventual independence. Authorities ignored his offer, and refused him entry into the Philippines.

Lopez hailed from the town of Balayan; he would learn that his entire family was targeted. On December 13, 1901, three of his brothers were sent to a penal colony on the small island of Talim. The Lopez house and storehouses were seized, cattle shot, ranch house burned to the ground. Horrors leaked out: the father of a family friend "was thrown still alive on a fire, simply because his son was an insurgent and he had not been able to bring about his surrender." Women they knew were deported for being rebels' wives. Anyone rumored to aid guerrillas was targeted.

Then one of their own was killed. On December 25, 1901, Isabelo Capacia—the aged superintendent of the Lopez holdings—was dragged from his jail cell to locate fifty guns intended for rebels that were buried on their plantation. This was a rumor, Capacia said: there were no guns. Under torture, he revealed one gun owned by the family, "a broken and useless Mauser rifle of the Spanish type." The next day, an American lieutenant, a police inspector, and a squad of Macabebes "took Isabelo to the bank of the River Matauanak, where, after having wrapped him in a carabao skin and attached a stone to his belt as a weight, they threw him in the water, allowing him to be entirely submerged," a friend wrote to Clemencia. When it seemed that Capacia no longer breathed, his torturers dragged him to the bank, "where they terminated their torture by jumping on his body, until blood burst from his mouth, nose, eyes, and ears; finally breaking some of his ribs." He was thrown unconscious into a wagon and taken back into jail. His wife pleaded to see him and was allowed in his cell. As she wept beside him, he said he knew he was dying and begged her not to leave. But U.S. soldiers dragged her off. Soon afterward, he died.

Cholera raced through the *zonas*. On March 23, 1902, Julia Lopez wrote Clemencia that several Balayan friends had died. In the town of Abra de Ilog, the sick refused to see U.S. doctors, convinced that "Americans were paying to have Filipinos poisoned." The Filipinos even distrusted American cures: "As soon as the medicine was taken, the patient died, even although he had not been fatally ill."

By the time these letters reached Clemencia, the war in Batangas had peaked. In Samar, it was over: on February 18, 1902, Vicente Lukbán was captured. One of the last holdouts, he was disgusted with war. That left Malvar as the last active Filipino general, and he was weakening, too. By March, armed resistance was all but over; only Malvar's capture remained. Soldiers chased the general and his last comrades over mountains and from valley to valley; they killed all domestic animals encountered, burned crops and houses, shot natives. Malvar's last troops were sick, starving, and almost out of cartridges; his wife fell dangerously ill. That may have been the trigger: on April 4, he penned a letter to Bell asking for a suspension in fighting to discuss terms. Bell promised fair treatment, and on April 16 Malvar surrendered. His loyalists trickled from the mountains. By May, the war in Batangas had ended.

In explaining his surrender, Malvar pointed to the *zonas*; one of his officers said that without them, the war would have dragged on another three years. Yet privately, Malvar was convinced that the Americans would resort to mass murder if he'd kept fighting. If farmers had not been allowed to plant rice in May, famine would sweep the province. It probably would anyway, since Bell's scorched-earth policy had devastated their farms and fields.

Batangas divides historians. Some American scholars, like John Morgan Gates, called Bell's campaign "a credit to the American Army in the Philippines and a masterpiece of counter-guerrilla warfare." Most Filipinos, like Reynaldo Ileto and Teodoro Kalaw, call it genocide. Bell's reports declared Batangas pacified, with 163 rebels killed, 209 wounded, 3,626 captured or surrendered, and 2,893 firearms seized. He did not mention the 54,000 who died in the first months of *reconcentrado*. On April 17 Roosevelt wired congratulations to Bell.

That same day, the army released everyone held in the *zonas*. They returned to what the historian Glenn A. May called "ecological devastation on a massive scale." Brian Linn called Bell's destruction so "enormous" that it contributed to "the appalling cholera and fever epidemics that killed thousands of Batanguenos." All agriculture screeched to a halt; livestock and draft animals were reduced to a tenth of their prewar numbers. Few records remain, but a 1906 report released by the Anti-Imperialist League gave a glimpse, comparing pre- and postwar conditions in the towns of Balayan, Tuy, and Calatagan. In 1896, 41,308 people lived there; in 1905, 13,924. In 1896, 19,500 hectares of land were cultivated; in 1905, 1,700. Rice production dropped from 39,020 units to 12,500; sugar from 520,000 to 12,300; maize from 110,000 to 10,000. The number of wagons and carts available for shipping dropped from 3,550 to 71. Livestock deaths were astounding: 10,000 oxen in 1896 dropped to 427 in 1905; 5,460 *carabao* dropped to 525; 4,800 horses fell to 616; hogs and hens fell from 107,000 to 7,800.

The Batangans brought cholera from the zones. The disease had swept Luzon before: the epidemic of 1882–83 killed hundreds of thousands; Clara Maass had seen cases in 1899, as well as Helen Taft in 1900. It came on quickly, often at night, first as shivers that turned into convulsions. Next came violent diarrhea, vomiting, severe pains in the stomach, and agonizing cramps in the legs, feet, and abdomen. Fluid loss was so great that one's blood thickened; the body turned cold and blue or purple; one's eyes sank beneath their brows. Death could occur within two hours, though more often within a day. As Batangans fled their doomed province by ship, they brought cholera to Manila, the hub. By summer, Manila saw seventy to eighty new cases a day. Burials were banned for fear of infecting the water table: only hermetically sealed metal coffins were permitted, something the poor could not afford. So people buried their dead in their backyards or threw them into rivers, poisoning the water further. The 1902–1903 cholera epidemic accounted for 150,000 documented cases, 109,461 of them fatal—4,386 in Manila alone.

Batangas exploded into a human and environmental cataclysm of unprecedented scale. But how many people actually died? Specifics may never be known. U.S. commanders tended to cover up accurate death counts in the *zonas*; in the country, officers failed to mention the "unsavoury aspects of the fighting," Glenn May found. But if army records were silent, parish records were not: the *libros de entierros*, or "books of burials," recorded the deceased's name, age, and place of residence; the dates of their death and interment; cause of death; and the name of the decedent's spouse. Parish records showed that "excess" deaths over standard historical levels were abnormally high during those four months of *zonas* captivity, but they exploded in the months following release, which then turned into the early months of the cholera epidemic. In the town of Lipa, an average of 291 people died per month in normal times. But in April, 558 died; in May, 762; in June, an astonishing 1,329. In Batangas City, site of a huge *zona*, an average of 392 people died per month, but after they were released in April, 637 died.

May discovered a disturbing "150,000 missing" Batangans during and after Bell's campaign. The medical historian Ken De Bevoise goes further: During the four months of *reconcentrado*, Batangas may have had the highest mortality rate in the world. When the 1902 census was published, statisticians estimated the death rate as 132.9 per thousand, or one out of eight. Taft realized belatedly that the devastation had gone far beyond anything they'd ever imagined. "The severity with which the inhabitants have been dealt with would not look well if a complete history of it were written out," he said, and he hoped it never would.

The United States had learned, as do all conquerors, that Empire and Death go hand in hand.

By March 1902 the war in Luzon was practically over. In the United States, a moral reckoning began.

It started in January, when a Senate committee finally held hearings on the atrocity reports that had been piling up for years. Though Chairman Henry Cabot Lodge tried to downplay accounts as infrequent or inaccurate, the testimony of witnesses to the water cure, to villages being burned and villagers hung, released an onslaught of horrors that continued through summer and pummeled the American conscience as thoroughly as the My Lai Massacre in Vietnam. What had been sold as a civilizing campaign looked more like a dirty war of subjugation. True, such reports had leaked earlier, but these were isolated and scattered, confined to the letters by local heroes or to such regional controversies as Kansan reactions to Funston's misdeeds. Before, most accounts had been collected in Anti-Imperialist publications, which Americans tended to disregard. Now the sheer weight of revelation could not be ignored. Roosevelt and Elihu Root tried to defend the army, but realized they must make a show of cleaning up army excesses if the administration hoped to salvage its future. Root decided that example would be Littleton Waller, still mending from his ordeal.

Waller was truly shocked when he was charged with murder. When his marines were relieved on February 26, 1902, Jake Smith wired, "You are as fine a group of soldiers as has ever served under my command and I have been an officer for forty years." They'd boarded the *Lawton* for Manila: naval vessels dipped their colors as they passed. Waller led his men ashore amid cheering crowds. He reported to his commanding officer, who said he was under arrest and must surrender his sword.

Waller's court-martial embodied more than the alleged crimes of one feverish major. It symbolized the brutal entirety of the Philippine War. But was Waller a scapegoat or genuinely guilty? Certainly his acts in Samar were brutal, but that brutality had been sanctioned at every level—all the way up to Roosevelt, who'd said that Filipinos should be dealt with as "savages." But now Roosevelt said that Waller's acts "sullied the American name." In this way, he certainly was a scapegoat, and for this, many historians would call him an "honorable warrior" abandoned to sacrifice. Yet Waller had not been in the field when he ordered those eleven executions; he could not, as had Funston and others, plead the exigencies of combat when he condemned the porters without giving them a trial. For that, he had blood on his hands.

Waller's trial opened in a Manila army barracks on March 17, 1902, and lasted through April 12. Officers of the court represented the army and the marines. The coverage was extensive. He confessed to ordering the deaths, but based his defense on General Order 100. Seeking to protect his superior officer, he assumed full responsibility. But six days later, when Jake Smith took the stand, the general did nothing to repay the favor. Smith claimed that his orders called for captives to be treated humanely; his officers must respect "the laws of war." Littleton Waller did not reflect the attitudes of the men fighting in the Philippines, Smith claimed. The major had gone rogue.

Waller was incensed. Smith's betrayal put his career and even his life in jeopardy. He returned to the stand for "redirect" and revealed for the first time Smith's exact words—from his orders to execute children to his wish that Samar become a "howling wilderness" where one must "kill and burn." He admitted to disobeying orders by not killing children. Suddenly the show trial became a stunning embarrassment: the court acquitted Waller of all charges. He returned to command; although in time he would make major general, the taint remained. When Taft became president, he passed over Waller for the job of Marine Corps commandant: the man dubbed "the butcher" symbolized too nakedly the American way of "civilizing" the globe.

In the midst of this circus, deep rifts opened in Roosevelt's political kingdom. His image was one of bold action: he'd already enraged Southern whites by inviting Booker T. Washington to dine at the newly dubbed "White House," vexed Big Business by calling for a congressional investigation of trusts, and delighted imperialists by promising more battleships and a strategic canal slicing across Central America. Yet he could not control Commanding General Nelson A. Miles. Roosevelt had never liked Miles: he was not a team player. His revelations about "embalmed beef" at the end of the Dodge Commission threatened to derail McKinley's reelection while sinking careers. As more atrocities dripped forth, Miles asked to investigate, a request Roosevelt denied. In mid-March, Miles told the reporter Henry Watterson about the denial, and Watterson wondered aloud in *The Washington Post* what further dark secrets might be exposed. Miles "could, and would, bring order out of chaos if sent to Manila," he wrote, but his request "sleeps in some pigeonhole." Roosevelt called Miles an "intriguer," and considered firing him. The two sniped back and forth in competing papers until Miles leaked a March 24 letter hinting at the administration's cover-up of "marked severities" in Batangas, quoting internal documents, including the letter from Taft to Root describing the horrors unleashed by Bell. Root dressed Miles down: such charges, he said, should not be revealed "against our countrymen whom we have sent to labor and fight under our flag on the other side of the world." But Roosevelt left Miles alone, fearing the political backlash that would come with his firing.

The court of public condemnation began on the day of Waller's acquittal. The Philadelphia *North American* screamed in bold print, "Butcher Waller Testifies to Dastardly Crimes." Hearst's *Evening Journal* ran a cartoon depicting American soldiers shooting women and children; its entire front page on April 8 led with the headline "'KILL ALL': Major Waller Ordered to Massacre the Filipinos!" The Baltimore *Herald* said that Smith's order to turn Samar into a wasteland had no precedent in "the annals of civilized warfare"; *The Indianapolis News* and *The Buffalo Express* saw in the whole sorry episode proof of failed U.S. policy. The *New York Evening Post* went further, declaring that U.S. troops pursued "a policy of wholesale and deliberate murder," a characterization one small step below genocide.

Many narratives today decry the "feeding frenzy" that ripped through the nation's papers in April–May 1902. But it can also be seen as a reaction to three years of censorship, falsification, and downright lies, the same pattern repeated in later wars. Americans always want to believe the best of the military and its daily serving of heroes, yet when such accounts pierce the fog, someone must pay before the self-willed, cozy veil lowers again. In this case, Jake Smith, Edwin Glenn, and several lower-ranking officers were sacrificed, not Chaffee, Robert Hughes, Taft, Elihu Root, or Roosevelt, the top-level sources of the murderous directives. Howling Jake never stood a chance: Roosevelt demanded action, Root told Chaffee to press matters "forcefully," and Chaffee filed charges against his old friend. "It looks as if Jake Smith is going to be in the soup, too," Chaffee told his wife. Smith denied his guilt, but even the most rabid imperialists abandoned him. "Nothing can justify the use of torture or inhuman conduct" by U.S. troops, declaimed Roosevelt, who just a year earlier discredited such accusations as the lies of Democrats, Anti-Imperialists, and their traitorous mouthpieces. Smith was court-martialed and found guilty, and Roosevelt ordered him retired from active service immediately. The embittered Glenn was court-martialed, found guilty, and reprimanded. He learned the truth of colonial conflict: all are expendable, not just the enemy.

Even as the trials played out, Bell's Batangan campaign hit the papers. The first salvo was the leaked documents Root had tried to conceal. One included a complaint by Cornelius Gardener, now governor of Tabayas Province, claiming that Bell made war on the entire province, not just guerrillas. At least 100,000 were dead, and the "bitter hatred" produced by his actions would work against the United States for decades. Chaffee forwarded the letter to Root, who filed it and forgot it. But someone leaked Gardener's report after Roosevelt had congratulated Bell.

A second leak exposed Bell's *zonas* policy, which unleashed nationwide condemnation. Howling Jake's call for child murder had been bad enough, but at least Waller showed the good sense to disobey and Smith could be dismissed as a madman. Batangas was different: its conception, planning, and execution were systemic, approved at every level of the military and government, and most papers called it a crime. Papers that once supported U.S. policy mourned what the nation had become. *The*

Detroit Journal compared Bell to "Butcher Weyler"; the *Baltimore American* lamented that "we have actually come to do the thing we went to war to banish" in Cuba. The Philadelphia *Public Ledger* reminded readers of McKinley's statement that reconcentration "was not civilized warfare."

Who was responsible for this corruption of American values? To damn the army meant damning American boys, which suggested that the taint lay in Americans themselves. But there must be a culprit. As yet, they did not blame Roosevelt, but did so in proxy by targeting his close ally Elihu Root. Each revelation exposed the secretary's "attempts to gild the hideous truth," mocked the *Springfield Republican.* Were the "superpatriots in Washington so drunk on this new wave of imperialism that they complacently think they can settle all these things in their own private enclaves and keep Congress and the American people in the dark?" asked the *New York Evening Post.* In May 1902 the Anti-Imperialist League released *Secretary Root's Record: "Marked Severities" in Philippine Warfare.* The most famous of their "atrocity pamphlets," it laid the carnage directly at the feet of Roosevelt and Root by quoting their own words.

At this very moment, "Fighting Fred" Funston entered the fray. In mid-November 1901 he'd been felled by chronic ulcerative appendicitis and sent to Manila's military hospital. He failed to improve and was sent to San Francisco for a second operation in January 1902. His recuperation was fitful, and over the next six months, he'd be readmitted for his Cuban malaria and a third operation to clean an infected cavity in his appendectomy scar.

Convalescence did not still his tongue. Like celebrities before and since, he missed the limelight, and sick leave offered ample means for correction. He gave sold-out lectures and wrote a fall 1901 serialized magazine account of "Aggie's" capture. Dinner invitations abounded, and during the postprandial speeches he'd attack Taft's "misguided" Benevolence: "The Filipino doesn't love us a bit," he sneered. "He doesn't know what gratitude is. He has no sense of appreciation, and I believe he'd like us better if we dealt more severely with him."

Funston headed east, first to Iola, then on a cross-country speaking tour rivaling Roosevelt's in 1900. The whistle-stops paraded political intent: he lectured in uniform, using the colonel's same "bully" tone.

Editors dusted off rumors of a 1904 Roosevelt-Funston ticket; thanks to his father's tutelage, he knew that a colorful quote drove a story to the front page. By now, it was February 1902. Lodge's committee was mired in damning testimony, including that of Edmund Boltwood, former captain in the Twentieth Kansas. Boltwood said that Funston personally administered the water cure to suspects and on several occasions ordered his men "to take no prisoners." Accompanying affidavits corroborated his words. Lodge hustled Boltwood out as fast as possible, and Roosevelt privately called the water cure "an old Filipino method of mild torture" that could not approach the "incredible tortures" they'd inflicted "on our people."

Funston swept into New York City like a *derecho*, the straight-line gales screaming across the Great Plains. On March 9 he headlined a gala dinner at Fifth Avenue's Lotos Club, one of America's oldest upper-class gentlemen's clubs. William Randolph Hearst was a member, as were Andrew Carnegie and Mark Twain. The guest list that night is uncertain, but not long afterward, Twain mercilessly satirized the "Little Guy."

Funston began his speech mildly enough, chiding fellow citizens for a lack of fortitude in dragging out the war, a theme upon which Roosevelt would soon expound. "It is perfectly proper for us to have all sorts of opinions as to what we should do with the Philippines, but for heaven's sake let us keep them to ourselves until every square inch of that territory recognizes the sovereignty of the United States," he said. Then he lowered the boom. The current outrage over summary execution was sheer nonsense: he boasted of personally hanging thirty-five *insurrectos*, and told of twenty-four Americans who'd joined the enemy "and who were afterward captured and executed as traitors"—a number that quadrupled from six deserters when he first spoke in San Francisco two months earlier. "What was all the fuss over Waller's 'dispatching' a few 'treacherous savages'?" he stormed. He aimed his choicest barbs at "prattlers" who fed the Senate "outright lies" just to discredit the army. "The whole lot" should be hung for treason: "If there had been more Smiths and Wallers, the war would have been over long ago. Impromptu domestic hanging might also hasten the end of the war. For starters, all Americans who had recently petitioned Congress to sue for peace in the Philippines should be dragged out of their houses and lynched."

This was strong stuff, though calls for political lynchings still persist today. The audience didn't know what hit them: some cried "That's right!" Others sat in silence, stunned.

But Funston was only getting warmed up. During his return to San Francisco, he'd emerge at whistle-stops and yell "Bully for Waller!" and "Hooray for Smith!" to the crowds. During a Chicago banquet, he said, "There is no room for any American who calls himself a patriot to have other than one opinion about our present position in the Philippines." He suggested again that "impromptu domestic hangings" might shorten the war. In a Kansas stop, when his old friend Charles Scott suggested that he cool his language, Funston confided that the president had said, "I am glad you made that speech. I was all right. But I think it would be well for you to be a little more careful about speech making hereafter." On March 8, in Topeka, Funston spoke at a Republican dinner for three minutes "and didn't say a thing," Scott said.

It didn't take Funston long to backslide. On March 12 in Colorado Springs, he listed several candidates for his noose, including senators, prominent citizens, "the presidents of nearly all American universities, and the leading clergymen of all denominations." After the septuagenarian Senator George Hoar took the floor to scold him, Funston mocked Hoar for his "overheated conscience." According to rumor, he planned to catch a train to Boston, where he'd recommend the senator for his "noose party." In response, Hoar told the Harvard Republican Club that he would not be intimidated by "some microscopic general who knows as much about the rules of civil government as he does about the rules of civilized warfare."

The episode would be the general's undoing. Everyone but Funston seemed to realize that he'd crossed a line. After an April 6 speech in Denver, reporters asked if he'd not gone too far. "The idea that an army officer must keep his mouth always shut is a hallucination," Funston snapped. "I have a mouth, I use it for two purposes. One is to eat and the other is to talk, and when I talk I mean what I say, because I know what I am talking about." He added that he had "great contempt" for men who, at the start of the war, would have taken everything from Spain, but now were "playing peanut politics and gambling in the blood of their countrymen."

Perhaps Funston sensed that the damage was done. As he headed back to San Francisco, the *Call* suggested he would "do well to repair his inflated condition and sheathe his unruly mouth." When a *Call* reporter caught him on arrival, Funston declared that his paper's publisher and editor "ought to be strung up to the nearest lamppost." Friends worried. His malarial fever had returned two days before the Denver speech, and they feared delirium. Worse, William Allen White and Vernon Kellogg feared that "Timmy" had returned to hard drinking. White was on the West Coast when Roosevelt wired him to talk to their friend: "He must quit talking, or the President would have to rebuke him publicly," White wrote in his autobiography. "When I told my message, Timmy looked at me and grinned. 'Oh Billy, look not upon the gin rickey when it is red, and giveth color in the cup, for it playeth hell and repeat with poor Timmy.'" He seemed to have listened: at a banquet at the Palace Hotel held in his honor, he raised the number of prisoners he'd personally executed to fifty, but said nothing "about hanging Boston's finest citizens." Instead, he lectured on the futility of making war against "unruly savages."

But the expiation came too little, too late. On April 21 a small article about Funston's Denver speech and criticism of Senator Hoar ran in a Washington newspaper under the headline "Gamble in Country's Blood." Funston's excesses finally hit home. All talk of Funston's political future ended at that moment as Roosevelt picked up a pen:

> To the Secretary of War:
>
> I call your attention to the enclosed report of a speech by General Funston. The reference to the senior Senator from Massachusetts is entirely improper in a general of the army. I think that General Funston will have to be requested not to make any more public speeches. I appreciate to the full his great service and I am in cordial sympathy with his general view of the Philippines, but he expresses himself at times in a way that is very unfortunate.

Elihu Root was not so kind. Three days later, on April 24, 1902, the secretary wired Funston: "I am directed by the President to instruct you that he wishes you to cease all further discussion of the situation in the Philippines," an official reprimand reproduced on front pages across the nation.

All further talk must cease. All furloughs were canceled. The muzzled Funston must return to Nueva Ecija, where he would sit out the remainder of the war.

Funston might be gone, the Smith and Waller courts-martial might be over, but the Lodge hearings roared on. Funston had barely stepped on the boat for Manila when the Reverend W. H. Walker, who ran a Boston school for missionaries, released to *The Boston Journal* a letter from his son in Batangas describing the systematic execution of thirteen hundred prisoners. According to Walker's son, a native priest had been called to hear the condemneds' final confessions. This took days. When all confessions were heard, the priest was hung in full view of the prisoners. Next, they dug their own graves. This took another six days, after which some of the men were gunned down. By now, it was the Sabbath, so those left rested. On Monday, the process started again. The mass execution took weeks: the men would have starved to death anyway, explained the younger Walker, owing to the army's efficiency in decimating the land. "To keep the prisoners would necessitate the placing of the soldiers on short rations if not starving them," he wrote. "There was nothing to do but kill them."

On April 16, 1902, Pulitzer's *World* ran a eulogy for a bygone nation. "The American public eats its breakfast and reads in its newspapers of our doings in the Philippines," the lead editorial began. "It sips its coffee and reads of its soldiers administering the 'water cure' to rebels . . . and remarks, 'how very unpleasant.' It then butters its bread and reads of the ingenious Major Waller who murdered his defenseless victims . . . and remarks, 'how distressing!' It cracks an egg and reads of the orders of General Smith 'to kill and burn' . . . and thinks to itself 'Rather extreme,' perhaps with mild disapproval, perhaps turning aside with disgust":

> But where is that vast national outburst of astounded horror which an old fashioned America would have predicted at reading such news? Is it lost somewhere in the 8,000 miles that divide us from these abominations? Is it led astray by the darker skins of the alien race among

which these abominations are perpetrated? Or is it rotted away by that inevitable demoralization which the wrongdoing of a great nation must inflict on the consciences of the least of its citizens?

The editorial crystallized something in Mark Twain. He rarely mentioned sources, but three days later, on April 19, he spoke at Princeton University. He cited the war's casualties, then read a U.S. decree making it a crime for any Filipino to defend independence for his country. He paused, cocking his head as he always did before launching into the heart of the matter. "If I were in the Philippines, I could be imprisoned a year for publicly expressing the opinion that we ought to withdraw and give those people their independence—an opinion which I desire to express right now," he told the silent crowd. "On these terms I am quite willing to be called a traitor—quite willing to wear that honorable badge—and not willing to be affronted with the title of Patriot and classed with the Funstons, when so help me God I have done nothing to deserve it."

Privately, he despaired. He mourned the loss of something fundamental in America, but did not know how and when it disappeared. Maybe he'd been abroad too long. After his return, he began writing a series of historical fantasies about an empire where books were banned and libraries destroyed as history was wholly rewritten to glorify conquest in foreign lands, pieces that would not come out until after his death. One read like the obituary for the country he'd satirized and loved: "It was impossible to save the Great Republic," he wrote: "She was rotten to the heart. Lust of conquest had long ago done its work. Trampling upon the helpless abroad had taught her, by a natural process, to endure with apathy the like at home; multitudes who had applauded the crushing of other peoples' liberties, lived to suffer this mistake in their own persons." The only patriotism left, he concluded, was that "of the pocket."

In May, Twain published "A Defense of General Funston" in the *North American Review.* Most commentators focus on Twain's "defense" of Funston's begging Aguinaldo for food before capturing him at gunpoint: It would be "clearly unfair" to blame Funston for bad faith, he writes, "because his conscience leaked through one of his pores when he was little." But this "defense" was not about Funston: it was about the kind of nation that turned Funston into a model "to teach us children what Patriotism is!" The nation had built him up until "Funstonism" was everywhere. Funston's example had bred "many ghastly additions to our history: the torturing of Filipinos by the awful 'water-cure' . . . to make them confess—what? Truth?" Maybe he was even to blame for Krakatoa's eruption that killed millions, but "no, that could not have been Funston's example; I remember now, he was not born then."

Twain's crazy hyperbole implied that Americans no longer listened or cared. This war had gone on too long. The costs had been too great, both in lives and in lost ideals. Twain imagined that the annual Independence Day parade snaking down Broadway would include floats heaped with the bodies of dead patriots called "rebels." The new national flag that led off the march could be inscribed with the words "Oh, you will get used to it, brother. I had sentimental scruples myself at first." It was easier to forget and turn away.

Lodge concluded his Senate hearing in late May without issuing a report. One week later, at noon on May 30, 1902, Theodore Roosevelt rode from the White House by carriage to Arlington Cemetery for his traditional Memorial Day address to the nation. Thirty thousand people hearkened to his words. He paid homage to the warriors around him, living and dead. He segued to the topic threatening his presidency. The war in the Philippines would soon end, "a small but peculiarly trying and difficult war in which is involved not only the honor of the flag but the triumph of civilization over forces which stand for the black chaos of savages and barbarism." Our soldiers had fought "under terrible difficulties and have received terrible provocations from a very cruel and very treacherous enemy." True, there had been "acts of cruelty," and he'd launched a "determined and unswerving effort" to ensure that it never happened again. "For every act of cruelty by our men," he said, "there have been innumerable acts of forbearance, magnanimity, and generous kindness." How ungrateful were those Americans who, "walking delicately" in the "soft places of the earth," would attack those brave men engaged in this great act of redemption.

He stepped back from the podium. The applause rolled over the green hills and white graves. It would be his only public statement about the war's well-documented atrocities. The honor of the army reflected the honor of the nation, as it still does, and then as now "occasional" acts of cruelty were easily forgotten by inevitable waves of national pride.

On July 1, 1902, Congress passed the Philippine Organic Act, which put into law actions already taken by Roosevelt and Taft, thus creating a legal structure to hold the islands forever. The next day, Elihu Root wired that since organized resistance had ended with the surrenders of Lukbán and Malvar, and since provincial governments had been established through most of the islands, the office of the military government was herewith terminated. Chaffee handed power in Luzon and the Visayas over to Taft, but in May, he had convinced Roosevelt to let him attack Islamic "Moros" farther south in the islands of Jolo and Mindanao—a campaign that continued until 1913. On July 4 Roosevelt ended the war with the stroke of a pen. His proclamation thanked American soldiers for their "self-control, patience, and magnanimity." Not only was the Philippine War over, but it had been the most glorious war in the nation's history, he said.

Roosevelt's edict was not the first time the authorities declared the war over. Nor was it the second time. *The Washington Post* reminded readers that two years earlier, Taft announced the "fourth and final termination of hostilities," and still it went on. "The war has been brought to an end on six different occasions since."

Hopefully this was the last. "A bad thing cannot be killed too often," the paper said.

The "war" would drag on for another decade under another name. Samar's Dios-Dios sect emerged resurgent and harassed U.S. garrisons for years. In Northern Luzon, the mountain Igorots staged headhunting raids against Americans and the Philippine Constabulary. Uprisings in Mindanao and Jolo arose throughout the first decades of the American Century, and still do today. John J. Pershing made his name fighting the Moros: the war's "final" end most often cited by Philippine historians refers to a June 1913 attack Pershing led against a redoubt in an extinct volcano named Bud Bagsak, resulting in the death of 200 to 500 Moros, including women and children, and 15 Americans. Even today, violence arises there in the name of freedom.

The "official" war that Roosevelt ended on July 4, 1902, lasted forty-one months—126,468 American soldiers participated, though never more than 69,000 at one time. They fought in 2,811 recorded engagements. Final casualties were tallied at 2,818 wounded and 4,234 dead: 1,073 in battle, 589 to accidents and other causes, 2,572 to disease. By comparison, 379 Americans were officially lost in combat during the Cuban campaign. But neither count includes the thousands who died back home of diseases contracted on the islands, their numbers never recorded. U.S. deaths in the "dirty little war" were high by the standards of the time; most were buried in the Philippines, their bodies never recovered. Some historians believe that 10,000 American troops died or succumbed to disease, many suffering effects for the rest of their short lives.

The Philippine War would be America's most quickly forgotten war, the one least celebrated in song or legend, the one least memorialized. By Memorial Day 1903, many monuments to the Spanish-American dead had chiseled on their base a brief reminder of those who served their country in the "Philippine Insurrection." But that was all. The war cost the United States some $600 million, or $17.65 billion in 2019 dollars. Newspaper coverage of the war's end was skimpy and noncommittal, "flat in tone," according to the historian Leon Wolff, and soon after Roosevelt's fiat, *The Chicago Record-Herald* reported the price tag at $170 million, a severe miscalculation but still astounding for the era. "But think of the glory!" the paper jeered.

The Filipino cost was much higher, though still unknown. American commanders counted 16,000 rebel corpses in their reports to Manila, but most studies today believe the actual number exceeded 20,000. Civilians fared far worse. On May 2, 1901, J. Franklin Bell told *The New York Times* that war and disease had killed one-sixth of Luzon's population, or 600,000 people, based on his estimate that "perhaps 10 percent of the population died" in an 1898 population thought to be 6 million. The Philippine historian Resil Mojares estimates that another 100,000 people died on the island of Cebu, about one-sixth of its population, during the underreported war there from 1898 to 1906. The historians James H. Blount in 1913, Leon Wolff in 1960, and Henry F. Graff in 1989 were more conservative, listing the number of civilians dead from disease, famine, and cruelties from both sides at 200,000 to 250,000. The historian Ken De Bevoise calculates that from 1899 to 1903, the death rate hung at 50 per 1,000 people—a total mortality of 1.7 million, or an "excess" of 775,000 over normal mortality if there'd been no war at all.

It may have been worse: a statistical profile of the 1918 population reveals 400,000 "missing" people who should have been born in 1904–1908. When combined with the "excess" deaths, "it appears that the American war contributed directly or indirectly to the loss of more than a million persons" from a base population of 7 million. That is an astounding number—more deaths than in the American Civil War, more than were killed or died of mistreatment during the three and a half centuries of Spanish rule. "If the Apocalypse never arrived," De Bevoise concluded, "its agents had stalked the Philippine island world for forty years."

The islands had been decimated, in every sense of the word. Even animals suffered. *Carabao* were reduced by 90 percent from slaughter and rinderpest, or "cattle plague," a highly contagious disease that is almost always fatal. Without these beasts of burden, rice, the islands' staple, could not be cultivated. Atrocities continued without recourse: a Filipino priest died after being given the water cure by a "Captain Royal" who was tried but acquitted after the army made it clear that torture could not occur when the end of the war had already been declared.

Instead, "war" was redefined. Instead of organized resistance, authorities fought "irregular" bands, many led by former rebel officers, others by new messiahs. Whatever their names, all opposed American rule and its enforcers, the Constabulary. Authorities called them *ladrones*, or bandits. They numbered in the thousands, many swearing allegiance to a "New Katipunan" centered in Manila, their stated purpose to continue the revolution. Malvar's "class war" had come of age, and much of the peasantry saw this group as the new rebels, or Robin Hoods. According to the Philippine historian Renato Constantino, "The people, minus the *ilustrados*, now confronted the Americans."

Taft fought back with the November 1902 Brigandage Act, which called further resistance banditry. Violence continued, but "war" no longer existed, defined instead as "police action." U.S. troops could go home, transferring power to the Constabulary and Philippine Scouts. Any *ladrone* captured was not due the rights of a combatant, but could be tried and hung.

On October 30, 1902, three hundred *ladrones* under the former rebel chief Faustino Guillermo attacked a Constabulary patrol near the northern town of Novaliches. The police inspector in charge was Charles J. Bates, a former Twenty-Fourth Infantry lieutenant who'd inherited Fagen's old company when James Moss moved on. Bates scratched an urgent note to Lieutenant De Rubio in nearby Polo. "I had a big scrap this afternoon," he wrote: "I am about surrounded." During the battle, Bates had spotted a man leading the enemy whom he recognized—an African American who'd once been a soldier. Bates survived, and within two weeks, the rumor spread to Manila: "American Negros Reported in League with Ladrones," proclaimed *The Manila American* on November 14, 1902:

> From the province of Bulacan comes information to the effect that there are about 300 ladrones led by an American Negro who propose to wipe out the Constabulary and that a few miles out from the town of Caloocan four American negros are actively engaged in teaching a large number of highway men the rudiments of military tactics and how to handle a firearm.

That was all, and Bates kept the name of the man under wraps. After all, the United States had proudly proclaimed him dead. But soon after the *American*'s report, more "renegade" sightings surfaced. Those who saw him knew he was not a ghost. He seemed to possess all body parts, including his head.

David Fagen and his war raged on.

31

Exiles

On July 1, 1905, Richard Harding Davis stood again on San Juan Hill.

Much had changed in seven years. On May 20, 1902, the occupation ended with bombast and ceremony: Leonard Wood handed over the government to Tomás Estrada Palma, now Cuba's first elected president. The Cuban flag flew overhead. "It shall be my aim to strengthen the friendly feeling which exists between Cuba and the United States," Estrada Palma declared. Since then, Davis had rushed to cover South Africa's Boer War, steamed up the Congo River, and packed his rubber bathtub and revolver to chronicle a dustup between Russia and Japan. But now, as he stood here amid old memories, he felt that this had been the last, best war.

Most Americans believed that they'd liberated the island. Cuba "owes us her birth," Roosevelt proclaimed in 1902, the same year he "ended" the Philippine War. "We gave [Cuba] liberty," he said one year later. "We are knit to her by the memories of the blood and courage of our soldiers who fought for her in war; by the memories of the wisdom and integrity of our administrators." Newspapers echoed the catechism: "Freedom was presented to Cuba, not won by Cuba," claimed the *Brooklyn Eagle*, "and has been accepted not wholly with gratitude or with grace by Cuba herself."

As the *Eagle* noted, many Cubans disagreed. In America's narrative, she'd liberated Cuba and handed over sovereignty. But many knew better. The Platt Amendment of March 2, 1901, passed as part of that year's

Army Appropriations Act, had gutted the Cuban Republic of any real independence. Conceived by War Secretary Root, Governor-General Leonard Wood, and Senator Orville H. Platt, chair of the Senate Committee on Relations with Cuba, this was a tool for control. It delineated seven conditions for the withdrawal of U.S. troops, plus an eighth requiring Cuba to sign a treaty accepting those seven. Three months later, on June 12, 1901, the Cuban assembly amended its new constitution to contain those demands word for word. Cuba had two choices: accept the amendment or be annexed. The angry Republic capitulated.

In essence, Platt—which replaced the earlier Teller Amendment—denied Cuba the freedom for which she'd struggled for more than three decades. "There is, of course, little or no independence left in Cuba under the Platt Amendment," Wood bragged to Roosevelt soon after its passage. "It is quite apparent that she is absolutely in our hands." Though it did stipulate the eventual withdrawal of U.S. troops, it also created infringements on Cuban sovereignty that defined U.S. and Cuba relations until its 1934 repeal by Franklin Delano Roosevelt. The amendment prohibited Cuba from entering into any international arrangements, such as treaties or foreign debts, that the U.S. believed compromised the island's independence or allowed foreign powers to use the island for military purposes; the United States could intervene at any time "to protect life, property, and individual liberty." Cuba agreed to sell or lease territory that the U.S. could use for coaling and naval stations, a clause that ultimately led to the perpetual lease at Guantánamo Bay. If American interests seemed threatened, she could deploy the marines, giving legal basis to interventions in 1906, 1912, 1917, and 1920. Maximo Gómez grasped the implications early; when offered the presidency, he declined, knowing all was not well. "The Republic will surely come," he told a friend, "but not with the absolute independence we had dreamed about," echoing the resignation and hope that defined his country in the coming years.

The United States, until its eviction in 1959, owned Cuba lock, stock and barrel. By 1898 Americans had invested $50 million; by 1902 another $30 million; by 1906, $80 million more. At first much of this was in sugar. In 1902 U.S. interests produced 13 percent of the nation's sugar crop, but such hegemony also spread to other industries: mining, tobacco, agriculture. In 1902 U.S. capital totaled more than $100 million, and by 1905, when Davis returned, nearly thirteen thousand Americans had bought up nearly 10 percent of the country's land.

Davis preferred the past, but it played tricks on him. Distance warped: he'd thought that the jungle trek to Kettle Hill stretched three-quarters of a mile, when in fact it was seventy-five yards; the bloody trail to Las Guásimas seemed to take forever. He remembered the "amateur colonel" he'd admired, but now that colonel was commander in chief, and Davis regretted reports that he "too generously [gave] offices and promotions to the friends he made in Cuba." Nothing stays clean.

He remembered the dead. The first had been the young rebel Adolfo Rodriguez, who stood erect and fixed "his eyes immovably on the morning light" peeking above the hills. That was a good death. He'd heard of the young nurse named Clara Maass who'd died in the yellow fever tests and was eventually given a hero's burial back home—that was good, too. But few signs remained of the soldiers who'd died on these heights; the sun and rain and creeping foliage leeched away all trace. Though Americans had erected a monument by the main blockhouse atop San Juan Hill, this, too, was "rapidly falling to pieces."

He remembered Stephen Crane. Maddening, brilliant Crane, dead now of tuberculosis after checking in to a German health spa at the edge of the Black Forest. He pictured that day when several Rough Riders dug into the hillside and Crane walked on the crest, standing out "as sharply outlined as a semaphore." That brought Mauser fire on all. "You're drawing the fire on these men," Wood screamed. Even in the terrific heat, Crane wore a long "India-rubber rain-coat" and seemed as cool as if he gazed "down from a box at a theatre." Davis knew that "to Crane, anything that savored of a pose was hateful," so he yelled out, "You're not impressing anyone by doing that, Crane," and the writer dropped to his knees. When he crawled over, Davis said, "I knew that would fetch you."

"Oh, was that it?" Crane answered, then grinned.

Davis knew that he himself had changed. Cuba had been the high point of his career. Now he was married, rich, the author of successful plays and novels, but somehow the Davis of Cuba had been left behind. While the American Voice had grown darker, his works still promoted optimism and confidence—"safe stuff" to feed to the young. He'd become a genteel symbol of a bygone world, where war was a fair contest, like football. Such notions no longer mattered: just look at the Philippines. He was not proud of the army; it was no coincidence he did not cover that war—"because we are rightly ashamed of it." This was not his America.

These days, Carlos Portuondo and his wrinkled wife guarded San Juan Hill. The old man said he'd fought during the Ten Years' War, not in 1898: Why, Davis asked, was he in the blockhouse if he'd not fought here? "To keep the cows out of the park," Portuondo replied. When Davis asked where the Americans had camped, the old man pointed out the back door to his garden, which would have been within range of Spanish guns. When Davis tried to correct him, the old man "politely but unmistakably showed that he thought I was a liar."

One found such revisionism everywhere. Davis had been driven from his Santiago hotel by "old Casanova" and his sixteen-year-old son. This elder, "like most Cubans," did not give Americans much credit for winning the war: "Had the Americans left us alone a few weeks longer, we would have ended the war," old Casanova said.

Davis was too tired to argue. People believe what they want: "lack of knowledge and jealousy" always win. San Juan Hill, like Davis, had been left behind. "It is a pity," he said. "The place where so many of our men fought and fell, and still lie, should not disappear."

It deserved more than a backdoor garden and "Cuban pig-pens."

Upon entering Arlington National Cemetery and strolling to the green interior, one passes monuments to the Splendid War. The first is a memorial to the 385 soldiers killed in action, a tall round plinth made of buff marble and capped by a globe. An eagle sits astride it, holding in its talons the arrows of war. A few steps away rises a second, to the USS *Maine*; past that, a low, rough-hewn spike chopped from gray stone. This memorializes the dead of Roosevelt's "Rough Riders." No such monument along this route honors the 4,234 killed in the archipelago.

The Philippine "police action" dragged on. There would be many "police actions" in the American Century, an Orwellian euphemism for the nation's unpleasantries. In Luzon, former rebels like Faustino Guillermo and Luciano San Miguel gathered their men. The sheer numbers engaged in open revolt made ludicrous the American fiction. In 1904 Dios-Dios cultists on Samar rebelled in such numbers that fighting continued for two years. In February 1906 Moros on Sulu declared independence and fled to Bud Dajo, an extinct volcano. Leonard Wood, now governor, ordered eight hundred soldiers to crush them. In four days of fighting in early March, U.S. troops killed all but six: a March 11, 1906, *New York Times* photo showed soldiers standing over dead Moros piled five deep. Wood assured War Secretary Taft: "No man, woman, or child was wantonly killed." A second rebellion in December 1911 saw Moros surrounded again in Bud Dajo, but John Pershing, now governor, negotiated peace, and most went home.

This was the age of image makers, beginning with Taft, who served as governor of the Philippines from 1901 to 1903, after which Roosevelt named him war secretary. The invasion was "the best possible thing that could have happened to the Filipino people," Taft said in February 1902. But for Americans, "it probably would be better that chance had not thrown the Filipino people under our guidance and protection." Five years later he admitted that the tab came to $300 million, plus another $14 million to fund the scouts and 12,000 soldiers overseeing 8 million natives, hundreds of thousands of whom had been "gotten rid of" in ways still undocumented. Though Congress continued to investigate atrocities, news coverage focused on "assimilation." Americans read of Igorot children learning to read, of the first Filipino to attend a U.S. college. Filipinos were "the best of the Asiatic races," lauded the *San Francisco Chronicle*, looking to that day when "all would point with pride to the glorious history of our common country." As Thomasites taught English, natives could "write their orders for goods so that American merchants can read them," ensuring that they too would soon partake of the "American Dream."

Yet the Dream had not turned out as planned. On the morning of December 15, 1901, Manila was struck by an earthquake that lasted a minute and twenty seconds "and of greater force than any which has occurred within the memory of the present generation," wrote the reporter Stephen Bonsal. The "massive medieval walls" of the Old City "cracked like gingerbread, the great stone monument to Magellan swayed to and fro like a sapling, the lofty images fell from their vaulted niches, and the bells in the church tower tolled their peals of alarm." In the aftermath, "some barrier not of masonry had been broken down," and "men spoke with a frankness I had missed before." An unnamed general wished that a tidal wave would "sweep with overwhelming force" through areas where rebellion still raged. An unidentified governor said that Americanization rested solely "upon the bayonets of our soldiers." Taft loved to say "the Philippines for the Filipinos," but privately he called the country a "deplorable" sink of cholera, rinderpest, famine, religious cults, and bandit gangs.

War's end was proving a beleaguered fiction, not a hopeful one. Southern Luzon was not quiet, and Taft's 1903 Reconcentration Act returned tens of thousands of peasants to the *zonas*. When resistance resurged in 1905, the provinces and southern islands reverted to full military authority. When fighting ended in 1913, it was mostly a result of exhaustion.

America had turned her largest colony into a land of exiles. From May to October 1903, the Michigan lawyer Gustavus Ohlinger traveled outside Manila. The land was empty of life. He visited a ruined monastery in Guadalupe where, around the rifled tombs of friars, "bones lay scattered," and one churchman's skull and ribs lay in the debris. A huge nest of bats made their home in a prison. In Nueva Ecija, a Constabulary sergeant joined the rebels and attacked the barracks of his men; a Thomasite said that while his town held five hundred school-age children, only eighty enrolled. Ohlinger said that as he rode through Batangas, where peasants still starved in the *zonas*, he met a man who'd ridden "through groves of oranges" and plucked "fruit from the trees." In Cavite, he and a friend paddled to the site of Dewey's triumph, where they crawled into the red-rusted gunboat *Marques del Duero* and found an "uncommunicative Filipino" cooking rice in the galley's remains. The old man gazed at them in hatred; he seemed more comfortable with the dead.

Why should America regret the devastation, asked General Samuel B. M. Young at Washington's Church of the Epiphany on November 13, 1902. "War is a game, after all," he declared. Every game has winners and losers, and he'd been one of the winners after that enthusiastic meal with Roosevelt at the Metropolitan Club. He'd been promoted from brigadier general in the volunteers to major general in the Regulars; when he retired in 1904, he'd be the army's first chief of staff at the rank of lieutenant general. America treated Filipinos too gently, he claimed: "If it had not been for the intense desire of the American people to carry on an easy, persuasive war with the Filipinos, and the good faith in which the American officers acted to carry out that desire," the war "would have been shorter because it would have been far more ruthless and devastating." Those great powers hoping to fill Spain's shoes would not have been so kind. "I feel confident our little Jap friends would have stopped the pattering of bare feet of our 'little brown brothers' through the jungle in a very short time, and that the aggressive Army of our German friends would not have viewed with equanimity the burying alive of their friends as did our soldiers in obedience to the home sentiment."

On February 26, 1903, Apolinario Mabini came home. He was sick, and seven months earlier, he had written his will, thinking he'd die in Guam. When Roosevelt ended the war, he'd granted amnesty to every exile who took the oath. All did so except Mabini and Artemio Ricarte, so both remained in Guam. In December 1902 Senator Hoar petitioned Roosevelt to bring the invalid home, but Root claimed that Mabini was a threat to peace and his return could spark a new revolution. "His physical condition as a helpless paralytic and his gentle and courteous manner have served to place him in the attitude of a martyr," Taft warned. But Hoar introduced a Senate resolution for Mabini's benefit that passed unopposed, forcing the administration's hand.

Mabini took the oath when helped off the boat; he felt "completely disoriented" and "almost overcome by disease and suffering." Ricarte witnessed his oath, but refused it himself and continued on to Hong Kong. The Filipinos rejoiced at Mabini's return: he was thirty-eight, he was tired, and he accepted the inevitable. "Let us stop the Revolution in order that the people may rest," he wrote to the New Katipunan's Luciano San Miguel, but the general died before the letter reached him. Mabini moved to Tanauan, his birthplace in northern Batangas. All he wished for in his little time left was to "be of some use, unless I have returned to the islands for the sole purpose of dying."

He'd always excelled at foretelling the future. On May 11, 1902, he drank some unpasteurized goat's milk and seventeen hours later came down with cholera. His skin turned blue. Diarrhea and vomiting followed; his eyes sank in his head. On May 12 he wrote to Tanauan's *presidente* requesting a certificate of residence, or *cedula*, since he'd been in exile too long and just wanted a home. It would be his last letter. His old comrade Dr. Justo Lukbán hurried to his bedside and at midnight on May 13, 1902, pronounced him dead.

Aguinaldo outlived Mabini by sixty-one years. He outlived almost everyone in the Philippine tragedy, dying of a heart attack one month before his ninety-fifth birthday, February 6, 1964. Despite attempts otherwise, he was exiled to irrelevance, a "walking anticlimax" to what might have been. He tried to sell Aladdin kerosene lamps from his Manila office on Juan Luna Street, but the venture never caught on. In 1935, when presidential elections were held as part of a ten-year transition to full independence, he ran for office against the popular Manuel L. Quezon. It was a tumultuous campaign: Aguinaldo's surrender to Funston, his cooperation with Taft and Wood, his involvement in the deaths of Bonifacio and Luna—all came back to haunt him. He lost to Quezon, garnering a mere 17.5 percent of the vote. Yet Quezon was not free of taint: he stole ballots in areas where votes were not counted, and Aguinaldo called the election rigged. He came home to Cavite, the only province he won.

His bitterness grew. When the Japanese invaded the islands ten hours after the attack on Pearl Harbor, Aguinaldo served as their mouthpiece, urging Douglas MacArthur to surrender. Japan promises us independence, he broadcast: she was the "protector of all the weak peoples of Asia." He was arrested after Japan's defeat and charged with treason. Yet the 1948 amnesty absolved him, and he was never tried.

He returned to his mansion in Kawit, no longer a menace, instead a cult figure for those who worshipped the lost elegance of *ilustrados*. He rambled through his dark house, adding passages until it became an echoing labyrinth rising above a sea of huts. His health faded. Every day, he could peer from the windows to the mountain where Bonifacio died. He wrote his memoirs, published in the year of his death, recalling betrayals, rewriting history. In 1963 he donated the mansion as a shrine to the 1896 Little Republic, the purest revolt, when his people rejoiced and all seemed possible.

In December 1903 Fagen's nemesis James Moss rode through Pampanga, Pangasinan, and Nueva Ecija—provinces that had been occupied by his Twenty-Fourth Infantry from 1899 to 1902. The last time he visited, "I heard nothing but the tramp of the infantry, the clatter of cavalry, the rumble of artillery." Now the land seemed empty: the population of Natividad, for example, had dropped from 20,000 to 7,000. He found "neglect and gloominess" everywhere. Fields lay fallow; roads were torn up. Of the twenty-three bridges his men had built, six were still intact, the rest cannibalized for building material. Houses used by army commanders had been burned or torn down. "The American flag was conspicuous by its absence," he said. He smiled at passing natives, but "I don't think more than a dozen spoke to me." He ended his trip certain that most Filipinos "have absolutely no use" for Americans. For them, "we can not get out of the islands any too soon."

Yet one group seemed happy—Buffalo Soldiers who'd stayed after discharge, choosing self-exile from their native land. In the summer and fall of 1902, Taft engineered the early transfer of black regiments back to the States, still fearing their too-easy rapport with natives. As the end of "our term of enlistment was drawing near," wrote the veteran Richard Johnson, soldiers were told that "all who desired to remain in the islands were permitted to do so." About 20 in his company stayed: about 1,000 in total took this option, and one report put the number at 1,200—nearly one-fifth of the 6,000 African Americans who'd served in the Philippines.

Official reports suggested that the black exiles did not flourish, and the December 23, 1902, *Manila American* supported this view: after carousing in Manila, veterans returned to their old garrison towns to live "off the female population" or become public nuisances. *The Manila American* was often racist, but the transition may have been hard: census figures tracked diminishing numbers of black veterans. Where the 1903 census listed 505 "foreign born" blacks in the Philippines, the 1918 survey counted 185. The Bureau of Insular Affairs passed the 1903 Dissolute Americans and Vagrancy Act, which targeted "dissolute, drunken, and lawless Americans" and allowed for deportation.

But eyewitness evidence painted a different picture. During his ride, Moss discovered thirteen of his former soldiers. They included Abraham Morse, who married a native woman and kept a saloon in Bautista; Robert Scott, a police sergeant in Dupay; Henry Johnson, Joseph Bunch, and Thomas White, all dabbling in San Quintin politics; and Albert Sims, who had a Filipina wife and children, owned a couple of *carabao*, and farmed a small rice field in San Jose. Others became well-known and respected: Walter H. Loving served as bandleader of the famous Philippine Constabulary Band; T. N. McKinney of Texas worked his way through civil service and owned the U.S. Philippine Commission house. Why should he go home, asked Sergeant Major T. Clay Smith in the October 1902 *Savannah Tribune.* Old soldiers like him were doing well: he knew "several school teachers, one lawyer and one doctor of medicine." Smith thought, "everything considered, that the Philippines offer our people the best opportunities of the century."

Smith's advice was tempting, as the lives of American blacks only grew worse after the war. In 1903 the black novelist Charles Chestnutt wrote, "The rights of the negroes are at a lower ebb than at any time during the thirty-five years of their freedom, and the race prejudice is more intense and uncompromising." That certainly applied in the military: between 1902 and World War I, the navy excluded blacks from seamen's billets, restricting them to steward's positions. National Guard units in the South prohibited blacks entirely. The army banned blacks from "technical" units like the artillery, claiming they lacked the intelligence and mechanical skills. In August 1906 black soldiers rioted against segregation in Brownsville, Texas; a white bartender was killed, a white policeman injured. Roosevelt dishonorably discharged 167 men—three entire companies—even when evidence against them proved flawed.

One exile returned from abroad. Three months after his February 1901 discharge, John Calloway steamed back to Manila, reunited with Mamerta and their child, Juanita, took a job as watchman in the army quartermaster's department, and wrote pleas for a fair trial. They were always denied. In August, Moss encountered him on the street and engineered a second deportation. He came back in 1902; the War Department had a watch list and warned Adna Chaffee that the "dangerous" Calloway had returned. But Manila was now under civil control, and Chaffee could not touch him. Calloway got a job with the Bureau of Public Printing and moved into Manila's Quiapo district, in time fathering fourteen children with Mamerta: one of the girls, Maggie, became a silent-film star. Calloway died in 1934 at age sixty-three, probably of a stroke; *The Manila Times* noted his passing in the story "Old Timer Dies."

The fate of one exile became legendary: despite every effort to kill him, evidence suggests that David Fagen still lived.

The first hint surfaced during the near annihilation of Charles Bates and his scouts on October 30, 1902. This battle remained secret until November 14, when *The Manila American* ran its brief teaser about the "American negro" and his "300 ladrones" who tried to "wipe out the Constabulary." A number of U.S. papers ran the Manila story in December 1902.

The campaign against former guerrillas in Central and Northern Luzon rekindled interest in Fagen's ultimate fate, and soon many rumors swirled that he still lived. On February 10, 1903, he was reported alive in Manila: "A former member of the 25th Infantry [*sic*], the regiment from which Fagan [*sic*] deserted, claims that Fagan was in Manila for several days last week." The old comrade housed him for two nights, as well as the woman "supposed to be his wife." Fagen hoped to make his way to Batangas, then Cebu or Iloilo, where he might book passage to Hong Kong or Singapore. He no longer seemed his old cocky self, his friend claimed: years on the run had left him "nervous and restless," and he lived "in constant fear of capture." When the man was asked why he did not call the police, he said that Fagen had been good to him when he was a rookie, and he "did not mean to go back on him now that [he] needed friends."

Though the tale might be of whole cloth, some details ring true: the Filipino wife who'd stuck from the beginning; the loyalty and sympathy of old comrades. With this story, Fagen drops from sight for three years. The constant wife never appears again.

During this time, war expanded everywhere against *ladrones*, religious cults, New Katipunan, self-proclaimed messiahs, Moros, and reborn Dios-Dios. On February 5, 1903, 400 *ladrones* nearly wipe out 35 constables in Leyte; three days later, constables battle 300 fighters in Luzon under Faustino Guillermo and Luciano San Miguel. The latter will die in battle and Guillermo is eventually captured and hung, but others fill their shoes. In 1904, in a place called Dolores River in Samar, forty-seven Constabulary Scouts are ambushed by a thousand Dios-Dios cultists and nearly eradicated. In January 1905, three hundred *ladrones* attack the town of San Francisco de Malabon, and among the attackers were seen "two American Negros."

The sighting again sparked speculation that Fagen lived. "The name most dreaded in the ears of American soldiers" was David Fagen, "the most brilliant and dangerous of the Filipino chieftains," recalled the April 20, 1905, *New York Age*: "How much of this reputation Fagan [*sic*] owed to his exploits, and how much to the mythmaking faculty natural to mankind, we do not pretend to calculate; but his name did excite vividly among our soldiers a spontaneous terror similar to that which made awful among Saracens the name of Richard the Lion-Hearted."

He'd become legend, like Bernardo Carpio or Robin Hood. During this period, a charismatic figure known as Apong Ipe led a militant religious sect in a vast area stretching from southern Bulacan to Pangasinan; he preached a socialist doctrine, promising followers "ownership of the land and many other benefits if they overthrew the government," said the historian George Coats. Ipe's real name was Felipe Salvadore: he kept his headquarters atop Mount Arayat and disappeared into the Candaba Swamp when pressed—areas Fagen knew well. On April 16, 1906, eighty of Ipe's men attacked constables in Malabon, killing three and taking rifles and ammo. Similar attacks occurred throughout Central Luzon that same night. On May 10 dozens of papers reported Ipe's raid on Malasiqui, a town of nine thousand.

During this chaos, Fagen rose from the dead. "Fagan [*sic*] Comes to Life," announced the May 19, 1906, *Manila Times* on page one. A purported photo of the "notorious renegade" accompanied the story—the one taken in Manila in 1899. He was the "'big chief' of a band of cattle rustlers of his own color," specializing in the theft of valuable *carabao* of Australian lineage worth 12,000 pesos a head. Again he eluded pursuit, due partly to the fact that his cattle rustling provisioned Apong Ipe. Army officials still denied Fagen's presence, but on June 28, 1906, *The Washington Post* and other papers reprinted "Fagan Comes to Life," a story bolstered by reports from the Bureau of Internal Affairs.

Then he vanished again, this time forever. Fagen's biographer Michael Morey makes the case that scouts finally killed him that summer. After the raids and Fagen's unveiling, they had little choice but to hunt down the rustlers, and they may have succeeded where Funston failed. A July 27, 1906, report from Governor Isabelo Artacho to the U.S. Philippine Commission claimed that "municipal police and rural guards have been able to bring about the death of one thief in the hills of Nueva Ecija." Three years later, Kansas newspapers reported the retirement of Colonel James G. Harbord, the Constabulary's assistant chief from 1903 to 1909. "In the northern part of the Island of Luzon, a band of ladrones held forth for some years, and gave the constabulary great trouble," Harbord said in an interview: "The band was supposed to have been headed by a renegade negro named Fagan [*sic*], who had deserted from the Twenty-fifth [*sic*] Infantry, U.S.A. Fagan was a hard man to kill, but after the Manila papers had reported his death in 25 different places in the space of two years, the constabulary finally succeeded in silencing him."

If Fagen died in 1906, he was twenty-eight years old. That year, the Brownsville riot exploded in Texas among units he'd hunted in Nueva Ecija; that year, his old nemesis Funston helped quell a threatened Cuban revolt. Unlike them, Fagen never moved out or moved on. In the end, he died as he lived—a symbol of rage. And a mystery.

Some like to think he remained alive and free. The Buffalo Soldier scholar Anthony Powell contends that Fagen survived into his sixties, and points to the chronicles of Major Edwin Price Ramsey, a white American cavalry officer who fought a guerrilla war against the Japanese during World War II. As Ramsey ranged the jungles of Mindoro, he came upon a "tall, skinny black man dressed in native clothing, well into his sixties, his skin deeply wrinkled and his hair all white." He identified himself as Sergeant White of the Tenth Cavalry, come to the Philippines in 1907 to fight Moros with John Pershing. He'd lived thirty years in the jungle, married several Philippine women, raised dozens of children, and had not seen another American for years. Believers in Fagen's survival contend this was a false name.

Ramsey asked if he wanted to go home. The old man gazed back, close to tears. "But I'm at peace, Major," he said. "I have my home here, and I'll die among my family." He grew silent, as if remembering lost days. "That's what we fight for, ain't it, Major?" he finally said. "To die in peace in our home, among our own people."

In late summer 1902 Captain Frederick S. Wild came home. On August 1 he'd been court-martialed for refusing orders to punish two soldiers who'd torched Lingayen's cockpit; their bunkmate had been killed by *amigos*, and Wild sided with their revenge. Chaffee censured Wild, stalling his career. By the end of the month, Wild was posted on Angel Island in San Francisco Bay, the West Coast's Ellis Island. "Had I remained in the Philippines, I believe I would have been insane in a few months," he wrote on August 30: "I was right and [Chaffee] was wrong, but I had to be sacrificed to appease the clamor of the civil authorities." Still there two years later, Wild guessed he would remain through the end of his career.

By 1904 the army noticed a strange rootlessness among Philippine veterans, blaming the "climactic influences" they'd contracted in the islands—as if they no longer belonged anywhere. On July 3, 1904, the twenty-eight-year-old artillery lieutenant Guilford S. Garber—recently posted to Honolulu's Camp McKinley—hosted a dinner for his brother officers. He was engaged to be married the following year in Madison, Wisconsin; he planned to study engineering and had everything to live for, friends said. But the Philippines had changed him, and that night, after all guests departed, he scribbled "I cannot stop drinking," stuck his Colt army revolver in his mouth, and pulled the trigger. An army investigation concluded that Gerber was "another of the numerous victims of the Philippine climate," the closest they ever got to publicly addressing the rash of unexplained suicides. Only then did they release the fact that Frederick Wild also shot himself to death three weeks earlier, on June 10, 1904. His court-martial was not mentioned in the report, nor was his lingering anger. "No positive explanation has been offered for the act of either one of these officers in taking his life," said *The Pacific Commercial Advertiser.* "Both were young, able, vigorous, and ambitious," yet they battled despair alone and went under. Their comrades all knew of the "Philippine disease" plaguing many, but would not speak of it. The silence was "making the army people ask 'Who next?'"

Mark Twain feared that something fundamental had broken in his country. For all his fierce words and public protests, he felt a stranger in this new world. He privately wrote stories that questioned the nature of reality. In these tales, a man wakes to find himself on a voyage where every fellow passenger is dead or insane; a man voyages in a drop of water and becomes a parasite floating in God's bowels. The tales rang of responsibility and hidden guilt, of extremes that destroy identity. During this period, he also wrote *The Mysterious Stranger*, his most bitter dream. "It is true," says Satan to the narrator, "there is no God, no universe, no human race, no heaven, no hell: It is all a dream—a grotesque and feverish dream. Nothing exists but you. And you are but a *thought*—a vagrant thought, a useless thought, a homeless thought, wandering forlorn among the empty eternities!"

In 1905 Twain crafted "The War Prayer" for *Harper's Bazaar*. The parody could take place in any white Protestant church in America: Christians sing praises to war; soldiers believe their crusade holy; the American flag invokes a mystical sense of Right and Good. But then enters an "aged stranger" who might be angel, ghost, demon, or all in one. He speaks of a prayer the congregants know but dare not voice—a victory prayer that demands the enemy's death. The unspoken prayers address a Deity who is a nationalist and a murderer.

On March 22, 1905, *Harper's Bazaar* rejected "War Prayer" on the grounds that it was "not quite suited to a woman's magazine." Because he had an exclusive contract with Harper and Brothers, Twain could not publish "War Prayer" elsewhere. "None but the dead are permitted to tell the truth," he told his friend Dan Beard. One month later, the same publisher rejected *King Leopold's Soliloquy*, Twain's evisceration of the Belgian king's murderous reign in the Congo, this time on the grounds that they doubted the "commercial wisdom" of addressing genocide. His publisher was "so situated, by the contract between us, that I cannot make them do right," he told Edmund D. Morel, head of the British Congo Reform Association. The censorship begun by the U.S. Army in the Philippines had infiltrated commercial strategy back home. "In America—as elsewhere—free speech is confined to the dead," Twain wrote privately in 1905. "War Prayer" and other writings like it remained unpublished until 1923, thirteen years after he died of a heart attack on April 21, 1910, at age seventy-four.

The year Twain died was the year that Sandburg changed his name back to "Carl," the name his parents had given him—the name of his father, a proud working man. By then, he was a full-fledged socialist, writing for the *Milwaukee Sentinel*, the *Milwaukee Journal*, *The Milwaukee Daily News*, and the weekly *Social Democratic Herald* as he also worked as district organizer for the Social Democratic Party. The Splendid War meant to spread freedom overseas had not spread freedom at home. Labor violence had only grown worse since 1898: violent strikes tore from coast to coast in mills, factories, and mines. Socialists like him believed in a looming working-class revolution that would replace the capitalist system, and radicals in the International Workers of the World—a group Sandburg joined in 1915—pressed for shattering change. His father had believed that hard work got one ahead, but nowadays hard work turned you into a "wage slave."

Sandburg left Lombard College in 1902 before graduation, determined to either "be a writer—or a bum!" But he had to survive. He sold Underwood & Underwood stereoscopic photos, peddled poems, made speeches in lecture halls: "There are ten men in me," he said, "and I do not know or understand one of them." He came to believe that the freedom vaunted by politicians was the freedom to ask for a job and be turned down. Wherever he went, he encountered unemployed veterans, often behind bars. In 1904 he was thrown into the Allegheny County Jail for ten days. He'd nailed an eastbound drag out of Pittsburgh, but two bulls caught him and five others and took them to a justice of the peace. The man heard before him was an Antietam veteran. "It seems every old man brought in here fought in the Union Army," mocked the judge. Did the old man have written proof of his Union service? He did not. "Stand to one side."

Sandburg was next: "Well, five years ago I was in the 6th Illinois Regiment and went through a campaign in Porto Rico under General Miles." The judge winked at the deputies, said, "We have young soldiers and old here today," and sentenced them all to six to ten days in jail.

With this, Sandburg entered the timeless ranks of angry veterans. If the army had taught him anything, it was how to shoot, and he imagined an army of unemployed workers shouldering arms and charging the "scabs, strikebreakers, gunmen, and thugs" he saw everywhere. The vision arose during Roosevelt's national tour urging America's entry into World War I. When T.R. suggested that the U.S. adopt the Swiss draft system, Sandburg realized that Roosevelt had not thought out the consequences. When "each workingman is given his own gun and belt of cartridges," Sandburg wrote in September 1915, the march for equality would begin.

By then, he'd moved to Chicago with his wife, Lilian, and his sense of betrayal had grown. Man's greatest enemy, he decided, "has been man." His Chicago and war poems written in this period overflow with images of violence and despair. The faces of workers riding the Halsted Street trolley are "Tired of wishes / Empty of dreams." The soldier is always a killer: "I come from killing. /I go to more. / I drive red joy ahead of me from killing." The poor wait silently for their reckoning: "I am the undertow . . . / I am the crumbler: tomorrow." Blacks, women, orphans, prostitutes, the homeless: all wait in anger and exile.

On April 17, 1917, Sandburg covered Roosevelt's pro-war speech in Chicago's Union Stock Yards. The former corporal found it hard to swallow anything said by "the horse-teeth patriot and politician from Oyster Bay." Yet Roosevelt was a national force, and on November 8, 1904, he'd been elected by a landslide for his second term. He grew into the job, reining in Big Business, safeguarding unregulated food and drugs, creating national monuments and parks, and promoting the conservation of national resources. He'd thought he was finished with politics and had groomed Bill Taft to succeed him, but he did not like Taft's conservatism and in 1912 ran again, splitting the Republican vote to usher the Democrat Woodrow Wilson into the presidency. The embittered Roosevelt embarked upon the two-year Amazon expedition that nearly killed him.

Through all these various personas, foreign policy remained his deep passion. He liked to quote the old African proverb "Speak softly and carry a big stick" that he'd learned on a well-publicized safari, but his extension of America's grasp was anything but quiet or subtle. In November 1903 he signed a Panama Canal treaty that made America's naval reach global. In 1905 he issued the Roosevelt Corollary to the Monroe Doctrine, which claimed that America had the right to wield power throughout the Western Hemisphere, not just in Puerto Rico and Cuba. On December 16, 1907, he dispatched sixteen battleships, called the "Great White Fleet," on a 43,000-mile round-the-world cruise that paraded American power. He welcomed the fleet back on February 22, 1909, less than a month before handing the presidency to his chosen successor.

As Sandburg covered Roosevelt's 1917 stockyard speech, he realized that none of this would have been possible if not for the personality cult embracing the man. Crowd members interrupted his script, and Roosevelt joked back as if they were old friends. This was the man who'd shaped the nation Sandburg no longer knew—the "big stick" nation that worshipped raw power. Yet uncertainty gripped his listeners: the United States had declared war against Germany three weeks earlier, on April 6, and Sandburg remembered the same feeling nineteen years earlier, when he'd marched off to war. "We fight for our own rights," Roosevelt cried, urging young men to sign up and others to buy Liberty Bonds. "We fight for the rights of mankind." Then, without the slightest touch of irony, he added, "The free people who govern themselves are lined up against the governments which deny freedom to those people." The Great American Amnesia had set in.

Roosevelt's words inflamed Sandburg. The colonel was sick, with less than two years to live; even so, less than a month after this speech, he offered to lead a new division of Rough Riders to the Western Front. Wilson turned him down. Even now, in Chicago, he dreamed of past glories. "It wasn't much of a war," he said of the splendid abattoir he'd helped engineer, "but it was all the war there was." Sandburg's memories were less romantic: the war he remembered was "a nightmare of blood, fever, and blunders."

Sandburg's anger launched him on a lifelong query: Could one person matter in such a world of pain and greed? As an Illinois boy steeped in Lincoln mythology, the immersion led finally to his six-volume Pulitzer Prize–winning biography of the war president. Growing up, he'd watched Civil War veterans march past: "I listened to stories of old-timers," and when he fought his own war, his uniform was "the same light blue trousers and dark blue jackets" they'd worn, too—as if, in America, the wars never ended, but blended into one. "America whither?" Sandburg wrote "as Lincoln began his winding journey to Washington." The questions were always the same: How did we get here? Where are we going?

It was a New World, as new as that day Columbus gazed upon Hispaniola and dreamed of empire. The first rays shone on those accused of war crimes. Atrocity could be good for one's career. "Howling Jake" Smith became popular in veterans' circles, hailed as a hero sacrificed to political gain. Adna Chaffee was named army chief of staff until his 1906 retirement; his successor, J. Franklin Bell, held the post until 1910. Littleton Waller would be named a lead marine field officer in U.S. interventions in Panama, Cuba, Haiti, and Mexico; he retired in 1920 as a major general. The torturer Edwin Glenn led U.S. troops during World War I before retiring in 1919 as a major general.

But no one profited like the "Little Guy." Funston's career had stalled after Roosevelt's rebuke, but once again Fate stepped in. He'd been sent to San Francisco in hopes that he'd fade away when, at 5:12 a.m. on April 18, 1906, the Great San Francisco Earthquake struck. Eda and he had a family by then; they lived on Washington Street, halfway up Knob Hill. Funston was the senior officer on duty, commanding seventeen hundred Regulars in and around the city. "It was a beautiful morning with no wind," he wrote, but as he ran to the summit, he saw fires coalescing into a "sinister column of smoke [mounting] a thousand feet into the air." The water mains had broken; the unchecked conflagration would cover four square miles.

The fire burned for three days: 28,188 buildings were destroyed and 225,000 people made homeless out of a registered 400,000 population. Though the official death toll was 500, it is believed that more than 3,000 died. It would have been worse without Funston: he declared martial law, used troops and his own authority to blast buildings in the fire's path, set up guards against looting, and organized aid stations. The greatest criticism involved his shoot-to-kill order, since innocent people returning home for their possessions were allegedly killed. Funston did not apologize. "I have no doubt," he wrote in his May 17, 1906, report, that if not for armed guards, "the saloons would have been broken into and then, the crowd becoming turbulent, would have begun sacking the banks and jewelry stores." Most city officials agreed. He was "the man that saved San Francisco," rising like a phoenix from the crackling ruins.

Four months later, Funston took part in a drama that foreshadowed

U.S. police actions in the Caribbean. The revolution had never really ended in Cuba: old resentments lingered, ready to boil over given the right trigger. The 1904 National Assembly elections had been marred by fraud; Estrada Palma was reelected president in 1905 after forcing his opponent to withdraw. The losing Liberal Party, packed with ex-*mambisi*, fought back, and by August 1906, fifteen thousand rebels cut communications throughout the island. There was no standing army, just the small Rural Guard. Palma wired for help, and Roosevelt sent Taft to head off what was now being called the August Revolution. Taft took Funston with him and gave him command of the two thousand marines who landed in Havana on September 29, 1906. Taft told Roosevelt that the elected Cuban government had "proven to be nothing but a house of cards," and he hammered out a peace treaty with the political antipodes. But peace in the country was complicated, exacerbated by the fact that Taft got along with Funston about as well as he had with MacArthur.

One sticking point was horses: insurgents grabbed them where they found them, with no record of ownership. As Funston ranged through the country trying to keep peace, his solution seemed logical enough, considering that eight thousand horses were at issue. He vested temporary possession of a horse to the man who held it and issued him a certificate deeming "ownership to be determined later." He grasped the rural reality: horses were as important to Cuban farmers as *carabao* had been to Filipinos, and time and the courts could resolve ownership one by one. But Taft felt that this did not pay proper respect to property rights, and when they argued the point, Funston admitted he "rather indiscreetly" gave Taft "a piece of my mind." The Second U.S. Occupation stayed in place until 1909, but Funston was not part of it; Taft had sent him back to San Francisco.

Though the August Revolution tainted Funston's chances for promotion, he still received the appointments typical of any upwardly mobile general. From 1908 to 1910, he headed the Army Service Schools at Fort Leavenworth; while Eda was away, a man broke into their house and started shooting. But Funston kept a revolver under his pillow and fired back; no one was hit, and the man got away. The intruder was later identified as "Mr. Dunawald," whom Funston had sent to Alcatraz in an earlier court-martial. In 1910 Funston returned to Manila for three years as commander of the Department of Luzon; in 1911 he published *Memories of Two Wars.* He told Leonard Wood, by now the army chief of staff, that the "national backbone" had weakened, as shown by the public's desire for peace. Like Roosevelt, he believed that war alone kept a nation strong.

At age forty-six, he'd become a cranky old man. Photos show him fat, florid, and balding; he drank too much, suffered from an ulcer, and had a heart condition. Rage consumed him. He'd given his life to the army but felt he'd been passed over for promotion eight times since becoming brigadier general. On July 13, 1912, he told U.S. senator Charles Curtis that "some sinister work" was at play. The occasion was the April 12 death of Frederick Dent Grant, the former president's first son: this vacated the slot of major general, still the highest rank in the army. Many top brass anticipated war in Europe, and the army's major general would lead U.S. forces in the epoch-making conflict that would cement his reputation for all time.

Throughout 1912–1913, Funston wrote increasingly bitter pleas to Washington. At first he blamed the seniority system, but then the letters turned petty. He'd lobbied President Taft, who politely noted that others lay ahead in the lists. "I am inclined to think that personal dislike of me by [President Taft] is the whole thing," Funston said. When Senator Joseph Bristow of Kansas became his chief advocate, Funston bombarded the man with screeds. "The list of our general officers is a sorry lot when it comes to considering war service in command of the higher units," he wrote in a gigantic missive dated September 28, 1912. Since Pershing *did* have experience, he called him "a cold-blooded, selfish, unscrupulous schemer" who was "without doubt the most detested officer in the Army today." He accused Pershing of keeping a Filipina mistress, having two children by her, and spiriting them "out of the way." This was a presidential year: Taft, the Republican, versus Democrat Woodrow Wilson, and Roosevelt as third-party nominee. Funston wrote to Wilson, Bristow, Chaffee, and others as if he had nothing better to do.

Wilson won on November 5, 1912, with 42 percent of the vote, beating Roosevelt's 27 percent and Taft's 23. Five days later, Funston lobbied Wilson through his Kansas proxies. A letter to U.S. representative James Hay abused Wilson's predecessors. "Mr. Roosevelt has always regarded me with disfavor," he wrote, forgetting professions of friendship on both sides; the cause—"a mean and petty feeling of jealousy against one whose war record makes his look like what it is—buncombe." Taft was distant because he'd been a MacArthur favorite, a fact spotlighting Taft's "shriveled soul." He said he had lots of dirt on Taft from their days together in Cuba, and when it came out, his "stock will be worth about two cents on the dollar."

In 1913 Funston was sent to Hawaii in hopes that the tropics might mellow his rage. It worked: as he improved the island's defenses, the acid letters slowed. On January 22, 1914, he hurried to San Antonio to command the U.S. forces massing on the Mexican border: the election of President Victoriano Huerta threw Mexico into revolt, and several U.S. Marines had been captured. Wilson told Funston to take Veracruz after a German ship loaded with arms was reported heading there. A brief fight left seventeen Americans and two hundred Mexicans dead; Funston secured the city, and there he stayed as military governor.

For once, Funston showed restraint. He kept order, distributed rations, dealt with the Mexican authorities, and several times refrained from starting a war. When Huerta was forced out of office in July 1914 and fled to Jamaica, Funston was praised. On November 17, 1914, he finally got his promotion to major general, along with an appointment as commander of the Southern Department, which covered most of the border with Mexico. The Yankees left Veracruz on November 23, and Funston set up headquarters in San Antonio.

William Allen White saw him during this time: he'd come home to visit, and they chatted in White's Emporia home. The restraint under fire had galled him, he groused, and the memory unleashed such "dazzling, wrathful profanity" that both recalled college and started laughing. As Funston left, "he turned back on the sidewalk, saw me lingering at the door, and waved his hand and gave me the old gay smile." White yelled, "God bless you, old-timer!" Funston yelled back, "Same to you, Billy, you old hell-raiser!" It was the last time White saw him alive.

Even as Funston's ambitions bore fruit, he grew sicker. On March 9, 1916, Francisco "Pancho" Villa raided the New Mexican town of Columbus, killing seventeen Americans; Funston wanted to lead the campaign himself, but instead, he sent Pershing, now a brigadier general but still his subordinate, on his famous "Punitive Expedition." Funston's other officers on the border included Douglas MacArthur, soon to be promoted to major, and Lieutenants George Patton and Dwight Eisenhower, all shapers of the martial century to come. As the army planned for the Big Show in Europe, Wilson's war secretary Newton D. Baker said he intended to make Funston commander of all U.S. forces should war begin. Eda moved back to California with their three children; Freddie wrote long letters about his deteriorating health. He blamed indigestion and went to the hospital repeatedly. He neglected to tell Eda about a mistress on the side.

On the night of February 19, 1917, Funston relaxed in the lobby of San Antonio's St. Anthony's Hotel. The orchestra played "The Blue Danube Waltz." According to family lore, he sat at the table with the mistress and lifted six-year-old Inez Harriet Silverberg onto his lap. "How beautiful it is," he said, turning to his lover. "You know, there is no music as sweet as the old tunes." He drew a sharp breath, slumped in his chair, and died. A telegram to Eda dated 11:52 p.m. that night said, "General Funston died here to-night very suddenly heart failure."

Funston was fifty-one. Douglas MacArthur manned the War Department's night watch when the news arrived at ten p.m. Wilson and War Secretary Baker were dining at Baker's home, and he'd left notice not to disturb them unless something important occurred. MacArthur looked at his friend Peyton March, also on duty, and both agreed that this qualified. MacArthur arrived at the secretary's house and heard the tinkle of glass and soft laughter from the dining room. As he pushed past the butler, Wilson spotted him. "Come in," he said. "There are no secrets here." MacArthur clicked his heels, saluted, and "barked in a drill-sergeant tone, 'Sir, I regret to report that General Funston has just died.'" The room fell quiet, a silence that seemed "that of death itself," and all one could hear was the sound "of your own breathing."

Wilson and Baker took the young major into an adjacent room as they composed a note for Eda Funston. "What now, Newton, who will take the army over?" Wilson asked his war secretary. Baker glanced at MacArthur. "Who do you think the Army would choose, Major?"

MacArthur hesitated: "I cannot, of course, speak for the Army, but for myself the choice would unquestionably be General Pershing." Wilson cast MacArthur "a long inquisitive look, and then said quietly, 'It would be a good choice.'"

Two months later, America entered the war. The man Funston called the "most detested officer in the Army" stole his place in history, as he had feared. Pershing would go to war as commander of the American Expeditionary Forces and go down in history. "Only a breath of wind," William White wrote, "the flutter of a heart," kept "Timmy" out of "Pershing's place in the World War." Ten thousand people filed past as the Little Guy lay in state at the Alamo; he was buried at the Presidio in full-dress uniform on a hill overlooking the city he'd saved.

And today, like the war that defined him, he is exiled from memory.

EPILOGUE

The Reckoning

Historians tend to see 1898–1902 as a mistake: a period when patriotism catalyzed to jingoism and the United States craved empire; when America changed and "went wrong." Traditionalists blame a "momentary fall from grace"; Progressives, an instant when "the forces of evil triumphed over the forces of good"; Centrists, "a burst of imperial missionary zeal." The reasons behind mass behavior remain as enigmatic for historians as they do for psychologists; one is reminded of the famous, somewhat confounded observation in Charles Mackay's *Extraordinary Popular Delusions and the Madness of Crowds*: "Men, it has been well said, think in herds: it will be seen that they go mad in herds, while they only recover their senses slowly, and one by one."

At the very least, the nation changed. After 1898–1902, interventionist fever seized the United States over and over. After assuming the presidency in 1909, Taft ordered the overthrow of regimes in Nicaragua and Honduras to protect American businesses. Woodrow Wilson sent U.S. troops to Cuba, Haiti, the Dominican Republic, Mexico, and Russia, promising to leave when they elected "good men." No other president invaded more countries: "America is the only idealistic nation in the world," he often claimed. After World War I, Calvin Coolidge returned troops to Cuba, Haiti, Nicaragua, and the Dominican Republic in the name of "stability" while edging the Philippines toward "self-rule." Herbert Hoover told Americans that in large parts of the earth, people believed the United States a "new imperial power intent upon dominating the destinies and freedoms of other people." That must stop, he warned—an assertion an American president had never made before and never would again.

During those days, a "large policy" acolyte unbosomed his sins. The Marine Corps veteran Smedley Butler led troops in Cuba and the Philippines; fought Boxers in China and Mexicans under Funston; invaded Nicaragua, Haiti, Honduras, and the Dominican Republic; and made Panama safe to build the canal. For this he won two Medals of Honor and was promoted to general; in the 1920s the marines sent him on a nationwide recruitment tour. But suddenly, during the journey, he experienced a conversion as profound and unexpected as Saul's on the road to Damascus, and he denounced U.S. imperialism. When the marines forced him from active duty, he barnstormed the nation alone. His patriotism had made him a "high-class muscle man for big business," he confessed; his purpose in life, to protect the dominion of American "petro," the National City Bank, Wall Street, U.S. fruit and sugar, and above all else, Standard Oil. He'd transformed from a simple believer into a "gangster for capitalism," and he could have given Al Capone some pointers. "The best [Capone] could do was operate his racket in three districts," Butler said. "I operated in three continents." He'd glimpsed a hard truth: changing regimes by coercion would come back to haunt you. But Americans like quick results, and they paid little heed.

U.S. history is haunted by a ruthlessness often shackled to professed idealism. Freeing Cuba from Spain led to a half century of exploitation and the emergence of a bitter anti-American regime. Dewey's victory in Manila Bay launched waves of hope—then disbelief and hatred. Philippine and American statesmen would extol the two countries' closeness after World War II, but the conflict took a heavy toll: the historian Daniel Immerwahr in his *How to Hide an Empire* estimates 1.6 million Japanese, American, and mostly Filipino dead, much of that from American carpet-bombing of Philippine population centers: "It was by far the most destructive event to ever take place on U.S. soil," he writes. Most Americans turn a blind eye: it is hard to defend the annihilation of those you've come to save. To the water cure and *zonas* would be added the execution of Vietnamese villagers, torture of Iraqi prisoners, or the "collateral damage" of unlucky citizens of Afghanistan. An Afghan shopkeeper recalled the April 2019 day when a U.S. air strike meant for the Taliban instead leveled his shop and killed twelve neighbors. Though Americans introduced women's rights and other freedoms to urban hubs, death was the legacy in the countryside. U.S. soldiers "murdered civilians and committed atrocities," the shopkeeper said, a claim that had been made in Batangas 125 years earlier.

"I do not think I like your country," a young Cuban mother said. Her judgment took me by surprise: this was exams week at the University of Havana, and on the notes-strewn table before her lay a text on modern Caribbean history, opened to the Wilson years. When traveling abroad for research, I try to keep a low profile. But wherever you go, you *are* your native land. Prejudices always catch up; old angers lay coiled. Cubans sense that when the American juggernaut rolled through their history, something was lost that must be regained. Even non-Cubans sting like the Cuban black wasp *avispa negra*. "We are *all* Americans!" an Argentine vacationer screamed on the Cuban beach where Funston had landed 120 years earlier. I'd been staring across the Florida Straits, and I hadn't seen this coming. Behind us, a cinder-block Guardia Frontiera tower watched for invaders from the north, or Cubans chancing tricky currents to reach the far shore. The blockhouse stood empty, a monument to a Cold War that seems to have no end.

I flew into Havana from Fort Lauderdale on June 10, 2018, at a time when the Trump administration had reinstated the decades-old trade embargo but before further travel restrictions clamped down. One could still fly into almost any large Cuban city from South Florida; cruise ships filled with Americans squeezed into Havana harbor on Mondays and Tuesdays, a leftover from Barack Obama's opening relations in May 2016. It was the most popular way for U.S. tourists to visit, and on those days, the Old City's brick streets and sidewalk cafés came to life, packed with cigar sellers, *samba* bands, and old widows selling palm crosses and cheap toys.

Cuba is haunted by history, and in no place more than Havana. Sections of the Old City wall snake along modern lanes; Morro Castle guards the harbor like an ancient sentinel. Every nation handpicks its memories, and except in Havana's necropolis, hints of the United States are rare. The old monument to the *Maine* near the harbor entrance has been changed to one honoring the 1959 Revolution; no mention exists in the harbor itself. Instead, José Martí is everywhere: in the names of streets, statues in plazas, the rock quarry where he caught TB. His statue faces the Hotel Inglaterra, where he was arrested. Murals repeat his famous lines:

There are two paths for people when they are born.
The path of slavery—it crushes and decays.
And the path of the star—it illuminates, but kills.

A first glimpse of life in present-day Cuba can be had in South Florida. Although the vast majority of Cubans are still allowed to visit the United States only once a year, friends and relations in South Florida have no such restrictions, and they wheel into customs the giant blue airport-plastic-wrapped bundles filled with everything Cubans can't get at home: Air Jordans, titanium white house paint, 40-to-50-inch LED TVs—and buried deep inside, U.S. currency. Though some restrictions have loosened, the U.S. embargo is still in place and has been so since 1962. Few other nations support it, and every year since 1992, the U.N. General Assembly has voted for its end. In a secret April 6, 1960, memo, the U.S. State Department spelled out its purpose: to "bring about hunger, desperation and overthrow of government." Twenty years later, CIA analysts concluded that it "[had] not met any of these objectives." Castro's government survived, as did his people.

Hard times continued under President Miguel Díaz-Canel, who in 2018 became Cuba's first leader in nearly sixty years from outside the Castro clan. He enacted currency reform and invited Chinese tourism, construction, and investment, but despite such measures the economy has grown worse since 2018. The embargo was bad enough: COVID and reimposed U.S. sanctions were crippling. The nation imports 70 percent of its food and has run short of cash for such basics as cooking oil, chicken, milk, and feed for dairy cows. The milk shortage hits hard: Castro came from a dairy farm north of Santiago, and when he assumed power, he promised a daily supply of milk to every child under seven. Every month, families received baskets of powdered milk, beans, rice, cooking oil, and diapers and baby formula for parents with infants. Those I met were often proud of these baskets, and despite all the other privations saw them as somehow emblematic of what it meant to be "Cuban."

Yet now those needs aren't being met, and Cuba is suffering its worst economic crisis in decades. At one point, a two-pound sack of powdered milk cost $50—a week's salary—on the black market. Mass protests broke out in mid-2021 over high prices; in Havana, 1,300 demonstrators were detained, and by September 2022 hundreds had been sentenced to prison for as long as twenty-five years. In 2022 nearly 225,000 Cubans were stopped at the U.S.-Mexico border, the largest flight of exiles since 125,000 arrived during the 1980 Mariel boatlift.

There is an old saying in Cuba: "Live today—tomorrow, we'll see." One heard it during the "Special Period in the Time of Peace" of 1989–1991, when the old Soviet Union pulled out, taking with it up to $5 billion a year in subsidies. Tales of starvation were common, especially in the country. One hears that saying again. But that does not mean Cubans will seek relief by being "Americanized." Now, as in 1898, many of them are proud to play David against the northern Goliath. It is part of their identity.

One does not ask Cubans about politics, even after Fidel Castro's death, in 2016. Though I found a loosening of censorship in Havana, many Cubans are still circumspect, and artists and writers were among the first to be jailed after the mass protests that began on July 11, 2021. In the conservative east, expression is more tightly controlled. I stopped counting the number of times I saw "Yo Soy Fidel" painted on walls and billboards, a phrase with a history: during the 1959 revolution, Batista's soldiers asked rebels "Where is Fidel?" before they shot them. A rebel's last words were often "I am Fidel." In the east, Committees for the Defense of the Revolution—the neighborhood arm of the Communist Party—still served as watchdogs. People were curious about an American wandering off the beaten track, but when committee members filmed me once or twice from the side or from behind, my escorts grew careful. An old friend (and army officer) told my guide, "I don't know how it is in Havana, but out here I can't be seen with an American." After the July 2021 protests, surveillance intensified: if you work for the government, you're expected to report even mild dissent. If you're a teacher or professor, you're expected to turn in student hotheads. "Most people I know aren't doing it," one friend said. "You don't do that to friends and family."

After a week in Havana, our party climbed into a gleaming blue-and-white 1955 Ford Fairlane and motored east in the footsteps of Funston and Calixto García. Our final destination was Santiago and San Juan Hill, but we passed through lonely, forgotten sites rarely mentioned in U.S. histories: Ciego de Ávila; Camaguey; Las Tunas, and Bayamo; Nuevitas, where Funston landed; the coastal resort of Manzanillo, shelled by the U.S. Navy; Guáimaro, where the all-American *mambi* Winchester Dana Osgood died. The Ford was my age: a curbside cabochon with a recycled Kia engine under the buffed hood.

Everything is recycled here: Cuba's is a culture of shortage, much as Depression-era America, where you learn to do everything from hanging drywall to rebuilding an engine. When you don't know something, you find someone who does. Two-thirds of the way to Santiago, in Holguin, the clutch gave out; in need of a replacement gearbox, we visited a secondhand dealer in the dead of night far out of town. Along the way, we came upon a tree sticking out of the road. The workmen had run out of road fill and asphalt, so they'd thrown a tree into the hole as a warning until material arrived. "Cuba!" Our guide laughed. "You've got to love it."

In Santiago, the end of our journey, I watched the half-hourly changing of the guard at Castro's tomb, a ritual attended by continuous busloads of people. That same day, I got sucked into a block-long conga line; uniformed Guardia tried to move the line forward by swinging batons against the backs of dancers' knees. But the line, like the island, dances at its own speed.

Later that summer, my wife, Kathy, and I followed Carl Sandburg's footsteps in Puerto Rico; then a few months later, I flew to the Philippines. In both places, the anger against America was more palpable than Cuba's; and these were, ostensibly, allies. In Puerto Rico, we stayed in the central highlands, nearly a year after Category 4 Hurricane Maria roared through on September 20, 2017. Roads were still washed out, houses gutted, gashes creasing the landscape where homes and their occupants slid down a mountainside. Entire sections of Utuado looked shelled. The death toll first reported by Puerto Rico's government and then adopted by the United States was sixty-four; one year later, the Milken Institute School of Public Health at George Washington University reported that number closer to 2,975.

Four years later, in September 2022, Hurricane Fiona slammed into the island, dropping thirty-two inches of rain and again crashing the grid. At least a thousand people needed rescue, four people died, and more than half the island lost power and water. Mariangy Hernandez, of mountainous Cayey, surveyed her street where floods swept away beds, dressers, and refrigerators. "Puerto Rico is not prepared for this," she lamented, "or for anything," even after 120 years of American rule.

Betrayal and anger is more complex in the Philippines. When I flew to Manila in March 2019, the country was in turmoil. I'd been warned by Filipino friends that Northern Luzon's drug gangs kidnapped Americans for ransom; my friends traveled with an armed bodyguard when visiting family. In Mindanao, the Moro rebellion dragged on, making it the world's longest continuing revolt. To the east, the Communist-led National Democratic Front of the Philippines (NDFP) celebrated its fiftieth birthday by attacking a rural police station, resulting only in dead, wounded, and captured attackers. Security guards stand at the glass doors of malls armed with pump shotguns. Uniformed policemen direct traffic with submachine guns slung over their shoulders. Journalists I met said that their papers pay for their weapons training in response to a mass killing of journalists at a Mindanaoan rally years earlier.

McKinley, Taft, and Roosevelt hoped to recast the archipelago "in our image." Considering America's current number of mass killings, they succeeded. Yet many Philippine murders were political and ideological, not stemming from the free-floating anger rampant in her former ruler. Shortly before I arrived, President Rodrigo Duterte responded to a crystal meth epidemic by releasing a "narco-list" filled with political opponents, journalists, and clergy who'd criticized his policies. Inclusion could be deadly. Assassinations were carried out through "extra-judicial killings," or EJKs, usually involving two gunmen astride a motorbike who worked with police in Duterte's "war on drugs." According to the Philippine Drug Enforcement Agency, 4,949 suspected drug dealers and users were killed between July 2016 and September 2018, but according to human rights organizations, that number was really more than 20,000, including dozens of children whom Duterte shrugged off as "collateral damage."

For centuries, Filipinos have known a continual flux of reinvention: Spanish colony, U.S. possession, independent nation with a "special relationship" to America; hotbed of Duterte's anti-Americanism; the dictatorship of Ferdinand Marcos; his ouster by Maria "Cory" Aquino following her husband's assassination; the landslide election of Ferdinand "Bongbong" Marcos Jr., who in his own campaign whitewashed his father's plunder. On May 25, 2022, Marcos was sworn in as the archipelago's seventeenth president, as was his vice president, Duterte's daughter Sara, a win that analysts said bespoke their predecessors' popularity.

A large part of that depends upon the malleability of historical "truth" and memory. While I was there, the Philippines seemed caught again in an identity crisis, but this time focused on Aguinaldo as a national metaphor. Was he a tragic hero, a flawed founding father, or a weak man who sold his ideals? What did the new nation stand for? What does its history *mean*? It did not help that he was linked to the deaths of Andrés Bonifacio and Antonio Luna. It would be easier if he'd just been a martyr, said Jesus Crispin Remulla, then governor of Cavite, where an international conference on Aguinaldo's legacy was held on his 150th birthday. "If Aguinaldo had died in the Philippine Revolution, he would have been venerated," he said. Death defines heroism, but more than that, "Death defines *us*," he exclaimed.

One can follow José Rizal's walk to death these days. The route starts at his cell in Fort Santiago, where he married Josephine Bracken; follows his red-painted footsteps through mood music piped into the prison gardens, past signs that warn WATCH FOR FALLING FRUIT plummeting from branches above. The steps wend past San Agustin Church, where on weekends weddings start every forty-five minutes: the giant wooden doors swing open, and the bride stands, eyes downcast, before a backdrop of white roses and greenery. Rizal marches on, down cobblestone streets, through the Old City's south gates, over Padre Burgos Street, onto the parade ground, where he died. An effigy stands where a dog danced around him as he faced the firing squad. He is dressed in frock coat, black tie, wide-brimmed bowler, the very image of *ilustrado* respectability, staring, as the sword dropped, at blue Manila Bay.

Before leaving the Aguinaldo conference, I walk through the surrounding town, past a boy leading the family *carabao* by rope, past fields burned brown by drought. The worst drought in recent memory had struck Luzon that season: this turned into a water shortage in sprawling, dystopian Metro Manila, and in panic the state declared a "state of calamity." I strolled down a crumbling street bordered by a culvert so deep that if I fell in, no one would know. Vendors' stands line the road; the right-of-way choked to a standstill with Jeepneys, bikes with no pedals, motorbikes with sidecars. I pass folding tables loaded with fish, octopus, paper fans, mints, posters of the film *Heneral Luna*, posters of Rambo, mysterious tubers. As I stop to inspect a package of dried squid, a personal fave, an old vendor in a Miami Dolphins ball cap emerges from his tent in the back and grins.

"You United States?" he asks, his rough English 500 percent better than my nonexistent Tagalog. I smile and answer, "Virginia," near the huge navy base in Norfolk. His eyes grow wide. Through a Babel of phrases, gestures, and a twenty-six-year-old atlas kept in the back of his stall, we piece together that his sister is a nurse who lives somewhere in the Tidewater area, and from experience I know that she, or someone in her family, probably married into the navy. In the coming months, several Filipino nurses pass through my life as Kathy and I heal in the hospital from a near-fatal crash; in all probability, they help save our lives. I wish I could tell that old vendor now. He turns to an old woman seated back in the shadows and says something in Tagalog. She snorts and makes a comment. He laughs and translates: "Maybe we family."

I laugh, too. Shoppers glance at the Yank and Filipino who can barely converse but nonetheless act crazy in tandem. They carefully squeeze past, hoping they don't get infected.

I buy two packs of squid—one more than planned. I munch in contentment and weave through the curious crowd.

"And now we see that the abyss of history is deep enough to bury all the world," Paul Valéry wrote one year after the War to End All Wars. At its start, the Great War was as popular as America's recent adventures in Cuba and the Philippines had been; Europeans believed it would be quick and glorious, as did Americans. Valéry had celebrated European civilization as history's apex, "the pearl of the sphere, the brain of a vast body" that would save mankind. Instead, that civilization almost snuffed itself out in four years. He saw that every era spawns lies that advance careers, subvert ideals, and change the course of history. The art and science he revered had been replaced by the horrors of the trench, the reality of rotting flesh, the constant terror of waiting to die. The empires of Elam, Nineveh, and Babylon had once been splendid constructs, but they had passed into ash: the names "France, England, Russia," were also splendid, but "the illusion of a European culture has been lost . . . called to account for its dreams."

By the time Valéry wrote these words, Clara Barton had passed on, dying at age ninety of double pneumonia on April 12, 1912, in her Glen Echo home. She was tired. In 1900, she'd rushed to Galveston, Texas, in the wake of the hurricane that killed, injured, and displaced thousands; but when she came home, the internal campaign against her mounted, led by the rumormongering Mabel Boardman. Her account of the Red Cross in the Splendid War would excise all mention of Barton, just as Walter Reed excised mention of Clara Maass in his account of the yellow fever trials. Barton resigned in 1904. On January 5, 1905, Congress created a new corporation, signed by President Roosevelt, one of her chief critics, who apparently forgot that day in Siboney when Barton gave him free delicacies for his exhausted Rough Riders. As usual, Miss B did not retaliate. "It is," she wrote, "an unfortunate trait in the human character to assail or asperse others engaged in the performance of humanitarian acts."

But the attacks took their toll. In the year of her resignation, she contemplated suicide—as she had before, though she apparently never made the attempt. More and more she fought back the "thin black snakes" of sadness as they closed in. In 1907 she published her autobiography, and in it she recalled 1861, the beginning of her career. As Captain Stephen Barton lay on his deathbed, he granted his daughter's wish to serve on the battlefield. "Go," he said, "it is your duty to go."

As pneumonia set in, she felt herself ready to go. On April 10, two nights before her death, she groaned and opened her eyes. "I dreamed I was back in battle," she said:

> I waded in blood up to my knees. I saw death as it is on the battlefield. The poor boys with arms shot off and legs gone, were lying on the cold ground, with no nurses and no physicians to do anything for them. I saw the surgeons coming, too much needed by all to give special attention to any one. Once again I stood by them and witnessed those soldiers bearing their soldier pains, limbs being sliced off without opiates being taken, or even a bed to lie on. I crept around once more, trying to give them at least a drink of water to cool their parched lips, and I heard them at last speak of mothers and wives and sweethearts, but never a murmur of complaint.

She woke one last time, at nine o'clock on a spring morning. "Let me go," she cried, as she'd implored her father five decades earlier. She was very tired. Tired of a world where nations forever made the same mortal choices. Tired of the ruin wrought by each new liberator. Tired of what Henry Adams once called every individual's "education among the carnivores."

She thrashed, and whispered "Let me go" one last time. Then breathed out, releasing herself to what she'd always known would be her "sweetest hour."

Notes

In the course of my research, I spent time in many national archives and libraries, and many of the sources cited in my notes come from the following.

After the first reference, those resources frequently cited will be abbreviated as follows:

ACHS: Allen County Historical Society & Research Archives, Iola, KS.

CS: University of Illinois Rare Books and Manuscripts Collection, Urbana-Champaign, IL; Carl Sandburg Papers (Connemara Accession), 1898–1967.

ILL: Illinois Historical and Lincoln Collection, University of Illinois, Urbana-Champaign, IL.

KHS: Kansas Historical Society, Topeka, KS.

KX: Knox College Archives, Galesburg, IL.

LC/MS: Library of Congress, Manuscript Division, Washington, D.C.

MAC: MacArthur Memorial Library and Archives, Norfolk, VA.

NARA: National Archives and Records Administration, Washington, D.C.

Philip, "A Volunteer of 1898": USAMH: Spanish American War Veterans Survey Collection: Box 64: "U.S. Volunteer Cavalry—1st, 2nd, 3rd, and 11th Regiments": Folder 4: "U.S. Volunteer Cavalry—1st Regiment [1898-W-60], Hoffman, Philip, Co. A.": Herman Hoffman Philip, "A Volunteer of 1898" [typescript].

RIZ: Rizal Library Special Collections, Ateneo de Manila University, Quezon City, Philippines.

Taylor, *The Philippine Insurrection*: John R. M. Taylor, ed., *The Philippine Insurrection Against the United States: A Compilation of Documents with Notes and Introduction by John R. M. Taylor*, vols. 1–5 (Pasay City, PI: Eugenio Lopez Foundation, 1971).

UM: University of Miami Special Collections, Coral Gables, FL.

USAMH: U.S. Army Military History Institute, Carlisle, PA.

U.S. Congress, *Commission on the Conduct of the War*: U.S. Congress, *Report of the Commission Appointed by the President to Investigate the Conduct of the War Department in the War with Spain.* 56th Congress, 1st Session (Washington, D.C.: Government Printing Office, 1900).

USF: University of South Florida: Florida Studies Center, Tampa, FL.

USMCHC: U.S. Marine Corps Historical Center, Quantico, VA.

U.S War Department, *Correspondence Relating to the War with Spain*: U.S. Department of War, *Correspondence Relating to the War with Spain, and Conditions Growing Out of the Same, Including the Insurrection in the Philippine Islands and the China Relief Expedition, Between the Adjutant-General of the Army and Military Commanders in the United States, Cuba, Porto Rico, China, and the Philippine Islands, from April 15, 1898, to July 30, 1902*, 2 vols. (Washington, D.C.: Government Printing Office, 1902).

UVA: University of Virginia Claude Moore Health Sciences Library, Charlottesville, VA.

Villa, "Flight and Wanderings": Simeon A. Villa, "The Flight and Wanderings of Emilio Aguinaldo, from His Abandonment of Bayambang Until His Capture in Palanan," in U.S. Senate, *Affairs in the Philippine Islands: Hearings Before the Committee on the Philippines of the United States Senate.* 57th Congress, 1st Session, Doc. No. 331, Part 3 (Washington, D.C.: Government Printing Office, 1902).

PROLOGUE: "HAD THE NATION GONE MAD?"

3 *At 9:39 p.m. on February 15*: Sources for the Prologue on pages 3 to 11 include: "Clara Barton and the American Red Cross in Cuba and Tampa During the Spanish American War," *Clara Barton, Founder of the Red Cross*, www.tampapix.com/barton2.htm; Stephen B. Oates, *A Woman of Valor: Clara Barton and the Civil War* (New York: Free Press, 1994); Library of Congress Manuscript Division, Washington, D.C. (hereafter LC/MS), Clara Barton Papers: Barton to Bernard Vassall, July 28, 1860; David H. Burton, *Clara Barton: In the Service of Humanity* (Westport, CT: Greenwood Press, 1995), 23; John C. Reilly Jr. and Robert L. Scheina, *American Battleships 1886–1923: Predreadnought Design and Construction* (Annapolis, MD: Naval Institute Press, 1980), 20–48, 258; W. A. Swanberg, *Citizen Hearst: A Biography of William Randolph Hearst* (New York: Charles Scribner's Sons, 1961), 134; Clara Barton, *The Red Cross: A History of This Remarkable International Movement in the Interest of Humanity* (Washington, D.C.: American National Red Cross, 1898), 515, 521; Charles Dwight Sigsbee, "Personal Narrative of the 'Maine': Part I, Our Reception in Havana," *Century Illustrated Magazine*, 57:1 (November 1898), 83, and "Personal Narrative of the 'Maine': Part II, The Explosion," *Century Illustrated Magazine*, 57:2 (December 1898), 241; Percy H. Epler, *The Life of Clara Barton* (New York: MacMillan, 1915), 284–85; Trumbull White, *Pictorial History of Our War with Spain for Cuba's Freedom* (Freedom Publishing, 1898), 136, 402; Mildred Tengborn, *No Greater Love: The Gripping Story of Nurse Clara Maass* (St. Louis, MO: Concor-

dia, 1978), 21, 25, 49, 54; Kansas Historical Society, Topeka (hereafter KHS), Ms. Coll. 33, Frederick Funston Collection, box 3, "Miscellaneous Papers, Clippings, 1892–1932, Undated," folder: "Clippings, 1892–1898": "Fred Funston in New York," Jan. 11, 1898, reprint from New York paper in unidentified Kansas paper; Leon Wolff, *Little Brown Brother* (New York: History Book Club, 2006; 1st pub. 1961), 37–38; Frank Norris, *Collected Letters*, ed. Jesse S. Crisler (San Francisco: Book Club of California, 1986), 52–53; Stephen Crane, "War Memories," in *The War Dispatches of Stephen Crane* (New York: New York University Press, 1964), 258; Carl Sandburg, *Always the Young Strangers* (New York: Harcourt, Brace, 1952), 375–76, 403; Philip R. Yannella, *The Other Carl Sandburg* (Jackson, MI: University Press of Mississippi, 1996), xiv; U.S. Army Military History Institute, Carlisle, PA (hereafter USAMH), Samuel B. M. Young Papers, box 10, folder: "Correspondence, primarily with Presidents McKinley and Roosevelt": Letter, Young to Theodore Roosevelt, Feb. 12, 1899; *La Catastrofe del Maine* (Havana: El Figaro, 1898), 6–7; Edmund Morris, *The Rise of Theodore Roosevelt* (New York: Ballantine Books, 1979), 625; Paul Fussell, "The Culture of War," in *The Costs of War: America's Pyrrhic Victories*, ed. John V. Denson (New Brunswick, NJ: Transaction Press, 1999, 2nd edition), 417, 421; Evan Thomas, *The War Lovers: Roosevelt, Lodge, Hearst, and the Rush to Empire* (New York: Back Bay Books, 2011; 1st pub. 2010), 12; Richard White, *"It's Your Misfortune and Not My Own": A New History of the American West* (Norman, OK: University of Oklahoma Press, 1993), 73; James C. Bradford, ed., *Crucible of Empire: The Spanish-American War and Its Aftermath* (Annapolis, MD: Naval Institute Press, 1993), xv; T. E. Lawrence, *Seven Pillars of Wisdom: A Triumph* (New York: Penguin, 1978; 1st pub. 1926, privately), 27; Max Boot, *The Savage Wars of Peace: Small Wars and the Rise of American Power* (New York: Basic Books, 2002), 120, 284; James W. Loewen, *Lies Across America: What Our Historic Sites Get Wrong* (New York: New Press, 2019), 142; Arthur A. Ekirch Jr., *Progressivism in America: A Study of the Era from Theodore Roosevelt to Woodrow Wilson* (New York: New Viewpoints, 1974), 200; Martin van Creveld, *The Culture of War* (New York: Presidio Press, 2008), 292; Anand Gopal, "Clean Hands," *New Yorker*, Dec. 21, 2020, 77; "List of Wars Involving United States," *Wikipedia*; Paul Atwood, "War IS the American Way of Life," *New England Journal of Public Policy*, 19:1 (Fall 2003), 183; John V. Denson, "War and American Freedom," in John V. Denson, ed., *The Costs of War: America's Pyrrhic Victories*, 33; Louis A. Perez Jr., *Cuba in the American Imagination: Metaphor and the Imperial Ethos* (Chapel Hill, NC: University of North Carolina Press, 2008), 7; Richard Slotkin, *Regeneration Through Violence: The Mythology of the Frontier, 1600–1860* (Middletown, CT: Wesleyan University Press, 1973), 4–5.

1. MARTYRS

15 *caves—where the mythic freedom fighter*: Sources for the introduction to Chapter 1 on pages 15 to 16 include: Reynaldo Clemena Ileto, *Pasyon and Revolution: Popular Movements in the Philippines, 1840–1910* (Quezon City, PI: Ateneo de Manila

University Press, 1979), 99; "Martyrs," *Encyclopedia of Death and Dying*, www.deathreference.com/Ke-Ma/Martyrs.html; Erik Erikson, *Gandhi's Truth: On the Origins of Militant Nonviolence* (New York: Norton, 1969), 197; John Barrett, "The Cuba of the Far East," *North American Review*, 164:483 (February 1897), 78; George B. Waldron, "The Commercial Promise of Cuba, Porto Rico, and the Philippines," *McClure's Magazine*, 11:5 (September 1898), 482.

16 *Spain was a shadow*: Sources for the life and death of José Martí on pages 16 to 25 include: Hal Klepak, *Churchill Comes of Age: Cuba 1895* (Stroud, U.K.: History Press, 2015), 27; Mark 1:15; John Lawrence Tone, *War and Genocide in Cuba, 1895–1898* (Chapel Hill, NC: University of North Carolina Press, 2006), 30, 31–32, 37, 78, 79; Jerry A. Sierra, "Jose Marti: Apostle of Cuban Independence, Part 1," *historyofcuba.com*, www.historyofcuba.com/history/marti/marti2.htm; "Oriente Province," *Wikipedia*; Clifford L. Staten, *The History of Cuba* (New York: Palgrave MacMillan, 2005), 22–24, 28–29, 32–35; Louis A. Perez Jr., *Cuba and the United States: Ties of Singular Intimacy* (Athens, GA: University of Georgia Press, 2003, 3rd edition), 16–17, 19–20, 59–61; Trumbull White, *Pictorial History of Our War with Spain for Cuba's Freedom*, 155, 160–61, 171, 199–203, 206–207; interview with Carlos Osquel Céspedes Leyra, director, Museo Parque Nacional La Damajagua, Oct. 21, 2018; *José Martí Reader*, ed. Deborah Shnookal and Mirta Muñiz (New York: Ocean Press, 1999): José Martí, "Political Prison in Cuba," 35; "With All, for the Good of All," 140; "The Spanish Republic and the Cuban Revolution," 41–42; "Campaign Diary," 198–200; Letter, Martí to Maximo Gomez, Oct. 20, 1884, 209; Letter, Martí to Federico Henríquez y Carvajal, March 25, 1895, 225; Letter, Martí to mother, March 25, 1895, 227; Letter, Martí to José Martí y Zayer Bazán, April 1, 1895, 228; Letter, Martí to Carmen Miyares de Mantilla, April 16, 1895, 230; Letter, Martí to Manuel Mercado, May 18, 1895, 243; Walter Millis, *The Martial Spirit: A Study of Our War with Spain* (New York: Literary Guild of America, 1931), 14–15; Frederick Funston, *Memories of Two Wars: Cuban and Philippine Experiences* (New York: Charles Scribner's Sons, 1914), 31; "Antonio Maceo Grajoles," *Wikipedia*; Michael Clodfelter, *Warfare and Armed Conflicts: A Statistical Encyclopedia of Casualty and Other Figures, 1492–2007* (Jefferson, NC: McFarland, 2008, 3rd edition), 330–31; Vicki Huddleston, *Our Woman in Havana: A Diplomat's Chronicle of America's Long Struggle with Castro's Cuba* (New York: Overlook Press, 2018), 50–57; Joyce Milton, *The Yellow Kids: Foreign Correspondents in the Heyday of Yellow Journalism* (New York: Harper Perennial, 1989), 52; José H. Hernandez, "Cuba in 1898," *Library of Congress Research Guides: World of 1898: Perspectives on the Spanish American War*; Stefan Collini, "The Enlightened Vote," *London Review of Books*, Dec. 19, 2019, 10; "José Martí," *Wikipedia*; Vicki L. Ruiz, "Nuestra America: Latino History as United States History," *Journal of American History*, 93:3 (December 2006), 662; U.S. Treasury Department, *Report of Commissioner of Internal Revenue, 1628* (1892), 30, and *Report of Commissioner of Internal Revenue, 1902* (1895), 37; John C. Appel, "The Unionization of Florida Cigarmakers and the Coming of the War with Spain," *The Hispanic American Historical Review*, 36:1 (February 1956), 40; Susan Greenbaum,

"Patriots in Exile: Afro-Cubans in Tampa 1886–1909," in *Soldiers and Patriots: Buffalo Soldiers and Afro-Cubans in Tampa, 1898* [USF Anthropology Studies in Historical Archaeology, no. 2], ed. Brent R. Weisman (Tampa, FL: Florida Division of Historical Resources, July 1999), 104; Geoffrey Mohlman, "'An Insult and a Blow': The Buffalo Soldiers in Tampa Bay," in *Soldiers and Patriots*, 19, 33; Jose S. Arcilla, "The Enlightenment and the Philippine Revolution," *Philippine Studies*, 39:3 (Third Quarter 1991), 370; interview, Mario Rafael Guerrero, professor of history, Camaguey, June 11, 2018.

26 *three new animal species*: Sources for the life and death of José Rizal on pages 25 to 34 include: "Chapter Eight: Jose P. Rizal's Exile in Dapitan (1892–1896)," https://bshjoserizal.weebly.com/our-hero-jose-rizal/chapter-eight-jose-p-rizals-exile-in-dapitan-1892-1896 (the three species were: *Draco rizoli*, a flying dragon; *Apegonia rizoli*, a small beetle; and *Rhacophorus rizoli*, a rare frog), 3, 4; Ambeth R. Ocampo, *Two Lunas, Two Mabinis: Looking Back 10* (Mandaluyong City, PI: Anvil Publishing, 2015), 16–17, 53; Stanley Karnow, *In Our Image: America's Empire in the Philippines* (New York: Ballantine Books, 1989), 15, 51–52, 67, 71–72, 73–74, 76; Augusto de Viana, *Stories Rarely Told: the Hidden Stories and Essays on Philippine History* (Quezon City, PI: New Day Publishers, 2013): "Statement of Josephine Bracken," 11; "Rizal's Own Story of His Life," 6, 14, 15, 16–19; "Confession of Antonio Luna to Judge Advocate Col. Don Francisco de Olive, Manila, Nov. 12, 1897," 62–66; Philippine Information Society, *Facts About Filipinos, 1900–1902* (Boston: Philippine Information Society, 1901), 26, 27, 47; Nick Joaquin, *A Question of Heroes: Essays in Criticism on Ten Keys Figures of Philippine History* (Manila: Ayala Museum Press, 1977), 40–41, 93–95; Carlos Quirino, "Rizal and Bonifacio," *Philippine Magazine*, 35:11 (November 1935), 519; "La Solidaridad," *Wikipedia*; Ronald E. Dolan, ed., *Philippines, a Country Study* (Washington, D.C.: Federal Research Division, Library of Congress, 1993), 18; C. O. Resurreccion, "A Second Look at Rizal's Martyrdom," *Philippine Historical Association Historical Bulletin*, 6:4 (December 1962), 419, 422; José Rizal, *Noli Me Tángere (Touch Me Not)*, trans. Harold Augenbrum (New York: Penguin, 2006; 1st pub. 1887), xxi–xxii; Jose S. Arcilla, "The Enlightenment and the Philippine Revolution," *Philippine Studies*, 39:3 (Third Quarter 1991), 369–70, 372; Ferdinand Blumentritt, "Biography of Dr. Jose Rizal, The Distinguished and Talented Scholar and Patriot, Infamously Shot in Manila on December 30, 1896," *International Archives of Ethnology* (Special Supplement: vol. X, 1897), trans. Howard W. Bray (Singapore: Lelly & Walsh, Ltd., 1898), 5, 14; "Andres Bonifacio," *Philippine Magazine*, 22:5 (October 1925), 227; Eric Hobsbawm, *Primitive Rebels: Studies in Archaic Forms of Social Movements in the Nineteenth and Twentieth Centuries* (London: Abacus, 2017; 1st pub. 1959), xxi–xxii; Teodoro A. Agoncillo, *The Revolt of the Masses: the Story of Bonifacio and the Katipunan* (Quezon City, PI: University of the Philippines Press, 1956), 85; Teodoro M. Kalaw, *The Philippine Revolution* (Kawilihan, PI: Jorge B. Vargas Filipiniana Foundation, 1969; 1st pub. 1924), 22; Sol. H. Gwekoh, "Andres Bonifacio," *Philippine Magazine*, 25:6 (November 1928), 307–309; Santiago V. Alvarez, *Recalling the Revolution: Memoirs*

of a Filipino General, trans. Paula Carolina S. Malay (Madison, WI: University of Wisconsin Press, 1992; 1st pub. 1927–28), 29–32, 91; John R.M. Taylor, ed., *The Philippine Insurrection Against the United States: A Compilation of Documents with Notes and Introduction by John R.M. Taylor*, vols. 1–5 (Pasay City, PI: Eugenio Lopez Foundation, 1971), 237–38 (hereafter Taylor, *The Philippine Insurrection*); T. H. Pardo de Tavera, "The Character of Rizal," *Philippine Review*, 2:6 (June 1917), 50, 52–53; Augusto V. de Viana, ed., *The I Stories: The Philippine Revolution and the Filipino-American War as Told by Its Eyewitnesses and Participants* (Manila: University of Santa Tomas, 2006), 85–89; Joseph Earle Stevens, "An American in Manila," *McClure's Magazine*, 11:2 (June 1898), 186; "José Rizal," *Wikipedia*.

2. WATCHMEN

35 *Martí's dreams of* Cuba Libre: Sources for the first days of *Cuba Libre* on pages 35 to 37 include: John Lawrence Tone, *War and Genocide in Cuba, 1895–1898*, 1–3, 58–60, 60–61, 81, 88, 90–91, 108, 111; "More Men: Gen. Campos Says He Needs Them in Cuba," *Louisville Courier-Journal* (Louisville, KY), June 28, 1895, 8; Hal Klepak, *Churchill Comes of Age: Cuba 1895*, 41–42, 44–45, 61–62, 81, 97, 98, 107–109, 128–29, 242; "Maximo Gomez," *Wikipedia*; Richard Harding Davis, *Cuba in War Time* (Lincoln, NE: University of Nebraska Press, 2000; 1st pub. 1898), 78–79; Paul S. Scarlata, "Whatever Its Other Deficiencies, the Spanish Army in Cuba Had One of the World's Best Infantry Weapons in 1898," *Military History*, 15:2 (June 1998), 26; Eric Hobsbawm, *Primitive Rebels: Studies in Archaic Forms of Social Movements in the Nineteenth and Twentieth Centuries* (London: Abacus, 2017; 1st pub. 1959), 6–7, 17; Max Boot, *The Savage Wars of Peace: Small Wars and the Rise of American Power*, 112; Joyce Milton, *The Yellow Kids*, xii, 57.

37 *Sylvester "Harry" Scovel*: Sources for the arrival of the correspondents on pages 37 to 42 include: "Sylvester H. Scovel," *Wikipedia*; Milton, *The Yellow Kids*, xii, 47–50, 53, 57–59, 67–68, 69, 70–77, 79–80; George Bronson Rea, *Facts and Fakes About Cuba: A Review of the Various Stories Circulated in the United States Concerning the Present Insurrection* (New York: George Munro's Sons, 1897), 111, 151, 153, 173–74, 174–75, 177, 236–37, 261–63; Marisa L. Ambio, "Cuba's 'Laborante': The Worker as Revolutionary Identity," *Latin American Research Review*, 50:3 (2015), 157; Charles H. Brown, *The Correspondents' War: Journalists in the Spanish-American War* (New York: Charles Scribner's Sons, 1967), 10–11, 14–15, 28–29, 31, 129–30; W. A. Swanberg, *Citizen Hearst: A Biography of William Randolph Hearst*, 54, 79–80; Don Carlos Seitz, *Joseph Pulitzer: His Life and Letters* (New York: Simon & Schuster, 1924), 52; Arthur Lubow, *The Reporter Who Would Be King: A Biography of Richard Harding Davis* (New York: Charles Scribner's Sons, 1992), 129.

42 *"but I have scruples"*: Sources for the beginning of Cuba's *reconcentrado* policy on pages 42 to 46 include: G.J.A. O'Toole, *The Spanish War: An American Epic—1898* (New York: W.W. Norton, 1984), 55–56, 57–58 ff58; Trumbull White, *Pictorial History of Our War with Spain for Cuba's Freedom*, 226–28, 230–31, 238, 264; Tone, *War and Genocide*, 153–55, 164, 193–94, 209–10, 223; Milton, *The Yellow Kids*, 82–83,

84–86, 89, 95; Brad K. Berner, ed., *The Spanish-American War: A Documentary History with Commentaries* (Lanham, MD: Fairleigh Dickinson University Press, 2014), 12, 26–27, 33–34; Fitzhugh Lee, "Cuba Under Spanish Rule: Personal Impressions of the Island, the People; of the Government, and the War for Freedom," *McClure's Magazine*, 11:2 (June 1898), 10; Rea, *Facts and Fakes*, 112; David Haward Bain, *Sitting in Darkness: Americans in the Philippines* (New York: Penguin, 1986; 1st pub. 1984), 51–52; Evan Thomas, *The War Lovers: Roosevelt, Lodge, Hearst, and the Rush to Empire*, 69–70, 132–33; *Congressional Record*, 54th Congress, 1st Session, 1971–72; Louis A. Perez Jr., *Cuba in the American Imagination: Metaphor and the Imperial Ethos* (Chapel Hill, NC: University of North Carolina Press, 2008), 50–51, 69–70; Clifford L. Staten, *The History of Cuba*, 38; Leonard W. Levy and Merrill D. Peterson, *Major Crises in American History*, vol. 2 (New York: Harcourt, Brace, 1962), Spanish report cited page 166; *The Statesmen's Yearbook. 1900* (London, 1900), 1196; *Report of the Census of Cuba, 1899* (Washington, D.C.: Government Printing Office, 1900), 179; "Genocide," *Wikipedia*.

3. THE WANDERER

47 *"of hunger and exhaustion"*: Sources for the first discovery of Spanish atrocities on pages 47 to 49 include: John Lawrence Tone, *War and Genocide in Cuba, 1895–1898*, 164; Trumbull White, *Pictorial History of Our War with Spain for Cuba's Freedom*, 231–32; Joyce Milton, *The Yellow Kids*, 90, 92–93, 94–97; "The War Angel of Ayoleta," *Galveston Daily News*, April 13, 1896, 1; Gonzalo de Quesada and Henry Davenport Northrop, *The War in Cuba: Being a Full Account of Her Great Struggle for Freedom* (Liberty Publishing, 1896), 172–73; Gonzalo de Quesada, *The History of the War* (Washington, D.C.: Publishers Union, 1896), 558, 566–68; "Some Men Who Have Reported the War," *The Cosmopolitan*, 25:5 (September 1898), 556; "James Creelman," *Wikipedia*; Charles H. Brown, *The Correspondents' War: Journalists in the Spanish-American War*, 35, 37; James Creelman, *On the Great Highway* (Boston: Lothrop Publishing, 1901), 167; Marcus M. Wilkerson, *Public Opinion and the Spanish-American War: A Study in War Propaganda* (Baton Rouge, LA: Louisiana State University Press, 1932), 32; *New York World*, May 17, 1896, 1, and May 29, 1896, 7.

49 *through the flag-bedecked hall*: Sources for Frederick Funston joining the Cuban Junta on pages 49 to 51 include: G.J.A. O'Toole, *The Spanish War: An American Epic—1898*, 60–61, 62, 63; Thomas W. Crouch, *A Yankee Guerrillero: Frederick Funston and the Cuban Insurrection, 1896–1897* (Memphis, TN: Memphis State University Press, 1975), 1, 10–12, 18–19, 32–33; Frederick Funston, *Memories of Two Wars: Cuban and Philippine Experiences*, 3–4, 26–27, 30; David Haward Bain, *Sitting in Darkness: Americans in the Philippines*, 16, 17–19, 27, 34–35, 37–38; George W. Auxier, "The Propaganda Activities of the Cuban Junta in Precipitating the Spanish-American War, 1895–1898," *Hispanic American Historical Review*, 19:3 (August 1939), 294–96; Frederick Funston, "To Cuba as a Filibuster," *Scribner's Magazine*, 48:3 (September 1910), 306–307, 308–11, 313–14, 315–17; William Allen White, *The Autobiography of William Allen White* (New York: Macmillan, 1946),

142–43; H. O'Hara, "Major-General Funston, Soldier of Fortune," *Pearson's Magazine*, 35–36 (September 1916), 265; interview, July 27, 2018: Kurtis Russell, director, Allen County Historical Society & Research Archives (henceforth ACHS), Iola, KS; Neil R. Peirce and Jerry Hagstrom, *The Book of America: Inside Fifty States Today* (New York: Warren Books, 1984), 585–87.

51 *"ultimate triumph of good over evil"*: Sources for Theodore Roosevelt and the American frontier on pages 51 to 53 include: John Fiske, "Manifest Destiny," *Harper's Monthly Magazine*, March 1888, 587–88, 590; Theodore Roosevelt, *Works*, National Edition, ed. Herman Hagedorn (New York: Scribner's, 1926), vol. 8, 57–58 (the first two volumes came out in 1889, the last in 1896); Edmund Morris, *The Rise of Theodore Roosevelt*, 477; Joe Jackson, *Black Elk: The Life of an American Visionary* (New York: Farrar, Straus & Giroux, 2016), 173; Richard Slotkin, *Gunfighter Nation: The Myth of the Frontier in Twentieth-Century America* (Norman, OK: University of Oklahoma Press, 1998; 1st pub. 1992), 29; Frederick Jackson Turner, *Frontier and Section: Selected Essays*, ed. Ray Allen Billington (New York: Prentice-Hall, 1961), 61; George Beard, *American Nervousness* (New York: G.P. Putnam and Sons, 1881), "Author's Preface"; Evan Thomas, *The War Lovers*, 54–56 ff58, 59, 90; Kathleen Dalton, *Theodore Roosevelt: A Strenuous Life* (New York: Vintage, 2002), 166; Elting E. Morison, *The Letters of Theodore Roosevelt*, vol. 1 (Cambridge, MA: Harvard University Press, 1951), 436.

53 *always ready to fight*: Sources for Funston's early days on pages 53 to 55 include: Thomas W. Crouch, "Frederick Funston of Kansas: His Formative Years, 1865–1891," *Kansas Historical Quarterly*, 40:2 (Summer 1974), 7, 179–80, 181, 188; Crouch, *A Yankee Guerrillero*, 16–18; "MG Frederick Funston," *Museum of the Kansas National Guard, Medal of Honor*, http://www.kansasguardmuseum.org/dispmoh.php?id=2; ACHS: Frederick Funston Collection: Section A: Early Life: Eckdall Collection: "Correspondence of Frederick Funston and a Letter by His Grandfather, James Mitchell": Letter, Funston to Mother, Feb. 1, 1890, Death Valley, CA., no. 121; Letter, Funston to Charles Scott, July 16, 1896; folder: "Batch 2, Early Years": Records of County Superintendent of Public Instruction, Allen Co., KS, 35; Section B: Cuba: folder, "George Rudolph Voss: Partial Diary of Alaska, Fred Funston"; folder: "Funston—Cuba": "Fred Funston's Coffee Company," n.d., n.p.; Eckdall Scrapbook III, 4: Vernon Kellogg, "Fred Funston and the Mountain Lion," *Atlantic Monthly*, n.d., n.p.; Funston, "Storm Bound Above the Clouds," *St. Nicholas Magazine*, July 1891, 657–63; William Allen White, "Funston and the Bear," *New England Home Magazine*, Sept. 17, 1899, 567; KHS, Ms. Coll. 33, Frederick Funston Collection: box 1, "Correspondence, 1890–1911; Report on Expedition to Alaska," folder 1: "Correspondence, 1890–1894, Report on Expedition to Alaska": Letter, Funston to "Brick," March 8, 1891, Death Valley, CA; Funston, "Death Valley," *Iola Register*, Sept. 11, 1891; Frank F. Eckdall, "'Fighting' Fred Funston of Kansas," *Kansas Historical Quarterly*, 22:1 (Spring 1956), 80; H. O'Hara, "Major-General Funston, Soldier of Fortune," *Pearson's Magazine*, 35–36 (Septem-

ber 1916), 263; "Brigadier-General Funston," *The World's Work: A History of Our Time*, 2 (May–October 1901), 697; Funston, "Over the Chilkoot Pass to the Yukon," *Scribner's Magazine*, 20:5 (November 1896), 572–85; Frank F. Eckdall, "'Fighting' Fred Funston of Kansas," *Kansas Historical Quarterly*, 22:1 (Spring 1956), 80; Bain, *Sitting in Darkness*, 36–37.

56 *impressed by his zeal*: Sources for Funston's expedition to Cuba aboard the *Dauntless* on pages 56 to 60 include: Crouch, *A Yankee Guerrillero*, 20–23, 25–33, 111–12; O'Toole, *The Spanish War*, 58–59, 60–62; Auxier, "The Propaganda Activities of the Cuban Junta," 288–89, 290; Funston, "To Cuba as a Filibuster," 306–308, 309–11, 313–17; *New York Herald*, June 3, 1896, 7; Wilkerson, *Public Opinion and the Spanish-American War*, 35; "Fred Funston Gone to Cuba," *Iola Register*, July 10, 1896; "Scott Family," *Kansaspedia: Kansas Historical Society*, www.kshs.org/kansaspedia/scott-family/17656; Jackson, *Black Elk*, 334–35; Richard V. Rickenbach, "Filibustering with the Dauntless," *Florida Historical Quarterly*, 28:4 (April 1950), 231, 236–37, 252 ff252; "Mayor General Calixto García Íñiguez: Mapa Histórico-Biografico" (Havana: Ediciones GEO, 2004); author's notes, June 17, 2019; Funston, *Memories of Two Wars*, 26–27, 30.

4. MAKING GOOD

61 *"plebian, instinctive, and in vain"*: Sources for the rise of Emilio Aguinaldo and the "Little Republic" on pages 61 to 68 include: Nick Joaquin, *A Question of Heroes: Essays in Criticism on Ten Key Figures of Philippine History*, 10, 105–106, 111, 122–23, 124–26; Stanley Karnow, *In Our Image: America's Empire in the Philippines*, 74–75, 78; "Saint Emilius the Martyr," *CatholicSaints.Info*, https://catholicsaints.info/saint-emilius-the-martyr; Opening comments, Jesus Crispin C. Remalla, governor of Cavite, and Dr. Rene R. Escalante, National Historical Commission of the Philippines, March 19, 2019, *International Conference on the 150th Birth Anniversary of Emilio Aguinaldo*, Lyceum of the Philippine University, Cavite; Oscar King Davis, "The Real Aguinaldo," *Everybody's Magazine*, 5:24 (August 1901), 141–44; Augusto V. de Viana, ed., *Stories Rarely Told 2: Threads from Philippine History* (Quezon City, PI: New Day Publishers, 2018), 94; Edwin Wildman, *Aguinaldo: A Narrative of Filipino Ambitions* (Boston: Lothrop, 1901), 19; Reynaldo Clemena Ileto, *Pasyon and Revolution: Popular Movements in the Philippines, 1840–1910*, 14, 25, 26–27, 115–16; Taylor, *The Philippine Insurrection*, vol. 1, 65–71, 283–84, 287–88, 289–94, and vol. 2, 121, 175; interview with Dr. Fernando A. Santiago Jr., Department of History, De La Salle University, Manila, March 18, 2019; David Haward Bain, *Sitting in Darkness: Americans in the Philippines*, 45, 162–63, 167; Philippine Information Society, *Facts About Filipinos, 1900–1902* (Boston: Philippine Information Society, 1901), 19–20; Leon Wolff, *Little Brown Brother*, 25, 35; "The Philippine Revolution from the Eyes of Nozaleda," *The Baratillo Pamphlet*, https://baratillo.net/2011/08/the-philippine-revolution-from-the-eyes-of-nozaleda; Carlos Quirino, "The Spanish Colonial Army," *Philippine Studies*, 36:3 (Third Quarter 1988), 382–

84, 385, 386; Brad K. Berner, ed., *The Spanish-American War: A Documentary History with Commentaries*, 18–19; "Camilio Garcia de Polavieja," *Wikipedia*; Santiago V. Alvarez, *Recalling the Revolution: Memoirs of a Filipino General*, trans. Paula Carolina S. Malay (Madison, WI: University of Wisconsin Press, 1992; 1st pub. 1927–28), 86–87, 90–91, 96–97; Robert Peckham, "Hong Kong Junk: Plague and the Economy of Chinese Things," *Bulletin of the History of Medicine*, 90:1 (Spring 2016), 48; E. G. Pryor, "The Great Plague of Hong Kong," *Journal of the Hong Kong Board of the Royal Asiatic Society*, 15 (1975), 61–70.

69 *McKinley promised stability*: Sources for the rise of William McKinley on pages 68 to 73 include: Edmund Morris, *The Rise of Theodore Roosevelt*, 576, 577; Karnow, *In Our Image*, 85–87, 91, 93; W. A. Swanberg, *Citizen Hearst*, 86–88; Gerald F. Linderman, *The Mirror of War: American Society and the Spanish-American War* (Ann Arbor, MI: University of Michigan Press, 1974), 11–13, 14–15, 18–20, 22–23; Robert W. Merry, *President McKinley: Architect of the American Century* (New York: Simon & Schuster, 2017), 3–5, 33, 111–19, 159, 162–65; Joseph A. Fry, "William McKinley and the Coming of the Spanish-American War: A Study of the Besmirching and Redemption of an Historical Image," *Diplomatic History* 3 (Winter 1979), 77; Wolff, *Little Brown Brother*, 12–13; Charles S. Olcott, *The Life of William McKinley*, vol. 1 (Boston: Houghton Mifflin, 1916), 309–26; Lewis Gould, *The Presidency of William McKinley* (Lawrence, KS: Regents Press of Kansas, 1986), 66–67, 104; Elting E. Morison, ed., *The Letters of Theodore Roosevelt*, vol. 1, letters, Roosevelt to Anna Roosevelt Cowles, March 9 and 30, 1896, 521, 522; Theodore Roosevelt, *Letters from Theodore Roosevelt to Anna Roosevelt Cowles, 1870–1918* (New York: Charles Scribner's Sons, 1924), letters, Roosevelt to Anna Roosevelt Cowles, Apr. 5, 1896, and Jan. 2, 1897, 180, 201; Oscar M. Alfonzo, *Theodore Roosevelt and the Philippines, 1897–1909* (Quezon City, PI: University of the Philippines Press, 1970), 22–23; James Ford Rhodes, *The McKinley and Roosevelt Administrations, 1897–1909* (New York: MacMillan, 1922), 41.

73 *thrown in with a poor lot*: Sources for Funston's first days as a *mambi* on pages 73 to 78 include: Thomas W. Crouch, *A Yankee Guerrillero: Frederick Funston and the Cuban Insurrection, 1896–1897* (Memphis, TN: Memphis State University Press, 1975), 50–51, 53 ff51, 57, 70–71, 77, 129–32, 134; Frederick Funston, *Memories of Two Wars: Cuban and Philippine Experiences*, 33–34, 36–38, 40–41; John Lawrence Tone, *War and Genocide in Cuba, 1895–1898*, 1, 4, 5–6, 8–9; Funston, "Cascorra, The First Cuban Siege," *Scribner's Magazine*, 48:4 (October 1910), 388, 390, 392, 393; Jean de Bueil, Guy Sajer, and Michael Herr are all quoted in Martin van Creveld, *The Culture of War* (New York: Presidio Press, 2008), 107, 108, 109, 112; "Calixto García," *Wikipedia*; Funston, "The Fall of Guaimaro," *Scribner's Magazine*, 48:5 (November 1910), 579–80, 589, 595; interview with Yonilaysi Ortiz, director, Colectivo del Museo Casa Natal "Calixto García Íñiguez," Holguin, Cuba, June 19, 2019; KHS: Ms. Coll. 33, Frederick Funston Collection: box 1, "Correspondence, 1890–1911; Report on Expedition to Alaska," folder 2: "Correspondence. 1896–1898," Letter, Funston to Charles Scott, Nov. 9, 1896.

5. THE VOICE OF AMERICA

79 *neither could Maceo leave*: Sources for the death of Antonio Maceo on pages 79 to 81 include: G.J.A. O'Toole, *The Spanish War: An American Epic—1898*, 72–73, 76–77; Larry Daley, "The Death of Cuban General Antonio Maceo," *The Spanish American War Centennial Website*; "Antonio Maceo, The Bronze Titan," *Monthly Review*, https://monthlyreview.org; "Antonio Maceo Grajales," *Wikipedia*; Thomas W. Crouch, *A Yankee Guerrillero: Frederick Funston and the Cuban Insurrection, 1896–1897* (Memphis, TN: Memphis State University Press, 1975), 45; Horatio S. Rubens, "The Insurgent Government in Cuba," *North American Review*, 166:498 (May 1898), 568.

81 *jewel-encrusted sword*: Sources for the rush of reporters to Cuba on pages 81 to 90 include: Charles H. Brown, *The Correspondents' War: Journalists in the Spanish-American War*, 63–64, 65, 69, 72–73, 77, 78, 85–86; W. A. Swanberg, *Citizen Hearst: A Biography of William Randolph Hearst*, 91, 103–104, 111–13, 161; "Rebels Never More Hopeful," *New York World*, Jan. 7, 1897, 1; Joyce Milton, *The Yellow Kids: Foreign Correspondents in the Heyday of Yellow Journalism*, 108, 110–13, 115, 129, 136, 141, 142–49; Arthur Lubow, *The Reporter Who Would Be King: A Biography of Richard Harding Davis*, 136–37, 138, 139, 140, 142–44; Paul Sorrentino, *Stephen Crane: A Life of Fire* (Cambridge, MA: Belknap Press, 2014), 165–66; Christian W. McMillen, *Discovering Tuberculosis: A Global History, 1900 to the Present* (New Haven, CT: Yale University Press, 2015), 8–9; Joseph J. Kwiat, "Stephen Crane, Literary-Reporter: Commonplace Experience and Artistic Transcendence," *Journal of Modern Literature*, 8:1 (1980), 130–31; O'Toole, *The Spanish War*, 78–79; Michael Robertson, *Stephen Crane, Journalism, and the Making of Modern American Literature* (New York: Columbia University Press, 1997), 58; "The Open Boat," *Wikipedia*; Stephen Crane, "Stephen Crane's Own Story," *New York Post*, Jan. 7, 1897, 1; Ralph W. Stallman, *Stephen Crane: A Biography* (New York: Generic, 1968), 256; Stephen Crane's Seawreck in Daytona," Jan. 3, 1897, quoted in *Volusia History*, https://volusiahistory.wordpress.com; "Stephen Crane," *Wikipedia*; Stephen Crane, "The Open Boat," in *The Bride Comes to Yellow Sky and Other Stories* (New York: Avon, 1956; 1st pub. 1889), 22, 25; Michael Robertson, *Stephen Crane, Journalism, and the Making of Modern American Literature* (New York: Columbia University Press, 1997), 19; Stephen Crane, *The War Dispatches of Stephen Crane*, ed. R. W. Stallman and E. R. Hagemann (New York: New York University Press, 1964), 3; Linda H. Davis, *Badge of Courage: The Life of Stephen Crane* (New York: Houghton Mifflin, 1998), 200, 204; John Berryman, *Stephen Crane* (New York: Meridian, 1962), 178, 184; Christopher Benfey, *The Double Life of Stephen Crane* (New York: Knopf, 1992), 202; Peggy and Harold Samuels, *Frederic Remington: A Biography* (Garden City, NJ: Doubleday and Co., 1982), 245; John Seelye, *War Games: Richard Harding Davis and the New Imperialism* (Amherst, MA: University of Massachusetts Press, 2003), 236–37, 240; James Creelman, *On the Great Highway* , 158, 162, 168; Richard Harding Davis, *Cuba in War Time* (Lincoln, NE: University of Nebraska Press, 2000; 1st pub. 1898), 47, 50, 53, 54, 55, 59–60, 62, 65–73, 78, 112; "Does Our Flag

Shield Women?," *New York Journal*, Feb. 12, 1897, 1–2; George W. Auxier, "Middle Western Newspapers and the Spanish American War, 1895–1898," *Mississippi Valley Historical Review*, 26:4 (March 1940), 524, 530.

92 *Dr. Ricardo Ruiz*: Sources for the jailing of Scovel, Ricardo Ruiz, and other U.S. citizens on pages 91 to 94 include: Joseph B. Kelly, John T. Kelly, and Kiernan Kelly, "Dr. Ricardo Ruiz de Ugerrio Salvador," from *The New York Journal*, March 6, 1897, *historyofcuba.com*, www.historyofcuba.com/history/ruiz1.htm; *Report of the Committee on Foreign Relations, United States Senate, Relative to Affairs in Cuba* (Washington, D.C.: Government Printing Office, 1898), 258–67; "The War Must Be Ended," *New York World*, Feb. 13, 1897 (editorial usually attributed to Joseph Pulitzer); Milton, *The Yellow Kids*, 148, 149, 152; Marcus M. Wilkerson, *Public Opinion and the Spanish-American War: A Study in War Propaganda* (Baton Rouge, LA: Louisiana State University Press, 1932), 10, 84; "Sylvester H. Scovel," *Wikipedia*.

6. THE YOUNG AND THE RESTLESS

95 *A strange lull*: Joyce Milton, *The Yellow Kids*, 173; Robert W. Merry, *President McKinley: Architect of the American Century*, 183, 188; Marcus M. Wilkerson, *Public Opinion and the Spanish-American War: A Study in War Propaganda* (Baton Rouge, LA: Louisiana State University Press, 1932), 39.

95 *"new American"*: Sources for Theodore Roosevelt and the expansionists on pages 95 to 104 include: Henry Adams, *The Education of Henry Adams: An Autobiography* (New York: Modern Library, 1996; 1st pub. 1918), 349, 355–56, 417, 425; Merry, *President McKinley*, 165–66, 223–24, 228–29; Ivan Musicant, *Empire by Default: The Spanish-American War and the Dawn of the American Century* (New York: Holt, 1998), 11; Edmund Morris, *The Rise of Theodore Roosevelt*, 424–25, 592–94, 596, 602, 608–12; William Allen White, "Theodore Roosevelt," in *Masks in a Pageant* (New York: Macmillan, 1928), 17–20, 25, 283–326; Morton Keller, ed., *Theodore Roosevelt: A Profile* (New York: Hill and Wang, 1967), 20; Evan Thomas, *The War Lovers: Roosevelt, Lodge, Hearst, and the Rush to Empire*, 45–46, 148–50, 171–74, 180–81, 183–85; John C. Reilly Jr. and Robert L. Scheina, *American Battleships, 1886–1923: Predreadnought Design and Construction* (Annapolis, MD: Naval Institute Press, 1980), 20–21; G.J.A. O'Toole, *The Spanish War: An American Epic*, 85–86, 96–100, 102–107; Gregg Jones, *Honor in the Dust: Theodore Roosevelt, War in the Philippines, and the Rise and Fall of America's Imperial Dream* (New York: New American Library, 2012), 25–26, 26–27; Elting E. Morison, ed., *The Letters of Theodore Roosevelt*, vol. 1, 655; *New York Sun*, Aug. 23, 1897; "Metropolitan Club," *Wikipedia*; Richard Slotkin, *Gunfighter Nation: The Myth of the Frontier in Twentieth-Century America* , 37–38; J. H. Hitchman, "The American Touch in Imperial Administration: Leonard Wood in Cuba, 1898–1902," *The Americas*, 24:4 (April 1968), 394; Paul Andrew Hutton, *The Apache Wars: The Hunt for Geronimo, the Apache Kid, and the Captive Boy Who Started the Longest War in American History* (New York: Broadway Books, 2016), 382; Marshall Everett, ed., *Exciting*

Experiences in Our Wars with Spain and the Filipinos: The Life of Admiral Dewey (Chicago: Book Publishers Union, 1899), 402; William Allen White, "What's the Matter with Kansas?," *Emporia Daily Gazette*, Aug. 15, 1896; NARA: Microcopy T20, "Despatches from U.S. Consuls in Havana, 1783–1906": "Consular Despatch Oct. 27, 1897"; Theodore Roosevelt, *An Autobiography* (New York: Macmillan, 1913), 231; James Ford Rhodes, *The McKinley and Roosevelt Administrations, 1897–1909* (New York: MacMillan, 1922), 69.

104 *desperate to be a real American*: Sources on Carl Sandburg on pages 104 to 108 include: Carl Sandburg, *Always the Young Strangers* (New York: Harcourt, Brace & Co., 1952), 77–79, 80, 102–108, 152, 253, 280, 287, 375–77, 381, 382–400, 400–402; Penelope Niven, *Carl Sandburg: A Biography*, 4–5, 19–27, 32–33, 35–36; Knox College Archives, Galesburg, IL (hereafter KX): Sandburg Collection, MSS 169, box 1, folder, "Biographical and Anecdotal, General": "Carl Sandburg, Poet, Life Told by His Brother," *Elmwood (IL) Gazette*, June 26, 1936, n.p.; folder: "CAS's Boyhood Neighborhood, CAS in Galesburg": Rex Cherrington, "Carl Sandburg's Galesburg: A Tour Prepared for the Illinois State Historical Society Convention held April 24 & 25, 1987" (typescript), 1; "Carl Sandburg: A Driving Tour of Historic Sites in Galesburg, IL" (Galesburg, IL: Carl Sandburg State Historic Site, 2011); CS: Carl Sandburg Papers, box 30, "Manuscripts": 30-002-006 [typescript for *Always the Young Strangers*], folder: "More Loose Items": "Some notes related to his hobo travels," 18-10-3; Michael Lesy, *Wisconsin Death Trip* (New York: Doubleday, 1973), n.p.: "1885–86," "1890," "1896," and "1897"; Jacob Riis, *The Making of an American* (New York: Macmillan, 1947; 1st pub. 1901), 21–79; Josiah Flynt, *Tramping with Tramps* (New York: Century, 1899), 303; B. A. Botkin and Alvin F. Harlow, eds., *A Treasury of Railroad Folklore: The Stories, Tall Tales, Traditions, Ballads, and Songs of the American Railroad Man* (New York: Bonanza Books, 1953), ff222; Jack London, *The Road* (New York: Macmillan, 1907), 128; Glen H. Mullin, *Adventures of a Scholar Tramp* (New York: Century, 1925), 286–87.

108 *Clara Louise Maass*: Sources on Clara Maass on pages 108 to 111 include: NARA: RG112, Records of the Office of the Surgeon General-Army, Entry 149: "Personal Data Cards on Women Contract Nurses, 1898–1917," box 4, MAD-REED: "Maass, Clara Louise"; John T. Cunningham, *Clara Maass: A Nurse—A Hospital—A Spirit* (Cedar Grove, NJ: Rae Publishing Co., 1968), 8–13, 23–28, 32–34, 35–38, 44; Martha M. Libster and Sr. Betty Ann McNeil, *Enlightened Charity: The Holistic Nursing Care, Education, and ADVICES CONCERNING THE SICK of Sister Matilda Coskery, 1799–1870* (Neenah, WI: Golden Apple Publications, 2009), 310–16; Mildred Tengborn, *No Greater Love: The Gripping Story of Nurse Clara Maass* (St. Louis, MO: Concordia, 1978), 20–21, 46–47, 52–53, 223–24; Rosary S. Gilheany, "Early Newark Hospitals," *Proceedings of the New Jersey Historical Society*, 83 (1965), 20–21; "A Humanitarian Without Peer," *West Essex Tribune*, Dec. 19, 1985, 14.

111 *world had grown more complicated*: Letter, Mary B. Lave to Senator George F. Hoar, Apr. 16, 1898, quoted in Kristin L. Hoganson, *Fighting for American Manhood: How Gender Politics Provoked the Spanish-American and Philippine-American Wars*

(New Haven, CT: Yale University Press, 1998), 57; "The Passing of Maceo," *American Home Magazine*, 1 (January 1897), 3.

111 *woman of influence*: Sources on Clara Barton and Evangelina Cisneros on pages 111 to 113 include: "The Cuban Girl Martyr," *New York Journal*, Aug. 17, 1897, 1; "Clara Barton Papers: Diaries and Journals: 1897, Sept. 10–1898, Jan. 19": Sept. 26, Oct. 10, 11, 14, 15, 21, and Nov. 5, 1897, https://www.loc.gov/item/mss119730046; Swanberg, *Citizen Hearst*, 119–20, 122–23, 124–25, 128–29; *New York Journal*, Aug. 17, 18, and 27, 1897; Hoganson, *Fighting for American Manhood*, 58–59; Willis J. Abbott, *Watching the World Go By* (Boston: Little, Brown), 193, 215–16; *New York Journal*, Oct. 14 & 17, 1897.

113 *it was black America*: Sources for David Fagen and Jim Crow on pages 113 to 117 include: Willard B. Gatewood Jr., *Black Americans and the White Man's Burden, 1893–1903* (Chicago: University of Illinois Press, 1975), 2–3, 16–19; *Omaha Enterprise*, June 26, 1897; Benjamin Brawley, *A Social History of the American Negro* (New York: Macmillan, 1921), 297; Jay Corzine, James Creech, and Lin Corzine, "Black Concentration and Lynchings in the South: Testing Blalock's Power-Threat Hypothesis," *Social Forces*, 61:3 (March 1983), 774–96; Bob Herbert, "The Blight That Is Still with Us," *New York Times*, Jan. 27, 2008; James C. Clark, "Lynching: Florida's Brutal Distinction," *Orlando Sentinel*, March 7, 1993; *Richmond Planet*, Jan. 1, 1897, 5; Michael Morey, *Fagen: An African American Renegade in the Philippine-American War* (Madison, WI: University of Wisconsin Press, 2019), 10, 13–14, 42; Robert P. Ingalls, "Lynching and Establishment Violence in Tampa, 1858–1935," *Journal of Southern History*, 53:4 (November 1987), 613–14, 620–21, 623–24; Frank Schubert, "Seeking David Fagen: The Search for a Black Rebel's Florida Roots," *Tampa Bay History*, 22 (2008), 20–21, 22–24, 25, 27; "David Fagin," *Salt Lake City Herald*, Oct. 30, 1900; Jose Alejandrino, *The Price of Freedom: Episodes and Anecdotes of Our Struggles for Freedom* (Manila: M. Colcol, 1949), trans. Jose M. Alejandrino, 175; NARA: RG 94: Records of the Adjutant General's Office 1780s–1917: box 1241, AGO File 431081: letters and memos concerning "Information Slip on David Fagen, Deserter"; Entry 91: Enlistment Papers, US Army, 1894–1912: Faatz-Failer: "David Fagen," no. 901; Joe Knetsch and Nick Wynne, *Florida in the Spanish-American War* (Charleston, SC: History Press, 2011), 18–19; Paul Ortiz, "'Like Water Covered the Sea': The African-American Freedom Struggle in Florida, 1877–1920" [a dissertation in partial fulfillment of a Ph.D. in history, Duke University, 2000], 118–19; "Harmon Murray," *Wikipedia*.

7. "I WAS A REBEL ONCE, TOO"

118 *"Lost Eden"*: Sources for the "Lost Eden" on pages 118 to 124 include: Reynaldo Clemena Ileto, *Pasyon and Revolution: Popular Movements in the Philippines, 1840–1910*, 108–109, 110–11, 112; Ambeth R. Ocampo, *Two Lunas, Two Mabinis: Looking Back 10*, 56–60; Augusto V. de Viana, ed., *Stories Rarely Told: The Hidden Stories and Essays on Philippine History* (Quezon City, PI: New Day Publishers, 2013), 8–10 (San Francisco de Malabon is today called General Trias); Nick Joaquin, *A*

Question of Heroes: Essays in Criticism on Ten Key Figures of Philippine History, 100–101, 102–103, 189–91, 192–94, 195; Sixto Y. Orosa, "Gregorio H. del Pilar," *Philippine Historical Association Historical Bulletin*, 4:3 (1960), 83; Santiago V. Alvarez, *Recalling the Revolution: Memoirs of a Filipino General*, trans. Paula Carolina S. Malay (Madison, WI: University of Wisconsin Press, 1992; 1st pub. 1927–1928), 103, 104–108, 110–12, 117, 120–21, 122–23, 128–29, 132–35, 142–43, 149; David Haward Bain, *Sitting in Darkness: Americans in the Philippines*, 165–66, 171–73; Emilio Aguinaldo, *Memoirs of the Revolution*, vol. I, trans. Luz Colendrino-Bucu (Manila: Cristina Aguinaldo, Sunray, 1967), 186–88; Taylor, *The Philippine Insurrection*, vol. 1, 426–27.

124 *"How I hate yams!"*: Sources for Funston's final days in Cuba on pages 124 to 131 include: Thomas W. Crouch, *A Yankee Guerrillero: Frederick Funston and the Cuban Insurrection, 1896–1897* (Memphis, TN: Memphis State University Press, 1975), 88–91 ff88–89, 98–103, 107–10, 113–14, 125, 129–31; Funston, "A Defeat and a Victory," *Scribner's Magazine*, 48:6 (December 1910), 736, 740–42, 741–55; Frank F. Eckdall, "'Fighting' Fred Funston of Kansas," *Kansas Historical Quarterly*, 22:1 (Spring 1956), 81; KHS, Ms. Coll. 33, Frederick Funston Collection: box 1, "Correspondence, 1890–1911; Report on Expedition to Alaska," folder 2: "Correspondence. 1896–1898": letter, Funston to Charles Scott, Nov. 9, 1896; letter, Funston to father, March 5, 1897; letters, Funston to Ella Funston, March 5 and 14, 1897; letter, Funston to Ella Funston, March 10, 1897; letter, Funston to Charles Scott, May 10, 1897; letter, Funston to Charles Scott, Aug. 31, 1897; letter, Funston to Charles Scott, Jan. 13, 1898; box 3, "Miscellaneous Papers, Clippings, 1892–1932, Undated," folder: "Clippings, 1892–1898": "Funston Starving," *Iola Register*, May 20, 1897, n.p.; ACHS: Frederick Funston Collection: Section B: Cuba: folder: "Funston—Cuba": Thomas White Steep, "Funston's Comrade Tells of Fighter's Days in Rags," *Topeka Capital*, Jan. 12, 1898, n.p.; Horatio S. Rubens, "The Insurgent Government in Cuba," *North American Review*, 166:498 (May 1898), 564, 565–66; Joe Jackson, *The Thief at the End of the World: Rubber, Power, and the Seeds of Empire* (New York: Viking Penguin, 2008), 122.

8. THE SPARK

135 *Funston watched Havana recede*: Sources for Funston's return to New York on pages 135 to 137 include: Thomas W. Crouch, "The Making of a Soldier: The Career of Frederick Funston, 1865–1902" [a dissertation in partial fulfillment of a Ph.D. in history, University of Texas at Austin, 1969], 130 130ff1; KHS, Ms. Coll. 33, Frederick Funston Collection: box 3, "Miscellaneous Papers, Clippings, 1892–1932, Undated": folder: "Clippings, 1892–1898": "Fred Funston in New York," Jan. 11, 1898, unidentified Kansas paper reprinted in a New York paper; "MG Frederick Funston," *Museum of the Kansas National Guard, Medal of Honor*, http://www.kansasguardmuseum.org/dispmoh.php?id=2.

137 *odd-looking ship*: Sources for the arrival of the *Maine* in Havana harbor on pages 137 to 139 include: Musicant, *Empire by Default*, 116–17; 118–19; John C. Reilly

Jr. and Robert L. Scheina, *American Battleships, 1886–1923: Predreadnought Design and Construction* (Annapolis, MD: Naval Institute Press, 1980), 19–32; Walter Millis, *The Martial Spirit: A Study of Our War with Spain*, 94; Morris, *The Rise of Theodore Roosevelt*, 618–20, 624–25; USAMH, Samuel B. M. Young Papers: box 10: folder: "Correspondence, primarily with Presidents McKinley and Roosevelt," letter, Young to Roosevelt, Feb. 12, 1899.

139 *"Why has homicide increased"*: Sources on a murderous America on pages 139 to 140 include: Cesare Lombroso, "Why Homicide Has Increased in the United States: I," *North American Review*, 165:493 (December 1897), 642–43, and "Why Homicide Has Increased in the United States: II, Barbarism and Civilization," *North American Review*, 166:494 (January 1898), 3–4, 6–7.

140 *his new, angry homeland*: KHS, Ms. Coll. 33, Frederick Funston Collection: box 1, folder 2: letter, Funston to "My dear old Boy," presumably Charles Scott, Jan. 18, 1898; letter, Funston to Scott, Jan. 24, 1898.

140 *the* Maine *to Havana*: Sources for the growing turmoil in Havana on pages 140 to 145 include: G.J.A. O'Toole, *The Spanish War: An American Epic—1898*, 115–17, 121, 122–23, 123–24; Robert W. Merry, *President McKinley: Architect of the American Century*, 252–53, 253–54; Robert Gardiner, ed., *Conway's All the World's Fighting Ships, 1860–1905* (New York: Mayflower Books, 1979), 382; Lawrence Shaw Mayo, ed., *America of Yesterday: As Reflected in the Journal of John Davis Long* (Boston: Atlantic Monthly Press, 1923), 153, 155; author's observations; Millis, *The Martial Spirit*, 95–96; Trumbull White, *Pictorial History of Our War with Spain for Cuba's Freedom*, 134–35; W. A. Swanberg, *Citizen Hearst*, 134; Musicant, *Empire by Default*, 126–30; Charles Dwight Sigsbee, "Personal Narrative of the 'Maine': Part I, Our Reception in Havana," *Century Illustrated Magazine*, 57:1 (November 1898), 84–86; "Our Flag in Havana at Last," *New York Journal*, Jan. 26, 1898, 1; Margaret Leech, *In the Days of McKinley* (New York: Harper & Bros., 1959), 165; Stanley Karnow, *In Our Image: America's Empire in the Philippines*, 100; Rhoda E. A. Hackler, "The United States Presence in the Northern Philippines Prior to 1898 (II)," *Bulletin of the American Historical Collection: The American Era in the Philippines*, vol. 18, 1:70 (January–March 1990), 61–67; William Allen White, *The Autobiography of William Allen White*, 306; ACHS, Frederick Funston Collection, Section B: Cuba: folder: "Funston—Cuba," newspaper advertisement for Funston's lectures, n.p., n.d., possibly from the *Iola Register*; Clara Barton, *The Red Cross: A History of This Remarkable International Movement in the Interest of Humanity*, 514–15, 516; Clara Barton, "Our Work and Observations in Cuba," *North American Review*, 166:498 (May 1898), 553–54; LC/MS: William McKinley Papers: Series 1: General Correspondence and Related Items, 1847–1902: Reel 3: "1897, Dec. 24—1898, June 23": Order by McKinley regarding Clara Barton, Feb. 4, 1898; "Clara Barton and the American Red Cross in Cuba and Tampa During the Spanish American War," *Clara Barton, founder of the Red Cross*, www.tampapix.com/barton2.htm, 2–8, 8–9; Marcus M. Wilkerson, *Public Opinion and the Spanish-American War: A Study in War Propaganda* (Baton Rouge, LA: Louisiana State University Press, 1932), 92–97.

146 *"felt more than heard" a blast*: Sources for the *Maine*'s explosion on pages 145 to 151 include: Millis, *The Martial Spirit*, 100–105; Joyce Milton, *The Yellow Kids: Foreign Correspondents in the Heyday of Yellow Journalism*, 217–20; Musicant, *Empire by Default*, 137–41, 142–43; Percy H. Epler, *The Life of Clara Barton*, 286–88; U.S. Senate, *Report of the Naval Court of Inquiry upon the Destruction of the United States Battle Ship Maine* (hereafter cited as *Naval Board of Inquiry*), 55th Congress, 2nd Session, doc. no. 207, 21, 119; NARA: RG 59, "General Records of the Department of State": T20, "Despatches From U.S. Consuls in Havana, Cuba, 1783–1906": Microroll 132, "Feb. 1, 1898–Dec. 11, 1902"; *New York World*, Feb. 17, 1898, 1; U.S. Senate, *Lives Lost by the Sinking of the U.S. Battle Ship Maine*, 55th Congress, 2nd Session, doc. no. 231, 2; *Clara Barton, founder of the Red Cross*, 16 of 77; Merry, *President McKinley*, 258–59; Mayo, *America of Yesterday*, 162; Swanberg, *Citizen Hearst*, 136–37.

9. "ALL I WANTED WAS MORE TIME"

152 *The keel had jackknifed up*: Sources for the Sampson Board and the "accident theory" on pages 152 to 157 include: Hyman G. Rickover, *How the Battleship Maine Was Destroyed* (Annapolis, MD: Naval Institute Press, 1995; 1st pub. 1976), 57, 91, 125; U.S. Senate, *Naval Board of Inquiry*, 55th Congress, 2nd Session, doc. no. 207, 11; Walter Millis, *The Martial Spirit: A Study of Our War with Spain*, 105–106, 107, 108–109; Ivan Musicant, *Empire by Default: The Spanish-American War and the Dawn of the American Century*, 143, 144–45, 670–71 ff48; Charles Dwight Sigsbee, "My Story of the *Maine*," *Cosmopolitan Magazine*, July 1912, 154; Lawrence Shaw Mayo, ed., *America of Yesterday*, 163–64; Robert W. Merry, *President McKinley: Architect of the American Century*, 260; W. A. Swanberg, *Citizen Hearst: A Biography of William Randolph Hearst*, 137–39; O'Toole, *The Spanish War*, 127–28, 128–29, 131; "Growing Suspicion That a Torpedo Was Used," *New York World*, Feb. 17, 1898, 2; Joyce Milton, *The Yellow Kids*, 221, 222–23, 235; Elting E. Morison, ed., *The Letters of Theodore Roosevelt*, vol. 1, 779–80; John Ault, "Rear Admiral William Sampson," *The Spanish American War Centennial Website*, www.spanamwar.com/sampson.htm; "William T. Sampson," *Wikipedia*; Evan Thomas, *The War Lovers: Roosevelt, Lodge, Hearst, and the Rush to Empire*, 213–14; John C. Reilly Jr. and Robert L. Scheina, *American Battleships, 1886–1923: Predreadnought Design and Construction* (Annapolis, MD: Naval Institute Press, 1980), 31–32; *Report of Board on Investigation of the Spontaneous Ignition of Coal, 27 January 1898*, in *Reports of the Efficiencies of Various Coals, 1896 to 1898* (Washington, D.C.: Government Publishing Office, 1906), 82; Thomas B. Allen, "A Special Report: What Really Sank the Maine?," *Naval History*, 12:2 (March/April 1998), 2–3, 30–43; S. Hansen and Robert S. Price, "The U.S.S. *Maine*: An Examination of the Technical Evidence Bearing on Its Destruction," Appendix A to Rickover, *How the Battleship Maine Was Destroyed*, 107–30; John Lawrence Tone, *War and Genocide in Cuba, 1895–1898*, 241; Edmund Morris, *The Rise of Theodore Roosevelt*, 627–28; Theodore Roosevelt, *An Autobiography* (New York: Macmillan, 1913), 212; Russell A. Alger,

The Spanish-American War (New York: Harper & Brothers, 1901), 4; Louis A. Perez Jr., "The Meaning of the Maine: Causation and the Historiography of the Spanish-American War," *Pacific Historical Review*, 58:3 (August 1989), 296–300.

157 *swayed more people*: Sources for Sen. Proctor's speech and its effects on pages 158 to 161 include: Michelle Bray Davis and Rollin W. Quimby, "Senator Proctor's Cuban Speech: Speculations on a Cause of the Spanish-American War," *Quarterly Journal of Speech* 55:2 (1969), 131, 134; Gerald F. Linderman, *The Mirror of War: American Society and the Spanish-American War*, 37–39, 40, 42–43, 44–45, 46, 49, 52–55, 56–57, 58–59; Clara Barton, *The Red Cross: A History of This Remarkable International Movement in the Interest of Humanity*, 527–31, 540–41, 544; Kenneth E. Hendrickson, *The Spanish-American War* (Westport, CT: Greenwood Press, 2003), "Primary Documents of the Spanish-American War: Document 2, Senator Redfield Proctor's Speech," 120; Musicant, *Empire by Default*, 164, 165–66; "Speech by Sen. Redfield Proctor (R, VT), About Conditions in Cuba," *Congressional Record*, 55th Congress, 2nd Session, vol. 31, part 3: 2916–19.

161 *He'd seen "the dead piled up"*: Sources for the final steps to war on pages 161 to 164 include: Linderman, *The Mirror of War*, 27–28, 29, 30–31, 184 ff53, 185 ff65; Merry, *President McKinley*, 246–47, 270–71; Mayo, *America of Yesterday*, 165, 169–70; Morris, *The Rise of Theodore Roosevelt*, 133, 622–33; Thomas, *The War Lovers*, 228, 229; Drew Gilpin Faust, *This Republic of Suffering: Death and the American Civil War* (New York: Vintage, 2008), 123, 271; H. H. Kohlsaat, *From McKinley to Harding: Personal Recollections of Our Presidents* (New York: Charles Scribner's Sons, 1923), 67; Joseph A. Fry, "William McKinley and the Coming of the Spanish-American War: A Study of the Besmirching and Redemption of an Historical Image," *Diplomatic History*, 3 (Winter 1979), 77–97; O'Toole, *The Spanish War*, 136–37, 141, 142; Millis, *The Martial Spirit*, 112, 113, 116–17; LC/MS: Theodore Roosevelt Papers: Correspondence: Series 1: Reel 1: letter, Roosevelt to George Dewey, Feb. 25, 1898; *El Pais* [Madrid], March 1, 1898, quoted in Brad K. Berner, ed., *The Spanish-American War: A Documentary History with Commentaries*, 47–48, and "España no se asusta," *El Imparcial*, March 15, 1898, 31; Morison, *The Letters of Theodore Roosevelt*, vol. 1, 789: Roosevelt to friend, March 6, 1898.

164 *they were not trained in analysis*: Sources for the Sampson Board's conclusions on pages 164 to 166 include: Tone, *War and Genocide in Cuba*, 242; Patrick McSherry, "Ensign Wilfred Van Nest Powelson, U.S.N.," www.spanamwar.com/powelson.htm; U.S. Senate, *Report of the Naval Court of Inquiry upon the Destruction of the United States Battle Ship Maine* (hereafter cited as *Naval Board of Inquiry*), 55th Congress, 2nd Session, doc. no. 207; O'Toole, *The Spanish War*, 137, 138, 148; U.S. Congress, *Papers Relating to the Foreign Relations of the United States with the Annual Message of the President Transmitted to Congress, December 5, 1898* (Washington, D.C.: Government Printing Office, 1901), 1044–45.

166 *What really happened to the* Maine*?*: Sources for an explanation to the *Maine*'s explosion on pages 166 to 167 include: Louis Fisher, "Destruction of the *Maine* (1898)," *The Law Library of Congress* (monograph, August 4, 2009); Rickover, *How*

the Battleship Maine Was Destroyed, ix, xvii, 27, 46, 55, 91, 95, 114–15; Thomas B. Allen, "A Special Report: What Really Sank the Maine?" *Naval History*, 12:2 (March/April 1998), 30–43; Lewis L. Gould, *The Spanish-American War and President McKinley* (Lawrence, KS: University Press of Kansas, 1982), 35; John L. Offner, *An Unwanted War: The Diplomacy of the United States and Spain Over Cuba, 1895–1898* (Chapel Hill, NC: University of North Carolina Press, 1992), 127; Marrion Wilcox, *A Short History of the War with Spain* (New York, 1898), 73; James Morton Callahan, *Cuba and International Relations: A Historical Study in American Diplomacy* (Baltimore: Johns Hopkins University Press, 1899), 485; Charles S. Campbell, *The Transformation of American Foreign Relations, 1865–1900* (New York: Harper, 1976), 257; Louis A. Perez Jr., "The Meaning of the Maine: Causation and the Historiography of the Spanish-American War," *Pacific Historical Review*, 58:3 (August 1989), 313–14.

167 *three Spanish ministers*: Sources for the declaration of war on pages 167 to 171 include: Millis, *The Martial Spirit*, 130, 131; Tone, *War and Genocide in Cuba*, 253–56; "The Great Powers Notes," U.S. Congress, *Papers Relating to the Foreign Relations of the United States*, 740–41; LC/MS: Clara Barton Papers: "Clara Barton Papers: Diaries and Journals": April 6, 7, 8, 9, 11, 15, 1898; Morris, *The Rise of Theodore Roosevelt*, 635, 638; Thomas, *The War Lovers*, 228, 235–36, 236–37, 240–41; Elias Canetti, *Crowds and Power* (New York: Penguin, 1992; 1st pub. in German, 1960), trans. Carol Stewart, 23–24, 82–84; "President William McKinley's War Message to Congress," in Berner, *The Spanish-American War*, 58–60, 63–64; John L. Offner, "McKinley and the Spanish–American War," *Presidential Studies Quarterly*, 34:1 (March 2004), 60; *London Times*, April 14, 1898; Benjamin R. Beede, ed., "The War of 1898, and U.S. Interventions, 1898–1934: An Encyclopedia," *Military History of the United States* (New York: Garland Publishing, 1994), 120; O'Toole, *The Spanish War*, 120; Margaret Leech, *In the Days of McKinley*, 188; Linderman, *The Mirror of War*, 35; *New York Times*, Sept. 1, 1912.

10. PROMISES

172 *two U.S. naval squadrons*: George Dewey, *Autobiography of George Dewey: Admiral of the Navy* (New York: Charles Scribner's Sons, 1913), 192; Walter Millis, *The Martial Spirit: A Study of Our War with Spain*, 145; Leon Wolff, *Little Brown Brother*, 36; "Secretary of the Navy John D. Long to Commodore George Dewey, Commander, Asiatic Squadron, 4/24/1898," *Documentary Histories: Spanish American War*, www.history.navy.mil/research/publications/documentary-histories/united-states-navy-s/the-battle-of-manila.

172 *he was an "intelligence officer"*: Sources on Consul Oscar Williams in Manila on pages 172 to 176 include: Joseph Earle Stevens, "An American in Manila," *McClure's Magazine*, 11:2 (June 1898), 186–88; Rhoda E. A. Hackler, "The United States Presence in the Northern Philippines Prior to 1898 (II)," *Bulletin of the American Historical Collection: The American Era in the Philippines*, vol. 18, 1:70 (January–March 1990), 61–67; LC/MS, George Dewey Papers: box 4: folder 7, "I Jan.–31 Mar.

1898," letter, Dewey to Williams, Feb. 17, 1898; letters, Williams to H. H. Caldwell, March 10 and 12, 1898; letter, Williams to Dewey, March 26, 1898; letter, Dewey to Secretary Long, March 31, 1898; 8: "Apr. 1–13, 1898," letter, Williams to Dewey, April 10, 1898.

176 *wither and die*: Sources on U.S. officials contacting Aguinaldo on pages 176 to 183 include: Nick Joaquin, *A Question of Heroes: Essays in Criticism on Ten Key Figures of Philippine History* (Manila: Ayala Museum Press, 1977), 86, 130; Ronald Kenneth Bell, "The Filipino *Junta* in Hong Kong, 1898–1903: History of a Revolutionary Organization" [a thesis in partial fulfillment of an M.A. in Asian studies, San Diego State University, 1974], 31, 49, 50–53, 150; Augusto V. de Viana, ed., *Stories Rarely Told: The Hidden Stories and Essays on Philippine History* (Quezon City, PI: New Day Publishers, 2013), 75, 94–95; David Haward Bain, *Sitting in Darkness: Americans in the Philippines*, 173–74, 175–76; Antonio A. Torres, "Centenarians of 1968," *Philippines Free Press*, Jan. 13, 1968, 63–64; U.S. War Department, Philippine Division, *Philippine Insurgent Records 1896–1901 with Associated Records of the United States War Department, 1900–1906* [NARA: Microcopy #M254, 10.10, 54.9 (PIR)]; Taylor, *The Philippine Insurrection*, vol. 1, 93–94, 445, 449, 453; Teodoro Agoncillo, *Malolos: The Crisis of the Republic* (Quezon City, PI: University of the Philippines Press, 1960), 73–74, 82–84; Emilio Aguinaldo, *True Version of the Philippine Rebellion* (Ann Arbor, MI: University of Michigan Library, 2005; 1st pub. 1899), 280–85; Stanley Karnow, *In Our Image: America's Empire in the Philippines*, 110–11; Brad K. Berner, ed., *The Spanish-American War: A Documentary History with Commentaries*, 21–23, 23–24; Emilio Aguinaldo and Vicente A. Pacis, *A Second Look at America* (New York: Robert Speller & Sons, 1957), 30–31, 32–33; Wolff, *Little Brown Brother*, 46–47; G.J.A. O'Toole, *The Spanish War: An American Epic—1898*, 21–23, 23–24; Emilio Aguinaldo, "Appeal to the Civilized Nations, and Especially to the Great North American Republic," September 23, 1899, in Marrion Wilcox, ed., *Harper's History of the War in the Philippines* (New York: Harper, 1900), 85; H. W. Brands, *Bound to Empire: The United States and the Philippines* (New York: Oxford University Press, 1922), 46; Millis, *The Martial Spirit*, 181–82, 182–83; Apolinario Mabini, *The Letters of Apolinario Mabini* (Manila: National Historical Institute, 1999, 1st printing 1965), 39–42; Stuart Creighton Miller, *"Benevolent Assimilation": The American Conquest of the Philippines, 1899–1903* (New Haven, CT: Yale University Press, 1982), 36.

183 *Dewey sipped cold tea*: Sources for the Battle of Manila Bay on pages 183 to 191 include: O'Toole, *The Spanish War*, 178–79, 179–80, 182–83, 183–89; Millis, *The Martial Spirit*, 184–86, 186–87, 188–98; George Dewey, "*Official Report to the Secretary of the Navy, May, 1898*," in *Autobiography of George Dewey* (Appendix B), 204–208, 297–300, 301–307; French Ensor Chadwick, *The Relations of the United States and Spain: The Spanish-American War*, vol. 1 (New York: Charles Scribner's Sons, 1911), 158–60, 167–68; John Lawrence Tone, *War and Genocide in Cuba, 1895–1898*, 258–60, 261–62, 267, 268; Charles H. Brown, *The Correspondents' War: Journalists in the*

Spanish-American War, 188; Karnow, *In Our Image*, 103–104; Berner, *The Spanish-American War*, 163; Jose S. Arcilla, "The Fall of Manila: Excerpt's from a Jesuit's Diary," *Philippine Studies*, 37:2 (Second Quarter 1989), 193–94, 194–96; James Ford Rhodes, *The McKinley and Roosevelt Administrations, 1897–1909* (New York: MacMillan, 1922), 72; Laurin Hall Healy and Luis Kutner, *The Admiral* (New York: Ziff-Davis, 1994), 174–75; Ivan Musicant, *Empire by Default: The Spanish-American War and the Dawn of the American Century*, 216–34; Joseph L. Stickney, *The Life and Glorious Deeds of Admiral Dewey* (New York: n.p., 1899), 44–65; U.S. Marine Corps Historical Center, Quantico, VA (hereafter USMCHC): COLL/3016: John Twiggs Myers Collection: box 1: folder 2: "Personal Correspondence, 1898," Letter from Lt. William Winder to his mother, Abby (Dewey's sister), May 1, 1898, pp. 2, 5.

191 *200,000 cartridges at $33.50 per thousand*: Aguinaldo, *True Version of the Philippine Rebellion*, 287–88; Wolff, *Little Brown Brother*, 50–51; Bell, "The Filipino *Junta* in Hong Kong," 68.

11. GATHERING TRIBES

193 *first news of Dewey*: Sources for the world learning of Dewey's victory on pages 193 to 195 include: Walter Millis, *The Martial Spirit: A Study of Our War with Spain*, 196–97, 198–99; G.J.A. O'Toole, *The Spanish War: An American Epic—1898*, 190–91; Ivan Musicant, *Empire by Default: The Spanish-American War and the Dawn of the American Century*, 190–91, 232–33, 233–34; Edmund Morris, *The Rise of Theodore Roosevelt*, 643–44; Robert W. Merry, *President McKinley: Architect of the American Century*, 289–90; Margaret Leech, *In the Days of McKinley*, 206; USMCHC: COLL/3016: John Twiggs Myers Collection: box 1: folder 2: "Personal Correspondence, 1898," letter from Lt. William Winder to his mother, Abby (Dewey's sister), May 4, 1898, p. 9; Joyce Milton, *The Yellow Kids*, 265; John Lawrence Tone, *War and Genocide in Cuba, 1895–1898*, 257–58; Joseph R. Stromberg, "The Spanish-American War as Trial Run, or Empire for Its Own Justification," in John V. Denson, ed., *The Costs of War: America's Pyrrhic Victories* (New Brunswick, NJ: Transaction Press, 1999, 2nd ed), 175; Charles Denby, "Shall We Keep the Philippines?," *Forum*, Nov. 1898, 279.

195 *The U.S. Army of April 1, 1898*: Sources for the state of the army and gathering of officers on pages 195 to 198 include: O'Toole, *The Spanish War*, 197; Tone, *War and Genocide in Cuba*, 258–59; Graham A. Cosmas, *An Army for Empire: The United States Army in the Spanish-American War* (Shippensburg, PA: White Mane Publishing, 1994, 2nd edition), 1–2, 9, 10–11, 14–15; Leech, *In the Days of McKinley*, 102–103, 201–202, 229; Merry, *President McKinley*, 285–86; Charles G. Dawes, *A Journal of the McKinley Years*, ed. Bascom N. Timmons (Chicago: R. R. Donnelley & Sons, 1950), May 5, 1898, 158; Musicant, *Empire by Default*, 237; *Army and Navy Journal*, May 28, 1898; Nelson A. Miles, "The War with Spain," Part 1, *North American Review*, May 1899, 516; Milton, *The Yellow Kids*, 309–10; John D. Miley, *In Cuba with Shafter* (New York: Charles Scribner's Sons, 1899), 70; Graham A.

Cosmas, "San Juan Hill and El Caney, 1–2 July 1898," in Charles E. Heller and William A. Stofft, eds., *America's First Battles, 1776–1965* (Lawrence, KS: University of Kansas Press, 1986), 115; Steven L. Ossad, "Henry Ware Lawton: Flawed Giant and Hero of Four Wars," *Army History* (Winter 2007), 13, 17; Stanley Karnow, *In Our Image: America's Empire in the Philippines*, 149; LC/MS: Henry T. Allen Papers: box 1: "Diaries," folder: "1898: H. T. Allen's Diary," June 3, 1898; box 6: "Correspondence," folder: "1898, Jan.–June": letter, Allen to Nelson Miles, March 22, 1898; letter. Miles to Allen, April 1, 1898; letter, Maj. Gen. Wesley Merritt to Allen, Apr. 5, 1898; letter, Allen to Jeanine Allen, Apr. 21, 1898; "Henry Tureman Allen," *Wikipedia*.

198 *beyond its experience or means*: Sources for the recruitment of Carl Sandburg and other volunteers on pages 198 to 202 include: Gerald F. Linderman, *The Mirror of War: American Society and the Spanish-American War*, 61–62, 63, 80–81, 89; Musicant, *Empire by Default*, 244, 249–51, 644–47; Millis, *The Martial Spirit*, 152–53, 185, 200–201; letter, William James to Francis Pillon, in Henry James, ed., *The Letters of William James*, vol. 2 (Boston: Atlantic Monthly Press, 1920), 73–74; Theophilus G. Steward, *Buffalo Soldiers: The Colored Regulars in the United States Army* (Philadelphia: AME Book Concern, 1904), 172; David F. Trask, *The War with Spain in 1898* (Lincoln, NE: University of Nebraska Press, 1996), 156; Charles Johnson Post, *The Little War of Private Post: The Spanish-American War Seen Up Close* (Lincoln, NE: University of Nebraska Press, 1999; 1st pub. 1960), v–vi, 3, 4–6; Carl Sandburg, *Always the Young Strangers* (New York: Harcourt, Brace, 1952), 404–407, 408, 409; NARA: RG 94: Records of the Adjutant General's Office 1780s–1917: Spanish-American War Regimental Books: Sixth Illinois Infantry, Descriptive and Clothing Book, NCS/Band/Companies A to F, vol. 1 of 4, "Charles A. Sandburg"; Sixth Illinois Infantry, Morning Reports, Co. C: May & June, 1898; *Galesburg Weekly Mail*: April 28, 1898, 1; "Scared by Dynamite," May 5, 1898, 1; "Boys En Route to Washington," May 19, 1898, 1; "Soldier Dies in Camp," May 20, 1898; "Life at Camp Alger" and "Swan Bohman Insane," June 2 and 9, 1898; Illinois Historical and Lincoln Collection, University of Illinois, Urbana-Champaign, IL (hereafter ILL): MS 794, O. Batson Hinman Collection: box 1: folder: Corporal O. B. Hinman, "A Soldier's Diary," April 30 to May 26, 1898; Cloth Packet, "Soldier's Housewife"; CS: folder: "Sandburg-Connemara": letter, Carl Sandburg to home, May 1, 1898.

202 *One camp ran like silk*: Sources for the training of the Rough Riders on pages 202 to 207 include: Morris, *The Rise of Theodore Roosevelt*, 640–41, 642, 643, 648–49, 652, 869 ff98; LC/MS, Leonard Wood Papers: box 26: "General Correspondence. 1825–1898": File: "1898," no. 1: letter, Alger to Wood, Apr. 28, 1898; letter, Roosevelt to Wood, May 9, 1898; letter, Leonard Wood to "Lon" Wood, May 22, 1898; letter, Leonard Wood to wife, Louise, June 4, 1898; Evan Thomas, *The War Lovers: Roosevelt, Lodge, Hearst, and the Rush to Empire*, 262–63, 264–65, 266–67, 268; Dale L. Walker, *The Boys of '98: Theodore Roosevelt and the Rough Riders* (New York: Tom Doherty Associates, 1998), 113, 114–16, 118–20, 122–23, 125; Millis, *The Martial*

Spirit, 218–20; Dixon Weeter, "Rough Rider," in Morton Keller, ed., *Theodore Roosevelt: A Profile* (New York: Hill and Wang, 1967), 93; Richard Slotkin, *Gunfighter Nation: The Myth of the Frontier in Twentieth-Century America*, 102–103, 104; Theodore Roosevelt, *The Rough Riders* (Mineola, NY: Dover, 2006; 1st pub. 1899), 6, 9–15, 17, 149–81, Appendix A; Theodore Roosevelt, *Pocket Diary, 1898: Theodore Roosevelt's Private Account of the War with Spain*, ed. Wallace Finley Dailey (Cambridge, MA: Harvard University Press, 1998), May 6, 1898, May 15, 1898; Elting E. Morison, ed., *The Letters of Theodore Roosevelt*, vol. 1, 108; USAMH: Spanish-American War Veterans Survey Collection: box 64: "U.S. Volunteer Cavalry—1st, 2nd, 3rd, and 11th Regiments": folder 2: "U.S. Volunteer Cavalry—1st Regiment [SAWS-W-1842], Hamner, George P., Troop F"; folder 4: "U.S. Volunteer Cavalry—1st Regiment [1898-W-60], Hoffman, Philip, Co. A.": Herman Hoffman Philip, "A Volunteer of 1898" [typescript] (hereafter Philip, "A Volunteer of 1898"); John Dudley, "Crane's Dispatches from Cuba: The Dynamics of Race, Class, and Professionalism in 'The Correspondents' War.'" *Stephen Crane Studies* 11:2 (Fall 2002), 11–12, 16; KHS: Allen M. Coville Collection, #319, [6–2]: Allen M. Coville, "A Rough Rider's Story" [typescript], 13–14. (The men who deserted during this period, often without explanation, were: Sergeants Alfred E. Lewis and John E. Jackson of the staff, Privates Henry Crowley of Troop D, Charles Thompson of Troop F, Samuel T. McCulloch of Troop G, Samuel Miller of Troop H, John Brown and Fred P. Farrell of Troop I, and Frank Stanley and "Curzon" of Troop K.)

12. THE PLEASURE DOME

208 *War creates opportunities*: Sources for Tampa on pages 208 to 210 include: "The War That Launched Tampa," *Tampa Bay Times*, Sept. 30, 2005; Joe Knetsch and Nick Wynne, *Florida in the Spanish-American War* (Charleston, SC: History Press, 2011), 93, 97; University of South Florida: Florida Studies Center, Tampa, FL (hereafter USF): Leland Hawes Collection: box 27: folder: "Spanish-American War, a Chronology—Compiled by Paul Eugen Camp," 1, 4, 11, 12, 13, 14, 16; folder: "Henry Dobson Letters—Spanish-American War," letters, Henry Dobson to "Mama," June 6, 18, 1898; Alexandra Frye, "'Waiting for War to Begin,' News Dispatches from the Tampa Bay Hotel," *Sunland Tribune: Journal of the Tampa Historical Society*, 24 (1998), n.p.; Charles Johnson Post, *The Little War of Private Post*, 61; Alicia Addeo, "'Tampa Is a Bum Place': The Letters of First Sergeant Henry A. Dobson in 1898," *Tampa Bay History*, 20:1 (Spring/Summer 1998), 49, 50.

210 *army's great vulnerability*: Sources on the army's medical woes on pages 210 to 211 include: Ingrid Gessner, "Heroines of Health: Examining the Other Side of the 'Splendid Little War'," *European Journal of American Studies*, 10:1 (2015), 4, 5–6, 10, 13; Spencer C. Tucker, *The Encyclopedia of the Spanish-American and Philippine-American Wars: A Political, Social, and Military History*, vol. 2 (Santa Barbara: CA: ABC-CLIO, 2009), 390, 392; "Dr. Anita Newcomb McGee," *Changing the Face of Medicine*, https://efmedicine.nlm.nih.gov/physicians/biography_216.html; Knetsch and Wynne, *Florida in the Spanish-American War*, 88.

211 *If one person glimpsed the future*: Sources on Clara Barton's arrival in Florida on pages 211 to 215 include: Ann K. Frantz, "Nursing Pride: Clara Barton in the Spanish-American War," *American Journal of Nursing*, 98:10 (October 1998), 39–40; A. G. Ramsay, "92-year-old Mary Nelson in a reminiscent mood as she breezes in Washington, D.C.," *Red Cross Courier*, Nov. 1948, 10–12; "Mallory Steamship Company—Mallory Line—Frank A. Young," www.timetableimages.com/maritime/images/young.htm; Clara Barton, *The Red Cross*, 370, 373, 552; LC/MS: Clara Barton Papers, "Clara Barton Papers: Diaries and Journals": April 23, 1898; May 9, 1898; May 23, 1898; Christine Ardalan, "Clara Barton's 1898 Battles in Cuba: A Reexamination of Her Nursing Contributions," *Florida Atlantic Comparative Studies Journal* 12.1 (2010), 7; George Kennan, *Campaigning in Cuba* (New York: Century Company, 1899), 1–4, 5; LC/MS: George Kennan Papers: box 22: Diaries, Letters, & Notebooks, 1897–1906: Cuban Notebook no. 1, Santiago Campaign, May 5 to July 12, 1898 (hereafter *George Kennan Diary*): May 6, 1898; May 7, 1898; May 9, 1898, 24–26; Lani Friend, "Fantasy Land for a Gilded Age: Henry Bradley Plant's Tampa Bay Hotel," *Journal of Florida Studies*, 1:8 (2019), 9–11, 13–15; "The War that Launched Tampa," *Tampa Bay Times*; Evan Thomas, *The War Lovers*, 278; Knetsch and Wynne, *Florida in the Spanish-American War*, 97, 99; Charles H. Brown, *The Correspondents' War: Journalists in the Spanish-American War*, 170.

215 *"It was an army of occupation"*: Sources on the "Rocking Chair" war on pages 215 to 217 include: Richard Harding Davis, *The Cuban and Porto Rican Campaigns* (New York: Charles Scribner's Sons, 1898), 45–50, 55; Walter Millis, *The Martial Spirit: A Study of Our War with Spain*, 169–70, 170–71; French Ensor Chadwick, *The Relations of the United States and Spain: The Spanish-American War*, vol. 1 (New York: Charles Scribner's Sons, 1911), 234–35; Brad K. Berner, *The Spanish-American War: A Documentary History with Commentaries*, 186–87; Jon Ault, "Rear Admiral William Sampson," *The Spanish American War Centennial Website*, www.spanamwar.com/sampson.htm; Arthur Lubow, *The Reporter Who Would Be King: A Biography of Richard Harding Davis*, 160–65; Friend, "Fantasy Land for a Gilded Age," 22; Brown, *The Correspondents' War*, 209–20; "The War that Launched Tampa," *Tampa Bay Times*, Sept. 30, 2005; Knetsch and Wynne, *Florida in the Spanish-American War*, 156; Stephen Crane, *The War Dispatches of Stephen Crane*, ed. R. W. Stallman and E. R. Hagemann (New York: New York University Press, 1964), 120–23; Frank Norris, *The Letters of Frank Norris*, ed. Franklin Walker (San Francisco: Book Club of California, 1956), 10–18.

217 *Lieutenant Andrew S. Rowan*: Sources for Andrew Rowan's mission to Cuba on pages 217 to 219 include: Andrew S. Rowan, "My Ride Across Cuba: The Story of a Secret Mission to the Cuban Leaders," *McClure's Magazine*, 11:4 (August 11, 1898), 377–78; G.J.A. O'Toole, *The Spanish War: An American Epic—1898*, 203; John Lawrence Tone, *War and Genocide in Cuba, 1895–1898*, 271; USAMH: Nelson A. Miles Papers: box 5: "Spanish-American War, 1898": folder 1: "Spanish-American

War—preparations and Cuba campaign": Confidential Report, Lt. Col. A. S. Rowan to Miles, Nov. 2, 1898; Tone, *War and Genocide in Cuba*, 11, 270–71.

219 *four regiments of black Regulars*: Sources for the arrival of Buffalo Soldiers on pages 219 to 221 include: Willard B. Gatewood Jr., *Black Americans and the White Man's Burden, 1893–1903*, 42–43. 44–47, 48–49; Michael Morey, *Fagen: An African American Renegade in the Philippine-American War* (Madison, WI: University of Wisconsin Press, 2019), 19; Arlen Fowler, *The Black Infantry in the West, 1869–1891* (Westport, CT: Greenwood, 1971), 87, 97, 137; *Washington Bee*, March 5, 1895; "Negroes Eager to Fight Spain Should Also Fight Southern Brutes," *Omaha Afro-American Sentinel*, April 2, 1898; Rev. H. H. Proctor, "The Negro and the War: A Sermon on the War" (Atlanta, GA: a sermon self-published by the author, 1898); "The Colored Brother and the War," *Richmond Planet*, May 7, 12, and 14, and June 18, 1898; Maurice Duke and Daniel P. Jordan, eds., *A Richmond Reader: 1733–1983* (Chapel Hill, NC: University of North Carolina Press, 1983), 327–28; George W. Prioleau to H. C. Smith, May 13, 1898, in the *Cleveland Gazette*, May 21, 1898; Brent R. Weisman, ed., *Soldiers and Patriots: Buffalo Soldiers and Afro-Cubans in Tampa, 1898* [USF Anthropology Studies in Historical Archaeology, no. 2] (Tampa, FL: Florida Division of Historical Resources, July 1999), 127; Willard B. Gatewood Jr., "Negro Troops in Florida, 1898," *Florida Historical Quarterly* 49:1 (July 1970), 2, 15; *Tampa Morning Tribune*, May 5, 7, 10, and 12, 1898; *Florida Times Union and Citizen* (Jacksonville), May 31, 1898; Charles Johnson Post, *The Little War of Private Post: The Spanish-American War Seen Up Close*, 55–56; *Savannah Tribune*, April 1, 1899; *Iowa State Bystander* (Des Moines), March 24, 1899.

221 *Funston entered the Pleasure Dome*: Sources on Funston's arrival in Tampa on pages 221 to 224 include: KHS: Ms. Coll. 33, Frederick Funston Collection: box 1, "Correspondence, 1890–1911; Report on Expedition to Alaska": folder 2: "Correspondence. 1896–1898," letter, Funston in Tampa to Charles Scott, May 25, 1898; Order from Adjutant General's Office, War Department, to Funston, May 8, 1898; Knetsch and Wynne, *Florida in the Spanish-American War*, 158–59; ACHS: Frederick Funston Collection: Section B: Cuba: folder: "Funston—Cuba": ad for Funston lectures, *Iola Register*, no date or page but probably March 1898; Engagement Contract with James A. Young, Kansas City, MO, to appear in Maryville, KS, April 12, 1898; letter, Dr. Charles Arand to Kansas State Historical Society, Sept. 25, 1936, re: Funston's lectures; "Here's to Col. Fred," *Iola Register*, May 12 or 13, 1898; Thomas W. Crouch, *A Leader of Volunteers: Frederick Funston and the 20th Kansas in the Philippines, 1898–1899* (Lawrence, KS: Coronado Press, 1984), 5–6, 11–13 34ff2; Frederick Funston, *Memories of Two Wars: Cuban and Philippine Experiences*, 156–57; Louis Albert Banks, *Capital Stories About Famous Americans* (New York: The Christian Herald, 1905), 189; Jon Ault, "Rear Admiral William Sampson," *The Spanish American War Centennial Website*; Robert W. Merry, *President McKinley: Architect of the American Century*, 296; Funston, "The Making of a Regiment," *Scribner's Magazine*, 49:6 (June 1911), 645.

224 *frenzy of preparation*: Sources on the rush to load the ships include: Merry, *President McKinley*, 298–99; Ivan Musicant, *Empire by Default: The Spanish-American War and the Dawn of the American Century*, 270–72; Post, *The Little War of Private Post*, 75–77.

224 *Rough Riders arrived in the middle of this*: Sources on the Rough Riders' arrival in Tampa on pages 224 to 226 include: LC/MS: Leonard Wood Papers: box 2: "Diaries": File: "Diary—May 29, 1898—July 15, 1898" (hereafter *Leonard Wood Diary)*, June 2, 3, 8, & 9, 1898; Theodore Roosevelt, *Pocket Diary, 1898: Theodore Roosevelt's Private Account of the War with Spain*, ed. Wallace Finley Dailey (Cambridge, MA: Harvard University Press, 1998), June 5, 1898; Thomas, *The War Lovers*, 276–77, 279, 280–81; James W. Covington, "The Rough Riders in Tampa," *Sunland Tribune: Journal of the Tampa Historical Society*, 3:1 (November 1977), n.p., ff11; Lubow, *The Reporter Who Would Be King*, 163, 166–69; Philip, "A Volunteer of 1898"; Harvard University, Houghton Library, Theodore Roosevelt Collection: letter, Edith Roosevelt to Emily Carrow, June 3, 1898; Covington, "The Rough Riders in Tampa," n.p.; Dale L. Walker, *The Boys of '98: Theodore Roosevelt and the Rough Riders* (New York: Tom Doherty Associates, 1998), 143–44; Edmund Morris, *The Rise of Theodore Roosevelt*, 656–57.

226 *last possible minute, David Fagen became*: Sources on the enlistment of David Fagen on pages 226 to 229 include: NARA: RG 94: Records of the Adjutant General's Office 1780s–1917: Entry 91: Enlistment Papers, US Army, 1894–1912: Callahan-Calumno: "John Calloway"; Faatz-Failer, "David Fagen"; NARA Microfilm M665, Roll 249: Returns from Regular Army Infantry Regiments, June 1821–December 1911: Twenty-Fourth U.S. Infantry, January 1898–December 1899, June & July 1898 Regimental Returns; box 111, AGO File 17043: John W. Calloway, Co. F, 24th US Infantry; Morey, *Fagen*, 23, 42; Frank Schubert, "Seeking David Fagen: The Search for a Black Rebel's Florida Roots," *Tampa Bay History*, 22 (2008), 24; William T. Bowers, William M. Hammond, and George L. MacGarrigle, *Black Soldier, White Army: The 24th Infantry Regiment in Korea* (Washington, D.C.: Center of Military History, 1996), 8; Marvin Fletcher, "The Negro Soldier and the United States Army, 1891–1917" [a dissertation in partial fulfillment of a Ph.D. in history, University of Wisconsin, 1968], 192, 193–94; Timothy D. Russell, "African Americans and the Spanish-American War and Philippine Insurrection: Military Participation, Recognition, and Memory, 1898–1904" [a dissertation in partial fulfillment of a Ph.D. in history, University of California, Riverside, 2013], 135; Weisman, *Soldiers and Patriots*, 52–53; Gatewood Jr., *Black Americans and the White Man's Burden*, 52; *Tampa Morning Tribune*, June 8 and 25, 1898; *Atlanta Constitution*, June 11, 1898; Morris, *The Rise of Theodore Roosevelt*, 658–59; Thomas, *The War Lovers*, 281–82; John J. Pershing, *My Life Before the World War, 1860–1917: A Memoir*, ed. John T. Greenwood (Lexington, KY: University Press of Kentucky, 2013), 106–107; Musicant, *Empire by Default*, 272.

230 *most famous story about the mad rush*: Sources on the tale of the *Yucatan* on pages 230 to 231 include: Theodore Roosevelt, *The Rough Riders*, 34–35; Frank Freidel,

The Splendid Little War (Short Hills, NJ: Burford Books, 2002; 1st pub. 1958), 54; Morris, *The Rise of Theodore Roosevelt*, 658, 659; Post, *The Little War of Private Post*, 82–83; LC/MS: Wood, *Leonard Wood Diary*, June 8, 1898; O'Toole, *The Spanish War*, 243.

13. INVADERS

235 *"either of ignorance or of hypocrisy"*: Charles Norton, *Public Opinion*, 24 (June 23, 1898), 775–76.

235 *beneath Faneuil's high ceiling*: *Boston Evening Transcript*, *Boston Daily Globe*, *Boston Journal*, and *New York Times*, June 16, 1898; Stephen Kinzer, *The True Flag: Theodore Roosevelt, Mark Twain, and the Birth of the American Empire* (New York: Henry Holt, 2017), 5–7.

235 *"necessary act of surgery"*: Walter Hines Page, "The War with Spain and After," *Atlantic Monthly*, June 1898, 727.

236 *"three colored women and a pathetic group of perspiring stevedores"*: Sources on the invasion convoy on pages 236 to 238 include: Frank Freidel, *The Splendid Little War*, 34, 55, 56–57; Robert W. Merry, *President McKinley: Architect of the American Century*, 299; LC/MS: Leonard Wood Papers: box 26: "General Correspondence. 1825–1898": File: "1898," no. 1: letter, Wood aboard the USS *Yorktown* to his wife, Louise, June 18, 1898; Charles H. Brown, *The Correspondents' War: Journalists in the Spanish-American War*, 276–77, 278–79; Franklin Walker, *Frank Norris* (Garden City, NY: Doubleday, Doran & Co., 1932), 181; Charles Johnson Post, *The Little War of Private Post*, 98–99, 106–107; Ivan Musicant, *Empire by Default: The Spanish-American War and the Dawn of the American Century*, 355, 357–61, 364; John Lawrence Tone, *War and Genocide in Cuba, 1895–1898* (Chapel Hill, NC: University of North Carolina Press, 2006), 274, 277; John J. Pershing, *My Life Before the World War, 1860–1917: A Memoir*, 107–108; Theodore Roosevelt, *The Rough Riders*, 38; David F. Trask, *The War with Spain in 1898* (Lincoln, NE: University of Nebraska Press, 1996), 194.

238 *the month of invasions*: Sources for the Battle of Guantánamo Bay on pages 238 to 241 include: Tone, *War and Genocide in Cuba*, 274–75; Musicant, *Empire by Default*, 348; Bradley M. Reynolds, "Guantanamo Bay: A Doubly Important Advanced Base," *Marine Corps Gazette*, Nov. 1982, 64; "Battle of Guantanamo Bay," *Wikipedia*; USMCHC: COLL/653: Spanish-American War Collection: box 1: folder 1: "Letters, w/Index, 1–9, 1898": letter, Commander B. H. McCalla to Commander in Chief, June 12 and 13, 1898; folder 3: "Letters, 15–21," letter, Capt. M. C. Goodnell to Commandant Heywood, Oct. 6, 1898, "Report on Landing"; folder 8: "'Marines at Cusco Hill,' Howbert Billman, 1898" [typescript]; folder 11: "Articles/Extracts": John William Mitchell, "With the Marines at Guantanamo," *Home Magazine*, n.d., 524; COLL/1957: Robert W. Huntington Papers: box 1: folder 10: "Personal Notes, 1861–1899": Trevor K. Plante, "'New Glory to Its Already Gallant Record': The First Marine Battalion in the Spanish American War," *NARA Bulletin*, 30:1 (Spring 1998), n.p.; "The Journal of Frank Keeler," *Marine Corps Letters Series*,

n.d., 7; Joyce Milton, *The Yellow Kids: Foreign Correspondents in the Heyday of Yellow Journalism* (New York: Harper Perennial, 1989), 304; Stephen Crane, "War Memories of Guantanamo," *Marine Corps Gazette*, vol. 1, 1916, 409, 410; "Battle of Guantanamo Bay," *Wikipedia*; Frank Keeler, *Guantanamo Bay, Cuba, 1898: The Journal of Frank Keeler* (Marine Corps Paper Series, no. 1), ed. Carolyn A. Tyson, 9, 11, 13; John H. Clifford, "My Memories of Cuba," *The Leatherneck*, June 1929, 7; Stephen Crane, "Marines Signaling Under Fire at Guantanamo," *McClure's Magazine*, 12:4 (February 1899), 335–36; "The Red Badge of Courage Was His Wig-Wag Flag," *New York World*, July 1, 1898; Charles H. Brown, *The Correspondents' War: Journalists in the Spanish-American War*, 286–87, 287–88; G.J.A. O'Toole, *The Spanish War: An American Epic—1898*, 248–49.

241 *no rest for Crane*: Sources for U.S.-Cuban War Council on pages 241 to 244 include: Milton, *The Yellow Kids*, 306–308, 309–10; Ralph D. Paine, *Roads of Adventure* (Boston: Houghton Mifflin Co., 1922), 246; Crane, *War Dispatches*, 277–79; John D. Miley, *In Cuba with Shafter* (New York: Charles Scribner's Sons, 1899), 70; Swanberg, *Citizen Hearst*, 151–52; Brown, *The Correspondents' War*, 22–23, 302–305; LC/MS: Clara Barton Papers: "Clara Barton Papers: Diaries and Journals," June 20, 1898; George Kennan, *Campaigning in Cuba* (New York: Century Company, 1899), 52–54, 77–78; Smith College, Northampton, MA: Sophia Smith Collection: Clara Barton Papers: Series II, "Correspondence": box 2, folder 5, "General J. C. Breckinridge, 1898," letter, Barton to Breckinridge, June 21, 1898; Richard Harding Davis, "Shafter and Sampson Go Ashore to Confer with General Garcia," *New York Herald*, June 22, 1898; O'Toole, *The Spanish War*, 255, 256, 265; Richard Harding Davis, *The Cuban and Porto Rican Campaigns* , 103–12; *New York Herald*, June 22, 1898; John Seelye, *War Games: Richard Harding Davis and the New Imperialism* (Amherst, MA: University of Massachusetts Press, 2003), 276–77; Musicant, *Empire by Default*, 362.

244 *delayed a day due to rough seas*: Sources for the Daiquirí landing on pages 244 to 247 include: Musicant, *Empire by Default*, 366–67, 370, 371–73; Brown, *The Correspondents' War*, 304–305; O'Toole, *The Spanish War*, 265, 266–67; Steward, *Buffalo Soldiers*, 121–22; Stanley Westheim, "The Yellow Kids: Frank Norris and Stephen Crane," *Frank Norris Studies*, 27 (Spring 1999), 3; Kennan, *Campaigning in Cuba*, 79; Roosevelt, *The Rough Riders*, 42, 44; Davis, *The Cuban and Porto Rican Campaigns*, 116, 136–37; author's notes on Daiquirí; Crane, *War Dispatches*, 140, 279–80; LC/MS: Henry T. Allen Papers: box 1: "Diaries": "1898: H. T. Allen's Diary," June 24, 1898; A. B. Feuer, *The Santiago Campaign of 1898: A Soldier's View of the Spanish-American War* (Westport, CT: Praeger, 1993), 23.

247 *third invasion*: Sources for the invasion of Guam on pages 247 to 249 include: Leslie W. Walker, "Guam's Seizure by the United States in 1898," *Pacific Historical Review*, 14:1 (March 1945), 2–3, 3–4, 7–8, 9; Robert Gardiner, ed., *Conway's All the World's Fighting Ships, 1860–1905* (New York: Mayflower Books, 1979), 151; Stephen Kinzer, "Cruel Realities: The American Conquest of Guam," *World Policy Journal*, 23:2 (Summer 2006), 100–101, 102; Kinzer, *The True Flag*, 51; Anne Perez Hattori, "Colonialism, Capitalism and Nationalism in the US Navy's Expulsion of

Guam's Spanish Priests, 1898–1900," *Journal of Pacific History*, 44:4 (December 2009), 283 ff11.

14. THE ROYAL ROAD

250 *dawn broke suddenly*: Sources for the Battle of Las Guásimas on pages 250 to 257 include: Anastasio Azoy, *Charge: The Story of the Battle of San Juan Hill* (New York: Layman's, 1961), 40; Edmund Morris, *The Rise of Theodore Roosevelt*, 668, 672–73; Ivan Musicant, *Empire by Default*, 375–76, 381–85; Dale L. Walker, *The Boys of '98: Theodore Roosevelt and the Rough Riders* (New York: Tom Doherty Associates, 1998), 98–99, 171–81; Evan Thomas, *The War Lovers: Roosevelt, Lodge, Hearst, and the Rush to Empire*, 202, 205, 299, 301, 302–303, 305; LC/MS: William R. Shafter Papers, 1862–1938: Correspondence, June 2–August 3, 1898: Microfilm Reels I–VI: letter, Lawton to Shafter, June 23, 1898; Philip, "A Volunteer of 1898," 6–7; Theodore Roosevelt, *The Rough Riders*, 46–47, 50–59, 61–62; Herman Hagedorn, *Leonard Wood: A Biography*, vol. 1 (New York: Harper and Bros., 1931), 162, 168–69; LC/MS: Leonard Wood Papers: box 2: "Diaries": File: "Diary—May 29, 1898—July 15, 1898": "Las Guásimas, June 1898," 7–8; Charles Johnson Post, *The Little War of Private Post: The Spanish-American War Seen Up Close*, 115, 120–24; Jose Muller y Tejeiro, "Battles and Capitulation of Santiago de Cuba," in *Proceedings of the United States Naval Institute*, 25:1 (March 1899), 77–79; author observations and interview with Angelina Ramos Blanco, director of the Museo de la Guerra Hispano-Cubano-Norteamericana; Charles H. Brown, *The Correspondents' War: Journalists in the Spanish-American War*, 312–20, 321; Stephen Crane, "Stephen Crane at the Front for the World," in *The War Dispatches of Stephen Crane*, ed. R. W. Stallman and E. R. Hagemann (New York: New York University Press, 1964), 154–59; Arthur Lubow, *The Reporter Who Would Be King: A Biography of Richard Harding Davis*, 173–75, 177; Edward Marshall, *The Story of the Rough Riders, 1st U.S. Volunteer Cavalry* (New York: G.W. Dillingham Co., 1899), 95–100, 103, 104, 111–12, 115, 116, 119; Richard Harding Davis, "How Hamilton Fish and Allyn Capron Died, Fighting Bravely," *New York Herald*, June 26, 1898; A. B. Feuer, *The Santiago Campaign of 1898: A Soldier's View of the Spanish-American War* (Westport, CT: Praeger, 1993), 25, 27, 29; Theophilus G. Steward, *Buffalo Soldiers: The Colored Regulars in the United States Army*, 130–31; O'Toole, *The Spanish War: An American Epic—1898*, 275; Edward Marshall, "A Wounded Correspondent's Recollections of Guasimas," *Scribner's*, 24 (1898), 273–82; David F. Trask, *The War with Spain in 1898* (Lincoln, NE: University of Nebraska Press, 1996), 222; Walter Millis, *The Martial Spirit: A Study of Our War with Spain*, 274; Graham A. Cosmas, *An Army for Empire: The United States Army in the Spanish-American War*, 209; Joyce Milton, *The Yellow Kids: Foreign Correspondents in the Heyday of Yellow Journalism*, 315–16; Stephen Crane, *The War Dispatches of Stephen Crane*, 157–59, 159–60; Crane, "Roosevelt's Rough Riders' Loss Due to a Gallant Blunder," *New York World*, June 26, 1898.

257 *A string of blockhouses and trenches*: Cosmas, *An Army for Empire*, 209.

257 *"The officers and others were sitting round"*: Frederick W. Ramsden, "Diary of the British Consul at Santiago During Hostilities, Part I," *McClure's Magazine*, 11:6 (October 1898), 588; ibid., Part II, *McClure's Magazine*, 12:1 (November 1898), 63.

257 *Damage control set in*: Sources on the first stages of disparaging Cubans on pages 257 to 261 include: LC/MS: Henry T. Allen Papers: box 1: "Diaries": "1898," July 20, 1898; box 6: "Correspondence": folder: "1898, Jan.–June": Letter, Allen to wife, June 30, 1898; Post, *The Little War of Private Post*, 115–16 ff116, 130; Feuer, *The Santiago Campaign of 1898*, 29; Milton, *The Yellow Kids*, 316, 317–18, 318–19; Walker, *The Boys of '98*, 197; Thomas, *The War Lovers*, 306–307; letter, Roosevelt to William Todd, Boston, MA, July 19, 1898, in Alexander K. McClure and Charles Morris, *The Authentic Life of William McKinley, Our Third Martyr President: Together with a Life Sketch of Theodore Roosevelt* (Washington, D.C.: W. E. Scull, 1901), 479; Lubow, *The Reporter Who Would Be King*, 178–79; Brown, *The Correspondents' War*, 321; letter, Richard Harding Davis to Charles Davis, June 6, 1898, in Charles Belmont Davis, *Adventures and Letters of Richard Harding Davis* (New York: Charles Scribner's Sons, 1917), 247–52; Louis A. Perez Jr., *Cuba and the United States: Ties of Singular Intimacy*, 203; USAMH: Nelson A. Miles Papers: box 5: "Spanish-American War, 1898": folder 1: "Spanish-American War—preparations and Cuba campaign": Lt. Col. A. S. Rowan to Miles, "Confidential Report," November 2, 1898; Michael Robertson, *Stephen Crane, Journalism, and the Making of Modern American Literature* (New York: Columbia University Press, 1997), 161–62; University of Miami Special Collections, Coral Gables, FL (hereafter UM): V. Hansen Papers, 1899: "typescript manuscript of V. Hansen of Co. A, 13th U.S. Infantry Regiment," 12–13; Louis A. Perez Jr., "Cuba Between Empires, 1898–1899," *Pacific Historical Review*, 48:4 (November 1979), 473–500; Louis A. Perez Jr., *Cuba in the American Imagination: Metaphor and the Imperial Ethos*, 175, 178–80; author's notes: interview with Professor Francisca López Civeira, Department of History, University of Havana, June 14, 2019; John Lawrence Tone, *War and Genocide in Cuba, 1895–1898*, 283.

261 *breathing the same air*: Sources on after the Battle of Las Guásimas on pages 261 to 265 include: W. A. Swanberg, *Citizen Hearst: A Biography of William Randolph Hearst*, 152–54; Thomas, *The War Lovers*, 309–11, 312–13; *New York Evening Journal*, June 29, 1898; Brown, *The Correspondents' War*, 325–26, 326–27; David S. Pierson, "What the Rough Riders Lacked in Military Discipline, They Made Up for with Patriotic Fervor and Courage," *Military History*, 15:2 (June 1998), 10; Valery Havard, *The Santiago Campaign* (Richmond, VA: Williams Printing Co., 1927), 217–19; George Kennan, *Campaigning in Cuba* (New York: Century Company, 1899), 83–84, 84–85, 88–100; Cosmas, *An Army for Empire*, 88; Gerald F. Linderman, *The Mirror of War: American Society and the Spanish-American War* (Ann Arbor, MI: University of Michigan Press, 1974), 104; Morris, *The Rise of Theodore Roosevelt*, 678; LC/MS: George Kennan Papers: box 22: Diaries, Letters, & Notebooks, 1897–1906: Cuban Notebook no. 1, Santiago Campaign, May 5 to July 12, 1898: Monday, June 27, 1898, 132–36; Azoy, *Charge: The Story of the Battle of San Juan Hill*, 132.

15. THE HEIGHTS

266 *"desperate ground"*: Sources on the Battle of El Caney on pages 266 to 270 include: Evan Thomas, *The War Lovers*, 312–13; William R. Shafter, "The Capture of Santiago de Cuba," *Century Magazine* 57:4 (February 1899), 612–30; G.J.A. O'Toole, *The Spanish War: An American Epic—1898*, 293–94, 294–95; Steven L. Ossad, "Henry Ware Lawton: Flawed Giant and Hero of Four Wars," *Army History* (Winter 2007), 14, 15, 16; Jose Muller y Tejeiro, "Battles and Capitulation of Santiago de Cuba," *Proceedings of the United States Naval Institute*, 25:1 (March 1899), 86–92; "Allyn Capron," *Wikipedia*; Frank Norris, "With Lawton at El Caney," *The Century*, 58:2 (June 1899), 304–309; Marshall Everett, ed., *Exciting Experiences in Our Wars with Spain and the Filipinos: The Life of Admiral Dewey* (Chicago: Book Publishers Union, 1899), 126; LC/MS: Henry T. Allen Papers: box 6: "Correspondence": folder: "1898: July–August," letter, Allen to wife, July 9, 1898, from El Caney; Brian McAllister Linn, *The Philippine War, 1899–1902* (Lawrence, KS: University Press of Kansas, 2000), 101; George Clarke Musgrave, *Under Three Flags in Cuba: A Personal Account of the Cuban Insurrection and Spanish-American War* (Boston: Little, Brown and Co., 1899), 308–309; John D. Miley, *In Cuba with Shafter* (New York: Charles Scribner's Sons, 1899), 111–12; Swanberg, *Citizen Hearst*, 155–56; Willard B. Gatewood Jr., ed., *"Smoked Yankees" and the Struggle for Empire: Letters from Negro Soldiers, 1898–1902* (Urbana, IL, 1971), 55–57; Stanley Wertheim, "Two Yellow Kids: Frank Norris and Stephen Crane," *Frank Norris Studies*, 27 (Spring 1999), 3; Frank Norris, *Collected Letters*, ed. Jesse S. Crisler (San Francisco: Book Club of California, 1986): letter, Norris to Ernest Peixalto, August 1898.

270 *The Battle of San Juan Heights*: Sources on the Battle of San Juan Heights on pages 270 to 273 and 274 to 279 include: O'Toole, *The Spanish War*, 302–21; Graham A. Cosmas, *An Army for Empire: The United States Army in the Spanish-American War*, 131–44, 210–18; Ivan Musicant, *Empire by Default: The Spanish-American War and the Dawn of the American Century*, 398–99, 400–401, 409–23; Henry Chandler Christy, "An Artist at El Pozo," *Scribner's* (1898), 283–84; R. A. Alger, *The Spanish-American War*, 154–55; Howard A. Giddings, *Exploits of the Signal Corps in the War with Spain* (Kansas City, MO: Hudson-Kimberly Publishing Co., 1900), 59–61; Stephen Crane, *The War Dispatches of Stephen Crane*, ed. R. W. Stallman and E. R. Hagemann (New York: New York University Press, 1964), 176, 282–83; Richard Harding Davis, "The Battle of San Juan Hill," *Scribner's*, Oct. 1898, 387–403; Charles Johnson Post, *The Little War of Private Post: The Spanish-American War Seen Up Close*, 164–80; letter, Cpl. John R. Conn to sister, *Evening Star* (Washington, D.C.), Sept. 17, 1898, in Gatewood, *"Smoked Yankees,"* 65–71; Joyce Milton, *The Yellow Kids*, 325–30; "How a War Balloon Came Down After Being Pierced More Than Two Hundred Times," in Trumbull White, *Pictorial History of Our War with Spain for Cuba's Freedom*, 554–55; John J. Pershing, *My Life Before the World War, 1860–1917: A Memoir*, ed. John T. Greenwood, 114–16; Theodore Roosevelt, *The Rough Riders*, 72–86; Dale L. Walker, *The Boys of '98: Theodore Roosevelt and the Rough Riders* (New York: Tom

Doherty Associates, 1998), 210–11; Norm Tessman, "Captain William Owen 'Bucky' O'Neill," *Spanish American War Centennial Website*, www.spanamwar.com/Oneill.htm; Philip, "A Volunteer of 1898," 9; Richard Holmes, *Acts of War: The Behavior of Men in Battle* (New York: Free Press, 1985), 156–57, 215–16, 232; "Conduct of 71st New York at Charge of San Juan," *New York World*, July 16, 1898; Brad K. Berner, ed., *The Spanish-American War: A Documentary History with Commentaries*, 129–30; Theophilus G. Steward, *Buffalo Soldiers: The Colored Regulars in the United States Army*, 208–19; Stephen Bonsal, "The Fight for Santiago: The Account of an Eye-Witness," *McClure's Magazine*, 11:6 (October 1898), 15–16; Charles H. Brown, *The Correspondents' War: Journalists in the Spanish-American War*, 359–62; Richard Harding Davis, *The Cuban and Porto Rican Campaigns*, 218; Edmund Morris, *The Rise of Theodore Roosevelt*, 685–87; Peggy Samuels and Harold Samuels, *Teddy Roosevelt at San Juan Hill: The Making of a President* (College Station, TX: Texas A&M University Press, 1997), 269–70, 305; Gerald F. Linderman, *The Mirror of War: American Society and the Spanish-American War*, 106; letter, Roosevelt to Henry Cabot Lodge, July 19, 1898, in Elting E. Morison, *The Letters of Theodore Roosevelt*, vol. 2, 853; Sylvia Jukes Morris, *Edith Kermit Roosevelt: Portrait of a First Lady* (New York: Modern Library, 2001; 1st pub. 1980), 181; Thomas, *The War Lovers*, 324–29; LC/MS: George Kennan Papers: box 22: Diaries, Letters, & Notebooks, 1897–1906: Cuban Notebook no. 1, Santiago Campaign, May 5 to July 12, 1898: July 1, 1898, 150; author's observations; Charles E. Heller and William A. Stofft, eds., *America's First Battles, 1776–1965*, 124–57; interview with Angelina Ramos Blanco, director of the Museo de la Guerra Hispano-Cubano-Norteamericana at Guásimas, Cuba; Graham A. Cosmas, "San Juan Hill and El Caney, 1–2 July 1898," in Heller and Stofft, eds., *America's First Battles*, 130.

274 *"caused the loss of many lives"*: Sources on the fate of the Signal Corps balloon on pages 273 to 274 include: LC/MS: Leonard Wood Papers: box 2: "Diaries": File: "Diary—May 29, 1898—July 15, 1898": July 1, 1898, 7; Trumbull White, *Pictorial History of Our War*, 554–55; Walter W. Ward, *Springfield in the Spanish American War* (Easthampton, MA: Enterprise Printing Co., 1899), 186–87. (Though Boone said he did not "notice the pain" from his fall, he died of his injuries in Springfield on March 19, 1899.)

279 *"great wave sweeping slowly in from the sea"*: Stephen Bonsal, "The Night After San Juan: Stories of the Wounded on the Field and in the Hospital," *McClure's Magazine*, 12:2 (December 1898), 118.

281 *account beggars belief*: Sources on Roosevelt's questionable account of the charge on pages 280 to 283 include: Milton, *Yellow Kids*, 329; Paul T. Arnold, "Negro Soldiers in the U.S. Army," *Magazine of History with Notes and Queries*, 11 (January–June, 1910), 120; "Black Americans in the U.S. Military from the American Revolution to the Korean War: The Spanish-American War and the Philippine Insurgency," *New York State Military Museum and Veterans Research Center; NYS Division of Military and Naval Affairs*, http://dmna.state.ny.us/historic/articles/blacksmilitary

/BlacksMilitarySpanAm.htm; Roosevelt, *The Rough Riders*, 85 (this follows nearly verbatim his 1899 *Scribner's* account of the Santiago campaign); Steward, *Buffalo Soldiers*, 327; Willard B. Gatewood Jr., *Black Americans and the White Man's Burden, 1893–1903*, 59, 103; Davis, *The Cuban and Porto Rican Campaigns*, 244; John Seelye, *War Games: Richard Harding Davis and the New Imperialism* (Amherst, MA: University of Massachusetts Press, 2003), 299–300.

283 *charge had ended, but not the battle*: Sources on the aftermath of the charge up San Juan Hill on pages 283 to 285 include: O'Toole, *The Spanish War*, 319; Heller and Stofft, eds., *America's First Battles*, 144–45; Stephen Bonsal, *The Fight for Santiago: The Story of the Soldier in the Cuban Campaign, from Tampa to the Surrender* (New York: Doubleday & McClure, 1899), 141; Cosmas, "San Juan Hill and El Caney," 141; Musicant, *Empire by Default*, 423; Michael Clodfelter, *Warfare and Armed Conflicts: A Statistical Encyclopedia of Casualty and Other Figures, 1492–2015* (Jefferson, NC: McFarland, 2017, 4th edition), 255; Fernando Redondo Diaz, *Historia de las Fuerzas Armadas*, vol. 1 (Zaragosa: Ediciones Palafox, S.A., 1983); Cosmas, *An Army for Empire*, 218; Morison, ed., *The Letters of Theodore Roosevelt*, vol. 2, 846.

16. THE ALTAR OF VANITY

286 *Thus began the dreaded siege*: Sources on the beginning of the siege of Santiago on pages 286 to 287 include: Evan Thomas, *The War Lovers*, 337, 338–39; Edmund Morris, *The Rise of Theodore Roosevelt*, 688; Theodore Roosevelt, *The Rough Riders*, 101, 104, 145; Roosevelt, *An Autobiography* (New York: Macmillan, 1913), 265–67; Ivan Musicant, *Empire by Default: The Spanish-American War and the Dawn of the American Century*, 425, 426–27; NARA: Microfilm M665, Roll 249: Returns from Regular Army Infantry Regiments, June 1821–December 1911: Twenty-Fourth U.S. Infantry, January 1898–December 1899, "July 1898 Regimental Returns"; Charles E. Heller and William A. Stofft, eds., *America's First Battles, 1776–1965*, 144–45; Philip, "A Volunteer of 1898," 11; Frank Freidel, *The Splendid Little War*, 136–37; W.A.M. Goode, "The Destruction of Cervera's Fleet, Part II," *McClure's Magazine*, 11:5 (September 1898), 423; George Kennan, *Campaigning in Cuba* (New York: Century Company, 1899), xx; Stephen Bonsal, "The Night After San Juan: Stories of the Wounded on the Field and in the Hospital," *McClure's Magazine*, 12:2 (December 1898), 120–23; LC/MS: George Kennan Papers: box 22: Diaries, Letters, & Notebooks, 1897–1906: Cuban Notebook no. 1, Santiago Campaign, May 5 to July 12, 1898, 150–51.

287 *"I fear I have underestimated today's casualties"*: Sources on Shafter's doubts on pages 287 to 289 include: Robert W. Merry, *President McKinley: Architect of the American Century*, 302–303; Musicant, *Empire by Default*, 427–29; Jose Muller y Tejeiro, "Battles and Capitulation of Santiago de Cuba," in *Proceedings of the United States Naval Institute*, 25:1 (March 1899), 123; Freidel, *The Splendid Little War*, 143–44, 191; Department of the Navy, *Annual Report, 1898* (Washington, D.C.: Government Printing Office, 1899), Appendix A, 504; USAMH: Nelson A. Miles

Papers: box 5: "Spanish-American War, 1898": folder 1: "Spanish-American War—preparations and Cuba campaign": "Conversation Between U.S. Captain Mondoza and General Torel [*sic*], Sat., Aug. 27, 1898, 4 p.m."

289 *Resurrection of Hoffman Philip*: Sources for the Resurrection of Hoffman Philip on pages 289 to 295 include: Hoffman Philip, "A Volunteer of 1898" [transcript], 12–19; Kennan, *Campaigning in Cuba*, 134–37; "Hoffman Philip (1872–1951)," U.S. State Department, Office of Historian, https://history.state.gov/departmenthistory/people/philip-hoffman; Michael Clodfelter, *Warfare and Armed Conflicts: A Statistical Encyclopedia of Casualty and Other Figures, 1492–2007* (Jefferson, NC: McFarland & Co., 2008, 3rd edition), 255; "William Astor Chanler," *Wikipedia*; Bonsal, "The Night After San Juan," 123–24; Roosevelt, *The Rough Riders*, 115–16; Morris, *The Rise of Theodore Roosevelt*, 688.

295 *Pascual Cervera donned his pressed uniform*: Sources for the destruction of the Spanish fleet on pages 295 to 304 include: Manuel Cervera, Wayne A. Lydick, and Angel L. Cervera, "Admiral D. Pascual Cervera," *SpanAm War Centennial Website*, http://spanamwar.com/cervera.htm; Gregg Jones, *Honor in the Dust: Theodore Roosevelt, War in the Philippines, and the Rise and Fall of America's Imperial Dream*, 81–86; Freidel, *The Splendid Little War*, 149–77; telegram, Cervera to Gov.-General Ramon Blanco, July 2, 1898, quoted in O'Toole, *The Spanish War: An American Epic*, 285, 328–339; Musicant, *Empire by Default*, 439–66; Admiral Pascual Cervera, "The Last Address to the Spanish Squadron," *SpanAm War Centennial Website*, www.spanamwar.com/Cerveraquote.htm; Victor M. Concas y Palau, *The Squadron of Admiral Cervera* (Washington, D.C.: Government Printing Office, 1900), 71–84; Robley D. Evans, *A Sailor's Log* (New York, 1908), 443–50; Pascual Cervera y Topete, *A Collection of Documents Relative to the Squadron Operations in the West Indies* (Washington, D.C.: Government Printing Office, 1899), 123–34; Winfield Scott Schley, *Forty-Five Years Under the Flag* (New York, 1904), 297–310, 323–31; George E. Graham, "The Destruction of Cervera's Fleet, Part I," *McClure's Magazine*, 11:5 (September 1898), 4–24; George E. Graham, *Schley and Santiago* (Chicago, 1902), 287–330, 293; W. T. Sampson, "Destruction of Admiral Cervera's Fleet" (including a copy of Sampson's report to Secretary Long, July 15, 1898), in *The Great Republic*, vol. 4 (New York: Lippincott, 1901), 55–64; author's notes of field of battle; Walter Millis, *The Martial Spirit: A Study of Our War with Spain*, 305–12; Goode, "The Destruction of Cervera's Fleet, Part II," 423–33; John C. Philip, "Story of the Captains," *Century Magazine* (May 1899), 90–91.

17. THE FEAR

305 *"fleet under my command"*: Sources on the response to the defeat of the Spanish fleet on pages 305 to 307 include: Walter Millis, *The Martial Spirit: A Study of Our War with Spain*, 311–13, 314, 316, 317; Frank Freidel, *The Splendid Little War*, 176–77; Pascual Cervera y Topete, *A Collection of Documents Relative to the Squadron Operations in the West Indies* (Washington, D.C.: Government Printing Office, 1899), 134; Brad K. Berner, ed., *The Spanish-American War: A Documentary History*

with Commentaries, 77–79; Robert W. Merry, *President McKinley: Architect of the American Century*, 304; *New York Times*, July 3, 1898, 3, and July 4, 1898, 4.

307 *Sickness was already there*: Sources on the spreading sickness on pages 307 to 309 include: Freidel, *The Splendid Little War*, 182, 183; Ivan Musicant, *Empire by Default: The Spanish-American War and the Dawn of the American Century*, 468; Joyce Milton, *The Yellow Kids: Foreign Correspondents in the Heyday of Yellow Journalism*, 342; *New York World*, July 5, 1898; Ann K. Frantz, "Nursing Pride: Clara Barton in the Spanish-American War," *American Journal of Nursing*, 98:10 (October 1998), 40–41; LC/MS: Clara Barton Papers: "Clara Barton Papers: Diaries and Journals," July 2 and 3, 1898; Clara Barton, *The Red Cross: A History of This Remarkable International Movement in the Interest of Humanity*, 564–65, 569–75; Percy H. Epler, *The Life of Clara Barton*, 296–97, 299–300; "USS Reina Mercedes," *Wikipedia*; Henry Wattterson, "Significance of the Fall of Santiago," in *The Great Republic*, vol. 4 (New York: Lippincott, 1901), 83–102; John J. Turner, "The Campaign in Cuba as Remembered by Sergeant John J. Turner, USV (Part 3)," *The Spanish American War Centennial Website*, www.spanamwar.com, 3–4.

309 *town was built around a plaza*: Sources on the disaster at El Caney on pages 309 to 310 include: Frederick W. Ramsden, "Diary of the British Consul at Santiago During Hostilities," *McClure's Magazine*, 12:1 (November 1898), 67–68; LC/MS: Henry T. Allen Papers: box 1: "Diaries": entries for July 11, 12, 13, 14, 16, 18, and 20; box 6: "Correspondence": folder: "1898: July-Aug.": letters, Allen to wife, Jeannine, July 6, 9, and 12; folder: "1898" (news clippings): "Major Allen and Caney," no source, July 1898, 4; Milton, *The Yellow Kids*, 280–81, 343; Stephen Crane, "Spanish Deserters Among the Refugees at El Caney," in *The War Dispatches of Stephen Crane* (New York: New York University Press, 1964), 183–86; Frank Norris, "Comida: An Experience in Famine," *The Atlantic*, 83 (March 1899), 343–45; David Scott Kramer, "The Spanish-American War as a Bourgeois Testing Ground: Richard Harding Davis, Frank Norris, and Stephen Crane," *War, Literature, and the Arts: An International Journal of the Humanities* (2015), 1; UM: V. Hansen Papers, 1899: "typescript manuscript of V. Hansen of Co. A, 13th U.S. Infantry Regiment," 6; LC/MS: Leonard Wood Papers: box 2: "Diaries": File: "Diary—May 29, 1898—July 15, 1898" (hereafter *Leonard Wood Diary*) July 8, 1898; Arthur Lubow, *The Reporter Who Would Be King: A Biography of Richard Harding Davis*, 190; French Ensor Chadwick, *The Relations of the United States and Spain: The Spanish-American War*, vol. 1 (New York: Charles Scribner's Sons, 1911), 234, 253; John D. Miley, *In Cuba with Shafter* (New York: Charles Scribner's Sons, 1899), 146.

310 *"Yellow Jack"*: Sources on the growing fears of yellow fever on pages 310 to 312 include: NARA: RG 112: Records of the Office of the Surgeon General—Army: Entry 230: Anita Newcomb McGee's Office Files, box 2: File: "Spanish American War Nurses, Letters, Lists, Reports, from Dr. McGee": "Turner Memories" [typescript], 1; Mildred Tengborn, *No Greater Love: The Gripping Story of Nurse Clara Maass* (St. Louis, MO: Concordia, 1978), 140–41; Margaret Humphreys, "No Safe Place: Disease and Panic in American History," *American Literary History*, 14:4 (Winter

2002), 845–46, 853; George Kennan, *Campaigning in Cuba* (New York: Century Company, 1899), 214; Barton, *The Red Cross*, 568–69; Epler, *The Life of Clara Barton*, 299–300, 306–307; "Eben Brewer," *The Cincinnati Enquirer*, July 17, 1898, 2 (Brewer died of yellow fever on July 15, 1898); USAMH: Nelson A. Miles Papers: box 6: "Spanish-American War, 1898": folder 2: "Spanish-American War, diary of Lieutenant Colonel Marion P. Maus; annotations by General Miles, 1898" (hereafter *Maus Diary)*, 20; Charles Johnson Post, *The Little War of Private Post: The Spanish-American War Seen Up Close*, 253, 257–59; USF: Leland Hawes Collection: box 27: folder: "Henry Dobson Letters—Spanish-American War," letter, Henry Dobson to "Mama," Aug. 1, 1898; Letter, S. A. Dobson to son Will, Sept. 20, 1898.

313 *"Not since the campaign of Crassus"*: Sources on Shafter's "poker game" with Toral on pages 313 to 315 include: Elting E. Morison, *The Letters of Theodore Roosevelt*, vol. 2, 324–25, 849; Theodore Roosevelt, *Selections from the Correspondence of Theodore Roosevelt and Henry Cabot Lodge, 1884–1918*, vol. 1 (New York: Scribner's, 1925), 316–20, 324–25; Millis, *The Martial Spirit*, 320–21; Charles H. Brown, *The Correspondents' War: Journalists in the Spanish-American War*, 397–98, 398–99; Kenneth Harris, "Shrapnel, Dynamite, and Shell," *The Chicago Record's War Stories* (Chicago, 1898), 113–14; Ramsden, "Diary of the British Consul at Santiago During Hostilities," 71; LC/MS: William R. Shafter Papers, 1862–1938: Correspondence, June 2–August 3, 1898: Microfilm Reels I–VI: letter, Joe Wheeler to Shafter, July 10, 1898; cable, Shafter to Miles, July 16, 1898; John Lawrence Tone, *War and Genocide in Cuba, 1895–1898*, 277–78; Merry, *President McKinley*, 305–307; Maus, *Diary*, 12–15, 16; Joseph Wheeler, *The Santiago Campaign, 1898* (Port Washington, NY: Kennikat, 1971), 128–29; O'Toole, *The Spanish War*, 349, 350; author's notes; Thomas, *The War Lovers*, 350; David F. Trask, *The War with Spain in 1898* (Lincoln, NE: University of Nebraska Press, 1996), 315; Chadwick, *The Relations of the United States and Spain*, 245–47.

315 *it felled Stephen Crane*: Sources on "disease panic" on pages 315 to 318 include: Scott C. Osborn, "The 'Rivalry-Chivalry' of Richard Harding Davis and Stephen Crane," *American Literature*, 28:1 (March 1956), 55–56, 58; Crane, "Yellow Fever," in *The War Dispatches of Stephen Crane*, 291–95; Milton, *The Yellow Kids*, 345, 353; John Berryman, *Stephen Crane: A Critical Biography* (New York: Farrar, Straus & Giroux, 1962; 1st pub. 1950), 221, 223, 225; Thomas Beer, *Stephen Crane: A Study in American Letters* (New York: Knopf, 1923), 193–94; Clara Barton, *The Red Cross in Peace and War* (Washington, D.C.: American Historical Press, 1904), 569–75; Chadwick, *The Relations of the United States and Spain*, 234, 252; LC/MS: Clara Barton Papers: *Clara Barton Diaries*, July 11, 12, & 13, 1898; "The Women Who Gave Their Lives," http://userpages.aug.com/captbarb.lives.html; Smith College, Northampton, MA.: Sophia Smith Collection: Clara Barton Papers, Series II, "Correspondence": box 2: Letter, W. Wood to Clara Barton, July 14, 1898; LC/MS: George Kennan Papers: box 22: Diaries, Letters, & Notebooks, 1897–1906: Cuban Notebook no. 2, Santiago Campaign, July 14 to August 17, 1898; "Clara Barton's Whereabouts During the Red Cross Relief for Cuba," www.tampapix.com/barton3.htm, July 11–17, 1898.

318 *One nurse left voluntarily*: Sources for Janet Jennings and the *Seneca* on pages 318 to 321 include: John Evangelist Walsh, "Forgotten Angel: The Story of Janet Jennings and the Seneca," *Wisconsin Magazine of History*, 81:4 (Summer 1998), 267–93; *Harper's Bazaar*, Aug. 6, 1898, 662–68; *New York Times*, July 21, 22, 23 & 25, 1898; *New York World*, July 21 & 22, 1898; *Dodge Commission Report*, Sen. doc. 221, 1900, vol. 7, 3539–41; Post, *The Little War of Private Post*, 28–32; "The Medical Department Scandals," *New York Times*, Aug. 4, 1898; *New York Evening Post*, July 22, 1898; *New York World*, July 25, 1898; LC/MS: Henry T. Allen Papers: box 1: "Diaries": "1898: H. T. Allen's Diary," July 24–Aug. 27, 1898; box 6: "Correspondence," folder: "1898, July–Aug.": news clipping, "Victims on the Concho," Aug. 1, 1898, n.s., n.p.; "Major Henry T. Allen," Aug. 1, 1898, n.s., n.p.; letter, Allen to wife, Jeannine, Aug. 23, 1898; folder: "1898": "Concho an Unfit Ship," n.s., n.d., n.p.

321 *army turned to "Immunes"*: Sources on David Fagen and the "fever camp" on pages 321 to 323 include: Roger D. Cunningham, Lt. Col., "The Black 'Immune' Regiments in the Spanish-American War," *National Museum of the United States Army*, https://armyhistory.org/the-black-immune-regiments-in-the-spanish-american-war; William G. Muller, *The Twenty-Fourth Infantry: Past and Present* (Fort Collins, CO: Old Army Press, 1972), 20–21; USAMH: Spanish-American War Veterans Survey Collection: box 60: "U.S. Hospital Corps—Alsover to Norvell": folder 30: "Harger, Charles E.": "The Times of Cuba," 1:13 (August 15, 1898), "The Arrival of the Immunes," 1; Michael Morey, *Fagen: An African American Renegade in the Philippine-American War*, 28, 30–31; "Unparalleled: A Tribute to the Heroes of the Twenty-Fourth Regiment," *Piqua* (OH) *Daily Call*, Sept. 20, 1898, 1; L. Albert Scipio II, *Last of the Black Regulars: A History of the 24th Infantry Regiment, 1869–1951* (Silver Spring, MD: Roman Publications, 1983), 27; Stephen Bonsal, "The Negro Soldier in War and Peace," *North American Review*, 185 (June 7, 1907), 324–25; *Piqua* (OH) *Daily Call*, Sept. 20, 1898; Stephen Bonsal, *The Fight for Santiago: The Story of the Soldier in the Cuban Campaign, from Tampa to the Surrender* (New York: Doubleday & McClure Co., 1899), 455, 466; NARA: RG 94: Records of the Adjutant General's Office 1780s–1917: AGO File 215561: Names of soldiers who performed duty as nurses or cooks in camp at Siboney; Entry 530: Carded Medical Records, Regular Army, 24th US Infantry: Ewing-Gibson: "Fagen, David"; Microfilm M665, Roll 249: Returns from Regular Army Infantry Regiments, June 1821–December 1911: "Twenty-Fourth U.S. Infantry, January 1898–December 1899": "Record of Events," Regimental returns, 24th Inf., Co. H and Co. I, July & Aug. 1898; Morey, *Fagen*, 30–31; Phillip W. Hoffman, *David Fagen: Turncoat Hero* (Staunton, VA: American History Press, 2017), 104–105.

18. "WE ARE NOT SAVAGES"

324 *Americans amazed and confounded Calixto García*: Sources on the surrender of Santiago on pages 324 to 329 include: LC/MS: William R. Shafter Papers, 1862–1938: Correspondence, June 2–August 3, 1898: Microfilm Reels I–VI: letters, García to Shafter, July 12, 15, 19, 1898; John Lawrence Tone, *War and Genocide in*

Cuba, 1895–1898, 284; "William Ludlow," *Wikipedia*; Eugene McAndrews, "Custer's Engineer—William Ludlow," *Military Engineer*, 61:401 (May–June 1969), 200–202; USAMH: Nelson A. Miles Papers: box 5: "Spanish-American War, 1898": folder 1: "Spanish-American War—preparations and Cuba campaign": letter, Ludlow to García, July 15, 1898; John J. Turner, "The Campaign in Cuba as Remembered by Sergeant John J. Turner, USV (Part 3)," *The Spanish American War Centennial Website*, www.spanamwar.com, 3–4; Joyce Milton, *The Yellow Kids: Foreign Correspondents in the Heyday of Yellow Journalism*, 347, 348–49, 350–51; Charles H. Brown, *The Correspondents' War: Journalists in the Spanish-American War*, 399–401, 401–402, 402–405; Evan Thomas, *The War Lovers: Roosevelt, Lodge, Hearst, and the Rush to Empire*, 350, 351; James J. Archibald, "What I Saw of the War," *Leslie's Weekly*, Feb. 2, 1899; Frank Freidel, *The Splendid Little War*, 195–200; Ivan Musicant, *Empire by Default*, 502–504; John J. Pershing, *My Life Before the World War, 1860–1917: A Memoir*, 120–21; George Clarke Musgrave. *Under Three Flags in Cuba: A Personal Account of the Cuban Insurrection and Spanish-American War* (Boston: Little, Brown and Co., 1899), 347–56; Charles Johnson Post, *The Little War of Private Post: The Spanish-American War Seen Up Close*, 248; Frederick W. Ramsden, "Diary of the British Consul at Santiago During Hostilities," *McClure's Magazine*, 12:1 (November 1898), 71 ff71; *New York Herald*, Aug. 10, 1898; Louis A. Perez Jr., "Cuba Between Empires, 1898–1899," *Pacific Historical Review*, 48:4 (November 1979), 482, 488; author's notes; phone interview with Maria Isabel Colón, July 23, 2021; "On San Juan Hill, U.S. Glory Meant Cuban Humiliation," *New York Daily News*, Oct. 27, 2008; U.S. War Department, *Correspondence Relating to the War with Spain, and Conditions Growing Out of the Same, Including the Insurrection in the Philippine Islands and the China Relief Expedition, Between the Adjutant-General of the Army and Military Commanders in the United States, Cuba, Porto Rico, China, and the Philippine Islands, from April 15, 1898, to July 30, 1902*, 2 vols. (Washington, D.C.: Government Printing Office, 1902), Letter: Shafter to Alger, July 29, 1898, 185 (hereafter U.S. War Department, *Correspondence Relating to the War with Spain*); U.S. Congress, *Report of the Commission Appointed by the President to Investigate the Conduct of the War Department in the War with Spain*, 56th Congress, 1st Session, doc. no. 3859-3866, II (Washington, D.C.: Government Printing Office, 1900), 1032: Letter, Shafter to Adjutant General, Aug. 16, 1898 (hereafter U.S. Congress, *Commission on the Conduct of the War*); "Cuba—the New Klondike," & "Better Than Klondike," *Galesburg Weekly Mail*, July 28, 1898, 10; Trumbull White, *The United States in a War with Spain and the History of Cuba, a Thrilling Account* (Chicago, IL: International Publishing Co., 1898), 411–12.

330 *he'd never leave Camp Alger alive*: Sources on Carl Sandburg's invasion of Puerto Rico on pages 330 to 336 include: author's notes; KX: Local History Collection, Accession no. 994.76.15: box 5: "Local History Series: Wars 1870s–1890s": folder: "Illinois Co. C 1898, Spanish American War, 1898 Wars"; "Knox County at War," *Galesburg Register Mail*, April 26, 1898, n.p.; "The Volunteer Army Chaplain," *Lombard Review*, 17:6 (February 1901), 96–97; *Galesburg Weekly Mail*: "Life in

Camp Alger," June 23, 1898; "False Alarm Given," June 30, 1898; "Sham Battle Is Real," June 30, 1898; "Surrounds the City," "Capt. McGirr Sends Fare Well," and "Sixth to Santiago," July 14, 1898; "Galesburg Soldiers Suffer at the Front," August 11, 1898; USAMH: Nelson A. Miles Papers: box 5: "Spanish-American War, 1898": folder 1: "Spanish-American War—preparations and Cuba campaign": letter, Miles to Alger, July 25, 1898; folder 2: "Spanish-American War—Puerto Rico Campaign": Capt. Jose Jerez, "Notes Regarding the Island of Puerto Rico and the Spanish Forces Therein"; box 6: "Spanish-American War, 1898": folder 2: "Spanish-American War, diary of Lieutenant Colonel Marion P. Maus," July 28, 1898, 50–51, 60; box 7: "Commanding General, Personal Correspondence, Retirement, 1898–1925": letter, Felix M. Bernier to Miles, July 26, 1898; Spanish-American War Veterans Survey Collection: box 5: "Illinois Infantry—4th, 5th, 6th, 7th, 8th, and 9th Regiments": folder 20: "5th Regiment. Illinois Infantry [1898-W-302], Cochran, Timothy, Co. A": Anonymous, "A Cultured People": folder 31: "6th Regiment, Illinois Infantry, Petersen, Nels, Co. F"; folder 32: "6th Regiment, Illinois Infantry, Teitz, Frank W., Co. B"; O'Toole, *The Spanish War: An American Epic—1898*, 352, 353, 354–55; Luis E. González Vales, "The Puerto Rican Campaign Revisited: 'A Splendid Little War'" (November 1998, The Caribbean Institute and Study Center for Latin America, San Germain, Puerto Rico), 5–10; U.S. War Department, *Correspondence Relating to the War with Spain*: letter, McKinley to Miles, June 4, 1898, 263; Virginia Weisel Johnson, *The Unregimented General: A Biography of Nelson A. Miles* (Boston: Houghton Mifflin, 1962), 324–25, 327; Karl Waggenheim and Olga Jiménez de Waggenheim, eds., *The Puerto Ricans: A Documentary History* (Princeton, NJ: Markus Wiener Pub., 1994), 1, 19, 99; Trumbull White, *The Philippines, Puerto Rico, and Other Spanish Colonies* (Chicago, IL: International Publishing, 1898), 402–403, 505, 506–507, 548–51; J. B. Foraker, "The United States and Puerto Rico," *North American Review*, 170:521 (April 1900), 464–71; *New York Times*, July 11, 1898, 6; Alger, *The Spanish-American War*, 42; Graham A. Cosmas, *An Army for Empire: The United States Army in the Spanish-American War*, 233–34; Carl Sandburg, *Always the Young Strangers* (New York: Harcourt, Brace, 1952), 412–15; Freidel, *The Splendid Little War*, 202–203, 205, 208–209, 212–13, 263–64; NARA: RG 94: Records of the Adjutant General's Office 1780s–1917: Spanish-American War Regimental Books: 6th Illinois Infantry, Descriptive and Clothing Book: 6th Illinois Infantry, Morning Reports, Co. C: May, June, July, August, and September 1898; Sixth Illinois Infantry, Regimental Letters Sent & Received: Regimental Orders—Order Books Companies B to L: "General Field Order no. 3"; Brown, *The Correspondents' War*, 409–10; Penelope Niven, *Carl Sandburg: A Biography*, 41; Richard Harding Davis, *The Cuban and Porto Rican Campaigns*, 303; "El desembarco en Guernica 25 de julio de 1898," http://home.cogni.net/sarrasin/desembarco.guanica.htm; CS: Carl Sandburg, "Spanish-American War Diary, 25 July to 12 August, 1898," July 25, 26, July 30–Aug. 10, Aug. 16–26, 1898 (hereafter *Sandburg War Diary*); Karl Stephen Herrmann, *From Yauco to Las Marias: Being a Story of the Recent Campaign in Western Puerto Rico by the Independent Regular Brigade,*

Under Command of Brigadier-General Schwan (Boston: Richard G. Badger, 1900), 36–37; Christine Duffy Ponsa, "When Statehood Was Autonomy," in *Reconsidering the Insular Cases: The Past and Future of American Empire*, ed. Gerald L. Numan and Tomiko Brown-Nagin (Cambridge, MA: 2015), 25; Daniel Immerwahr, *How to Hide an Empire: A History of the Greater United States* (New York: Farrar, Straus & Giroux, 2019), 108; Berbusse, *The United States in Puerto Rico*, 66; Brad K. Berner, *The Spanish-American War: A Documentary History with Commentaries*, 95–96; French Ensor Chadwick, *The Relations of the United States and Spain: The Spanish-American War*, vol. 2 (New York: Charles Scribner's Sons, 1911), 297; Office of the Commonwealth of Puerto Rico, *Documents on the Constitutional History of Puerto Rico* (Washington, D.C.: Government Printing Office, 1964, 2nd ed.) 55, 56–57; Albert Gardner Robinson, *The Porto Rico of To-Day, Pen Pictures of the People and the Country* (New York: Charles Scribner's Sons, 1899), 29–30; Freidel, *The Splendid Little War*, 208–209; White, *The Philippines, Puerto Rico, and Other Spanish Colonies*, 506–507; "The Recent Events," *La Nueva Era* (Ponce), July 28, 1898.

336 *Stephen Crane rose from his sickbed*: Sources on Crane and Davis in Puerto Rico include: Milton, *The Yellow Kids*, 355–56, 359; Richard Harding Davis, "How Stephen Crane Took Juana Diaz," in *The War Dispatches of Stephen Crane* (New York: New York University Press, 1964), 194–96, 197; Stephen Crane, "The Porto Rican 'Straddle,'" *New York Journal*, Aug. 18, 1898.

337 *marched through the city center*: Sources on Sandburg from Ponce until leaving Puerto Rico on pages 336 to 340 include: *Galesburg Weekly Mail*: "Life on the Guard Lines," "Too Ill to Write," "Will Write His Story," "Regaining His Health," and "Their Health Is Excellent," Aug. 25, 1898; "Tells Graphic Story" and "Drag Weary Feet Up Mountain Paths," Sept. 1, 1898; *The Spanish American War: The Events of the War Described by Eye Witnesses* (Chicago and New York: Herbert Stone, 1899), 192–98; Herrmann, *From Yauco to Las Marias*, 70; Vales, "The Puerto Rican Campaign Revisited," 7; *Sandburg War Diary*, Aug. 2, 3, 4–10, 16–26, 1898; Sandburg, *Always the Young Strangers*, 416–17; Rafael J. Mirabel Linares, *Puebleto de Las Adjuntas, de Puerto Rico: Entre Fotos y Palabras* (Puerto Rico: Imprenta Llorens, 2005), 146–52; Robinson, *The Porto Rico of To-Day*, 67–92; "Utuado, Puerto Rico," *Wikipedia*; Charles I. Bevans, ed., *Treaties and Other International Agreements of the United States of America, 1776–1949*, vol. 11 (Washington, D.C.: Government Printing Office, 1974), 613–14; Bevans, *Treaties and Other International Agreements of the United States of America, 1776–1949*, vol. 11, 613–14; Mark R. Barnes, "The American Army Moves on Puerto Rico, Part 4," www.spanamwar.com/puertoland4.htm.

19. COMING HOME

341 *our own "natives"*: Walter Millis, *The Martial Spirit: A Study of Our War with Spain*, 361.

341 "What ought we to do?": Arthur S. Link, ed., *The Papers of Woodrow Wilson, 1896–1898*, vol. 10 (Princeton, NJ: Princeton University Press, 1971), 574–76.

341 *Get us out of here!*: Sources on the "round-robin" letter on pages 341 to 346 include: O'Toole, *The Spanish War: An American Epic*, 358, 360; USAMH: Spanish-American War Veterans Survey Collection: folder 28: "Regiment, Illinois Infantry, Johnson, Charles A., Co. A": "To Prevent Yellow Fever"; Charles Johnson Post, *The Little War of Private Post*, 260, 282–83; Millis, *The Martial Spirit*, 346–47; John J. Pershing, *My Life Before the World War, 1860–1917: A Memoir*, 121; Christopher Varela and Patrick McSherry, "A Brief History of the 9th U.S. Volunteer Infantry," *The Spanish American War Centennial Website*, www.spanamwar.com; Ivan Musicant, *Empire by Default: The Spanish-American War and the Dawn of the American Century*, 511–12; John D. Miley, *In Cuba with Shafter* (New York: Charles Scribner's Sons, 1899), 215–16; Graham A. Cosmas, *An Army for Empire: The United States Army in the Spanish-American War*, 258, 259–60, 261; U.S War Department, *Correspondence Relating to the War with Spain*, 200–201, 203–207, 261; Edmund Morris, *The Rise of Theodore Roosevelt*, 691, 722; Alger, *The Spanish-American War*, 255–59, 259–61, 264–65, 269–73; letter, Roosevelt to Alger, July 23, 1898, and Roosevelt to Lodge, July 31, 1898, in Elting E. Morison, ed., *The Letters of Theodore Roosevelt*, vol. 2, 859, 861–64; Joseph Wheeler, *The Santiago Campaign, 1898* (Port Washington, NY: Kennikat, 1971), 347–48; *Army and Navy Journal*, June 25, 1898; Spencer C. Tucker, *The Encyclopedia of the Spanish-American and Philippine-American Wars: A Political, Social, and Military History*, vol. 2 (Santa Barbara: CA: ABC-CLIO, 2009), vol. 3, Adna Chaffee's notes on 873–75; Theodore Roosevelt, *The Rough Riders*, 126, 190–93; Theodore Roosevelt, *An Autobiography* (New York: Macmillan, 1913), 75–76; Ralph D. Paine, *Roads of Adventure* (Boston, 1925), 269–70; Charles H. Brown, *The Correspondents' War: Journalists in the Spanish-American War*, 436–37; Lawrence Shaw Mayo, ed., *America of Yesterday*, 212; *Army and Navy Journal*, Aug. 13, 1898; French Ensor Chadwick, *The Relations of the United States and Spain: The Spanish-American War*, vol. 2 (New York: Charles Scribner's Sons, 1911), 259–61.

347 *Responsibility for Santiago fell to Leonard Wood*: Sources on cleaning up Santiago on pages 347 to 350 include: Musicant, *Empire by Default*, 509–10; Ann K. Frantz, "Nursing Pride: Clara Barton in the Spanish-American War," *American Journal of Nursing*, 98:10 (October 1998), 41; author's notes; interview, Professor Francisca López Civeira by author, June 14, 2018, in her living room in Havana, Cuba; Post, *The Little War of Private Post*, 277–78, 282; Clara Barton, *The Red Cross: A History of This Remarkable International Movement in the Interest of Humanity*, 578–79; Herman Hagedorn, *Leonard Wood: A Biography*, vol. 1 (New York: Harper and Bros., 1931), 187–89, 192, 198; Marshall Everett, ed., *Exciting Experiences in Our Wars with Spain and the Filipinos: The Life of Admiral Dewey* (Chicago: Book Publishers Union, 1899), 135–38; Mrs. Bryan Wells Collier, *Biographies of Representative Women of the South, 1861–1927*, vol. 4 (self-published, 1927), 37–43; Mildred Tengborn, *No Greater Love: The Gripping Story of Nurse Clara Maass* (St. Louis, MO: Concordia, 1978), 83; LC/MS: Clara Barton Papers: *Clara Barton Diaries*, August 2 and 9, 1898; telegram, Barton to War Department, August 18, 1898; Leonard Wood Papers: box 26: "General Correspondence, 1825–1898": File: "1898," letter,

Wood to wife, July 21, 1898; USAMH: Spanish-American War Veterans Survey Collection: box 60: "U.S. Hospital Corps—Alsover to Norvell": folder 30: "U.S. Hospital Corps, Harger, Charles E.": "The Times of Cuba," 1:13 (August 15, 1898), "The Street Cleaning Department," 1; "The Times of Cuba," 1:13 (August 15, 1898), advertisement, 3; Juan C. Santamaria, "The Cuba Company and the Expansion of American Busines in Cuba, 1898–1915," *Business History Review*, 74:1 (Spring 2000), 41–45; letter, Shafter to Adjutant General, Aug. 16, 1898, in U.S. Congress, *Commission on the Conduct of the War*, 1052; *New York Times*, Aug. 1, 1898, 6; Millis, *The Martial Spirit*, 361–62; Wood quoted in Louis A. Perez Jr., *Cuba in the American Imagination: Metaphor and the Imperial*, 11, 101, 103, 105; Thomas G. Paterson, "United States Intervention in Cuba, 1898: Interpretations of the Spanish-American–Cuban-Filipino War," *The History Teacher*, 29:3 (May 1996), 354.

351 *he placed Henry Lawton in charge*: Sources on Henry Lawton's appointment on pages 351 to 353 include: NARA: RG 94: Records of the Adjutant General's Office 1780s–1917: AGO File 116542: letter, Lawton to Adj. Gen. H. C. Corbin, Aug. 16, 1898; letter, H. C. Corbin to Lawton, Aug. 26, 1898; U.S Department of War, *Correspondence Relating to the War with Spain*, 231; Louis A. Perez Jr., "Cuba Between Empires, 1898–1899," *Pacific Historical Review*, 48:4 (November 1979), 483–84; Warren Zimmerman, "Jingoes, Goo-Goos, and the Rise of America's Empire," *Wilson Quarterly*, 22:2 (Spring 1998), 60–61; Charles R. Gill, M.D., "A Ride into Cuba for the Red Cross," *Scribner's Magazine*, 25 (January–June 1899), 111–18; Steven L. Ossad, "Henry Ware Lawton: Flawed Giant and Hero of Four Wars," *Army History* (Winter 2007), 10; LC/MS: Henry Ware Lawton Papers: box 3: folder 12: "Death of Lawton, printed matter": "Let Us Have a Definite Policy," *New York Journal and Advertiser*, Oct. 15, 1899, 26; Michael E. Shay, *Henry Ware Lawton: Union Infantryman, Frontier Soldier, Charismatic Warrior* (Columbia, MO: University of Missouri Press, 2016), 175, 177; "Henry Ware Lawton," *Wikipedia*; Anthony Starr, *Churchill's Black Dog, Kafka's Mice, and Other Phenomena of the Human Mind* (New York: Ballantine Books, 1990); Brian McAllister Linn, *The Philippine War, 1899–1902*, 101–102; Stanley Karnow, *In Our Image: America's Empire in the Philippines*, 148–49.

353 *it ground down Clara Barton*: Sources on Americans and Spaniards leaving Santiago on pages 353 to 359 include: LC/MS: Clara Barton Papers: telegram, Barton to War Department, August 18, 1898; *Clara Barton Diaries*, August 7, 1898; George Kennan Papers: box 11: Letterbooks—"Letterbook May 1892 to Dec. 1900": letter, Kennan to Charles Kinney, Philadelphia, Oct. 8, 1898; letter, Kennan to Clerk of Tichfield Hotel, Port Antonio, Jamaica, Nov. 7, 1898; Percy H. Epler, *The Life of Clara Barton*, 312–13; George Kennan, *Campaigning in Cuba* (New York: The Century Company, 1899), 220–21; Franklin Walker, *Frank Norris* (Garden City, NY: Doubleday, Doran, 1932), 201; Millis, *The Martial Spirit*, 348–49, 362–63; Evan Thomas, *The War Lovers: Roosevelt, Lodge, Hearst, and the Rush to Empire*, 362–63; Elizabeth Brown Pryor, *Clara Barton: Professional Angel* (Philadelphia: University of Pennsylvania Press, 1987), 334, 341; Christine Ardalan, "Clara

Barton's 1898 battles in Cuba: A Reexamination of Her Nursing Contributions," *Florida Atlantic Comparative Studies Journal* 12:1 (2010), 10–11; "Mabel Thorp Boardman," *Wikipedia;* Angela Howard and Frances M. Kavenik, *Handbook of American Women's History* (New York: Garland, 1990), 61–62; A. B. Feuer, *The Santiago Campaign of 1898*, 723–24; Roosevelt, *The Rough Riders*, 126; Dale L. Walker, *The Boys of '98: Theodore Roosevelt and the Rough Riders* (New York: Tom Doherty Associates, 1998), 263; Post, *The Little War of Private Post*, 293–300; Musicant, *Empire by Default*, 507; A. Holloway, *Hero Tales of the American Soldier and Sailor* (Philadelphia: Elliott, 1899), 127–28; USAMH: Nelson A. Miles Papers: box 5: "Spanish-American War, 1898": folder 1: "Spanish-American War—preparations and Cuba campaign": "Conversation Between Capt. Mondoza and Gen. Torel [*sic*]," Sat. Aug. 27, 1898, 4 p.m."; *El Trabajo Nacional*, Aug. 5, 1898, in Brad K. Berner, *The Spanish-American War: A Documentary History with Commentaries*, 78–79; U.S. War Department, *Correspondence Relating to the War with Spain*, vol. 1, 211–14, 216, 219–21, 224–26, 232–35, 237, 239–45, 248–49, 253, 255, 382, 384, 395, 402; Alger, *The Spanish-American War*, 278–79; Miley, *In Cuba with Shafter*, 228; Post, *The Little War of Private Post*, 291–96; Wheeler, *The Santiago Campaign*, 205, 267–69; NARA: Microfilm M665, Roll 249: Returns from Regular Army Infantry Regiments, June 1821–December 1911: Twenty-Fourth U.S. Infantry, August 1898; Stephen Bonsal, *The Fight for Santiago: The Story of the Soldier in the Cuban Campaign, from Tampa to the Surrender* (New York: Doubleday & McClure Co., 1899), 434, 457.

359 *Camp Wikoff was still under construction*: Sources for the return to Camp Wikoff on pages 359 to 361 include: U.S. War Department, *Correspondence Relating to the War with Spain*, vol. 1, 225, 227–29, 241–42, 257; "Barbarism at Montauk," *Harper's Weekly*, XLII, 890; W. A. Rogers, "Camp Wikoff," *Harper's Weekly*, XLII, 890; Alger, *The Spanish-American War*, 425–29; Post, *The Little War of Private Post*, vi, 324–25, 327–29, 336–40; Wheeler, *The Santiago Campaign*, 206, 208–12, 219–21; *Army and Navy Journal*, Aug. 16, 1898, Sept. 10 & 24, 1898, Oct. 8, 1898, Nov. 5, 1898; Cosmas, *An Army for Empire*, 263–64, 265; Thomas, *The War Lovers*, 358; Morison, *The Letters of Theodore Roosevelt*, vol. 2, 869; Kathleen Dalton, *Theodore Roosevelt: A Strenuous Life* (New York: Vintage, 2002), 179; Edmund Morris, *The Rise of Theodore Roosevelt*, 672–74; Jacob Riis, *Theodore Roosevelt, the Citizen* (New York: Johnson, Wynne Co., 1904), 199–200; O'Toole, *The Spanish War*, 374–75, 378.

361 *Not all were lucky*: Sources for the death of Henry Dobson on pages 361 to 362 include: Alicia Addeo, "'Tampa Is a Bum Place': The Letters of First Sergeant Henry A. Dobson in 1898," *Tampa Bay History*, 20:1 (Spring/Summer 1998), 55–57; USF: Leland Hawes Collection: box 27: folder: "Henry Dobson Letters—Spanish-American War": letter, Dr. Hervie Dobson to William Dobson, September 20, 1898.

362 *Shafter docked at Montauk Point on September 1*: Sources for the return of the Buffalo Soldiers on pages 362 to 363 include: Theophilus G. Steward, *Buffalo Soldiers: The Colored Regulars in the United States Army*, 224–25; NARA: Microfilm M665,

Roll 249: Returns from Regular Army Infantry Regiments, June 1821–December 1911: Twenty-Fourth U.S. Infantry, August and September 1898 returns; RG 94: Records of the Adjutant General's Office 1780s–1917: Entry 530: Carded Medical Records, Regular Army, 24th US Infantry: Ewing-Gibson: "Fagin, David"; Michael Morey, *Fagen: An African American Renegade in the Philippine-American War*, 30–31; Phillip W. Hoffman, *David Fagen: Turncoat Hero* (Staunton, VA: American History Press, 2017), 114–15.

363 *Camp Wikoff had become a ghost town*: Sources for the final casualty figures on pages 363 to 364 include: U.S. Congress, *Commission on the Conduct of the War*, vol. 1, 219; vol. 4, 1274; vol. 5, 1894–1895; Roosevelt, *The Rough Riders*, 228–29; Wheeler, *The Santiago Campaign*, 212–13, 222–27; U.S. War Department, *Report of the War Department, 1898* (Washington, D.C.: Government Printing Office, 1899), vol. 1, pt. 2, 244–45; LC/MS: Lewis W. Colson Papers: box 3: folder 1: "Notes: Historical Sketches of the War with Spain and Resultant Campaigns in the Philippine Islands at the Far East, Book 1, 1898–1900."

364 *Private Charles August Sandburg came home*: Sources on Sandburg's return on pages 364 to 365 include: NARA: RG 94: Records of the Adjutant General's Office 1780s–1917: Spanish-American War Regimental Books: 6th Illinois Infantry, Descriptive and Clothing Book: 6th Illinois Infantry, Morning Reports, Co. C, September 1898; Carl Sandburg, *Always the Young Strangers* (New York: Harcourt, Brace, 1952), 419–21; "Knox County at War," *Galesburg Register Mail*, April 26, 1898; "Charges for McGirr," *Galesburg Weekly Mail*, Sept. 22, 1898; CS: Carl Sandburg Papers (Connemara Accession), 1898–1967: Letters to and from Fellow Soldiers: Correspondence: "McGirr, Clinton J.": 3a-023-38; KX: Sandburg Collection, MSS 169: box 1: folder: "Biographical and Anecdotal, General": folder: "CAS's Boyhood Neighborhood, CAS in Galesburg": "Carl Sandburg, Poet, Life Told by His Brother," *Elmwood* (IL) *Gazette*, June 26, 1936, n.p.; Penelope Niven, *Carl Sandburg: A Biography*, 44.

PART IV: THE AMERICAN CENTURY

367 *How do I know*: CS: folder: "More Loose Items": "Untitled Poem," 18–10-8.

20. THE OTHER WAR

369 *Memory has not been kind*: Sources on Dewey's promises to Aguinaldo on pages 369 to 371 include: John W. Chambers, *The Oxford Companion to American Military History* (Oxford, U.K.: Oxford University Press, 1999), 849; Joseph P. McCallus, *Forgotten Under a Tropical Sun: War Stories by American Veterans in the Philippines, 1898–1913* (Kent, OH: Kent State University Press, 2017), 1–2; Walter Millis, *The Martial Spirit: A Study of Our War with Spain*, 224–25; Emilio Aguinaldo, *True Version of the Philippine Rebellion* (Ann Arbor, MI: University of Michigan Library, 2005; 1st pub. 1899), 288–89, 290; Leon Wolff, *Little Brown Brother*, 66, 69, 70; Oscar King Davis, "The Real Aguinaldo," *Everybody's Magazine*, 5:24 (August 1901), 142; Christopher A. Vaughan, "The 'Discovery' of the Philippines by the U.S.

Press, 1878–1902," *The Historian*, 57:2 (December 1995), 306; David Haward Bain, *Sitting in Darkness: Americans in the Philippines*, 177.

371 *News of his return tore through the provinces*: Sources on Aguinaldo's return and the Second Philippine Revolution on pages 371 to 379 include: Brad K. Berner, ed., *The Spanish-American War: A Documentary History with Commentaries*, 170–71, 173–74; Wolff, *Little Brown Brother*, 70–73, 74–75, 86; Jose S. Arcilla, "The Fall of Manila: Excerpts from a Jesuit's Diary," *Philippine Studies*, 37:2 (Second Quarter 1989), May 31, June 1, July 6–19, 1898, 203–204, 207, 211 ff30; Charles H. Brown, *The Correspondents' War: Journalists in the Spanish-American War*, 416–20, 421–22; Millis, *The Martial Spirit*, 222, 223, 355; Vaughan, "The 'Discovery' of the Philippines," 306–307; Bain, *Sitting in Darkness*, 178; Joseph Stickney, "Aguinaldo Declares the Independence of the Philippines" and "Gradually Closing in on Manila," *San Francisco Chronicle*, June 7, 13, 17, 1898, in Augusto V. De Viana, ed., *Stories Rarely Told: The Hidden Stories and Essays on Philippine History* (Quezon City, PI: New Day Publishers, 2013), 125–26, 139–41; "Lieutenant X" (Aime Ernest Motsch), *The Diary of a French Officer on the War in the Philppines, 1898*, trans. Marietta Enriquez-de la Haye Jousselin (Manila: National Historical Institute, 1994), xiii, 5–6, 19, 33, 42, 58; Nick Joaquin, *A Question of Heroes: Essays in Criticism on Ten Key Figures of Philippine History*, 131–33; "Act of the Proclamation of Independence of the Filipino People," https://en.wikisource.org/wiki/Philippine-Declaration-of-Independence; Jose George, *Our army and navy in the Orient, giving a full account of the operations of the army and navy in the Philippines, together with accurate detail of the organization of the expeditionary forces, their voyage across the Pacific, and a full account of Spanish misrule on the islands* (Manila, 1899), 69; *Literary Digest*, 17 (1898), 24–26; Stanley Karnow, *In Our Image: America's Empire in the Philippines* (New York: Ballantine Books, 1989), 116–17; LC/MS: John R. Thomas Papers, 1876–1933 (Philippine Insurrection Collection): File 10: "Correspondence Aguinaldo, 1898, Jan.–June": letters, Spencer Pratt to Aguinaldo, June 10 and 11, 1898; letters, Rounsevelle Wildman to Aguinaldo, June 28 and July 25, 1898; letter, Wildman to Aguinaldo, July 25, 1898; letter, Henry T. Mirtha to Aguinaldo, June 14, 1898; Luis Camara Dery, *When the World Loved the Filipinos, and Other Essays on Philippine History* (Manila: University of Santa Tomas Publishing House, 2005), 73; Ambeth R. Ocampo, *101 Stories of the Philippine Revolution* (Pasig City, PI: Anvil Publishing, 2009), 162–63; Horatio de la Costa, S.J., "Initial Contacts Between American Officials and Philippine Revolutionary Leaders, 1898–1899: A Problem in Diplomatic History," *Bulletin of the American Historical Collection: The American Era in the Philippines*, vol. 5, 1:18 (January 1977), 16; James H. Blount, *The American Occupation of the Philippines, 1898–1912* (New York: G. P. Putnam's Sons, 1912), 13–14, 15; Frank Freidel, *The Splendid Little War*, 223; "Aguinaldo Talked to Prince Henry," *California Call*, May 18, 1899; Bernhard von Bulow, *Memoirs of Prince von Bulow: From Secretary of State to Imperial Chancellor, 1897–1903*, vol. 1 (Boston: Little, Brown, 1931), 254–56; Karl-Heinz Wionzek, ed., *Germany, the Philippines, and the Spanish-American War: Four Accounts by Officers of the Imperial*

German Navy (Manila: National Historical Commission of the Philippines, 2012), trans. Thomas Clark, xvi–xvii.

380 *Germans irritated the commodore*: Sources on Dewey and the German navy include: Commander Nathan Sargent, USN, ed., *Admiral Dewey and the Manila Campaign* (Washington D.C.: Naval Historical Foundation, 1947), 69–73; "Footnotes to History: Admiral Dewey and the German Fleet," *Bulletin of the American Historical Collection: The American Era in the Philippines*, vol. 5, 1:18 (January 1977), 82–96; Wionzek, ed., *Germany, the Philippines*, xiv–xxi; Leon Ma Guerrero, "The Kaiser and the Philippines," *Philippine Studies*, 9:4 (October 1961), 585–87.

380 *Philippine and American forces interacted warmly*: Sources on the U.S. occupation of Manila on pages 380 to 382 include: Thomas A. Anderson, "Our Rule in the Philippines," *North American Review*, 170:519 (February 1900), 277, 278, 279; Oscar King Davis, "Dewey's Capture of Manila," *McClure's Magazine*, 13:2 (June 1899), 174, 176, 183; Karnow, *In Our Image*, 117, 122–23, 124; Motsch, *The Diary of a French Officer*, Aug. 1–3, 1898, 93, 99–100; Arcilla, "The Fall of Manila," 211 ff30; USMCHC COLL/3016: John Twiggs Myers Collection: box 1: folder 2: "Personal Correspondence, 1898": letter, "Jack" Myers to "Heywood," Aug. 15, 1898; Millis, *The Martial Spirit*, 357–60.

21. THE REPUBLIC OF SELF-RESTRAINT

383 *An uneasy truce filled*: Sources on the U.S. reign of terror in Manila on pages 383 to 386 include: Stanley Karnow, *In Our Image: America's Empire in the Philippines*, 130–31; Paul A. Kramer, "Race-Making and Colonial Violence in the U.S. Empire: The Philippine-American War as Race War," *Diplomatic History*, 30:2 (April 2006), 172; Michael Morey, *Fagen: An African American Renegade in the Philippine-American War* (Madison, WI: University of Wisconsin Press, 2019), 50; Frederick Palmer, "White Man and Brown Man in the Philippines," *Scribner's*, 27 (January 1900), 80; William Thaddeus Sexton, *Soldiers in the Sun: An Adventure in Imperialism* (Harrisburg, PA: Military Service Publishing Co., 1939), 81–82; Russell Roth, "Forgotten Soldiers, Part I: With the 13th Minnesota Volunteers at Manila, 1898–99," *Bulletin of the American Historical Collection*, 14:1 (January–March 1986), 74–75; "Bateman on Drunkenness," *Manila Times*, Feb. 26, 1900, 1; Howard Middleton, "California Regulars in the Philippines (I): from the Correspondence of Howard Middleton, 1898–1899," *Bulletin of the American Historical Collection*, 26:1 (January–March 1998), ed., Harold F. Taggart, 52, 55; Gregg Jones, *Honor in the Dust: Theodore Roosevelt, War in the Philippines, and the Rise and Fall of America's Imperial Dream*, 97; Brian Linn, "The U.S. Army and the Philippine-American War," speech given at the Philippine-American War: 125th Anniversary remembrance event, MacArthur Memorial, Norfolk, VA, Feb. 3, 2024; William Oliver Trafton, *We Thought We Could Whip Them in Two Weeks* (Quezon City, PI: New Day Publishers, 1990), 61; Leon Wolff, *Little Brown Brother*, 142; Stuart Creighton Miller, *"Benevolent Assimilation": The American Conquest of the Philippines, 1899–1903*, 58–59; Willard B. Gatewood Jr., ed., *"Smoked Yankees" and the*

Struggle for Empire: Letters from Negro Soldiers, 1898–1902, 179; "Lieutenant X" (Aime Ernest Motsch), *The Diary of a French Officer on the War in the Philppines, 1898*, trans. Marietta Enriquez-de la Haye Jousselin (Manila: National Historical Institute, 1994), 93; Richard Brinsley Sheridan, *The Filipino Martyrs: A Story of the Crime of February 4, 1899* (London: John Lane, The Bodley Head, 1900), 6–7, 180, 181; Thomas A. Anderson, "Our Rule in the Philippines," *North American Review*, 170:519 (February 1900), 282; Rene Escalante, "Collapse of the Malolos Republic," *Philippine Studies*, 46:4 (Fourth Quarter 1998), 457–62; Taylor, *The Philippine Insurrection*, 2:92, 3:372–73; Datu Bandara, "Some American Traits," *Bulletin of the American Historical Collection: The American Era in the Philippines*, vol. 4, 4:10 (October 1976), 88–92.

386 *he readied for war*: Sources on Aguinaldo's preparation for war on pages 386 to 388 include: James H. Blount, *The American Occupation of the Philippines, 1898–1912*, 73–74; Sen. doc. 62, 1898, 379–80; Karnow, *In Our Image*, 131–32; Wolff, *Little Brown Brother*, 139, 143–44, 147, 148; David Healy, *U.S. Expansionism: The Imperialist Urge in the 1890s* (Madison, WI: University of Wisconsin Press, 1970), 128–29; Walter L. Williams, "United States Indian Policy and the Debate Over Philippine Annexation: Implications for the Origins of American Imperialism," *Journal of American History*, 66:4 (March 1980), 811–12, 822, 825; Henry Pratt Judson, "Our Federal Constitution and the Government of Tropical Territories," *Review of Reviews*, XIX (January 1899), 74; *Nation*, March 16, 1899, 201; "Aguinaldo's Indians," *Harper's Weekly*, May 13, 1899, 485; Russell Roth, *Muddy Glory: America's "Indian Wars" in the Philippines, 1899–1935* (West Hanover: MA: The Christopher Publishing House, 1981), 16; Sexton, *Soldiers in the Sun*, 85–88; Oscar King Davis, "The Real Aguinaldo," *Everybody's Magazine,* 5:24 (August 1901), 142; Edwin Wildman, "General Emilio Aguinaldo—A Character Sketch," *Harper's Weekly*, Jan. 25, 1899, 197; Augusto V. de Viana, ed., *The I Stories: The Philippine Revolution and the Filipino-American War as Told by Its Eyewitnesses and Participants* (Manila: University of Santa Tomas Publishing House, 2006), 104; Esteban A. Ocampo, with Alfredo B. Saulo, *First Filipino Diplomat: Felipe Agoncillo (1859–1941)* (Manila: National Historical Institute, 1977), 83; "Felipe Agoncillo," *Wikipedia*; Hector DeLeon, *Textbook of the Philippine Constitution* (Quezon City, PI: Rex Printing Co., 2008), 20; John Barrett, "Some Phases of the Philippine Situation," *Review of Reviews*, 20 (July 1899), 65.

388 *Part Two of his "civilizing project"*: Sources on the Malolos Constitution on pages 388 to 390 include: Hector DeLeon, *Textbook of the Philippine Constitution* (Quezon City, PI: Rex Printing Co., 2008), 20; John Barrett, "Some Phases of the Philippine Situation," *Review of Reviews*, 20 (July 1899), 65; Wolff, *Little Brown Brother*, 147; *Report of the Philippine Commission to the President*, vol. 1 (Washington, D.C.: Government Printing Office, 1900), 91; Lance D. Collins, "Approaching the State: How to Study the Ideas of the Malolos Constitution," *Filipinas Journal of the Philippine Studies Association* (2020), 86, 99–101; Jose Amiel P. Angeles, "As Our Might Grows Less: The Philippine-American War in Context" [a dissertation in partial

fulfillment of a Ph.D. in history, University of Oregon, 2013], 147–48; "Pronunciamiento," *Wikipedia*; Karnow, *In Our Image*, 131–32; Morey, *Fagen*, 51–52; Cesar Adib Majul, *Mabini and the Philippine Revolution* (Quezon City, PI: University of Philippines Press, 1996; 1st pub. 1960), 45–48, 193; Teodoro A. Agoncillo, *Malolos: The Crisis of the Republic* (Quezon City, PI: University of the Philippines Press, 1960), x, 308.

390 *Aguinaldo's house lay in disorder*: Sources on McKinley's certainties on page 390 to 391 include: O'Toole, *The Spanish War: An American Epic—1898*, ff385; Musicant, *Empire by Default: The Spanish-American War and the Dawn of the American Century*, 603–604; U.S. Congress, *Papers Relating to the Foreign Relations of the United States with the Annual Message of the President Transmitted to Congress, December 5, 1898* (Washington, D.C.: Government Printing Office, 1901), 904–908; Charles S. Olcott, *The Life of William McKinley*, vol. 1, 108–11.

391 *his puny if polished voice*: Sources on Agoncillo's journey on pages 391 to 392 include: Ocampo, *First Filipino Diplomat*, 83–85, 86; "Francis Winston Greene," *Wikipedia*; "Wesley Merritt," *Wikipedia*; Kramer, "Race-Making and Colonial Violence," 176; Felipe Agoncillo, *Memorial to the Senate of the United States* (Washington, D.C.: Government Printing Office, 1899), 2, 7; Frederick G. Hoyt, "Agoncillo's Mission to America: Reality Confronts Mythology," *Bulletin of the American Historical Collection: The American Era in the Philippines*, vol. 7, 1:26 (January–March 1979), 32–36.

392 *One need only look to Cuba*: Sources on the state of Cuba during the early occupation on pages 392 to 394 include: Walter Millis, *The Martial Spirit: A Study of Our War with Spain*, 365, 370; A. B. Feuer, *The Santiago Campaign of 1898: A Soldier's View of the Spanish-American War* (Westport, CT: Praeger, 1993), 135–36; U.S. Congress, *Commission on the Conduct of the War*, vol. 7 (Washington, D.C.: Government Printing Office, 1900), 3540–42; John Evangelist Walsh, "Forgotten Angel: The Story of Janet Jennings and the Seneca," *Wisconsin Magazine of History*, 81:4 (Summer 1998), 289–92; Robert W. Merry, *President McKinley: Architect of the American Century*, 351–52, 352–58; U.S. Senate, *Food Furnished to Troops in Cuba and Porto Rico*, pt. 3, serial no. 3872 (Washington, D.C.: Government Printing Office, 1900), ff1913; Clifford L. Staten, *The History of Cuba*, 40; Michael Clodfelter, *Warfare and Armed Conflicts: A Statistical Encyclopedia of Casualty and Other Figures, 1492–2015* (McFarland: 2017, 4th edition), 330–31; Swanberg, *Citizen Hearst: A Biography of William Randolph Hearst*, 167–68, 167 ff14, 168 ff16.

394 *time to settle her affairs*: Sources on Clara Maass in Cuba on pages 394 to 395 include: Spencer C. Tucker, "Medicine, Military," *The Encyclopedia of the Spanish-American and Philippine-American Wars: A Political, Social, and Military History*, vol. 2 (Santa Barbara: CA: ABC-CLIO, 2009), 390–92; NARA: RG 112: Records of the Office of the Surgeon General—Army: Entry 103, box 3: "Historical Files of the Army Nurse Corps, 1898–1947": File: Spanish American War Nurses, Certificate of Service: "Clara Maas [*sic*]": File: Spanish American War Nurses—Historical Mate-

rial: Letter, Anita Newcomb McGee, June 1931; Mildred Tengborn, *No Greater Love: The Gripping Story of Nurse Clara Maass* (St. Louis, MO: Concordia, 1978), 39–40, 66, 70–71, 76–77; Ingrid Gessner, "Heroines of Health: Examining the Other Side of the 'Splendid Little War,'" *European Journal of American Studies*, 10:1 (2015), 13.

395 *city geared for war*: Sources on Funston taking command of the Twentieth Kansas on pages 395 to 396 include: Simon Winchester, *A Crack in the Edge of the World: America and the Great California Earthquake of 1906* (New York: Harper Perennial, 2006), 206, 216–17, 225–29, 233; Lt. Dave Young, "MG Frederick Funston," *Museum of the Kansas National Guard*, www.kansasguardmuseum.org; ACHS: Frederick Funston Collection: Section A: Early Life: Eckdall Scrapbook II: "Major General Frederick Funston, by Ella Funston Eckdall, 1948 (Excerpts Concerning Major General Frederick Funston from Newspapers, Magazines, and Letters)": "Kansas Topics: Colonel Funston and the Twentieth," *Kansas City Journal*, April 1899, n.p.; Thomas W. Crouch, *A Leader of Volunteers: Frederick Funston and the 20th Kansas in the Philippines, 1898–1899* (Lawrence, KS: Coronado Press, 1984), 23–25, 28–29; KHS: Ms. Coll. 836, Henry C. Ruppenthal papers: folder: "Diary of Henry C. Ruppenthal of Russel Co., Kan.": June 16, 1898, 25; July 3, 1898, 29; July 11,1898, 37; *The "Fighting Twentieth": History and Official Souvenir of the Twentieth Kansas Regiment* (Topeka, KS: W. Y. Morgan, 1899), 23–31; Ms. Coll. 33, Frederick Funston Collection: box 1: folder 2: "Correspondence. 1896–1898," letter, Funston to Charles Scott, Sept. 14, 1898; LC/MS: Lewis W. Colson Papers: box 1: folder 1: "Diaries, vol. 1, 1898–1900," May 19, 1898, June 1, 1898; Frederick Funston, "The Making of a Regiment," *Scribner's Magazine*, 49:6 (June 1911), 649.

396 *stepped into a mob of reporters*: Sources on Agoncillo meeting McKinley on pages 396 to 400 include: Oscar V. Campomanes, "The Japanese Analogy as Liminal Crisis-Effect in Initial Filipino-American Encounters, 1898–1899," in *The Philippines and Japan in America's Shadow*, ed. Kiichi Fujiwara and Yoshiko Nagano (Singapore: NUS Press, 2011), 79–80, 89, 94, 95, 96; NARA: RG 94: Records of the Adjutant General's Office 1780s–1917: Microcopy 254, Reel 28: Philippine Insurgent Records (PIR) 451.6: telegram, Agoncillo to Aguinaldo, Oct. 22, 1898; Raymond Williams, *Keywords: A Vocabulary of Culture and Society* (Milton Park, U.K.: Routledge, 2011; 1st pub. 1976), 223; Hoyt, "Agoncillo's Mission to America," 32–38, 38–39, 39–40, 40–42; *Chicago Daily News*, Sept. 29, 1898; *Boston Globe*, Oct. 1, 1898; Wolff, *Little Brown Brother*, 161–62; Merry, *President McKinley*, 336; Ocampo, *First Filipino Diplomat*, 87–88; Ocampo, *101 Stories of the Philippine Revolution*, 69–71; Musicant, *Empire by Default*, 613–15; William McKinley, *Speeches and Addresses of William McKinley, from March 1, 1897, to May 30, 1900* (New York: Doubleday and McClure Co., 1900), 131–34; U.S. Congress, *Papers Relating to the Foreign Relations of the United States*, 937–38; *Spanish Diplomatic Correspondence and Documents, 1896–1900* (Washington, D.C.: Government Printing Office, 1905), 310, 311–12; Frederic Bancroft, ed., *Speeches, Correspondence and Political Papers of Carl Schurz*, vol. 5 (New York: G. P. Putnam's Sons, 1913), ff77; Brad K. Berner, ed., *The Spanish-*

American War: A Documentary History with Commentaries, 247–49; O'Toole, *The Spanish War*, 386–87; Elting E. Morison, *The Letters of Theodore Roosevelt*, vol. 2, letter, Roosevelt to Lodge, Jan. 26, 1899, 923–24.

400 *To such drumbeats, Funston fell in love*: Crouch, *A Leader of Volunteers*, 31–33; ACHS: Frederick Funston Collection: Section A: Early Life: Eckdall Scrapbook I, "Note About Frederick Funston's Father Edward Hogue Funston"; David Haward Bain, *Sitting in Darkness: Americans in the Philippines*, 75–76.

400 *Agoncillo and Lopez haunted Paris*: Sources on the Treaty of Paris on pages 400 to 403 include: Campomanes, "The Japanese Analogy," 90; LC/MS: Rounsevelle Wildman and Edwin Wildman Papers, 1896–1923: box 1: Subject File: "Filipino Leaders": File: "General Correspondence, RW Oct. 2, 1897–Dec. 17, 1898": letter, Wildman to Porter, Oct. 18, 1898; reply letter, Porter to Wildman, Nov. 21, 1898; Musicant, *Empire by Default*, 624–25; Olcott, *The Life of William McKinley*, vol. 2, 128; Merry, *President McKinley*, 340–341; Millis, *The Martial Spirit*, 391, 406; William Graham Sumner, "The Conquest of the United States by Spain," *Yale Law Journal*, 8:4 (January 1899), 168; Wolff, *Little Brown Brother*, 173, 175; Julian W. Richards, *A Handbook of the Spanish-American War of 1898 and the Insurrection in the Philippines* (Cedar Rapids, IA: The Republican Printing Co., 1899), 24–26; Teodoro M. Kalaw, *The Philippine Revolution* (Kawilihan, PI: Jorge B. Vargas Filipiniana Foundation, 1969; 1st pub. 1924), 162–63; Davis, "The Real Aguinaldo," 143–44; LC/MS: Theodore Roosevelt Papers: Correspondence: Series 1: Reel 2—1898 June–1899 July: "Aguinaldo Pleading with His Brother Filipinos" [typescript of an undelivered speech], Dec. 25, 1898.

403 *One last transition occurred*: Perez, "Cuba Between Empires," 489; "Calixto García," *Wikipedia*.

22. "MY PRINCIPLES ARE YOURS"

405 *Eda Funston hated the roaches*: Sources on Funston's life in Manila before the war on pages 405 to 409 include: KHS: Ms. Coll. 33, Frederick Funston Collection: box 1, "Correspondence, 1890–1911; Report on Expedition to Alaska": folder 2: "Correspondence. 1896–1898," letter, Eda Funston to family, Dec. 11, 1898; letter, Frederick Funston to mother, Dec. 25, 1898; folder 3: "Correspondence, 1899": Eda Funston, "Rough Sketch of Manila" [edited transcript of magazine article about her arrival in Manila]; Ms. Coll. 836, *Henry Ruppenthal Diaries*, Dec., 8, 1898, 69; Jan. 18, 1899, 86; USAMH: Spanish-American War Veterans Survey Collection: box 8: "Kansas Infantry—20th, 21st, 22nd, and 23rd Regiments": folder 10: "20th Regiment, Kansas Infantry, Jamieson, John T., Co. E": "Army Service Questionnaire"; Thomas W. Crouch, *A Leader of Volunteers: Frederick Funston and the 20th Kansas in the Philippines, 1898–1899* (Lawrence, KS: Coronado Press, 1984), 39–43, 45–47; Augusto de Viana, *Stories Rarely Told: The Hidden Stories and Essays on Philippine History* (Quezon City, PI: New Day Publishers, 2013), 119–23; *Manila Times*, Nov. 29, 1898, 1, 4; Frederick Funston, *Memories of Two Wars: Cuban and Philippine Experiences*, 176; U.S. Senate, *Affairs in the Philippine Islands: Hearings*

Before the Committee on the Philippines of the United States Senate, 57th Congress, 1st Session, doc. no. 331 (Washington, D.C.: Government Printing Office, 1902), 884; John B. B. Trussell Jr., "A Pennsylvanian in the Philippines: Extracts from the Letters of Corporal William S. Christner, 1898–1899," *Pennsylvania History: A Journal of Mid-Atlantic Studies*, 44:2 (April 1977), 132; Leon Wolff, *Little Brown Brother*, 181–83, 200–205, 206–207; James H. Blount, *The American Occupation of the Philippines, 1898–1912*, 88–89, 107–20, 139; Michael Morey, *Fagen: An African American Renegade in the Philippine-American War*, 52–53; Henri Turet, "The War in the Philippines," in E. Aguilar Cruz, trans., *The War in the Philippines: As Reported by Two French Journalists in 1899* (Manila: National Historical Institute, 1985), 49; Stanley Karnow, *In Our Image: America's Empire in the Philippines*, 132–33; Rizal Library Special Collections, Ateneo de Manila University, Quezon City, PI (hereafter RIZ): T. H. Pardo de Tavera Collection: box 5: folder 1: "Correspondence Incoming": letters, de Tavera to Otis, Sept. 21 and Oct. 18, 1898; box 8B: "Correspondence Outgoing": File 11.31: letter, Otis to de Tavera, Oct. 1, 1898; cable, Otis to McKinley, undated; Julian W. Richards, *A Handbook of the Spanish-American War of 1898 and the Insurrection in the Philippines* (Cedar Rapids, IA: Republican Printing Co., 1899), 24–26; Teodoro M. Kalaw, *The Philippine Revolution*, 156, 164; interview, Oscar V. Campomanes, Professor of American and Philippine history, Ateneo de Manila University, Quezon City, PI, April 2019; "The Big Scare," unknown Manila newspaper, Jan. 24, 1899, in Daniel Immerwahr, *How to Hide an Empire: A History of the Greater United States* (New York: Farrar, Straus & Giroux, 2019), 90; LC/MS: Rounsevelle Wildman and Edwin Wildman Papers, 1896–1923: box 1: Subject File: "Filipino Leaders": File: "General Correspondence," letters, T. S. Woods to Rounsevelle Wildman, Jan. 25 and 26, 1899; Miscellaneous Manuscripts Collection: "Aguinaldo, Emilio, 1869–1964": Proclamation on "rules of war"; "From Over the Sea Comes Brave Mrs. Funston to the Home of her Childhood," *San Francisco Examiner*, Oct. 12, 1899; Russell Roth, "Forgotten Soldiers, Part I: With the 13th Minnesota Volunteers at Manila, 1898–99," *Bulletin of the American Historical Collection*, vol. 14, 1:54 (January–March 1986), 73–91; Frederick Funston, "The Making of a Regiment," *Scribner's Magazine*, 49:6 (June 1911), 652–53.

409 *warm, moonless night*: Sources on the first shots of the war on pages 409 to 413 include: Brian McAllister Linn, *The Philippine War, 1899–1902*, 44–46; Percy G. McDonnell, "The Battle of the Block-Houses: The War with the Insurgents in Manila," *Scribner's*, 25:66 (June 1899), 658; Isagani R. Medina, *Espionage in the Philippines (1896–1902) and Other Essays*, ed. Mirana Medina (Manila: UST Publishing House, 2002), 30–35, 40–41 (statement of Lt. Burt Wheedon), 44–45 (quoting three Filipino affidavits from Philippine Insurgent Records (PIR): Exhibit 818, in Spanish, PIR 65,4; "Testimony of Division General Artemio Ricarte y Garcia," Exhibit 818, in Spanish, PIR 65,4: "Letter of 'Commander Serapio,' Feb. 5, 1899," Exhibit 812, in Spanish, PIR 2018.8); Nebraska Historical Society, State Archives, Lincoln, NE: William Grayson Papers: Special Order 170, Muster Roll, Co. D; Medical Records 0919, 1004, 1087, 1168, 1271, 1352, 1436; Benito J. Legarda Jr., *The Hills*

of Sampaloc: The Opening Actions of the Philippine-American War, February 4–5, 1899 (Makati City, PI: Bookmark, 2001), 45; August 5, 1899, statement by William Grayson in Ora Williams, *Oriental America: Official and Authentic Records of the Dealings of the United States with the Natives of Luzon and Their Former Rulers* (Chicago: Oriental America Pub. Co., 1899), 79; Charles E. Russell, *The Outlook for the Philippines* (New York: Century Co., 1922), ff93; Crouch, *A Leader of Volunteers*, 63; Funston, *Memories of Two Wars*, 177–78; KHS: Ms. Coll. 67, Wilder S. Metcalf Papers (Diaries and Correspondence): box 1: "Diaries 1887–1904," Feb. 4, 1899; ACHS: Frederick Funston Collection: Section A: Early Life: Eckdall Collection: "Correspondence of Frederick Funston and a Letter by His Grandfather, James Mitchell": folder: "State Historical Society #1 (Misc.)": "Letters from the Wife of General Funston That Give a Vivid Idea of Her Life in Manila," Feb. 4, 1899, n.s.; Bain, *Sitting in Darkness*, 78; William McKinley, *Speeches and Addresses of William McKinley, from March 1, 1897, to May 30, 1900* (New York: Doubleday and McClure Co., 1900), 211–17; letter, Roosevelt to Lodge, Feb. 7, 1899, in Elting E. Morison, ed., *The Letters of Theodore Roosevelt*, vol. 2, 935; O'Toole, *The Spanish War: An American Epic*, 388–89; David B. Schirmer, *Republic or Empire: American Resistance to the Philippine War* (Cambridge, MA: Schenkman, 1972); Joshua E. Polster, *Stages of Engagement: U.S. Theatre and Performance* (Milton Park, U.K.: Routledge, 2015), 25; Esteban A. Ocampo, with Alfredo B. Saulo, *First Filipino Diplomat: Felipe Agoncillo (1859–1941)* (Manila: National Historical Institute, 1977), 91; Paolo E. Coletta, "McKinley, the Peace Negotiations, and the Acquisition of the Philippines," *Pacific Historical Review*, 30 (November 1961), 348.

413 *Such wars were necessary*: Sources for Rudyard Kipling's "White Man's Burden" on pages 413 to 414 include: Rudyard Kipling, "The White Man's Burden," *McClure's Magazine*, 12:4 (February 1899), 4; Mark D. Van Ells, "Assuming the White Man's Burden: The Seizure of the Philippines, 1898–1902," *Philippine Studies*, 43:4 (Fourth Quarter 1995), 607; Denis Judd, "Diamonds Are Forever: Kipling's Imperialism; Poems of Rudyard Kipling," 47:6 (June 1997), 37, 41–42; Rudyard Kipling, *The Letters of Rudyard Kipling*, vol. 2, ed. Thomas Pinney (London: MacMillan, 1990), 350; "The White Man's Burden," *Wikipedia*; Karnow, *In Our Image*, 142; John F. Bass, "The Philippine Revolt—Manila's Night of Terror," *Harper's Weekly*, 43:2209 (April 22, 1899), 401.

414 *Dewey's ships came to life with devastating accuracy*: Sources for the first days of the war on pages 414 to 418 include: Wolff, *Little Brown Brother*, 219, 221, 223–27; Crouch, *A Leader of Volunteers*, 71; Funston, "The Making of a Regiment," 656; USMCHC: COLL/3016: John Twiggs Myers Collection: box 1: folder 3: "Personal Correspondence, 1899": letter, Myers to brother Heywood, Feb. 7, 1899; Stuart Creighton Miller, *"Benevolent Assimilation": The American Conquest of the Philippines, 1899–1903*, 67; Van Ells, "Assuming the White Man's Burden," 618 (quoting the "Diary of Lt. Frederick Sladen," Feb. 8, 1899); "American Soldiers in the Philippines Write Home About the War": letter, Burr Ellis to his brother John, Feb. 8, 1899, www.historymatters,gmu.edu/d/58; Henri Turet, "The War in the Philip-

pines," 35, 46, 47; Immerwahr, *How to Hide an Empire*, 91–92, 92–93; Karnow, *In Our Image*, 144–45; U.S. Secretary of War, *Annual Report, 1900*, pt. 4, 560; Moorfield Storey and Marcial P. Lichauco, *The Conquest of the Philippines, 1898–1925* (New York: G. P. Putnam's Sons, 1926), 92–93; Maj.-Gen. E. S. Otis, *Report on Military Operations and Civil Affairs in the Philippine Islands, 1899*, vol. 1, pt. 4 (Washington, D.C.: Government Printing Office, 1899), 92, 95–96; Nick Joaquin, *A Question of Heroes: Essays in Criticism on Ten Key Figures of Philippine History*, 175; Roth, "Forgotten Soldiers," 77–78; Richard O'Connor, *Pacific Destiny: An Informal History of the U.S. in the Far East, 1776–1968* (Boston: Little Brown, 1969), xx.

419 *"There goes Kansas"*: Sources for the execution of prisoners on pages 419 to 423 include: KHS: Ms. Coll. 836, *Henry Ruppenthal Diaries*, March 1, 1899, 111–16; Bain, *Sitting in Darkness*, 79–81, 86–87; Blount, *The American Occupation of the Philippines*, 195, 200–201; Philip S. Foner and Richard Winchester, eds., *The Anti-Imperialist Reader: A Documentary History of Anti-Imperialism in the United States*, vol. 1 (New York: Holmes & Meier, 1984), 316–23; Crouch, *A Leader of Volunteers*, 86–88, 220–21; John F. Bass, "The Philippine Revolt—The Campaign in the North," *Harper's Weekly*, July 1, 1899, 648–50; Bain, *Sitting in Darkness*, 81, 83–84, 86–87; Karnow, *In Our Image*, 145–46, 148; KHS: Ms. Coll. 67, Wilder S. Metcalf Papers (Diaries and Correspondence): MS 1111 (Microfilm): newspaper article: "Filing of the Charges: Caustic Letter to Gen. Corbin Accompanies the Allegations," n.s., n.d.; newspaper article: "Impugning the Integrity of Gen. Funston," Jan. 9 or 10, 1900, n.s., n.p.; Ms. Coll. 836, *Henry Ruppenthal Diaries*, March 1, 2, 23, 1899, 116, 123, 135; U.S. Senate, *Affairs in the Philippine Island*, doc. 331, vol, 2, pt. 2, 1436, 1447, 1448, & pt. 3, 1428; "Spanish-American War: The 20th Kansas Volunteer Infantry," *Museum of the Kansas National Guard*, www.kansasguardmuseum.com; G. H. Fitch, "General Funston on Philippine Problems," *Harper's Weekly*, Nov. 11, 1899, 1143; U.S. Senate, *Affairs in the Philippine Islands*, doc. 331, pt. 2, 1436, 1447, 1448. (In 1912, the Judge Advocate General wrote, "I am not convinced from a careful reading of this report, that Private Brenner has made a false charge against Captain Bishop," and by extension Funston.)

423 *Some wondered about that decency*: Sources on the conduct of U.S. soldiers on pages 423 to 428 include: KHS: Ms. Coll. 33, Frederick Funston Collection: box 1, folder 3: "Correspondence, 1899": Eda Funston, "Rough Sketch of Manila" [edited transcript], 21–22; letter, Eda Funston to sister Elizabeth, June 4, 1899; box 3, "Miscellaneous Papers, Clippings, 1892–1932, Undated": folder, "Clippings, 1900–1910": "When Frederick Funston Was Neither Alive nor Dead," *Philadelphia Saturday Evening Post*, n.d., n.p.; Ms. Coll. 349, Garrett Collection: folder: "Diary of W. R. Smith, Philippine Insurrection," April 3 & 4–9, May 5 & 24, and June 12, 1899; Ms. Coll. 836, *Henry Ruppenthal Diaries*, June 2, 1899, 197; ILL: MS 394, Frederick S. Wild Papers: folder: "Correspondence, 1898–1899," letter, Wild to mother and father, April 20, 1899; May 27, 1899; Christopher R. Browning, *Ordinary Men: Reserve Police Battalion 101 and the Final Solution in Poland* (New York: Harper Perennial, 1998; 1st pub. 1993), 161; Ervin Staub, *The Roots of Evil: The Origins of Genocide*

and Other Group Violence (Cambridge: Cambridge University Press, 1989), 250–51 ff4; Funston, *Memories of Two Wars*, 266, 282, 285–87, 292–93, 295–96; "Spanish-American War: The 20th Kansas Volunteer Infantry," *Museum of the Kansas National Guard*; Bain, *Sitting in Darkness*, 91–92, 93; Marshall Everett, ed., *Exciting Experiences in Our Wars with Spain and the Filipinos: The Life of Admiral Dewey* (Chicago: Book Publishers Union, 1899), 486–87; Blount, *The American Occupation of the Philippines*, 193, 196, 206; Miller, "*Benevolent Assimilation*," 72–73; NARA: RG 94: Records of the Adjutant General's Office 1780s–1917: Spanish-American War Regimental Books: 20th Kansas Infantry, Morning Reports, Co. G to M, vol. 15: July–August 1899; E. S. Martin, "This Busy World," *Harper's Weekly*, July 15, 1899, 689; Crouch, *A Leader of Volunteers*, 194–95; LC/MS: Theodore Roosevelt Papers: Correspondence: Series 2: Reel 321—Apr. 28, 1899–Sept. 2, 1899: letter, Roosevelt to Funston, July 22, 1899.

23. THE FAR SIDE OF THE WORLD

429 *Lawton packed his wife, son, and three daughters*: Sources on doubts about Otis on pages 429 to 432 include: Steven L. Ossad, "Henry Ware Lawton: Flawed Giant and Hero of Four Wars," *Army History* (Winter 2007), 17–18, 18–19; Stanley Karnow, *In Our Image: America's Empire in the Philippines*, 147–48, 148–50, 152; Leon Wolff, *Little Brown Brother*, 239–40, 240–41, 241–44; LC/MS: Henry Ware Lawton Papers: box 3: folder 8: "Death of Lawton, printed matter": "General Lawton Killed at San Mateo," *Philadelphia Public Ledger*, Dec. 20, 1899, n.p.; Robert Dexter Carter, *A Civilian in Lawton's 1899 Philippine Campaign: The Letters of Robert D. Carter*, ed. Michael E. Shay (Columbia, MD: University of Maryland Press, 2013), 4–5; William Dinwiddie, "General Lawton in the Field," *Harper's Weekly*, July 29, 1899, 756; John F. Bass, "The Philippine Revolt—The Santa Cruz Expedition," *Harper's Weekly*, May 27, 1899, 616; Brian McAllister Linn, *The Philippine War, 1899–1902*, 106–15, 116; USAMH: Spanish-American War Veterans Survey Collection: box 8: "Kansas Infantry—20th, 21st, 22nd, and 23rd Regiments": folder 3: "20th Regiment, Kansas Infantry [1898-W-1078], Buchanan, Charles M., Co. D": "Experience with Censors," newspaper account from Summer 1899, n.d., n.p., n.s.

432 *outright victory was impossible*: Sources on the death of Antonio Luna on pages 432 to 436 include: Wolff, *Little Brown Brother*, 245, 246; Augusto de Viana, *Stories Rarely Told: The Hidden Stories and Essays on Philippine History* (Quezon City, PI: New Day Publishers, 2013), 62–66; Nick Joaquin, *A Question of Heroes: Essays in Criticism on Ten Key Figures of Philippine History*, 157, 177–78, 180–81, 181–83; Stuart Creighton Miller, *"Benevolent Assimilation": The American Conquest of the Philippines, 1899–1903*, 75–76; Carlos Quirino, "The Death of Luna," *Philippines Free Press*, Dec. 12, 1953, 20–21; Michael Morey, *Fagen: An African American Renegade in the Philippine-American War*, 80; Karnow, *In Our Image*, 156; Taylor, *The Philippine Insurrection*, vol. 4, 656–58; Augusto V. de Viana, ed., *The I Stories: The Philippine Revolution and the Filipino-American War as Told by Its Eyewitnesses and Participants* (Manila: University of Santa Tomas Publishing House, 2006), 106–109;

Teodoro A. Agoncillo, *Malolos: The Crisis of the Republic* (Quezon City, PI: University of the Philippines Press, 1960), 526–28; David Haward Bain, *Sitting in Darkness: Americans in the Philippines*, 189–90; Ambeth R. Ocampo, *Two Lunas, Two Mabinis: Looking Back 10*, 28–38, 39–44; Alfredo Saulo, *Emilio Aguinaldo Generalissimo and President of the First Philippine Republic* (Quezon City, PI: Phoenix Publishing House, 1983), 392; Ambeth R. Ocampo, *101 Stories of the Philippine Revolution*, 109.

436 *The rain fell in sheets*: Sources for Fagen and the Buffalo Soldiers after leaving Montauk Point on pages 436 to 442 include: Morey, *Fagen*, 45, 55–56, 65–66, 81–84, 86–87; Wolff, *Little Brown Brother*, 250–51; NARA: RG 94: Records of the Adjutant General's Office 1780s–1917: box 111, AGO File 17043 (filed with AGO 356 799): John W. Calloway, Co. F, 24th U.S. Infantry; AGO File 215561: Names of soldiers who performed duty as nurses or cooks in camp at Siboney; Entry 91: Enlistment Papers, U.S. Army, 1894–1912: Enlistment Papers, U.S. Army, 1894–1912: Faatz-Failer: "David Fagen": no. 901, 1898; no. 232, 1899; Microfilm M665, Roll 249: Returns from Regular Army Infantry Regiments, June 1821–December 1911: Twenty-Fourth U.S. Infantry, Co. H, January 1898–December 1899: Sept.–Oct., 1898; Nov. 25, 1898; Jan.–Feb. 1899; March 25, 1899; July–August 1899, 1899; Co. I, May–June 1899, "To forfeit to U.S. $5 per S.C. sentence June 7, '99," Sept. 11 and 22, 1899, Sept.–Oct. 1899; Theophilus Steward, *Buffalo Soldiers: The Colored Regulars in the United States Army*, 224–25; *Salt Lake Herald*, "Negro Troops to the Rescue," March 12, 1899; "They Knew Gen. Fagin," Oct. 30, 1900; *Salt Lake Tribune*, Oct. 8, 1898; "Will Reduce the 24th," Jan. 26, 1899; "Fever," May 1, 1899; Frank Schubert, "Seeking David Fagen: The Search for a Black Rebel's Florida Roots," *Tampa Bay History*, 22 (2008), 27; Willard B. Gatewood Jr., *Black Americans and the White Man's Burden, 1893–1903*, 111, 145–46; *Richmond Planet*: July 3, 1898; "A Vain Hope," Aug. 27, 1898; *Indianapolis Freeman*, Oct. 29, 1898; "James Alfred Moss, Colonel, United States Army," www.arlingtoncemetery.net/jamoss.htm; Francis B. Heitman, *Historical Register and Dictionary of the United States Army*, vol. 1 (Washington, D.C.: Government Printing Office, 1903), 732; U.S. War Department, *Correspondence Relating to the War with Spain*, 1018; *San Francisco Chronicle*, March 14, June 30, Oct. 20, Nov. 22 & 23, 1899; Feb. 18, 1900; "Blacks Should Not Enlist," *Broad-Ax* (Salt Lake City, UT), Aug. 7, 1899; Gatewood Jr., *Black Americans and the White Man's Burden*, 184; *Washington Bee*, Sept. 9, 1899; Richard E. Miller, "Black American Troops in the Philippines," *Bulletin of the American Historical Collection: The American Era in the Philippines*, 8:4 (October–December 1980), 76–77; Joseph P. McCallus, ed., *Gentleman Soldier: John Clifford Brown and the Philippine-American War* (College Station, TX: Texas A&M University Press, 2004), 40, 75, 101, 232–33, 267 ff14; *Army and Navy Journal*, 38 (April 13, 1901), 797; Willard B. Gatewood Jr., *"Smoked Yankees" and the Struggle for Empire: Letters from Negro Soldiers, 1898–1902*, 241–43, 251–55; Michael C. Robinson and Frank N. Schubert, "David Fagen: An Afro-American Rebel in the Philippines," *Pacific Historical Review*, 44:1 (February 1975), 71; "A Little Story from Manila," *Army and Navy Journal*, Nov. 11, 1899, 259; testimony of General Robert P. Hughes in Senate

Document 331, 57th Congress, 1st Session, *Hearings Before the Senate Committee on the Philippines*, vol. 1, 647; Stephen Bonsal, "The Negro Soldier in War and Peace," *North American Review*, 185 (June 7, 1907), 325; *Manila Times*, May 19, 1906.

442 *a reception none ever imagined*: Sources on Funston returning to the United States on pages 442 to 445 include: Crouch, *A Leader of Volunteers*, 186–88, 195–96, 202–209, 218–20, 227; *Harper's Weekly*: May 20, 1899, cover: "The Fighting Colonel of the 20th Kansas Volunteers, Who Has Been Promoted for Bravery"; "This Busy World," July 15, 1899, 689; "General Funston on Philippine Problems," Nov. 11, 1899, 1143; ACHS: Frederick Funston Collection: Section A: Early Life: Eckdall Scrapbook II: "How the Philippines Should Be Governed," *The Sunday Call*, n.d.; "Funston as a Professor" and "Would Make His Son a Senator," unattributed and undated news clippings; LC/MS: Theodore Roosevelt Papers: Correspondence: Series 1: Reel 3—1899 Aug.–1899 Dec.: letter, Funston in San Francisco to Roosevelt in Albany, New York, Nov. 23, 1899; Series 2: Reel 322—Sept. 2 1899–Jan. 31 1900: letter, Roosevelt to Funston, Oct. 17, 1899; letter, Roosevelt to Henry Cabot Lodge, July 1, 1899; Elting E. Morison, ed., *The Letters of Theodore Roosevelt*, vol. 2, 1023; Edmund Morris, *The Rise of Theodore Roosevelt*, 741; *Emporia Gazette*, June 26, 1899; KHS: Ms. Coll. 33, Frederick Funston Collection: box 3, "Miscellaneous Papers, Clippings, 1892–1932, Undated": folder: "Clippings, 1900–1910": "The Funston Club," n.d., n.s.; *San Francisco Call*, Nov. 2, 1899; *Chicago Tribune*, Nov. 3, 1899; *Iola Register*, Nov. 4, 1899, 4.

445 *autumn months of Funston's apotheosis*: Sources on Fagen's arrival in the Philippines on pages 445 to 449 include: Sanford M. Thomas, *War in the Philippines: A True Story* (Sanford Thomas, 1903), 14–15; NARA: RG 94: Records of the Adjutant General's Office 1780s–1917: box 1241, AGO File 431081: Letters and memos concerning "David Fagen, Deserter": "Information Slip on David Fagan [*sic*], Deserter"; RG 395/2133: box 3, LS593: letter, AAG Smith to AG Manila, Feb. 19, 1901; Microfilm M665, Roll 249: Returns from Regular Army Infantry Regiments, June 1821–December 1911: Twenty-Fourth U.S. Infantry, Co. I, Sept.-Oct. 1899, Nov. 1899; Karnow, *In Our Image*, 156–57; McCallus, *Gentleman Soldier*, 108; War Department, *Annual Report, 1901* (Washington, D.C.: Government Printing Office, 1902); Morey, *Fagen*, 91, 103–105, 106, 107, 108–109; Gatewood Jr., "*Smoked Yankees*," 248–49; "Suicide of a Sentry," *Manila Times*, Oct. 7, 1899; Gregg Jones, *Honor in the Dust: Theodore Roosevelt, War in the Philippines, and the Rise and Fall of America's Imperial Dream*, 128–29; William Thaddeus Sexton, *Soldiers in the Sun: An Adventure in Imperialism*, 180; *New York Herald*, March 17, 1912; Linn, *The Philippine War*, 145; *Richmond Planet*: April 29, Oct. 14, Nov. 11, 1899; *Indianapolis Freeman*, May 6, 1899; May 11, 1901 (William Simms letter); *Indianapolis Recorder*, May 7, 1899; Gatewood Jr., *Black Americans and the White Man's Burden*, 198–99; *St. Louis Post-Dispatch*, April 16, 1902.

24. PURSUED

450 *Otis's pinchers drew tighter*: Sources on Aguinaldo's flight through Tirad Pass on pages 450 to 459 include: Stanley Karnow, *In Our Image: America's Empire in the*

Philippines, 156–57, 158–59; Gregg Jones, *Honor in the Dust: Theodore Roosevelt, War in the Philippines, and the Rise and Fall of America's Imperial Dream*, 130–34, 136; William Thaddeus Sexton, *Soldiers in the Sun*, 180, 184, 188, 198; David Haward Bain, *Sitting in Darkness: Americans in the Philippines* (New York: Penguin, 1986; 1st pub. 1984), 192–94, 196–97; Sixto Y. Orosa, "Gregorio H. del Pilar," *Philippine Historical Association Historical Bulletin*, 4:3 (1960), 83–84, 85; Augusto de Viana, *Stories Rarely Told: The Hidden Stories and Essays on Philippine History* (Quezon City, PI: New Day Publishers, 2013), 91–93, 96, 97; Teodoro M. Kalaw, *An Acceptable Holocaust: The Life and Death of a Boy General* (Manila: National Historical Commission, 1999), 28, 48–54, 57, 61; Nick Joaquin, *A Question of Heroes: Essays in Criticism on Ten Key Figures of Philippine History*, 197–98, 201–206; Orlino A. Ochero, *"Bandoleros": Outlawed Guerrillas of the Philippine-American War, 1903–1907* (Quezon City, PI: New Day Publishers, 1995), 23; Brian McAllister Linn, *The Philippine War, 1899–1902*, 128, 148–51, 156; David R. Sturtevant, *Popular Uprising in the Philippines, 1840–1940* (Ithaca, NY: Cornell University Press, 1976), 96–97; Simeon A. Villa, "The Flight and Wanderings of Emilio Aguinaldo, from His Abandonment of Bayambang Until His Capture in Palanan," in U.S. Senate, *Affairs in the Philippine Islands: Hearings Before the Committee on the Philippines of the United States Senate*, 57th Congress, 1st Session, doc. no. 331, Part 3 (Washington, D.C.: Government Printing Office, 1902), 1987–1999, 2026 (hereafter Villa, "Flight and Wanderings"); Moorfield Storey and Marcial P. Lichauco, *The Conquest of the Philippines, 1898–1925* (New York: G. P. Putnam's Sons, 1926), 106–10; John T. McCutcheon wrote two accounts of the battle: "Aguinaldo's Rear Guard," in *Harper's History of the War in the Philippines* (New York: Harper, 1900), 317–21, and *Drawn from Memory* (Indianapolis: Bobbs-Merrill, 1950), 161–65; James H. Blount, *The American Occupation of the Philippines, 1898–1912*, 249; Telesforo Carrasco y Perez, *A Spaniard in Aguinaldo's Army: The Military Journal of Telesforo Carrasco y Perez*, trans. Nick Joaquin (Manila: Solar Publishing Corp., 1986), 45–46; Philippine Information Society, "The Luzon Campaign," *Facts About Filipinos*, 1:7 (August 1, 1902), 62, 63; John T. McCutcheon, *Stories of Filipino Warfare* (Menasha, WI: Banta, 1900), 27, 63.

459 *"Sublime Paralytic"*: Sources on the capture of Mabini on pages 459 to 461 include: Augusto V. de Viana, ed., *The I Stories: The Philippine Revolution and the Filipino-American War as Told by Its Eyewitnesses and Participants* (Manila: University of Santa Tomas Publishing House, 2006), 116–19; "Chasing Aguinaldo Through the Clouds," *New York Times*, Dec. 14, 1899, 1; Apolinario Mabini, "A Filipino Appeal to the People of the United States," *North American Review*, 170:518 (January 1900), 59–60; Morey, *Fagen*, 115.

461 *Otis raged*: Sources on the death of Henry Lawton on pages 461 to 463 include: U.S. War Department, *Correspondence Relating to the War with Spain*, vol. 2, 1107, 1113–14; *Leslie's Weekly*, June 16, 1900, 462; Sturtevant, *Popular Uprising in the Philippines*, 115–16; Jones, *Honor in the Dust*, 138–39; "Gen. Lawton's Advice," *New York Evening Post*, Sept. 16, 1899; Ossad, "Henry Ware Lawton," 5, 20; William

Dinwiddie, "General Lawton's Last Fight, San Mateo, Dec. 19, 1899," *Harper's Weekly*, Feb. 24, 1900, 175–76; Karnow, *In Our Image*, 159; "General Lawton Dead," *The Citrograph* (Redlands, CA), 25:23 (December 23, 1899), 1; Linn, *The Philippine War*, 160–61; "General Lawton Killed in San Mateo," *Philadelphia Public Ledger*, Dec. 20, 1899, 1; "Giant of Generals Laughed at Death," *New York Journal*, Dec. 20, 1899, 2; O. O. Howard, "Gen. Henry W. Lawton: A Sketch of His Long Service," *Bulletin of the American Historical Collection: The American Era in the Philippines*, vol. 26, 2:103 (April–June 1998), 7–11; "Lawton's Last Words," *American Heritage*, 33:5 (August/September 1982).

463 *Thousands lined Lawton's funeral procession*: Sources on Lawton's funeral on pages 463 to 464 include: Ossad, "Henry Ware Lawton," 21; "Funeral of General Lawton," *New York Times*, Dec. 31, 1899; George Hamlin Fitch, "Arrival of Gen. Lawton's Body," *Harper's Weekly*, Feb. 17, 1900, 150; Karnow, *In Our Image*, 159–60; LC/MS: Henry Ware Lawton Papers: Box 3, Folder 9: "Death of Lawton, printed matter," Unattributed cartoon; Folder 10: "Death of Lawton, printed matter," "Lawton, the Hero," unattributed clipping from Arizona newspaper.

464 *what of the man who shot him?*: "Licerio Geronimo," *Wikipedia*; "Luna's Sharpshooters," *Wikipedia*; LC/MS: Henry Ware Lawton Papers: Box 3, Folder 8: "Death of Lawton, printed matter"; Folder 10, "Lawton and the Filipinos," unattributed; "Death of General Lawton," *The Tribune* (Manila), Dec. 21, 1899, 1; letter from Daniel H. Dizon, History of Angeles, Villa Gloria, Angeles City, in "Tiradores de la Muerte" ("Shooters of Death"), *Philippine Defense Forces Forum*, http://webcache.googleusercontent.com.

464 *Aguinaldo's fate was a mystery*: Sources on Aguinaldo's flight through the mountains on pages 464 to 466 include: Epifanio de los Santos, ed., "The Flight and Wandering of Emilio Aguinaldo, from His Abandonment of Baymabang Until His Capture at Palanan," *Philippine Magazine* 23:1 (June 1926), 6–7; Bain, *Sitting in Darkness*, 276–77; Villa, "The Flight and Wanderings," 1991–97, 1999–2000.

25. THE AMERICAN CENTURY

467 *the United States had by accident*: "America at the Turn of the Century," www.loc.gov/collection/early-films-of-new-york-1898-to-1906/articles-and-essays/; "The American Experience: America 1900," www.pbs.org/wgbh/pages/amex/1900/timeline/index.html.

467 *"crossing the divide"*: Judy Crichton, *America 1900: The Turning Point* (New York: Henry Holt, 1998).

468 *Clara Maass reapplied*: Sources on Clara Maass in the Philippines on pages 467 to 470 include: NARA: RG 112: Records of the Office of the Surgeon General—Army: Entry 103, box 3: "Historical Files of the Army Nurse Corps, 1898–1947": File: "Philippine Islands": Emma Ruthfus, "A Nurse's Impression of the Philippine Islands," *The Dietetic and Hygienic Gazette*, n.d., 59–61; Entry 149, Personal Data Cards on War Contract Nurses, 1898–1917: box 4, MAD-REED: "Maass, Clara Louise"; Entry 230: Anita Newcomb McGee's Office Files: box 3: File: "Philippine

Islands": Mrs. E. C. Hemill and Ida D. Pipperti, "Shall We Fear Leprosy?" [typescript address]; Entry 26, box 303: File 52030: "Maass": Letter, Maass to Surgeon General Office, March 24, 1900; Michael Morey, *Fagen: An African American Renegade in the Philippine-American War*, 119–20; John Bass, "The Situation in Luzon," in *Harper's History of the War in the Philippines*, ed. Marrion Wilcox (New York: Harper, 1900), 218–22; Gregg Jones, *Honor in the Dust: Theodore Roosevelt, War in the Philippines, and the Rise and Fall of America's Imperial Dream*, 141–42, 146–47; Fred R. Brown, *History of the Ninth U.S. Infantry, 1799–1909* (Chicago: R. R. Donnelley and Sons, 1909), 441; Brian McAllister Linn, *The U.S. Army and Counterinsurgency in the Philippine War, 1899–1902* (Chapel Hill, NC: University of North Carolina Press, 1989), 53–54; U.S. War Department, *Annual Report, 1900*, vol. 1 (Washington, D.C.: Government Printing Office, 1901), 284–90; U.S. War Department, *Correspondence Relating to the War with Spain*, vol. 2: letter, Otis to AGO, Feb. 17, 1900, 1145; letter, Otis to AGO, March 26, 1900, 1153; letter, Otis to AGO, Jan. 8–10, 1900, 1130–31; Brigadier General George W. Davis, *Report on the Military Government of the City of Manila* (Manila: Headquarters Division of the Philippines, 1901), 37–39; MacArthur Memorial Library and Archives, Norfolk, VA (hereafter MAC): RG-20 Papers of General Arthur MacArthur, 1845–1912: Series 1: Official Correspondence: box 1: letter, Lt. Col. L. M. Maus to MacArthur, Jan. 21, 1905; Ken De Bevoise, *Agents of Apocalypse: Epidemic Disease in the Colonial Philippines* (Quezon City, PI: New Day Publishers, 2002; 1st pub. 1995), 12–13; Warwick Anderson, *Colonial Pathologies: American Tropical Medicines, Race, and Hygiene in the Philippines* (Manila: Ateneo de Manila University Press, 2007), 59, 60; John T. Cunningham, *Clara Maass: A Nurse—A Hospital—A Spirit* (Cedar Grove, NJ: Rae Publishing, 1968), 41; Laurie Garrett, *The Coming Plague: Newly Emerging Diseases in a World Out of Balance* (New York: Farrar, Straus & Giroux, 1994), 254–55.

470 *Charlie Sandburg's American Century*: Sources on Carl Sandburg's new century on pages 470 to 472 include: Penelope Niven, *Carl Sandburg: A Biography*, 45–53, 57–59, 51 ff716; "Carl Sandburg," *Twentieth Century Authors* (New York: H. W. Wilson, 1942), 1227–28; Carl Sandburg, *In Reckless Ecstasy* (Galesburg, IL: Asgard Press, 1904), 3; Philip R. Yannella, *The Other Carl Sandburg* (Jackson, MI: University Press of Mississippi, 1996), xv–xviii, 3–4, 6–8, 10–12; CS: folder: "Sandburg-Connemara": "Dr. Jekyll and Mr. Hyde" [typescript college assignment]; Carl Sandburg, *Ever the Winds of Chance* (Urbana, IL: University of Illinois Press, 1999; 1st pub. 1983), 49, 121, 158; Margaret Sandburg, ed., *The Poet and the Dream Girl* (Urbana, IL: University of Illinois Press, 1987), 74, 97, 112, 157; Carl Sandburg, "Timesweep," in *Honey and Salt: The Complete Poems of Carl Sandburg* (New York: Harcourt Brace Jovanovich, 1978), 758; Robert W. Merry, *President McKinley: Architect of the American Century*, 443–45.

472 *workshops for change*: Sources on Cuba under the military occupation on pages 472 to 474 include: Clifford L. Staten, *The History of Cuba*, 40–41, 42–43; U.S. Secretary of War, *Annual Report, 1900* (Washington, D.C.: Government Printing Office, 1901), 33; Charles S. Olcott, *The Life of William McKinley*, vol. 2, 203–205; *New*

York Times: "Gen. Wood at His Post," *New York Times*, Dec. 21, 1899, 4; "Banquet to Gen. Brooke," *New York Times*, Dec. 23, 1899, 5; Louis A. Perez Jr., *On Becoming Cuban* (Chapel Hill, NC: University of North Carolina Press, 1999), 106; interview, Francisca López Civeira, June 14, 2018; Hugh Thomas, *Cuba: The Pursuit of Freedom* (New York: Harper & Row, 1971), 466–68; 600; "History of Cuba," *Wikipedia*.

474 *the war's progress nor our own moral compass*: Sources on Funston's arrival in Central Luzon on pages 474 to 477 include: Brian McAllister Linn, *The Philippine War, 1899–1902*, 225, 255, 265–66; LC/MS: Henry T. Allen Papers: box 32: "Dept. of Visayas": letter, Arthur Murray to AGO, May 13, 1900; John A. Larkin, "Philippine History Reconsidered: A Socioeconomic Perspective," *American Historical Review*, 87:3 (June 1982), 612–13; Gerardo P. Sicat, "Crossroads Towards Philippine Economic and Social Progress," *Philippine Star*, Feb. 12, 2020; James H. Blount, *The American Occupation of the Philippines, 1898–1912*, 119n, 246; Morey, *Fagen*, 131–32; William Oliver Trafton, *We Thought We Could Whip Them in Two Weeks* (Quezon City, PI: New Day Publishers, 1990), 81, 82; Thomas W. Crouch, "The Making of a Soldier: The Career of Frederick Funston, 1865–1902" [a dissertation in partial fulfillment of a Ph.D. in history, University of Texas at Austin, 1969], 386–87; Frederick Funston, *Memories of Two Wars: Cuban and Philippine Experiences*, 314–15; Marshall McClennan, "Changing Human Ecology in the Central Luzon Plain: Nueva Ecija, 1705–1939," in *Philippine Social History*, ed. Alfred W. McCoy and Edward C. de Jesus (Quezon City, PI: Ateneo de Manila University Press, 1982), 57–91; Marshall McClennan, "Peasant and Hacendero in Nueva Ecija: The Socio-Economic Origins of a Philippine Rice-Growing Region" [a dissertation in partial fulfillment of a Ph.D. in history, University of California at Berkeley, 1973], 236–47.

477 *"quiet" did not mean "safe"*: Sources on the plight of black soldiers on pages 477 to 483 include: U.S. War Department, *Annual Report, 1900*, vol. 1, pt. 5, 133; pt. 3, 134; pt. 7, 505; NARA: RG 94: Records of the Adjutant General's Office 1780s–1917: Entry 91: Enlistment Papers, U.S. Army, 1894–1912: Duboc-Dudrey: "Edward A. DuBose" and Russell-Ruth: "Lewis Russell"; box 111, AGO File 17043 (also filed as 356 799): John W. Calloway, Co. F, 24th U.S. Infantry: Letter, John W. Calloway to Tomas Consunji, Feb. 5, 1900; RG 153: Office of the Judge Advocate General (Army): Entry 15: Court Martial Case Files, 1894–1917; RG 395/2282: Records of U.S. Army, Overseas Operations and Commands, 1898–1942: box 1, "TS Fifth District": letter, Gen. Grant to AG Manila, July 13, 1900; *St. Louis Post-Dispatch*, Feb. 16, 1902; Morey, *Fagen*, 114, 133–34, 210–11, 227; *Manila Freedom*, May 12, 1901; "The Charmed Class Ring," *Washington Post*, March 12, 1912, 3; Jonathan Dentler, "In the Shadow of the Black Man's Burden: Black Americans in and of the Philippines" [senior thesis, Columbia College, 12011], 46; Department of the Army, *Army Almanac: A Book of Facts Concerning the Army of the United States* (Washington, D.C.: Government Printing Office, 1950), 411; Gatewood Jr., ed., *"Smoked Yankees" and the Struggle for Empire: Letters from Negro Soldiers, 1898–1902*, 243, 244, 251–55; *Manila Times*: Aug. 26, Oct. 4, and Nov. 17, 1899, and May 11, 1900; Scot Ngozi-Brown, "African–

American Soldiers and Filipinos: Racial Imperialism, Jim Crow and Social Relations," *Journal of Negro History*, 82:1 (Winter 1997), 44–45, 50; Stuart Creighton Miller, "*Benevolent Assimilation*," 192, 193; *Cleveland Gazette*, Sept. 29, 1900; "A Fiery Response," *Richmond Planet*, Feb. 3, 1900, 1; Melvin G. Holli and Cornelius Gardner, "A View of the American Campaign Against 'Filipino Insurgents': 1900," *Philippine Studies*, 17:1 (January 1969), 97–99, 105, 109–10; "May the Soldiers Who Say 'Nigger' Get Killed," *Chicago Broad-Ax*, June 6, 1899; "May Negroes Who Volunteer Get Ball-Stung," *Helene (AR) Reporter*, Feb. 1, 1900; Stephen Bonsal, "The Negro Soldier in War and Peace," *North American Review*, 185 (June 7, 1907), 325–26; Christopher M. Redgraves, "African-American Soldiers in the Philippine War: An Examination of the Contributions of Buffalo Soldiers During the Spanish American War and Its Aftermath, 1898–1902" [a dissertation in partial fulfillment of a Ph.D. in history, University of North Texas at Austin, 2017], 93–95, 96; Luis Camara Dery, *When the World Loved the Filipinos, and Other Essays on Philippine History* (Manila: University of Santa Tomas Publishing House, 2005), 10–11; Telesforo Carrasco y Perez, *A Spaniard in Aguinaldo's Army: The Military Journal of Telesforo Carrasco y Perez*, trans. Nick Joaquin (Manila: Solar Publishing Corp., 1986), 94; Samuel K. Tan, *The Filipino-American War, 1899–1913* (Quezon City, PI: University of the Philippines Press, 2002), 249–50; James A. Leroy, "Race Prejudice in the Philippines," *Atlantic Monthly*, XC (July 1902), 104; T. Thomas Fortune, "The Filipino: A Social Study in Three Parts," *Voice of the Negro* I:3 (March 1904), 93–99.

483 *Aguinaldo's holiday in the plains of Nueva Vizcaya*: Sources on Aguinaldo consolidating power on pages 483 to 484 include: Villa, "Flight and Wanderings," 2006–29; David Haward Bain, *Sitting in Darkness: Americans in the Philippines*, 285; "Rebel Atrocities in Nueva Ecija," *Manila Times*, March 17, 1900, 2; Linn, *The Philippine War*, 196, 211–13, 260; Isagani R. Medina, *Espionage in the Philippines (1896–1902) and Other Essays*, ed. Mirana Medina (Manila: UST Publishing House, 2002), 24–25.

484 *atrocities are no longer surprising or rare*: Sources on increasing numbers of U.S. atrocities on pages 484 to 487 include: USAMH: Spanish-American War Veterans Survey Collection: box 69: "U.S. Volunteer Infantry—32nd and 33rd Regiments": folder 26: "U.S. Volunteer Infantry—33rd Regiment [1898-W-856], Nixon, Milton G., Co. G" [typescript memoir], March 25, April 22, and May 6, 1900; box 214: folder: "Wm. Eggenberger [1898-120], Co. K, U.S. 3rd Inf, 3rd Regiment": letter, William Eggenberger to "Dear Mother and all," March 26, 1900; Richie Routt Papers: box 1: folder 2: "E. C. Adams 17th Infantry, letter to his brother-in-law, Ed Gardner," May 28, 1900; Trafton, *We Thought We Could Whip Them in Two Weeks*, 83, 91; Leon Wolff, *Little Brown Brother*, 304–307, 366; *New York World*, July 26, 1900; *Washington Post*, Sept. 28, 1900; Crouch, "The Making of a Soldier," 400–401, 402–404; John W. Ganzhorn, *I've Killed Men* (London: Robert Hale Limited, 1910), 168–169; Funston, *Memories of Two Wars*, 319, 323–34; James A. LeRoy, *The Americans in the Philippines; a History of the Conquest and First Years of Occupation*,

vol. 2 (New York: Houghton Mifflin, 1914), 27 ff1; *New York Times*, July 22, 1900, 3; NARA: RG 94: Records of the Adjutant General's Office 1780s–1917: Entry 117: "41st Inf Letters Sent Book": letter, Clarence S. Nettles to Commanding Officer, Co. L, Guagua, PI, March 23, 1900; RG 395: Records of U.S Army, Overseas Operations and Commands, 1898–1942: Entry 4330: "Letters Received": Adjutant General to Commanding Officer, Malolos, and Commanding Officer, Caloocan, March 22, 1900; Morey, *Fagen*, 227; Linn, *The Philippine War*, 211–13; U.S. War Department, *Annual Report, 1901*, vol. 1, pt. 4, 93.

487 *Americans employed various torture techniques*: Sources on the "Water Cure" on pages 487 to 488 include: Paul Kramer, "The Water Cure," *New Yorker*, Feb. 25, 2008, 38; "Talks of the Water Cure," *Wadesboro (NC) Messenger and Intelligencer*, April 24, 1902, 2; Edward E. Brown, "Philippine Diary Notebooks," Dept. of Special Collections, Morris Library, University of Delaware; Morey, *Fagen*, 133–34; Sen. doc. 331, 57th Congress, 1st Session, 1903, 1767–1768; Massachusetts Historical Society: *George Frisbie Hoar Papers*: "Philippine Islands, File 2"; Richard E. Welch Jr., "American Atrocities in the Philippines: The Challenge and the Response," *Pacific Historical Review*, 43 (May 1974), 234–36; Medina, *Espionage in the Philippines*, 24–25; U.S. War Department, *Annual Report, 1901*, Appendix C:3; Will Smiley, "Lawless Wars of Empire? The International Law of War in the Philippines, 1898–1903," *Law and History Review*, 36:3 (August 2018), 548; Ambeth R. Ocampo, *101 Stories of the Philippine Revolution*, 62.

26. THE WILL OF THE PEOPLE

489 *evil had befallen the Philippines*: Sources on evil in U.S. troops on pages 489 to 490 include: Robert W. Merry, *President McKinley: Architect of the American Century*, 397–98; "Cost of the Philippine War," *New York Times*, March 7, 1900; first-year casualties as a part of overall statistics in "Philippine-American War," *Wikipedia*; Glenn A. May, "Why the United States Won the Philippine-American War, 1899–1902," *Bulletin of the American Historical Collection: The American Era in the Philippines*, vol. 13, 1:50 (January–March 1985), 84; Leon Wolff, *Little Brown Brother*, 306–307; "War Department Expenditures, Fiscal Years 1789–1948," in Department of the Army, *Army Almanac: A Book of Facts Concerning the Army of the United States* (Washington, D.C.: Government Printing Office, 1950), 692; Henry C. Rowland, M.D., "Fighting Life in the Philippines," *McClure's Magazine*, 19:3 (July 1902), 241, 243, 244, 247; Paul A. Kramer, *The Blood of Government: Race, Empire, the United States, and the Philippines* (Chapel Hill, NC: University of North Carolina Press, 2006), 148–50; "Rules for Filipinos," *Washington Post*, Jan. 17, 1900.

490 *"ambitious, optimistic, diligent, and above all, big"*: Sources for Taft's acceptance of his Philippine post on pages 490 to 491 include: Stanley Karnow, *In Our Image: America's Empire in the Philippines*, 167; Michael Morey, *Fagen: An African American Renegade in the Philippine-American War*, 398–99; Wolff, *Little Brown Brother*, 307–308; Merry, *President McKinley*, 399–400; "Judge Taft on His Mission," *New York Times*, Feb. 8, 1900; Jonathan Lurie, *William Howard Taft: The*

Travails of a Progressive Conservative (Cambridge: Cambridge University Press, 2014), 39–40; Stephen Kinzer, *The True Flag: Theodore Roosevelt, Mark Twain, and the Birth of the American Empire*, 159–60; Karnow, *In Our Image*, 167–69; Helen Taft, *Recollection of Full Years* (New York: Dodd, Mead & Co., 1914), 39–40.

491 *Change was certain*: Sources on changing times on pages 491 to 492 include: Brian McAllister Linn, *The Philippine War, 1899–1902*, 206; Karnow, *In Our Image*, 177; Wolff, *Little Brown Brother*, 309–10; Kinzer, *The True Flag*, 161–62, 209; Marshall S. Shatz, ed., *The Essential Works of Anarchism* (New York: Bantam Books, 1971), xii; Merry, *President McKinley*, 478; "Another Anarchical Maniac," *Manila Times*, Nov. 20, 1900, 1.

492 *man who replaced Elwell Otis*: Sources on Arthur MacArthur on pages 492 to 495 include: Karnow, *In Our Image*, 170–71, 172–73, 178–79; Linn, *The Philippine War*, 208–14, 216; William Manchester, *American Caesar: Douglas MacArthur 1880–1964* (New York: Dell Books, 1978), 41–48, 48–49; John Morgan Gates, *Schoolbooks and Krags: The United States Army in the Philippines, 1898–1902* (Westport, CT: Greenwood Press, 1973), 140–49, 192–99; LC/MS: Samuel B. M. Young Papers: box 6, "Letters Received 258": letter, John G. Balance to Young, April 17, 1900; Henry Ware Lawton Papers: box 2, "Correspondence": letter, Dean C. Worcester to Mrs. Henry W. Lawton, Oct. 10, 1900; Wolff, *Little Brown Brother*, 311–12; MAC: RG-20 Papers of General Arthur MacArthur, 1845–1912: Series 1: Official Correspondence: box 1: folder 15: "News Clippings, 1900": "MacArthur Will Take the Field," n.d., n.s.; Quijano de Manila, "The MacArthurs in the Philippines," *Philippine Free Press*, 57:16 (April 18, 1964), 4–5; U.S. War Department: *Annual Report, 1900*, vol. 1, pt. 7, 557–59; *Annual Report, 1901*, vol. 1, 91–93; and *Correspondence Relating to the War with Spain*, vol. 2, letter, MacArthur to AG, Aug. 31, 1900, 2:1001 and 2:1203–1204; *Literary Digest*, 21 (1900), 605–606; *Springfield Republican*, Nov. 14, 1900; Stuart Creighton Miller, *"Benevolent Assimilation": The American Conquest of the Philippines, 1899–1903*, 150; Morey, *Fagen*, 227–28; Gregg Jones, *Honor in the Dust: Theodore Roosevelt, War in the Philippines, and the Rise and Fall of America's Imperial Dream*, 206–207.

495 *Taft arrived in Manila on June 3*: Sources for Taft's arrival in Manila on pages 495 to 497 include: Wolff, *Little Brown Brother*, 312–13; Karnow, *In Our Image*, 172–73; Linn, *The Philippine War*, 216–17; William McKinley, *Instructions of the President to Philippine Commission, April 7, 1900* (Washington, D.C.: Government Printing Office, 1900), 6; Helen Taft, *Recollections of Full Years*, 39–45, 80–82; LC/MS: Henry Ware Lawton Papers: box 2, "Correspondence": letter, Dean C. Worcester to Mrs. Henry W. Lawton, Oct. 10, 1900; William McKinley Papers: Series 1: General Correspondence and Related Items, 1847–1902: Reel 11: letter, Taft and Philippine Commissioners to Elihu Root, Aug. 21, 1900; William H. Taft Papers: Series 3: General Correspondence and Related Material, 1877–1941: Reel 30: "1887, June 6–1900, June 30": letters, John M. Harlan and Howard C. Hollister, June 30, 1900; Reel 31: "1900, July 2–1901, Jan. 31": letters: Taft to Elihu Root, July 14, Aug. 18, Sept. 4, and Nov. 6, 1900; to Helen Taft, July 22, 1900; to William R. Day, Aug. 16, 1900; to Samuel

Dickson, Aug. 16, 1900; to Theodore Roosevelt, Sept. 4, 1900; to Horace Taft, Sept. 8, 1900; to Henry M. Hoyt, Sept. 8, 1900; to Charlie Taft, Nov. 6, 1900; Manchester, *American Caesar*, 45–47; Ralph E. Minger, "Taft, MacArthur and the Establishment of Civil Government in the Philippines," *Ohio Historical Quarterly*, 70:4 (October 1961), 308–31; Charles P. Taft, "Charlie—Baby Taft—in the Philippines," *Bulletin of the American Historical Collection: The American Era in the Philippines*, vol. 2, 3:8 (July 1974), 16–17; Merry, *President McKinley*, 438–39; "Report by Taft," *Washington Post*, Sept. 20, 1900; Oscar M. Alfonso, "Taft's Views on 'The Philippines for the Filipinos,'" *Asian Studies*, 6 (1968), 239–40.

497 *war wasn't ending soon*: Sources on effect of war on soldiers on pages 497 to 500 include: Merry, *President McKinley*, 439; "The Situation in the Philippines," *The Nation*, Aug. 16, 1900; Karnow, *In Our Image*, 171; Wolff, *Little Brown Brother*, 315; MAC: RG-20 Papers of General Arthur MacArthur, 1845–1912: Series 1: Official Correspondence: box 1: folder 15: "News Clippings, 1900": "A Soldier's Statement," *Baltimore Sun*, first reported in *Roanoke Dispatch*, n.d., n.p.; Melvin G. Holli and Cornelius Gardner, "A View of the American Campaign Against 'Filipino Insurgents': 1900," *Philippine Studies*, 17:1 (January 1969), 99, 103–14, 109; Lewis E. Gleeck Jr., "Lucban Besieged by Filipino Guerrillas (1899–1901)," *Bulletin of the American Historical Collection: The American Era in the Philippines*, 17:3 (July 1989), 79, 80 (although Gardener's name is often misspelled "Gardner" in newspapers and histories, it is "Gardener" in West Point records); ILL: MS 394, Frederick S. Wild Papers: folder: "Correspondence, 1898–1899": letters, Wild to Parents, April 20, 1899, May 27, 1899, Oct. 17, 1899; folder: "Correspondence, 1900": letters, Wild to Parents, Jan. 9, Jan. 31, May 7, & Oct. 2, 1900; Charles Francis Adams, *"Imperialism" and "The Tracks of Our Forefathers": A Paper Read by Charles Francis Adaams Before the Lexington, Massachusetts Historical Society* (Boston: D. Estes, 1899), 25.

500 *fear tripled the ranks of the Anti-Imperialist League*: Sources on Anti-Imperialists on pages 500 to 501 include: Bain, *Sitting in Darkness*, 182–83; Merry, *President McKinley*, 360–61; Joseph R. Stromberg, "The Spanish-American War as Trial Run, or Empire for Its Own Justification," in John V. Denson, ed., *The Costs of War: America's Pyrrhic Victories* (New Brunswick, NJ: Transaction Press, 1999, 2nd edition), 192–93; Philip S. Foner and Richard Winchester, *The Anti-Imperialist Reader: A Documentary History of Anti-Imperialism in the United States*, 235–36; Jennifer M. McMahon, *Dead Stars: American and Philippine Literary Perspectives on the American Colonization of the Philippines* (Quezon City, PI: University of the Philippines Press, 2011), 31–33; Kinzer, *The True Flag*, 133; William James, *Essays, Comments, and Reviews* (Cambridge, MA: Harvard University Press, 1987), 154–58.

501 *the one imperialists most feared*: Sources on Mark Twain on pages 501 to 502 include: David Zmijewski, "The Man in Both Corners: Mark Twain, the Shadowboxing Imperialist," *Hawaiian Journal of History*, 40 (2006), 55–73; Ron Powers, *Mark Twain: A Life* (New York: Free Press, 2006), 593; Albert Bigelow Paine, ed., *Mark Twain's Letters*, vol. 2 (New York: Harper & Brothers, 1917), 663; "Mark Twain Home, an Anti-Imperialist," *New York Herald*, Oct. 16, 1900, 4; Louis I. Budd, *Mark*

Twain: Social Philosopher (Bloomington, IN: Indiana University Press, 1962), 13; Helen Scott, "The Mark Twain They Didn't Teach Us About in School," *International Socialist Review*, 10 (Winter 2000), 61–65; Mark Twain, *Mark Twain's Speeches* (Charleston, SC: BiblioBazaar, 2007), 116; McMahon, *Dead Stars*, 35; Mark Twain, *Following the Equator and Anti-Imperialist Essays* (New York: Oxford University Press, 1996), 392; Mark Twain, "My Boyhood Dreams," *McClure's Magazine*, 14:3 (January 1900), 286; Joe Jackson, *A Furnace Afloat* (New York: Free Press, 2003), 216–17; Mark Twain, *The Mysterious Stranger*, in *Selected Shorter Writings of Mark Twain*, ed. Walter Blair (New York: Houghton Mifflin, 1962), 388.

502 *Redemption matters in an unjust world*: Sources on the election of 1900 on pages 502 to 504 include: Thomas A. Bailey, "Was the Presidential Election of 1900 a Mandate on Imperialism?," *Mississippi Valley Historical Review*, 24:1 (June 1937), 43, 45–46, 46–48; Karnow, *In Our Image*, 164–65; Merry, *President McKinley*, 378–80; *Harper's Weekly*, Oct. 13, 1900; Wolff, *Little Brown Brother*, 324–25; LC/MS: Leonard Wood Papers: box 28: "General Correspondence, 1900": folder: "April 1900": letter, Roosevelt to Wood, April 9, 1900; Elting E. Morison, ed., *The Letters of Theodore Roosevelt*, vol. 1, 1160; Theodore Roosevelt, *Works*, ed. Herman Hagedorn (New York: Scribner's, 1926), vol. 14, 342–45; Theodore Roosevelt, *An Autobiography* (New York: Macmillan, 1913), 127; Edmund Morris, *The Rise of Theodore Roosevelt*, 747–71; *Boston Evening Transcript*, Nov. 2, 1900; letter, Grover Cleveland to C. S. Hamlin, Sept. 13, 1900, in Allan Nevins, ed., *Letters of Grover Cleveland, 1850–1908* (Boston, 1933), 536; John W. Bailey Jr., "The Presidential Election of 1900 in Nebraska: McKinley Over Bryan," *Nebraska History*, 54 (1973), 579; *The Nation*, 171 (1900), 302.

504 *Aguinaldo promised far-flung guerrillas*: Sources of effects of election on guerrillas on pages 504 to 505 include: U.S. War Department, *Correspondence Relating to the War with Spain*, 1128–96; Bain, *Sitting in Darkness*, 202; Wolff, *Little Brown Brother*, 293, 322; Villa, "Flight and Wanderings," 2046–47; Gates, *Schoolbooks and Krags*, 163, 176, 189–90; Brian McAllister Linn, *The U.S. Army and Counterinsurgency in the Philippine War, 1899–1902*, 52, 58; "San Miguel Fight: Five Boys Killed, Seven Wounded," *Manila Freedom*, June 1, 1900, 1; NARA: RG 94: Records of the Adjutant General's Office 1780s–1917: AGO 459488, "Report of Capt. Charles D. Roberts to CO, 35th Inf., U.S.V., July 18, 1900."

505 *Funston and Fagen came to know each other well*: Sources on Funston vs. Fagen on pages 505 to 511 include: Thomas W. Crouch, "The Making of a Soldier: The Career of Frederick Funston, 1865–1902" [a dissertation in partial fulfillment of a Ph.D. in history, University of Texas at Austin, 1969], 408; Morey, *Fagen*, 108, 138, 139–42, 162–63, 166–68, 178, 411–12; *Davenport Weekly Leader*, July 24, 1900; Funston, *Memories of Two Wars*, 343, 351–53, 361–62, 364–73; *New York Times*, June 5, 1900; NARA: Microfilm M665, Roll 249: Returns from Regular Army Infantry Regiments, June 1821–December 1911: Fourth Cavalry, Troop H, August 1900, frame 151; Twenty-Second U.S. Infantry, January 1898–December 1899, Co. A, June 1900; RG395/2282: Records of US Army, Overseas Operations and Commands,

1898–1942: box 1, "Telegrams Sent": Funston to AG Manila, June 4, 1900; AG Manila to Plummer, Baliang, July 25, 1900; box 2, "Telegrams Sent and Received": A. H. Smith to Funston, San Miguel, Aug. 2, 1900; Funston to AG DNL, Aug. 6, 1900; RG 395: Records of U.S. Army, Overseas Operations and Commands, 1898–1942: LTR 1358, "Lieutenant David R. Stone," 22nd Inf., Co. F, Aug. 6, 1900," and "Sgt. H.D. Williams, Co. G, 34th Inf., USV, July 25, 1900"; "Filipinos Killed Deserter Fagin [*sic*]," *St. Louis Post-Dispatch*, April 16, 1902, 12; "Funston's Enemy," *Iola Register*, Apr. 23, 1902; *St. Louis Republic*, Feb. 5, 1902; Linn, *The Philippine War*, 270–71; U.S. War Department, *Annual Report, 1901*, vol. 1, pt. 7, 115–20, 370–73, 375–82; Ganzhorn, *I've Killed Men*, 167, 172–73, 175–77; Paul Dickson, *War Slang: American Fighting Words and Phrases from the Civil War to the Gulf War* (New York: Dover, 1994), 28; Redgraves, "African-American Soldiers in the Philippine War," 181–82; "Now a General in Filipino Army," *Caucasian* (Alexandria, LA), Nov. 1, 1900; "Now a General in Filipino Army," *Evening Star* (Washington, D.C.), April 24, 1902; "Funston's Enemy," *Topeka State Journal*, April 19, 1902; "Negro Deserter," *Cook County Herald* (Grand Marais, MN), Nov. 10, 1902; LC/MS: William H. Taft Papers: Series 8: "Philippine Commission, April 17, 1900–Oct. 12, 1903," Letter Book: letter, Taft to Elihu Root, July 14, 1900; *Manila Freedom*, July 26, 1900, 1; *New York World*, July 26, 1900; "He Was Fagin's [*sic*] Prisoner," *Piqua (OH) Daily Call*, Dec. 31, 1901; *Manila Times*, Aug. 3, 1900; "Lieut. Alstaetter's Ring," *Daily Herald* (Delphos, OH), Dec. 11, 1901, 3; "Lt. Alstaetter Talks of David Fagin [*sic*]," *New York Times*, Dec. 10, 1901; "Promoted for the Capture," *Leavenworth (KS) Times*, Dec. 10, 1904, 4.

511 *Funston found these victories intolerable*: Sources on Funston's growing anger on pages 511 to 512 include: NARA: RG 395/2282: box 2, "Telegrams Sent and Received": Funston to AG Dept. of Northern Luzon, Aug. 6, 1900; Funston to AG DNL, Aug. 12 and 18, 1900; AAG Alford to Funston, Aug. 18, 1900; Lt. Col. Keller to Funston, Aug. 16, 1900; Maj. Wheeler to AA Smith, Aug. 17, 1900; Funston to Wheeler, Aug. 28, 1900; box 3: Funston to AG DNL, Aug. 31, 1900; Taylor, *The Philippine Insurrection*, vol. 2, 276; "Talks of the Water Cure," *Messenger and Intelligencer* (Wadesboro, NC), April 24, 1902, 2; *Manila Times*, Sept. 3, 1900, 1; Morey, *Fagen*, 173; "Filipino Ingenuity," *Saint Paul (MN) Globe*, Sept. 29, 1900, 1; NARA: RG 94: Records of the Adjutant General's Office 1780s–1917: Microcopy 254, Reel 28: Philippine Insurgent Records (PIR), 658–54; *Philadelphia Inquirer*, Sept. 11, 1900.

512 *Sergeant Walter L. Washington of the Twenty-Fourth*: Sources for the attempted rescue and death of Sgt. Walter Washington on pages 512 to 514 include: NARA: Microfilm M665, Roll 249: Returns from Regular Army Infantry Regiments, June 1821–December 1911: Twenty-Fourth U.S. Infantry, 1895, 1898; RG 395/2261, box 3: "Letters Received": Funston to AG DNL, Sept. 14, 1900; Lt. Mitchell to AAG 4th District, Sept. 19, 1900 (including Mitchell's report of the action); RG 395/2263, box 3, "Telegrams Received": AA Smith to Morrison, Sept. 23, 1900; Michael C. Clark, "Improbable Ambassadors: Black Soldiers at Fort Douglas, 1896–99," in *Buffalo*

Soldiers in the West: A Black Soldier's Anthology, ed. Bruce A. Glasrud and Michael N. Searles (College Station, TX: Texas A&M University Press, 2007), 56; Ganzhorn, *I've Killed Men*, 172–73; *Manila Times*, Sept. 24, 1900, and Sept. 27, 1900, 1; *Kansas City Gazette*, Oct. 1, 1900, 1.

514 *Fagen became almost supernatural*: Sources on Fagen's demonization on pages 514 to 515 include: Joseph P. McCallus, *Forgotten Under a Tropical Sun: War Stories by American Veterans in the Philippines, 1898–1913*, 99–100; "The Renegade Fagan [*sic*]," *Manila Times*, May 14, 1901.

515 *the famous Lieutenant Alstaetter, held on Mount Corona*: Sources on the relationship between Fagen and Alstaetter on pages 515 to 516 include: "A Letter from Lieut. Frederick Alstaetter—His Gilded Cage," *Sandusky (OH) Daily Star*, Nov. 23, 1900; "Lieutenant Alstaetter Home," *Brooklyn Daily Eagle*, Sept. 12, 1901. 9; "He Was Fagin's [*sic*] Prisoner," *Piqua Daily Call*, Dec. 31, 1901; "Renegade Fagan [*sic*] in Town," *Manila Times*, Feb. 26, 1901, 1; "Funston's Enemy," *Iola Register*, April 23, 1902; Jose Alejandrino, *The Price of Freedom: Episodes and Anecdotes of Our Struggles for Freedom*, trans. Jose M. Alejandrino, 176; "Released Captive Joins His Corps," *Manila Times*, Nov. 17, 1900, 1.

516 *not good days to be a black soldier*: Sources on the army's treatment of black soldiers on pages 516 to 518 include: "Assaulted a Negro Ex-Soldier," *Manila Times*, May 11, 1900, 1; "A Negro Soldier's Lament," *Army and Navy Journal*, Feb. 2, 1901, 539; NARA: RG 395/1251, box 3, "Telegrams Received": Wheeler to AAG 4th District, Sept. 11, 1900; RG 395/2263, box 3, "Telegrams Sent": Funston to Freemana, Feb. 12, 1900; box 4, "Telegrams Received": Funston to AG DNL, Oct. 11, Oct. 25, & Oct. 26, 1900; RG 94, AGO 335956: Investigation of "Private Snyder" letter; AGO 403885, "Report by Capt. & Adj. J. B. Bachelor of investigation into ambush of Co. I, Oct. 10, 1900," Dec. 17, 1900; AGO 483885, Funston to AG 24th Infantry, Dec. 17, 1900; Microfilm M665, Roll 249: Returns from Regular Army Infantry Regiments, June 1821–December 1911: Twenty-Second U.S. Infantry, Troop A, Oct. 1900, frame 169; Morey, *Fagen*, 209–10, 239; *Manila Times*: "Recaptured from Insurgents," Oct. 16, Oct. 27, 1900; "Colored Troops in the Philippines," *Richmond Planet*, Sept. 30, 1899, 1; Funston, *Memories of Two Wars*, 343; *Salt Lake Herald*, Feb. 3, 1899; "Operator and Soldier Tells Rookie Story," *Lincoln (NE) Daily News*, June 8, 1914, 10; "American Deserter a Filipino General," *New York Times*, Oct. 29, 1900, 1.

518 *Sergeant Major John Calloway was among the first*: Sources on the fate of John Calloway on pages 518 to 521 include: NARA: RG 94, box 111, AGO File 17043 (also filed as AGO 365799): "John W. Calloway, Co. F, 24th US Infantry": letters, Capt. A. Williams, Provost Marshall, San Fernando, to Adj. San Fernando, Oct. 29, 1900; Freeman to Wheaton; Wheaton to MacArthur; Williams to AG of the Philippines, Dec. 12, 1900; "Report by Adj. C.H. Miller"; "Statement of John Calloway, Bilibid prison, December 11, 1900"; "John Calloway: 3rd Endorsement, Headquarters Division of the Philippines, Major General Arthur MacArthur, Commanding"; RG 153: Office of the Judge Advocate General (Army): Entry 15: Court-Martial Case Files,

1894–1917: Case #5077: John Calloway; Entry 15-AA-O, Oversized, Court Martials: Case #21757: John Calloway; Morey, *Fagen*, 213; Letter, John "Galloway" to *Richmond Planet*, published Dec. 30, 1899, in Gatewood Jr., *"Smoked Yankees,"* 251–55; Miller, *"Benevolent Assimilation,"* 299; U.S. Secretary of War, *Annual Report, 1900*, pt. 4, 630; Edward S. O'Reilly, *Roving and Fighting: Adventures Under Four Flags* (New York: Century Co., 1918), 102–104; McCallus, *Forgotten Under a Tropical Sun*, 95–97.

521 *Mark Twain had come home*: Sources on the homecoming of Mark Twain on pages 521 to 522 include: *New York World*, Oct. 6, 1900; Philip McFarland, *Mark Twain and The Colonel: Samuel L. Clemens, Theodore Roosevelt, and the Arrival of a New Century* (Lanham, MD: Rowman & Littlefield, 2012), 56, 62; *Chicago Tribune*, Oct. 15, 1900; *New York Herald*, Oct. 15, 1900; Kinzer, *The True Flag*, 179–80; Mark Zwonitzer, *The Statesman and the Storyteller: John Hay, Mark Twain, and the Rise of American Imperialism* (Chapel Hill, NC: Algonquin Press, 2016), 417; Bailey, "Was the Presidential Election of 1900 a Mandate on Imperialism?," 44; Wolff, *Little Brown Brother*, 332; Miller, *"Benevolent Assimilation,"* 148; LC/MS: Theodore Roosevelt Papers: Series 1: Reel 6—1900 June 27–1900 Nov. 16: letter, Funston to Roosevelt, Nov. 6, 1900; Reel 8—1900 Dec. 24–1901 Feb. 14: letter, Roosevelt to Funston, Dec. 24, 1900.

522 *McKinley won by about 861,000 votes*: Sources on the war through the end of 1900 on pages 522 to 526 include: Wolff, *Little Brown Brother*, 333–35; Bain, *Sitting in Darkness*, 203; Ambeth R. Ocampo, *Two Lunas, Two Mabinis: Looking Back 10*, 86–91; NARA: Microfilm M665, Roll 249: Returns from Regular Army Infantry Regiments, Twenty-Second Infantry, Co. A, Oct. 1900, frames 168, 169; RG 395/2263, box 3, "Telegrams Received": Wheeler to AA 4th District, Oct. 2, 1900; box 4, "Telegrams Sent,": Funston to AG DNL, Oct. 11, 1900; "News from San Isidro," *Manila Times*, Oct. 6, 1900; Alejandrino, *The Price of Freedom*, 176; "Fagan [*sic*] Is Slippery," *Manila Freedom*, Oct. 13, 1900, 1; Funston, *Memories of Two Wars*, 376, 380; Ganzhorn, *I've Killed Men*, 205, 206; KHS: Ms. Coll. 33, Frederick Funston Collection: box 1, folder 5: "Correspondence, 1901": letter, Magdalene Blankart to her mother, Dec. 26, 1900; letter, Eda Funston to family, San Isidro, Jan. 3, 1901; *Manila Times*, Dec. 14, 1900, 1; "Army Wife's Christmas," *Iola Register*, Dec. 24, 1906, 6.

27. WINNERS AND MARTYRS

527 *Every war has winners*: Edmund Morris, *The Rise of Theodore Roosevelt*, 776; USAMH: Samuel B. M. Young Papers, box 10, folder: "Correspondence, primarily with Presidents McKinley and Roosevelt," letter, Young to Roosevelt, Feb. 12, 1899.

528 *Edison had produced a series of films*: Sources on the PR war in the Philippines on pages 528 to 529 include: Nick Deocampo, "Imperialist Fictions: The Filipino in the Imperialist Imaginary," *Bulletin of the American Historical Collection Foundation*, 27:4 (October–December 1999), 47–50, 50–51; David Haward Bain, *Sitting in Darkness: Americans in the Philippines*, 216–17; KHS: Ms. Coll. 33, Frederick

Funston Collection: box 1, folder 2: "Correspondence. 1896–1898": Eda Funston to Elizabeth Cullen, Manila, Dec. 17, 1898; Frederick Funston, *Memories of Two Wars: Cuban and Philippine Experiences*, 398–99; NARA: RG 395/2263: Records of US Army, Overseas Operations and Commands, 1898–1942: box 5, "Telegrams Sent and Received": telegram, Funston to AG DNL, Jan. 5 & 6, Feb. 12, 1901; Michael Morey, *Fagen: An African American Renegade in the Philippine-American War*, 229, 232, 234–36; Frederick Funston, "Guerrilla Warfare in the Philippines," *Colliers Weekly*, 28:25, March 22, 1902, 5; John W. Ganzhorn, *I've Killed Men*, 187; U.S. Secretary of War, *Annual Report, 1901*, vol. 1, pt. 3 (Washington, D.C.: Government Printing Office, 1902), 155–56; *Manila Times*: "An Irresponsible Critic of 'Our American Cousins,'" Feb. 17, 1901, 1; "Renegade Fagan [*sic*] in Town" & "Closing in on Fagan [*sic*]," Feb. 26, 1901, 1; "The Mentality of Manila," March 6, 1901, 1; Ken De Bevoise, *Agents of Apocalypse: Epidemic Disease in the Colonial Philippines*, 13.

529 *Twain emerged as the premier Anti-Imperialist*: Sources on Twain as an Anti-Imperialist on pages 529 to 532 include: Paul Fatout, ed., *Mark Twain Speaking* (Iowa City, IA: University of Iowa Press, 1976), 369, 394; Stephen Kinzer, *The True Flag: Theodore Roosevelt, Mark Twain, and the Birth of the American Empire*, 180–81, 184–85; Randolph S. Churchill, *Winston S. Churchill: Youth, 1874–1900* (Boston: Houghton Mifflin: 1966), 524–25; *New York Herald*, Dec. 30, 1900; Morton N. Cohen, "Mark Twain and the Philippines: Containing an Unpublished Letter," *Journal of the Central Mississippi Valley American Studies Association*, 1:2 (Fall 1960), 29; Mark Twain, *Mark Twain's Weapons of Satire: Anti-Imperialist Writings on the Philippine-American War*, ed. Jim Zwick (Syracuse, NY: Syracuse University Press, 1992), xxii; Mark Twain, "To the Person Sitting in Darkness," in *Selected Shorter Writings of Mark Twain*, ed. Walter Blair, 298–99, 303–305; Leon Wolff, *Little Brown Brother*, 335–36, 336–38; Jim Zwick, "Mark Twain's Anti-Imperialist Writings in the 'American Century,'" in *Vestiges of War: The Philippine-American War and the Aftermath of an Imperial Dream, 1899–1999*, ed. Angel Velasco Shaw and Luis H. Francia (New York: New York University Press, 2002), 42–43; Albert Bigelow Paine, ed., *Mark Twain's Letters*, vol. 3 (New York: Harper & Brothers, 1917), 1113; *Springfield Daily Republican*, Feb. 3, 1901.

532 *One martial fantasy rarely changes*: Sources on the early plot to catch Aguinaldo on pages 532 to 535 include: James H. Blount, *The American Occupation of the Philippines, 1898–1912*, 332, 333, 338; USAMH: Spanish-American War Veterans Survey Collection: box 69: "U.S. Volunteer Infantry—32nd and 33rd Regiments": folder 26: "U.S. Volunteer Infantry—33rd Regiment [1898-W-856], Nixon, Milton G., Co. G": "Campaign diary," June 13, 1900; Villa, "Flight and Wanderings," 2019, 2039–60; Lazaro Segovia, *The Full Story of Aguinaldo's Capture* (Manila, 1902), x, 19, 23–24, 92, 140–42, 146–47, 153 ff1; Bain, *Sitting in Darkness*, 292–94, 296, 361–67; Emilio Aguinaldo, "The Story of My Capture," *Everybody's Magazine*, 5:24 (August 1901), 131–40; William Thaddeus Sexton, *Soldiers in the Sun: An Adventure in Imperialism*, 260, 261–64; Wolff, *Little Brown Brother*, 340–46; Funston, *Memories of Two Wars: Cuban and Philippine Experiences*, 384–426; KHS: Ms.

Coll. 33, Frederick Funston Collection: box 1, folder 5: "Correspondence, 1901": letters, Jan. 13 & 14, 1901; "Translated copies of captured orders from Emilio Aguinaldo and other Filipino insurgent leaders"; William F. Zornow, "Funston Captures Aguinaldo," *American Heritage*, 9:2 (February 1958), 24; G. B. Lang, "Funston and Aguinaldo," *Foreign Service* 3:8 (December 1914), 5–7; Emilio Aguinaldo and Vicente A. Pacis, *A Second Look at America* (New York: Robert Speller & Sons, 1957), 126–27, 128–29.

535 *That night, Funston couldn't sleep*: Sources on Aguinaldo's capture on pages 535 to 543 includes: NARA: RG 395/2263: Records of U.S. Army, Overseas Operations and Commands, 1898–1942: box 5, "Telegrams Sent and Received": telegram, Funston to AG DNL (Funston's Official Account), 122–30; *Manila Times*, March 28, 1901, 1; Morey, *Fagen*, 243–47; LC/MS: Theodore Roosevelt Papers: Correspondence: Series 1: Reel 13: "Capture of Aguinaldo," April 27, 1901; Frederick Funston, "How Aguinaldo Was Captured: Report of Brig. Gen. Frederick Funston, May 6, 1901," *Army and Navy Journal*, July 20, 1901, 1141–42; KHS: Ms. Coll. 33, Frederick Funston Collection: box 1, folder 5: letter, Magdalene Blankart to mother, Feb. 17, 1901; letters, Eda Funston to family, Feb. 26, March 9, 1901; Antonio K. Abad, "The Betrayal of General Aguinaldo," *Aguinaldo in Retrospect*, ed. Mauro Garcia (Manila: Philippine Historical Association, 1969), 211–12, 231–32, 233, 234–35; Samuel K. Tan, *The Filipino-American War, 1899–1913* (Quezon City, PI: University of the Philippines Press, 2002), 17; Blount, *The American Occupation of the Philippines*, 338; Taylor, *The Philippine Insurrection*, vol. 2, 32; "From the Islands," *Army and Navy Journal*, June 15, 1901, 1025; "General Aguinaldo and General Funston," *Bulletin of the American Historical Collection: The American Era in the Philippines*, 26:1 (January–March 1998), 81–82.

543 Vicksburg *sailed for three days*: Sources on Aguinaldo's return to Manila on pages 543 to 548 include: Jose Alejandrino, *The Price of Freedom: Episodes and Anecdotes of Our Struggles for Freedom*, 177; Karnow, *In Our Image*, 176–77; Dorothy Wickenden, "Late Harvest," *New Yorker*, Feb. 28, 2022, 37; Aguinaldo, "The Story of My Capture," 140; Stuart Creighton Miller, *"Benevolent Assimilation": The American Conquest of the Philippines, 1899–1903*, 168–69, 169–70; *San Francisco Call*, March 24, 25, 28, 29, and April 6, 1901; "Dewey and Aguinaldo," *New York Evening Post*, March 28, 1901, 1; *Baltimore Sun*, March 28, 1901; *San Francisco Chronicle*, March 29, 1901; *New York Times*, March 29, 1901; *New York Evening Journal*, March 28, 1901; "Funston's Nerve Took Wily Filipinos Off Their Guard," *New York Evening Journal*, March 28, 1901, 1; David Brody, *Visualizing American Empire: Orientalism and Imperialism in the Philippines* (Chicago: University of Chicago Press, 2010), 61–63; Wolff, *Little Brown Brother*, 346–47; *Springfield Republican*, March 29 & 30, 1901; *Literary Digest*, 22 (1901), 467–68; KHS: Ms. Coll. 33, Frederick Funston Collection: box 1, folder 5: telegram, Roosevelt to Funston, March 30, 1901; letters, Magdalene Blankart to family, April 2 & 15, 1901; *Literary Digest*, 22 (1901), 402–403; "Aguinaldo in Jail," *New York Evening Post*, March 28, 1901, 1; Karnow, *In Our Image*, 184; "Mail Items from the Philippines," *Army and Navy Journal*, Aug. 10,

1901, 345; William Manchester, *American Caesar: Douglas MacArthur 1880–1964* (New York: Dell Books, 1978), 47–48.

548 *Nature abhors an empire*: Herodotus, *History of the Greek and Persian War*, trans. George Rawlinson (New York: Washington Square Press, 1963; 1st pub. in Greek, circa 440 BCE), Book 7: 35, 263.

548 *conquerors strove against an invisible foe*: Sources on the campaign against yellow fever on pages 548 to 551 include: William H. McNeill, *Plagues and Peoples* (Garden City, NY: Anchor Books, 1976), 247; Joe Jackson, *The Thief at the End of the World: Rubber, Power, and the Seeds of Empire* (New York: Viking Penguin, 2008), 38–40; Laurie Garrett, *The Coming Plague: Newly Emerging Diseases in a World Out of Balance* (New York: Farrar, Straus & Giroux, 1994), 66–67 ff23, 628; Mildred Tengborn, *No Greater Love: The Gripping Story of Nurse Clara Maass* (St. Louis, MO: Concordia, 1978), 40–47, 76, 112–14, 115–17, 119–20; Enrique Chaves-Carbollo, M.D., "Carlos Finley and Yellow Fever: Triumph Over Adversity," *Military Medicine*, vol. 170, 10:881 (October 2005), 882–89; Manuel A. Jusino, "Nursing Imperialism: Clara Maass, Yellow Fever, and U.S. Ambitions in Cuba, 1898–1901" [a thesis in partial fulfillment of a M.A. in history, Rutgers University, 2012], 29–30; Mariola Espinosa, "A Fever for Empire: U.S. Disease Eradication in Cuba as Colonial Public Health," in *Colonial Crucible: Empire in the Making of the Modern American State*, ed. Alfred W. McCoy and Francisco A. Scarano (Manila: Ateneo de Manila Press, 2010), 289–90; U.S. Senate, *Yellow Fever: A Compilation of Various Publications*, 61st Congress, 2nd Session, doc. no. 520 (Washington, D.C.: Government Printing Office, 1911); Daniel Liebowitz, "Carlos Finley, Walter Reed, and the Politics of Imperialism in Early Tropical Medicine," *Pharos*, 75:1 (Winter 2012), 16–22; Walter Reed, James Carroll, Aristedes Agramonte, and Jesse W. Lazear, "The Etiology of Yellow Fever: A Preliminary Note," presented at the annual meeting of the American Public Health Association, Indianapolis, IN, Oct. 24, 1900, reprinted in *Military Medicine*, 166 (2001), Supplement 1, 29–36; University of Virginia Claude Moore Health Sciences Library, Charlottesville, VA (hereafter UVA): Philip S. Hench Walter Reed Yellow Fever Collection circa 1800–circa 1998 bulk 1863–1974: "Letter from Leonard Wood to Mabel H. Lazear, Nov. 4, 1900"; "Letter from Leonard Wood to the Adjutant-General, United States Army, November, 1900," http://yellowfever.lib.virginia.edu/reed.

551 *Clara Maass had recuperated in East Orange*: NARA: RG 112: Records of the Office of the Surgeon General—Army: Entry 103, box 3: "Historical Files of the Army Nurse Corps, 1898–1947": letter, Lt. Col. Mary G. Philips to Josiah C. Trent, March 23, 1947; John T. Cunningham, *Clara Maass: A Nurse—A Hospital—A Spirit* (Cedar Grove, NJ: Rae Publishing Co., 1968), 42–43, 44; Tengborn, *No Greater Love*, 115–17.

551 *Cuba had changed since January 1899*: LC/MS: Leonard Wood Papers: box 28: "General Correspondence, 1900": folder: "April 1900": letter, Wood to McKinley, April 12, 1900; ILL: MS 794, O. Batson Hinman Collection: box 1: folder: "Cuban Service Photograph Book"; "From the Islands," *Army and Navy Journal*, June 15,

1901, 1025; J. H. Hitchman, "The American Touch in Imperial Administration: Leonard Wood in Cuba, 1898–1902," *The Americas*, 24:4 (April 1968), 397; Philip C. Jessup, *Elihu Root, 1845–1909*, vol. 1 (New York: Dodd, Mead & Co., 1938), 304–305; Jack C. Lane, "Instrument for Empire: The American Military Government in Cuba, 1899–1902," *Science & Society*, 36:3 (Fall 1972), 322.

552 *Maass reported to Las Animas Hospital*: Sources on the life and death of Maass in Cuba on pages 552 to 556 include: U.S. Senate, "Report of the Yellow Fever Board," in *Yellow Fever: A Compilation of Various Publications*; Tengborn, *No Greater Love*, 119–22, 129–30, 134–35, 136–42; John R. Pierce, "'In the Interest of Humanity and the Cause of Science': The Yellow Fever Volunteers," *Military Medicine*, 168:11 (November 2003), 857, 861; *New York World*, Aug. 26, 1901; Leopoldine Guinther, "A Nurse Among the Heroes of the Yellow-Fever Conquest," *American Journal of Nursing*, 32:2 (February 1932), 176; UM: Cuban Heritage Collection: CHC5207—Fernando Lopez Fernandez Collection: "Clara Maass clippings"; Katja Wuestenbecker, "Maass, Clara Louise," *The Encyclopedia of the Spanish-American and Philippine-American Wars: A Political, Social, and Military History*, ed. Spencer C. Tucker, vol. 2: M-Z (Santa Barbara: CA: ABC-CLIO, 2009), 351–52; NARA: RG 112: Records of the Office of the Surgeon General—Army: Entry 26: box 303: File 52030: "Maass"; Entry 103, box 3: "Historical Files of the Army Nurse Corps, 1898–1947": File: Spanish American War Nurses, Certificate of Service: "Clara Maas [*sic*]"; box 733: File 108147: "Memorandum for the Secretary of War"; Entry 149, Personal Data Cards on War Contract Nurses, 1898–1917: box 4, MAD-REED: "Maas [*sic*], Clara Louise"; Entry 230: Anita Newcomb McGee's Office Files: box 2: File: "Spanish American War Nurses, Letters, Lists, Reports, from Dr. McGee": "Turner Memoir" (about conditions at Las Animas); "Brave Nurse Third Victim of the Yellow Fever," *New York Journal*, Aug. 26, 1901, 1; *New York World*, Aug. 26, 1901; Enrique Chaves-Carbollo, M.D., "Clara Maass, Yellow Fever and Human Experimentation," *Military Medicine*, vol. 178, 5:557 (2013), 559; W. C. Gorgas, *Sanitation in Panama* (New York: D. Appleton & Co., 1916), 40–51; UVA: Philip S. Hench Walter Reed Yellow Fever Collection circa 1800—circa 1998 bulk 1863–1974: Series III: Walter Reed Papers: "Fever Chart of Clara Louise Maass, August 14, 1901"; letter, Philip Hench to George A. Kellogg, Feb. 20, 1941: re: death of Maass; Series IV: Philip S. Hench Papers and Correspondence: "The Conquest of Yellow Fever" (typescript); letter, John R. Taylor to Philip S. Hench, Dec. 5, 1941, re: yellow fever tests; Series VI: Alphabetical Files: "Biographical Sketch of Clara Louise Maass."

556 *story of Clara Maass's death on the front page*: *New York Times*, Aug. 26, 1901, 1.

557 *symbols and rhetoric of martyrdom*: Lacey Baldwin Smith, "Martyrs," *Encyclopedia of Death and Dying*, www.deathreference.com/Kc-Ma/Martyrs.html.

558 *But not unforeseen*: Sources on the assassination of William McKinley on pages 558 to 562 include: Charles G. Dawes, *A Journal of the McKinley Years*, ed., Bascom N. Timmons, Aug. 3, 1900, 239–43; Kinzer, *The True Flag*, 209, 210–11; H. Wayne Morgan, *William McKinley and His America* (Syracuse, NY: Syracuse University Press, 1963), 520–21; Robert W. Merry, *President McKinley: Architect of the*

American Century, 478, 479, 481–82; Margaret Leech, *In the Days of McKinley*, 592–93, 595–96, 597–98, 600–601; "Career of Assassin," *Washington Post*, Sept. 8, 1901; *Chicago Daily News*, Sept. 8, 1901; *New York Times*, Oct. 30, 1901; *New York Tribune*, Sept. 7, 1901; Charles S. Olcott, *The Life of William McKinley*, vol. 2, 315–17; David Nasaw, *The Chief: The Life of William Randolph Hearst* (Boston: Houghton Mifflin, 2000), 156; *New Yorker*, Sept. 26, 1901; "The Martyred President," *Wikipedia*.

28. "BETWEEN THEM AND US IS A CHASM"

563 *Roosevelt took the oath of office*: Sources on Theodore Roosevelt, William Taft, and the Philippines on pages 563 to 566 include: Jacob Riis, *Theodore Roosevelt, the Citizen* (New York: Johnson, Wynne Co., 1904), 76; Edmund Morris, *The Rise of Theodore Roosevelt*, 778–80; Margaret Leech, *In the Days of McKinley*, 602; *New York Tribune*, Sept. 14, 1901; *New York Evening Post*, Sept. 14, 1901; Robert W. Merry, *President McKinley: Architect of the American Century*, 483; Leon Wolff, *Little Brown Brother*, 19, 349, 353; Oscar M. Alfonso, *Theodore Roosevelt and the Philippines, 1897–1909* (Quezon City, PI: University of the Philippines Press, 1970), 5, 34–37, 39–40, 45–47, 105; LC/MS: William H. Taft Papers: Series 3: General Correspondence and Related Material, 1877–1941: Reel 30: "1887, June 6–1900, June 30": letter, Taft to John M. Harlan, June 30, 1900; Reel 31: "1900, July 2–1901, Jan. 31": letter, Taft to Charlie Taft, Nov. 6, 1900; Series 8: "Philippine Commission, April 17, 1900–Oct. 12, 1903," Letter Book: letter, Taft to Root, Nov. 14, 1900; Theodore Roosevelt Papers: Correspondence: Series 1 & 2: letter, Sherrard Coleman to Roosevelt, May 16, 1900; letter, Funston to Roosevelt, Sept. 2, 1901; letter, Major General Adna Chaffee to Roosevelt, Dec. 1, 1902; Elihu Root Papers: "General Correspondence, 1870–1937": box 176: letter, Root to Sen. John T. Morgan, July 8, 1902; "Special Correspondence," B1, B162: letter, Roosevelt to Root, March 17, 1902; *Letter Book 15*, Red box 175: letter, Root to Lodge, May 5, 1902; Theodore Roosevelt, *Selections from the Correspondence of Theodore Roosevelt and Henry Cabot Lodge, 1884–1918*, vol. 1 (New York: Scribner's, 1925), 25; Mark Sullivan, *Our Times, 1900–1925* (New York: Charles Scribner's Sons, 1935), vol. 3, 16–18; Stanley Karnow, *In Our Image: America's Empire in the Philippines*, 199–200; *Senate Committee on the Philippines*, Sen. doc. 331, 57th Congress, 1st Session, part 4, 75, 77; Tacitus, *Agricola* (New York: Penguin, 1975; 1st pub. AD 98), 30.4; Theodore Roosevelt, *The Winning of the West* (Lincoln, NE: University of Nebraska Press, 1995), vol. 3, 44–45; Walter Lafeber, "'The Lion in the Path': The U.S. Emergence as a World Power," *Political Science Quarterly*, 101:5 (1986), 710, 712, 714; Stuart Creighton Miller, *"Benevolent Assimilation": The American Conquest of the Philippines, 1899–1903*, 71, 171, 174–75; "From the Islands," *Army and Navy Journal*, June 15, 1901, 1025; Michael Morey, *Fagen: An African American Renegade in the Philippine-American War*, 254; *Hazel Green (KY) Herald*, July 4, 1901, 1; KHS: Ms. Coll. 33, Frederick Funston Collection: box 1, folder 5: "Correspondence, 1901": letter, Magdalene Blankart to mother, May 20 & 27, 1901; *Literary Digest*, 23 (1901), 3; *Public Opinion*, 30 (1901), 885.

566 *The real target was the next generation*: Sources on the Thomasites on pages 566 to 568 include: Karnow, *In Our Image*, 196, 197; Edilberto P. Dagot, "American Teacher in Paraguay," *Bulletin of the American Historical Collection: The American Era in the Philippines*, vol. 12, 3:48 (July–September 1984), 82; Geronimo T. Pecson and Maria Racelis, eds., *Tales of American Teachers in the Philippines* (Manila: Carmilo & Bauermann, 1959); Eric Gamalinda, "English Is Your Mother Tongue/ Ang Ingles Ay ang Tongue ng Ina Mo," in *Vestiges of War: The Philippine-American War and the Aftermath of an Imperial Dream, 1899–1999*, ed. Angel Velasco Shaw and Luis H. Francia, 247, 248, 252; Ronald P. Gleason, ed., *The Log of the Thomas* (Publisher not specified, 1901), 11; Joe Jackson, *Black Elk: The Life of an American Visionary* (New York: Farrar, Straus & Giroux, 2016), 202–203, 398–99; Reynaldo Clemena Ileto, *Knowledge and Pacification: On the U.S. Conquest and the Writing of Philippine History*, 133, 251–57; Ileto, "The Philippine-American War: Friendship and Forgetting," in *Vestiges of War*, 13; Price W. Cooper, "The Life and Death of an Ilocos Public School Teacher (1901–1903)," *Bulletin of the American Historical Collection: The American Era in the Philippines*, vol. 10, 1:38 (January–March 1982), 45; "Remarks by U.S. Embassy Chargé d'Affaires Michael E. Malinowski in Honor of the Thomasites Centennial Memorial Program, August 26, 2001," *Peace Corps Online*, Feb. 17, 2003, www.peacecorpsonline.org/messages/messages/467/1011987 .html. (Though some sources say that 600 teachers arrived aboard the *Thomas*, most say the number was 540.)

568 *malaise swept through army ranks*: Sources on malaise and murder in the ranks on pages 568 to 570 include: *Army and Navy Journal*, June 15, 1901, 125; Aug. 2, 1902, 1217; *Honolulu Advertiser*, Nov. 13, 1901; Miller, "*Benevolent Assimilation*," 171, 196–97; USAMH: Papers of Major (Brigadier General) William A. Koble: "Diary of Field Service in the Philippines, 1898–1901," 42; *San Francisco Call*, Oct. 22, 1899; Anthony L. Powell, "Through My Grandfather's Eyes: Ties That Bind: African American Soldiers in the Filipino War for Liberation," *Sentenaryo/Centennial: The Philippine Revolution and Philippine-American War*, Jim Zwick, 4, http: //boondocksnet.com/centennial/sctexts/powell98a_d.html; ILL: MS 394, Frederick S. Wild Papers: folder: "Correspondence, 1902–1903": letters, Wild to parents, Jan. 4 & 8, 1902; "18 Reprimanded by Chaffee," *Barrington (IL) Review*, Aug. 1, 1902, 6; "Many Crimes in Philippines," *Rochester (NY) Democrat & Chronicle*, Oct. 23, 1901; "Victim Swung and Roasted," *Atlanta Constitution*, Oct. 27, 1901; Dennis Edward Flake, *The White Bandit: The 1901 Trial and Execution of George A. Raymond in Angeles Town, Philippines* (Angeles, PI: Holy Angel University Press, 2013), 33–42, 128–29; Karnow, *In Our Image*, 187; Brian McAllister Linn, *The U.S. Army and Counterinsurgency in the Philippine War, 1899–1902*, 219; William H. Carter, *The Life of Lt. General Chaffee* (Chicago: University of Chicago Press, 1917); LC/ MS: Henry Clark Corbin Papers, 1864–1980: box 1, "General Correspondence": File: "Chafee [*sic*], Adna Romanza, 1900–1904," letter, Chaffee to Corbin, Sept. 2, 1901"; U.S. War Department, *Annual Report, 1901*, vol. 1, pt. 7, 10–11; Frederick Funston, *Memories of Two Wars: Cuban and Philippine Experiences*, 436–37.

570 *shook American complacency*: Sources on the background of "Bloody Samar" on pages 570 to 574 include: Brian McAllister Linn, *The Philippine War, 1899–1902*, 223, 253, 306–309, 309–10; Bruce Cruikshank, "The Settlement of Samar in the Nineteenth Century," *Leyte-Samar Studies*, 12:1 (1978), 49; James H. Blount, *The American Occupation of the Philippines, 1898–1912*, 384; Rolando O. Borrinaga, *The Balangiga Conflict Revisited* (Quezon City, PI: New Day Publishers, 2003), 1–3, 5–6, 7–9, 22–40, 59, 63, 64–65, 173–74 ff38; Karnow, *In Our Image*, 189; Joseph P. McCallus, *Forgotten Under a Tropical Sun: War Stories by American Veterans in the Philippines, 1898–1913*, 131, 132–34; ILL: J. H. Grant Collection (privately held: J. H. Grant, "A Short Synopsis of the Military Service of Captain Joseph H. Grant" [typescript diary of Grant's service on Samar, 1901–1902], 6A; Taylor, *The Philippine Insurrection*, vol. 2, 426–38; Donald Chaput, "The American Press and General Vincente Lukban, Hero of Samar," *Leyte-Samar Studies*, 8:1 (1974), 22; Eugenio Daza, "Some Revolutionary Documents of the Philippine-American War in Samar," *Leyte-Samar Studies*, 17:2 (1983), 173; Gregg Jones, *Honor in the Dust: Theodore Roosevelt, War in the Philippines, and the Rise and Fall of America's Imperial Dream*, 139–40, 151–52, 210–14, 219–20, 226, 227, 229; "The Hemp Scheme," *Sunday Washington Globe*, Dec. 15, 1901, 2; U.S. Senate Report, "Col. H.O.S. Heistand," *Congressional Record*, 57th Congress, 1st Session, no. 91; Brian McAllister Linn, "The Struggle for Samar," in James C. Bradford, ed., *Crucible of Empire: The Spanish-American War and Its Aftermath*, 162; Rosario Nabong-Cabardo, "Balangiga!," *Samar Day*, Aug. 11, 1997 (Commemorative book published by Samar Provincial Historical Committee, 1997), 49 ff15; Donald Chaput, "Leyte Leadership in the Revolution: The Mayica-Lukban Issue," *Leyte-Samar Studies*, 9:1 (1975), 5 ff1; Joseph L. Schott, *The Ordeal of Samar* (New York: Bobbs-Merrill, 1964), 25–26, 27–28; U.S. Secretary of War, *Annual Report, 1902*, vol. 1, pt. 9, "Final report of Brig. Gen. Robert B. Hughes, U.S. Army, Commanding the Dept. of the Visayas," Nov. 30, 1901, 594; NARA: RG 153: Office of the Judge Advocate General (Army): Entry 15: Court-Martial Case Files, 1894–1917: Case # 34401, Edwin F. Glenn: testimony of George W. Davis, Feb. 16, 1903; RG 395: Records of U.S. Army, Overseas Operations and Commands, 1898–1942: Entry 2483, box 28: letter, Robert Hughes to AG, May 14, 1901; letter, Robert P. Hughes to J. E. Downes, Sept. 28, 1901; box 34: "Report of Operations for the Garrison of Laguan, Samar, P.I., for the month of June 1901"; box 49: letter, Mark L. Herseey to AG, Dept. of Visayas, July 7, 1901; Entry 2550, box 1: letter, Hughes to AG, June 3, 1901; box 36: "Statement of Sergeant C. Denning, Company H, 1st Infantry, June 30, 1901," in letter, John J. O'Connell to Commanding General, June 30, 1901; same letter—"Statement of Private Luther Jessup"; Entry 2551: letter, Robert Noble to AG, Sept. 10, 1901; U.S. Senate, *Affairs in the Philippine Islands: Hearings Before the Committee on the Philippines of the United States Senate*, 57th Congress, 1st Session, doc. no. 331, pt. 3 (Washington, D.C.: Government Printing Office, 1902), 1527–47, 2767; Robert Couttie, Jean Wall-Fee, and Rolando Borrinaga, "British Traders and Atrocities," *Balangiga Research Group: A Summary Interim Report of Inquiry, Sept. 28, 2001*, http://balangiga.bobcouttie.com.

574 *seventy-four men of Company C, Ninth Infantry*: Sources on the "Balangiga Massacre" on pages 574 to 580 include: Taylor, *The Philippine Insurrection*, exhibit 1350; Wolff, *Little Brown Brother*, 354–57; letters, Lt. Bumpus to "my dear father," Aug. 28 & Sept. 6, 1901, in Everitt C. Bumpus, *In Memoriam* (Norwood, MA: Norwood Press, 1902), 81, 82–83; Borrinaga, *The Balangiga Conflict Revisited*, 59–60, 65–66, 68–73, 73–83, 90–92, 93–118, 62 ff25, 168–69 ff8, 172 ff26, 173–74 ff38; Augusto V. de Viana, ed., *The I Stories: The Philippine Revolution and the Filipino-American War as Told by Its Eyewitnesses and Participants* (Manila: University of Santa Tomas Publishing House, 2006), 135–45; Miller, *"Benevolent Assimilation,"* 200, 201–205; Pedro Duran's account appears in Fr. Richard Arens, SVD, "The Early Pulahan Movement in Samar," *Leyte-Samar Studies*, 11:2 (1977), 61; Marconi M. Dioso, *A Trilogy of Wars: The Philippine Revolutionary Wars of 1896–1897, the Spanish-American War in the Philippines in 1898, and the Filipino-American War, 1899–1902* (Pittsburgh: Dorrance Publishing Co., 2004), 601, 602–603; Daza, "Some Revolutionary Documents of the Philippine-American War in Samar," 174–76; Robert Couttie, "What Went Wrong in Balangiga?," *Philippine Daily Inquirer*, Sept. 22, 2001, A12; Rolando O. Borrinaga, "Filipino Victory in Balangiga Recalled," *Philippine Daily Inquirer*, Sept. 28, 2001, A16; "Pvt. Adolph Gamlin's Account," in James O. Taylor, ed., *The Massacre of Balangiga: Being an Authentic Account by Several of the Few Survivors* (Joplin, MO: McCarn Printing Co., 1931), 1–16, 42–43, 25 ff1; G. E. Meyer, "The Massacre at Balangiga," and Col. E. G. Peyton, "Facts Concerning the Massacre of Company C, Ninth Infantry, at Balangiga, Samar, September 28, 1901," in James O. Taylor, ed., *The Massacre of Balangiga*, 1–16, 42–43; Capt. Edwin V. Bookmiller, "Report of the Action at Balangiga on September, 28th, 1901," dated Oct. 1, 1901, in "The Bookmiller Pages," http://balangiga.bobcouttie.com, 2; Karnow, *In Our Image*, 189–91; Jones, *Honor in the Dust*, 232–35; Reynaldo H. Imperial, "Balangiga and After," Paper Presented at the Balangiga Roundtable Conference, Tacloban, PI, Nov. 27–28, 1998; "The Terrible Massacre at Balangiga," *National Tribune*, Oct. 16, 1926; Fred R. Brown, *History of the Ninth Infantry, 1799–1909* (Chicago: R. R. Donnelly & Sons, 1909), 587–92; McCallus, *Forgotten Under a Tropical Sun*, 138–41; Linn, *The Philippine War*, 310–11; NARA: RG 395: Records of U.S. Army, Overseas Operations and Commands, 1898–1942: Entry 2076: "Returns of Casualties: Company C, 9th U.S. Infantry, Action in Balangiga, Samar, 28 September 1901"; Elam L. Stewart, "The Massacre of Balangiga," *Infantry Journal*, 30 (April 1927), 407–14; *San Francisco Call*, Sept. 30, 1901; Senate doc. 331, 57th Congress, 1st Session, 1591–99, 2284–310; Hosea 8:7.

29. "THE BETTER YOU WILL PLEASE ME"

581 *No single event in the Philippine War*: Sources on reaction to Balangiga on pages 581 to 583 include: Helen Taft, *Recollection of Full Years*, 225–26; *San Francisco Call*, Sept. 30, Oct. 21, & Nov. 16, 1901; *Public Opinion*, 31 (1901), 549; *Nation*, 73 (1901), 2; Stuart Creighton Miller, *"Benevolent Assimilation": The American Conquest of the Philippines, 1899–1903*, 205, 206; LC/MS: Stephen Bonsal Papers: box 7, "Subject

File": File: "Notebooks, Correspondence, Philippines, 1901–1945, Balangiga": letter, Jacob H. Smith to Bonsal, Nov. 29, 1901; Henry T. Allen Papers: box 7: "Correspondence, 1900–1902": Allen to Arthur Murray, Feb. 1, 1902; Allen to William Taft, Jan. 16 & Feb. 7, 1902; Elihu Root Papers: "General Correspondence, 1870–1937": box 23, S-T: letter, Taft to Root, Sept. 26, 1901; LC/MS: Henry Clark Corbin Papers, 1864–1980: box 1, "General Correspondence": File: "Chafee [*sic*], Adna Romanza, 1900–1904": letter, Chaffee to Corbin, Sept. 30, 1901; Gregg Jones, *Honor in the Dust: Theodore Roosevelt, War in the Philippines, and the Rise and Fall of America's Imperial Dream*, 236–40; Brian McAllister Linn, *The Philippine War, 1899–1902*, 312, 313, 315, 396 ff21, ff22; "Jacob H. Smith," *Wikipedia*; David L. Fritz, "Before the 'Howling Wilderness': The Military Career of Jacob Hurd Smith, 1862–1902," *Military Affairs*, 43:4 (December 1979), 186–90; NARA, RG 94, AGO File 425353Q: Telegram, Chaffee to AGO, May 5, 1902; RG 395, Entry 2065: letter, H. O. Heistand to Chaffee, Dec. 26, 1902 (although the phrase "howling wilderness" is usually ascribed to Smith, Heistand suggests that Chaffee was its author, and Smith would later say they were Chaffee's words); "The Struggle for Samar," in James C. Bradford, ed., *Crucible of Empire: The Spanish-American War and Its Aftermath*, 171; Teodoro M. Kalaw, *The Philippine Revolution*, 191.

583 *"Rape of Samar" began in Balangiga*: Sources on the "Rape of Samar" on pages 583 to 587 include: Marconi M. Dioso, *A Trilogy of Wars*, 605, 609–10, 610–11; Jones, *Honor in the Dust*, 241–43; U.S. Secretary of War, *Annual Report, 1902*, vol. 1, pt. 9, 188; "Littleton Waller's Testimony," Senate doc. 213, 57th Congress, 2nd Session (1903), 11; Joseph P. McCallus, *Forgotten Under a Tropical Sun: War Stories by American Veterans in the Philippines, 1898–1913*, 141; Linn, *The Philippine War*, 315–16, 319; Kalaw, *The Philippine Revolution*, 191–92; Jonathan Shay, *Achilles in Vietnam: Combat Trauma and the Undoing of Character* (New York: Scribner's, 1994), 3–21; Richard Holmes, *Acts of War: The Behavior of Men in Battle* (New York: The Free Press, 1985), 387–89; "'We Will Go Heavily Armed': The Marines' Small War on Samar, 1901–1902," in Stephen S. Evans, ed., *U.S. Marines and Irregular Warfare, 1898–2007: Anthology and Selected Bibliography* (Quantico, VA: Marine Corps University, 2008), 45; Stanley Karnow, *In Our Image: America's Empire in the Philippines*, 191; Andrew Pohlman, *My Army Experiences* (New York: Broadway Publishing, 1906), 67–68, 106–107; April 21, 1902, AP dispatch quoted in *The Philippine Review*, 2 (May 1902), 242; Richard E. Welch Jr., "American Atrocities in the Philippines: The Challenge and the Response," *Pacific Historical Review*, 43 (May 1974), 238 ff12; *Manila Times*, Oct. 26, 1901; Yates Stanley, *Sea Duty: The Memoirs of a Fighting Admiral* (New York: G. P. Putnam's & Sons, 1939), 76, 77,78–79; NARA: RG 153: Office of the Judge Advocate General (Army): Entry 15: Court Martial Case Files, 1894–1917: Case #34401: Edwin E. Glenn: George C. Davis testimony, Feb. 16, 1903; John N. Schumacher, *Revolutionary Clergy: The Filipino Clergy and the Nationalist Movement, 1850–1903* (Manila: Ateneo de Manila University Press, 1981), 144–46; ILL: J. H. Grant Collection (privately held): "Captain Joseph H. Grant Diary" [typescript diary of Grant's service on Samar, 1901–1902];

"Grant Leaving Post Owing to Ill Health of Family," n.d., n.s., 47; Secretary of War, *Annual Report, 1902*, vol. 1, pt. 9, 435–55, 612; Sen. doc. 213, 57th Congress, 1st Session, 14; Rolando O. Borrinaga, *The Balangiga Conflict Revisited*, 15, 17, 25–28, 30–31, 33–34, 39–40; James H. Blount, *The American Occupation of the Philippines, 1898–1912*, 490, 605–609, 615; telegram, Acting British Consul Sinclair to Home Secretary Lord Landsdowne, May 24, 1902, in Robert Couttie, Jean Wall-Fee, and Rolando Borrinaga, "British Traders and Atrocities," *Balangiga Research Group: A Summary Interim Report of Inquiry, Sept. 28, 2001*, http://balangiga.bobcouttie.com.

587 *"belt" the southern end of the island*: Sources for Waller's fatal "hike" across the southern end of Samar on pages 587 to 593 include: Dioso, *A Trilogy of Wars*, 614–15; Linn, "'We Will Go Heavily Armed,'" 46–48, 52 ff32; NARA: RG 153: Office of the Judge Advocate General (Army): Entry 15: Court Martial Case Files, 1894–1917: Case #10196: John A. Day; Case #30313: Littleton W. T. Waller; Testimony of Pvt. George Davis; RG 395, Entry 2070: General Order 93, Headquarters Division of the Philippines, May 7, 1902; Entry 2574, box 1: letter, Commander William Swift to Smith, Dec. 20, 1901; Entry 3451, box 1: letter, Waller to Smith, Nov. 19, 1901; Schott, *The Ordeal of Samar*, 104–106, 139, 142; USMCHC: COLL/719: Personal Papers, Hiram L. Bearss Collection: box 1: folder 3: "Typescript MSS of Unpublished Memoir," 285–86, 290–92, 297, 308–309; box 3: folder 5: "Samar, Philippine Islands: Research Material": letter, Frank Holford to Bearss, no date; COLL/1784: Personal Papers, Littleton W. T. Waller Sr. Collection: "Report of Maj. Littleton W. T. Waller" (1902), 43–48, 58, 60–64, 64–68, 76–77; Linn, *The Philippine War*, 316–17; COLL/2492: Joseph H. Hawkins Collection: folder: "Diary of Samar" (hereafter Hawkins Diary); Paul Melshen, "He Served on Samar," *Leatherneck: Magazine of the Marines*, 31:10 (October 1948), www.mca-marines.org/leatherneck/1948/10/he-served-samar; U.S. Senate, *Affairs in the Philippine Islands: Hearings Before the Committee on the Philippines of the United States Senate*, 57th Congress, 1st Session, doc. no. 331, pt. 3 (Washington, D.C.: Government Printing Office, 1902), 2341; Max Boot, *The Savage Wars of Peace: Small Wars and the Rise of American Power*, 121; Jones, *Honor in the Dust*, 166, 262, 264, 268; Joe Jackson, *A Furnace Afloat: The Wreck of the Hornet and the Harrowing 4,300-mile Voyage of Its Survivors* (New York: Free Press, 2003), 163; "Report of Lieutenant Kenneth P. Williams," in U.S. Secretary of War, *Annual Report, 1902*, vol. 1, pt. 9, 446.

593 *carnage was never blamed on Americans*: Sources on common themes of betrayal on pages 593 to 594 include: U.S. War Department, *Correspondence Relating to the War with Spain*, vol. 2, 1297; NARA: RG 153: Office of the Judge Advocate General (Army): Entry 15: Court-Martial Case Files, 1894–1917: Case #30313: Littleton W. T. Waller; Miller, "*Benevolent Assimilation*," 205; Dioso, *A Trilogy of Wars*, 617; Raymond L. Bridgman, *Loyal Traitors: A Story of Friendship for the Filipinos* (Boston: J. H. West, 1903), 95, 101; Perry E. Gianakos, "The Spanish-American War and the Double Paradox of the Negro American," *Phylon (1960–)*, 26:1 (First Quarter, 1965), 38–39; NARA: RG 153: Office of the Judge Advocate General (Army): Entry

15: Court-Martial Case Files, 1894–1917: Case #25594, "Pvt. Leonard Wilmore"; Case #42127, "Garth Shores"; Case #29958, "Garth Shores"; Case #15647, "John Dalrymple"; Case #22809, "William Victor"; Anthony L. Powell, "Through My Grandfather's Eyes: Ties That Bind: African American Soldiers in the Filipino War for Liberation," *Sentenaryo/Centennial: The Philippine Revolution and Philippine-American War*, Jim Zwick, ed., 4 parts, http://boondocksnet.com/centennial/sctexts/powell98a_d.html.

594 *greatest failure was the continued survival of David Fagen*: Sources on the "death" of David Fagen on pages 594 to 601 include: Miller, "*Benevolent Assimilation*," 205; Michael Morey, *Fagen: An African American Renegade in the Philippine-American War*, 252–54, 261–69; Linn, *The U.S. Army and Counterinsurgency in the Philippine War*, 86; Frederick Funston, *Memories of Two Wars: Cuban and Philippine Experiences*, 431–32, 434, 435; Jose Alejandrino, *The Price of Freedom: Episodes and Anecdotes of Our Struggles for Freedom*, 172–74, 174–76; Michael C. Robinson and Frank N. Schubert, "David Fagen: An Afro-American Rebel in the Philippines," *Pacific Historical Review*, 44:1 (February 1975), 78–79, 80–81; San Juan Jr., "An African-American Soldier in Philippine Revolution: A Homage to David Fagen," *Cultural Logic: An Electronic Journal of Marxist Theory and Practice*, 23; *Manila Times*, May 12, May 14, May 18, June 24, Sept. 18, Oct. 15, & Dec. 17, 1901; *Army and Navy Journal*, 38 (June 15, 1901), 1025; *San Francisco Chronicle*, Aug. 16 & 17, 1901; NARA: Microfilm M665, Roll 249: Regimental Returns, "Records of Events," Twenty-Fourth U.S. Infantry, Co. I, Sept.-Oct. 1899, November 1901, November–December 1901; NARA: RG 94: Records of the Adjutant General's Office 1780s–1917: box 1241, AGO File 431081: Letters and memos concerning "David Fagen, Deserter": "Report of Lt. R. C. Corliss to AG Second Separate Brigade, San Fernando, P.I., Dec. 6, 1901"; James A. Moss, "Information Slip on David Fagen, Deserter: letter, Corliss to AGO, Dec. 6, 1901; RG 391: Entry 1753, "Press Copies of Letters Sent to 24th U.S. Infantry," vol. 1: letter, Capt. E. B. Gose to Commanding General, Dec. 10, 1901; John W. Ganzhorn, *I've Killed Men*, 210–11; Frank Schubert, "Seeking David Fagen: The Search for a Black Rebel's Florida Roots," *Tampa Bay History*, 22 (2008), 31; *Indianapolis Freeman*, Dec. 14, 1901; "Fagan [*sic*] Reported Dead Just Once More," *Manila American*, Dec. 7, 1901, 1; *Leavenworth Times*, Jan. 19, 1902.

30. WAR BY ANY NAME

602 *The American people were tired*: Sources on General J. Franklin Bell on pages 602 to 604 include: Brian McAllister Linn, *The Philippine War, 1899–1902*, 219, 296–99, 299–304; LC/MS: Henry Clark Corbin Papers, 1864–1980: box 1, "General Correspondence": File: "Chafee [*sic*], Adna Romanza, 1900–1904," letter, Chaffee to Corbin, Sept. 2 & 30, 1901; letter, Chaffee to Corbin, Jan. 10, 1902; Elihu Root Papers: "General Correspondence, 1870–1937": box 164, letter, Taft to Root, Oct. 14, 1901; Charles P. Taft Papers: box I:23: "Family Correspondence, Taft Family, Helen (Herron) Taft (Mrs. William H.), 1875–1923": letter, Helen Taft to John Herron, Nov. 17, 1901; "J. Franklin Bell," *Wikipedia*; Stuart Creighton Miller, "Our Mylai of

1900: Americans in the Philippine Insurrection," *Transaction*, 19 (September 1970), 25; Paul A. Kramer, *The Blood of Government: Race, Empire, the United States, and the Philippines* (Chapel Hill, NC: University of North Carolina Press, 2006), 34–35; letter, James F. Bell to Apolinario Mabini, Aug. 28, 1900, & letter, Mabini to Bell, Aug. 31, 1900, in Apolinario Mabini, *The Letters of Apolinario Mabini* (Manila: National Historical Institute, 1999, 1st printing 1965), 259–60, 265–66; James H. Blount, *The American Occupation of the Philippines, 1898–1912*, 384; Glenn A. May, "The 'Zones' of Batangas," *Philippine Studies*, 29:1 (First Quarter 1981), 90–92, 94, 94 ff16 & ff17, 96, 103; Stanley Karnow, *In Our Image: America's Empire in the Philippines*, 188; Miguel Malvar, "Provisions and Instructions Issued by the Supreme Commander of Southern Luzon for Observation of This Department," Exhibits 1156, 1161, and 1168, in Taylor, *The Philippine Insurrection*, vol. 5, 329–33, 339–40; Reynaldo Clemena Ileto, *Pasyon and Revolution: Popular Movements in the Philippines, 1840–1910*, 163–65; Luis Camara Dery, *The Army of the First Philippine Republic, and Other Historical Essays* (Manila: De La Salle University Press, 1995), 123–29, 130–32, 140.

604 *issued "circulars" outlining the coming campaign*: Sources on Bell's campaign in Batangas on pages 604 to 610 include: Glenn A. May, *Battle for Batangas: A Philippine Province at War* (Quezon City, PI: New Day Press, 1993), 252; LC/MS: William H. Taft Papers: Series 3: General Correspondence and Related Material, 1877–1941: Reel 31: "1900, July 2–1901, Jan. 31": letter, Taft to Elihu Root, July 14, 1900; Henry T. Allen Papers: box 7: letter, Allen to Chaffee, Feb. 2, 1902; Dery, *The Army of the First Philippine Republic*, 123–24; Ambeth R. Ocampo, *101 Stories of the Philippine Revolution*, 54–55; Leon Wolff, *Little Brown Brother*, 358; Samuel K. Tan, *The Filipino-American War, 1899–1913* (Quezon City, PI: University of the Philippines Press, 2002), 86–87; Reynaldo Clemena Ileto, "The Philippine-American War: Friendship and Forgetting," in *Vestiges of War : The Philippine-American War and the Aftermath of an Imperial Dream, 1899–1999*, ed. Angel Velasco Shaw and Luis H. Francia, 15, 17; Canning Eyot, ed., *The Story of the Lopez Family: A Page from the History of the War in the Philippines* (Manila: Platypus Publishing, 2001; 1st pub. 1904, J. H. West Co. of Boston), foreword by Jim Zwick, 5–6, 7–9: letters, Juliana to Clemencia Lopez, Feb. 14 & 25, March 23, May 22, 1902, 78–80, 86, 95–97, 127–28; letter, Ignacio Laires to Clemencia Lopez, Aug. 1, 1902, 129–33; Sixto Lopez, "Christmas Letter to the President and People of the United States," *The Advocate of Peace*, 63:1 (January 1901), 21; Stuart Creighton Miller, *"Benevolent Assimilation": The American Conquest of the Philippines, 1899–1903*, 233; *Springfield Republican*, April 11, 1902; *Louisville Courier-Journal*, May 5, 1902; Marconi M. Dioso, *A Trilogy of Wars: The Philippine Revolutionary Wars of 1896–1897, the Spanish-American War in the Philippines in 1898, and the Filipino-American War, 1899–1902*, 615, 619–20; Michael Morey, *Fagen: An African American Renegade in the Philippine-American War*, 271–72; NARA: RG 94: Records of the Adjutant General's Office 1780s–1917: AGO 421607: Testimonies of Miguel Malvar, Eustacio Maloles, Noberto Mayo, Genero Brillante, and others; John Morgan Gates, *Schoolbooks and Krags:*

The United States Army in the Philippines, 1898–1902, 260–63; Daniel Immerwahr, *How to Hide an Empire: A History of the Greater United States* (New York: Farrar, Straus & Giroux, 2019), 101–102; A.V.H. Hartendorp, "Cholera," *Philippine Magazine*, 27:3 (August 1930), 172–74; Helen Taft, *Recollection of Full Years*, 253; Charles Engel, M.D., "Health Problems in the Philippine Islands in the American Era," *Bulletin of the American Historical Collection: The American Era in the Philippines*, vol. 4, 3:16 (July 1976), 20–21; Glenn May, "150,000 Missing Filipinos: A Demographic Crisis in Batangas, 1887–1903," *Annales de Démographie Historique* (1985), 215–43; Ken De Bevoise, "The Compromised Host: The Epidemiological Context of the Philippine-American War" [a dissertation in partial fulfillment of a Ph.D. in history, University of Oregon, 1986]; *Boston Journal*, May 5, 1902.

610 *moral reckoning began*: Sources on Waller's court-martial and its consequences on pages 610 to 614 include: Philip McFarland, *Mark Twain and The Colonel: Samuel L. Clemens, Theodore Roosevelt, and the Arrival of a New Century*, 202; Boot, *The Savage Wars of Peace*, 122–23; NARA: RG 94: Records of the Adjutant General's Office 1780s–1917: box 3069, AGO File 431056: "Court Martial and Trial of Littleton Waller, Genl. Order no. 93, Manila, Philippine Islands, May 7, 1902"; RG 153: Office of the Judge Advocate General (Army): Entry 15: Court- Martial Case Files, 1894–1917: Case #34401 (Edwin F. Glenn), box 17: letter, Edwin F. Glenn to Matthew F. Steele, Feb. 10, 1903; Rolando O. Borrinaga, *The Balangiga Conflict Revisited*, 16; Miller, "*Benevolent Assimilation*," 227; "'We Will Go Heavily Armed': The Marines' Small War on Samar, 1901–1902," in Stephen S. Evans, ed., *U.S. Marines and Irregular Warfare, 1898–2007: Anthology and Selected Bibliography* (Quantico, VA: Marine Corps University, 2008), 48; Joseph L. Schott, *The Ordeal of Samar* (New York: Bobbs-Merrill, 1964), Chapter 9; Paul Melshen, "He Served on Samar," *Leatherneck: Magazine of the Marines*, 31:10 (October 1948), www.mca-marines.org/leatherneck/1948/10/he-served-samar; Miller, "*Benevolent Assimilation*," 227, 232–33; Karnow, *In Our Image*, 193; *Washington Post*: "Republicans at Sea," March 15, 1902, and "Rebuff for Miles," March 17, 1902; Edmund Morris, *Theodore Rex* (New York: Random House, 2002), 97; Jones, *Honor in the Dust*, 296–97; *Evening Times*: "Gen. Miles' Retirement Has Been Decided Upon," March 22, 1902; "Gen. Miles Philippine Plan and the Correspondence," March 29, 1902; Richard E. Welch Jr., *Response to Imperialism: The United States and the Philippine-American War, 1899–1902* (Chapel Hill, NC: University of North Carolina Press, 1979), 138–41; *Manila Times*, Jan. 7, 1903; Linn, *The Philippine War*, 320–21; *Springfield Republican*, April 11, 1902; *New York Evening Post*, April 11, 1902.

614 *"Fighting Fred" Funston entered the fray*: Sources on Funston's Intemperate Tongue on pages 614 to 619 include: *San Francisco Call*, Jan. 19, 1901; March 9, 10, 11, 12, & 30, 1902; *San Francisco Call Sunday Magazine*, Jan. 26, 1902; Miller, "*Benevolent Assimilation*," 234–35, 239; David Haward Bain, *Sitting in Darkness: Americans in the Philippines*, 391–92; Elting E. Morison, *The Letters of Theodore Roosevelt*, vol. 3: Roosevelt to Speck von Sternberg, July 19, 1902, 298; *New York Sun*, March 10, 1902, 1; *New York Tribune*, March 9 & 12, 1902; ACHS: Eckdall Collection: folder:

"State Historical Society #1 (Misc.)": "An Embryonic Despot," March 20, 1902, n.s.; William F. Zornow, "Funston Captures Aguinaldo," *American Heritage*, 9:2 (February 1958), 24; KHS: Ms. Coll. 67, Wilder S. Metcalf Papers (Diaries and Correspondence): MS 1111 (Microfilm): letter, Charles F. Scott to Wilder Metcalf, March 17, 1902; *Colorado Springs Weekly*, March 12, 1902; *New York Times*, April 10, 1902; *Winnipeg Free Press*, April 6, 1902; William Allen White, *The Autobiography of William Allen White*, 501; LC/MS: Theodore Roosevelt Papers: Correspondence: letter, Roosevelt to Root, April 21, 1902; "Teddy and Freddy," *New York World*, April 24, 1902; *Boston Journal*, May 5, 1902; Sen. doc. 331, pt. 3, 2262–66; *New York World*, April 16, 1902.

619 *crystallized something in Mark Twain*: Sources on Twain's outspokenness on pages 619 to 620 include: Mark Foner, *Mark Twain, Social Critic* (New York: International Press, 1958), 377; Jim Zwick, *Confronting Imperialism: Essays on Mark Twain and the Anti-Imperialist League* (West Conshohocken, PA: Infinity Publishing Co., 2007), 155; John Sutton Tuckey, *The Devil's Race-Track: Mark Twain's Dark Writings* (Berkeley, CA: University of California Press, 1966), 376; Mark Twain, "A Defense of General Funston," *North American Review*, 174:156 (May 1902), 621, 622, 623, 624; Wolff, *Little Brown Brother*, 362–63; Robert L. Beisner, *Twelve Against Empire: The Anti-Imperialists, 1898–1900* (New York: McGraw-Hill, 1968), 81.

620 *Thirty thousand people hearkened to his words*: Sources on Roosevelt declaring an end to the war on pages 620 to 621 include: Welch, *Response to Imperialism*, 144–45; Theodore Roosevelt, *Presidential Addresses and State Papers*, vol. 1 (New York: The Review of Reviews, 1910), 56–67; Kramer, *The Blood of Government*, 55; *Boston Morning Journal*, May 31, 1902; Stephen Kinzer, *The True Flag: Theodore Roosevelt, Mark Twain, and the Birth of the American Empire*, 226; Miller, "*Benevolent Assimilation*," 250–51; "It Must Be Over Now," *Wahington Post*, May 6, 1902.

621 *"war" would drag on for another decade under another name*: Sources for the war's costs on pages 621 to 624 include: Immerwahr, *How to Hide an Empire*, 103–107; Wolff, *Little Brown Brother*, 360; Welch, *Response to Imperialism*, 148; Walter Lafeber, *The New Cambridge History of American Foreign Relations, Volume 2: The American Search for Opportunity, 1865–1913* (New York: Cambridge University Press, 2013), 165; Karnow, *In Our Image*, 194; *New York Times*, May 2, 1901, 1; Stephen Shalom, "Death in the Philippines," *New York Review of Books*, Dec. 17, 1981; Ken De Bevoise, *Agents of Apocalypse: Epidemic Disease in the Colonial Philippines*, 12–13, 158, 195 ff16; Resil B. Mojares, *The War Against the Americans: Resistance and Collaboration in Cebu, 1899–1906* (Quezon City, PI: Ateneo de Manila University Press, 1999), 135; Kinzer, *The True Flag*, 225; Drew Gilpin Faust, *This Republic of Suffering: Death and the American Civil War* (New York: Vintage, 2008), xi–xii; Miller, "Our Mylai of 1900," 28; Renato Constantino, *The Philippines: A Past Revisited*, vol. 1 (Manila: Constantino, 1975), 256; Morey, *Fagen*, 272–73; Kramer, *The Blood of Government*, 155; Zwick, *Confronting Imperialism*, 156–57; Victor Hurley, *Jungle Patrol: The Story of the Philippines Constabulary* (New York: E. P. Dutton

and Company, Inc., 1938), 76–77; "American Negro in League," *Manila American*, Nov. 14, 1902.

31. EXILES

625 *Much had changed in seven years*: Sources on the military occupation of Cuba and Richard Harding Davis on pages 625 to 628 include: "Thomas Estrada Palma: The First President of Cuba," *Richmond Planet*, May 10, 1902; Matt Huculak, "Davis, Richard Harding (1864–1916)," *Modernist Journals Project*, www.modjourn.org/biography/davis-richard-harding-1864-1916; Richard Harding Davis, "A War Correspondent's Kit," *Scribner's*, April 1905; Louis A. Perez Jr., *Cuba in the American Imagination: Metaphor and the Imperial Ethos*, 187, 195; G.J.A. O'Toole, *The Spanish War: An American Epic—1898*, 399; J. H. Hitchman, "The American Touch in Imperial Administration: Leonard Wood in Cuba, 1898–1902," *The Americas*, 24:4 (April 1968), 398 ff9, 398–99; Clifford L. Staten, *The History of Cuba*, 42–43; Richard Harding Davis, "The Passing of San Juan Hill," *Scribner's Magazine*, 38 (August 1905), 142, 144, 146, 148–49, 152–53; Davis, "The Death of Rodriguez," in *Cuba in War Time* (Lincoln, NE: University of Nebraska Press, 2000; 1st pub. 1898), 66; John Seelye, *War Games: Richard Harding Davis and the New Imperialism* (Amherst, MA: University of Massachusetts Press, 2003), 309; Scott C. Osborn, "Richard Harding Davis: Critical Background," *American Quarterly*, 12:1 (Spring 1960), 88, 92.

628 *The Philippine "police action" dragged on*: Sources on the postwar Philippines on pages 628 to 632 include: Michael Morey, *Fagen: An African American Renegade in the Philippine-American War*, 272–73, 291, 293; David R. Sturtevant, *Popular Uprisings in the Philippines 1840–1940* (Ithaca, NY: Cornell University Press, 1976), 118; Renato Constantino, *The Philippines: A Past Revisited*, vol. 1 (Manila: Constantino, 1975), 260; Brian McAllister Linn, "The Struggle for Samar," in James C. Bradford, ed., *Crucible of Empire: The Spanish-American War and Its Aftermath*, 175; Paul A. Kramer, *The Blood of Government: Race, Empire, the United States, and the Philippines* (Chapel Hill, NC: University of North Carolina Press, 2006), 154–55, 215–20; "Women and Children Killed in Moro Battle," *New York Times*, March 11, 1906; Jack C. Lane, *Armed Progressive: General Leonard Wood* (San Francisco: Presidio Press, 1978), 128; "Second Battle of Bud Dajo," *Wikipedia*; James H. Blount, *The American Occupation of the Philippines, 1898–1912*, 600; James Ford Rhodes, *The McKinley and Roosevelt Administrations, 1897–1909* (New York: Macmillan, 1922), 212–13, 212 ff2; Christopher A. Vaughan, "The 'Discovery' of the Philippines by the U.S. Press, 1878–1902," *The Historian*, 57:2 (December 1995), 313; *San Francisco Chronicle*, June 14, 1900; Stephen Bonsal, "The Philippines: After an Earthquake," *North American Review*, 174:544 (March 1902), 410, 417; LC/MS: William H. Taft Papers: Series 3: General Correspondence and Related Material, 1877–1941: Reel 37: "1902 Aug. 23–Dec. 31": letter, Taft to Jose del Vina, Juste Lucban, Leon Guerrero, and Alberto Barretto, Nov. 7, 1902; Oscar M. Alfonso, "Taft's Views on 'The

Philippines for the Filipinos,'" *Asian Studies*, 6 (1968), 240; Gustavus Ohlinger, "The Philippines in 1903," with notes by Mauro Garcia, *Philippine Historical Association Historical Bulletin*, 14:3–4 (September–December 1970), 217–18, 234, 242, 245; USAMH: Samuel B. M. Young Papers: box 10: folder: "Speech: Our Soldiers in the Philippines," 1, 6 [typescript speech before the Men's Club of the Church of the Epiphany, Washington, D.C., Nov. 13, 1902]; Honesto A. Villanueva, "Apollonario Mabini—His Exile in Guam," *Philippine Historical Association Historical Bulletin: Mabini Centenary Issue*, 8:2–3 (June–September 1964), 89–91; Augusto V. de Viana, ed., *Stories Rarely Told 2: Threads from Philippine History* (Quezon City, PI: New Day Publishers, 2018), 200–201; "The Case of General Aguinaldo," *Philippine Magazine*, 11:331 (November 1935), 540–41; "General Aguinaldo and General Funston," *Bulletin of the American Historical Collection: The American Era in the Philippines*, 26:1 (January–March 1998), 81–82; Satoshi Ara, "Emilio Aguinaldo Under American and Japanese Rule: Submission for Independence?," *Philippine Studies: Historical and Ethnographic Viewpoints*, 63:2 (June 2015), 167–69, 176–77, 184–85; Nick Joaquin, *A Question of Heroes: Essays in Criticism on Ten Key Figures of Philippine History*, 140; author's notes, March 20, 2019. The massacre of Moros at Bud Dajo is detailed in the recent Kim A. Wagner, *Massacre in the Clouds: An American Atrocity and the Erasure of History* (New York: Hachette Book Group, 2024).

632 *James Moss rode*: Sources on the postwar fate of Buffalo Soldiers in the Philippines on pages 632 to 634 include: KHS: Ms. Coll. 33, Frederick Funston Collection: box 1, folder 6: "Correspondence, 1902–1909": Capt. James A. Moss, 24th U.S. Infantry, "Journal of a Trip Through the Provinces of Pampanga, Nueva Ecija and Pangasinan, Covering Nearly All the Territory Occupied by the 24th Infantry from September, 1899, to June, 1902," 1–7; Willard B. Gatewood Jr., *Black Americans and the White Man's Burden, 1893–1903*, 272, 292; 313–34, 323 ff3; Rene G. Ontal, "Fagen and Other Ghosts: African-Americans and the Philippine-American War," in *Vestiges of War*, 129; Richard Johnson, "My Life in the U.S. Army, 1899–1922," in Anthony L. Powell, "Through My Grandfather's Eyes," pt. 5, *Sentenaryo/Centennial: The Philippine Revolution and Philippine-American War*; "Worthless Renegades," *Manila American*, Dec. 23, 1902, 1; U.S. Census Bureau, *Census of the Philippine Islands, 1903* (Washington, D.C.: U.S. Bureau of Census, 1905), 246; *Statistical Bulletin of the Philippine Islands, 1923* (Manila: Bureau of Printing, 1924), 3; NARA: RG94: box 111, AGO File 17043: John W. Calloway, Co. F, 24th US Infantry; RG 391: Records of U.S. Regular Army Mobile Units, 1821–1942: Entry 1753: Press Copies of Letters Sent to 24th US Infantry, vol. 1.: letter, Commander of 24th Infantry to Chief of Police, Manila, July 11, 1902; *Report of the Philippine Commission, 1903*, pt. 1 (Washington, D.C.: Government Printing Office, 1904), 397; *Manila Times*: July 11 & 13, 1906; "In the Philippines," *The Crisis*, 4 (April 1918), 279; Era Bell Thompson, "Veterans Who Never Came Home," *Ebony*, XXVII (October 1972), 104–106, 108–15; Gatewood Jr., *"Smoked Yankees" and the Struggle for Empire: Letters from Negro Soldiers, 1898–1902*, 316; C. Vann Woodward, *The Strange Career of Jim Crow* (New York: Oxford University Press, 2001; 1st pub. 1971), 96; John D.

Weaver, *The Brownsville Raid* (New York: W. W. Norton, 1970), 121; "Maggie Calloway," *Wikipedia*.

635 *first hint surfaced*: Sources on the ultimate fate of David Fagen on pages 635 to 638 include: Victor Hurley, *Jungle Patrol: The Story of the Philippines Constabulary*, 77; "American Negroes in League," *Manila American*, Nov. 14, 1902, 3; Morey, *Fagen*, 277–78, 282–83, 286–90, 332 ff16; "Renegade Fagan [*sic*] Last Seen in Manila," *Leavenworth Times*, March 17, 1903, 3; *Manila Freedom*, Feb. 5, 1903; *Manila Times*, Feb. 9, 1903, 1; "Renegades There: American Negroes Aided in Attack," *Evening Herald* (Ottawa, KS), Jan. 26, 1905; *New York Age*, April 20, 1905; George Yarrington Coats, "The Philippine Constabulary: 1901–1917" [a dissertation in partial fulfillment of a Ph.D. in history, Ohio State University, 1968], 205–206; John A. Larkin, "Philippine History Reconsidered: A Socioeconomic Perspective," *American Historical Review*, 87:3 (June 1982), 623; John A. Larkin, *The Pampangans: Colonial Society in a Philippine Province* (Berkeley, CA: University of California Press, 1972), 235–39; "Alarming Disaffection Spreading in Northern Luzon," *Manila American*, May 19, 1906, 1; "Fuzzy-Wuzzies on Warpath," *Manila Times*, May 9, 1906, 1; "Fagan [*sic*] Comes to Life," *Manila Times*, May 19, 1906, 1; "Fagan [*sic*] Again on Warpath," *Washington Post*, June 28, 1906, 1; *Report of the Philippine Commission, 1906*, pt. 1, 420; "Oust Island Bandit," *Rossville (KS) Reporter*, April 2, 1909, 3; Edwin Price Ramsey and Stephen J. Rivele, *Lieutenant Ramsey's War: From Horse Soldier to Guerrilla Commander* (New York: Knightside Publishing, 1990), 228–30; Ontal, "Fagen and Other Ghosts," 129.

638 *Captain Frederick S. Wild came home*: Sources on the "rootlessness" of veterans on pages 638 to 639 include: ILL: MS 394, Frederick S. Wild Papers: folder: "Correspondence, 1902–1903": letter, Wild to parents in Chicago, Aug. 30, 1902; "Reprimanded by Chaffee," *Barrington (IL) Review*, Aug. 1, 1902, 1; *Army and Navy Journal*, Aug. 2, 1902, 1217; *Daily Pacific Commercial Advertiser* (Honolulu): "Regular Army Officer Takes His Own Life," July 4, 1904; "Presidio Hears of Lt. Garber's Death," July 16, 1904; "Suicide Was Not Premeditated," *Hawaiian Star* (Honolulu), Aug. 10, 1904; *Seymour Daily Republican*, June 10, 1904, 1.

638 *Twain feared that something fundamental had broken*: Souces on the fate of Mark Twain on pages 639 to 640 include: Joe Jackson, *A Furnace Afloat: The Wreck of the Hornet and the Harrowing 4,300-mile Voyage of Its Survivors* (New York: Free Press, 2003), 216–17; Mark Twain, *The Mysterious Stranger*, in *Selected Shorter Writings of Mark Twain*, 388; Jim Zwick, ed., *Mark Twain's Weapons of Satire: Anti-Imperialist Writings on the Philippine-American War*, xxvii, 12–13, 23–39; Edward J. Blum, "God's Imperialism: Mark Twain and the Religious War Between Imperialists and Anti-Imperialists," *Journal of Transnational American Studies*, 1:1 (February 16, 2009), 35; Jim Zwick, *Confronting Imperialism: Essays on Mark Twain and the Anti-Imperialist League* (West Conshohocken, PA: Infinity Publishing Co., 2007), 164–66.

639 *the year that Sandburg changed his name back to "Carl"*: Sources on the anger of Carl Sandburg on pages 640 to 643 include: Penelope Niven, *Carl Sandburg: A Biog-*

raphy, 2, 65, 338–39; Philip R. Yannella, *The Other Carl Sandburg* (Jackson, MI: University Press of Mississippi, 1996), xv–xvi, 13–14, 42, 43, 47; Carl Sandburg, *Ever the Winds of Chance* (Urbana, IL: University of Illinois Press, 1999; 1st pub. 1983), 121, 131–32; CS: folder: "Sandburg-Connemara": "Notes: Systems and Milwaukee documents: (typed notes on pocket notebook pages, "Inventory Notes 20-8-1a," 1909–1911; "Notes: Systems and Milwaukee documents: 2-002-009"; "Looking 'Em Over," *International Socialist Review*, 16 (September 1915), 132–37; Carl Sandburg, *Chicago Poems* (New York: Dover, 1994; 1st pub. 1916): "Halstead Street Car," 4; "Fight," 40; "Under," 49–50; LC/MS: Theodore Roosevelt Papers: Series 5: Speeches and Executive Orders, 1899–1918; Subseries 5A: Speeches and Executive Orders, 1899–1918: Reel 423: 1912, Aug. 6–1918, Feb. 24: "Speech of Theodore Roosevelt at Dexter Pavilion, Union Stock Yards, Chicago, April 28, 1917"; Carl Sandburg, *Always the Young Strangers* (New York: Harcourt, Brace, 1952), 418; Carl Sandburg, *Abraham Lincoln: The Prairie Years* (New York: Harcourt Brace Jovanovich, 1982; 1st pub. 1925), 17; Carl Sandburg, *Abraham Lincoln: The War Years* (New York: Harcourt, Brace & Co., 1939), 9.

643 *"It was a beautiful morning with no wind"*: Sources on Frederick Funston's postwar fortunes on pages 643 to 648 include: Frederick Funston, "How the Army Worked to Save San Francisco," *Cosmopolitan*, 41:3 (July 1906), 239–48; Simon Winchester, *A Crack in the Edge of the World: America and the Great California Earthquake of 1906*, 301–302; KHS: Ms. Coll. 33, Frederick Funston Collection: box 1, folder 6: Funston, *Report to the Secretary of War*, May 17, 1906, 3; box 2, folder 1, "Correspondence, 1912–1913": letter, Funston to U.S. Senator Charles Curtis, July 13, 1912; letter, Funston to U.S. Senator Joseph Bristow, Sept. 28, 1912, 19, 24; letter, Funston to U.S. Rep. James Hay, Nov. 13 & 15, 1912; letter, Funston to Leonard Wood, Aug. 25, 1913; letter, Funston to Leonard Wood, Dec. 1, 1913; folder 4: "Correspondence, 1917": letter, Funston to Eda Funston, Feb. 15, 1917; telegram, Fitzhugh Lee to Eda Funston, Feb. 19, 1917, 11:52 p.m."; CHS: Frederick Funston Collection: Section A: Early Life: Eckdall Collection: "Correspondence of Frederick Funston and a Letter by His Grandfather, James Mitchell": folder: "State Historical Society #1 (Misc.)": letter, Gov. George E. Pardee to Funston, June 4, 1906; Section C: Philippines: Dave Young, "Maj. Gen. Frederick Funston, Kansas National Guard's Greatest Soldier," *Plains Guardsman*, Oct. 1997, n.p.; : Staten, *The History of Cuba*, 46–47, 47–48; Allan Reed Millett, *The Politics of Intervention: The Military Occupation of Cuba, 1906–1909* (Columbus, OH: Ohio State University Press, 1968), 66–67, 106–107; LC/MS: Theodore Roosevelt Papers: Series 1: Letters and Related Material, 1759–1919: Reel 69: 1906, Oct. 1–Nov. 6: letter, Taft to Roosevelt, Oct. 8, 1906; "Funston in Duel with Burglar," *The Congregationalist* (Boston), April 27, 1912; William Allen White, *The Autobiography of William Allen White*, 502, 532; interview, Kurtis Russell, director, Allen County Historical Society & Research Archives, Iola, KS.; Douglas MacArthur, *Reminiscences* (Annapolis, MD: Naval Institute Press, 2012; 1st pub. 1964), 47.

EPILOGUE: THE RECKONING

649 *Historians tend to see 1898–1902 as a mistake*: Sources on historical analysis of era on pages 649 to 651 include: Charles Mackay, *Extraordinary Popular Delusions and the Madness of Crowds* (New York: Harmony Books, 1980; 1st pub. London: Richard Bentley, 2nd edition, 1852), xx; Edward P. Crapol, "Coming to Terms with Empire: The Historiography of Late-Nineteenth Century American Foreign Relations," *Diplomatic History*, 16 (Fall 1992), 577–78; "Soul," *The New Shorter Oxford English Dictionary: On Historical Principles*, N–Z, vol. 2, ed. Lesley Brown (Oxford: Clarenden Press, 1993; 1st pub. 1933), 2954; Stephen Kinzer, *The True Flag: Theodore Roosevelt, Mark Twain, and the Birth of the American Empire*, 231–35, 241–43, 251–52; Harley A. Notter, *The Origins of the Foreign Policy of Woodrow Wilson* (New York: Russell & Russell, 1965), 274; Herbert Hoover, *The Ordeal of Woodrow Wilson* (Washington, D.C.: Woodrow Wilson Center, 1992; 1st pub. 1958), 18; Mark Strecker, *Smedley D. Butler, USMC: A Biography* (Jefferson, NC: McFarland, 2011), 153; Richard E. Welch Jr., "American Atrocities in the Philippines: The Challenge and the Response," *Pacific Historical Review*, 43 (May 1974), 251–52; Sudarsan Raghavan, "Everyone Hated the Americans," *The Week*, Oct. 21, 2021, 40–41, 1st pub. in *Washington Post.*

652 *U.S. embargo is still in place*: Sources on current-day Cuba on pages 651 to 654 include: author's travel notes; Clifford L. Staten, *The History of Cuba*, 9, 126–31; "Day 5, Day 9, Day 16: Responses to the Invasion of Ukraine," *London Review of Books*, 44:6 (March 24, 2022), 8 (CIA report); "Cubans Denounce 'Misery' in Biggest Protests in Decades," *New York Times*, July 21, 2021; Mary Beth Sheridan, "In Cuba, A Frantic Search for Milk," *Washington Post Weekly*, May 29, 2022, 10–16; "Economy, Political Woes Fuel Flight from Cuba," *Virginian-Pilot*, Sept. 1, 2022; *Soy Cuba* (I Am Cuba), Mikhail Kalatozov, dir. (Moscow: Mosfilm, 1964); "Ex-Cuban Judge Hits Country's Legal System," *Virginian-Pilot*, Jan. 14, 2020, 4; interview with informant requesting anonymity due to family back in Cuba, July 23, 2021.

655 *number closer to 2,975*: Sources on current-day Puerto Rico on pages 654 to 655 include: author's travel notes; "Hurricane Maria death toll controversy," *Wikipedia*; "Puerto Rico: Worst Since Maria," *The Week*, Sept. 30, 2022, 7.

656 *"Death defines* us,*" he exclaimed*: Sources on current-day Philippines on pages 655 to 657 include: author's travel notes; Opening remarks by Governor Jesus Crispin Remulla, International Confrence on Emilio Aguinaldo, March 19–21, 2019, Lyceum of the Philippines University, Cavite.

657 *"abyss of history is deep enough to bury all the world"*: Paul Valéry, "The Crisis of the Mind" (1919), in *The History Guide: Lectures on Twentieth Century Europe*, www.historyguide.org/europe/valery.html; "The Age of Anxiety: Europe in the 1920s (1)," www.tfo.upm.es/docencia/ArtDeco/Europe20s/htm.

658 *"unfortunate trait in the human character"*: Sources on the death of Clara Barton on pages 658 to 659 include: LC/MS: Clara Barton Papers: letter, Clara Barton to "the Public," Oct. 6, 1900; *Clara Barton Diaries*, Feb. 3, 1904; Melinda Henneberger,

"Red Cross Founder Clara Barton Fought 'Thin Black Snakes' of Depression by Springing into Action," *Washington Post*, April 6, 2012, www.washingtonpost.com/lifestyle/magazine/clara-bartons-enemy-depression/2012/04/04/gIQAdryXzS_story.html; Elizabeth Brown Pryor, *Clara Barton, Professional Angel* (Philadelphia: University of Pennsylvania Press, 1987), 340–41; Percy H. Epler, *The Life of Clara Barton*, 34, 433; Christine Ardalan, "Clara Barton's 1898 Battles in Cuba: A Reexamination of Her Nursing Contributions," *Florida Atlantic Comparative Studies Journal* 12:1 (2010), 10–12; Blanche Colton Williams, *Clara Barton, Daughter of Destiny* (Philadelphia: Lippincott, 1941), 63; Mabel Boardman, *Under the Red Cross Flag at Home and Abroad* (Philadelphia: Lippincott, 1915), 98.

659 *"education among the carnivores"*: Henry Adams, *The Education of Henry Adams: An Autobiography* (New York: Modern Library, 1996; 1st pub. 1918), 505.

Acknowledgments

What would a writer do without the patience and kindness of strangers? For four decades now, I've appeared out of the blue at their homes or their offices, asking all kinds of questions, taking up time, first as a journalist and now as an author. I've found that if you're honest about your interest in their lives or activities, more often than not they'll open up to you. For this long work, I repeated the formula, but this time in two foreign countries whose languages I barely spoke, if at all; the United States; and a recently devastated U.S. territory. Again, people were more than gracious. A serious accident intervened in the writing that slowed me down considerably and probably made them wonder whether I'd dropped off the face of the earth; I've reconnected where possible, and will continue to do so as time passes. Don't worry, oh my enlighteners—I haven't forgotten you.

When I started *Splendid Liberators*, I thought it was about the development of "national character," and what better place to start than a war that indelibly linked four emerging lands—the United States, Cuba, the Philippines, and Puerto Rico. Over time, that theme took a dark turn, focusing more on the road where idealism transforms to brutality—but perhaps it's not that far afield. In the United States, my quest started with Dr. Aprilfaye Manalang at Norfolk State University and Jeff Acosta at Tidewater Community College, both well-versed in the Philippines and its wars. Dr. Luisa Igloria at the MFA program at Old Dominion University introduced me to her friends and former colleagues at De La Salle University in Manila. James Zobel, the archivist at the MacArthur Memorial Museum in Norfolk, also guided me through the Philippine War. Kurtis Russell, director of the Allen County Historical Society and research archives in Iola, Kansas, helped me with the complicated life and times of Frederick Funston, while Andy Huse, special collections librarian at the University of South Florida in Tampa, eased my way for a similar trip through the life of Funston's nemesis, David Fagen. George Krepps popped up out of nowhere with the diaries and papers of his ancestor Joseph H. Grant, one of the few provincial governors to stand up to sanctioned murder in Samar. Jarrett Robinson provided needed insight into Funston's activities, while the biographer Michael Morey did the same with David Fagen. The archivist Mary McAndrew at Knox College in Galesburg, Illinois, dug up ephemera on the former student Carl Sandburg, while the archivists at the Library of Congress Manuscript Division, the National Archives, the Marine Corps History Division in Quantico, Virginia., the Illinois Historical and Lincoln Collection, and the U.S. Army Heritage and Education Center in Carlisle, Pennsylvania, worked their wonders as always.

Cuba can be a challenge for an American researcher, but I was lucky to have a father-son team act as my translators and guides. Professor Benito Albisa Novo at the University of Havana served as my pilot through Havana; after a week, I took off cross-country with his father, Benito Albisa Valdés, a former government official who seemed to know everyone across the length of the island, while our driver, Maikel Diaz, seemed to know every road. Thanks to their combined efforts, I explored the sites Funston, Fagen, García, and Gómez trod, and interviewed the following: Carlos Osquel Céspedes Leyra, director of the Museo Parque Nacional La Damajagua; Mario Rafael Guerrero, professor of history at the University of Camaguey; Yonilaysi Ortiz, director of the Colectivo del Museo Casa Natal "Calixto García Íñiguez" in Holguín; Angelina Ramos Blanco, director of the Museo de la Guerra Hispano-Cubano-Norteamericana at Guásimas on the Royal Road; Professora Francisca López Civeira in the department of history at the University of Havana; the historian Desiderio Borroto Fernández; and Omar López Rodríguez, director general of the Santiago Provincial House. For those I forgot, forgive me. I later had a phone interview with Maria Isabel Colón about her childhood in Central

Cuba, and talked with others about Cuba's current "troubles," some of whom requested anonymity to protect relatives back home.

In Puerto Rico, my wife, Kathy, and I followed the footsteps of the uncertain invader Carl Sandburg through the southern half of the island. This entailed piling into a sturdy vehicle driven by our former, now retired veterinarian Allan Adair, plus the amateur historians Juan Luis and Angel Luis Brito López. It had to be sturdy, because half of the country and its roads were still washed away by Hurricane Marie. In Ponce, I interviewed Gladys Tormes González, director of the Archivo Histórico de Ponce, considered Puerto Rico's most comprehensive historical archive, and in Adjuntas, the local historian and author Rafael J. Mirabal Linares. In addition, my exterminator, Puerto Rico–born David Perez, made sure I was well-versed in current affairs.

Next I spent a month in the Philippines, both in extensive archives throughout Manila and in spots outside the city where the revolts against the Spanish and American empires occurred. I used as my base Manila's De La Salle University, where I also did some graduate advising and taught a seminar. I wouldn't have grasped what I did if not for the wisdom of the following professors in the history and literature departments: Shirley O. Lua, Ronald Baytan, Jose Victor Z. Torres, and Fernando A. Santiago Jr., who also introduced me to the scholar and author Reynaldo Ileto. During that time, I was also invited to a roundtable with other writers at the bookstore Solidaridad, owned by the novelist and journalist F. Sionil José. I met him three years before his death at the age of ninety-seven in 2022; he was still writing, and sharp as a tack even then. To live so long, be able to write about it, and write about it so well is probably every writer's dream. At least it's mine.

As always, I'd like to thank my literary agent, Noah Lukeman, who kept me honest and steadily working during all the years of our partnership; he's evolved now to a new professional existence, so I'll miss you, brother. And I want to thank my long-suffering editors at Farrar, Straus and Giroux, involved in this work in different ways from conception to release: Jonathan Galassi, Alexander Star, and Eliza Rudalevige, all of whom slogged with me through the dark, messy recesses of the Spanish- and Philippine-American wars.

Index

A Note About the Author

Joe Jackson is the author of eight previous books, including *The Thief at the End of the World: Rubber, Power, and the Seeds of Empire*, one of *Time*'s Top Ten Books of 2008, and *Atlantic Fever: Lindbergh, His Competitors, and the Race to Cross the Atlantic.* His last book, *Black Elk: The Life of an American Visionary*, won the PEN/Jacqueline Bograd Weld Award for Biography, the Society of American Historians' Francis Parkman Prize, and the Western Writers of America's Spur Award and was named the best biography of 2016 by *True West* magazine. A former investigative journalist, he holds an MFA from the University of Arkansas and lives in Virginia Beach, Virginia.